SCRIPTURE BY TOPIC

SCRIPTURE BY TOPIC

Originally titled
The Divine Armory of Holy Scripture

Compiled and edited by
Rev. Kenelm Vaughan
and
Rev. Newton Thompson, S.T.D.

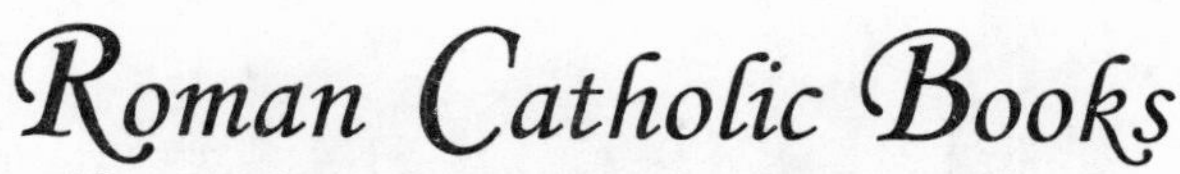

A Division of Catholic Media Apostolate, Harrison, New York
Business office: Post Office Box 2286, Fort Collins, CO 80522

NIHIL OBSTAT

Sti. Ludovici, die 24. Februarii, 1943

JOANNES P. CODY,

Censor Deputatus

IMPRIMATUR

Sti. Ludovici, die 24. Februarii, 1943

JOANNES J. GLENNON,

Archiepiscopus

ISBN 0-912141-51-4

Scripture By Topic

The sheer size and detail of Sacred Scripture intimidates most readers. Many passages have confounded scholars through the centuries. As for laymen, most simply don't know how to read the Bible. The trick is to read it in organized fashion, with Catholic teaching ever in mind. That's impossible to do, on your own.

But it never used to be a problem. This "topical Bible" was once available, right through the World War II years. "The Divine Armory," as it was then known, sat beside Scripture itself on the shelves of priests, religious, and active laymen. Now, Roman Catholic Books brings it back to print.

No other Catholic reference book — no encyclopedia or dictionary, no study of the Bible — does what this volume does: speed you immediately to *all* the Scripture passages for most commonly discussed topics.

CONTENTS

PART I

GOD

PART II

OUR LAST END

PART III

THE THEOLOGICAL AND CARDINAL VIRTUES AND THEIR CONTRARY VICES

PART IV

THE WORD OF GOD

PART V

SIN, JUSTIFICATION, MERIT

PART VI

THE FOUR LAST THINGS

PART I

GOD

I

THE ONE GOD

1. NAMES OF GOD

God said to Moses: I am who am. He said: Thus shalt thou say to the children of Israel: He who is hath sent me to you. And God said again to Moses: Thus shalt thou say to the children of Israel: The Lord God of your fathers, the God of Abraham, the God of Isaac, and the God of Jacob, hath sent me to you: This is my name forever, and this is my memorial unto all generations. Ex. 3:14 f.

My name Adonai I did not show them. Ex. 6:4.

Almighty is his name. Ex. 15:3.

Adore not any strange God: the Lord his name is jealous. He is a jealous God. Ex. 34:14.

Our Redeemer, the Lord of hosts is his name, the Holy One of Israel. Is. 47:4.

They shall know that my name is the Lord. Jer. 16:21.

The Lord is his name. Amos 5:8.

2. HIS ESSENCE AND EXISTENCE

I am who am. He said: Thus shalt thou say to the children of Israel: He who is hath sent me to you. Ex. 3:14.

I, I am he. Jer. 7:11.

If it be not he, who is it, then? Job 9:24.

Thou art from everlasting. Ps. 92:2.

He is before all time. Ecclus. 1:1.

Before Abraham was made, I am. John 8:58.

He that cometh to God must believe that he is. Heb. 11:6.

The fool said in his heart: There is no God. Ps. 52:1.

3. HIS SPIRITUAL NATURE

God is a spirit. John 4:24.

God is light, and in him there is no darkness. John 1:5.

To whom, then, have you likened God? or what image will you make of him? Is. 40:18.

We must not suppose the Divinity to be like unto gold, or silver, or stone, the graving of art, and device of man, Acts 17:29.

Professing themselves to be wise, they became fools. They changed the glory of the incorruptible God into the likeness of the image of a corruptible man, and of birds, and of four-footed beasts, and of creeping things. Rom. 1:22 f.

4. HIS UNITY

Our God is one Lord. Deut. 6:4.

See ye that I alone am, and there is no other God besides me. I will kill, and I will make to live; I will strike, and I will heal: and there is none that can deliver out of my hand. Deut. 32:39.

They gave the incommunicable name to stones and wood. Wis. 14:21.

Before me there was no God formed, and after me there shall be none. Is. 43:10.

I am the first, and I am the last, and besides me there is no God. Is. 44:6.

I am the Lord, and there is none else: there is no God besides me. Is. 45:5.

I will not give my glory to another, nor my praise to graven things. Is. 42:8.

I am the Lord thy God from the land of Egypt: and thou shalt know no God but me, and there is no savior besides me. Osee 13:4.

Who is God but the Lord? Ps. 17:32.

There is no other God but thou. Wis. 12:13.

One Lord, one faith, one baptism. One God, and Father of all. Eph. 4:5 f.

5. GOD, TRUTH AND LIFE

But the Lord is the true God. Jer. 10:10.

God is faithful, and without any iniquity. Deut. 32:4.

God is not as man, that he should lie; nor as the son of man, that he should be changed. Hath he said, then, and will he not do? hath he spoken, and will he not fulfil? Num. 23:19.

Let all fear the God of Daniel, for he is the living God. Dan. 6:26.

We hope in the living God. 1 Tim. 4:10.

It is a fearful thing to fall into the hands of the living God. Heb. 10:31.

In him was life. John 1:3.

I am the way, the truth, and the life. John 14:6.

All thy ways are truth. Ps. 118:151.

Just and true are thy ways, O King of ages. Apoc. 15:3.

6. HIS GOODNESS

None is good but God alone. Luke 18:19.

How good is God to Israel, to them that are of a right heart! Ps. 73:1.

Thou art good. Ps. 118:68.

The Lord is good to those who hope in him, so souls who seek him. Lam. 3:25.

Doth it seem good to thee that thou shouldst calumniate me, and oppress me, the work of thy own hands, and help the counsel of the wicked? Job 10:3.

Doth God pervert judgment, or doth the Almighty overthrow that which is just? Job 8:3.

Say not: It is through God that she [Wisdom] is not with me: for do not thou the things that he hateth. Say not: He hath caused me to err: for he hath no need of wicked men. The Lord hateth all abomination of error, and they that fear him shall not love it. Ecclus. 15:11.

Let no man, when he is tempted, say that he is tempted by God. For God is not a tempter of evils, and he tempteth no man. Jas. 1:13.

Thy eyes are too pure to behold evil, and thou canst not look on iniquity. Why lookest thou upon them that do unjust things, and holdest thy peace when the wicked devoureth the man that is more just than himself? Haba. 1:13.

Who can search out his ways? or who can say to him: Thou hast wrought iniquity? Job 36:23.

One is good, God. Mat. 19:17.

7. HIS PERFECTION

Great is the Lord, and greatly to be praised. Ps. 144:3.

All my bones shall say: Lord, who is like to thee? Ps. 34:10.

This is our God, and there shall no other be accounted of in comparison of him. Bar. 3:36.

Who shall not fear thee, O Lord, and magnify thy name? For thou only art holy: for all nations shall come, and shall adore in thy sight, because thy judgments are manifest. Apoc. 15:4.

There is none holy as the Lord is: for there is no other beside thee, and there is none strong like our God. 1 K. 2:2.

O Lord God, Creator of all things, dreadful and strong, just and merciful, who alone art the good king, who alone art gracious, who alone art just, and almighty, and eternal, who deliverest Israel from all evil, who didst choose the fathers, and didst sanctify them. 2 Mac. 1:24.

Who is the blessed and only mighty, who only hath immortality. Tim. 6:16.

I will show thee all good. Ex. 33:19.

He that planted the ear, shall he not hear? or he that formed the eye, doth he not consider? In me is all grace of the way and of the truth, in me is all hope of life and of virtue. Ecclus. 24:25.

Shall not I, that make others to bring forth children, myself bring forth? saith the Lord. Shall I, that give generation to others, be barren? saith the Lord thy God. Is. 66:9.

In him was life. John 1:3.

Be ye therefore perfect, as your heavenly Father is perfect. Mat. 5:48.

8. HIS INFINITY

Behold, God is high in his strength, and none is like him among the lawgivers. Bar. 3:25.

Of his greatness there is no end. Ps. 144:3

It is great, and hath no end; it is high and immense. Job 36:22.

Behold, the Gentiles are as a drop of a bucket, and are counted as the smallest grain of a balance: behold, the islands are as a little dust. And Libanus shall not be enough to burn, nor the beasts thereof sufficient for a burnt offering. All nations are before him as if they had no being at all, and are counted to him as nothing and vanity. Is. 40:15.

The whole world before thee is as the least grain of the balance, and as a drop of the morning dew, that falleth down upon the earth. Wis. 11:23.

I shall be satisfied when thy glory shall appear. Ps. 16:15.

9. HIS IMMENSITY

There shall be no flight for them, and he that shall flee of them shall not be delivered. Though they go down even to hell, thence shall my hand bring them out: and though they climb up to heaven, thence will I bring them down. And though they be hid in the top of Carmel, I will search and take them away from thence: and though they hide themselves from my eyes in the depth of the sea, there will I command the serpent, and he shall bite them; and if they go into captivity before their enemies, there will I command the sword, and it shall kill them. And I will set my eyes upon them for evil, and not for good. Amos 9:1-4.

Am I, think ye, a God at hand, saith the Lord, and not a God afar off? Shall a man be hid in secret places, and I not see him? saith the Lord. Do not I fill heaven and earth? saith the Lord. Jer. 23:23.

Whither shall I go from thy spirit? or whither shall I flee from thy face? If I ascend into heaven, thou art there: if I descend into hell, thou art present. If I take my wings early in the morning, and dwell in the uttermost parts of the sea: even there also shall thy hand lead me, and thy right hand shall hold me. And I said: Perhaps darkness shall cover me: and night shall be my light in my pleasures. But darkness shall not be dark to thee, and night shall be light as the day: the darkness thereof, and the light thereof, are alike to thee. For thou hast possessed my reins: thou hast protected me from my mother's womb. Ps. 138:7-13.

Heaven is my throne, and the earth my footstool: what is this house that you will build to me? and what is this place of my rest? Is. 66:1.

He is not far from every one of us; for in him we live and move and are. Acts 17:28.

The Spirit of the Lord hath filled the whole world; and that which containeth all things hath knowledge of the voice. Wis. 1:7.

All the earth is full of his glory. Is. 6:3.

Peradventure thou wilt comprehend the steps of God, and wilt find out the Almighty perfectly? He is higher than heaven, and what wilt thou do? He is deeper than hell, and how wilt thou know? The measure of him is longer than the earth, and broader than the sea. Job 11:7-9.

Dost not thou think that God is higher than heaven and is elevated above the height of the stars? Job 22:12.

If heaven and the heavens of heavens cannot contain thee, how much less this house which I have built? 3 K. 8:27.

Walk before me, and be perfect. Gen. 17:1.

I set the Lord always in my sight: for he is at my right hand, that I be not moved. Ps. 15:8.

10. HIS IMMUTABILITY

In the beginning, O Lord, thou foundedst the earth; and the heavens are the works of thy hands. They shall perish, but thou remainest; and all of them shall grow old like a garment: and as a vesture thou shalt change them, and they shall be changed. But thou art always the selfsame, and thy years shall not fail. Ps. 101:26.

What seest thou, Jeremias? And I said: I see a rod watching. And the Lord said to me: Thou hast seen well; for I will watch over my word to perform it. Jer 1:11.

Heaven and earth shall pass, but my words shall not pass. Mat. 24:35.

Wherein God, meaning more abundantly to show to the heirs of the promise the immutability of his counsel, interposed an oath: that by two immutable things, in which it is impossible for God to lie, we may have the strongest comfort, who have fled for refuge to hold fast the hope set before us. Heb. 6:17.

Thou shalt know that the Lord thy God, he is a strong and faithful God, keeping his covenant and mercy to them that love him, and to them that keep his commandments, unto a thousand generations. Deut. 7:9.

He that hath received his testimony hath set to his seal that God is true. For he whom God hath sent speaketh the words of God. John 3:33.

The triumpher in Israel will not spare, and will not be moved to repentance: for he is not a man that he should repent. 1 K. 15:29.

God is true, and every man a liar. Rom. 3:4.

If we deny him, he will also deny us: if we believe not, he continueth faithful: he cannot deny himself. 2 Tim. 2:12.

He is faithful, who hath called you, who will also do it. 1 Thess. 5:24.

God is faithful, who will strengthen and keep you from evil. 2 Thess. 3:3.

Every best gift, and every perfect gift, is from above, coming down from the Father of lights, with whom there is no change, nor shadow of alteration. Jas. 1:17.

God is not as a man that he should lie, nor as the son of man that he should be changed. Hath he said then, and will he not do? hath he spoken, and will he not fulfil? Num. 23:19.

I am the Lord, and I change not. Mal. 3:6.

11. HIS ETERNITY

Knowest thou not, or hast thou not heard? The Lord is the everlasting God, who hath created the ends of the earth. He shall not faint nor labor, neither is there any searching out of his wisdom. Is. 40:23.

Before the mountains were made, or the earth and the world was formed; from eternity and to eternity thou art God. Ps. 89:2.

Thy years are unto generation and generation. Ps. 101:25.

The Lord shall reign forever and forever. Ex. 15:11.

The number of his years is inestimable. Job 36:26.

Thus saith the High and the Eminent that inhabiteth eternity. Is. 57:15.

The mercy of the Lord is from eternity. Ps. 102:17.

His power is an everlasting power. Dan. 7:14.

I was set up from eternity. Prov. 8:23.

Thy word, O Lord is forever. Ps. 118:142.

12. HIS INCOMPREHENSIBILITY

Who among men is he who can know the counsel of God? or who can think what the will of God is? Wis. 9:13.

And hardly do we guess aright at things that are upon the earth: and with labor do we find the things that are before us. But the things that are in heaven, who shall search out? And who shall know thy thought, except thou give wisdom, and send thy Holy Spirit from above? Wis. 9:16.

Who can search out his ways? or who can say to him: Thou hast wrought iniquity? Remember that thou knowest not his work, concerning which men have sung. All men see him, every one beholdeth afar off. Behold, God is great, exceeding our knowledge; the number of his years is inestimable. Job 36:23-26.

Peradventure thou wilt comprehend the steps of God, and wilt find out the Almighty perfectly? Job 11:7.

O, how desirable are all his works! and what we can know is but a spark. Ecclus. 42:23.

Who first hath perfect knowledge of her, and a weaker shall not search her out. For her thoughts are more vast than the sea and her counsels more deep than the great ocean. Ecclus. 24:38 f.

As thou knowest not what is the way of the spirit, nor how the bones are joined together in the womb of her who is with child; so thou knowest not the works of God, who is the maker of all. Eccles. 11:5.

Lo, these things are said in part of his ways: and seeing we have heard scarce a little drop of his word, who shall be able to behold the thunder of his greatness? Job 26:14.

Who hath numbered the sand of the sea, and the drops of rain, and the days of the world? Who hath measured the height of heaven, and the breadth of the earth, and the depth of the abyss? Who hath searched out the wisdom of God that goeth before all things? To whom hath the discipline of wisdom been revealed and made manifest? and who hath understood the multiplicity of her steps? There is one most high Creator, almighty, and a powerful King, and greatly to be feared, who sitteth upon his throne, and is the God of dominion. He created her in the Holy Ghost, and saw her, and numbered her, and measured her. Ecclus. 1:2-9.

O the depth of the riches of the wisdom and of the knowledge of God! How incomprehensible are his judgments, and how unsearchable his ways! For who hath known the mind of the Lord? or who hath been his counsellor? Rom. 11:33 f.

Great in counsel, and incomprehensible in thought: whose eyes are open upon all the ways of the children of Adam, to render unto every one according to his ways, and according to the fruit of his devices. Jer. 32:19.

Who only hath immortality, and inhabiteth light inaccessible, whom no man hath seen, nor can see, to whom be honor and empire everlasting. Amen. 1 Tim. 6:16.

We know in part, and we prophesy in part. But when that which is perfect is come, that which is in part shall be done away. When I was a child, I spoke as a child, I understood as a child, I thought as a child. But when I became a man, I put away the things of a child. 1 C. 13:9-11.

13. HIS UNUTTERABLENESS

Thy judgments, O Lord, are great, and thy words cannot be expressed: therefore undisciplined souls have erred. Wis. 17:1.

Who is able to declare his works? For who shall search out his glorious acts? And who shall show forth the power of his majesty? or who shall be able to declare his mercy? Nothing may be taken away, nor added, neither is it possible to find out the glorious works of God. When a man hath done, then he shall begin; and when he leaveth off, he shall be at a loss. Ecclus. 18:2-6.

Cold cometh out of the north, and to God praise with fear. We cannot find him worthily: He is great in strength, and in judgment, and in justice, and he is ineffable. Therefore men shall fear him, and all that seem to themselves to be wise shall not dare to behold him. Job 37:22-24.

14. GOD KNOWN BY THE THINGS THAT ARE MADE

That which is known of God is manifest in them. For God hath manifested it unto them. For the invisible things of him, from the creation of the world, are clearly seen, being understood by the things that are made: His eternal power also and divinity: so that they are inexusable. Rom. 1:19 f.

By these good things that are seen they could not understand him that is, neither by attending to the works have acknowledged who was the workman. But have imagined either the fire or the wind, or the swift air, or the circle of the stars, or the great water, or the sun and moon, to be the gods that rule the world. With whose beauty, if they being delighted, took them to be gods: let them know how much the Lord of them is more beautiful than they; for the first Author of beauty made all those things. Or if they admired their power and their effects, let them understand by them that he that made them is mightier than they. For by the greatness of the beauty, and of the creature, the Creator of them may be seen, so as to be known thereby. Wis. 13:1-5.

If they were able to know so much, as to make a judgment of the world, how did they not more easily find out the Lord thereof? Wis. 13:9.

To know thee is perfect justice; and to know thy justice, and thy power, is the root of immortality. Wis. 15:3.

The sensual man perceiveth not these things that are of the Spirit of God. 1 C. 2:14.

15. THE BEATIFIC VISION

Blessed are the clean of heart, for they shall see God. Mat. 5:8.

Their angels in heaven always see the face of my Father who is in heaven. Mat. 18:10.

He that loveth me shall be loved of my Father: and I will love him, and will manifest myself to him. John 14:21.

We see now through a glass in a dark manner; but then face to face. Now I know in part; but then I shall know even as I am known. 1 C. 13:12.

We know that when he shall appear we shall be like to him: because we shall see him as he is. 1 John 3:2.

His servants shall serve him, and they shall see his face: and his name shall be on heir foreheads. Apoc. 22:4.

This is eternal life: that they may know thee, the only true God, and Jesus Christ, whom thou hast sent. John 17:3.

16. HIS KNOWLEDGE

O Lord, who hast the knowledge of all things. Esth. 14:14.

Shall any one teach God knowledge, who judgeth those that are high? Job 21:22.

Thy knowledge has become wonderful to me: it is high, and I cannot reach it. Ps. 138:6.

What man knoweth the things of a man, but the spirit of a man that is in him? So the things also that are of God no man knoweth, but the Spirit of God. 1 C. 2:11.

The spirit searcheth all things; yea, the deep things of God. 1 C. 2:10.

The eyes of the Lord behold all the earth. 2 Par. 16:9.

If thou say: I have not strength enough, he that seeth into the heart, he understandeth, and nothing deceiveth the keeper of thy soul, and he shall render to a man according to his works. Prov. 24:12.

Neither is there any creature invisible in his sight: but all things are naked and open to his eyes, to whom our speech is. Heb. 4:13.

God is greater than our heart, and knoweth all things. 1 John 3:20.

The eyes of the Lord are upon the just, and his ears unto their prayers. Ps. 33:16.

The searcher of hearts and reins is God. Ps. 7:10.

The heart of man is perverse above all things, and unsearchable. Who can know it? I am the Lord who search the heart and prove the reins; who give to every one according to his way, and according to the fruit of his devices. Jer. 17:9 f.

Thus saith the Lord, the holy one of Israel, his Maker: Ask me of things to come concerning my children, and concerning the work of my hands give ye charge to me. Is. 45:11.

Before I formed thee in the bowels of thy mother, I knew thee; and before thou camest forth out of the womb, I sanctified thee, and made thee a prophet unto the nations. Jer. 1:5.

O eternal God, who knowest hidden things, who knowest all things before they come to pass. Dan. 13:42.

If a man desire much knowledge, she knoweth things past, and judgeth of things to come: she knoweth the subtleties of speeches, and the solutions of arguments: she knoweth signs and wonders before they be done, and the events of times and ages. Wis. 8:8.

I know that the king of Egypt will not let you go, but by a mighty hand. Ex. 3:19.

I know their thoughts, and what they are about to do this day, before that I bring them into the land which I have promised them. Deut. 31:21.

My bone is not hidden from thee, which thou hast made in secret: and my substance in the lower parts of the earth. Thy eyes did see my imperfect being, and in thy book all shall be written: days shall be formed, and no one in them. Ps. 138:15 f.

He beholdeth the ends of the world, and looketh on all things that are under heaven. Job 28:24.

He hath searched out the deep, and the heart of man, and considered their crafty devices. For the Lord knoweth all knowledge, and hath beheld the signs of the world: he declared the things that are past, and the things that are to come, and revealeth the traces of hidden things. No thought escapeth him, and no word can hide itself from him. Ecclus. 42:18-20.

The wisdom of God is great, and he is strong in power, seeing all men without ceasing. The eyes of the Lord are towards them that fear him, and he knoweth all the work of man. Ecclus. 15:19 f.

Their ways are always before him, they are not hidden from his eyes. Over every nation he set a ruler. And Israel was made the manifest portion of God. And all their works are as the sun in the sight of God: and his eyes are continually upon their ways. Their covenants were not hid by their iniquity, and all their iniquities are in the sight of God. Ecclus. 17:13-17.

The works of all flesh are before him, and there is nothing hid from his eyes. He seeth from eternity to eternity, and there is nothing wonderful before him. Ecclus. 39:24.

His eyes are upon the ways of man, and he considereth all their steps. There is no darkness, and there is no shadow of death, when they may be hid who work iniquity. Job 34:21.

Who telleth the number of the stars, and calleth them all by their names. Great is our Lord, and great is his power; and of his wisdom there is no number. Ps. 146:4.

Who hath forwarded the spirit of the Lord? or who hath been his counsellor and hath taught him? With whom hath he consulted, and who hath instructed him, and taught him the path of justice, and taught him knowledge, and showed him the way of understanding? Why sayest thou, O Jacob, and speakest, O Israel: My way is hid from the Lord, and my judgment is passed over from my God? Knowest thou not, or hast thou not heard? The Lord is the everlasting God, who hath created the ends of the earth: He shall not faint nor labor, neither is there any searching out of his wisdom. Is. 40:13 f., 27 f.

Behold it is written before me: I will not be silent, but I will render and repay into their bosom. Is. 65:6.

My eyes are upon all their ways: they are not hid from my face, and their iniquity hath not been hid from my eyes. Jer. 16:17.

I know Ephraim, and Israel is not hid from me; for now Ephraim has committed fornication, Israel is defiled. Osee 5:3.

The Lord beholdeth the ways of man, and considereth all his steps. Prov. 5:21.

The eyes of the Lord in every place behold the good and the evil. Prov. 5:3.

Hell and destruction are before the Lord: how much more the hearts of the children of men! Prov. 15:11.

All the ways of a man are open to his eyes: the Lord is the weigher of spirits. Prov. 16:2.

Behold my witness is in heaven, and he that knoweth my conscience is on high. My friends are full of words; my eye poureth out tears to God. Job 16:20 f.

Thou sayest: What doth God know? and he judgeth as it were through a mist. The clouds are his covert, and he doth not consider our things, and he walketh about the poles of heaven. Dost thou desire to keep the path of ages, which wicked men have trodden? Job 22:13-15.

Say not: I shall be hidden from God, and who shall remember me from on high? In such a multitude I shall not be known: for what is my soul in such an immense creation? Behold, the heaven, and the heavens of heavens, the deep, and all the earth, and the things that are in them, shall be moved in his sight. The mountains also, and the hills, and the foundations of the earth: when God shall look at them, they shall be shaken with trembling. And in all these things the heart is senseless: and every heart is understood by him. Ecclus. 16:16-20.

Every man that passeth beyond his own bed, despising his own soul, and saying: Who seeth me? Darkness compasseth me about, and the walls cover me, and no man seeth me: whom do I fear? The Most High will not remember my sins. And he understandeth not that his eye seeth all things, for such a man's fear driveth from him the fear of God, and the eyes of men fearing him; and he knoweth not that the eyes of the Lord are far brighter than the sun, beholding round about all the ways of men, and the bottom of the deep, and looking into the hearts of men, into the most hidden parts. For all things were known to the Lord God before they were created; so also after they were perfected he beholdeth all things. Ecclus. 23:25-29.

Woe to you that are deep of heart to hide your counsel from the Lord; and their works are in the dark, and they say: Who seeth us, and who knoweth us? This thought of yours is perverse: as if the clay should think against the potter, and the work should say to the maker thereof: Thou madest me not: or the thing framed should say to him that fashioned it: Thou understandest not. Is. 29:15 f.

I made a covenant with my eyes, that I would not so much as think upon a virgin. For what part should God from above have in me, and what inheritance the Almighty from on high? Doth he not consider my ways, and number all my steps? Job 31:1 f., 4.

Blessed is the man that shall continue in wisdom, and that shall meditate in his justice, and in his mind shall think of the all-seeing eye of God. Ecclus. 14:22.

Lord, thou hast proved me, and hast known me: thou hast known my sitting down and my rising up. Thy knowledge is become wonderful to me: it is high, and I cannot reach to it. Whither shall I go from thy Spirit? or whither shall I flee from thy face? If I ascend into heaven, thou art there: if I descend into hell, thou art present. If I take my wings early in the morning, and dwell in the uttermost parts of the sea: even there also shall thy hand lead me, and thy right hand shall hold me. Ps. 138:1, 6-10.

17. HIS WILL

Fear not: can we resist the will of God? Gen. 50:19.

Who resisteth his will? Rom. 9:19.

God said: Be light made, and light was made. Gen. 1:3.

Our God is in heaven: he hath done all things whatsoever he would. Ps. 113:11.

He spoke, and they were made: he commanded, and they were created. Ps. 148:5.

By faith we understand that the world was framed by the word of God, that from invisible things visible things might be made. Heb. 11:3.

Thy power is at hand when thou wilt. Wis. 12:18.

I will heap evils upon them, and will spend my arrows among them. Deut. 32:24.

Good things and evil, life and death, poverty and riches, are from God. Ecclus. 11:14.

I form the light and create darkness, I make peace and create evil: I, the Lord, that do all these things. Is. 43:7.

Shall there be evil in a city, which the Lord hath not done? Amos 3:6.

Who is he that commanded a thing to be done, when the Lord commandeth it not? Shall not both evil and good proceed out of the mouth of the Highest? Why hath a living man murmured, man suffering for his sins? Let us search our ways, and seek and return to the Lord. Lam. 3:37-40.

God is faithful and without any iniquity, he is just and right. Deut. 32:4.

Is God unjust, who executeth wrath? God forbid; otherwise, how shall God judge this world? Rom. 3:5 f.

Thou shalt fly lying. The innocent and just person thou shalt not put to death, because I abhor the wicked. Ex. 23:7.

As long as they sinned not in the sight of their God, it was well with them: for their God hateth iniquity. Jdth. 5:21.

In the morning I will stand before thee, and will see: because thou art not a God that willest iniquity. Neither shall the wicked dwell near thee; nor shall the unjust abide before thy eyes. Thou hatest all the workers of iniquity: Thou wilt destroy all that speak a lie. Ps. 5:5-7.

Thou hast loved justice and hated iniquity: therefore God, thy God, hath anointed thee with the oil of gladness above thy fellows. Ps. 44:8.

The way of the wicked is an abomination to the Lord: he that followeth justice is beloved by him. Prov. 15:9.

To God the wicked and his wickedness are hateful alike. Wis. 14:9.

He will open his mouth in prayer, and will make supplication for his sins. For if it shall please the great Lord, he will fill him with the spirit of understanding. Ecclus. 39:7 f.

In whom we also are called by lot, being predestinated according to the purpose of him, who worketh all things according to the purpose of his will. Eph. 1:11.

The mercies of the Lord that we are not consumed, because his commiserations have not failed. Lam. 3:22.

If that nation against which I have

spoken shall repent of their evil, I also will repent of the evil that I have thought to do to them. And I will suddenly speak of a nation and of a kingdom, to build up and plant it. If it shall do evil in my sight, that it obey not my voice, I will repent of the good that I have spoken to do unto it. Jer. 18:8-10.

Who can tell if God will turn and forgive, and will turn away from his fierce anger, and we shall not perish? And God saw their works, that they were turned from their evil way: and God had mercy with regard to the evil which he had said he would do to them, and he did it not. Jon. 3:9 f.

Hast thou not seen Achab humbled before me? Therefore because he has humbled himself for my sake, I will not bring him the evil in his days, but in his son's days will I bring the evil upon his house. 3 K. 21:29.

The Lord of hosts hath sworn saying: Surely, as I have thought, so shall it be: and as I have purposed, so shall it fall out. This is the counsel that I have purposed upon all the earth, and this is the hand that is stretched out upon all nations. For the Lord of hosts hath decreed, and who can disannul it? And his hand is stretched out, and who shall turn it away? Is. 14:24, 26 f.

From the beginning I am the same, and there is none that can deliver out of my hand: I will work, and who shall turn it away? Is. 43:13.

My counsel shall stand, and all my will shall be done. Is. 46:10.

Refrain from these men, and let them alone: for if this counsel or this work be of men, it will come to naught. But if it be of God, you cannot overthrow it; lest perhaps you be found even to fight against God. And they consented to him. Acts 5:38 f.

The Lord bringeth to naught the counsels of nations; and he rejecteth the devices of people, and casteth away the counsels of princes. But the counsel of the Lord standeth forever: the thoughts of his heart to all generations. Ps. 32:10 f.

18. HIS OMNIPOTENCE

I am the almighty God: walk before me, and be perfect. Gen. 17:1.

O Lord almighty King, for all things are in thy power, and there is none that can resist thy will. Esth. 13:9.

At his word the waters stood as a heap, and at the words of his mouth the receptacles of waters: for at his commandment favor is shown, and there is no diminishing of his salvation. Ecclus. 39:22 f.

There is no wisdom, there is no prudence, there is no counsel against the Lord. The horse is prepared for the day of battle, but the Lord giveth safety. Prov. 21:30 f.

Many tyrants have sat on the throne, and he whom no man would think on hath worn the crown. Many mighty men have been brought down greatly, and the glorious have been delivered into the hand of others. Ecclus. 11:5 f.

O Adonai Lord, great art thou, and glorious in thy power, and no one can overcome thee. Let all thy creatures serve thee: because thou hast spoken, and they were made: thou didst send forth thy Spirit, and they were created, and there is no one that can resist thy voice. Jdth. 16:16 f.

Behold, the heaven, and the heavens of heavens, the deep, and all the earth, and the things that are in them, shall be moved in his sight; the mountains also, and the hills, and the foundations of the earth: when God shall look at them, they shall be shaken with trembling. Ecclus. 16:18 f.

The works of God are done in judgment from the beginning, and from the making of them he distinguished their parts, and their beginnings in their generations. He beautified their works forever; they have neither hungered nor labored, and they have not ceased from their works. Nor shall any of them straiten his neighbor at any time. Ecclus. 16:26 f.

He that liveth forever created all things together. God only shall be justified, and he remaineth an invincible King forever. Ecclus. 18:1.

He is alone, and no man can turn away his thought: and whatever his soul hath desired, that hath he done. Job 23:13.

Great power always belonged to thee alone; and who shall resist the strength of thy arm? For the whole world before thee is as the least grain of the balance, and as a drop of the morning dew that falleth down upon the earth. Wis. 11:22 f.

Thy power is at hand when thou wilt. Wis. 12:18.

It is thou, O Lord, that hast power of life and death, and leadest down to the gates of death, and bringest back again. But it is impossible to escape thy hand. Wis. 16:13-15.

Who shall say to thee: What hast thou done? or who shall withstand thy judgment? or who shall come before thee to be a revenger of wicked men? or who shall accuse thee if the nations perish which thou hast made? Wis. 12:12.

God, whose wrath no man can resist, and under whom they stoop that bear up the world. Job 9:13.

If he shall overturn all things, or shall press them together, who shall contradict him? Job 11:10.

He bringeth counsellors to a foolish end, and judges to insensibility. He looseth the belt of kings, and girdeth their lions with a cord. Job 12:17.

It is he that sitteth upon the globe of the earth, and the inhabitants thereof are as locusts: he that stretcheth out the heavens as nothing, and spreadeth them out as a tent to dwell in. He that bringeth the searchers of secrets to nothing, that hath made the judges of the earth as vanity. Lift up your eyes on high, and see who hath created these things: who bringeth out their host by number, and calleth them all by their names: by the greatness of his might, and strength, and power, not one of them was missing. Is. 40:22 f., 26.

I am the Lord that make all things, that alone stretch out the heavens, that establish the earth, and there is none with me. That make void the tokens of diviners, and make the soothsayers mad. That turn the wise backward, and that make their knowledge foolish. That raise up the word of my servant, and perform the counsel of my messengers, who say to Jerusalem: Thou shalt be inhabited; and to the cities of Juda: You shall be built, and I will raise up the wastes thereof. Who say to the deep: Be thou desolate, and I will dry up thy rivers. Who say to Cyrus: Thou art my shepherd, and thou shalt perform all my pleasure. Who say to Jerusalem: Thou shalt be built, and to the temple: Thy foundations shall be laid. Is. 44:24-28.

19. HIS JUSTICE

The Lord will reward every one according to his justice and his faithfulness. 1 K. 26:23.

I am the Lord who search the heart and prove the reins: who give to every one according to his way, and according to the fruit of his devices. Jer. 17:10.

The Almighty will look into the causes of every one. Job 35:13.

The wickedness of sinners shall be brought to naught, and thou shalt direct the just: the searcher of hearts and reins is God. Ps. 7:10.

God is faithful and without iniquity, he is just and right. Deut. 32:4.

Who keepeth truth forever: who executeth judgment for them that suffer wrong. Ps. 145:7.

I have seen those who work iniquity, and sow sorrows, and reap them, perishing by the blast of God, and consumed by the spirit of his wrath. Job 4:8 f.

Thou hast not given water to the weary, thou hast withdrawn bread from the hungry. Therefore art thou surrounded with snares, and sudden fear troubleth thee. Job 22:7, 10.

Many are the scourges of the sinner, but mercy shall encompass him that hopeth in the Lord. Ps. 31:10.

The countenance of the Lord is against them that do evil things, to cut off the remembrance of them from the earth. Ps. 33:17.

I know, O Lord, that thy judgments are equity: and in thy truth thou hast humbled me. Ps. 118:75.

God shall judge both the just and the wicked, and then shall be the time of everything. Eccles. 3:17.

For it is easy before God in the day of death to reward every one according to his ways. Ecclus. 11:28.

The Lord is just, and hath loved justice: his countenance hath beheld righteousness. Ps. 10:8.

Thou art just, O Lord, and thy judgment is right. Ps. 118:137.

Thy justice is justice forever. Ps. 118:142.

He will render to every man according to his works: to them indeed who, according to patience in good work, seek glory and honor and incorruption, eternal life; but to them that are contentious and who obey not the truth, but give credit to iniquity, wrath and indignation. Rom. 2:6-8.

We must all be manifested before the judgment seat of Christ, that every one may receive the proper things of the body, according as he hath done, whether it be good or evil. 2 C. 5:10.

I have finished my course, I have kept the faith. As to the rest, there is laid up for me a crown of justice, which the Lord, the just Judge, will render to me in that day; and not only to me, but to them also that love his coming. 2 Thess. 4:8.

Ye men of understanding, hear me: far from God be wickedness, and iniquity from the Almighty. For he will render to a man his work, and according to the ways of every one he will reward them. For in very deed God will not condemn without cause, neither will the Almighty pervert judgment. Job 34: 10-12.

If thou do well, shalt thou not receive? but if ill, shall not sin be forthwith present at the door? Gen. 4:7.

Give, and it shall be given to you: good measure and pressed down and shaken together and running over shall they give into your bosom. For with the same measure that you shall mete withal, it shall be measured to you again. Luke 6:38.

In the good day enjoy good things, and beware beforehand of the evil day: for God hath made both the one and the other, that man may not find against him any just complaint. Eccles. 7:15.

All things that are done, God will bring into judgment for every error, whether it be good or evil. Eccles. 12:14.

Before man is life and death, good and evil: that which he shall choose shall be given him. Ecclus. 15:18.

The Lord will not accept any person against a poor man, and he will hear the prayer of him that is wronged. And he will repay vengeance to the Gentiles, till he have taken away the multitude of the proud, and broken the scepters of the unjust. Till he have rendered to men according to their deeds, and according to the works of Adam, and according to his presumption. Till he have judged the cause of his people, and he shall delight the just with his mercy. Ecclus. 35:16, 23-25.

Because sentence is not speedily pronounced against the evil, the children of men commit evils without any fear. But though a sinner do evil a hundred times, and by patience be borne withal, I know from thence that it shall be well with them that fear God, who dread his face. Eccles. 8:11 f.

That servant who knew the will of his lord, and prepared not himself, and did not according to his will, shall be beaten with many stripes. But he that knew not and did things worthy of stripes shall be beaten with few stripes. Luke 12:47 f.

For we know that the judgment of

God is according to truth against them that do such things. Or despisest thou the riches of his goodness, and patience, and long-suffering? knowest thou not that the benignity of God leadeth thee to penance? But according to thy hardness and impenitent heart, thou treasurest up to thyself wrath against the day of wrath, and revelation of the just judgment of God. For whosoever have sinned without the law shall perish without the law: and whosoever have sinned in the law shall be judged by the law. For not the hearers of the law are just before God: but the doers of the law shall be justified. Rom. 2:2, 4 f., 12 f.

What things a man shall sow, those also shall he reap. For he that soweth in his flesh, of the flesh also shall reap corruption. But he that soweth in the Spirit, of the Spirit shall reap life everlasting. Gal. 6:8.

That which bringeth forth thorns and briars is reprobate, and very near unto a curse, whose end is to be burnt. Heb. 6:8.

See then the goodness and the severity of God: towards them indeed that are fallen, the severity; but towards thee, the goodness of God, if thou abide in goodness, otherwise thou also shalt be cut off. O the depth of the riches of the wisdom and of the knowledge of God! How incomprehensible are his judgments, and how unsearchable his ways! Rom. 11:22, 33.

The Lord knoweth how to deliver the godly out of temptation, but to reserve the unjust unto the day of judgment to be tormented. 2 Pet. 2:9.

He that shall lead into captivity shall go into captivity: he that shall kill by the sword must be killed by the sword. Apoc. 13:10.

Behold, I come quickly, and my reward is with me, to render to every man according to his works. Blessed are they that wash their robes in the blood of the Lamb: that they may have a right to the tree of life, and may enter in by the gates into the city. Apoc. 22:12, 14.

In very deed I perceive that God is not a respecter of persons. But in every nation, he that feareth him, and worketh justice, is acceptable to him. Acts 10:34 f.

He accepteth not the persons of princes: nor hath regarded the tyrant when he contended against the poor man, for all are the work of his hands. Job 34:19.

God will not except any man's person, neither will he stand in awe of any man's greatness: for he made the little and the great, and he hath equally care of all. Wis. 6:8.

Flee then from the face of the sword, for the sword is the revenger of iniquities: and know ye that there is a judgment. Job 19:29.

20. HIS MERCY

I am the Lord thy God, showing mercy unto thousands to them that love me and keep my commandments. Ex. 20:6.

O the Lord, the Lord God, merciful and gracious, patient and of much compassion, and true! Ex. 34:6.

The earth is full of the mercy of the Lord. Ps. 32:5.

He shall deliver the poor from the mighty, and the needy that had no helper. Ps. 71:12.

According to his greatness, so also is his mercy with him. Ecclus. 2:23.

Thy mercy is better than lives. Ps. 62:4.

The Lord is sweet to all, and his tender mercies are over all his works. Ps. 144:9.

The Lord delayeth not his promise, as some imagine; but dealeth patiently for your sake, not willing that any should perish, but that all should return to penance. 2 Pet. 3:9.

He endured with much patience vessels of wrath fitted for destruction. Rom. 9:22.

Showing mercy unto thousands to them that love me and keep my commandments. Ex. 20:6.

I am holy, saith the Lord, and I will not be angry forever. Jer. 3:12.

Shall I not spare Ninive, that great city, in which there are more than a hundred and twenty thousand persons that know not how to distinguish between their right hand and their left, and many beasts? Jon. 4:11.

When thou art angry, thou wilt remember mercy. Haba. 3:2.

The Lord is patient and full of mercy. Num. 14:18.

Mercy shall encompass him that hopeth in the Lord. Ps. 31:10.

The Lord is compassionate and merciful, long-suffering and plenteous in mercy. For according to the height of the heaven above the earth, he hath strengthened his mercy towards them that fear him. The mercy of the Lord is from eternity and unto eternity upon them that fear him. Ps. 102:8, 11, 17.

Let the mercies of the Lord give glory to him, and his wonderful works to the children of men. Ps. 106:8.

The compassion of man is towards his neighbor; but the mercy of God is upon all flesh. He hath mercy, and teacheth, and correcteth, as a shepherd doth his flock. Ecclus. 18:12 f.

The Lord waiteth that he may have mercy on you: and therefore shall he be exalted sparing you. Is. 30:18.

For a small moment have I forsaken thee, but with great mercies will I gather thee. In a moment of indignation have I hid my face a little while from thee; but with everlasting kindness have I had mercy on thee, said the Lord thy Redeemer. Is. 54:7 f.

His mercy is from generation unto generations, to them that fear him. Luke 1:50.

He will have all men to be saved, and to come to the knowledge of the truth. 1 Tim. 2:4.

It is not the will of your Father, who is in heaven, that one of these little ones should perish. Mat. 18:14.

Return to me, saith the Lord, and I will receive thee. Jer. 3:1.

As a father hath compassion on his children, so hath the Lord compassion on them that fear him. For he knoweth our frame. He remembereth that we are dust. Man's days are as grass: as the flower of the field so shall he flourish. Ps. 102:13-15.

Thus saith the Lord God: It is not for your sake that I will do this, O house of Israel, but for my holy name's sake, which you have profaned among the nations whither you went. Ez. 36:22.

It is not for your sakes that I will do this, saith the Lord God, be it known to you: be confounded, and ashamed at your own ways, O house of Israel. Ez. 36:32.

How great is the mercy of the Lord, and his forgiveness to them that turn to him! For all things cannot be in men, because the son of man is not immortal, and they are delighted with the vanity of evil. What is brighter than the sun? yet it shall be eclipsed. Or what is more wicked than that which flesh and blood hath invented? and this shall be reproved. He beholdeth the power of the height of heaven: and all men are earth and ashes. Ecclus. 17:28-31.

What is man, and what is his grace? and what is his good, or what is his evil? The number of the days of man at the most are a hundred years: as a drop of water of the sea are they esteemed; and as a pebble of the sand, so are a few years compared to eternity. Therefore God is patient in them, and poureth forth his mercy upon them. He hath seen the presumption of their heart that it is wicked, and hath known their end that it is evil. Therefore hath he filled up his mercy in their favor, and hath shown them the way of justice. Ecclus. 18:7-11.

Mercy and judgment I will sing to thee, O Lord. Ps. 100:1.

All the ways of the Lord are mercy and truth. Ps. 24:10.

Mercy and wrath are with him. He is mighty to forgive and to pour out indignation. According as his mercy is, so his correction judgeth a man according to his works. The sinner shall not escape in his rapines, and the patience of him that showeth mercy shall not be put off. Ecclus. 16:12.

When thou art angry, thou wilt remember mercy. Haba. 3:2.

Mercy exalteth itself above judgment. Jas. 2:13.

Wrath is in his indignation, and life in his good will. In the evening weeping shall have place, and in the morning gladness. Ps. 29:6 f.

The Lord shall stand up as in the mountain of divisions; He shall be angry as in the valley which is in Gabaon; that he may do his work, his strange work; that he may perform his work, his work is strange to him. Is. 28:21.

The Lord will not cast off forever. For if he hath cast off, he will also have mercy, according to the multitude of his mercies. For he hath not willingly afflicted nor cast off the children of men. Lam. 3:31.

Ah! I will comfort myself over my adversaries; and I will be revenged of my enemies. Is. 1:24.

Say not: I have sinned, and what harm hath befallen me? for the Most High is a patient rewarder. And say not: The mercy of the Lord is great, he will have mercy on the multitude of my sins. For mercy and wrath quickly come from him, and his wrath looketh upon sinners. Ecclus. 5:4. 6 f.

Because sentence is not speedily pronounced against the evil, the children of men commit evils without any fear. Eccles. 8:11.

21. HIS LOVE FOR ALL, EVEN SINNERS

Thou hast mercy on all, because thou canst do all things, and overlookest the sins of men, for the sake of repentance. For thou lovest all things that are, and hatest none of the things which thou hast made: for thou didst not appoint or make anything, hating it. Wis. 11:24 f.

My father and my mother have left me; but the Lord hath taken me up. Ps. 26:10.

In thy mercy thou hast been a leader to the people which thou hast redeemed; and in thy strength thou hast carried them to thy holy habitation. Ex. 15:13.

In the wilderness (as thou hast seen) the Lord thy God hath carried thee, as a man is wont to carry his little son, all the way you have come, until you came to this place. Deut. 1:31.

In his love and in his mercy he redeemed them, and he carried them and lifted them up all the days of old. Is. 63:9.

The Lord thy God in the midst of thee is mighty, he will save: he will rejoice over thee with gladness, he will be silent in his love, he will be joyful over thee in praise. Soph. 3:17.

Thou sparest all, because they are thine, O Lord, who lovest souls. Wis. 11:27.

O how good and sweet is thy Spirit, O Lord, in all things! And therefore thou chastisest them that err, by little and little; and admonishest them, and speakest to them concerning the things wherein they offend; that leaving their wickedness, they may believe in thee, O Lord. Wis. 12:1 f.

Because thou art Lord of all, thou makest thyself gracious to all. Wis. 12:16.

Behold what manner of charity the Father has bestowed upon us, that we should be called and should be the sons of God. 1 John 3:1.

By this hath the charity of God appeared towards us, because God hath sent his only begotten Son into the world, that we may live by him. In this is charity, not as though we had loved God, but because he hath first loved us, and sent his Son to be a propitiation for our sins. In this is the charity of God perfected with us, that we may have confidence in the day of judgment; because as he is, we also are in this world. 1 John 4:9 f., 17.

Give praise, O ye heavens, and rejoice, O earth; ye mountains, give praise with jubilation: because the Lord hath comforted his people, and will have mercy on his poor ones. Is. 49:13.

As one whom the mother caresseth, so will I comfort you, and you shall be comforted in Jerusalem. Is. 66:13.

I will not leave thee, neither will I forsake thee. Heb. 13:5.

I, I myself will comfort you. Is. 51:12.

Can a woman forget her infant, so as not to have pity on the son of her womb? and if she should forget, yet will not I forget thee. Is. 49:15.

Even to your old age I am the same, and to your gray hairs I will carry you: I have made you, and I will bear, I will carry, and I will save. Is. 46:4.

Behold, I have graven thee in my hands. Is. 49:16.

I will feed my sheep: and I will cause them to lie down, saith the Lord God. I will seek that which was lost, and that which was driven away I will bring again: and I will bind up that which was broken, and I will strengthen that which was weak, and that which was fat and strong I will preserve: and I will feed them in judgment. Ez. 34:15 f.

I will draw them with the cords of Adam, with the bands of love. Osee 11:4.

I will deliver them out of the hand of death, I will redeem them from death. O death, I will be thy death; O hell, I will be thy bite. Osee 13:14.

He that toucheth you toucheth the apple of my eye. Zach. 2:8.

God so loved the world as to give his only begotten Son, that whosoever believeth in him may not perish, but may have life everlasting. For God sent not his Son into the world to judge the world, but that the world may be saved by him. John 3:16 f.

As the Father hath loved me, I also have loved you. Abide in my love. John 15:9.

The Father himself loveth you, because you have loved me, and have believed that I came out from God. John 16:27.

God commendeth his charity towards us: because when as yet we were sinners, according to the time, Christ died for us. Rom. 5:8 f.

He that spared not even his own Son, but delivered him up for us all, how hath he not also, with him, given us all things? Rom. 8:32.

22. GOD'S LOVE OF SINNERS

I have loved thee with an everlasting love; therefore have I drawn thee, taking pity on thee. Jer. 31:3.

I will heal their breaches, I will love them freely; for my wrath is turned away from them. Osee 14:5.

I am, I am he that blot out thy iniquities for my own sake, and I will not remember thy sins. Is. 43:25.

For my name's sake I will remove my wrath far off: and for my praise I will bridle thee, lest thou shouldst perish. Is. 48:9.

Even so there shall be joy in heaven upon one sinner that doth penance. more than upon ninety-nine just who need not penance. Luke 15:7.

23. GOD WILLS ALL MEN TO BE SAVED

He will have all men to be saved, and to come to the knowledge of the truth. 1 Tim. 2:4.

This is the will of the Father who sent me: that of all that he hath given me I should lose nothing, but should raise it up again in the last day. And this is the will of my Father that sent me: that every one who seeth the Son, and believeth in him, may have life everlasting, and I will raise him up in the last day. John 6:39 f.

To him who is able to do all things more abundantly than we desire or understand, according to the power that worketh in us; to him be glory in the Church and in Christ Jesus, unto all generations, world without end. Amen. Eph. 3:20 f.

God was in Christ, reconciling the world to himself. 2 C. 5:19.

24. THE PROVIDENCE OF GOD

He made the little and the great, and he hath equally care of all. Wis. 6:8.

His eyes are upon the ways of men, and he considereth all their steps. Job 34:21.

My lots are in thy hands. Ps. 30:16.

The Lord maketh poor and maketh rich; he humbleth and he exalteth. 1 K. 2:7.

Men and beasts thou wilt preserve, O Lord. Ps. 35:7.

Who covereth the heaven with clouds, and prepareth rain for the earth: who maketh grass to grow on the mountains, and herbs for the service of men. Who giveth to beasts their food: and to the young ravens that call upon him. Ps. 148:6-9.

All expect of thee that thou give them food in season. What thou givest to them they shall gather up: when thou openest thy hand, they shall all be filled with good. But if thou turnest away thy face, they shall be troubled: thou shalt take away their breath, and they shall fail, and shall return to their dust. Ps. 103:27-29.

Every man that eateth and drinketh, and seeth good of his labor, this is the gift of God. Eccles. 3:13.

Good things and evil, life and death, poverty and riches, are from God. Ecclus. 11:14.

The steps of man are guided by the Lord. Prov. 20:24.

The Lord loveth judgment, and will not forsake his saints: they shall be preserved forever. Ps. 36:28.

When I sent you without purse and scrip and shoes, did you want anything? But they said: Nothing. Luke 22:35 f.

Be not solicitous, therefore, saying: What shall we eat, or what shall we drink, or wherewith shall we be clothed? For after all these things do the heathens seek. For your Father knoweth that you have need of all these things. Mat. 6:31 f.

It is he who giveth to all life, and breath, and all things. And hath made of one all mankind, to dwell upon the whole face of the earth, determining appointed times and the limits of their habitation. That they should seek God. Acts 17:25-27.

We know that to them that love God, all things work together unto good to such as according to his purpose are called to be saints. Rom. 8:28.

She (Wisdom) reacheth from end to end mightily, and ordereth all things sweetly. Wis. 8:1.

Fire, hail, snow, ice, stormy winds, fulfil his word. Ps. 148:8.

O Lord, thy mercy is in heaven, and thy truth reacheth even to the clouds. Ps. 35:6.

He commandeth the sun, and it riseth not: and shutteth up the stars as it were under a seal. Job 9:7.

He hath made a decree, and it shall not pass away. Ps. 148:6.

Are not two sparrows sold for a farthing? and not one of them shall fall on the ground without your Father. Mat. 10:29.

Behold the birds of the air, for they neither sow, nor do they reap, nor gather into barns: and your heavenly Father feedeth them. Are not you of much more value than they? Mat. 6:26.

Consider the lilies of the field, how they grow: they labor not, neither do they spin. And if the grass of the field, which is today, and tomorrow is cast into the oven, God doth so clothe: how much more you, O ye of little faith! Mat. 6:28-30.

There is no other God but thou who hast care of all. Wis. 12:13.

Thy providence, O Father, governeth it. Wis. 14:3.

I will visit upon the men that are settled on their lees: that say in their hearts: The Lord will not do good, nor will he do evil. Soph. 1:12.

You have wearied the Lord with your words, and you said: Wherein have we wearied him? In that you say: Every one that doth evil is good in the sight of the Lord, and such please him: or surely where is the God of judgment? Mal. 2:17.

You have said: He laboreth in vain that serveth God, and what profit is it that we have kept his ordinances, and that we have walked sorrowful before the Lord of hosts? Wherefore now we call the proud people happy, for they that work wickedness are built up, and they have tempted God and are preserved. Mal. 3:14 f.

Give not thy mouth to cause thy flesh to sin; and say not before the angel: There is no providence: lest God be angry at thy words, and destroy all the works of thy hands. Eccles. 5:5.

Surely thou seest, O son of man, what the ancients of the house of Israel do in the dark, every one in private in his chamber; for they say: The Lord seeth us not, the Lord hath forsaken the earth. Therefore I also will deal with them in my wrath: my eye shall not spare them, neither will I show mercy: and when they shall cry to my ears with a loud voice, I will not hear them. Ez. 8:12-18.

The iniquity of the house of Israel, and of Juda, is exceeding great, and the land is filled with blood, and the city is filled with perverseness; for they have said: The Lord hath forsaken the earth, and the Lord seeth not. Therefore neither shall my eye spare, nor will I have pity: I will requite their way upon their head. Ez. 9:9 f.

Wherefore hath the wicked provoked God? for he hath said in his heart: He will not require it. Thou seest it, for thou considerest labor and sorrow, that thou mayest deliver them into thy hands. Ps. 9:13 f.

25. PREDESTINATION

He chose us in him before the foundation of the world. He hath predestinated us unto the adoption of children of God. Eph. 1:4 f.

We speak the wisdom of God which God ordained before the world. 1 C. 2:7.

Come, ye blessed of my Father, possess you the kingdom prepared for you from the foundation of the world. Mat. 25:34.

Whom he foreknew, he also predestinated to be made conformable to the image of his Son. Whom he predestinated, them he also called. And whom he called, them he also justified. And whom he justified, them he also glorified. Rom. 8:29 f.

Many are called, but few chosen. Mat. 20:16.

As many as were ordained to life everlasting, believed. Acts 13:48.

Fear not, little flock, for it hath pleased your Father to give you a kingdom. Luke 12:32.

He was taken away, lest wickedness should alter his understanding. Wis. 4:11.

For his soul pleased God. Wis. 4:14.

We know that to them that love God all things work together unto good, to such as according to his purpose are called to be saints. Rom. 8:28.

Unless those days had been shortened, no flesh should be saved; but for the sake of the elect those days shall be shortened. False prophets shall show great signs and wonders, insomuch as to deceive (if possible) even the elect. Mat. 24:22, 24.

So then it is not of him that runneth, but of God that showeth mercy. Rom. 9:16.

If by grace, it is not now by works; otherwise grace is no more grace. Rom. 11:6.

You have not chosen me, but I have chosen you; that you should go, and should bring forth fruit. John 15:16.

The wages of sin is death. But the grace of God, life everlasting. Rom. 6:23.

When the children were not yet born nor had done any good or evil (that the purpose of God according to election might stand), not of works, but of him that calleth, it was said to her: The elder shall serve the younger. As it is written: Jacob I have loved, but Esau I have hated. Rom. 9:11-13.

Hath not the potter power over the clay, of the same lump, to make one vessel unto honor, and another unto dishonor? Rom. 9:21.

Who distinguisheth thee? or what hast thou that thou hast not received? And if thou hast received, why dost thou glory, as if thou hadst not received it? 1 C. 4:7.

My sheep hear my voice: and I know them, and they follow me. John 10:27.

The sure foundation of God standeth firm, having this seal: the Lord knoweth who are his. 2 Tim. 2:19.

That he might show the riches of his glory on the vessels of mercy, which he hath prepared unto glory. Rom. 9:23.

Who then shall separate us from the love of Christ? Shall tribulation? or distress? or famine? or nakedness? or danger? or persecution? or the sword? But in all these things we overcome because of him who hath loved us. For I am sure that neither death, nor life, nor angels, nor principalities, nor powers, nor any other creature shall be able to separate us from the love of God, which is in Christ Jesus our Lord. Rom. 8:35, 37-39.

26. GOD REWARDS MEN ACCORDING TO MERIT

Come, ye blessed of my Father, possess you the kingdom prepared for you from the foundation of the world: For I was hungry, and you gave me to eat. Mat. 25:34 f.

Eye hath not seen, nor ear heard, neither hath it entered into the heart of man, what things God hath prepared for them that love him. 1 C. 2:9

Whatsoever you do, do it from the heart as to the Lord, and not to men; knowing that you shall receive of the Lord the reward of inheritance. Col. 3:23 f.

We are the sons of God, and if sons, heirs also: heirs indeed of God, and joint-heirs with Christ; yet so if we suffer with him, that we may be also glorified with him. Rom. 8:16 f.

I have fought a good fight. As to the rest, there is laid up for me a crown of justice, which the Lord the just Judge will render to me in that day. 2 Tim. 4:8.

He will keep the salvation of the righteous, and protect them that walk in simplicity; keeping the paths of justice, and guarding the ways of saints. Prov. 2:7 f.

I will be to it, saith the Lord, a wall of fire round about; and I will be in glory in the midst thereof. Zach. 2:5.

Sometimes I have been in danger of death for these things, and I have been delivered by the grace of God. The spirit of those that fear God is sought after, and by his regard shall be blessed. For their hope is on him that saveth them, and the eyes of God are upon them that love him. Ecclus. 34:13-15.

If there be no offence of this people in the sight of their God, we cannot resist them, because their God will defend them, and we shall be a reproach to the whole earth. Jdth. 5:25.

Wheresoever they went in without bow and arrow, and without shield and sword, their God fought for them and overcame. And there was no one that triumphed over this people but when they departed from the worship of the Lord their God. Jdth. 5:16 f.

How good is God to Israel to them that are of a right heart! Ps. 72:1

The eyes of the Lord are upon the just, and his ears unto their prayers. But the countenance of the Lord is against them that do evil things, to cut off the remembrance of them from the earth. Ps. 33:16 f.

God will not cast away the simple, nor reach out his hand to the evil doer. Until thy mouth be filled with laughter, and thy lips with rejoicing. They that hate thee shall be clothed with confusion, and the dwelling of the wicked shall not stand. Job 8: 20-22.

27. THE BOOK OF LIFE

Rejoice in this, that your names are written in heaven. Luke 10:20.

They that depart from thee shall be written in the earth. Jer. 17:13.

Let them (the wicked) be blotted out of the book of the living, and with the just let them not be written. Ps. 68:29.

Thy eyes did see my imperfect being, and in thy book all shall be written. Ps. 138:16.

Either forgive them this trespass, or if thou do not, strike me out of the book that thou hast written. He that hath sinned against me, him will I strike out of my book. Ex. 32:32 f.

I wished myself to be an anathema from Christ, for my brethren. Rom. 9:3.

28. REPROBATION

God made not death, neither hath he pleasure in the destruction of the living. Wis. 1:13.

I desire not the death of him that dieth, saith the Lord God: return ye and live. Ez. 18:32.

Destruction is thine own, O Israel: thy help is only in me. Osee 13:9.

They changed the truth of God into a lie, and worshipped and served the creature rather than the Creator. For this cause God delivered them up to shameful affections. As they liked not to have God in their knowledge, God delivered them up to a reprobate sense. Rom. 1:25-28.

Because they received not the love of the truth, that they might be saved, therefore God shall send them the operation of error. 2 Tim. 2:10.

You stiffnecked and uncircumcised in heart and ears, you always resist the Holy Ghost. Acts 7:51.

I called, and you refused. Prov. 1: 24.

How often would I have gathered thy children, as the hen doth gather her chickens under her wings, and thou wouldst not! Mat. 23:37.

Today, if you shall hear his voice, harden not your hearts. Ps. 94:8.

Tribulation and anguish upon every soul of man that worketh evil. Rom. 2:9.

Depart from me, ye cursed, into everlasting fire, which was prepared for the devil and his angels; for I was hungry, and you gave me not to eat. Mat. 25:41.

By one man sin entered into this world, and by sin, death. Rom. 5:12.

By the disobedience of one man many were made sinners. Rom. 5:19.

When the children were not yet born, nor had done any good or evil (that the purpose of God according to election might stand), not of works, but of Him that calleth, it was said to her: The elder shall serve the younger. As it is written: Jacob I have loved, but Esau I have hated. Rom. 9:11-13.

He hath mercy on whom he will; and whom he will he hardeneth. Rom. 9:18.

Hath not the potter power over the clay, of the same lump, to make one vessel unto honor, and another unto dishonor? Rom. 9:21.

God in times past suffered all nations to walk in their own ways. Acts 14:15.

The branches were broken off because of unbelief. Rom. 11:20.

29. THE NUMBER OF THE SAVED

Many are called, but few chosen. Mat. 20:16.

Wide is the gate and broad is the way that leadeth to destruction, and many there are who go in thereat. How narrow is the gate and strait is the way that leadeth to life; and few there are that find it! Mat. 7:13 f.

Strive to enter by the narrow gate: for many, I say to you, shall seek to enter, and shall not be able. Luke 13:24.

Know you not that they that run in the race, all run indeed, but one receiveth the prize? Every one that striveth for the mastery refraineth himself from all things: and they indeed that they may receive a corruptible crown, but we an incorruptible one. 1 C. 9:24 f.

The fruit thereof, that shall be left upon it, shall be as one cluster of grapes and as the shaking of the olive-tree: two or three berries in the top of a bough, or four or five upon the top of the tree, saith the Lord, the God of Israel. Is. 17:6.

In that day the Lord of hosts shall be a crown of glory and a garland of joy to the residue of his people. Is. 28:5.

The soul of my lord shall be kept as in the bundle of the living with the Lord thy God. 1 K. 25:29.

O Lord, divide them from the few of the earth. Ps. 16:14.

He that buildeth his ascension in heaven, and hath founded his bundle upon the earth, the Lord is his name. Amos 9:6.

Fear not, little flock, for it hath pleased your Father to give you a kingdom. Luke 12:32.

There shall come from the east and the west and the north and the south, and shall sit down in the kingdom of God. Luke 13:29.

I saw a great multitude, which no man could number, of all nations, and tribes, and peoples, and tongues; standing before the throne, and in sight of the Lamb, clothed with white robes, and palms in their hands. Apoc. 7:9.

You are come to Mount Sion, and to the city of the living God, the heavenly Jerusalem, and to the company of many thousands of angels. Heb. 12:22.

Thousands of thousands ministered to him, and ten thousand times a hundred thousand stood before him. Dan. 7:10.

Is there any numbering of his soldiers? and upon whom shall not his light arise? Job 25:3.

Thither did the tribes go up, the tribes of the Lord; the testimony of Israel, to praise the name of the Lord. Ps. 121:4.

II

THE MOST BLESSED TRINITY

1. THE TRINITY OF PERSONS

The heavens were opened to him, and he saw the Spirit of God descending as a dove, and coming upon him. And behold a voice from heaven, saying: This is my beloved Son, in whom I am well pleased. Mat. 3:16 f.

Going therefore, teach ye all nations: baptizing them in the name of the Father, and of the Son, and of the Holy Ghost. Mat. 28:19.

The Holy Ghost shall come upon thee, and the power of the Most High shall overshadow thee. And therefore the Holy which shall be born of thee shall be called the Son of God. Luke 1:35.

I will ask the Father, and he shall give you another Paraclete, that he may abide with you forever, the Spirit of truth. But the Paraclete, the Holy Ghost, whom the Father will send in my name, he will teach you all things. John 14:16, 26.

When the Paraclete cometh, whom I will send you from the Father, the Spirit of truth, who proceedeth from the Father, he will give testimony of me. John 15:26.

Jesus being exalted therefore by the right hand of God, and having received of the Father the promise of the Holy Ghost, he hath poured forth this which you see and hear. Acts 2:33.

The grace of our Lord Jesus Christ, and the charity of God, and the communication of the Holy Ghost be with you all. 2 C. 13:13.

Because you are sons, God hath sent the Spirit of his Son into your hearts, crying: Abba, Father. Gal. 4:6.

By the Son we have access both in one Spirit to the Father. Eph. 2:18.

I bow my knees to the Father of our Lord Jesus Christ, of whom all paternity in heaven and earth is named, that he would grant you, according to the riches of glory, to be strengthened by his Spirit with might unto the inward man. Eph. 3:14.

To the elect, according to the foreknowledge of God the Father, unto the sanctification of the Spirit, unto obedience and sprinkling of the blood of Jesus Christ, grace unto you and peace be multiplied. 1 Pet. 1:2.

In this we know that we abide in him and he in us: because he hath given us of his Spirit, and we have seen and do testify that the Father hath sent his Son to be the Savior of the world. 1 John 4:13.

It is the Spirit which testifieth that Christ is the truth. For there are three who give testimony in heaven, the Father, the Word, and the Holy Ghost. And these three are one. 1 John 5:6.

Praying in the Holy Ghost, keep

yourselves in the love of God, waiting for the mercy of our Lord Jesus Christ. Jude 20.

They rested not day and night, saying: Holy, Holy, Holy, Lord God Almighty, who was, and who is, and who is to come. Apoc. 4:8.

2. THE FATHER, TRUE GOD

I ascend to my Father and to your Father, to my God and your God. John 20:17.

This is eternal life: that they may know thee, the only true God, and Jesus Christ, whom thou hast sent. John 17:3.

The Word was with God. John 1:1.

I will bring them back in mercy, for I am a Father to Israel. Jer. 31:9.

From this time call to me: thou art my Father. Jer. 3:4.

Thou, O Lord, art our Father, from everlasting is thy name. Is. 63:16.

O Lord, thou art our Father, and we are clay. Is. 64:8.

Our Father who art in heaven. Mat. 6:9.

Is not he thy Father that had possessed thee, and made thee, and created thee? Deut. 32:6.

You have received the Spirit of adoption of sons, whereby we cry: Abba (Father). Rom. 8:15.

Blessed art thou, O Lord, the God of Israel, our Father from eternity to eternity. 1 Par. 29:10.

3. THE SON, TRUE GOD

The Lord hath said to me: Thou art my Son, this day have I begotten thee. Ps. 2:7.

The Lord said to my Lord: Sit thou at my right hand until I make thy enemies thy footstool. With thee is the principality in the day of thy strength, in the brightness of the saints: from the womb before the daystar I begot thee. Ps. 109:1-3.

Behold, a virgin shall conceive, and bear a Son, and his name shall be called Emmanuel. Is. 7:14.

A child is born to us, and a son is given to us, and the government is upon his shoulder: and his name shall be called Wonderful, Counsellor, God the Mighty, the Father of the world to come, the Prince of peace. Is. 9:6.

God himself will come and will save you; then shall the eyes of the blind be opened, and the ears of the deaf shall be unstopped; then shall the lame man leap as a hart, and the tongue of the dumb shall be free. Is. 35:4-6.

Thus saith the Lord: The labor of Egypt, and the merchandise of Ethiopia and of Sabaim, men of stature shall come over to thee, and shall be thine: they shall walk after thee, they shall go bound with manacles: and they shall worship thee and shall make supplication to thee: only in thee is God, and there is no God besides thee. Verily thou art a hidden God, the God of Israel, the Savior. Is. 45:14 f.

Behold the days come, saith the Lord, and I will raise up to David a just branch; this is the name that they shall call him: The Lord, our just one. Jer. 23:5.

This is our God, and there shall no other be accounted of in comparison of him. He found out all the way of knowledge, and gave it to Jacob his servant, and to Israel his beloved. Afterwards he was seen upon earth, and conversed with men. Bar. 3:36-38.

Jesus being baptized, forthwith came out of the water: and lo, the heavens were opened to him, and he saw the Spirit of God descending as a dove, and coming upon him. And behold a voice from heaven, saying: This is my beloved Son, in whom I am well pleased. Mat. 3:16.

Peter said: Thou art Christ, the Son of the living God. Mat. 16:16.

In the beginning was the Word, and the Word was with God, and the Word was God. The same was in the beginning with God. All things were made by him, and without him was made nothing that was made. John 1:1-3.

God so loved the world as to give his only begotten Son; that whosoever believeth in him may not perish, but may have life everlasting. John 3:16.

The Jews sought to kill Jesus, because he did not only break the Sabbath, but also said God was his Father, making himself equal to God. John 5:18.

Before Abraham was made, I am. John 8:58.

I and the Father are one. John 10:30.

You believe in God; believe also in me. John 14:1.

All things whatsoever the Father hath are mine. John 16:15.

Thomas said to Jesus: My Lord and my God. John 10:28.

The Holy Ghost hath placed you bishops, to rule the Church of God, which he hath purchased with his own blood. Acts 20:28.

Of whom is Christ according to the flesh, who is over all things, God blessed forever. Rom. 9:5.

Neither did I receive the gospel of man, nor did I learn it; but by the revelation of Jesus Christ. Gal. 1:12.

Christ Jesus being in the form of God, thought it not robbery to be equal with God. Phil. 2:6.

In him were all things created in heaven and on earth, visible and invisible, whether thrones, or dominations, or principalities, or powers; all things were created by him and in him. And he is before all, and by him all things consist. Col. 1:16 f.

Who being the brightness of his glory and the figure of his substance: for to which of the angels hath he said at any time: Thou art my Son, today have I begotten thee? Heb. 1:3, 5.

In this we have known the charity of God, because he hath laid down his life for us. 1 John 3:16.

There are three who give testimony in heaven, the Father, the Word, and the Holy Ghost. And these three are one. And we may be in his true Son. This is the true God and life eternal. 1 John 5:7, 20.

Holy, Holy, Holy, Lord God Almighty, who was, and who is, and who is to come. Thou art worthy, O Lord our God, to receive glory, and honor, and power. Apoc. 4:8, 11.

The Lamb shall overcome them, because he is Lord of lords and King of kings. Apoc. 17:14.

4. THE HOLY GHOST, TRUE GOD

Going therefore, teach ye all nations: baptizing them in the name of the Father, and of the Son, and of the Holy Ghost. Mat. 28:19.

Peter said: Ananias, why hath Satan tempted thy heart, that thou shouldst lie to the Holy Ghost? Thou hast not lied to men, but to God. Acts 5:3 f.

Know you not that your members ple of God, and that the Spirit of God dwelleth in you? But if any man violate the temple of God, him shall God destroy. For the temple of God is holy: which you are. 1 C. 3:16 f.

Know you not that your members are the temple of the Holy Ghost, who is in you? Glorify and bear God in your body. 1 C. 6:19 f.

The holy men of God spoke, inspired by the Holy Ghost. 2 Pet. 1:21.

At sundry times and in divers manners God spoke by the prophets. Heb. 1:1.

Take heed to yourselves, and to the whole flock, wherein the Holy Ghost hath placed you bishops, to rule the Church of God. Acts 20:28.

5. THE HOLY GHOST, PROCEEDING FROM THE FATHER AND THE SON

When the Paraclete cometh, whom I will send you from the Father, who proceedeth from the Father, he will give testimony of me. John 15:26.

He (the Holy Spirit) shall glorify me; because he shall receive of mine, and shall show it to you. John 16:14.

He (Jesus) breathed on them, and said to them: Receive ye the Holy Ghost. John 20:22.

You are not in the flesh, but in the spirit, if so be that the Spirit of God dwell in you. Now if any man have not the Spirit of Christ, he is none of his. Rom. 8:9.

All things whatsoever the Father hath are mine. John 16:15.

6. THE EQUALITY, MISSION, AND WORK OF THE THREE PERSONS

What things soever the Father doth, these the Son also doth in like manner. John 5:19.

When the fulness of the time was come, God sent his Son. Gal. 4:4.

Know you not that you are the temple of God, and that the Spirit of God dwelleth in you? 1 C. 3:16.

My doctrine is not mine, but his that sent me. John 7:16.

When they shall deliver you up, take no thought how or what to speak, for it shall be given you in that hour what to speak: for it is not you that speak, but the Spirit of your Father that speaketh in you. Mat. 10:19 f.

The Spirit himself giveth testimony to our spirit, that we are the sons of God. Rom. 8:16.

Let the unction which you have received from him abide in you. And you have no need that any man teach you, but as his unction teacheth you of all things, and is truth, and is no lie. And as it hath taught you, abide in him. 1 John 2:27.

I will give them one heart, and will put a new spirit in their bowels: and I will take away the stony heart out of their flesh, and will give them a heart of flesh: that they may walk in my commandments, and keep my judgments and do them: and that they may be my people, and I may be their God. Ez. 11:19 f.

It shall come to pass after this that I will pour out my Spirit upon all flesh: and your sons and your daughters shall prophesy, your old men shall dream dreams, and your young men shall see visions. Moreover, upon my servants and handmaids in those days I will pour forth my Spirit. Joel 2: 28 f.

There are diversities of graces, but the same Spirit. 1 C. 12:4.

The fruit of the Spirit is charity, joy, peace, patience, benignity, goodness, longanimity, mildness, faith, modesty, continency, chastity. Gal. 5: 22 f.

The Spirit of the Lod shall rest upon him: the Spirit of wisdom and of understanding, the Spirit of counsel and of fortitude, the Spirit of knowledge and of godliness. And he shall be filled with the Spirit of the fear of the Lord. Is. 11:2 f.

III

THE CREATURES OF GOD

1. GOD THE CREATOR

In the beginning God created heaven and earth. Gen. 1:1.

Be light made. Gen. 1:3.

God saw all the things that he had made, and they were very good. Gen. 1:31.

He made us, and not we ourselves. Ps. 99:3.

I am the Lord, that make all things, that alone stretch out the heavens, that establish the earth, and there is none with me. Is. 44:24.

Thou thyself, O Lord, alone, thou hast made heaven, and the heaven of heavens, and all the host thereof: the earth and all things that are in it: the seas and all that are therein: and thou givest life to all these things, and the host of heaven adoreth thee. 2 Es. 9:6.

Holy, holy, holy, the Lord God of hosts: all the earth is full of his glory. Is. 6:3.

His glory covered the heavens, and the earth is full of his praise. Haba. 3:3.

The works of God are perfect, and all his ways are judgments. Deut. 32:4.

He stretched out the north over the empty space, and hanged the earth upon nothing. Job 26:7.

The heavens show forth the glory of God, and the firmament declareth the work of his hands. Day to day uttereth speech, and night to night showeth knowledge. There are no speeches nor languages where their voices are not heard. Ps. 18:2-4.

In the beginning, O Lord, thou foundedst the earth: and the heavens are the works of thy hands. They shall perish, but thou remainest: and all of them shall grow old like a garment: and as a vesture thou shalt change them, and they shall be changed. But thou art always the selfsame, and thy years shall not fail. Ps. 101:26-28.

Thou hast given me, O Lord, a delight in thy doings: and in the works of thy hands I shall rejoice. Ps. 91:5.

Let all thy works, O Lord, praise thee; and let thy saints bless thee. They shall speak of the glory of thy kingdom, and shall tell of thy power. Ps. 144:10 f.

He set his eye upon their hearts to show the greatness of his works. Ecclus. 17:7.

He that maketh the earth by his power, that prepareth the world by his wisdom, and stretcheth out the heavens by his knowledge. At his voice he giveth a multitude of waters in the heaven, and lifteth up the clouds from the ends of the earth. He maketh lightnings for rain, and bringeth forth the wind out of his treasures. Jer. 10:12 f.

By his magnificence the clouds run hither and thither. Deut. 33:26.

He that liveth forever created all things together. God only shall be justified, and he remaineth an invincible king forever. Who is able to declare his works? For who shall search out his glorious acts? And who shall show forth the power of his majesty? or who shall be able to declare his mercy? Nothing may be taken away, nor added, neither is it possible to find out the glorious works of God. Ecclus. 18:1-5.

In the beginning was the Word, and the Word was with God, and the Word was God. The same was in the beginning with God. All things were made by him, and without him was made nothing that was made. John 1:1-3.

Great and wonderful are thy works, O Lord God Almighty: just and true are thy ways, O King of ages. Apoc. 15:3.

He hath made all things good in their time. Eccles. 3:11.

Lord, thou art he that didst make heaven and earth, the sea, and all things that are in them. Acts 4:24.

Of him, and by him, and in him are all things. Rom. 11:36.

Thy hands have made me and fashioned me wholly round about, and dost thou thus cast me down headlong on a sudden? Remember, I beseech thee, that thou hast made me as the clay, and thou wilt bring me into dust again. Job 10:8 f.

I am the Lord thy God, who trouble the sea, and the waves thereof swell: the Lord of hosts is my name. Is. 51:15.

I will behold thy heavens, the works of thy fingers: the moon and the stars which thou hast founded. Ps. 8:4.

Sing to our God upon the harp, who maketh grass to grow on the mountains, and herbs for the service of men; who giveth to beasts their food, and to the young ravens that call upon him. Ps. 146:8 f.

My Father worketh until now, and I work. John 5:17.

Every best gift, and every perfect gift, is from above, coming down from the Father of lights, with whom there is no change nor shadow of alteration. Jas. 1:17.

2. HIS WORKS PERFECT

I have learned that all the works which God hath made continue forever: we cannot add anything, nor take away from those things which God hath made that he may be feared. Eccles. 3:14.

Nothing may be taken away nor added, neither is it possible to find out the glorious works of God. Ecclus. 18:5.

Thou hast ordered all things in measure, and number, and weight. Wis. 11:21.

The Lord by wisdom hath founded the earth. hath established the heavens by prudence. By his wisdom the depths have broken out, and the clouds grow thick with dew. Prov. 3:19 f.

How great are thy works, O Lord! Thou hast made all things in wisdom; the earth is filled with thy riches. Ps. 103:24.

All wisdom is from the Lord God, and hath been always with him, and is before all time. Wisdom hath been created before all things, and the understanding of prudence from everlasting. He created her in the Holy Ghost, and saw her, and numbered her, and measured her. Ecclus. 1:1, 4, 9.

3. GOD THE RULER AND PRESERVER OF ALL THINGS

He may let loose his hand, and cut me off. Job 6:9.

That which containeth all things hath knowledge of the voice. Wis. 1:7.

How could anything endure, if thou wouldst not? or be preserved, if not called by thee? Wis. 11:26.

In him we live and move and are. Acts 17:28.

By him all things consist. Col. 1:17.

Upholding all things by the word of his power. Heb. 1:3.

Unless the Lord keep the city, he watcheth in vain that keepeth it. Ps. 126:2.

As one keeping a furnace in the works of heat, the sun three times as much burneth the mountains, breathing out fiery vapors, and shining with his beams, he blindeth the eyes. Ecclus. 43:4.

By thy ordinance the day goeth on; for all things serve thee. Ps. 118:91.

4. GOD AS COOPERATOR AND HELPER

My grace is sufficient for thee: for power is made perfect in infirmity. Gladly therefore will I glory in my infirmities, that the power of Christ may dwell in me. For when I am weak, then am I powerful. 2 C. 12:9.

Though our outward man is corrupted, yet the inward man is renewed day by day. 2 C. 4:16.

I can do all things in him who strengtheneth me. Phil. 4:13.

God is faithful, who will strengthen and keep us from evil. 2 Thess. 3:3.

The eyes of the Lord behold all the earth, and give strength to those who with a perfect heart trust in him. 2 Par. 16:9.

The strength of the upright is the way of the Lord. Prov. 10:29.

The Lord is good and giveth strength in the day of trouble, and knoweth them that hope in him. Nah. 1:7.

Fear not, for I am with thee: turn not aside, for I am thy God: I have strengthened thee and have helped thee, and the right hand of my just one hath upheld thee. Is. 41:10.

Not that we are sufficient to think anything of ourselves as of ourselves; but our sufficiency is from God. 2 C. 3:5.

Without me you can do nothing. John 15:5.

It is God who worketh in you both to will and to accomplish. Phil. 2:13.

Our God is our refuge in strength; a helper in troubles. Ps. 45:1.

God is our helper forever. Ps. 61:9.

The Lord strengtheneth the just. Ps. 36:17.

5. GOD AS SAVIOR AND REDEEMER

Save me, O God, by thy name. Ps. 53:3.

He is my God and my Savior. Ps. 61:3.

Behold, God is my Savior. Is. 12:2.

God himself will come and will save you. Is. 35:4.

Truly in the Lord our God is our salvation. Jer. 3:23.

Drop down dew, ye heavens, from above, and let the clouds rain the just: let the earth be opened, and bud forth a Savior: and let justice spring up together: I, the Lord, have created him. Is. 45:8.

Behold, I have given thee to be the light of the Gentiles, that thou mayst be my salvation even to the farthest part of the earth. Is. 49:6.

Unto you that fear my name the sun of justice shall arise, and health in his wings. Mal. 4:2.

This is the way, walk ye in it: and go not aside, neither to the right hand nor to the left. Is. 30:21.

Being consummated, he became the cause of eternal salvation to all that obey him. Heb. 5:9.

6. THE GOOD ANGELS

In him were all things created in heaven and on earth, visible and invisible, whether thrones or dominations. Col. 1:16.

Thou wast the seal of resemblance, full of wisdom and perfect in beauty. Ez. 28:12.

It came to pass that night that an angel of the Lord came, and slew in the camp of the Assyrians a hundred and eighty-five thousand. 4 K. 19:35.

The angel of the Lord having found Agar, said to her: Agar, handmaid of Sarai, whence comest thou? and whither goest thou? And she answered: I flee from the face of Sarai, my mistress. And the angel of the Lord said to her: Return to thy mistress, and humble thyself under her hand. I will multiply thy seed exceedingly, and it shall not be numbered for multitude. Gen. 16:7-10.

The Lord opened the eyes of Balaam, and he saw the angel standing in the way with a drawn sword; and he worshipped him, falling flat on the ground. Num. 22:31.

When Josue was in the field of the city of Jericho, he saw a man standing over against him, holding a drawn sword; and he went to him and said: Art thou one of ours, or of our adversaries? And he answered: No; but I am prince of the host of the Lord, and now I am come. Josue fell on his face to the ground; and worshipping said: What saith my Lord to his servant? Jos. 5:13-15.

Bless the Lord, all ye his angels: you that are mighty in strength, and execute his word, hearkening to the voice of his orders. Ps. 102:20.

O Lord my God, who makest thy angels spirits, and thy ministers a burning fire. Ps. 103:4.

Praise ye him, all his angels: praise ye him, all his hosts. Ps. 148:2.

Thousands of thousands ministered to him, and ten thousand times a hundred thousand stood before him. Dan. 7:10.

I am the angel Raphael, one of the seven who stand before the Lord. When I was with you, I was there by the will of God. I seemed indeed to eat and to drink with you: but I use an invisible meat and drink, which cannot be seen by men. It is time therefore that I return to him that sent me. And when he had said these things he was taken from their sight, and they could see him no more. Tob. 12:15, 18-21.

In the sixth month, the angel Gabriel was sent to a virgin espoused to a man whose name was Joseph. Luke 1:26.

Behold, an angel of the Lord stood by them (shepherds), and the brightness of God shone round about them. And the angel said to them: Behold, I bring you good tidings of great joy, For this day is born to you a Savior. And suddenly there was with the angel a multitude of the heavenly army, praising God, and saying: Glory to God in the highest: and on earth peace to men of good will. Luke 2:9 f., 13 f.

To which of the angels said he at any time: Sit on my right hand, until I make thy enemies thy footstool? Are they not all ministering spirits, sent to minister for them who shall receive the inheritance of salvation? Heb. 1:13 f.

You are come to the company of many thousands of angels. Heb. 12:22.

Christ being gone into heaven, the angels and powers and virtues being made subject to him. 1 Pet. 3:22.

I beheld, and I heard the voice of many angels round about the throne, and the living creatures and the ancients; and the number of them was thousands of thousands, saying with a loud voice: The Lamb that was slain is worthy to receive power and divinity and wisdom and strength and honor and glory and benediction. Apoc. 5:11 f.

God placed before the Paradise of pleasure cherubims, and a flaming sword, turning every way, to keep the way of the tree of life. Gen. 3:24.

I saw the Lord sitting upon a throne high and elevated: and his train filled the temple. Upon it stood the seraphims: the one had six wings, and the other had six wings: with two they covered his face, and with two they covered his feet, and with two they flew. And they cried one to another, and said: Holy, holy, holy, the Lord God of hosts. Is. 6:1.

Michael, one of the chief princes, came to help me. Dan. 10:13.

God the Father, raising Christ up from the dead, and setting him on his right hand in the heavenly places, above all principality, and power, and virtue, and dominion, and every name that is named not only in this world, but also in that which is to come. Eph. 1:20 f.

In him were all things created in heaven and on earth, visible and invisible, whether thrones, or dominations or principalities, or powers: all things were created by him and in him. Col. 1:16.

Being gone into heaven, the angels and powers and virtues are made subject to him. 1 Pet. 3:22.

When Michael the archangel, disputing with the devil, contended about the body of Moses, he durst not bring against him the judgment of reviling, but said: The Lord command thee. Jude 9.

Bless the Lord, all ye his hosts: you ministers of his that do his will. Ps. 102:21.

I will encompass my house with them that serve me in war, going and returning, and the oppressor shall no more pass through them. Zach. 9:8.

My angel shall go before thee, and shall bring thee in unto the Amorrhite. Ex. 23:23.

The angel of the Lord shall encamp round about them that fear him, and shall deliver them. Ps. 33:8

The angel of his presence saved them. Ps. 63:9.

My God hath sent his angel and hath shut up the mouths of the lions, and they have not hurt me. Dan. 6:22.

An angel of God, whose I am and whom I serve, stood by me this night. Acts 27:23.

It came to pass that the beggar died, and was carried by the angels into Abraham's bosom. Luke 16:22.

He hath given his angels charge over thee, to keep thee in all thy ways. In their hands they shall bear thee up, lest thou dash thy foot against a stone. Ps. 90:11 f.

See that you despise not one of these little ones: for I say to you, that their angels in heaven always see the face of my Father who is in heaven. Mat. 18:10.

My angel is with you. Bar. 6:6.

It is his angel. Acts 12:15.

Are they not all ministering spirits, sent to minister for them who shall receive the inheritance of salvation? Heb. 1:14.

There was a great battle in heaven: Michael and his angels fought with the dragon; and the dragon fought, and his angels: And they prevailed not, neither was their place found any more in heaven. And that great dragon was cast out, that old serpent, who is called the devil and Satan, who seduceth the whole world: and he was cast unto the earth, and his angels were thrown down with him. Apoc. 12:7-9.

Behold I will send my angel, who shall go before thee, and keep thee in thy journey, and bring thee into the place that I have prepared. Take notice of him, and heed his voice, and do not think him one to be contemned: for he will not forgive when thou hast sinned, and my name is in him. But if thou wilt hear his voice, and do all that I speak, I will be an enemy to thy enemies, and will afflict them that afflict thee. Ex. 23:20-22.

Behold a man wrestled with Jacob till morning, and said to him: Let me go, for it is break of day. He answered: I will not let thee go, except thou bless me. Gen. 32:24.

The angel that delivereth me from all evils, bless these boys: and let my name be called upon them. Gen. 48:16.

The Lord opened the eyes of Balaam, and he saw the angel standing in the way with a drawn sword; and he worshipped him, falling flat on the ground. Num. 22:31.

When Josue was in the field of the city of Jericho, he lifted up his eyes, and saw a man standing over against him, holding a drawn sword; and he went to him, and said: Art thou one of ours, or of our adversaries? And he answered: No; but I am prince of the host of the Lord, and now I am come. Josue fell on his face to the ground; and worshipping said: What saith my Lord to his servant? Loose, saith he, thy shoes from off thy feet, for the place whereon thou standest is holy. And Josue did as was commanded him. Jos. 5:13-16.

The angel of the Lord stood by the treshingfloor of Ornan the Jebusite. David, lifting up his eyes, saw the angel of the Lord standing between heaven and earth, with a drawn sword in his hand, turned against Jerusalem: and both he and the ancients clothed in haircloth fell down flat on the ground. 1 Par. 21:15 f.

Call now if there be any that will answer thee, and turn to some of the saints. Job 5:1.

In the womb Jacob supplanted his brother, and by his strength he had success with an angel; and he prevailed over the angel, and was strengthened: he wept, and made supplication to him: he found him in Bethel, and there he spoke with us. Osee 12:3 f.

The angel of the Lord answered and said: O Lord of hosts, how long wilt thou not have mercy on Jerusalem, and on the cities of Juda, with which thou hast been angry? This is now the seventieth year. And the Lord answered the angel that spoke in me, good words, comfortable words. Zach. 1:11 f.

The holy angel of the Lord be with you in your journey, and bring you through safe. Tob. 10:11.

The angel said to Tobias: When thou didst pray with tears, I offered thy prayer to the Lord. Tob. 12:12.

There shall be joy before the angels of God upon one sinner doing penance. Luke 15:10.

I saw seven angels standing in the presence of God; and there were given to them seven trumpets. And another angel came, and stood before the altar, having a golden censer: and there was given to him much incense, that he should offer of the prayers of all saints upon the golden altar, which is before the throne of God. And the smoke of the incense of the prayers of the saints ascended up before God from the hand of the angel. Apoc. 8:2-4.

7. THE BAD ANGELS

He (Behemoth) is the beginning of the ways of God. Job 40:14.

Thou wast in the pleasures of the Paradise of God: every precious stone was thy covering. Ez. 28:13.

His tail drew the third part of the stars of heaven. Apoc. 12:4.

God spared not the angels that sinned: but delivered them, drawn down by infernal ropes to the lower hell. unto torments, to be reserved unto judgment. 2 Pet. 2:4.

The angels who kept not their principality, but forsook their own habitation, he hath reserved under darkness in everlasting chains unto the judgment of the great day. Jude 6.

I saw Satan like lightning falling from heaven. Luke 10:18.

How art thou fallen from heaven, O Lucifer, who didst rise in the morning! how art thou fallen to the earth, that didst wound the nations! Is. 14:12.

Behold, they that serve him are not steadfast, and in his angels he found wickedness. Job 4:18.

The devil, who seduced them, was cast into the pool of fire and brimstone. Apoc. 20:9.

The devil said to him: All these will I give thee, if falling down thou wilt adore me. Mat. 4:9.

He beholdeth every high thing, he is king over all the children of pride. Job 41:25.

By the envy of the devil death came into the world: and they follow him that are of his side. Wis. 2:24.

The spirits besought him, saying: Send us into the swine, that we may enter into them. Mark 5:12.

When an unclean spirit is gone out of a man, he walketh through dry places seeking rest, and findeth none. Mat. 12:43.

He sleepeth under the shadow, in the covert of the reed, and in moist places. Job 40:16.

He was a murderer from the beginning, and he stood not in the truth, because truth is not in him. When he speaketh a lie, he speaketh of his own, for he is a liar, and the father thereof. John 8:44.

I will go forth, and be a lying spirit in the mouth of all his prophets. And the Lord said: Thou shalt deceive him, and shalt prevail; go forth and do so. 3 K. 22:22.

The devil led him [Christ] into a high mountain, and showed him all the kingdoms of the world in a moment of time. And he said to him: To thee will I give all this power, and the glory of them: for to me they are delivered, and to whom I will, I give them. If thou therefore wilt adore before me, all shall be thine. Luke 4:5-7.

Doth Job fear God in vain? Hast not thou made a fence for him and his house, and all his substance round about, blessed the works of his hands, and his possession hath increased on the earth? But stretch forth thy hand a little and touch all that he hath, and see if he blesseth thee not to thy face. Then the Lord said to Satan: Behold, all that he hath is in thy hand: only put not forth thy hand upon his person. Job 1:9-12.

No, you shall not die the death: for God doth know that in what day soever you shall eat thereof, your eyes shall be opened: and you shall be as gods, knowing good and evil. Gen. 3:45.

The dragon stood before the woman who was ready to be delivered, that, when she should be delivered, he might devour her Son. Apoc. 12:4.

Woe to the sea, because the devil is come down unto you, having great wrath, knowing that he hath but a short time! And when the dragon saw that he was cast unto the earth, he persecuted the woman who brought forth the man-child. Apoc. 12:12 f.

The serpent cast out of his mouth, after the woman, water as it were a river, that he might cause her to be carried away by the river. Apoc. 12:15.

They may recover themselves from the snares of the devil, by whom they are held captive at his will. 2 Tim. 2:26.

The dragon was angry against the woman, and went to make war with the rest of her seed, who keep the commandments of God, and have the testimony of Jesus Christ. Apoc. 12:17.

Your adversary the devil, as a roaring lion, goeth about seeking whom he may devour. 1 Pet. 5:8.

The devil put into the heart of Judas Iscariot to betray Jesus. John 13:2.

Behold, the devil will cast some of you into prison, that you may be tried: and you shall have tribulation ten days. Apoc. 2:10.

We would have come unto you, I Paul indeed, both once and again; but Satan hath hindered us. 1 Thess. 2:18.

Why hath Satan tempted thy heart, that thou shouldst lie to the Holy Ghost, and by fraud keep part of the price of the land? Acts 5:3.

The devil cometh, and taketh the word out of their heart, lest believing they should be saved. Luke 8:12.

When he was come on the other side of the water, into the country of the Gerasens, there met him two that were possessed with devils, coming out of the sepulchers, exceeding fierce, so that none could pass by that way. Mat. 8:28.

The Lord showed me Jesus the high priest standing before the angel of the Lord: and Satan stood on his right hand, to be his adversary. Zach. 3:1.

I have gone round about the earth, and walked through it. Job 1:7.

Satan went forth from the presence of the Lord, and struck Job with a very grievous ulcer from the sole of the foot even to the top of his head: and he took a potsherd and scraped the corrupt matter, sitting on a dunghill. Job 2:7.

Satan rose up against Israel, and moved David to number Israel. 1 Par. 21:1.

Behold, Satan hath desired to have you, that he may sift you as wheat. Luke 22:31.

You when you were dead in your offences and sins, wherein in time past you walked according to the course of this world, of the spirit that now worketh on the children of unbelief, were by nature children of wrath. Eph. 2:1 f.

The serpent said to the woman: Why hath God commanded you that you should not eat of every tree of Paradise? Gen. 3:1.

When the thousand years shall be finished, Satan shall be loosed out of his prison, and shall go forth, and seduce the nations. Apoc. 20:7.

If our gospel be also hid, it is hid to them that are lost; in whom the god of this world hath blinded the minds of unbelievers, that the light of the gospel of the glory of Christ, who is the image of God, should not shine unto them. 2 C. 4:3 f.

Satan himself transformeth himself into an angel of light. 2 C. 11:14.

If thou be the Son of God, cast thyself down; for it is written: That he hath given his angels charge over thee, and in their hands shall they bear thee up, lest perhaps thou dash thy foot against a stone. Mat. 4:6.

Behold, a black horse, and he that sat on him had a pair of scales in his hand. Apoc. 6:5.

There is no power upon earth that can be compared with him who was made to fear no one. Job 41:24.

Thou hast moved me against him, that I should afflict him without cause. Job 2:3.

The Lord said to Satan: The Lord rebuke thee, O Satan, and the Lord that chose Jerusalem rebuke thee: is not this a brand pluckt out of the fire? Zach. 3:2.

See thou hurt not the wine and the oil. Apoc. 6:6.

The Lord said to Satan: Behold, all that he hath is in thy hand: only put not forth thy hand upon his person. And Satan went forth from the presence of the Lord. Job 1:12.

They besought him that he would not command them to go into the abyss. There was there a herd of many swine feeding on the mountain; and they besought him that he would suffer them to enter into them. And he suffered them. Luke 8:31 f.

That wicked one shall be revealed whose coming is according to the working of Satan, in all power, and signs, and lying wonders, and in all seduction of iniquity to them that perish: because they received not the love of the truth that they might be saved. Therefore God shall send them the operation of error, to believe lying, that all may be judged who have not believed the truth, but have consented to iniquity. 2 Thess. 2:9-11.

There shall arise false Christs and false prophets, and shall show great signs and wonders, insomuch as to deceive (if possible) even the elect. Mat. 24:24.

The dragon gave him his own strength and great power. Apoc. 13:2.

The magicians with their enchantments practised in like manner to bring forth sciniphs, as well on men as on beasts. Ex. 8:18.

There are spirits that are created for vengeance, and in their fury they lay on grievous torments; in the time of destruction they shall pour out their force, and they shall appease the wrath of him that made them. Ecclus. 39: 33 f.

I hear that she hath been given to seven husbands, and they all died: moreover, I have heard that a devil killed them. Tob. 6:14.

He sent upon them the wrath of his indignation: indignation and wrath and trouble, which he sent by evil angels. Ps. 77:49.

8. THE BODY OF MAN

The Lord God formed man of the slime of the earth. Gen. 2:7.

Seeing I have once begun, I will speak to my Lord, whereas I am dust and ashes. Gen. 18:27.

Thy hands have made me, and fashioned me wholly round about; and dost thou thus cast me down headlong on a sudden? Remember, I beseech thee, that thou hast made me as the clay, and thou wilt bring me into dust again. Job 10:8 f.

He remembered that they are flesh: a wind that goeth and returneth not. Ps. 77:39.

Woe to him that gainsayeth his Maker, a sherd of the earthern pots! Shall the clay say to him that fashioneth it: What art thou making, and thy work is without hands? Is. 45:9.

The voice of one saying: Cry. And I said: What shall I cry? All flesh is grass, and all the glory thereof as the flower of the field. The grass is withered, and the flower is fallen, because the Spirit of the Lord hath blown upon it. Indeed, the people is grass: the grass is withered and the flower is fallen; but the word of our Lord endureth forever. Is. 40:6-8.

Hast thou not milked me as milk, and curdled me like cheese? Thou hast clothed me with skin and flesh: thou hast put me together with bones and sinews. Job 10:10 f.

We know, if our earthly house of this habitation be dissolved, that we have a building of God, a house not made with hands, eternal in heaven. 2 C. 5:1.

We have this treasure in earthen vessels. 2 C. 4:7.

Behold, they shall be as nothing. Is. 41:12.

Why is earth and ashes proud? Ecclus. 10:9.

He knoweth our frame, he remembereth that we are dust: Man's days are as grass, as the flower of the field so shall he flourish. Ps. 102:14 f.

Against a leaf, that is carried away with the wind, thou showest thy power, and thou pursuest a dry straw. Job 13:25.

He cometh forth like a flower, and is destroyed, and fleeth as a shadow, and never continueth in the same state. Job 14:2.

In the morning man shall grow up like grass, in the morning he shall flourish and pass away; in the evening he shall fall, grow dry, and wither. Ps. 89:6.

All men have one entrance into life, and the like going out. Wis. 7:6.

All things cannot be in men, because the son of man is not immortal, and they are delighted with the vanity of evil. Ecclus. 17:29.

God created man of the earth, and made him after his own image. And he turned him into it again, and clothed him with strength according to himself. Ecclus. 17:1.

All things that are of the earth shall return into the earth; so the ungodly shall from malediction to destruction. Ecclus. 41:13.

In his angels he found wickedness. How much more shall they that dwell in houses of clay, who have an earthly foundation, be consumed as with the moth! Job 4:18 f.

All flesh shall perish together, and man shall return into ashes. Job 34:15.

In the sweat of thy face shalt thou eat bread till thou return to the earth, out of which thou wast taken: for dust thou art, and into dust thou shalt return. Gen. 3:19.

The spirit shall pass in him, and he shall not be: and he shall know his place no more. Ps. 102:16.

Thou hast considered the steps of my feet, who am to be consumed as rottenness, and as a garment that is moth-eaten. Job 13:28.

9. THE SOUL OF MAN

The souls of the just are in the hand of God, and the torment of death shall not touch them. In the sight of the unwise they seemed to die, and their departure was taken for misery, and their going away from us for utter destruction: but they are in peace. And though in the sight of men they suffered torments, their hope is full of immortality. Wis. 3:1-4.

Fear ye not them that kill the body, and are not able to kill the soul; but rather fear him that can destroy both soul and body in hell. Mat. 10:28.

Let us make man to our image and likeness. Gen. 1:26.

These things they thought, and were deceived; for their own malice blinded them. And they knew not the secrets of God, nor hoped for the wages of justice, nor esteemed the honor of holy souls. Wis. 2:21 f.

What doth it profit a man if he gain the whole world, and suffer the loss of his own soul? Or what exchange shall a man give for his soul? Mat. 16:26.

10. MAN'S CONDITION BEFORE AND AFTER THE FALL

God made not death, neither hath he pleasure in the destruction of the living. For he created all things that they might be: and he made the nations of the earth for health: and there is no poison of destruction in them, nor kingdom of hell upon the earth. For justice is perpetual and immortal. But the wicked with works and words have called it to them, and esteeming it a friend have fallen away, and have made a covenant with it, because they are worthy to be of the part thereof. Wis. 1:13-16.

God created man incorruptible, and to the image of his own likeness he made him. Wis. 2:23.

By the envy of the devil death came into the world: and they follow him that are of his side. Wis. 2:24 f.

It is not in man's power to stop the spirit, neither has he power in the day of death, neither is he suffered to rest when war is at hand, neither shall wickedness save the wicked. Eccles. 8:8.

I know that thou wilt deliver me to death, where a house is appointed for every one that liveth. Job 30:23.

We all die, and like waters that return no more we fall down into the earth: neither will God have a soul to perish, but recalleth, meaning that he that is cast off should not altogether perish. 2 K. 14:14.

It is appointed unto men once to die, and after this the judgment. Heb. 9:27.

There is no man that liveth always, or that hopeth for this: a living dog is better than a dead lion. Eccles. 9:4.

Who is the man that shall live, and not see death? that shall deliver his soul from the hand of hell? Ps. 88:49.

Thou hast appointed his bounds, which cannot be passed. Job 14:5.

A mountain falling cometh to naught, and a rock is removed out of its place. Waters wear away the stones, and with inundation the ground by little and little is washed away: so in like manner thou shalt destroy man. Job 14:18 f.

11. THE CONDITION OF LABOR, PAYMENT, AND WAGES

The Lord God took man, and put him into the Paradise of pleasure, to dress it and to keep it. Gen. 2:15.

In the sweat of thy face shalt thou eat bread till thou return to the earth, out of which thou wast taken. And the Lord God sent him out of the Paradise of pleasure to till the earth from which he was taken. Gen. 3:19, 23.

Arise, then, and be doing, and the Lord will be with thee. 1 Par. 22:16.

If thou be dilligent, thy harvest shall come as a fountain, and want shall flee far from thee. Prov. 6:11.

The hand of the industrious getteth riches. Prov. 10:4.

The soul of them that work shall be made fat. Prov. 13:4.

In much work there shall be abundance; but where there are many words there is oftentimes want. Prov. 14:23.

Be not slothful. Heb. 6:12.

He that stole let him steal no more; but rather let him labor, working with his hand that which is good, that he may have to give to him who is in need. Eph. 4:28.

Whatsoever thy hand is able to do, do it earnestly. Eccles. 9:10.

Hate not laborious works, nor husbandry ordained by the Most High. Ecclus. 7:16.

I have showed you all things, how that so laboring you ought to support the weak. Acts 20:35.

Provide things good, not only in the sight of God, but also in the sight of men. Rom. 12:17.

We entreat you that you use your endeavor to be quiet, that you do your own business, and work with your own hands, as we commanded you; and that you walk honestly towards them that are without; and that you want nothing of any man's. 1 Thess. 4:11.

We labor, working with our own hands. 1 C. 4:12.

Neither did we eat any man's bread for nothing, but in labor and in toil we worked night and day, lest we should be chargeable to any of you. Not as if we had not power; but that we might give ourselves a pattern to you to imitate us. For also, when we were with you, we declared this to you: that if any man will not work, neither let him eat. For we have heard that there are some among you who walk disorderly, working not at all, but curiously meddling. Now we charge them that are such, and beseech them by the Lord Jesus Christ, that working with silence they would eat their own bread. 2 Thess. 3:8-12.

His servants shall serve him. Apoc. 22:3.

Thou shalt not refuse the hire of the needy and the poor, whether he be thy brother, or a stranger that dwelleth with thee in the land, and is within thy gates: But thou shalt pay him the price of his labor, lest he cry against thee to the Lord, and it be reputed to thee for a sin. Deut. 24: 14 f.

If any man hath done any work for thee, immediately pay him his hire, and let not the wages of thy hired servant stay with thee at all. Tob. 4: 15.

He that oppresseth the poor upbraideth his Maker; but he that hath pity on the poor honoreth him. Prov. 14:31.

He that oppresseth the poor, to increase his own riches, shall himself give to one that is richer, and shall be in need. Do no violence to the poor because he is poor, and do not oppress the needy in the gate: because the Lord will judge his cause, and will afflict them that have afflicted his soul. Prov. 22:16, 22 f.

Bow down thy ear cheerfully to the poor, and pay what thou owest, and answer him peaceable words with mildness. Ecclus. 4:8.

He that offereth sacrifice of the goods of the poor is as one that sacrificeth the son in the presence of his father. The bread of the needy is the life of the poor: he that defraudeth them thereof is a man of blood. He that taketh away the bread gotten by sweat is like him that killeth his neighbor. He that sheddeth blood, and he that defraudeth the laborer of his hire, are brothers. Ecclus. 34:24-27.

The Lord will not accept any person against a poor man, and he will hear the prayer of him that is wronged. Ecclus. 35:16.

Go to now, ye rich men, weep and howl in your miseries which shall come upon you. Your riches are corrupted, and your garments are moth-eaten. Your gold and silver is cankered: and the rust of them shall be for a testimony against you, and shall eat your flesh like fire. You have stored up to yourselves wrath against the last days. Behold the hire of the laborers, who have reaped down your fields, which by fraud has been kept back by you, crieth: and the cry of them hath entered into the ears of the Lord of sabaoth. Jas. 5:1-4.

To Adam he said: Because thou hast hearkened to the voice of thy wife, and hast eaten of the tree, whereof I commanded thee that thou shouldst not eat, cursed is the earth in thy work; with labor and toil shalt thou eat thereof all the days of thy life. Gen. 3:17.

Six days shalt thou labor, and shalt do all thy works. Ex. 20:9.

Anna his wife went daily to weaving work, and she brought home what she could get for their living by the labor of her hands. Tob. 2:19.

Thou shalt eat the labor of thy hands: blessed art thou, and it shall be well with thee. Ps. 127:2.

Go to the ant, O sluggard, and consider her ways, and learn wisdom; which, although she hath no guide, nor master, nor captain, provideth her meat for herself in the summer, and gathereth her food in the harvest. Prov. 6:6-8.

Where there are no oxen the crib is empty; but where there is much corn, there the strength of the ox is manifest. Prov. 14:4.

Solomon praises the valiant woman, saying: She hath sought wool and flax, and hath wrought by the counsel of her hands. And she hath risen in the night, and given a prey to her household, and victuals to her maidens. She hath looked well to the paths of her house, she hath not eaten her bread idle. Prov. 31:13, 15, 27.

Sleep is sweet to a laboring man, whether he eat little or much; but the fulness of the rich will not suffer him to sleep. Eccles. 5:11.

Better is the poor man's fare under a roof of boards than sumptuous cheer abroad in another man's house. Ecclus. 29:28.

The lord of the vineyard paid the hire of the laborers. Mat. 20:8.

Christ, seeing his disciples laboring in rowing, came to them on the sea. Mark. 6:48.

Simon Peter said to them [Nathanael and the sons of Zebedee]: I go a fishing. They say to him: We also come with thee. And they went forth and entered into the ship. They caught nothing. (Christ manifested himself to his disciples while they were laboring.) John 21:3, 6.

Paul came to Corinth, and, finding a certain Jew named Aquila, with Priscilla his wife, he came to them. Because he was of the same trade he remained with them, and wrought: (now they were tent-makers by trade,). Acts 18:2 f.

You yourselves know: for such things as were needful for me and them that are with me these hands have furnished. Acts 20:34.

We are fools for Christ's sake, but you are wise in Christ: we are weak, but you are strong: you are honorable, but we without honor. Even unto this hour we both hunger and thirst, and are naked, and are buffeted, and have no fixed abode. And we labor, working with our own hands. 1 C. 4: 10-12.

You remember, brethren, our labor and toil: working night and day lest we should be chargeable to any of you, we preached among you the gospel of God. 1 Thess. 2:9.

The Lord appeared to Isaac and said: Go not down into Egypt, but stay in the land that I shall tell thee. And sojourn in it, and I will be with thee, and will bless thee: for to thee and to thy seed I will give all these countries, to fulfil the oath which I swore to Abraham thy father. Gen. 26:2 f.

Isaac sowed in that land, and he found that same year a hundredfold: and the Lord blessed him. And the man was enriched, and he went on prospering and increasing till he became exceeding great. Gen. 26:12 f.

Laban said to Jacob: Let me find favor in thy sight. I have learned by experience that God hath blessed me for thy sake. Gen. 30:27.

Remember the Lord thy God, that he hath given thee strength, that he might fulfil his covenant, concerning which he swore to thy fathers, as this present day showeth. Deut. 8:18.

The Lord blessed the latter end of Job more than his beginning. And he had fourteen thousand sheep, and six thousand camels, and a thousand yoke of oxen, and a thousand she-asses. Job 42:12.

The blessing of the Lord maketh men rich; neither shall affliction be joined to them. Prov. 10:22.

In the morning sow thy seed, and in the evening let not thy hand cease: for thou knowest not which may rather spring up, this or that; and if both together, it shall be the better. Eccles. 11:6.

Thou shalt not muzzle the ox that treadeth out thy corn on the floor.

Hurt not the servant that worketh faithfully nor the hired man that giveth thee his life. Ecclus. 7:22.

Thou shalt not calumniate thy neighbor, nor oppress him by violence. The wages of him that hath been hired by thee shall not abide with thee until the morning. Lev. 19:13.

Woe to him that buildeth up his house by injustice, and his chambers not in judgment: that will oppress his friend without cause, and will not pay him his wages! Jer. 23:13.

I will come to you in judgment, and will be a speedy witness against sorcerers, and adulterers, and false swearers, and them that oppress the hireling in his wages, the widows, and the fatherless: and oppress the stranger, and have not feared me, saith the Lord of hosts. Mal. 3:5.

The workman is worthy of his meat. Mat. 10:10.

The laborer is worthy of his hire. Luke 10:7.

He that tilleth his land shall be satisfied with bread. Prov. 12:11.

It is written in the law of Moses: Thou shalt not muzzle the mouth of the ox that treadeth out the corn. 1 C. 9:9.

Thou shalt not muzzle the ox that treadeth out the corn; and the laborer is worthy of his reward. 1 Tim. 5:18.

Prepare thy work without, and diligently till thy ground, that afterwards thou mayst build thy house. Prov. 24:27.

He that tilleth his ground shall be filled with bread. Prov. 28:19.

Better is the poor man that provideth for himself than he that is glorious and wanteth bread. Prov. 12:9.

He that tilleth his land shall make a high heap of corn, and he that worketh justice shall be exalted. Ecclus. 20:30.

We beseech you, brethren, to know them that labor among you; and we admonish you that you esteem them more abundantly in charity for their work's sake. Have peace with them. 1 Thess. 5:12 f.

The thoughts of the industrious always bring forth abundance. Prov. 21:5.

12. IDLENESS

If any man will not work, neither let him eat. For we have heard there are some among you who walk disorderly, working not at all, but curiously meddling. 2 Thess. 3:10 f.

The hand of the valiant shall bear rule; but that which is slothful shall be under tribute. Prov. 12:24.

He that neglecteth his own way shall die. Prov. 19:16.

Love not sleep, lest poverty oppress thee: open thy eyes, and be filled with bread. Prov. 20:13.

He that followeth idleness shall be filled with poverty. Prov. 28:19.

The slothful hand hath wrought poverty; but the hand of the industrious getteth riches. Prov. 10:4.

He hat pursueth idleness is very foolish. Prov. 12:11.

The way of the slothful is a hedge of thorns. Prov. 15:19.

Slothfulness casteth into a deep sleep, and an idle soul shall suffer hunger. The slothful hideth his hand under his armpit, and will not so much as bring it to his mouth. Prov. 19:15, 24.

Thou wilt sleep a little, thou wilt slumber a little, thou wilt fold thy hands a little to rest: and poverty shall come to thee as a runner, and beggary as an armed man. Prov. 24: 33 f.

Linger not in the time of distress. Ecclus. 10:29.

Every sluggard is always in want. Prov. 21:5.

Because of the cold the sluggard would not plow: he shall beg therefore in the summer, and it shall not be given him. Prov. 20:4.

Idleness hath taught much evil. Ecclus. 33:29.

Thou wicked and slothful servant. Take ye away, therefore, the talent from him, and give to him that hath ten talents. And the unprofitable servant cast ye into the exterior darkness. There shall be weeping and gnashing of teeth. Mat. 25:26, 28, 30.

Become not slothful, but followers of them who through faith and patience shall inherit the promises. Heb. 6:12.

Withal, being idle, they learn to go about from house to house: and are not only idle, but tattlers also, and busybodies, speaking things which they ought not. 1 Tim. 5:13.

(God foretold through his prophet Aggeus that many evils would befall his people because they had not labored to rebuild the temple.) Agg. 1:10.

13. MAN'S MANY MISERIES

Man is born to labor and the bird to fly. Job 5:7.

The life of man upon earth is a warfare, and his days are like the days of a hireling. Job 7:1.

Man born of a woman, living for a short time, is filled with many miseries. Job 14:1.

All his days are full of sorrows and miseries; even in the night he doth not rest in mind: and is not this vanity? Eccles. 2:23.

Great labor is created for all men, and a heavy yoke is upon the children of Adam, from the day of their coming out of their mother's womb until the day of their burial into the mother of all. Their thoughts, and fears of the heart, their imagination of things to come, and the day of their end: From him that sitteth on a glorious throne unto him that is humbled in earth and ashes. Ecclus. 40:1-3.

14. MAN'S IGNORANCE

My foolish people have not known me; they are foolish and senseless children: they are wise to do evils, but to do good they have no knowledge. Jer. 4:22.

The lips of the just teach many; but they that are ignorant shall die in the want of understanding. Prov. 10:21.

There is a time and opportunity for every business, and great affliction for man: because he is ignorant of things past, and things to come he cannot know by any messenger. Eccles. 8: 6 f.

A man cannot tell what hath been before him: and what shall be after him, who can tell him? Eccles. 10:14.

As thou knowest not what is the way of the spirit, nor how the bones are joined together in the womb of her that is with child; so thou knowest not the works of God, who is the maker of all. Eccles. 11:5.

The thoughts of mortal men are fearful, and our counsels uncertain. Wis. 9:14.

Boast not for tomorrow, for thou knowest not what the day to come may bring forth. Prov. 27:1.

There are just men and wise men, and their works are in the hand of God; and yet man knoweth not whether he be worthy of love or hatred. But all things are kept uncertain for the time to come, because all things equally happen to the just and to the wicked, to the good and to the evil, to the clean and to the unclean, to him that offereth victims and to him that despiseth sacrifices, As the good is, so also is the sinner: as the perjured, so he also that sweareth truth. This is a very great evil among all things that are done under the sun, that the same things happen to all men: whereby also the hearts of the children of men are filled with evil and with contempt while they live, and afterwards they shall be brought down to hell. The race is not to the swift, nor the battle to the strong, nor bread to the wise, nor riches to the learned, nor favor to the skilful; but time and chance in all. Eccles. 9:1-3, 11.

Behold, now, you that say: Today or tomorrow we will go into such a city, and there we will spend a year, and will traffic, and make our gain. Whereas you know not what shall be on the morrow. Jas. 4:13 f.

It is not for you to know the times or moments, which the Father hath put in his own power. Acts 1:7.

What I do thou knowest not now, but thou shalt know hereafter. John 13:7.

They that are ignorant shall die in the want of understanding. Prov. 10:21.

The ox knoweth his owner, and the ass his master's crib; but Israel hath not known me, and my people hath not understood. Is. 1:3.

My people is led away captive, because they had not knowledge. Is. 5:13.

The priests did not say: Where is the Lord? And they that held the law knew me not. Jer. 2:8.

The heart is perverse above all things and unsearchable. Who can know it? Jer. 17:9.

My people have been silent, because they had no knowledge; because thou hast rejected knowledge I will reject thee, that thou shalt not do the office of priesthood to me. Osee 4:6.

Father, forgive them, for they know not what they do. Luke 23:34.

Neither me do you know, nor my Father: if you did know me, perhaps you would know my Father also. John 8:19.

He who saith that he knoweth him, and keepeth not his commandments, is a liar, and the truth is not in him. 1 John 2:4.

He that loveth not, knoweth not God. 1 John 4:8.

To know thee is perfect justice; and to know thy justice and thy power is the root of immortality. Wis. 15:3.

15. MAN'S PRONENESS TO EVIL

All things cannot be in men, because the son of man is not immortal, and they are delighted with the vanity of evil. What is brighter than the sun? yet it shall be eclipsed. Or what is more wicked than that which flesh and blood hath invented? and this shall be reproved. He beholdeth the power of the height of heaven: and all men are earth and ashes. Ecclus. 17:29-31.

God seeing that the wickedness of men was great on the earth, and that all the thought of their heart was bent upon evil at all times, it repented him that he had made man on the earth. Gen. 6:5.

The imagination and thought of man's heart are prone to evil from his youth: therefore I will no more destroy every living soul as I have done. Gen. 8:21.

I know that there dwelleth not in me (that is to say, in my flesh) that which is good. For to will is present with me; but to accomplish that which is good I find not. For the good which I will, I do not; but the evil which I will not, that I do. Rom. 7:18 f.

I see another law in my members, fighting against the law of my mind, and captivating me in the law of sin, that is in my members. Rom. 7:23.

With the mind I serve the law of God; but with the flesh, the law of sin. Rom. 7:25.

IV

CHRIST THE REDEEMER

1. THE MESSIAS PROMISED TO THE WORLD

In thy seed shall all the nations of the earth be blessed. Gen. 22:18.

In thy seed all the tribes of the earth shall be blessed. Gen. 28:14.

The scepter shall not be taken away from Juda, nor a ruler from his thigh, till he come that is to be sent, and he shall be the expectation of nations. Gen. 49:10.

Of the fruit of thy womb I will set upon thy throne. Ps. 131:11.

David was a prophet, and knew that God hath sworn to him an oath, that of the fruit of his loins one should sit upon his throne. Acts 2:30.

The lion of the tribe of Juda, the root of David, hath prevailed to open the book. Apoc. 5:5.

Jesus Christ the Son of God, who was made to him of the seed of David according to the flesh. Rom. 1:3.

2. CHRIST'S INCARNATION FORETOLD BY THE PROPHETS

Behold, a virgin shall conceive, and bear a son, and his name shall be called Emmanuel. Is. 7:14.

I will put enmities between thee and the woman, and thy seed and her seed: she shall crush thy head, and thou shalt lie in wait for her heel. Gen. 3:15.

The Lord hath created a new thing upon the earth: A woman shall compass a man. Jer. 31:22.

He shall come down like rain upon the fleece, and as showers falling gently upon the earth. Ps. 71:6.

O that thou wouldst rend the heavens, and wouldst come down! Is. 64:1.

Drop down dew, ye heavens, from above, and let the clouds rain the just: let the earth be opened, and bud forth a Savior. Is. 45:8.

I will raise up to David a just branch: and a king shall reign and shall be wise: and shall execute judgment and justice in the earth. Jer. 23:5.

The desired of all nations shall come. Agg. 2:8.

Show us, O Lord, thy mercy, and grant us thy salvation. Ps. 84:8.

3. HIS COMING IN PASSIBLE FLESH

It came to pass that when they were there, her days were accomplished that she should be delivered. And she brought forth her first-born Son, and wrapped him up in swaddling clothes, and laid him in a manger. Luke 2:6.

And the Word was made flesh. John 1:14.

He was made of the seed of David according to the flesh. Rom. 1:3.

When the fulness of the time was come, God sent his Son, made of a woman, made under the law. Gal. 4:4.

Being in the form of God, he thought it not robbery to be equal with God; but emptied himself, taking the form of a servant, being made in likeness of men, and in habit found as a man. Phil. 2:6.

There is one God, and one Mediator of God and men, the man Christ Jesus. 1 Tim. 2:5.

Because the children are partakers of flesh and blood, he also himself in like manner hath been partaker of the same: that through death he might destroy him who had the empire of death. For nowhere doth he take hold of the angels: but of the seed of Abraham he taketh hold; wherefore it behoved him in all things to be made like unto his brethren. Heb. 2:14, 16.

Christ died, being put to death in the flesh, but enlivened in the spirit. 1 Pet. 3:18.

Christ having suffered in the flesh, be you also armed with the same thought. 1 Pet. 4:1.

Every spirit which confesseth that Jesus Christ is come in the flesh is of God. 1 John 4:2.

Many seducers are gone out into the world, who confess not that Jesus Christ is come in the flesh. 2 John 7.

4. THE FIRST-BEGOTTEN, THE HEAD AND PRINCE OF ALL CREATURES

He is the image of the invisible God, the first-born of every creature. Col. 1:15.

You are filled in him, who is the head of all principality and power. Col. 2:10.

He hath made him head over all the Church. Eph. 1:22.

Who is he that shall condemn? Christ Jesus, that died, yea that is risen also again, who is at the right hand of God, who also maketh intercession for us. Rom. 8:34.

Doing the truth in charity, may we in all things grow up to him who is the head, even Christ. Eph. 4:15.

Christ is the head of the Church; He is the Savior of his body. Eph. 5:23.

He is the head of the body, the Church, who is the beginning. Col. 1:18.

5. CHRIST A MIGHTY KING

I am appointed king by him over Sion his holy mountain, preaching his commandment. Ps. 2:6.

Grace be unto you and peace from Jesus Christ, who is the Prince of kings of the earth. Apoc. 1:5.

He hath on his garment and on his thigh written: King of kings and Lord of lords. Apoc. 19:16.

All things are delivered to me by my Father. Mat. 11:27.

All power is given to me in heaven and on earth. Mat. 28:18.

Thou hast given him power over all flesh. John 17:2.

The Father loveth the Son: and he hath given all things into his hand. John 3:35.

He hath subjected all things under his feet. Eph. 1:22.

When a strong man armed keepeth his court, those things are in peace which he possesseth: but if a stronger than he come upon him and overcome him, he will take away all his armor wherein he trusted, and will distribute his spoils. Luke 11:21 f.

Gird thy sword upon thy thigh, O thou most mighty. Ps. 44:4.

Thy arrows are sharp: under thee shall people fall, into the hearts of the king's enemies. Ps. 44:6.

Who hath raised up the just one from the east, hath called him to follow him? He shall give the nations in his sight, and he shall rule over kings: he shall give them as the dust to his sword, as stubble driven by the wind to his bow. Is. 41:2.

6. CHRIST, THE SAVIOR OF THE WORLD

This day is born to you a Savior who is Christ the Lord. Luke 2:11.

Surely he hath borne our infirmities and carried our sorrows: and we have thought him as it were a leper, and as one struck by God and afflicted. But he was wounded for our iniquities, he was bruised for our sins: the chastisement of our peace was upon him, and by his bruises we are healed. Is. 53:4 f.

Behold, the Lord hath made it to be heard in the ends of the earth. Tell the daughter of Sion: Behold, thy Savior cometh: behold, his reward is with him, and his work before him. Is. 62:11.

In those days shall Juda be saved, and Israel shall dwell confidently: and this is the name that they shall call him: The Lord our just one. Jer. 23:6.

He is like a refining fire, and like the fuller's herb. Mal. 3:2.

Rejoice greatly, O daughter of Sion; shout for joy, O daughter of Jerusalem: behold, thy king will come to thee, the just and Savior: he is poor, and riding upon an ass, and upon a colt the foal of an ass. Zach. 9:9.

Thou shalt call his name Jesus. For he shall save his people from their sins. Mat. 1:21.

In his name the Gentiles shall hope. Mat. 12:21.

The Son of man is come to seek and to save that which was lost. Luke 19:10.

To enlighten them that sit in darkness and in the shadow of death: to direct our feet into the way of peace. Luke 1:29.

We ourselves have heard him, and know that this is indeed the Savior of the world. John 4:42.

Come to me, all you that labor and are burdened, and I will refresh you. Mat. 11:28.

They that are in health need not a physician, but they that are sick. I am not come to call the just, but sinners. Mat. 9:12 f.

The Son of man came not to destroy souls, but to save. Luke 9:56.

I am the door. By me if any man enter in, he shall be saved: and he shall go in and go out, and shall find pastures. I am the good Shepherd. The good Shepherd giveth his life for his sheep. I am the good Shepherd; I know mine, and mine know me. John 10:9, 11, 14.

I am the way and the truth and the life. No man cometh to the Father but by me. John 14:6.

And I, if I be lifted up from the earth, will draw all things to myself. I came not to judge the world, but to save the world. John 12:32, 47.

All that the Father giveth me shall come to me; and him that cometh to me I will not cast out. John 6:37.

Jesus spoke, and lifting up his eyes to heaven, he said. Father, the hour is come; glorify thy Son, that thy Son may glorify thee. As thou hast given him power over all flesh, that he may give eternal life to all whom thou hast given him. Now this is eternal life: that they may know thee, the only true God, and Jesus Christ, whom thou hast sent. John 17:1-3.

He that believeth in the Son of God hath the testimony of God in himself. And this is the testimony, that God hath given to us, eternal life. And this life is in his Son. 1 John 5:10 f.

Neither is there salvation in any other. For there is no other name under heaven giver to men whereby we must be saved. Acts 4:12.

To him all the prophets give testimony, that by his name all receive remission of sins who believe in him. Acts 10:43.

Who is over all things, God blessed forever. Amen. Rom. 9:5.

Let every one depart from iniquity who nameth the name of the Lord. 2 Tim. 2:19.

Giving thanks to God the Father, who hath made us worthy to be partakers of the lot of the saints in light. Who hath delivered us from the power of darkness, and hath translated us into the kingdom of the Son of his love, in whom we have redemption through his blood, the remission of sins. And he is the head of the body, the Church, who is the beginning, the first-born from the dead: that in all things he may hold the primacy: because in him it hath well pleased the Father that all fulness should dwell; and through him to reconcile all things unto himself, making peace through the blood of his cross, both as to the things on earth and the things that are in heaven. Col. 1:12-20.

For there is one God, and one Mediator of God and men, the man Christ Jesus, who gave himself a redemption for all. 1 Tim. 2:5 f.

7. HIS CHARITY, GRACE, KNOWLEDGE, AND BEAUTY

God doth not give the Spirit by measure. John 3:34.

We saw his glory, the glory as it were of the only begotten of the Father, full of grace and truth. John 1:14.

As the apple-tree among the trees of the woods, so is my beloved among the sons. Cant. 2:3.

I pray that he would grant you to know the charity of Christ, which surpasseth all knowledge. Eph. 3:19.

Him, that knew no sin, for us he hath made sin, that we might be made the justice of God in him. 2 C. 5:21.

Christ suffered for us, who did no sin, neither was guile found in his mouth. 1 Pet. 2:22.

You know that he appeared to take away our sins, and in him there is no sin. 1 John 3:5.

All the Churches shall know that I am he that searcheth the reins and hearts, and I will give to every one of you according to your works. Apoc. 2:23.

We know that thou knowest all things, and thou needest not that any man should ask thee. By this we believe that thou comest forth from God. John 16:30.

Lord thou knowest all things: thou knowest that I love thee. John 21:17.

The grace of God our Savior hath appeared to all men; instructing us that, denying ungodliness and wordly desires, we should live soberly, and justly, and godly in this world, looking for the blessed hope and coming of the glory of the great God and our Savior Jesus Christ. Titus 2:11-13.

Grace is poured abroad in thy lips. Ps. 44:3.

They wondered at the words of grace that proceeded from his mouth. Luke 4:22.

Never did man speak like this man. John 7:46.

The charity of Christ presseth us. 2 C. 5:14.

8. HIS POVERTY

The foxes have holes, and the birds of the air nests; but the Son of man hath not where to lay his head. Mat. 8:20.

O expectation of Israel, the Savior thereof in time of trouble, why wilt thou be as a stranger in the land, and as a wayfaring man turning in to lodge? Why wilt thou be as a wandering man, as a mighty man that cannot save? Jer. 14:8 f.

You know the grace of our Lord Jesus Christ, that being rich he became poor for your sakes, that through his poverty you might be rich. 2 C. 8:9.

I am poor and in labors from my youth; and being exalted have been humbled and troubled. Ps. 87:16.

There was no room for them in the inn. Luke 2:7.

9. CHRIST AS HIGH PRIEST, AND MEDIATOR BETWEEN GOD AND MAN

The Lord hath sworn, and he will not repent: Thou art a priest forever according to the order of Melchisedech. Ps. 109:4.

Christ did not glorify himself that he might be made a high priest; but he that said unto him: Thou art my Son, this day have I begotten thee. Heb. 5:5.

We have such an high priest, who is set on the right hand of the throne of majesty in the heavens, a minister of the holies; for every high priest is appointed to offer gifts and sacrifices: wherefore it is necessary that he also should have something to offer. Heb. 8:1, 3.

He hath delivered himself for us, an oblation and a sacrifice to God for an odor of sweetness. Eph. 5:2.

There is one God and one mediator of God and men, the man Christ Jesus, who gave himself a redemption for all. 1 Thess. 2:5.

All things are of God, who hath reconciled us to himself by Christ. 2 C. 5:18.

He is the mediator of the new testament: that by means of his death they that are called may receive the promise of eternal inheritance. Heb. 9:15.

Christ was offered once to exhaust the sins of many. Heb. 9:28.

10. CHRIST'S LOVE OF SUFFERING AND PERFECT OBEDIENCE

I have a baptism wherewith I am to be baptized; and how I am straitened until it be accomplished? Luke 12:50.

My meat is to do the will of him that sent me, that I may perfect his work. John 4:34.

Can you drink the chalice that I shall drink? Mal. 20:22.

Having joy set before him, he endured the cross, despising the shame. Heb. 12:2.

Why did Christ, when as yet we were weak, according to the time, die for the ungodly? For scarce for a just man will one die; yet perhaps for a good man some one would dare to die. But God commendeth his charity towards us, because when as yet we were sinners, Christ died for us. Rom. 5:6-8.

Whereas indeed he was the Son of God, he learned obedience by the things which he suffered. Heb. 5:8.

It became him, for whom are all things and by whom are all things, who had brought many children into glory, to perfect the author of their salvation by his passion. For both he that sanctifieth and they who are sanctified are all of one. For which cause he is not ashamed to call them brethren. Heb. 2:10 f.

Because the children are partakers of flesh and blood, he also himself in like manner hath been partaker of the same; that through death he might destroy him who had the empire of death, that is to say, the devil; and might deliver them, who through the fear of death were all their lifetime subject to servitude. Heb. 2:14 f.

It behoved him in all things to be made like unto his brethren, that he might become a merciful and faithful high priest before God, that he might be a propitiation for the sins of the people. For in that wherein he himself hath suffered and been tempted he is able to succor them also that are tempted. Heb. 2:17 f.

He humbled himself, becoming obedient unto death, even to the death of the cross; for which cause God also hath exalted him, and hath given him a name which is above all names: that in the name of Jesus every knee should bow, of those that are in heaven, on earth, and under the earth, and that every tongue should confess that the Lord Jesus Christ is in the glory of God the Father. Phil. 2:8-11.

11. HIS VICTORY AND TRIUMPH ON THE CROSS

Despoiling the principalities and powers, he hath exposed them confidently in open show, triumphing over them in himself. Col. 2:15.

Horns are in his hands: there is his strength hid; death shall go before his face, and the devil shall go forth before his feet. Haba. 3:4 f.

I, if I be lifted up from the earth, will draw all things to myself. John 12:32.

We preach Christ crucified, unto the Jews indeed a stumbling-block, and unto the Gentiles foolishness: but unto them that are called, both Jews and Greeks, Christ the power of God and the wisdom of God; for the foolishness of God is wiser than men, and the weakness of God is stronger than men. 1 C. 1:23-25.

A Child is born to us, and a Son is given to us, and the government is upon his shoulder. Is. 9:6.

I will go up into the palm-tree, and will take hold of the fruit thereof. Cant. 7:8.

If he shall lay down his life for sin, he shall see a long-lived seed, and the will of the Lord shall be prosperous in his hand. Because his soul hath labored, he shall see and be filled; by his knowledge shall this my just servant justify many, and he shall bear their iniquities. Therefore will I distribute to him very many, and he shall divide the spoils of the strong, because he hath delivered his soul unto death, and was reputed with the wicked; and he hath borne the sins of many, and hath prayed for the transgressors. Is. 53:10-12.

Christ having suffered in the flesh, be you also armed with the same thought: for he that hath suffered in the flesh hath ceased from sins, that now he may live the rest of his time in the flesh, not after the desires of men, but according to the will of God. 1 Pet. 4:1 f.

Of his fulness we all have received. John 1:16.

12. CHRIST'S MERIT, AND THE DIVINE EXPIATION

Unless the grain of wheat, falling into the ground, dieth, itself remaineth alone; but if it die, it bringeth forth much fruit. John 12:24.

Being consummated, he became, to all that obey him, the cause of eternal salvation. Heb. 5:9.

For all have sinned, and do need the glory of God. Being justified freely by his grace, through the redemption that is in Christ Jesus. Rom. 3:23 f.

He hath graced us in his beloved Son. In whom we have redemption through his blood, the remission of sins, according to the riches of his grace, which hath superabounded in us. Eph. 1:7.

Christ died for all. 2 C. 5:15.

He gave himself a redemption for all. 1 Tim. 2:6.

He is the propitiation for our sins: and not for ours only. but also for those of the whole world. 1 John 2:2.

Give glory to the Lord, for he is good, for his mercy endureth forever. Let them say so that have been redeemed by the Lord, whom he hath redeemed from the hand of the enemy, and gathered out of the countries. Ps. 106:1 f.

With the Lord there is mercy, and with him plentiful redemption. Ps. 129:7.

God was in Christ, reconciling the word to himself. 2 C. 5:19.

In him we have redemption through his blood, the remission of sins. Col. 1:14.

In him it hath well pleased the Father that all fulness should dwell: and through him to reconcile all things unto himself, making peace through the blood of his cross, both as to the things on earth and the things that are in heaven. Col. 1:19 f.

Blotting out the handwriting of the decree that was against us, which was contrary to us. And he hath taken the same out of the way, fastening it to the cross: and despoiling the principalities and powers, he hath exposed them confidently in open show, triumphing over them in himself. Col. 2:14 f.

13. CHRIST'S REDEMPTION OF SINNERS BY HIS BLOOD

In Christ Jesus you, who some time were afar off, are made nigh by the blood of Christ. For he is our peace, who hath made both one, and breaking down the middle wall of partition, the enmities in his flesh; making void the law of commandments contained in decrees, that he might make the two in himself into one new man, making peace, and might reconcile both to God in one body by the cross, killing the enmities in himself. Eph. 2:13-16.

You were not redeemed with corruptible things, as gold or silver, from your vain conversation of the tradition of your fathers, but with the precious blood of Christ, as of a lamb unspotted and undefiled. 1 Pet. 1:18 f.

Christ by his own blood entered once into the holies, having obtained eternal redemption. Heb. 9:12.

Thus saith the Lord: You were sold gratis, and you shall be redeemed without money. Is. 52:3.

I am, I am he that blot out thy iniquities for my own sake, and I will not remember thy sins. Is. 43:25.

For nothing shalt thou save them. Ps. 55:8.

You, when you were dead in your sins and the uncircumcision of the flesh, he hath quickened together with him, forgiving you all offences. Col. 2:13.

14. CHRIST, JUDGE OF THE LIVING AND THE DEAD

I am Alpha and Omega, the Beginning and the End, saith the Lord God, who is, and who was, and who is to come, the Almighty. Apoc. 1:8.

We shall all stand before the judgment-seat of Christ; for it is written: As I live, saith the Lord, every knee shall bow to me, and every tongue shall confess to God. Rom. 14:10 f.

We must all be manifested before the judgment-seat of Christ, that every one may receive the proper things of the body, according as he hath done, whether it be good or evil. 2 C. 5:10.

He commanded us to preach to the people, and to testify that it is he who was appointed by God to be judge of the living and of the dead. Acts 10: 42.

He hath appointed a day wherein he will judge the world in equity by the man whom he hath appointed, giving faith to all by raising him up from the dead. Acts 17:31.

The judgment sat and the books were opened. Dan. 7:10.

I beheld in the vision of the night, and lo, one like the Son of man came with the clouds of heaven, and he cave even to the Ancient of days, and they presented him before him; and he gave him power, and glory, and a kingdom: and all peoples, tribes, and tongues shall serve him: his power is an everlasting power that shall not be taken away, and his kingdom shall not be destroyed. Dan. 7:13 f.

They shall see the Son of man coming in the clouds of heaven with much power and majesty. Mat. 24:30.

I say to you: Hereafter you shall see the Son of man sitting on the right hand of the power of God, and coming in the clouds of heaven. Mat. 26:64.

Neither doth the Father judge any man; but hath given all judgment to the Son. John 5:22.

From his mouth came out a sharp two-edged sword. Apoc. 1:16.

He hath made my mouth like a sharp sword. Is. 49:2.

Thou shalt rule them with a rod of iron, and shalt break them in pieces like a potter's vessel. Ps. 2:9.

Thou art terrible, and who shall resist thee? Ps. 75:8.

Who is that shepherd that can withstand my countenance? Jer. 50:44.

He will do all that pleaseth him, and his word is full of power. Neither can any man say to him: Why dost thou so? Ecclus. 8:3 f.

The Lord of hosts hath decreed, and who can disannul it? and his hand is stretched out, and who shall turn it away? Is. 14:27.

Woe to them that desire the day of the Lord! to what end is it for you? the day of the Lord is darkness and not light. As if a man should flee from the face of a lion, and a bear should meet him: or enter into the house, and lean with his hand upon the wall, and a serpent should bite him. Amos 5:18 f.

What will you do in the day of visitation, and of the calamity which cometh from afar? to whom will ye flee for help? and where will ye leave your glory? Is. 10:3.

God, whose wrath no man can resist, and under whom they stoop that bear up the world. Job 9:13.

15. OUR LORD'S NAMES AND TITLES

I

Jesus saith to them: But whom do you say that I am? Simon Peter answered and said: Thou art the Christ, the Son of the living God. Mat. 16: 15 f.

We have seen and do testify that the Father hath sent his Son to be the Savior of the world. 1 John 4:14.

I saw, and I gave testimony, that this is the Son of God. John 1:34.

When the fulness of the time was come, God sent his Son, made of a woman. Gal. 4:4.

God so loved the world as to give his only-begotten Son, that whosoever believeth in him may not perish, but may have life everlasting. John 3:16.

He that believeth in him is not judged. But he that doth not believe is already judged, because he believeth not in the name of the only-begotten Son of God. John 3:18.

Grace be with you, mercy, and peace from God the Father, and from Christ Jesus, the Son of the Father, in truth and charity. 2 John 3.

The Word was made flesh, and dwelt among us (and we saw his glory, as it were of the only-begotten of the Father), full of grace and truth. John 1:14.

No man hath seen God at any time: the only-begotten Son, who is in the bosom of the Father, he hath declared him. John 1:18.

He is the image of the invisible God, the first-born of every creature. Col. 1:15.

He that spared not even his own Son, but delivered him up for us all, how hath he not also, with him, given us all things? Rom. 8:32.

A Child is born to us, and a Son is given to us, and the government is upon his shoulder: and his name shall be called Wonderful, Counsellor, God the Mighty, the Father of the world to come, the Prince of peace. Is. 9:6.

Therefore having yet one son most dear to him, he also sent him unto them last of all, saying: They will reverence my son. Mat. 12:6.

The Lord hath said to me: thou art my son; this day have I begotten thee. Ps. 2:7.

He hath delivered us from the power of darkness, and hath translated us into the kingdom of the Son of his love. Col. 1:13.

He shall be great, and shall be called the Son of the Most High, and the Lord God shall give unto him the throne of David his father, and he shall reign in the house of Jacob forever. Luke 1:32.

He held his peace and answered nothing. Again the high priest asked him, and said to him: Art thou the Christ, the Son of the Blessed God? Mark 14:61.

He answered him [Manue]: Why askest thou my name, which is Wonful? Judg. 13:18.

His name shall be called Wonderful. Is. 9:6.

As he was yet speaking, behold, a bright cloud overshadowed them. And lo, a voice out of the cloud, saying: This is my beloved Son, in whom I am well pleased: hear ye him. Mat. 17:5.

Do you say of him, whom the Father hath sanctified and sent into the world: Thou blasphemest, because I said, I am the Son of God? John 10:36.

The beginning of the Gospel of Jesus Christ, the Son of God. Mark 1:1.

The angel, answering, said to her: The Holy Ghost shall come upon thee, and the power of the Most High shall overshadow thee. And therefore also the Holy which shall be born of thee shall be called the Son of God. Luke 1:35.

I saw, and I gave testimony, that this is the Son of God. John 1:34.

These are written that you may believe that Jesus is the Christ, the Son of God; and that believing you may have life in his name. John 20:31.

Immediately he preached Jesus in the synagogues, that he is the Son of God. Acts 9:20.

They that were in the boat came and adored him, saying: Indeed thou art the Son of God. Mat. 14:33.

Nathanael answered him, and said: Rabbi, thou art the Son of God, thou art the King of Israel. John 1:49.

She saith to him: Yea, Lord, I have believed that thou art Christ, the Son of the living God, who art come into this world. John 11:27.

He, answering, said: I believe that Jesus Christ is the Son of God. Acts 8:37.

The centurion who stood over against him, seeing that crying out in this manner he had given up the ghost, said: Indeed this man was the Son of God. Mark 15:39.

The unclean spirits, when they saw him, fell down before him; and they cried, saying: Thou art the Son of God. Mark 3:11.

Crying with a loud voice, he said: What have I to do with thee, Jesus, the Son of the Most High God? Mark 5:7.

II

In the beginning was the Word, and the Word was with God, and the Word was God. John 1:1.

Behold, a virgin shall be with child, and shall bring forth a son, and they shall call his name Emmanuel, which being interpreted is, God with us. Mat. 1:23.

The voice of one crying in the desert: Prepare ye the way of the Lord, make straight in the wilderness the paths of our God. Is. 40:3.

Thy throne, O God, is forever and ever. Heb. 1:8.

A child is born to us, and a son is given to us, and the government is upon his shoulder: and his name shall be called Wonderful, Counsellor, God the Mighty. Is. 9:6.

Knowest thou not, or hast thou not heard? The Lord is the everlasting God, who hath created the ends of the earth: he shall not faint nor labor, neither is there any searching out of his wisdom. Is. 40:26.

We know that the Son of God is come: and he hath given us understanding, that we may know the true God, and may be in his true Son. This is the true God and life eternal. 1 John 5:20.

Thomas said to him: My Lord and my God. John 20:28.

My spirit hath rejoiced in God my Savior. Luke 1:47.

Christ is over all things, God blessed forever. Amen. Rom. 9:5.

He that made thee shall rule over thee, the Lord of hosts is his name: and thy Redeemer, the holy one of Israel, shall be called the God of all the earth. Is. 54:5.

Evidently great is the mystery of godliness, which was manifested in the flesh, was justified in the spirit, appeared unto angels, hath been preached unto the Gentiles, is believed in the world, is taken up in glory. 1 Tim. 3:16.

Simon Peter, servant and apostle of Jesus Christ, to them that have obtained equal faith with us in the justice of our God and Savior Jesus Christ. 2 Pet. 1:1.

Looking for the blessed hope and coming of the glory of the great God and our Savior Jesus Christ. Titus 2:13.

The Lord appeared to him in a flame of fire out of the midst of a bush; and he saw that the bush was on fire, and was not burnt. And Moses said: I will go and see this great sight, why the bush is not burnt. And when the Lord saw that he went forward to see, he called to him out of the midst of the bush, and said: Moses, Moses. And he answered: Here I am. And he said: Come not nigh hither: put off the shoes from thy feet, for the place whereon thou standest is holy ground. And he said: I am the God of thy father, the God of Abraham, the God of Isaac, and the God of

Jacob. Moses hid his face, for he durst not look at God. Ex. 3:2-6.

Thou, child, shalt be called the prophet of the Highest; for thou shalt go before the face of the Lord to prepare his ways. Luke 1:76.

Holy, holy, holy, the Lord God of hosts. Is. 6:3.

The voice of one crying in the desert: Prepare ye the way of the Lord, make straight in the wilderness the paths of our God. Is. 40:3.

Behold, the Lord God shall come with strength, and his arm shall rule: behold, the reward is with them, and his work is before him. Is. 40:10.

You shall flee to the valley of those mountains, for the valley of the mountains shall be joined even to the next, and you shall flee as you fled from the face of the earthquake in the days of Ozias King of Juda; and the Lord my God shall come, and all the saints with him. Zach. 14:5.

Say to the cities of Juda: Behold your God. Is. 40:9.

He prevailed over the angel, and was strengthened: he wept and made supplication to him: he found him in Bethel, and there he spoke with us. Even the Lord the God of hosts, the Lord is his memorial. Osee 12:4 f.

In those days shall Juda be saved, and Israel shall dwell confidently: and this is the name that they shall call him: The Lord our just one. Jer. 23:6.

Who is the king of glory? The Lord, who is strong and mighty: the Lord mighty in battle. Ps. 23:8.

Whosoever shall call upon the name of the Lord shall be saved. Rom. 10:13.

Every one that shall call upon the name of the Lord shall be saved: for in Mount Sion and in Jerusalem shall be salvation, as the Lord hath said, and in the residue whom the Lord shall call. Jon. 2:32.

We speak the wisdom of God, which none of the princes of this world knew; for if they had known it, they would never have crucified the Lord of glory. 1 C. 2:8.

As a vesture shalt thou change them, and they shall be changed: but thou art the selfsame, and thy years shall not fail. Heb. 1:12.

They shall perish, but thou remainest: and all of them shall grow old like a garment: and as a vesture thou shalt change them, and they shall be changed. But thou art always the selfsame, and thy years shall not fail. Ps. 101:27 f.

God said to Moses: I am who am. He said: Thus shalt thou say to the children of Israel: He who is hath sent me to you. Ex. 3:14.

If you believe not that I am he, you shall die in your sins. John 8:24.

Jesus said to them: Amen, amen, I say to you, before Abraham was made, I am. John 8:58.

Jesus said to them: Whom seek ye? They answered him: Jesus of Nazareth. Jesus said to them: I am he. As soon therefore as he had said to them: I am he, they went backward, and fell to the ground. John 18:4-6.

Jesus said to them: When you shall have lifted up the Son of man, then shall you know that I am he, and that I do nothing of myself; but as the Father hath taught me, these things I speak. John 8: 28.

Jesus said to her: I am the resurrection and the life: he that believeth in me, although he be dead shall live. John 11:25.

III

I am Alpha and Omega, the Beginning and the End, saith the Lord God, who is, and who was, and who is to come, the Almighty. Apoc. 1:8.

In him were all things created, in heaven and on earth, visible and invisible, whether thrones, or dominations, or principalities, or powers: all things were created by him and in him. Col. 1:16.

He, being the brightness of his glory and the figure of his substance, and upholding all things by the word of his power, making purgation of sins, sitteth on the right hand of the

Majesty on high. Heb. 1:3.

A child is born to us, and a son is given to us, and the government is upon his shoulder: and his name shall be called the Father of the world to come. Is. 9:6.

He is the head of the body, the Church, who is the beginning, the firstborn from the dead, that in all things he may hold the primacy. Col. 1:18.

When I had seen him, I fell at his feet as dead. And he laid his right hand upon me, saying: Fear not. I am the First and the Last. Apoc. 1:17.

The life was manifested: and we have seen, and do bear witness, and declare unto you the life eternal, which was with the Father, and hath appeared to us. 1 John 1:2.

We know that the Son of God is come. And he hath given us understanding, that we may know the true God, and may be in his Son. This is the true God, and life eternal. 1 John 5:20.

Behold, I am living forever and ever. Apoc. 1:18.

In the beginning was the Word, and the Word was with God, and the Word was God. John 1:1.

The Father, the Word, and the Holy Ghost are one. 1 John 5:7.

He was clothed with a garment sprinkled with blood: and his name is called: The Word of God. Apoc. 19:13.

That which was from the beginning, which we have heard, which we have seen with our eyes, which we have looked upon, and our hands have handled, of the Word of Life. 1 John 1:1.

The Word was made flesh, and dwelt among us (and we saw his glory, the glory as it were of the only begotten of the Father) full of grace and truth. John 1:14.

If our gospel be also hid, it is hid to them that are lost, in whom the god of this world hath blinded the minds of unbelievers, that the light of the gospel of the glory of Christ, who is the image of God, should not shine unto them. 2 C. 4:4.

He is the image of the invisible God, the firstborn of every creature. Col. 1:15.

He being the brightness of his glory and the figure of his substance, and upholding all things by the word of his power, making purgation of sins, sitteth on the right hand of the Majesty on high. Heb. 1:3.

I Wisdom dwell in counsel, and am present in learned thoughts. The Lord possessed me in the beginning of his ways, before he made anything from the beginning. Prov. 8:13, 22.

Unto them that are called, both Jews and Greeks, Christ the power of God and the wisdom of God. 1 C. 1:24.

Who is blind, but my servant? or deaf, but he to whom I have sent my messengers? Is. 42:19.

Behold, I send my angel, and he shall prepare the way before my face. And presently the Lord whom you seek, and the angel of the testament whom you desire, shall come to his temple. Mal. 3:1.

The angel of the Lord called to Abraham a second time from heaven. Gen. 22:15.

The angel of God said to me in my sleep: Jacob. And I answered: Here I am. And he said: Lift up thy eyes: I am the God of Bethel, where thou didst anoint the stone, and make a vow to me. Gen. 31:11-13.

The angel of God, who went before the camp of Israel, removing, went behind them; and together with him the pillar of the cloud, leaving the forepart. Ex. 14:19.

In all their affliction he was not troubled, and the angel of his presence saved them: in his love and in his mercy he redeemed them, and he carried them and lifted them up all the days of old. Is. 63:9.

IV

Jesus therefore came forth bearing the crown of thorns and the purple garment: and he [Pilate] saith to them: Behold the man. John 19:5.

There is one God and one mediator of God and men, the man Christ Jesus. 1 Tim. 2:5.

Ye men of Israel, hear these words: Jesus of Nazareth, a man approved of God among you by miracles, and wonders, and signs, which God did by him in the midst of you, as you also know. Acts 2:22.

The first man was of the earth, earthly: the second man from heaven, heavenly. 1 C. 15:47.

Behold, we go up to Jerusalem, and the Son of man shall be betrayed to the chief priests, and to the scribes and ancients, and they shall condemn him to death, and shall deliver him to the Gentiles. Mark 10:33.

The book of the generation of Jesus Christ, the son of David, the son of Abraham. Mat. 1:1.

Is not this the carpenter, the son of Mary, the brother of James, and Joseph, and Jude, and Simon? Are not also his sisters here with us? Mark 6:3.

We have found him of whom Moses in the law and the prophets did write, Jesus the son of Joseph. John 1:45.

I will put enmities between thee and the woman, and thy seed and her seed: she shall crush thy head, and thou shalt lie in wait for her heel. Gen. 3:15.

To Abraham were the promises made, and to his seed. He saith not, And to his seeds, as of many; but as of one, And to thy seed, which is Christ. Why then was the law? It was set because of transgressions, until the seed should come, to whom he made the promise, being ordained by angels in the hand of a mediator. Gal. 3:16–19.

His Son was made to him of the seed of David, according to the flesh. Rom. 1:3.

This shall be a sign unto you: you shall find the infant wrapped in swaddling clothes, and laid in a manger. Luke 2:12.

Before the child know to refuse the evil, and to choose the good, the land which thou abhorrest shall be forsaken of the face of her two kings. Is. 7:16.

Arise, and take the Child and his mother, and go into the land of Israel. For they are dead that sought the life of the Child. Mat. 2:20.

A child is born to us, and a son is given to us, and the government is upon his shoulder. Is. 9:6.

Having fulfilled the days, when they returned the child Jesus remained in Jerusalem. Luke 2:43.

She brought forth her firstborn Son, and wrapped him up in swaddling clothes. Luke 2:7.

Do you say of him, whom the Father hath sanctified and sent into the world: Thou blasphemest because I said: I am the Son of God? John 10:36.

Holy brethren, partakers of the heavenly vocation, consider the Apostle and High Priest of our confession, Jesus. Heb. 3:1.

Moses said: A prophet shall the Lord your God raise up unto you of your brethren, like unto me: him you shall hear according to all things whatsoever he shall speak to you. And it shall be that every soul which will not hear that prophet shall be destroyed from among the people. Acts 3:22 f.

A great prophet is risen up among us, and God hath visited his people. Luke 7:16.

The people said: This is Jesus the prophet, from Nazareth of Galilee. Mat. 21:11.

To whom he said: What things? And they said: Concerning Jesus of Nazareth, who was a prophet, mighty in work and word before God and all the people. Luke 24:19.

He emptied himself, taking the form of a servant, being made in the likeness of men, and in habit found as a man. Phil. 2:7.

Behold my servant whom I have chosen, my beloved in whom my soul hath been well pleased. I will put my Spirit upon him, and he shall show judgment to the Gentiles. Mat. 12:18.

Thou art my servant Israel, for in thee will I glory. Is. 49:3.

Hear, O Jesus, thou high priest, thou and thy friends that dwell before thee, for they are portending men; for behold, I will bring my servant the orient. Zach. 3:8.

Because his soul hath labored, he shall see and be filled: by his knowledge shall this my just servant justify many, and he shall bear their iniquities. Is. 53:11.

Thus saith the Lord, the Redeemer of Israel, his holy one, to the soul that is despised, to the nation that is abhorred, to the servant of rulers: Kings shall see, and princes shall rise up, and adore for the Lord's sake, because he is faithful, and for the holy one of Israel, who hath chosen thee. Is. 49:7.

Coming he dwelt in a city called Nazareth; that it might be fulfilled which was said by the prophets: That he shall be called a Nazarite. Mat. 2:23.

Is not this the carpenter? Mark 6:3.

Is not this the carpenter's Son? Is not his mother called Mary? Mark 13:55.

He humbled himself unto death. I am become a stranger to my brethren, and an alien to the sons of my mother. Ps. 68:9.

We have seen him, despised and the most abject of men, a man of sorrows and acquainted with infirmity. Is. 53:3.

I am a worm, and no man, the reproach of men, and the outcast of the people. Ps. 21:7.

He is accursed of God that hangeth on a tree. Deut. 21:23.

V

Thou shalt call his name Jesus. For he shall save his people from their sins. Mat. 1:21.

It came to pass that while they talked and reasoned with themselves, Jesus himself also drawing near went with them. Luke 24:15.

I Jesus have sent my angel to testify to you these things in the churches. Apoc. 22:16.

Of this man's seed God, according to his promise, hath raised up to Israel a Savior, Jesus. Acts 13:23.

We have seen and do testify that the Father hath sent his Son to be the Savior of the world. 1 John 4:14.

This day is born to you a Savior, who is Christ the Lord, in the city of David. Luke 2:11.

Jesus Christ is the faithful witness, the first begotten of the dead, and the prince of the kings of the earth, who hath loved us, and washed us from our sins in his own blood. Apoc. 1:5.

To the saints and faithful brethren in Christ Jesus. Grace be to you and peace from God our Father, and from the Lord Jesus Christ. Col. 1:2 f.

May our Lord Jesus Christ himself, and God, and our Father, who hath loved us, and hath given us everlasting consolation, and good hope in grace, exhort your hearts, and confirm you in every good work and word. 2 Thess. 2:15 f.

He commanded his disciples that they should tell no one that he was Jesus the Christ. Mat. 16:20.

Where sin abounded, grace did more abound. That as sin hath reigned to death, so also grace might reign by justice unto life everlasting, through Jesus Christ our Lord. Rom. 5:20 f.

My little children, these things I write to you that you may not sin. But if any man sin, we have an Advocate with the Father, Jesus Christ the Just. 1 John 2:1.

Jesus Christ, yesterday, and today, and the same forever. Heb. 13:8.

I [Paul] answered: Who art thou, Lord? And he said to me: I am Jesus of Nazareth, whom thou persecutest. Acts 22:8.

Be it known to you all, and to all the people of Israel, that by the name of our Lord Jesus Christ of Nazareth, whom you crucified, whom God hath raised from the dead, even by him this man standeth here before you whole. Acts 4:10.

They stoned Stephen, invoking and saying: Lord Jesus, receive my spirit. Acts 7:58.

A faithful saying, and worthy of all acceptation, that Christ Jesus came into this world to save sinners, of whom I am the chief. 1 Tim. 1:15.

Neither be ye called masters: for one is your Master, Christ. Mat. 23:10.

The woman saith to him: I know that the Messias cometh (who is called Christ); therefore when he is come, he will tell us all things. John 4:25.

The kings of the earth stood up, and the princes met together against the Lord and against his Christ. Acts 4:28.

From heaven also we look for the Savior, our Lord Jesus Christ. Phil. 3:20.

Serve ye the Lord Christ. Col. 3:24.

He said to them: But whom do you say that I am? Simon Peter answering said: The Christ of God. Luke 9:20.

He [Simeon] had received an answer from the Holy Ghost, that he should not see death before he had seen the Christ of the Lord. Luke 1:25.

The high priest said to him: Art thou the Christ, the Son of the blessed God? Mark 14:61.

They said to the woman: We now believe, not for thy saying, for we ourselves have heard him, and know that this is indeed the Savior of the world. John 4:42.

The Lamb that was slain is worthy to receive power, and divinity, and wisdom, and strength, and honor, and glory, and benediction. Apoc. 5:12.

John saw Jesus coming to him, and he saith: Behold the Lamb of God, behold him who taketh away the sin of the world. John 1:29.

You were not redeemed with corruptible things, but with the precious blood of Christ, as of a lamb unspotted and undefiled. 1 Pet. 1:18 f.

I saw; and behold, in the midst of the throne and of the four living creatures, and in the midst of the ancients, a lamb standing as it were slain, having seven horns and seven eyes: which are the seven Spirits of God, sent forth into all the earth. Apoc. 5:6.

The lamb, which is in the midst of the throne, shall rule them, and shall lead them to the fountains of the waters of life, and God shall wipe away all tears from their eyes. Apoc. 7:17.

Jesus said to them: Can the children of the bridegroom mourn as long as the bridegroom is with them? But the days will come when the bridegroom shall be taken away from them, and then they shall fast. Mat. 9:15.

There came one of the seven angels, who had the vials full of the seven last plagues, and spoke with me, saying: Come, and I will show thee the bride, the wife of the lamb. Apoc. 21:9.

I saw no temple therein. For the Lord God Almighty is the temple thereof, and the lamb. The city hath no need of the sun nor of the moon to shine in it. For the glory of God hath enlightened it, and the lamb is the lamp thereof. Apoc. 21:22 f.

These shall fight with the lamb, and the lamb shall overcome them, because He is Lord of lords and King of kings, and they that are with him are called, and elect, and faithful. Apoc. 17:14.

Other sheep I have, that are not of this fold: them also I must bring, and they shall hear my voice, and there shall be one fold and one Shepherd. John 10:16.

Awake, O sword, against my shepherd, and against the man that cleaveth to me, saith the Lord of hosts; strike the shepherd and the sheep shall be scattered; and I will turn my hand to the little ones. Zach. 13:7.

May the God of peace, who brought again from the dead, the great Pastor of the sheep, our Lord Jesus Christ, in the blood of the everlasting testament fit you in all goodness that you may do his will. Heb. 13:20.

Jesus saith to him: I am the way, and the truth, and the life. No man cometh to the Father but by me. John 14:6.

Jesus said to them again: Amen, amen, I say to you, I am the door of the sheep. John 10:7.

You were as sheep going astray, but you are now converted to the shepherd and bishop of your souls. 1 Pet. 2:25.

I am the good shepherd. The good shepherd giveth his life for his sheep. John 10:11.

When the Prince of pastors shall appear you shall receive a never-fading crown of glory. 1 Pet. 5:4.

VI

In that day the root of Jesse, who standeth for an ensign of people, him the Gentiles shall beseech, and his sepulcher shall be glorious. Is. 11:10.

One of the ancients said to me: Weep not; behold, the lion of the tribe of Juda, the root of David, hath prevailed to open the book, and to loose the seven seals thereof. Apoc. 5:5.

I Jesus have sent my angel to testify to you these things in the churches. I am the root and stock of David, the bright and morning star. Apoc. 22:16.

There shall come forth a rod out of the root of Jesse, and a flower shall rise up out of his root. Is. 11:1.

In that day the bud of the Lord shall be in magnificence and glory, and the fruit of the earth shall be high, and a great joy to them that shall have escaped of Israel. Is. 4:2.

In those days, and at that time, I will make the bud of justice to spring forth unto David, and he shall do judgment and justice in the earth. Jer. 33:15.

Behold, the days come, saith the Lord, and I will raise up to David a just branch; and a king shall reign, and shall be wise, and shall execute judgment and justice in the earth. Jer. 23:5.

I am the vine, you the branches: he that abideth in me, and I in him, the same beareth much fruit; for without me you can do nothing. John 15:5.

I am the true vine: and my Father is the husbandman. John 15:1.

He that hath an ear, let him hear what the Spirit saith to the churches: To him that overcometh I will give to eat of the tree of life, which is in the paradise of my God. Apoc. 2:7.

Amen, amen, I say to you: Unless the grain of wheat falling into the ground die, itself remaineth alone. John 12:24.

Jesus said to them: Amen, amen, I say to you: Moses gave you not bread from heaven; but my Father giveth you the true bread from heaven. The bread of God is that which cometh down from heaven and giveth life to the world. John 6:32 f.

The Jews murmured at him, because he had said: I am the living bread which came down from heaven. John 6:41.

This is the bread which cometh down from heaven: that if any man eat of it, he may not die. John 6:50.

Jesus said to them: I am the bread of life: he that cometh to me shall not hunger. John 6:35.

I am the living bread. John 6:51.

To him that overcometh I will give the hidden manna. Apoc. 2:17.

VII

Jesus said to them: Yet a little while, the light is among you. Walk whilst you have the light, that the darkness overtake you not. And he that walketh in darkness knoweth not whither he goeth. John 12:35.

That was the true light which enlighteneth every man that cometh into this world. John 1:9.

The people that walked in darkness have seen a great light: to them that dwelt in the region of the shadow of death light is risen. Is. 9:2.

I am come a light into the world, that whosoever believeth in me may not remain in darkness. John 12:46.

Jesus spoke to them, saying: I am the light of the world: he that followeth me walketh not in darkness, but shall have the light of life. John 8: 12.

In him was life, and the life was the light of men. John 1:4.

A light to the revelation of the Gentiles, and the glory of thy people Israel. Luke 2:32.

I have given thee for a covenant of the people, for a light of the Gentiles. Is. 42:6.

I shall see him, but not now: I shall behold him, but not near. A star shall rise out of Jacob, and a scepter shall spring up from Israel. Num. 24:17.

As I also have received of my Father; and I will give him the morning star. Apoc. 2:28.

I Jesus have sent my angel to testify to you these things in the churches. I am the root and stock of David, the bright and morning star. Apoc. 22:16.

We have the more firm prophetical word: whereunto you do well to attend, as to a light that shineth in a dark place, until the day dawn, and the day star arise in your hearts. 2 Pet. 1:19.

Through the bowels of the mercy of our God, in which the Orient from on high hath visiteth us. Luke 1:78.

Unto you that fear my name the Sun of justice shall arise, and health in his wings; and you shall go forth, and shall leap like calves of the herd. Mal. 4:2.

VIII.

The Lord shall roar out of Sion, and utter his voice from Jerusalem, and the heavens and the earth shall be moved: and the Lord shall be the hope of his people, and the strength of the children of Israel. Joel 3:16.

Thou hast been a strength to the poor. A strength to the needy in distress. Is. 25:4.

Thou hast been a refuge from the whirlwind, a shadow from the heat. For the blast of the Mighty is like a whirlwind beating against a wall. Is. 25:4.

A man shall be as when one is hid from the wind, and hideth himself from a storm, as rivers of water in drought, and the shadow of a rock that standeth out in a desert land. Is. 32:2.

The Lord shall be the hope of his people, and the strength of the children of Israel. Joel 3:16.

He hath raised up an horn of salvation to us, in the house of David his servant. Luke 1:69.

To thee have I cried from the ends of the earth: when my heart was in anguish, thou hast exalted me on a rock. Ps. 60:3.

They drank of the spiritual rock that followed them, and the rock was Christ. 1 C. 10:4.

This man was counted worthy of greater glory than Moses, by so much as he that hath built the house hath greater honor than the house. Heb. 3:3.

I say to thee: That thou art Peter; and upon this rock I will build my Church, and the gates of hell shall not prevail against it. Mat. 16:18.

Other foundation no man can lay but that which is laid, which is Christ Jesus. 1 C. 3:11.

Thus saith the Lord God: Behold, I will lay a stone in the foundations of Sion, a tried stone, a corner stone, a precious stone, founded in the foundation. Is. 28:16.

As newborn babes, desire the rational milk without guile, if so be you have tasted that the Lord is sweet, unto whom coming, as to a living stone, rejected indeed by men, but chosen and made honorable by God. 1 Pet. 2:2-4.

Behold, I lay in Sion a chief corner stone, elect, precious. And he that shall believe in him shall not be confounded. 1 Pet. 2:6.

The stone which the builders rejected, the same is become the head of the corner. Ps. 117:22.

According as thou sawest that the stone was cut out of the mountain without hands, and broke in pieces the clay, and the iron, and the brass, and the silver, and the gold, the great

God hath shown the king what shall come to pass hereafter, and the dream is true, and the interpretation thereof is faithful. Dan. 2:45.

A stone of stumbling, and a rock of scandal, to them who stumble at the word, neither do believe, whereunto also they are set. 1 Pet. 2:8.

IX

I saw no temple therein. For the Lord God Almighty is the temple thereof and the lamb. Apoc. 21:22.

We have a minister of the holies and of the true tabernacle, which the Lord hath pitched, and not man. Heb. 8:2.

Christ Jesus was minister of the circumcision for the truth of God, to confirm the promises made unto the fathers. Rom. 15:8.

Having a new and living way, which he hath dedicated for us through the veil, that is to say his flesh, let us draw near. Heb. 10:20.

We have an altar, whereof they have no power to eat who serve the tabernacle. Heb. 13:10.

It was fitting that we should have such a high priest who needeth not daily (as the other priests) to offer sacrifices first for his own sins, and then for the people's: for this he did once in offering himself. Heb. 7:27.

Walk in love, as Christ also hath loved us, and hath delivered himself for us, an oblation and a sacrifice to God for an odor of sweetness. Christ hath delivered himself for us, a sacrifice to God for an odor of sweetness. Eph. 5:2 f.

The Son of man is not come to be ministered unto, but to minister, and to give his life a redemption for many. Mark 10:45.

I saw a great multitude, which no man could number, of all nations, and tribes, and peoples, and tongues, standing before the throne, and in sight of the lamb, clothed with white robes, and palms in their hands. Apoc. 7:9.

All that dwell upon the earth adored him, whose names are not written in the book of life of the lamb, which was slain from the beginning of the world. Apoc. 13:8.

Within the veil the forerunner Jesus is entered for us, made a high priest forever, according to the order of Melchisedech. Heb. 6:20.

Whom God hath proposed to be a propitiation, through faith in his blood, to the showing of his justice, for the remission of former sins. Rom. 3:25.

As he saith also in another place: Thou art a priest forever, according to the order of Melchisedech. Heb. 5:6.

Wherefore, holy brethren, partakers of the heavenly vocation, consider the apostle and high riest of our confession, Jesus. Heb. 3:1.

Having a great high priest that hath passed into the heavens, Jesus the Son of God, let us hold fast our confession. Heb. 4:14.

There is one God, and one Mediator of God and men, the man Christ Jesus. 1 Tim. 2:5.

Always living to make intercession for us. Heb. 7:25.

If any man sin, we have an advocate with the Father, Jesus Christ the just. 1 John 2:1.

By so much is Jesus made a surety of a better testament. Heb. 7:22.

X

God so loved the world as to give his only begotten Son: that whosoever believeth in him may not perish, but may have life everlasting. John 3:16.

Jesus said to her: If thou didst know the gift of God, and who he is that saith to thee, Give me to drink, thou perhaps wouldst have asked of him, and he would have given thee living water. John 4:10.

Thanks be to God for his unspeakable gift. 2 C. 9:15.

Behold my servant whom I have chosen, my beloved in whom my soul hath been well pleased. Mat. 12:18.

Behold my servant, I will uphold him: my elect, my soul delighteth in him: I have given my Spirit upon him. Is. 42:1.

There assembled together in this city against thy holy child Jesus, whom thou hast anointed, Herod and Pontius Pilate, with the Gentiles and the people of Israel. Acts 4:27.

The people stood beholding, and the rulers with them derided him, saying: He saved others; let him save himself, if he be Christ, the elect of God. Luke 23:35.

Now dost thou dismiss thy servant, O Lord, in peace, because my eyes have seen thy salvation. Luke 2:30.

Behold, the Lord hath made it to be heard in the ends of the earth. Tell the daughter of Sion: Behold, thy Savior cometh: behold, his reward is with him, and his work before him. Is. 62:11.

There shall come a Redeemer to Sion, and to them that return from iniquity in Jacob, saith the Lord. Is. 59:20.

The scepter shall not be taken away from Juda, nor a ruler from his thigh, till he come that is to be sent, and he shall be the expectation of nations. Gen. 49:10.

Behold, there was a man in Jerusalem named Simeon, and this man was just and devout, waiting for the consolation of Israel. Luke 2:25.

Let his name be blessed for evermore, his name continueth before the sun. Ps. 71:17.

Thou shalt give him to be a blessing forever and ever; thou shalt make him joyful in gladness with thy countenance. Ps. 20:7.

Jesus saith to him: I am the way and the truth, and the life. No man cometh to the Father but by me. John 14:6.

I saw heaven opened, and behold, a white horse: and he that sat upon him was called faithful and true, and with justice doth he judge and fight. Apoc. 19:11.

I the Lord have called thee in justice, and taken thee by the hand, and preserved thee. And I have given thee for a covenant of the people, for a light of the Gentiles. Is. 42:6.

Where there is a testament, the death of the testator must of necessity come in. For a testament is of force after men are dead; otherwise it is as yet of no strength whilst the testator lives. Heb. 9:16 f.

Jesus Christ, who is the faithful witness, the first begotten of the dead, and the prince of the kings of the earth, who hath loved us, and washed us from our sins in his own blood. Apoc. 1:5.

To the angel of the Church of Laodicea write: These things saith the Amen, the faithful and true witness, who is the beginning of the creation of God. Apoc. 3:14.

Behold, I have given him for a witness to the people, for a leader and a master to the Gentiles. Is. 54:4.

Christ also died once for our sins, the just for the unjust: that he might offer us to God, being put to death indeed in the flesh, but enlivened in the Spirit. 1 Pet. 3:18.

Which of the prophets have not your fathers persecuted? And they have slain them who foretold of the coming of the Just One, of whom you have been now the betrayers and murderers. Acts 7:52.

Thou wilt not leave my soul in hell, nor suffer thy Holy One to see corruption. Acts 2:27.

You denied the Holy One and the Just, and desired a murderer to be granted unto you. Acts 3:14.

Thus saith the Lord, the Redeemer of Israel, his holy one, to the soul that is despised, to the nation that is abhorred, to the servant of rulers: Kings shall see, and princes shall rise up, and adore for the Lord's sake, because he is faithful, and for the holy one of Israel, who hath chosen thee. Is. 49:7.

What have we to do with thee, Jesus of Nazareth? art thou come to destroy us? I know who thou art, the Holy One of God. Mark 1:14.

They cried one to another, and said: Holy, holy, holy, the Lord God of hosts: all the earth is full of his glory. Is. 6:3.

These things said Isaias, when he saw his glory and spoke of him. John 12:41.

I will make him my firstborn, high above the kings of the earth. Ps. 88:28.

He is the head of the body, the Church, who is the beginning, the firstborn from the dead, that in all things he may hold the primacy. Col. 1:18.

Whom he foreknew he also predestinated to be made conformable to the image of his Son, that he might be the firstborn among many brethren. Rom. 8:29.

Christ is risen from the dead, the firstfruits of them that sleep. 1 C. 15:20.

The first man Adam was made into a living soul: the last Adam into a quickening spirit. 1 C. 15:45.

Jesus said to her: I am the resurrection and the life; he that believeth in me, although he be dead, shall live. John 11:25.

Doing the truth in charity, we may in all things grow up in him who is the head, even Christ. Eph. 4:15.

He is the head of the body, the Church. Col. 1:18.

He hath subjected all things under his feet, and hath made him head over all the Church. Eph. 1:22.

I would have you know that the head of every man is Christ: and the head of the woman is the man: and the head of Christ is God. 1 C. 11:3.

You are filled in him who is the head of all principality and power. Col. 2:10.

XI

Josue said: Art thou one of ours, or of our adversaries? And he answered: No; but I am prince of the host of the Lord, and now I am come. Jos. 5:13 f.

It became him, for whom are all things and by whom are all things, who had brought many children into glory, to perfect the Author of their salvation by his passion. Heb. 2:10.

Looking on Jesus the Author and Finisher of faith, who, having joy set before him, endured the cross, despising the shame, and now sitteth on the right hand of the throne of God. Heb. 12:2.

Behold, I have given him for a witness to the people, for a leader and a master to the Gentiles. Is. 55:4.

Thou, Bethlehem Ephrata, art a little one among the thousands of Juda: out of thee shall he come forth unto me that is to be the ruler in Israel; and his going forth is from the beginning, from the days of eternity. Mich. 5:2.

Thou Bethlehem, the land of Juda, art not the least among the princes of Juda: for out of thee shall come forth the Captain that shall rule my people Israel. Mat. 2:6.

All Israel should be saved as it is written: There shall come out of Sion he that shall deliver, and shall turn away ungodliness from Jacob. Rom. 11:28.

One of the ancients said to me: Weep not: behold, the lion of the tribe of Juda, the root of David, hath prevailed to open the book, and to loose the seven seals thereof. Apoc. 5:5.

In that day the root of Jesse, who standeth for an ensign of people, him the Gentiles shall beseech, and his sepulcher shall be glorious. Is. 11:10.

He hath made my mouth like a sharp sword: in the shadow of his hand he hath protected me, and hath made me as a chosen arrow: in his quiver he hath hidden me. Is. 49:2.

No man can say the Lord Jesus but by the Holy Ghost. 1 C. 12:3.

One Lord, one faith, one baptism. Eph. 4:5.

Let all the house of Israel know most certainly that God hath made both Lord and Christ, this same Jesus, whom you have crucified. Acts 2:36.

These shall fight with the Lamb, and the Lamb shall overcome them, because he is Lord of lords and King of kings. Apoc. 17:14.

To this end Christ died and rose again: that he might be Lord both of the dead and of the living. Rom. 14:9.

The Son of man is Lord also of the Sabbath. Luke 6:5.

The Lord of peace himself give you everlasting peace in every place. 1 Thess. 3:16.

God sent the word to the children of Israel, preaching peace by Jesus Christ (he is Lord of all). Acts 10:36.

There is no distinction of the Jew and the Greek: for the same is Lord over all. Rom. 10:12.

XII

Take notice that from the going forth of the word, to build up Jerusalem again, unto Christ the prince, there shall be seven weeks and sixty-two weeks. Dan. 9:25.

Him hath God exalted with his right hand to be Prince and Savior, to give repentance to Israel and remission of sins. Acts 5:31.

A child is born to us, and a son is given to us, and the government is upon his shoulder: and his name shall be called Wonderful, Counsellor, God the Mighty, the Father of the world to come, the Prince of peace. Is. 9:6.

There shall arise a king, and his heart shall be puffed up; and in the abundance of all things he shall kill many; and he shall rise up against the prince of princes, and shall be broken without hand. Dan. 8:23, 25.

Grace be unto you and peace from him that is; and from Jesus Christ, who is the faithful witness, the first begotten of the dead, and the Prince of the kings of the earth, who hath loved us, and washed us from our sins in his own blood. Apoc. 1:4 f.

I the Lord will be their God, and my servant David the prince in the midst of them. Ez. 34:24.

Now thou dost dismiss Thy servant, O Lord, according to thy word in peace. Because my eyes have seen thy salvation; which thou hast prepared before the face of all peoples: a light to the revelation of the Gentiles, and the glory of thy people Israel. Luke 2:29-32.

He hath subjected all things under his feet, and hath made him head over all the Church, which is his body, and the fulness of him who is filled all in all. Eph. 1:22 f.

He hath appointed a day wherein he will judge the world in equity by the man whom he hath appointed, giving faith to all, by raising him up from the dead. Acts 17:31.

As to the rest, there is laid up for me a crown of justice, which the Lord the just Judge will render to me in that day; and not only to me, but to them also that love his coming. 2 Tim. 4:8.

All they that shall be left of all nations that came against Jerusalem shall go up from year to year, to adore the king, the Lord of hosts, and to keep the feast of tabernacles. Zach. 14:16.

He hath on his garment and on his thigh written: king of kings and Lord of lords. Apoc. 19:16.

A star shall rise out of Jacob, and a scepter shall spring up from Israel. Num. 24:17.

Give to the king thy judgment, O God, and to the king's son thy justice. Ps. 71:1.

They shall serve the Lord their God, and David their king, whom I will raise up to them. Jer. 30:9.

Nathanael answered him and said: Rabbi, thou art the Son of God, thou art the King of Israel. John 1:49.

Fear not, daughter of Sion: behold, thy King cometh sitting on an ass's colt. John 12:15.

Where is he that is born king of the Jews? Mat. 2:2.

Pilate asked him: Art thou the king of the Jews? But he answering saith to him: Thou sayest it. Mark 15:2.

Pilate wrote a title also; and he put it upon the cross. And the writing was: Jesus of Nazareth, the King of the Jews. John 19:19.

I saw as it were a sea of glass mingled with fire, and them that had overcome the beast and his image and the number of his name, standing on the sea of glass, having the harps of God: and singing the canticle of Moses the servant of God, and the canticle of the Lamb, saying: Great and wonderful are thy works, O Lord God Almighty; just and true are thy ways, O King of ages. Apoc. 15:2 f.

The Lord shall be king over all the earth: in that day there shall be one Lord, and his name shall be one. Zach. 14: 9.

This Melchisedech was king of Salem, to whom also Abraham divided the tithes of all: who first indeed, by interpretation, is king of justice. Heb. 7:1.

Who is this King of glory? The Lord of hosts, he is the King of glory. Ps. 23:10.

His eyes shall see the king in his beauty; they shall see the land far off. Is. 33:17.

The Lord maketh the flood to dwell; and the Lord shall sit king forever. Ps. 28:10.

The soldiers, platting a crown of thorns, put it upon his head. John 19:2.

We see Jesus, who was made a little lower than the angels, for the suffering of death, crowned with glory and honor. Heb. 2:9.

Thou hast prevented him with sweetness: Thou hast set on his head a crown of precious stones. Ps. 20:3.

His eyes were as a flame of fire, and on his head were many diadems. Apoc. 19:12.

16. CHARACTERISTICS OF OUR LORD

He humbled himself, becoming obedient unto death, even to the death of the cross. Phil. 2:8.

Take up my yoke upon you, and learn of me, because I am meek and humble of heart; and you shall find rest to your souls. Mat. 11:29.

He did no sin, neither was guile found in his mouth. 1 Pet. 2:22.

We have not a high priest who cannot have compassion on our infirmities; but one tempted in all things like as we are, without sin. Heb. 4:15.

He was offered because it was his own will, and he opened not his mouth; he shall be led as a sheep to the slaughter, and shall be dumb as a lamb before his shearer, and he shall not open his mouth. Is. 53:7.

We have seen him despised and the most abject of men, a man of sorrows and acquainted with infirmity; and his look was as it were hidden. Is. 53:3.

Judas, who betrayed him, seeing that he was condemned, repenting himself, brought back the thirty pieces of silver to the chief priests and ancients, saying: I have sinned in betraying innocent blood. Mat. 27:3 f.

You have heard the blasphemy: what think you? Who all condemned him to be guilty of death. Mark 16:64.

When he was reviled, he did not revile; when he suffered, he threatened not. 1 Pet. 2:23.

Pilate took Jesus and scourged him. John 19:1.

Platting a crown of thorns, they put it upon his head, and a reed in his right hand. And bowing the knee before him, they mocked him, saying: Hail, King of the Jews. Mat.27:29.

He was wounded for our iniquities, he was bruised for our sins. Is. 53:5.

Surely he hath borne our infirmities and carried our sorrows; and we have thought him as it were a leper, and as one struck by God and afflicted. Is. 53:4.

After they had crucified him they divided his garments. Mat. 27:35.

O God, my God, look upon me: why hast thou forsaken me? Ps. 21:2.

It behoved him in all things to be made like unto his brethren, that he might become a merciful and faithful high priest before God, that he might be a propitiation for the sins of the people. Heb. 2:17.

It was fitting that we should have such a high priest, holy, innocent, undefiled, separated from sinners, and made higher than the heavens. Heb. 7:26.

Being consummated, he became, to all that obey him, the cause of eternal salvation. Heb. 5:9.

And now, saith the Lord, that formed me from the womb to be his servant, that I may bring back Jacob unto him, and Israel will not be gathered together; and I am glorified in the eyes of the Lord, and my God is made my strength. Is. 49:5.

Who is this that cometh from Edom, with dyed garments from Bosra, this beautiful one in his robe, walking in the greatness of his strength? I that speak justice, and am a defender to save. Is. 63:1.

Great is the mystery of godliness, which was manifested in the flesh, was justified in the Spirit, appeared unto angels, hath been preached unto the Gentiles, is believed in the world, is taken up in glory. 1 Tim. 3:16.

This Jesus hath God raised again, whereof all we are witnesses. Being exalted therefore by the right hand of God, and having received of the Father the promise of the Holy Ghost, he hath poured forth this which you see and hear. Acts 2:33.

He is not here, but is risen. Luke 24:6.

The God of Abraham, and the God of Isaac, and the God of Jacob, the God of our fathers, hath glorified his Son Jesus, whom you indeed delivered up and denied before the face of Pilate, when he judged he should be released. Acts 3:13.

He that made thee shall rule over thee: the Lord of hosts is his name. Is. 54:5.

A bundle of myrrh is my beloved to me. Cant. 1:13.

Grow in grace, and in the knowledge of our Lord and Savior Jesus Christ. 2 Pet. 3:18.

Paul, an apostle of Jesus Christ, according to the commandment of God our Savior, and of Christ Jesus our hope. 1 Tim. 1:1.

Whosoever shall do the will of God, he is my brother, and my sister, and mother. Mark 3:35.

The portion of Jacob is not like these: for it is he who formed all things. Jer. 10:16.

We may confidently say: The Lord is my helper: I will not fear what man shall do to me. Heb. 13:6.

Is there no balm in Galaad? or is there no physician there? Why then is not the wound of the daughter of my people closed? Jer. 8:22.

He went into a desert place apart: which when the people knew they followed him; and he received them, and spoke to them of the kingdom of God, and healed them who had need of healing. Luke 9:10 f.

He shall sit refining and cleansing the silver, and he shall purify the sons of Levi, and shall refine them as gold and as silver, and they shall offer sacrifices to the Lord in justice. Mal. 3:3.

You call me Master and Lord: and you say well, for so I am. John 13:13.

Blessed are those servants whom the Lord, when he cometh, shall find watching. Amen I say to you, that he will gird himself, and make them sit down to meat, and passing will minister unto them. Luke 12:37.

I have given you an example, that as I have done to you, so you do also. John 13:15.

This man [Nicodemus] came to Jesus by night, and said to him: Rabbi, we know that thou art come a teacher from God; for no man can do these signs which thou dost, unless God be with him. John 3:2.

The Lord ruleth me: and I shall want nothing. He hath set me in a place of pasture. Ps. 22:1 f.

While I was with them I kept them

in thy name. Those whom thou gavest me have I kept. John 17:12.

I will set up one shepherd over them, and he shall feed them, even my servant David: he shall feed them, and he shall be their shepherd. Ez. 34:23.

He shall feed his flock like a shepherd: he shall gather together the lambs with his arm, and shall take them up in his bosom; and he himself shall carry them that are with young. Is. 40:11.

The Lord ruleth me: he hath brought me up on the water of refreshment: he hath converted my soul. Ps. 22:2.

My people hath been a lost flock, their shepherds have caused them to go astray, and have made them wander in the mountains; they have gone from mountain to hill, they have forgotten their resting-place. Is. 50:6.

My flesh is meat indeed, and my blood is drink indeed. John 6:56.

Christ our Pasch is sacrificed. 1 C. 5:7.

You, who some time were afar off, are made nigh by the blood of Christ. For he is our peace. Eph. 2:13 f.

Of him are you in Christ Jesus, who of God is made unto us wisdom, and justice, and sanctification, and redemption. 1 C. 1:30.

Christ is all, and in all. Col. 3:11.

17. OUR LORD'S RESURRECTION

My flesh shall rest in hope, because thou wilt not leave my soul in hell; nor wilt thou give thy holy one to see corruption. Ps. 15:9 f.

As Jonas was in the whale's belly three days and three nights, so shall the Son of man be in the heart of the earth three days and three nights. Mat. 12:40.

They shall deliver him to the Gentiles to be mocked, and scourged, and crucified, and the third day he shall rise again. Mat. 20:19.

After I shall be risen again I will go before you into Galilee. Mark 14:28.

He charged them not to tell any man what things they had seen till the Son of man shall be risen again from the dead. And they kept the word to themselves, questioning together what that should mean: When he shall be risen from the dead. Mark 9:8 f.

Thus it is written, and thus it behoved Christ to suffer and to rise again from the dead the third day. Luke 24:46.

Destroy this temple, and in three days I will raise it up. But he spoke of the temple of his body. John 2:19, 21.

They said unto them: Why seek you the living with the dead? He is not here, but is risen. Remember how he spoke unto you when he was yet in Galilee, saying: The Son of man must be delivered into the hands of sinful men, and be crucified, and the third day rise again. Luke 24:5-7.

To whom also he showed himself alive after his passion by many proofs, appearing to them, and speaking to them, and speaking of the kingdom of God. Acts 1:3.

Jesus of Nazareth God hath raised up, having loosed the sorrows of hell, as it was impossible that he should be holden by it. Acts 2:24.

The Author of life you killed, whom God hath raised from the dead, of which we are witnesses. Acts 3:15.

Him God raised up the third day, and gave him to be made manifest, not to all the people, but to witnesses preordained by God, even to us who did eat and drink with him after he rose again from the dead. Acts 10:40 f.

David was laid unto his fathers, and saw corruption. But he whom God hath raised from the dead saw no corruption. Acts 13:36 f.

I stand unto this day saying no other thing than those which the prophets and Moses did say should come to pass: that Christ should suffer, and that he should be the first that should rise from the dead. Acts 26:22 f.

If we have been planted together in the likeness of his death, we shall be also in the likeness of his resurrection. Rom. 6:5.

Christ rising again from the dead, dieth now no more; death shall no more have dominion over him. Rom. 6:9.

Who is he that shall condemn? Christ Jesus that died, yea that is risen also again. Rom. 8:34.

If thou confess with thy mouth the Lord Jesus, and believe in thy heart that God hath raised him up from the dead, thou shalt be saved. Rom. 10:9.

He arose again the third day, according to the Scriptures. 1 C. 15:4.

Christ is risen from the dead, the first-fruits of them that sleep. 1 C. 15:20.

Be mindful that the Lord Jesus Christ is risen again from the dead, according to my gospel. 2 Tim. 2:8.

Whereunto baptism, being of the like form (with the water by which Noe was saved), now saveth you also by the resurrection of Jesus Christ. 1 Pet. 3:21.

Grace be unto you from Jesus Christ, who is the first-begotten of the dead. Apoc. 1:5.

I am alive and was dead, and behold, I am living forever and ever. Apoc. 1:18.

18. OUR LORD'S ASCENSION

The Lord Jesus, after he had spoken to them, was taken up into heaven, and sitteth on the right hand of God. Mark 16:19.

Ought not Christ to have suffered these things, and so to enter into his glory? Luke 24:26.

He led them as far as Bethania; and lifting up his hands, he blessed them. And it came to pass, whilst he blessed them he departed from them, and was carried up into heaven. Luke 24:50 f.

If, then, you shall see the Son of man ascending up where he was before. John 6:63.

Yet a little while I am with you, and then I go to him that sent me. John 7:33.

I go to prepare a place for you. John 14:2.

You have heard that I said to you: I go away, and I come unto you. If you loved me, you would indeed be glad because I go to the Father, for the Father is greater than I. John 14:28.

And now I go to him that sent me, and none of you asketh me: Whither goest thou? John 16:5.

It is expedient for you that I go. For if I go not, the Paraclete will not come to you: but if I go, I will send him to you. John 16:7.

I go to my Father, and you shall see me no longer. John 16:10.

A little while and now you shall not see me: and again a little while and you shall see me, because I go to the Father. John 16:16.

I came forth from the Father, and am come into the world: again I leave the world and go to the Father. John 16:28.

Glorify thou me, O Father, with thyself, with the glory which I had, before the world was, with thee. John 17:5.

Do not touch me, for I am not ascended to my Father: but go to my brethren, and say to them: I ascend to my Father and to your Father, to my God and to your God. John 20:17.

Lift up your gates, O ye princes, and be ye lifted up, O eternal gates, and the King of glory shall enter in. Ps. 23:7.

Thou hast ascended on high; thou hast led captivity captive. Ps. 67:19.

When he had said these things, while they looked on, he was raised up: and a cloud received him out of their sight. Acts 1:9.

Being exalted by the right hand of God, and having received of the Father the promise of the Holy Ghost, he hath poured forth this which you see and hear. Acts 2:33.

He shall send him, whom heaven indeed must receive until the times of the restitution of all things. Acts 3:20 f.

Him hath God exalted with his right hand to be Prince and Savior, to give repentance to Israel, and remission of sins. Acts 5:31.

Behold, I see the heavens opened, and the Son of man standing at the right hand of God. Acts 7:55.

He raised him up from the dead, and set him on his right hand in the heavenly places. Eph. 1:20.

He that descended is the same also that ascended above all the heavens, that he might fill all things. Eph. 4:10.

God hath also exalted him. Phil. 2:9.

He was manifested in the flesh. Great is the mystery of godliness which was manifested in the flesh, is taken up in glory. 1 Tim. 3:16.

We see Jesus, who was made a little lower than the angels, for the suffering of death, crowned with glory and honor. Heb. 2:9.

We have such an high priest, who is set on the right hand of the throne of majesty in the heavens. Heb. 8:1.

This man, offering one sacrifice for sins, forever sitteth on the right hand of God. Heb. 10:12.

Jesus, who having joy set before him endured the cross, despising the shame, and sitteth on the right hand of the throne of God. Heb. 12:2.

He is on the right hand of God, being gone into heaven. 1 Pet. 2:22.

To him that shall overcome I will give to sit with me in my throne: as I also have overcome, and am set down with my Father in his throne. Apoc. 3:21.

19. OUR LORD'S SECOND COMING

The Son of man shall come in the glory of his father with his angels: and then will he render to every man according to his works. Mat. 16:27.

As lightning cometh out of the east and appeareth even into the west, so shall also the coming of the Son of man be. Mat. 24:27.

And then shall appear the sign of the Son of man in heaven: and then shall all the tribes of the earth mourn; and they shall see the Son of man coming in the clouds of heaven with much power and majesty. And he shall send his angels with a trumpet and a great voice, and they shall gather together his elect from the four winds, from the farthest parts of the heavens to the utmost bounds of them. Mat. 24:31 f.

As in the days of Noe, so shall also the coming of the Son of man be. Mat. 24:37.

Watch ye, therefore, because you know not at what hour your Lord will come. Mat. 24:

At midnight there was a cry made: Behold, the bridegroom cometh: go ye forth to meet him. Mat. 25:6.

When the Son of man shall come in his majesty, and all the angels with him, then shall he sit upon the seat of his majesty. Mat. 25:31.

Watch ye, therefore, for you know not when the Lord of the house cometh: at even or at midnight, or at the cock-crowing or in the morning. Mark 13:35.

He that shall be ashamed of me and of my words, of him the Son of man shall be ashamed, when he shall come in his majesty, and that of his Father and of the holy angels. Luke 9:26.

Blessed are those servants whom the Lord, when he cometh, shall find watching. Luke 12:37.

The Son of man, when he cometh, shall he find, think you, faith on earth? Luke 18:8.

A certain nobleman went into a far country to receive for himself a kingdom and to return. Luke 19:12.

I will come again and take you to myself, that where I am, you also may be. John 14:3.

This Jesus, who is taken up from you into heaven, shall so come as you have seen him going into heaven. Acts 1:11.

Judge not before the time: until the Lord come, who both will bring to light the hidden things of darkness, and will make manifest the counsels of the hearts. 1 C. 4:5.

When Christ shall appear who is your life, then you also shall appear with him in glory. Col. 3:4.

The Lord himself shall come down from heaven with commandment, and with the voice of an archangel, and with the trumpet of God; and the dead who are in Christ shall rise first. 1 Thess. 4:15.

I charge thee that thou keep the commandment without spot, blameless, unto the coming of our Lord Jesus Christ. 1 Tim. 6:14.

When the Prince of pastors shall appear you shall receive a neverfading crown of glory. 1 Pet. 5:4.

Looking for and hasting unto the coming of the day of the Lord, by which the heavens being on fire shall be dissolved, and the elements shall melt with the heat of fire. 2 Pet. 3:12.

Little children, abide in him: that when he shall appear we may have confidence, and not be confounded by him at his coming. 1 John 2:28.

We know that when he shall appear we shall be like to him, because we shall see him as he is. 1 John 3:2.

Enoch, the seventh from Adam, prophesied, saying: Behold, the Lord cometh with thousands of his saints, to execute judgment upon all. Jude 14 f.

Behold, he cometh with the clouds, and every eye shall see him, and they also that pierced him. Apoc. 1:7.

Behold, I come quickly, and my reward is with me to render to every man according to his works. Apoc. 22:12.

He that giveth testimony of these things saith: Surely I come quickly; amen. Come, Lord Jesus. Apoc. 22:20.

20. THE WORSHIP OF OUR LORD

Come, let us adore and fall down and weep before the Lord that made us. Ps. 94:6.

Adore him, all you his angels. Sion heard, and was glad. Ps. 96:7.

Adore his footstool, for he is holy. Ps. 98:5.

They shall adore the King, the Lord of hosts. Zach. 14:16.

Falling down, they adored him; and opening their treasures, they offered him gifts: gold, frankincense, and myrrh. Mat. 2:11.

A leper came and adored him, saying: Lord, if thou wilt, thou canst make me clean. Mat. 8:2.

They that were in the boat came and adored him, saying: Thou art the Son of God. Mat. 14:33.

A woman of Canaan came and adored him, saying: Lord, help me. Mat. 15:25.

Jesus met them, saying: All hail. But they came up and took hold of his feet, and adored him. Mat. 28.9.

Seeing him, they adored him, but some doubted. Mat. 28:17.

Seeing Jesus afar off, he ran and adored him. Mark 5:6.

They that went before and they that followed cried, saying: Hosanna. Blessed is he that cometh in the name of the Lord. Mark 11:9 f.

They adoring went back into Jerusalem with great joy. Luke 24:52.

He who honoreth not the Son honoreth not the Father who hath sent him. John 5:23.

The true adorers shall adore the Father in spirit and in truth. John 4:23.

He said: I believe, Lord. And falling down, he adored him. John 9:38.

God hath given him a name above every name, that in the name of Jesus every knee should bow, of those that are in heaven, on earth, and under the earth, and that every tongue should confess that the Lord Jesus

Christ is in the glory of God the Father. Phil. 2:9-11.

When he bringeth in the first-begotten into the world, he saith: And let all the angels of God adore him. Heb. 1:6.

When he had opened the book, the four living creatures and the four-and-twenty ancients fell down before the Lamb, having every one of them harps, and golden vials full of odors, which are the prayers of saints. And they sang a new canticle, saying: Thou art worthy, O Lord, to take the book, and to open the seals thereof. Worthy is the Lamb to receive power and divinity, and wisdom and strength, and honor, and glory, and benediction. Apoc. 5:8 f., 12.

Every creature which is in heaven, and on the earth, and under the earth, and such as are in the sea, and all that are in them, I heard all saying: To him that sitteth on the throne, and to the Lamb, benediction, and honor, and glory, and power forever and ever. Apoc. 5:13.

And the four living creatures said: Amen. And the four-and-twenty ancients fell down on their faces, and adored him that liveth forever and ever. Apoc. 5:14.

They cried with a loud voice, saying: Salvation to our God, who sitteth upon the throne, and to the Lamb. Apoc. 7:10.

21. THE PARABLES OF OUR LORD

1. The sower. Mat. 13:3-8.
2. The cockle. Mat. 13:24-30.
3. The mustard-seed. Luke 13:18 f.
4. The leaven hid in three measures of meal. Mat. 13:33.
5. The net cast into the sea. Mat. 13:45 f.
6. The seed growing secretly. Mark 4:26-29.
7. The good shepherd giving his life for his sheep. John 10:11-18.
8. The prodigal son. Luke 15:11-32.
9. The groat that was lost. Luke 15:8-10.
10. The lost sheep. Mat. 18:12-14.
11. The Pharisee and the publican. Luke 18:9-14.
12. Strife for the first seats at the table. Luke 14:7-11.
13. The sheep and the goats. Mat. 25:31-46.
14. The hidden treasure. Mat. 13:44.
15. The merchant seeking good pearls. Mat. 13:45 f.
16. The two sons. Mat. 21:33-44.
17. The tower and the warring king. Luke 14:28-33.
18. The wedding garment. Mat. 22:1-14.
19. The great supper. Luke 14:15-24.
20. The true vine. John 15:1-8.
21. The wicked husbandmen. Mat. 21:33-44.
22. The talents. Mat. 25:14-30.
23. The barren fig-tree. Luke 13:6-9.
24. The laborers in the vineyard. Mat. 20:1-16.
25. The pounds. Luke 19:11-27.
26. The good Samaritan. Luke 10:30-37.
27. The creditor and the two debtors. Luke 7:41-43.
28. The door and the sheepfold. John 10:1-18.
29. The unprofitable servants. Luke 17:7-10.
30. The unjust steward. Luke 16:1-9.
31. The rich man and Lazarus. Luke 16:19-31.
32. The unmerciful servant. Mat. 18:23-35.
33. The ten virgins. Mat. 25:1-13.
34. The importunate widow. Luke 18:1-8.
35. The friend on his journey. Luke 11:5-10.
36. The servants waiting for their lord returning from the wedding. Luke 12:35-48.

22. EMBLEMS AND IMAGERIES IN THE NEW TESTAMENT

1. The mote and the beam. Mat. 7:3-5.
2. The narrow gate. Mat. 7:13 f.
3. The house built upon a rock. Mat. 7:24-27.
4. The birds of the air. Mat. 6:26.
5. The lilies of the field. Mat. 6:28.
6. The axe laid to the root of the tree. Mat. 3:10.
7. The fishers and their nets. Mat. 4:18.
8. Salt. Mat. 5:13.
9. A city seated on a mountain. Mat. 5:14.
10. A light under a bushel. Mat. 5:15.
11. The single eye. Mat. 6:22.
12. The two builders. Mat. 7:24.
13. The broad way. Mat. 7:13.
14. The strait way. Mat. 7:14.
15. The great physician. Mat. 9:10.
16. The keys of the kingdom of heaven. Mat. 16:19.
17. The little child. Mat. 18:2.
18. The sudden lightning. Mat. 24:27.
19. The thief in the night. Mat. 24:43.
20. The hen gathering her chickens. Mat. 23:37.
21. Perverse children. Luke 7:31.
22. Lambs among wolves. Luke 10:3.
23. The faithful and wise steward. Luke 12:42.
24. The stone crying out. Luke. 19:40.
25. The human temple. John 2:21.
26. Wind an emblem of the Holy Spirit. John 2:21.
27. Darkness an emblem of evil. John 3:12.
28. Fields white to harvest. John 4:35.
29. Christ the door. John 10:9.
30. The grain of wheat. John 12:24.
31. Christ the way. John 14:6.
32. The branches. John 15:5.
33. The pillar of the temple. Acts 3:12.
34. Adoption of sons. Rom. 8:15.
35. One body and many members. Rom. 12:4.
36. The judgment-seat. Rom. 14:10.
37. The sure foundation. 1 C. 3:10.
38. The earthly house of this tabernacle. 2 C. 5:1.
39. The pillar and ground of the truth. 1 Tim. 3:15.
40. The soldier of Christ. 2 Tim. 2:3.
41. The anchor of the soul. Heb. 6:19.
42. Running the race. Heb. 12:1.
43. The flower of the grass that perisheth. Jas. 1:11.
44. The faithful mirror. Jas. 1:23.
45. The helm of a ship. Jas. 3:4.
46. Pilgrims on earth. 1 Pet. 2:11.
47. The roaring lion. 1 Pet. 5:8.
48. The sow wallowing in the mire. 2 Pet. 2:22.
49. The dog returning to his vomit. 2 Pet. 2:22.
50. Light an emblem of God. 1 John 1:5.
51. Clouds without water. Jude 12.
52. Christ knocking at the door of the soul. Apoc. 3:20.

23. PARABLES, VISIONS, ETC., IN THE OLD TESTAMENT

1. Jacob's ladder. Gen. 28:12.
2. Joseph's dream. Gen. 37:5.
3. The burning bush. Ex. 3:2.
4. The trees that made a king to reign over them. Judg. 9:7.
5. A honeycomb in the carcass of a lion. Judg. 14:8.
6. The poor man's little ewe-lamb. 2 K. 12:1.
7. The two brothers that quarrelled. 2 K. 14:6.
8. The man that slipped away. 3 K. 20:19.
9. Micheas's vision. 3 K. 22:19.
10. The thistle of Libanus and a cedar-tree. 4 K. 14:9.
11. The vision of a spirit. Job 4:15.
12. The behemoth. Job 40:1.
13. The leviathan. Job 41:1.
14. The ant and the sluggard. Prov. 6:6.

15. The vineyard of wild grapes. Is. 5:1.
16. The vision of the throne of God. Is 6:1.
17. The parable of Lucifer fallen from heaven. Is. 14:12.
18. The rod watching. Jer. 1:11.
19. The boiling caldron. Jer. 1:13.
20. The linen girdle. Jer. 13:1.
21. The two baskets of figs. Jer. 24:1.
22. The cup of the wine of fury. Jer. 25:2.
23. The bands and chains. Jer. 27:2.
24. The chains of wood and of iron. Jer. 28:13.
25. The book cast into the Euphrates. Jer. 51:63.
26. Eating a book. Ez. 3:1.
27. The hair of the prophet. Ez. 5:1.
28. The vision of the temple. Ez. 8:1.
29. The thau-cross [T]. Ez. 9:4.
30. The coals of fire scattered over the city. Ez. 10:1.
31. The untempered mortar. Ez. 13:14.
32. The cushions and pillows of the prophetesses. Ez. 13:20.
33. The two eagles and the vine. Ez. 17:1.
34. The young lions taken in a pit. Ez. 19:1.
35. The vine plucked up and burnt. Ez. 19:10.
36. The boiling pot. Ez. 24:1.
37. The resurrection of dry bones. Ez. 37:1.
38. The two sticks that were joined together into one. Ez. 37:15.
39. Holy waters issuing out from under the Temple. Ez. 47:1.
40. Nabuchodonosor's dream of the great statue. Dan. 2:31.
41. Nabuchodonosor's dream of the great tree. Dan. 4:7.
42. The four beasts. Dan. 7:1.
43. The ram and the goat. Dan. 8:1.
44. The ivy that withered. John 4:6.
45. The locusts. Amos 7:1.
46. The fruit-hook. Amos 8:1.
47. The fire. Amos 7:4.
48. The mason's trowel. Amos 7:7.
49. The vision of the horses. Zach. 1:7.
50. The four horns and the four smiths. Zach. 1:18.
51. The golden candlestick and the seven lamps. Zach. 4:1.
52. The flying volume. Zach. 5:1.
53. The woman in the vessel. Zach. 5:5
54. The four war-chariots. Zach. 6:1.
55. The two rods. Zach. 11:10.
56. The foolish shepherd. Zach. 11:15.
57. The battle in the air. 2 Mac. 5:1.
58. The vision of Jeremias the prophet, environed with great beauty and majesty. 2 Mac. 15:13.
59. Thorns and thistles. Gen. 3:17.
60. The stars of light. Gen. 15:5.
61. The woody valleys. Num. 24:5.
62. Divine doctrine likened to rain. Deut. 32:2.
63. The eagle training her young. Deut. 32:11.
64. Sands on the seashore. 3 K. 4:29.
65. The hireling looking for the evening. Job 7:2.
66. The rush and the sedge-bush. Job 8:11.
67. The spider's web. Job 8:14.
68. Man fleeth as a shadow. Job 14:2.
69. The old tree springing up again at the scent of water. Job 14:9.
70. The dust driven away by the wind. Ps. 1:4.
71. The hart panting after the fountains of water. Ps. 41:1.
72. The mighty conqueror. Ps. 44:4.
73. Snow. Ps. 50:9.
74. Sparrows building near the sanctuary. Ps. 83:4.
75. The pelican of the wilderness. Ps. 101:7.
76. Rejuvenescence. Ps. 102:5.
77. The compassionate father. Ps. 102:13.
78. A cry from the great depths. Ps. 129:1.
79. The precious ointment and the dew of Hermon. Ps. 132:2.

80. The fowler's net. Prov. 1:17.
81. The dawning of day. Prov. 4:18.
82. The wandering bird. Prov. 4:18.
83. Iron sharpeneth iron. Prov. 27:17.
84. The face shining in the water. Prov. 27:19.
85. The threefold cord. Eccles. 4:12.
86. The neglected house. Eccles. 10:18.
87. Bread cast upon the waters. Eccles. 11:1.
88. The fallen tree. Eccles. 11:3.
89. The pitcher crushed at the fountain. Eccles. 12:6.
90. Words as goads and as nails, Eccles. 12:11.
91. White as wool. Is. 1:18.
92. The cords of vanity. Is. 5:18.
93. The oak-tree. Is. 6:13.
94. The wolf dwelling with the lamb. Is. 12:6.
95. The boundless sea. Is. 12:9.
96. The falling star. Is. 14:12.
97. The watchman of the city. Is. 21:11.
98. The key of the house of David. Is. 22:22.
99. A peg in a sure place. Is. 22:23.
100. The shaking of the olive-tree. Is. 24:13.
101. The desert as a Carmel. Is. 32:15.
102. The desert an impassable land. Is. 35:1.
103. Summer blossoms. Is. 40:7.
104. The bruised reed and the smoking flax. Is. 42:3.
105. Feeding on ashes. Is. 44:20.
106. The captive. Is. 52:3.
107. The lamb before his shearer. Is. 53:7.
108. The raging sea. Is. 57:20.
109. The royal diadem. Is. 62:3.
110. The fallen leaf. Is. 64:6.
111. The fountain of living water. Jer. 2:13.
112. The broken cisterns. Jer. 2:13.
113. The husbandry. Jer. 4:3.
114. The old paths. Jer. 6:16.
115. The horse rushing to the battle. Jer. 8:6.
116. The physician. Jer. 8:22.
117. The returning swallow. Jer. 8:7.
118. The Ethiopian and the leopard. Jer. 13:23.
119. The dark mountains. Jer. 13:16.
120. The graver's tool. Jer. 17:1.
121. The tamaric in the desert. Jer. 17:6.
122. The tree planted by the waters. Jer. 17:8.
123. Clay in the hand of the potter. Jer. 18:1.
124. The hammer that breaketh the rock in pieces. Jer. 23:29.
125. The watered garden. Jer. 31:12.
126. The bullock unaccustomed to the yoke. Jer. 31:18.
127. Rising early to work. Jer. 35:15.
128. Wine upon the lees. Jer. 48:11.
129. The espousals by faith. Osee 2:20.
130. The morning dew. Osee 6:4.
131. The brand plucked out of the fire. Zach. 3:2.
132. Gold in the furnace. Mal. 3:2.
133. The sun an emblem of our Lord. Mal. 4:3.

24. THE MIRACLES OF OUR LORD

1. The Incarnation. Luke 1:38.
2. Zachary's dumbness and cure. Luke 1:20.
3. The heavenly army of angels singing the "Gloria in Excelsis" at his birth. Luke 2:13.
4. His star in the east. Mat. 2:2.
5. Water changed into wine at Cana. John 2:1-11.
6. Healing of the ruler's son at Capharnaum. John 4:46-54.
7. Stilling of the storm on the Lake of Galilee. Mat. 8:23-27.
8. The miraculous draught of fishes. Luke 5:1-11.
9. The devils driven out of two demoniacs. Mat. 8:28-34.
10. The daughter of Jairus raised to life. Mat. 9:23-26.
11. Healing of the woman who was troubled for twelve years with an issue of blood. Mark 5:35-43.

12. Two blind men receive their sight. Mat. 11:27-31.

13. Healing of a dumb man possessed by the devil. Mat. 11:32 f.

14. Healing of one sick of the palsy. Mark 2:1-12.

15. Cleansing of the leper. Mat. 8:1-4

16. The centurion's servant healed at Capharnaum. Luke 7:1-10.

17. The unclean spirit driven out of a man in the synagogue at Capharnaum. Mark 1:23-26.

18. Peter's mother-in-law cured of fever. Mat. 8:14-17.

19. Healing a man who was a cripple thirty-eight years. John 5:1-16.

20. The water of the pond of Bethsaida troubled by an angel. John 5:4.

21. Feeding of five thousand with five loaves and two fishes at Decapolis. Luke 9:12-17.

22. The widow's son raised to life at Naim. Luke 7:11-16.

23. Jesus walks upon the Sea of Galilee. Mat. 14:22-33.

24. In Jerusalem the man born blind restored to sight. John 9:1-41.

25. Healing the withered hand. Mat. 12:9-13.

26. Healing one possessed with a devil, blind and dumb, so that he spoke and saw. Mat. 12:22 f.

27. Healing in Galilee a woman who had a spirit of infirmity eighteen years. Luke 13:11-17.

28. Healing of the dropsical man in Galilee. Luke 14:1-6.

29. Cleansing of the ten lepers in Samaria. Luke 17:11-19.

30. Cure of the daughter of the Syrophenician woman. Mat. 15:21-28.

31. Healing the man that was deaf and dumb at Decapolis. Mark 7:31-37.

32. Feeding of four thousand with seven loaves and a few fishes. Mat. 15:32-39.

33. He gives sight in Bethsaida to a blind man. Mark 8:22-26.

34. Cure of the lunatic child at Thabor. Mat. 17:14-21.

35. The fish with the tribute money in its mouth. Mat. 17:24-27.

36. Raising to life of Lazarus of Bethania after he had been dead four days. John 11:11-44.

37. Sight given to two blind men nigh to Jericho. Mat. 20:29-34.

38. Cursing the barren fig tree, which immediately withered away. Mark 11:12-14.

39. Institution of the Blessed Sacrament. Mat. 26:26.

40. Healing of Malchus's ear in the Garden of Gethsemani. Luke 22:49-51.

41. Darkness over the whole earth at our Lord's death. Mat. 27:45.

42. A great earthquake at our Lord's Resurrection. Mat. 28:2.

43. The second miraculous draught of fishes. John 21:1-23.

Miracles Not Specified

Jesus went about all the cities and towns, teaching in their synagogues and preaching the gospel of the kingdom, and healing every disease and every infirmity. Mat. 9:35.

There came the bind and the lame in the Temple, and he healed them. Mat. 21:14.

When it was evening, after sunset, they brought to him all that were ill and that were possessed with devils. And all the city was gathered together at the door. And he healed many that were troubled with divers diseases, and he cast out many devils. Mark 1:32-34.

Running through that whole country. they began to carry about in beds those that were sick where they heard he was. And whithersoever he entered into towns or into villages or cities, they laid the sick in the streets, and besought him that they might touch but the hem of his garment: and as many as touched him were made whole. Mark 6:55 f.

All the multitude sought to touch him, for virtue went out from him and healed all. Luke 6:19.

Other Miracles and Visions

1. The descent of the Holy Ghost at Pentecost in parted tongues of fire. Acts 2:2-4.
2. Our Lord appears to St. Stephen. Acts 7:55 f.
3. Our Lord appears to St. Paul. Acts 9:3-6.
4. Our Lord appears to Ananias. Acts 9:10.
5. An angel appears to Cornelius. Acts 10:3.
6. St. Peter's vision of the clean and unclean beasts. Acts 10:9-18.
7. Ananias appears in a vision to St. Paul. Acts 9:12.
8. A man of Macedonia appears in a vision to St. Paul. Acts 16:9.
9. St. Paul is caught up into Paradise. 2 C. 12:1-4.

25. MIRACLES OF THE OLD TESTAMENT

Wrought in Divine Mercy

1. Creation of the world out of nothing. Gen. 1:1-31.
2. The miraculous properties of the tree of life. Gen. 2:9.
3. The rainbow. Gen. 9:12.
4. A pillar of a cloud and of fire. Ex. 13:21.
5. Blossoming of Aaron's rod. Num. 17:8.
6. God gives quails and manna to the children of Israel in the wilderness. Ex. 16:8.
7. Preservation of the manna. Ex. 16:24.
8. The Jordan dried up for the passage of the children of Israel. Jos. 3:16.
9. The walls of Jericho fall down at the sounding of the trumpets by the priests. Jos. 6:20.
10. The sun and moon stand still at the prayer of Josue. Jos. 10:12.
11. Water issues out of a jaw-bone of an ass, to quench the thirst of Samson. Judg. 15:19.
12. Isaias heals Ezechias of sickness. Is. 38:21.
13. Sidrach, Misach, and Abdenago cast into the fiery furnace without being hurt. Dan. 3:23.
14. Daniel cast into the lions' den. The mouths of the lions closed by an angel. Dan. 6:22.
15. The ivy prepared by the Lord for Jonas. Jon. 4:10.
16. Ravens bring Elias bread and flesh to eat morning and evening. 3 K. 17:6.
17. The pot of meal belonging to the widow woman of Sarephta wasted not, and her cruse of oil diminished not. 3 K. 17:9.
18. The widow's son raised to life. 3 K. 17:17.
19. An angel feeds Elias with an hearth-cake and a vessel of water. 3 K. 19:6.
20. Elias forty days and forty nights without eating. 3 K. 19:8.
21. Eliseus divides the waters of the Jordan with the mantle of Elias. 4 K. 2:14.
22. The bad waters of Jericho healed by casting in salt. 4 K. 2:19.
23. Eliseus multiplies the widow's oil. 4 K. 4:1.
24. The Sunamitess's child raised to life. 4 K. 4:34.
25. Miracle of the meal and pottage. 4 K. 4:38.
26. Naaman the Syrian is cleansed of his leprosy by washing seven times in the Jordan. 4 K. 5:14.
27. The iron head of an axe floats upon the water. 4 K. 6:6.
28. A dead man is raised to life by touching the bones of Eliseus. 4 K. 13:21.
29. Those bitten by fiery serpents healed by the brazen serpent (a figure of Christ crucified). Num. 21:9.

Wrought in Divine Vengeance

30. The Deluge. Gen. 7:11.
31. The confusion of tongues. Gen. 11.7.
32. The destruction of the cities of the plain. Gen. 19:24.

33. The plagues of Egypt. Ex. 7:20—11:4.

34. The waters of the Red Sea come upon the Egyptians, and the Lord shut them up in the midst of the waves. Ex. 14:27.

35. Nadab and Abiu burnt by fire for offering strange fire. Lev. 10:2.

36. Israelites burnt by fire at Taberah for murmuring against God. Num. 10:1.

37. Josue overcomes the five kings of the Amorrhites. Jos. 10:10.

38. Dagon twice falls before the ark. 1 K. 5:3.

39. For curiously looking into the ark 50,070 were slain. 1 K. 6:19.

40. Thunder and rain sent in punishment of sin. 1 K. 12:17.

41. Samson slays a thousand men with a jaw-bone. Judg. 15:15.

42. The people punished with pestilence, which David stops by offering sacrifice of expiation on the threshing floor of Ornan. 1 Par. 21:15.

43. Withering of Jeroboam's hand for offering violence to the prophet. 3 K. 13:4.

44. The waters of Moab turned into blood. 4 K. 3:22.

45. The panic in the Syrian camp. 4 K. 7:6.

46. An angel of the Lord slew of Sennacherib's army 85,000 men. 4 K. 19:35.

47. Elias shuts up the heaven from raining three years and six months. 3 K. 17:1.

48. Elias causes fire to come from heaven to consume two captains and their companies. 4 K. 1:10.

49. Eliseus smites with blindness the Syrian soldiers sent to apprehend him. 4 K. 6:18.

50. The handwriting on the wall—Mane, Thecel, Phares. Dan. 5:5.

Other Miracles

51. Aaron's rod turned into a serpent. Ex. 7:10.

52. Balaam's ass speaks. Num. 22:28.

53. Gedeon's fleece. Judg. 6:37 ff.

54. The shadow in the dial of Achaz goes ten degrees backward. 4 K. 20:11.

55. The tempest ceases on Jonas being cast into the sea. Jon. 1:15.

56. Jonas in the whale three days and three nights. Jon. 2:1.

57. The law given on Mount Sinai in thunder and lightning. Ex. 19:9.

58. The earthquake and fire at Horeb. 3 K. 19:11.

59. Elias divides the waters of the Jordan with his mantle. 4 K. 2:8.

60. Elias is taken up by a whirlwind into heaven in a fiery chariot. 4 K. 2:11.

61. Fire from heaven consumed the holocaust of Elias, and the wood and the stones and the dust, and licked up the water that was in the trench. 3 K. 18:38.

62. Fire came from the Lord upon the altar. Lev. 9:24.

63. An angel causes fire to arise from the rock to consume Gedeon's holocaust. Judg. 6:20.

64. Manue's holocaust consumed by fire from heaven. Judg. 13:19.

65. Fire comes from heaven to consume the sacrifices of Solomon. 2 Par. 7:1.

26. VISIONS AND SYMBOLS OF THE APOCALYPSE

1. Our Lord walking in the midst of the golden candlesticks. 1:12-19.

2. The seven stars and the seven churches. 1:20.

3. Messages to the seven churches of Asia. 2:1—3:22.

4. A door opened in heaven. 4:1.

5. A rainbow round about the throne. 4:2 f.

6. Four-and-twenty ancients seated around the throne. 4:4.

7. Seven lamps burn before the throne. 4:5.

8. Before the throne as it were a sea of glass. 4:6.

9. The four living creatures. 4:6-8.

10. The book sealed with seven seals, and opened by the Lamb. 5:1-5.

11. Golden vials full of odors. 3:8.

12. The opening of the seven seals.
(1-4) The four horses. 6:1-8.
(5) The souls of them that were slain for the word of God. 6:9-11.
(6) Earthquake and convulsion of the heavenly bodies. 6:12-14.
(7) The seven angels with their trumpets. 8:2.

13. Four angels holding the four winds. 7:1.

14. The signing of the 144,000. 7:2-8.

15. Silence in heaven for half an hour. 8:1.

16. Incense offered on the golden altar. 8:5.

17. The seven angels sounding the seven trumpets. 8:6.
1st Trumpet. Hail and fire mingled with blood cast upon the earth. 8:7.
2nd Trumpet. A burning mountain cast into the sea. 8:8 f.
3rd Trumpet. A star from heaven, burning like a torch, falls upon the third part of waters. 8:10 f.
4th Trumpet. The third part of the sun, moon, and stars darkened. 8:12.
5th Trumpet. A star falls from heaven. 9:1.
The opening of the bottomless pit. 9:2.
Locusts like unto horses. 9:3-11.
6th Trumpet. Four angels loosed from the river Euphrates to kill the third part of men. 9:14.
An army of horsemen twenty thousand times ten thousand. 9:16-19.
An angel having a little book opened. 10:2.
Seven thunders utter their voices. 10:3 f.
7th Trumpet. The mystery of God finished. The book eaten. 10:9 f.

18. Measurement of the temple. 11:1 f.

19. The two witnesses clothed in sackcloth. 11:3.

20. The court of the temple given to the Gentiles. 11:2.

21. The two olive trees and two candlesticks. 11:4.

22. The beast ascending out of the abyss. 11:7.

23. Fall of the tenth part of the city. 11:13.

24. The second woe and the third woe. 11:14.

25. The temple of God opened in heaven. 11:19.

26. The woman clothed with the sun, birth of a man child. 12:1-6.

27. The red dragon with seven heads and ten horns. 12:3-17.

28. St. Michael and his angels fight a great battle with the dragon and his angels. 12:7-9.

29. The woman flees into the desert from the face of the serpent. 12:14.

30. A beast comes up out of the sea. 13:1.

31. A beast comes out of the earth with two horns like a lamb. 13:11-18.

32. The Lamb on Mount Sion, and with him the 144,000. 14:1-5.

33. The angel flying through heaven having the everlasting gospel. 14:6 f.

34. The angel proclaims the fall of Babylon. 14:8-13.

35. The Son of man having on his head a crown of gold, and in his hand a sharp sickle. 14:14-16.

36. An angel coming out of the temple. 14:17.

37. The angel reaping the harvest and gathering in the clusters of the vineyard. 14:18.

38. The vine of the earth cast into the great press of the wrath of God. 14:19.

39. Seven angels with seven last plagues. 15:1.

40. A sea of glass mingled with fire. 15:2.

41. The temple of the tabernacle of the testimony opened. 15:5.

42. The seven angels pour out the seven vials of God's wrath.

(1) A grievous wound falling upon men who have the character of the beast. 16:2.
(2) Sea turned into blood. 16:3.
(3) The rivers and springs become blood. 16:4-6.
(4) Men scorched with great heat. 16:9.
(5) The kingdom of the beast becomes dark, and they gnaw their tongues for pain. 16:10 f.
(6) The waters of the Euphrates dry up. 16:12.
    Three unclean spirits like frogs. 16:13 f.
    The kings of the earth gather at Armagedon to battle against the great day of the Almighty God. 16:15 f.
(7) A great earthquake, such an one as never hath been since men were upon earth, and great hail from heaven. 16:17-21.
    The earthquake divides the great city of Babylon in three parts. 16:19 f.

43. The woman on the scarlet-colored beast with seven heads and ten horns. 17:1-18.

44. The fall of Babylon. Kings and merchants lament over her. 18:1-20.

45. A stone like a great millstone cast into the sea by an angel. 18:21.

46. Christ's victory over the beast. 19:1-10.

47. The Word of God riding on a white horse. 19:11-16.

48. An angel standing in the sun. 19:17-21.

49. The birds gather to eat the flesh of the slain army. 19:18.

50. The beast and false prophet cast alive in the pool of fire burning with brimstone. 19:20.

51. Satan bound for a thousand years. 20:1-3.

52. The souls of the martyrs reign with Christ a thousand years. 20:4.

53. The first resurrection. 20:5.

54. Satan, loosed out of his prison, seduces the nations. 20:7-10.

55. Gog and Magog encompass the camp of the saints. 20:8 f.

56. The devil cast into the pool of fire. 20:10.

57. The great white throne. 20:11.

58. The opening of the book of life. 20:12.

59. Hell and death cast into the pool of fire. 20:14.

60. St. John's vision of the New Jerusalem, coming down out of heaven from God. 21:1.

61. The length, height, and breadth thereof. 21:16.

62. The exceeding riches, splendor, and glory thereof. 21:1-11.

63. The walls thereof are of jasper stone, the twelve gates of pearls. 21:12.

64. The twelve foundations thereof are of precious stones. 21:19 f.

65. The streets thereof of pure gold. 21:21.

66. The brightness and eternal felicity thereof. 21:22-27.

67. The river of the water of life. 22:1.

68. The tree of life bearing twelve kinds of fruit. 22:2.

69. The angel's words to St. John. 22:8.

70. Our Lord calls upon us to yearn after the possession of heaven. 22:17.

71. He that giveth testimony of these things saith: Surely I come quickly. Amen. 22:20.

27. OUR LORD'S SEVEN LAST WORDS

1

Jesus said: Father forgive them, for they know not what they do. Luke 23:34.

2

Jesus said to him: Amen I say to thee, this day thou shalt be with me in paradise. Luke 23:43.

3

When Jesus had seen his mother and the disciple standing whom he loved, he saith to his mother: Woman, behold thy son. After that he saith to the disciple: Behold thy mother. And from that hour the disciple took her to his own. John 19: 26 f.

4

From the sixth hour there was darkness over the whole earth until the ninth hour. And about the ninth hour Jesus cried with a loud voice, saying: Eli, Eli, lamma sabacthani? that is, My God, my God, why hast thou forsaken me? Mat. 27: 45 f.

5

Jesus knowing that all things were now accomplished, that the Scripture might be fulfilled, said: I thirst. John 19: 28.

6

When Jesus had taken the vinegar, he said: It is consummated. John 19: 3.

7

Jesus crying with a loud voice said· Father, into thy hands I commend my spirit. Luke 23: 48.

28. THE SEVEN BLOOD-SHEDDINGS OF OUR LORD

1. In His Circumcision

After eight days were accomplished that the Child should be circumcised, his name was called Jesus. Luke 2: 21.

2. In His Agony

There appeared to him an angel from heaven strengthening him. And being in an agony, he prayed the longer. And his sweat became as drops of blood trickling down upon the ground. Luke 22: 43 f.

3. In His Scourging

Having scourged Jesus, [Pilate] delivered him unto them to be crucified. Mat. 27: 26.

4. In His Crowning with Thorns

The soldiers platting a crown of thorns, put it upon his head. John 19: 2.

5. In the Stripping of His Garments

Stripping him, they put a scarlet cloak about him. Mat. 27: 28.

6. In His Crucifixion

It was the third hour, and they crucified him. Mark 15: 25.

7. In the Opening of His Side

One of the soldiers with a spear opened his side, and immediately there came out blood and water. John 19: 34.

29. EJACULATIONS IN HIS PRAISE AND LOVE

I love Thee, O Lord my strength. Ps. 17: 1.

What have I in heaven? and besides thee what do I desire upon earth? For thee my flesh and my heart hath fainted away. Thou art the God of my heart, and the God that is my portion forever. Ps. 72: 25 f.

Lord, thou knowest all things: thou knowest that I love thee. John 21: 17.

We give thee thanks, O Lord God Almighty, who art, and who wast, and who art to come: because thou hast taken to thee thy great power, and thou hast reigned. Apoc. 11: 17.

Great and wonderful are thy works, O Lord God Almighty; just and true are thy ways, O King of ages. Who shall not fear thee, O Lord, and magnify thy name? For thou only art holy: for all nations shall come and shall adore in thy sight, because thy judgments are manifest. Apoc. 15: 3 f.

Thou art worthy, O Lord our God, to receive glory and honor and power: because thou hast created all things, and for thy will they were and have been created. Apoc. 4: 11.

To thee, O God of our fathers, I give thanks, and I praise thee: because thou hast given me wisdom and strength. Dan. 2:23.

Praise the Lord, O my soul: in my life I will praise the Lord, I will sing to my God as long as I shall be. Ps. 145:1.

I will extol thee, O God my King; and I will bless thy name forever, yea forever and ever. Every day I will bless thee, and I will praise thy name forever, yea forever and ever. Ps. 144:1 f.

We thy people, and the sheep of thy pasture, will give thanks to thee forever. We will show forth thy praise unto generation and generation. Ps. 78:13.

I will praise thee, O Lord my God, with my whole heart, and I will glorify thy name forever. Ps. 85:12.

I will praise thee forever because thou hast done it. Ps. 51:11.

O God, my God, to thee do I watch at break of day. For thee my soul hath thirsted: for thee my flesh, O how many ways! Ps. 62:2.

In the daytime the Lord hath commanded his mercy; and a canticle to him in the night. With me is prayer to the God of my life; I will say to God: Thou art my support. Ps. 41:9 f.

My soul doth magnify the Lord, and my spirit had rejoiced in God my Savior. Luke 1:46 f.

V

THE BLESSED VIRGIN MARY
ST. JOSEPH
ST. JOHN THE BAPTIST

A. The Blessed Virgin

1. THE ANNUNCIATION AND VISITATION

In the sixth month, the angel Gabriel was sent from God into a city of Galilee called Nazareth, to a virgin espoused to a man whose name was Joseph, of the house of David; and the virgin's name was Mary. And the angel being come in, said to her: Hail, full of grace: the Lord is with thee: blessed art thou among women. Who having heard, was troubled at his saying, and thought within herself what manner of salutation this should be. And the angel said to her: Fear not, Mary, for thou hast found grace with God. Behold, thou shalt conceive in thy womb, and shalt bring forth a Son; and thou shalt call his name Jesus. He shall be great and shall be called the Son of the Most High, and the Lord God shall give unto him the throne of David his father; and he shall reign in the house of Jacob forever. And of his kingdom there shall be no end. And Mary said to the angel: How shall this be done? because I know not man. And the angel answering said to her: The Holy Ghost shall come upon thee, and the power of the Most High shall overshadow thee. And therefore also the Holy [One] which shall be born of thee shall be called the Son of God. And behold, thy cousin Elizabeth, she also hath conceived a son in her old age; and this is the sixth month with her that is called barren: because no word shall be impossible with God. And Mary said: Behold the handmaid of the Lord: be it done to me according to thy word. And the angel departed from her. Luke 1:26-38.

When his mother Mary was espoused to Joseph before they came together, she was found with child of the Holy Ghost. Whereupon Joseph her husband, being a just man, and not willing publicly to expose her, was minded to put her away privately. But while he thought on these things, behold an angel of the Lord appeared to him in his sleep, saying: Joseph, son of David, fear not to take unto thee Mary thy wife, for that which is conceived in her is of the Holy Ghost. And she shall bring forth a Son: and thou shalt call his name Jesus. For he shall save his people from their sins. Mat. 1:18-21.

Mary, rising up in those days, went into the hill country with haste into a city of Juda. And she entered into the house of Zachary, and saluted Elizabeth. And it came to pass that when Elizabeth heard the salutation of Mary, the infant leaped in her womb. And Elizabeth was filled with the Holy Ghost, and she cried out with a loud voice and said: Blessed art thou among women, and blessed is the fruit of thy womb. And whence is this to me, that the mother of my Lord should come to me? For behold, as soon as the voice of thy salutation sounded in my ears, the infant in my womb leaped for joy. And blessed art thou that hast believed, because those things shall be accomplished that were spoken to thee by the Lord. Luke 1:39-45.

And Mary said:

The Magnificat

My soul doth magnify the Lord,

And my spirit hath rejoiced in God my Savior.

Because he hath regarded the humility of his handmaid: for behold, from henceforth all generations shall call me blessed.

Because he that is mighty hath done great things to me: and holy is his name.

And his mercy is from generation unto generations, to them that fear him.

He hath shown might in his arm: he hath scattered the proud in the conceit of their heart.

He hath put down the mighty from their seat, and hath exalted the humble.

He hath filled the hungry with good things, and the rich he hath sent empty away.

He hath received Israel his servant, being mindful of his mercy.

As he spoke to our fathers, to Abraham and to his seed forever. Luke 1:46-55.

And Mary abode with her about three months, and she returned to her own house. Luke 1:56.

Behold, he cometh leaping upon the mountains, skipping over the hills (to verse 14). Cant. 2:8.

When the fulness of the time was come, God sent his Son, made of a woman. Gal. 4:4.

He that made me rested in my tabernacle. Ecclus. 24:12.

By me his handmaid he hath fulfilled his mercy which he promised to the house of Israel. Judg. 13:18.

2. THE BIRTH OF HER DIVINE SON

Joseph went up from Galilee out of the city of Nazareth into Judea, to the city of David which is called Bethlehem, because he was of the house and family of David, to be enrolled with Mary his espoused wife, who was with child. Luke 2:4 f.

And it came to pass that when they were there, her days were accomplished that she should be delivered. And she brought forth her first-born Son, and wrapped him up in swaddling clothes, and laid him in a manger, because there was no room for them in the inn. Luke 3:6 f.

And there were in the same country shepherds watching and keeping the night-watches over their flock. And behold, an angel of the Lord stood by them, and the brightness of God shone round about them, and they feared with a great fear. And the angel said to them: Fear not: for behold, I bring you good tidings of great joy, that shall be to all the people: For this day is born to you a Savior, who is Christ the Lord, in the city of David. And this shall be a sign unto you: you shall find the Infant wrapped in swaddling clothes, and laid in a manger. And suddenly there was with the angel a multitude of the heavenly army, praising God and saying: Glory to God in the highest: and on earth peace to men of good will. And it came to pass, after the angels departed from them into heaven, the shepherds said one to another: Let us go over to Bethlehem, and let us see this word that is come to pass, which the Lord hath showed to us. And they came with haste, and they found Mary and Joseph, and the Infant lying in the manger. And seeing, they understood the word that had been spoken concerning this Child. And all that heard wondered, and at those things that were told them by the shepherds. Luke 2:8-18.

3. PRESENTATION OF HER SON IN THE TEMPLE

After the days of her purification according to the law of Moses were accomplished, they carried him to Jerusalem, to present him to the Lord. As it is written in the law of the Lord: Every male opening the womb shall be called holy to the Lord. And to offer a sacrifice according as it is written in the law of the Lord, a pair of turtle-doves or two young pigeons. And behold, there was a man in Jerusalem named Simeon, and this man was just and devout, waiting for the consolation of Israel, and the Holy Ghost was in him. And he had received an answer from the Holy Ghost, that he should not see death before he had seen the Christ of the Lord. And he came by the Spirit into the temple. And when his parents brought in the Child Jesus to do for him according to the custom of the law, he also took him into his arms, and blessed God, and said:

The Nunc dimittis

Now thou dost dismiss thy servant, O Lord, according to thy word, in peace.

Because my eyes have seen thy salvation,

Which thou hast prepared before the face of all people:

A light to the revelation or the Gentiles, and the glory of thy people Israel.

And his father and mother were wondering at these things which were spoken concerning him. And Simeon blessed them, and said to Mary his mother: Behold, this Child is set for the fall and for the resurrection of many in Israel, and for a sign which shall be contracted. And thy own soul a sword shall pierce, that out of many hearts thoughts may be revealed. Luke 2:22-35.

4. THE VISIT OF THE WISE MEN; THE FLIGHT INTO EGYPT

Behold, the star which they [the Magi] had seen in the east went before them, until it came and stood over where the Child was. And seeing the star, they rejoiced with exceeding great joy. And entering into the house, they found the Child with Mary his mother; and falling down, they adored him; and opening their treasures, they offered him gifts: gold, frankincense, and myrrh. Mat. 2:9-11.

After they [the Magi] were departed, behold an angel of the Lord appeared in sleep to Joseph, saying: Arise, and take the Child and his mother, and fly into Egypt, and be there until I shall tell thee. For it will come to pass that Herod will seek the Child to destroy him. Who arose, and took the Child and his mother by night and retired into Egypt: and he was there until the death of Herod: that it might be fulfilled which the Lord spoke by the prophet [Osee], saying: Out of Egypt have I called my Son. Mat. 2:13-15.

But when Herod was dead, behold an angel of the Lord appeared in sleep to Joseph in Egypt, saying: Arise, and take the Child and his mother, and go into the land of Israel: for they are dead that sought the life of the Child. Who arose, and took the Child and his mother and came into the land of Israel. But hearing that Archelaus reigned in Juda in the room of Herod his father, he was afraid to go thither; and being warned in sleep, retired into the quarters of Galilee. Mat. 2:19-22.

5. THE RETURN TO NAZARETH

And coming, he dwelt in a city called Nazareth. Mat. 2:23.

His parents went every year to Jerusalem, at the solemn day of the Pasch. And when he was twelve years old, they going up into Jerusalem according to the custom of the feast, and having fulfilled the days, when they returned, the Child Jesus remained in Jerusalem; and his parents knew it not. And thinking that he was in the company, they came a day's journey, and sought him among their kinsfolks and acquaintance. And not finding him, they returned into Jerusalem, seeking him. And it came to pass, that after three days they found him in the temple, sitting in the midst of the doctors, hearing them and asking them questions. And all that heard him were astonished at his wisdom and his answers. And seeing him, they wondered. And his mother said to him: Son, why hast thou done so to us? Behold, thy father and I have sought thee sorrowing. And he said to them: How is it that you sought me? Did you not know that I must be about my father's business? And they understood not the word that he spoke unto them. Luke 2:41-50.

And he went down with them, and came to Nazareth, and was subject to them. And his mother kept all these words in her heart. Luke 2:51.

Mary kept all these words, pondering them in her heart. Luke 2:19.

His father and mother were wondering at these things which were spoken concerning him. Luke 2:33.

6. JESUS' FIRST MIRACLE, AT CANA

There was a marriage in Cana of Galilee; and the mother of Jesus was there.. And Jesus also was invited, and his disciples, to the marriage. And the wine failing, the mother of Jesus saith to him: They have no wine. And Jesus said to her: Woman, what is it to me and to thee? My hour is not yet come. His mother saith to the waiters: Whatsoever he shall say to you, do ye. Now there were set there six water-pots of stone, according to the manner of the purifying of the Jews, containing two or three measures apiece. Jesus saith to them: Fill the water-pots with water. And they filled them up to the brim. And Jesus saith to them: Draw out now and carry to the chief steward of the feast: and they carried it. And when the chief steward had tasted the water made wine, and knew not whence it was [but the waiters knew who had drawn the water], the chief steward calleth the bridegroom, and said to him: Every man at first setteth forth good wine, and when men have well drunk, then that which is worse: but thou hast kept the good wine until now. This beginning of miracles did Jesus in Cana of Galilee; and he manifested his glory, and his disciples believed in him. John 2:1-11.

7. MARY AT THE CRUCIFIXION; AFTER THE RESURRECTION

There stood by the cross of Jesus, his mother, and his mother's sister, Mary of Cleophas, and Mary Magdalen. When Jesus therefore had seen his mother and the disciple standing whom he loved, he saith to his mother: Woman, behold thy son. After that, he saith to the disciple: Behold thy mother. And from that hour the disciple took her to his own. John 19:25-27.

O all ye that pass by the way, attend, and see if there be any sorrow like to my sorrow. Lam. 1:12.

The apostles were persevering with one mind in prayer with the women, and with Mary the mother of Jesus, and with his brethren. Acts 1:14.

A great sign appeared in heaven: A woman clothed with the sun, and the moon under her feet, and on her head a crown of twelve stars. Apoc. 12:1.

8. HER VIRTUES

Blessed art thou that hast believed. Luke 1:45.

I am the mother of holy hope. Ecclus. 24:24.

I am the mother of fair love. Ecclus. 24:24.

Put me as a seal upon thy heart, as a seal upon thy arm; for love is strong as death, jealousy as hard as hell, the lamps thereof are fire and flames. Many waters cannot quench charity, neither can the floods drown it: if a man should give all the substance of his house for love, he shall despise it as nothing. Cant. 8:6 f.

As the vine I have brought forth a pleasant odor: and my flowers are the fruit of honor and riches. Ecclus. 24:23.

Thou hast done manfully, and thy heart has been strengthened: therefore also the hand of the Lord hath strengthened thee, and therefore thou shalt be blessed forever. Jdth. 15:11.

Grace is poured abroad in thy lips: therefore hath God blessed thee forever. Ps. 44:3.

The Lord hath blessed thee by his power, because by thee he hath brought our enemies to naught. Jdth. 13:22.

Blessed art thou, O daughter, by the Lord the Most High God, above all women upon the earth. Jdth. 13:23.

He hath so magnified thy name this day that thy praise shall not depart out of the mouth of men, who shall be mindful of the power of the Lord forever; for that thou hast not spared thy life by reason of the distress and tribulation of thy people, but hast prevented our ruin in the presence of God. Jdth. 13:25.

Mary hath chosen the best part, which shall not be taken from her. Luke 10:42.

Mary rising up in those days went into the hill-country with haste, into a city of Juda, and she entered into the house of Zachary, and saluted Elizabeth. Luke 1:39 f.

The wine failing, the mother of Jesus saith to him: They have no wine. John 2:3.

His parents went every year to Jerusalem, at the solemn day of the Pasch. Luke 2:41.

Joseph went up to Bethlehem, to be enrolled with Mary. Luke 2:4.

Behold, I have sought thee sorrowing. Luke 2:48.

After the days of Mary's purification according to the law of Moses were accomplished, they carried Jesus to Jerusalem, to present him to the Lord. Luke 2:22.

My soul doth magnify the Lord. Luke 1:46.

Thou art beautiful, O my love, sweet and comely as Jerusalem: terrible as an army set in array. Cant. 6:3.

God hath girt me with strength, and made my way blameless. Ps. 17:33.

Thou art the glory of Jerusalem, thou art the joy of Israel, thou art the honor of our people. Jdth. 15:10.

Blessed art thou, O daughter, by the Lord the Most High God, above all women of the earth. Jdth. 13:23.

Many daughters have gathered together riches; thou hast surpassed them all. Prov. 31:29.

Behold the handmaid of the Lord: be it done to me according to thy word. Luke 1:38.

A great sign appeared in heaven: a woman clothed with the sun. On her head was a crown of twelve stars. Apoc. 12:1.

I am the mother of fear and of knowledge. Ecclus. 24:24.

All the glory of the king's daughter is within, in golden borders clothed around about with varieties. Ps. 44:15-17.

9. PROPHETIC TYPES AND FIGURES OF THE BLESSED VIRGIN

In the Old Testament

1. The second Eve. Gen. 3:20.
2. Mother of all the living. Gen. 3:20.
3. The woman that crushed the serpent's head. Gen. 3:15.
4. Rachel, mother of Joseph. Gen. 29:17.
5. The burning bush. Ex. 3:2.
6. The ark of the covenant. Num. 10:33.
7. The star of Jacob. Num. 24:17.
8. The blooming of Aaron's rod. Num. 17:8.
9. Gedeon's fleece. Judg. 6:37.
10. Debbora the prophetess. Judg. 4:4.

11. Jahel. Judg. 4:21.
12. The daughter of Jephte the Galaadite. Judg. 11:37.
13. Ruth the Moabite. Ruth 1:4.
14. Anna, the mother of Samuel (her canticle). 1 K. 1:20.
15. The ivory throne of Solomon. 2 K. 10:18.
16. Vessel of gold. 2 K. 10:25.
17. The glory of Jerusalem. Jdth. 15:10.
18. Judith (her canticle). Jdth.16:1.
19. Edissa or Esther. Esth. 2:7.
20. Set up from eternity. Prov. 8:23.
21. The valiant woman. Prov. 31:10.
22. Surpassing all the daughters of men. Prov. 21:29.
23. The unspotted mirror. Wis. 7:26.
24. The morning star in the midst of a cloud. Ecclus. 50:6.
25. Cedar of Libanus. Ecclus. 24:17.
26. Palm-tree of Cades. Ecclus. 24:13.
27. The first-born before all creatures. Ecclus. 24:5.
28. The flower of the field. Cant. 2:1.
29. The lily of the valleys. Cant. 2:1.
30. The lily among thorns. Cant.2:2.
31. The honeycomb. Cant. 4:11.
32. The garden enclosed. Cant. 4:12.
33. A fountain sealed up. Cant. 4:12.
34. The well of living waters. Cant. 4:15.
35. The morning rising. Cant. 6:9.
36. Bright as the sun. Cant. 6:9.
37. Terrible as an army set in array. Cant. 6:9.
38. Tower of ivory. Cant. 7:4.
39. Foretold by the prophets. Is.7:14.
40. The earth that budded forth a Savior. Is. 45:8.
41. The woman that compassed a man. Jer. 31:22.
42. The gate passed through by the prince alone. Ez. 44:2.
43. The stone cut out of a mountain without hands. Dan. 2:34.
44. The mother of the Machabees. 2 Mac. 7:1.

In the New Testament

1. Born of the race of David. Mat. 1:1.
2. Espoused to St. Joseph. Mat. 1:8.
3. Saluted by an angel. Luke 1:26.
4. Visited by the shepherds. Luke 2:16.
5. Visited by the wise men. Mat. 2:11.
6. Her flight into Egypt. Mat. 2:13.
7. Her inviolable virginity. Luke 1:34.
8. Handmaid of the Lord. Luke 1:38.
9. Full of grace. Luke 1:28.
10. Blessed among women. Luke 1:28.
11. Overshadowed by the Holy Ghost. Luke 1:35.
12. The mother of the Lord. Luke 1:43.
13. Called "Blessed" by all generations. Luke 1:48.
14. Mother of sorrows. Luke 2:35.
15. Vessel of honor. Rom. 9:21.
16. The woman clothed with the sun. Apoc. 12:1.
17. The tabernacle of God with men. Apoc. 21:3.

10. THE SEVEN SORROWS OF THE BLESSED VIRGIN

1. The Prophecy of Holy Simeon

Simeon blessed them, and said to Mary his mother: Behold, this Child is set for the fall and for the resurrection of many in Israel, and a sign which shall be contradicted: And thy own soul a sword shall pierce, that out of many hearts thoughts may be revealed. Luke 2:34 f.

2. The Flight into Egypt

Behold, an angel of the Lord appeared in sleep to Joseph, saying: Arise, and take the Child and his mother, and fly into Egypt, and be there until I shall tell thee: for it will come to pass that Herod will seek the Child to destroy him. Who arose, and took the Child and his mother by night, and retired into Egypt: and he was there until the death of Herod. Mat. 2:13 f.

3. The Losing of the Child Jesus

They came a day's journey, and sought him among their kinsfolks and acquaintance. And not finding him, they returned to Jerusalem seeking him. Luke 2:44 f.

4. The Meeting of Jesus Carrying the Cross

Bearing his own cross, he went forth to that place which is called Calvary, but in Hebrew Golgotha. Where they crucified him, and with him two others, one on each side, and Jesus in the midst. John 19:17 f.

From the sole of the foot unto the top of the head there is no soundness therein: wounds and bruises and swelling sores: they are not bound up, nor dressed, nor fomented with oil. Is. 1:6.

5. Witnessing the Sufferings and Death of Her Divine Son

There stood by the cross of Jesus his mother. When Jesus therefore had seen his mother and the disciple standing whom he loved, he saith to his mother: Woman, behold thy son. After that he saith to the disciple: Behold thy mother. And from that hour the disciple took her to his own. John 19:25-27.

6. The Taking Down of Her Dead Son from the Cross

When it was evening there came a certain rich man of Arimathea, named Joseph, who also himself was a disciple of Jesus. He went to Pilate, and asked the body of Jesus. Then Pilate commanded that the body should be delivered. And Joseph taking the body, wrapped it up in a clean linen cloth. Mat. 25:27-59.

7. Jesus is Laid in the Sepulcher

They took the body of Jesus, and bound it in linen cloths with the spices, as the manner of the Jews is to bury. Now there was in the place where he was crucified a garden, and in the garden a new sepulcher, wherein no man yet had been laid. There therefore, because of the Parasceve of the Jews, they laid Jesus, because the sepulcher was nigh at hand. John 19:40-42.

11. THE ROSARY OF THE BLESSED VIRGIN

The Joyful Mysteries

1. The Incarnation of Our Lord

The Word was made flesh, and dwelt among us. John 1:14.

2. The Visitation

Mary rising up in those days went into the hill-country with haste, into a city of Juda. And she entered into the house of Zachary, and saluted Elizabeth. Luke 1:39 f.

3. The Nativity of Our Lord

She brought forth her first-born Son, and wrapped him up in swaddling clothes, and laid him in a manger. Luke 2:7.

4. The Presentation of Our Lord in the Temple

After the days of her purification according to the law of Moses were accomplished, they carried him to Jerusalem, to present him to the Lord. Luke 2:22.

5. The Finding of Our Lord in the Temple

It came to pass that after three days they found him in the temple, sitting in the midst of the doctors, hearing them and asking them questions. Luke 2:46.

The Sorrowful Mysteries

1. The Agony in the Garden

Going out, he went according to his custom to the Mount of Olives. And kneeling down, he prayed, saying: Father, if thou wilt, remove this chalice from me: but yet not my will but thine be done. And there appeared to him an angel from heaven strengthening him. And being in an agony, he prayed the longer. And his sweat became as drops of blood trickling down upon the ground. Luke 22:39, 41-44.

2. The Scourging at the Pillar

Then Pilate took Jesus and scourged him. John 19:1.

3. The Crowning with Thorns

The soldiers platting a crown of thorns, put it upon his head, and they put on him a purple garment. And they came to him and said: Hail, King of the Jews. And they gave him blows. Pilate therefore went forth again, and saith to them: Behold, I bring him forth unto you that you may know that I find no cause in him. (Jesus therefore came forth bearing the crown of thorns and the purple garment.) And he saith to them: Behold the Man. John 19:1-5.

4. The Carrying of the Cross

They took Jesus and led him forth. And bearing his own cross, he went forth to that place which is called Calvary, but in Hebrew Golgotha. John 19:16 f.

And there followed him a great multitude of people, and of women who bewailed and lamented him. But Jesus turning to them, said: Daughters of Jerusalem, weep not over me, but for yourselves and for your children. Luke 23:27 f.

If any man will come after me, let him deny himself and take up his cross daily and follow me. Luke 9:23.

God forbid that I should glory, save in the cross of our Lord Jesus Christ, by whom the world is crucified to me, and I to the world. Gal. 6:14.

5. The Crucifixion of Our Lord

Pilate spoke again to them, desiring to release Jesus. But they cried again, saying: Crucify him, crucify him. Luke 23:20 f.

Pilate delivered him unto them to be crucified. Mat. 27:26.

They took Jesus and led him forth to that place which is called Calvary, where they crucified him. John 19:17 f.

Jesus bowing his head, gave up the ghost. John 19:30.

They that are Christ's have crucified their flesh with the vices and concupiscences. Gal. 5:24.

With Christ I am nailed to the cross. Gal. 2:19.

The Glorious Mysteries

1. The Resurrection of Our Lord

The angel said to the women: Fear not you: for I know that you seek Jesus, who was crucified. He is not here, for he is risen, as he said. Mat. 28:5 f.

You are buried with him in baptism, in whom also you are risen again by the faith of the operation of God. Col. 2:12.

If you be risen with Christ, seek the things that are above. Col. 3:1.

2. The Ascension of Our Lord

He led them out as far as Bethania, and lifting up his hands he blessed them. And whilst he blessed them he departed from them, and was carried up into heaven. Luke 24:50 f.

3. The Desent of the Holy Ghost

I will ask the Father, and he shall give you another Paraclete, that he may abide with you forever: the Spirit of truth, whom the world cannot receive. John 4:16 f.

It is expedient to you that I go; for if I go not, the Paraclete will not come to you: but if I go, I will send him to you. He will teach you all truth. John 16:7, 13.

When the days of the Pentecost were accomplished, they were all together in one place. And suddenly there came a sound from heaven, as of a mighty wind coming, and it filled the whole house where they were sitting. And there appeared to them parted tongues, as it were of fire, and it sat upon every one of them: and they were filled with the Holy Ghost; and they began to speak with divers tongues, according as the Holy Ghost gave them to speak. Acts 2:1-4.

4. The Assumption of the Blessed Virgin

A throne was set for the king's mother, and she sat on his right hand. 3 K. 2:19.

In the Holy City I rested, and my power was in Jerusalem. And I took root in an honorable people, and my abode is in the full assembly of the saints. Ecclus. 24:15 f.

5. Her Coronation

Thou art all fair, O my love, and there is no spot in thee. Come from Libanus, my spouse, come from Libanus, come: Thou shalt be crowned from the top of Amana. Cant. 4:7 f.

A great sign appeared in heaven: a woman clothed with the sun, and the moon under her feet, and on her head a crown of twelve stars. Apoc. 12:1.

B. St. Joseph

1. EVENTS RECORDED IN THE GOSPELS

The book of the generation of Jesus Christ, the Son of David, the son of Abraham. Abraham begot Isaac. And Mathan begot Jacob. And Jacob begot Joseph, the husband of Mary, of whom was born Jesus, who is called Christ. Mat. 1:1 f., 15 f.

And Joseph, rising up from sleep, did as the angel of the Lord had commanded him, and took unto him his wife. Mat. 1:24.

The angel Gabriel was sent from God to a virgin espoused to a man whose name was Joseph, of the house of David. Luke 1:26 f.

When his mother was espoused to Joseph, before they came together, she was found with child of the Holy Ghost. Mat. 1:18.

Whereupon Joseph her husband, being a just man, and not willing publicty to expose her, was minded to put her away privately. Mat. 1:19.

But while he thought on these things, behold the angel of the Lord appeared to him in his sleep, saying: Joseph, son of David, fear not to take unto thee Mary thy wife, for that which is conceived in her is of the Holy Ghost. Mat. 1:20.

They wondered at the words of grace that proceeded from his mouth, and they said: Is not this the son of Joseph? Luke 4:22.

Philip findeth Nathanael, and saith to him: We have found him of whom Moses in the law and the prophets did write, Jesus the son of Joseph of Nazareth. John 1:45.

Joseph also went up from Galilee out of the city of Nazareth into Judea, to the city of David which is called Bethlehem, because he was of the house and family of David, to be enrolled wih Mary his espoused wife, who was with child. And it came to pass that when they were there her days were accomplished that she should be delivered. Luke 2:4-6.

They came with haste, and they found Mary and Joseph, and the Infant lying in the manger. Luke 2:16.

After the days of her purification according to the law of Moses were accomplished they carried him to Jerusalem, to present him to the Lord. Luke 2:22.

When his parents brought in the Child Jesus, to do for him according to the custom of the law, he [Simeon] also took him into his arms, and blessed God, and said: Now thou dost dismiss thy servant, O Lord, according to thy word, in peace. And his father and mother were wondering at these things which were spoken concerning him. Luke 2:27, 29, 33.

After they had performed all things according to the law of the Lord they returned into Galilee, into their city Nazareth. Luke 2:39.

After they were departed, behold an angel of the Lord appeared in sleep to Joseph, saying: Arise and take the Child and his mother, and fly into Egypt, and be there until I shall tell thee. For it will come to pass that Herod will seek the Child to destroy him. Who arose, and took the Child and his mother by night, and retired into Egypt. Mat. 2:13 f.

When Herod was dead, behold an angel of the Lord appeared in sleep to Joseph in Egypt, saying: Arise, and take the Child and his mother, and go into the land of Israel. For they are dead that sought the life of the Child. Who arose, and took the Child and his mother, and came into the land of Israel. But hearing that Archelaus reigned in Judea in the room of Herod his father, he was afraid to go thither: and being warned in sleep, retired into the quarters of Galilee. And coming, he dwelt in a city called Nazareth. Mat. 2:19-23.

His parents went every year to Jerusalem at the solemn day of the Pasch. And when he was twelve years old, they going up to Jerusalem according to the custom of the feast, and having fulfilled the days, when they returned the Child Jesus remained in Jerusalem; and his parents knew it not. And thinking that he was in the company, they came a day's journey, and sought him among their kinsfolks and acquaintance. And not finding him, they returned into Jerusalem, seeking him. Luke 2:41-45.

And it came to pass that after three days they found him in the temple, sitting in the midst of the doctors, hearing them and asking them questions. And all that heard him were astonished at his wisdom and his answers. And seeing him, they wondered. And his mother said to him: Son, why hast thou done so to us? Behold, thy father and I have sought thee sorrowing. Luke 2:46, 48.

2. SACRED TEXTS ACCOMMODATED TO ST. JOSEPH

He taught them in their synagogues, so that they wondered and said: How came this man by this wisdom and these mighty works? Is not this the carpenter's son? Mat. 13:54 f.

The Jews murmured at him because he had said: I am the living bread which came down from heaven. And they said: Is not this Jesus the son of Joseph, whose father and mother we know? How then saith he, I came down from heaven? John 6:41 f.

Joseph her husband being a just man. Mat. 1:19.

His parents went every year to Jerusalem at the solemn day of the Pasch. Luke 1:41.

Behold, thy father and I have sought thee sorrowing. Luke 2:48.

The just shall flourish like the palm-tree. He shall grow up like the cedar of Libanus. They that are planted in the house of the Lord shall flourish in the courts of the house of our God. Ps. 91:13 f.

Praise the Lord, O Jerusalem, because he hath strengthened the bolts of thy gates, he hath blessed thy children within thee. Ps 147:12 f.

Blessed is the man that feareth the Lord: he shall delight exceedingly in his commandments. His seed shall be mighty upon earth: the generation of the righteous shall be blessed. Ps. 111:1 f.

My truth and my mercy shall be with him: and in my name shall his horn be exalted. Ps. 88:25.

The Lord is our helper and protector. For in him our heart shall rejoice: and in his holy name we have trusted. Ps. 32:20 f.

Thou that rulest Israel: thou that leadest Joseph as a sheep. Ps. 79:2.

Israel shall spring as a lily, and his root shall shoot as that of Libanus. Osee 14:6.

My beloved feedeth among the lilies. Cant. 2:16.

The young man shall dwell with the virgin. And the bridegroom shall rejoice over the bride. And thy God shall rejoice over thee. Is. 62:5.

Beloved of God and men, whose memory is in benediction. He made him like the saints in glory, and magnified him in the fear of his enemies, and with his words he made prodigies to cease. He glorified him in the sight of kings, and gave him commandments in the sight of his people, and showed him his glory. He sanctified him in his faith and meekness, and chose him out of all flesh. For he heard him and his voice, and brought him into a cloud. And he gave him commandments and a law of life and instruction. Ecclus. 45:1-6.

The Lord made him blessed in glory. He clothed him with a robe of glory. Ecclus. 45:9.

C. St. John the Baptist

1. BEFORE HIS PUBLIC MINISTRY

Behold, I send my angel, and he shall prepare the way before my face. Mal. 3:1.

Behold, I will send you Elias the prophet before the coming of the great and dreadful day of the Lord. And he shall turn the heart of the fathers to the children, and the heart of the children to their fathers: lest I come, and strike the earth with anathema. Mal. 4:5 f.

The voice of one crying in the desert: Prepare ye the way of the Lord, make straight in the wilderness the paths of our God. Every valley shall be exalted, and every mountain and hill shall be made low, and the crooked shall become straight, and the rough ways plain. And the glory of the Lord shall be revealed, and all flesh together shall see that the mouth of the Lord hath spoken. Is. 4:3-5.

There was in the days of Herod the king of Judea a certain priest named Zachary, of the course of Abia, and his wife was of the daughters of Aaron, and her name Elizabeth. And they were both just before God, walking in all the commandments and justifications of the Lord without blame. Luke 1:5 f.

And there appeared to him an angel of the Lord, standing on the right side of the altar of incense. And Zachary seeing him was troubled, and fear fell upon him. But the angel said to him: Fear not, Zachary, for thy prayer is heard, and thy wife Elizabeth shall bear thee a son, and thou shalt call his name John: And thou shalt have joy and gladness, and many shall rejoice in his nativity. For he shall be great before the Lord, and shall drink no wine nor strong drink: and he shall be filled with the Holy Ghost, even from his mother's womb. And he shall convert many of the children of Israel to the Lord their God. And he shall go before him in the spirit and power of Elias: that he may turn the hearts of the fathers unto the children, and the incredulous to the wisdom of the just, to prepare unto the Lord a perfect people. Luke 1:11-17.

Mary, rising up in those days, went into the hill-country with haste into a city of Juda. And she entered into the house of Zachary, and saluted Elizabeth. And it came to pass that when Elizabeth heard the salutation of Mary, the infant leaped in her womb. And Elizabeth was filled with the Holy Ghost. And she cried out with a loud voice, and said: Blessed art thou among women, and blessed is the fruit of thy womb. And whence is this to me that the mother of my Lord should come to me? For behold, as soon as the voice of thy salutation sounded in my ears, the infant in my womb leaped for joy. Luke 1:39:44.

Before I formed thee in the bowels of thy mother, I knew thee: and before thou camest forth out of the womb, I sanctified thee. Jer. 1:5.

Give ear, ye islands, and hearken, ye people from afar. The Lord hath called me from the womb: from the bowels of my mother he hath been mindful of my name (to verse 7). Is. 49:1.

Behold, I have given thee to be the light of the Gentiles, that thou mayst be my salvation even to the farthest part of the earth. Is. 49:6.

Now Elizabeth's full time of being delivered was come, and she brought forth a son. And her neighbors and kinsfolks heard that the Lord had showed his great mercy towards her, and they congratulated with her. Luke 1:57 f.

And it came to pass that on the eighth day they came to circumcise the child, and they called him by his father's name Zachary. And his mother answering, said: Not so, but he shall be called John. And they said to her: There is none of thy kindred that is called by this name. And they made signs to his father, how he would have him called. And demanding a writing-table, he wrote, saying: John is his name. And they all wondered. Luke 1:59-63.

And immediately his mouth was opened, and his tongue loosed, and he spoke, blessing God. And fear came upon all their neighbors; and all these things were noised abroad over all the hill-country of Judea. And all they that had heard them laid them up in their heart, saying: What an one, think ye, shall this child be? For the hand of the Lord was with him. And Zachary his father was filled with the Holy Ghost: and he prophesied, saying: Luke 1:64-67.

The Benedictus

Blessed be the Lord God of Israel: because he hath visited and wrought the redemption of his people.

And hath raised up a horn of salvation to us, in the house of David his servant.

As he spoke by the mouth of his holy prophets, who are from the beginning:

Salvation from our enemies, and from the hand of all that hate us.

To perform mercy to our fathers, and to remember his holy testament.

The oath which he swore to Abraham our father, that he would grant to us,

That, being delivered from the hand of our enemies, we may serve him without fear.

In holiness and justice before him, all our days.

And thou, child, shalt be called the prophet of the Highest: for thou shalt go before the face of the Lord to prepare his ways.

To give knowledge of salvation to his people, unto the remission of their sins.

Through the bowels of the mercy of our God, in which the Orient, from on high, hath visited us.

To enlighten them that sit in darkness and in the shadow of death: to direct our feet into the way of peace. Luke 1:68-79.

And the child grew, and was strengthened in spirit; and was in the deserts until the day of his manifestation to Israel. Luke 1:80.

And John was clothed with camel's hair, and a leathern girdle about his loins: and he ate locusts and wild honey. Mark 1:6.

He shall drink no wine nor strong drink; and he shall be filled with the Holy Ghost. Luke 1:15.

John the Baptist came neither eating nor drinking wine, and you say: He hath a devil. Luke 7:33.

And when they went their way, Jesus began to say to the multitudes concerning John: What went you out into the desert to see? a reed shaken with the wind? But what went you out to see? a man clothed in soft garments? Behold, they that are clothed in soft garments are in the houses of kings. But what went you out to see? a prophet? Yea, I tell you, and more than a prophet. For this is he of whom it is written: Behold, I send my angel before thy face, who shall prepare thy way before thee.

Amen I say to you, there hath not risen among them that are born of women a greater than John the Baptist; yet he that is the lesser in the kingdom of heaven is greater than he. And from the days of John the Baptist until now the kingdom of heaven suffereth violence, and the violent bear it way. For all the prophets and the law prophesied until John: and if you will receive it, he is Elias that is to come. He that hath ears to hear, let him hear.

But whereunto shall I esteem this generation to be like? It is like to children sitting in the market-place, who, crying to heir companions, say: We have piped to you, and you have not danced: we have lamented, and you have not mourned.

For John came neither eating nor drinking; and they say: He hath a devil. The Son of man came eating and drinking, and they say: Behold a man that is a glutton and a wine-drinker, a friend of publicans and sinners. And wisdom is justified by her children. Mat. 11:7-19.

He was a burning and a shining light, and you were willing for a time to rejoice in his light. John 5:35.

I meditated on thy commandments, which I loved. Ps. 118:47.

The just shall flourish like the palm tree: he shall grow up like the cedar of Libanus. Ps. 91:13.

Israel shall spring as the lily, and his root shall shoot forth as that of Libanus. Osee 14:6.

2. HIS PUBLIC MINISTRY

In those days cometh John the Baptist preaching in the desert of Judea, and saying: Do penance: for the kingdom of heaven is at hand. For this is he that was spoken of by Isaias the prophet, saying: A voice of one crying in the desert: Prepare ye the way of the Lord, make straight his paths. Mat. 3:1-3.

John was in the desert, baptizing and preaching the baptism of penance unto remission of sins. And there went out to him all the country of Judea, and all they of Jerusalem, and were baptized by him in the river Jordan, confessing their sins. Mark 1:4 f.

In the fifteenth year of the reign of Tiberius Caesar, Pontius Pilate being governor of Judea, and Herod being tetrarch of Galilee, and Philip his brother tetrarch of Iturea and the country of Trachonitis, and Lysanias tetrarch of Abilina, under the high priests Annas and Caiphas, the word of the Lord was made unto John the son of Zachary, in the desert.

And he came into all the country about the Jordan, preaching the baptism of penance for the remission of sins. As it was written in the book of the sayings of Isaias the prophet: A voice of one crying in the wilderness: Prepare ye the way of the Lord, make straight his paths. Every valley shall be filled, and every mountain and hill shall be brought low: and the crooked shall be made straight, and the rough ways plain. And all flesh shall see the salvation of God. Luke 3:1-6.

He said to the multitudes that went forth to be baptized by him: Ye offspring of vipers, who hath showed you to flee from the wrath to come? Bring forth therefore fruits worthy of penance, and do not begin to say: We have Abraham for our father. For I say unto you, that God is able of these stones to raise up children to Abraham. For now the axe is laid to the root of the trees. Every tree therefore that bringeth not forth good fruift shall be cut down, and cast into the fire.

And the people asked him, saying: What then shall we do? And he answering said to them: He that hath two coats, let him give to him that hath none; and he that hath meat, let him do in like manner.

And the publicans also came to be baptized, and said to him: Master, what shall we do? But he said to them: Do nothing more than that which is appointed you.

And the soldiers also asked him, saying: And what shall we do? And he said to them: Do violence to no man, neither calumniate any man; and be content with your pay.

And as the people were of opinion and all were thinking in their hearts of John, that perhaps he might be the Christ, John answered, saying unto all: I indeed baptize you with water; but there shall come one mightier than I, the latchet of whose shoes I am not worthy to loose; he shall baptize you with the Holy Ghost and with fire: whose fan is in his hand, and he will purge his floor; and will gather the wheat into his barn, but the chaff he will burn with unquenchable fire.

And many other things exhorting did he preach to the people. Luke 3:7-18.

Then went out to him Jerusalem and all Judea, and all the country about Jordan: and were baptized by him in the Jordan, confessing their sins. Mat. 3:5 f.

Having a mind to put him to death, he feared the people, because they esteemed him as a prophet. Mat. 14:5.

John came to you in the way of justice, and you did not believe him. But the publicans and the harlots believed him: but you seeing it did not even afterwards repent, that you might believe him. Mat. 21:32.

The baptism of John, was it from heaven or from men? Answer me. But they thought with themselves, saying: If we say, From heaven, he will say, Why then did you not believe him? If we say, From men, we fear the people. For all men counted John that he was a prophet indeed. And they answering say to Jesus: We know not. And Jesus answering saith to them: Neither do I tell you by what authority I do these things. Mark 11:30-33.

And this is the testimony of John, when the Jews sent from Jerusalem priests and Levites to him, to ask him: Who art thou? And he confessed and did not deny: and he confessed, I am not the Christ. And they asked him: What then? Art thou Elias? And he said: I am not. Art thou the prophet? And he answered: No.

They said therefore unto him: Who art thou, that we may give an answer to them that sent us? what sayest thou of thyself? He said: I am the voice of one crying in the wilderness: Make straight the way of the Lord, as said the prophet Isaias. And they that were sent were of the Pharisees.

And they asked him, and said to him: Why then dost thou baptize, if thou be not Christ, nor Elias, nor the prophet? John answered them, saying: I baptize with water; but there hath stood one in the midst of you whom you know not. The same is he that shall come after me, who is preferred before me, the latchet of whose shoe I am not worthy to loose.

These things were done in Bethania beyond the Jordan, where John was baptizing. John 1:19-28.

Many resorted to him, and they said: John indeed did no sign. John 10:41.

The disciples of John used to fast. Mark 2:18.

Lord, teach us to pray, as John also taught his disciples. Luke 11:1.

There was a man sent from God, whose name was John. This man came for a witness, to give testimony of the Light, that all men might believe through him. He was not the Light, but was to give testimony of the Light. John 1:6-8.

There cometh after me one mightier than I, the latchet of whose shoes I am not worthy to stoop down and loose. I have baptized you with water; but he shall baptize you with the Holy Ghost. Mark 1:7 f.

The next day again John stood, and two of his disciples. And beholding Jesus walking, he saith: Behold the Lamb of God. And the two disciples heard him speak, and they followed Jesus.

And Jesus turning, and seeing them following him, saith to them: What seek you? Who said to him, Rabbi (which is to say, being interpreted, Master), where dwellest thou? He saith to them: Come and see. They came, and saw where he abode, and they stayed with him that day: now it was about the tenth hour. And Andrew the brother of Simon Peter was one of the two who had heard from John, and followed him. John 1:35-40.

John beareth witness of him, and crieth out, saying: This was he of whom I spoke: He that shall come after me is preferred before me, because he was before me. John 1:15.

The next day John saw Jesus coming to him, and he saith: Behold the Lamb of God; behold him who taketh away the sin of the world. This is he of whom I said: After me there cometh a man who is preferred before me, because he was before me, and I knew him not; but that he may be made manifest in Israel, therefore am I come batizing with water.

And John gave testimony, saying: I saw the Spirit coming down as a dove from heaven, and he remained upon him. And I knew him not: but he who sent me to baptize with water said to me: He upon whom thou shalt see the Spirit descending and remaining upon him, he it is that baptizeth with the Holy Ghost. And I saw, and I gave testimony, that this is the Son of God. John 1:29-34.

And they came to John, and said to him: Rabbi, he that was with thee beyond the Jordan, to whom thou gavest testimony, behold he baptizeth, and all men come to him.

John answered and said: A man cannot receive anything unless it be given him from heaven. You yourselves do bear me witness that I said, I am not Christ, but that I am sent before him. He that hath the bride is the bridegroom: but the friend of the bridegroom, who standeth and heareth him, rejoiceth with joy because of the bridegroom's voice. This my joy therefore is fulfilled. He must increase, but I must decrease.

He that cometh from above is above all. He that is of the earth, of the earth he is, and of the earth he speaketh. He that cometh from heaven is above all. And what he hath seen and heard, that he testifieth: and no man receiveth his testimony. He that hath received his testimony hath set to his seal that God is true. For he whom God hath sent speaketh the words of God: for God doth not give the Spirit by measure.

The Father loveth the Son: and he hath given all things into his hand. He that believeth in the Son hath life everlasting: but he that believeth not the Son shall not see life, but the wrath of God abideth on him. John 3:26-36.

There is another that beareth witness of me: and I know that the witness which he witnesseth of me is true. You sent to John: and he gave testimony to the truth. John 5:32 f.

And he went again beyond the Jordan into that place where John was baptizing first; and there he abode. And many resorted to him, and they said: John indeed did no sign. But all things whatsoever John said of this man were true. And many believed in him. John 10:40-42.

John first preaching before his coming the baptism of penance to all the people of Israel. And when John was fulfilling his course, he said: I am not he whom you think me to be: but behold there cometh one after me, the shoes of whose feet I am not worthy to loose. Acts 13:24 f.

They were baptized by him in the river of Jordan, confessing their sins. Mark 1:5.

These things were done in Bethania beyond the Jordan, where John was baptizing. John 1:28.

John was baptizing in Ennon near Salim, because there was much water there. John 3:23.

He who sent me to baptize with water said to me: He upon whom thou shalt see the Spirit descending and remaining upon him, he it is that baptizeth with the Holy Ghost. John 1:33.

I indeed baptize you in water unto penance: but he that shall come after me is mightier than I, whose shoes I am not worthy to bear: he shall baptize you in the Holy Ghost and fire. Mat. 3:11.

I have baptized you with water, but he will baptize you with the Holy Ghost. Mark 1:8.

He upon whom thou shalt see the Spirit descending and remaining upon him, he it is that baptizeth with the Holy Ghost. John 1:33.

John indeed baptized with water, but you shall be baptized with the Holy Ghost not many days hence. Acts 1:5.

I remembered the word of the Lord, how that he said: John indeed baptized with water, but you shall be baptized with the Holy Ghost. Acts 11:16.

Then cometh Jesus from Galilee to the Jordan, unto John, to be baptized by him. But John stayed him, saying: I ought to be baptized by thee and comest thou to me? And Jesus answering said to him: Suffer it to be so now, for so it becometh us to fulfil all justice. Then he suffered him.

And Jesus being baptized, forthwith came out of the water: and lo, the heavens were opened to him, and he saw the Spirit of God descending as a dove, and coming upon him. And behold a voice from heaven, saying: This is my beloved Son, in whom I am well pleased. Mat. 3:13-17.

For all the prophets prophesied until John: And if you will receive it, he is Elias that is to come. Mat.11:13 f.

And his disciples asked him, saying: Why then do the scribes say that Elias must come first? But he answering said to them: Elias indeed shall come, and restore all things. But I say to you that Elias is already come, and they knew him not, but have done unto him whatsoever they had a mind. So also the Son of man shall suffer from them. Then the disciples understood that he had spoken to them of John the Baptist. Mat. 17:10-13.

3. HIS DEATH

Now Herodias laid snares for him, and was desirous to put him to death, and could not. For Herod feared John, knowing him to be a just and holy man, and kept him: and when he heard him, did many things: and he heard him willingly. Mark 6:19 f.

Herod the tetrarch, when he was reproved by him for Herodias his brother's wife, and for all the evils which Herod had done, he added this also above all, and shut up John in prison. Luke 3:19 f.

Herod had apprehended John and bound him, and put him into prison, because of Herodias his brother's wife. For John said to him: It is not lawful for thee to have her. And having a mind to put him to death, he feared the people, because they esteemed him as a prophet. Mat. 14:3-5.

Now when John had heard in prison the works of Christ, sending two of his disciples, he said to him: Art thou he that art to come, or look we for another? Mat. 11:2 f.

And in that same hour he cured many of their diseases, and hurts, and evil spirits: and to many that were blind he gave sight. Luke 7:31.

And Jesus making answer, said to them: Go and relate to John what you have heard and seen: the blind see, the lame walk, the lepers are cleansed, the deaf hear, the dead rise again, the poor have the gospel preached to them. And blessed is he that shall not be scandalized in me. Mat. 11:4-7.

And when a convenient day was come, Herod made a supper for his birthday, for the princes, and tribunes, and chief men of Galilee. And when the daughter of the same Herodias had come in, and had danced, and pleased Herod, and them that were at table with him, the king said to the damsel: Ask of me what thou wilt, and I will give it thee. And he swore to her: Whatsoever thou shalt ask I will give thee, though it be the half of my kingdom. Who, when she was gone out, said to her mother: What shall I ask? But she said: The head of John the Baptist. And when she was come in immediately with haste to the king, she asked, saying: I will that forthwith thou give me in a dish the head of John the Baptist.

And the king was struck sad. Yet because of his oath, and because of them that were with him at table, he would not displease her; but, sending an executioner, he commanded that his head should be brought in a dish. And he beheaded him in the prison, and brought his head in a dish, and gave it to the damsel, and the damsel gave it to her mother. Which his disciples hearing, came, and took his body, and laid it in a tomb. Mark 6:21, 29.

At that time Herod the tetrarch heard the fame of Jesus. And he said to his servants: This is John the Baptist: he is risen from the dead, and therefore mighty works show forth themselves in him. Mat. 14:1 f.

And Jesus came into the quarters of Caesarea Philippi: and he asked his disciples, saying: Whom do men say that the Son of man is? But they said: Some John the Baptist, and other some Elias, and others Jeremias or one of the prophets. Mat. 16:13 f.

PART II

OUR LAST END AND THE MEANS OF ITS ATTAINMENT

I

FINAL END AND BEATITUDE OF MAN

1. GOD THE FINAL END OF ALL THINGS

The Lord hath made all things for himself, the wicked also for the evil day. Prov. 16:4.

Who hath forwarded the spirit of the Lord? or who hath been his counsellor, and hath taught him? Is. 40:13.

Who hath known the mind of the Lord? Or who hath first given to him, and recompense shall be made him? For of him, and by him, and in him are all things. Rom. 11:34 f.

I have created him for my glory, I have formed him and made him. I am the Lord your Holy One, the Creator of Israel, your King. Is. 43:7,15.

All the nations thou hast made shall come and adore before thee, O Lord, and they shall glorify thy name. Ps. 85:9.

I am Alpha and Omega, the Beginning and the End, saith the Lord. Apoc. 1:8.

What doth the Lord thy God require of thee, but that thou fear the Lord thy God, and walk in his ways, and love him, and serve the Lord thy God with all thy heart and with all thy soul? Deut. 10:12.

I am the Lord your God. Lev. 18:2.

Know ye that the Lord he is God. We are his people, and the sheep of his pasture. Ps. 99:3.

Thou hast created all things, and for thy will they were and have been created. Apoc. 4:11.

Adore not any strange god. The Lord his name is Jealous. He is a jealous God. Ex. 34:14.

2. GOD ALONE THE OBJECT OF ETERNAL BLISS

Let Israel rejoice in him that made him, and let the children of Sion be joyful in their King. Ps. 149:2.

Fear not, Abram, I am thy protector, and thy reward exceeding great. Gen. 15:1.

What have I in heaven? and besides thee what do I desire upon earth? For thee my flesh and my heart hath fainted away; thou art the God of my heart, and the God that is my portion forever. Ps. 72:25 f.

It is good for me to adhere to my God, to put my hope in the Lord God. Ps. 72:28.

Vanity of vanities, and all is vanity. Eccles. 1:2.

Love not the world nor the things which are in the world. 1 John 2:15.

I have seen the trouble which God hath given the sons of men, to be exercised in it. He hath made all things good in their time, and hath delivered the world to their consideration, so that man cannot find out the work which God hath made from the beginning to the end. Eccles. 3:10 f.

All things are hard; man cannot explain them by word. The eye is not filled with seeing, neither is the ear filled with hearing. Eccles. 1:8.

I understood that man can find no reason of all those works of God that are done under the sun; and the more he shall labor to seek, so much less shall he find; yea, though the wise man should say that he knoweth it, he shall not be able to find it. Eccles. 8:17.

I have given my heart to know prudence, and learning, and errors, and folly; and I have perceived that in these also there was labor, and vexation of spirit, because in much wisdom there is much indignation; and he that addeth knowledge, addeth also labor. Eccles. 1:17 f.

3. BEATITUDE IN THE INTELLECT

His eyes shall see the king in his beauty, they shall see the land far off. Is. 33:17.

Alleluia shall be sung in its streets. Tob. 13:22.

After these things I heard as it were the voice of much people in heaven, saying: Alleluia, salvation, and glory, and power is to our God. Apoc. 19:1.

The high praises of God shall be in their mouth. Ps. 149:6.

Blessed are they that dwell in thy house, O Lord; they shall praise thee forever and ever. Ps. 83:5.

Show me thy face, that I may know thee. Ex. 33:13.

With thee is the fountain of life, and in thy light we shall see light. Ps.35:10.

The Lord will give grace and glory. Ps. 83:12.

The grace of God is life everlasting. Rom. 6:23.

The things that are of God no man knoweth, but the Spirit of God. 1 C. 2:11.

The glory of God hath enlightened it. Apoc. 21:23.

My sheep hear my voice; and I know them, and they follow me. And I give them life everlasting. John 10:27.

Lord, show us the Father, and it is enough for us. John 14:8.

Passing, He will minister unto them. Luke 12:37.

4. JOY OF THE BLESSED IN THE WILL

Well done, good and faithful servant: because thou hast been faithful over a few things, I will place thee over many things; enter thou into the joy of thy Lord. Mat. 25:21.

I dispose to you, as my Father hath disposed to me, a kingdom; that you may eat and drink at my table in my kingdom; and may sit upon thrones, judging the twelve tribes of Israel. Luke 22:29 f.

I will see you again, and your heart shall rejoice; and your joy no man shall take from you. John 16:22.

The kingdom of God is not meat and drink; but justice, and peace, and joy in the Holy Ghost. Rom. 14:17.

They shall be inebriated with the plenty of thy house, and thou shalt make them drink of the torrent of thy pleasures. Ps. 35:9.

Thou hast made known to me the ways of life, thou shalt fill me with joy with thy countenance; at thy right hand are delights even to the end. Ps. 15:11.

The dwelling in thee is as it were of all rejoicing. Ps. 86:7.

The Lord of hosts shall make unto all people in this mountain a feast of fat things, a feast of wine, of fat things full of marrow, of wine purified from the lees. Is. 25:6.

As one whom the mother caresseth, so will I comfort you, and you shall be comforted in Jerusalem. You shall see and your heart shall rejoice, and your bones shall flourish like a herb: and the hand of the Lord shall be known to his servants, and he shall be angry with his enemies. Is. 66:13 f.

The saints shall rejoice in glory; they shall be joyful in their beds. Ps. 149:5.

Everlasting joy shall be upon their heads: they shall obtain joy and gladness, and sorrow and mourning shall flee away. Ps. 35:10.

You shall be glad and rejoice forever in those things which I create; for behold, I create Jerusalem a rejoicing, and the people there of joy. Is. 65:18.

You shall have a song as in the night of the sanctified solemnity and joy of heart, as when one goeth with a pipe to come into the mountain of the Lord to the Mighty One of Israel. Is. 30:29.

The passage of the rod shall be strongly grounded, which the Lord shall make to rest upon him with timbrels and harps. Is. 30:32.

5. QUALITIES OF A GLORIFIED BODY

The just shall shine, and shall run to and fro like sparks among the reeds. Wis. 3:7.

Then shall the just shine as the sun in the kingdom of their Father. Mat. 13:43.

It is sown in corruption, it shall rise in incorruption. It is sown in dishonor, it shall rise in glory. It is sown in weakness, it shall rise in power. It is sown a natural body, it shall rise a spiritual body. If there be a natural body, there is also a spiritual body. 1 C. 15:42-44.

They that are learned shall shine as the brightness of the firmament; and they that instruct many to justice, as stars for all eternity. Dan. 12:3.

We look for the Savior, our Lord Jesus Christ, who will reform the body of our lowness, made like to the body of his glory, according to the operation whereby also he is able to subdue all things unto himself. Phil. 3:20 f.

This corruptible must put on incorruption, and this mortal must put on immortality. 1 C. 15:53.

They that hope in the Lord shall renew their strength: they shall run and not be weary, they shall walk and not faint. Is. 40:31.

Unto you that fear my name the sun of justice shall arise, and health in his wings; and you shall go forth, and shall leap like calves of the herd. Mal. 4:2.

They shall receive double in their land. Is. 61:7.

6. KINGLY DIGNITY OF THE BLESSED

His servants shall reign forever and ever. Apoc. 22:5.

Blessed are the poor in spirit, for theirs is the kingdom of heaven. Mat. 5:3.

Blessed are they that suffer persecution for justice' sake, for theirs is the kingdom of heaven. Mat. 5:10.

Come, ye blessed of my Father, possess you the kingdom prepared for you from the foundation of the world. Mat. 25:34.

To him that shall overcome I will give to sit with me in my throne; as I also have overcome and am sat down with my Father in his throne. Apoc. 3:21.

If we suffer, we shall also reign with him. 2 Tim. 2:12.

I, John, am your brother, and your partner in tribulation and in the kingdom. Apoc. 1:9.

God hath chosen the poor in this world rich in faith, and heirs of the kingdom which God hath promised to them that love him. Jas. 2:5.

7. POWER, HONOR, AND GLORY OF THE BLESSED

Blessed is that servant whom when his Lord shall come he shall find so doing. Amen I say to you, he shall place him over all his goods. Mat. 24:46 f.

Blessed are those servants whom the Lord when he cometh shall find watching. Amen I say to you, that he will gird himself, and make them sit down to meat, and passing will minister to them. Luke 12:37.

I have fought a good fight, I have finished my course, I have kept the faith. As to the rest, there is laid up for me a crown of justice, which the Lord the just judge will render to me in that day; and not only to me, but to them also that love his coming. 2 Tim. 4:7 f.

When the Prince of pastors shall appear, you shall receive a never-fading crown of glory. 2 Pet. 5:4.

Blessed is the man that endureth temptation; for when he hath been proved, he shall receive the crown of life, which God hath promised to them that love him. Jas. 1:12.

They are equal to the angels, and are the children of God, being the children of the resurrection. Luke 20:36.

Thither did the tribes go up, the tribes of the Lord: the testimony of Israel, to praise the name of the Lord. Because their seats have sat in judgment, seats upon the house of David. Ps. 121:4 f.

8. SPLENDOR AND BEAUTY OF OUR HEAVENLY COUNTRY

The gates of Jerusalem shall be built of sapphire and of emerald, and all the walls thereof round about of precious stones. All its streets shall be paved with white and clean stones, and Alleluia shall be sung in its streets. Tob. 13:21 f.

The building of the wall thereof was of jasper-stone; but the city itself pure gold, like to clear glass. Apoc. 21:18.

The foundations of the wall of the city were adorned with all manner of precious stones. Apoc. 21:19.

The twelve gates are twelve pearls, one to each; and every several gate was of one several pearl. And the street of the city was pure gold, as it were transparent glass. Apoc. 21:21.

They shall bring the glory and honor of the nations into it. Apoc. 21:25.

The kingdom of heaven is like unto a treasure. Mat. 13:44.

The kingdom of heaven is like to a merchant seeking good pearls, who, when he had found one pearl of great price, went his way and sold all that he had, and bought it. Mat. 13:45 f.

9. MAGNITUDE AND MULTITUDE OF CELESTIAL GOODS

They shall be inebriated with the plenty of thy house, and thou shalt make them drink of the torrent of thy pleasure. Ps. 35:9.

We know if our earthly house of this habitation is dissolved, that we have a building of God, a house not made with hands, eternal in heaven. 2 C. 5:1.

That which is at present momentary and light of our tribulation worketh for us above measure exceedingly an eternal weight of glory, while we look not at the things which are seen, but at the things which are not seen. For the things which are seen are temporal; but the things which are not seen are eternal. 2 C. 4:17 f.

My eyes shall see Jerusalem, a rich habitation, a tabernacle that cannot be removed, neither shall the nails thereof be taken away forever, neither shall any of the cords thereof be broken. Is. 33:20.

He that spoke with me had a measure of a reed of gold. Apoc. 21:15.

He looked for a city that hath foundations, whose builder and maker is God. Heb. 11:10.

O how great is the multitude of thy sweetness, O Lord, which thou hast hidden for them that fear thee! Which thou hast wrought for them that hope in thee, in the sight of the sons of men! Ps. 30:20.

Eye hath not seen, nor ear heard, neither hath it entered into the heart of man, what things God hath prepared for them that love him. 1 C. 2:9.

10. VARIETY OF REWARD FOR VARIETY OF LABOR

The Lord will reward me according to my justice, and will repay me according to the cleanness of my hands. Ps. 17:21.

He that shall do and teach, he shall be called great in the kingdom of heaven. Mat. 5:19.

Your reward is very great in heaven. Mat. 5:12.

He will render to every man according to his works. Rom. 2:6.

Every man shall receive his own reward, according to his own labor. 1 C. 3:8.

In my Father's house there are many mansions. John 14:2.

One is the glory of the sun, another the glory of the moon, and another the glory of the stars. For star differeth from star in glory. So also is the resurrection of the dead. 1 C. 15:41 f.

He who soweth sparingly shall also reap sparingly; and he who soweth in blessings shall also reap blessings. 2 C. 9:6.

He that is the lesser in the kingdom of heaven is greater than he. Mat. 11:11.

To sit on my right or left hand is not mine to give to you, but to them for whom it is prepared by my Father. Mat. 20:23.

I will give to them in my house, and within my walls, a place, and a name better than sons and daughters: I will give them an everlasting name which shall never perish. Is. 56:5.

No man could say the canticle but those hundred and forty-four thousand, who were purchased from the earth. Apoc. 14:3.

11. ENJOYMENT WITHOUT WEARINESS OF ETERNAL LIFE

I have inebriated the weary soul, and I have filled every hungry soul. Jer. 31:25.

It shall come to pass in that day that the mountains shall drop down sweetness, and the hills shall flow with milk; and water shall flow through all the rivers of Juda, and a fountain shall come forth of the house of the Lord. Joel 3:18.

There remaineth therefore a day of rest for the people of God. Heb. 4:9.

Glorious things are said of thee, O City of God. Ps. 86:3.

He hath blessed thy children within thee. Ps. 147:2.

He satisfieth thy desire with good things; thy youth shall be renewed like the eagle's. Ps. 102:5.

I shall be satisfied when thy glory shall appear. Ps. 16:15.

Show us the Father, and it is enough for us. John 14:8.

I saw the Holy City, the New Jerusalem, coming down out of heaven from God, prepared as a bride adorned for her husband. And I heard a great voice from the throne, saying: Behold the tabernacle of God with men, and he will dwell with them, and they shall be his people; and God himself with them shall be their God. Apoc. 21:2 f.

Better is one day in thy courts above thousands. Ps. 83:11.

Every one that hath left house, or brethren, or sisters, or father, or mother, or wife, or children, or lands, for my name's sake, shall receive an hundredfold, and shall possess life everlasting. Mat. 19:29.

12. PURITY OF HEAVENLY JOY WITHOUT ADMIXTURE OF SORROW

There shall no evil come to thee, nor shall the scourge come near thy dwelling. Ps. 90:10.

God shall wipe away all tears from their eyes; and death shall be no more, nor mourning, nor crying, nor sorrow shall be any more, for the former things are passed away. Apoc. 21:4.

They shall no more hunger nor thirst, neither shall the sun fall on them, nor any heat. For the Lamb, which is in the midst of the throne, shall rule them, and shall lead them to the fountains of the waters of life, and God shall wipe away all tears from their eyes. Apoc. 7:16 f.

He shall destroy in this mountain the face of the bond with which all people were tied, and the web that he began over all nations. Is. 25:7.

He shall cast death down headlong forever; and the Lord shall wipe away tears from every face, and the reproach of his people he shall take away from off the whole earth; for the Lord hath spoken it. Is. 25:8.

The redeemed of the Lord shall come into Sion with praise, and everlasting joy shall be upon their heads. They shall obtain joy and gladness, and sorrow and mourning shall flee away. Is. 35:10.

I will rejoice in Jerusalem, and joy in my people, and the voice of weeping shall no more be heard in her, nor the voice of crying. Is. 65:19.

Iniquity shall no more be heard in thy land, wasting nor destruction in thy borders, and salvation shall possess thy walls, and praise thy gates. Is. 60:18.

Thou shalt no more have the sun for thy light by day, neither shall the brightness of the moon enlighten thee; but the Lord shall be unto thee for an everlasting light, and the days of thy mourning shall be ended. Is. 60:19 f.

Give praise, O daughter of Sion: shout, O Israel: be glad and rejoice with all thy heart, O daughter of Jerusalem. Soph. 3:14.

Winter is now past, the rain is over and gone, the flowers have appeared in our land. Cant. 2:11.

I will clothe her priests with salvation, and her saints shall rejoice with exceeding great joy. Ps. 131:16.

13. SAFETY WITHOUT ANXIETY

The gates thereof shall not be shut by day; for there shall be no night there. Apoc. 21:25.

Thy gates shall be open continually: they shall not be shut day nor night, that the strength of the Gentiles may be brought to thee, and their kings may be brought. Is. 60:11.

He shall dwell on high, the fortifications of rocks shall be his highness; bread is given him, his works are sure. Is. 33:16.

Israel is saved in the Lord with an eternal salvation: you shall not be confounded, and you shall not be ashamed forever and ever. Is. 45:17.

He showed me the holy city Jerusalem; and it had a wall great and high. Apoc. 21:10-12.

The city lieth in a foursquare, and the length thereof is as great as the breadth: and he measured the city with a golden reed for twelve thousand furlongs, and the length, and the height, and the breadth thereof are equal. Apoc. 21:16.

The city itself was pure gold, like to clear glass. Apoc. 21:18.

I will be to it, saith the Lord, a wall of fire round about; and I will be in glory in the midst thereof. Zach. 2:5.

They shall feed and shall lie down, and there shall be none to make them afraid. Soph. 3:13.

The Lord hath turned away thy enemies: the King of Israel the Lord is in the midst of thee, thou shalt fear evil no more. Soph. 3:15.

He has strengthened the bolts of thy gates. Ps. 147:2.

He hath placed peace in thy borders. Ps. 147:3.

He that shall overcome I will make him a pillar in the temple of my God: and he shall go out no more: and I will write upon him the name of my God, and the name of the city of my God, the New Jerusalem which cometh down out of heaven from my God, and my new name. Apoc. 3:12.

14. SURE WAY OF OBTAINING ETERNAL LIFE

Follow peace with all men, and holiness, without which no man shall see God. Heb. 12:14.

Through many tribulations we must enter into the kingdom of God. Acts 14:21.

If thou wilt enter life, keep the commandments. Mat. 19:17.

He that shall lose his life for me shall find it. Mat. 10:39.

Know you not that they that run in the race all run indeed, but one winneth the prize? So run that you may obtain. 1 Cor. 9:24.

Be you also as living stones built up, a spiritual house. 1 Pet. 2:5.

Our feet were standing in thy courts, O Jerusalem: Jerusalem, which is built as a city which is compact together. Ps. 121:2 f.

Go out quickly into the streets and

lanes of the city, and bring in hither the poor, and the feeble, and the blind, and the lame. Luke 14:21.

He showed me the holy city Jerusalem. It had twelve gates, and names written thereon which are the names of the twelve tribes of the children of Israel. Apoc. 21:12.

Unless your justice abound more than that of the scribes and Pharisees, you shall not enter into the kingdom of heaven. Mat. 5:20.

Not every one that saith to me, Lord, Lord, shall enter into the kingdom of heaven; but he that doth the will of my Father who is in heaven, he shall enter into the kingdom of heaven. Mat. 7:21.

If by the Spirit you mortify the deeds of the flesh, you shall live. Rom. 8:13.

Labor the more, that by good works you may make sure your calling and election. For doing these things, you shall not sin at any time. 2 Pet. 1:10.

15. ETERNAL LIFE THE REWARD OF LABOR, AND NOT BESTOWED WITHOUT GRACE

The Lord knoweth the days of the undefiled, and their inheritance shall be forever. Ps. 36:18.

The just shall inherit the land, and shall dwell therein for evermore. Ps. 36:29.

He that reapeth recieveth wages, and gathereth fruit unto life everlasting. John 4:36.

The just shall live for evermore, and their reward is with the Lord, and the care of them with the Most High. Wis. 5:16.

Behold, I come quickly; and my reward is with me, to render to every man according to his works. Apoc. 22:12.

Whatsoever you do, do it from the heart, as to the Lord, and not to men; knowing that you shall receive of the Lord the reward of inheritance. Serve ye the Lord Christ. Col. 3:23 f.

To him that thirsteth I will give of the fountain of the water of life freely. Apoc. 21:6.

I reckon that the sufferings of this time are not worthy to be compared with the glory to come, that shall be revealed in us. Rom. 8:18.

Come ye, buy wine and milk without money and without any price. Is. 55:1.

He that thirsteth, let him come; and he that will, let him take the water of life freely. Apoc. 22:17.

16. ETERNAL LIFE NOT TO BE OBTAINED ON EARTH, TO BE WON BY COMBAT

Man shall not see me and live. Ex. 33:20.

We who have believed shall enter into rest. Heb. 4:3.

Man born of a woman, living for a short time, is filled with many miseries. Job. 14:1.

We see now through a glass in a dark manner; but then face to face. Now I know in part; but then I shall know, even as I am known. 1 C. 13:12.

While we are in the body we are absent from the Lord. (For we walk by faith, and not by sight.) But we are confident, and have a good will to be absent rather from the body, and to be present with the Lord. And therefore we labor, whether absent or present, to please him. 2 C. 5:6-8.

He is not crowned who does not strive lawfully. 2 Tim. 2:5.

The life of man upon earth is a warfare, and his days are like the days of a hireling. Job. 7:1.

We have not here a lasting city, but we seek one that is to come. Heb. 13:14.

God hath regenerated us unto a lively hope, by the resurrection of Jesus Christ from the dead. Unto an inheritance incorruptible, and undefiled, and that cannot fade, reserved in heaven for you, who are kept by faith unto salvation. 1 Pet. 1:3 f.

17. ETERNAL LIFE TO BE WON WHEN LIFE'S COMBAT IS HAPPILY OVER

This day thou shalt be with me in paradise. Luke 23:43.

Behold, I see the heavens opened, and the Son of man standing on the right hand of God. Acts 7:55.

Lord Jesus, receive my spirit. Acts 7:59.

Ascending on high, he led captivity captive; he gave gifts to men. Eph.4:8.

To me to live is Christ, and to die is gain. And if to live in the flesh, this is the fruit of labor, and what I shall choose I know not. But I am straitened between two, having a desire to be dissolved, and to be with Christ. Phil. 1:21-23.

The Holy Ghost signifying this: that the way into the holies was not yet made manifest, whilst the former tabernacle was yet standing. Heb. 9:8.

You are come to Mount Sion, and to the city of the living God, the heavenly Jerusalem, and to the company of many thousands of angels. And to the church ot the first-born, who are written in the heavens, and to God the judge of all, and to the spirits of the just made perfect. Heb. 12:22 f.

White robes were given to every one of them one: and it was said to them that they should rest for a little time, till their fellow servants and their brethren, who are to be slain even as they, should be filled up. Apoc. 6:11.

18. ETERNAL LIFE IS PROMISED TO THOSE WHO FIGHT AND WIN LAWFULLY

Do you take courage, and let not your hands be weakened: for there shall be a reward for your work. 2 Par. 15:7.

We are the children of saints, and look for that life which God will give to those that never change their faith in him. Tob. 2:18.

To him that overcometh I will give to eat of the tree of life, which is in the paradise of my God. Apoc. 2:7.

Be thou faithful unto death, and I will give thee the crown of life. Apoc. 2:10.

The meek shall inherit the land, and shall delight in abundance of peace. Ps. 36:11.

To him that overcometh I will give the hidden manna, and will give him a white counter, and in the counter a new name written, which no man knoweth but he that receiveth it. Apoc. 2:17.

Blessed are the dead who die in the Lord. From henceforth now, saith the Spirit, that they may rest from their labors: for their works follow them. Apoc. 14:13.

He that shall overcome, and keep my works unto the end, I will give him power over the nations. And he shall rule them with a rod of iron; and as the vessel of a potter they shall be broken. As I also have received of my Father; and I will give him the morning star. Apoc. 2:26-28.

He that shall overcome shall thus be clothed in white garments, and I will not blot his name out of the book of life, and I will confess his name before my Father and before his angels. Apoc. 3:5.

He that shall overcome shall possess these things, and I will be his God, and he shall be my son. Apoc. 21:7.

If you be willing, and will hearken to me, you shall eat the good things of the land. Is. 1:19.

Whom he justified, them he also glorified. Rom. 8:30.

They shall oring the glory and honor of the nations into it. Apoc. 21:26.

Thy people shall be all just, they shall inherit the land forever, the branch of my planting, the work of my hand, to glorify me. Is. 60:21.

19. COWARDS, UNBELIEVERS, AND WICKED MEN FORFEIT ETERNAL LIFE

The fearful and unbelieving, and the abominable, and murderers, and whoremongers, and sorcerers, and idolaters, and all liars, they shall have their portion in the pool burning with fire and brimstone, which is the second death. Apoc. 21:8.

There shall not enter into it anything defiled or that worketh abomination or maketh a lie, but they that are written in the book of life of the Lamb. Apoc. 21:27.

Without are dogs, and sorcerers, and unchaste, and murderers, and servers of idols, and every one that loveth and maketh a lie. Apoc. 22:15.

If they hear not they shall pass by the sword, and shall be consumed in folly. Job 35:12.

I have seen those who work iniquity, and sow sorrows and reap them, perishing by the blast of God, and consumed by the spirit of his wrath. Job 4:8 f.

The enemies of the Lord, presently after they shall be honored and exalted, shall come to nothing and vanish like smoke. Ps. 36:20.

The unjust shall be punished, and the seed of the wicked shall perish. Ps. 36:29.

I will visit upon you according to the fruit of your doings, saith the Lord: and I will kindle a fire in the forest thereof, and it shall devour all things round about it. Jer. 21:14.

Henceforth the uncircumcised and unclean shall no more pass through thee. Is. 52:1.

Jerusalem shall be holy, and strangers shall pass through it no more. Jon. 3:17.

Envy not them that work iniquity, for they shall shortly wither away as grass, and as the green herbs shall quickly fall. Ps. 36:1 f.

He shall rain snares upon sinners, fire and brimstone: and storms of winds shall be the portion of their cup. Ps. 10:7.

Behold, thy enemies, O Lord, shall perish: and all the workers of iniquity shall be scattered. Ps. 91:10.

Except you will be converted, he will brandish his sword. He hath bent his bow, and made it ready. And in it he hath prepared the instruments of death. He hath made ready his arrows for them that burn. Ps. 7:13 f.

Friend, how camest thou in hither not having on a wedding garment? But he was silent. Then the king said to the waiters: Bind his hands and feet, and cast him into the exterior darkness; there shall be weeping and gnashing of teeth. Mat. 22:12 f.

At last came also the other virgins, saying: Lord, Lord, open to us. But he answering said: Amen I say to you, I know you not. Mat. 25:11 f.

And he shall say to you: I know you not whence you are: depart from me, all ye workers of iniquity. Luke 13:27.

The angels shall go out, and shall separate the wicked from among the just. And shall cast them into the furnace of fire; there shall be weeping and gnashing of teeth. Mat. 13:49 f.

20. YEARNING AFTER OUR HEAVENLY COUNTRY

I look for thy salvation, O Lord. Gen. 49:18.

If I forget thee, O Jerusalem, let my right hand be forgotten. Let my tongue cleave to my jaws, if I do not remember thee; if I make not Jerusalem the beginning of my joy. Ps. 136:5 f.

Be not silent; for I am a stranger with thee, and a sojourner, as all my fathers were. Ps. 38:13.

What have I in heaven? and besides thee what do I desire upon earth? Ps. 72:25.

I have longed for thy salvation, O Lord. Ps. 118:174.

Upon the rivers of Babylon there we sat and wept, when we remembered Sion. Ps. 136:1.

Our conversation is in heaven. Phil. 3:20.

Thou that dwellest in the gardens, the friends hearken: make me hear thy voice. Cant. 8:13.

All those died according to faith, not having received the promises, but beholding them afar off, and saluting them, and confessing that they are pilgrims and strangers on the earth. For they that say these things do signify that they seek a country. And truly if they had been mindful of that from whence they came out, they had doubtless time to return. But now they desire a better, that is to say a heavenly country. Heb. 11:13-16.

Unhappy man that I am, who will deliver me from the body of this death! Rom. 7:24.

Bring my soul out of prison, that I may praise thy name; the just wait for me until thou reward me. Ps. 141:8.

In a desert land, and where there is no way and no water; so in the sanctuary have I come before thee, to see thy power and thy glory. Ps. 62:3.

I have gone round, and have offered up in his tabernacle a sacrifice of jubilation; I will sing and recite a psalm to the Lord. Ps. 26:6.

21. EJACULATIONS OF THE SOUL ARDENTLY DESIRING THE GLORY OF HEAVEN

[O, when shall be given] to the mourners of Sion a crown for ashes, the oil of joy for mourning, a garment of praise for the spirit of grief! Is. 61:3.

One thing I have asked of the Lord, this will I seek after: that I may dwell in the house of the Lord all the days of my life. That I may see the delight of the Lord, and may visit his temple. Ps. 26:4.

As the hart panteth after the fountains of water, so my soul panteth after thee, O God. My soul hath thirsted after the strong living God: when shall I come and appear before the face of God? Ps. 41:1 f.

Who will give me wings like a dove, and I will fly and be at rest? Ps. 54:7.

Who will bring me into the strong city? Ps. 59:11.

If I have found favor in thy sight, O Lord, show me thy face. Ex. 33:13.

How lovely are thy tabernacles, O Lord of hosts! my soul longeth and fainteth for the courts of the Lord. Ps. 83:1.

Blessed are they that dwell in thy house, O Lord; they shall praise thee for ever and ever. Ps. 83:5.

Better is one day in thy courts above thousands. Ps. 83:11.

Woe is me that my sojourning is prolonged! my soul has been long a sojourner. Ps. 119:5.

My soul hath fainted after thy salvation. Ps. 118:81.

For thee my flesh and my heart hath fainted away: thou art the God of my heart, and the God that is my portion forever. Ps. 72:26.

For thee my flesh hath thirsted; for thee my flesh, O how many ways! Ps. 62:2.

Open ye to me the gates of justice: I will go into them, and give praise to the Lord. Ps. 117:19.

O Lord, save me: O Lord, give good success. Ps. 117:25.

O Lord, we have patiently waited for thee: thy name and thy remembrance are the desire of the soul. Is. 26:8.

My soul hath desired thee in the night: yea and with my spirit within me in the morning early I will watch to thee. Is. 26:9.

Lord all my desire is before thee, and my groaning is not hidden from thee. Ps. 37:10.

Who will grant that my request may come: and that God may give me what I look for? Job 6:8.

II

MAN'S USE OF FREE WILL

1. USE OF FREE WILL IN PURSUIT OF GOOD OR EVIL, VIRTUE OR VICE

God made man from the beginning, and left him in the hand of his own counsel. Ecclus. 15:14.

He added his commandments and precepts; if thou wilt keep them, they will preserve thee. Ecclus. 15:15 f.

Before man is life and death, good and evil: that which he shall choose shall be given him. Ecclus. 15:18.

Consider that I have set before thee this day life and good, and on the other hand death and evil; that thou mayst love the Lord thy God, and walk in his ways, and keep his commandments. Deut. 30:15 f.

I call heaven and earth to witness this day that I have set before you life and death, blessing and cursing. Deut. 30:19.

Choose therefore life, that both thou and thy seed may live, and that thou mayst love the Lord thy God, and obey his voice. Deut. 30:20.

Destruction is thy own, O Israel: thy help is only in me. Osee 13:9.

If we sin wilfully after having received the knowledge of the truth, there is now left no sacrifice for sins, but a certain dreadful expectation of judgment, and the rage of a fire which shall consume the adversaries. Heb. 10:26 f.

I will freely sacrifice to thee, and will give praise, O God, to thy name because it is good. Ps. 53:8.

It shall depend on the will of her husband whether she shall do it or not do it. Num. 30:14.

Behold, I set before you the way of life and the way of death. Jer. 21:8.

Behold, thou hast spoken and hast done evil things, and hast been able. Jer. 3:5.

If it seem evil to you to serve the Lord, you have your choice; choose this day that which pleaseth you. Jon. 24:15.

If thou do well, shalt thou not receive? but if ill, shall not sin forthwith be present at the door? But the lust thereof shall be under thee, and thou shalt have dominion over it. Gen. 4:7.

He that hath determined, being steadfast in his heart, having no necessity, but having power of his own will. 1 C. 7:37.

Without thy counsel I would do nothing; that thy good deed might not be as it were of necessity, but voluntary. Philem. 14.

If you be willing, and will hearken to me, you shall eat the good things of the land; but if you will not, and will provoke me to wrath, the sword shall devour you. Is. 1:19 f.

It depends on the will of a man whether he shall do or not do. Num. 30:14.

Because I called, and you refused, I stretched out my hand, and there was none that regarded. You have despised all my counsel, and have neglected my reprehensions. I also will laugh in your destruction, and will mock when that shall come to you which you feared. Prov. 1:24-26.

How often would I have gathered together thy children, as the hen doth gather her chickens under her wings, and thou wouldst not! Mat. 23:37.

You have been called unto liberty: only make not liberty an occasion to the flesh, but by charity of the Spirit serve one another. Gal. 5:13.

You are bought with a price: be not made the bondslaves of men. 1 C. 7:23.

2. INCENTIVES TO THE PRACTICE OF GOOD WORKS

Sow for yourselves in justice and reap in the month of mercy, break up your fallow ground; but the time to seek the Lord is when he shall come that shall teach you justice. Osee 10:12.

Speak ye truth every one to his neighbor; judge ye truth and judgment of peace in your gates. Zach. 8:16.

I have appointed you that you should go, and should bring forth fruit, and your fruit should remain. John 15:16.

What things a man shall sow, those also shall he reap. For he that soweth in the flesh, of the flesh also shall reap corruption. But he that soweth in the Spirit, of the Spirit shall reap life everlasting. Gal. 6:8.

In doing good let us not fail, for in due time we shall reap, not failing. Therefore, whilst we have time let us work good to all men, but especially to those who are of the household of the faith. Gal. 6:9 f.

Labor the more, that by good works you may make sure your calling and election. For doing these things, you shall not sin at any time. For so an entrance shall be ministered to you abundantly into the everlasting kingdom of our Lord and Savior Jesus Christ. 1 Pet. 1:10 f.

3. PRECEPTS AS TO GOOD WORKS

From me is thy fruit found. Osee 14:9.

Work your work before the time, and he will give you your reward in his time. Ecclus. 51:38.

Decline from evil and do good, and dwell forever and ever. Ps. 36:27.

The beginning of a good way is to do justice: and this is more acceptable with God than to offer sacrifices. Prov. 16:5.

Lord, who shall dwell in thy tabernacle? or who shall rest in thy holy hill? He that walketh without blemish and worketh justice. Ps. 14:1 f.

Remember me, O my God, for this thing, and wipe not out my kindness, which I have done relating to the house of my God and his ceremonies. 2 Es. 13:14.

He that feareth God will do good. Ecclus. 15:1.

I was an eye to the blind and a foot to the lame. I was the father of the poor: and the cause which I knew not I searched out most diligently. Job 29:15 f.

Turn away from evil and do good. Ps. 33:15.

Judge for the needy and fatherless: do justice to the humble and the poor. Ps. 81:3.

Do not withhold him from doing good who is able: and if thou art able, do good thyself also. Prov. 3:27.

My son, in thy good deeds make no complaint; and when thou givest anything, add not grief by an evil word. Ecclus. 18:15.

Eat thy bread with the hungry and the needy, and with thy garments cover the naked. Tob. 4:17.

The fruit of good labors is glorious. Wis. 3:15.

Lay up for yourselves treasures in heaven, where neither the rust nor the moth doth consume, and where thieves do not break through nor steal. For where thy treasure is there is thy heart also. Mat. 6:80 f.

By the fruit the tree is known. Mat. 12:33.

Every good tree yieldeth good fruit. Mat. 7:17.

He spoke also this parable: A certain man had a fig tree planted in his vineyard, and he came seeking fruit on it, and found none. And he said to the dresser of the vineyard: Behold, these three years I come seeking fruit on this fig tree, and I find none. Cut it down, therefore: why cumbereth it the ground? Luke 13:6 f.

I am the vine; you the branches. He that abideth in me, and I in him, the same beareth much fruit: for without me you can do nothing. In this is my Father glorified: that you bring forth very much fruit and become my disciples. John 15:5-8.

Having your conversation good among the Gentiles: that whereas they speak against you as evildoers, they may, by the good works which they shall behold in you, glorify God in the day of visitation. 1 Pet. 2:12.

Other foundation no man can lay but that which is laid, which is Christ Jesus. Now if any man build upon this foundation, gold, silver, precious stones, wood, hay, stubble, every man's work shall be manifest: for the day of the Lord shall declare it, because it shall be revealed in fire: and the fire shall try every man's work, of what sort it is. If any man's work abide which he hath built thereupon, he shall receive a reward. 1 C. 3:11-14.

Cornelius, thy prayer is heard, and thy alms are had in remembrance in the sight of God. Acts 10:31.

We are his workmanship, created in Christ Jesus in good works, which God hath prepared that we should walk in them. Eph. 2:10.

Filled with the fruit of justice through Jesus Christ, unto the glory and praise of God. Phil. 1:11.

[Jesus Christ] who gave himself for us, that he might redeem us from all iniquity, and purify unto himself a people acceptable, pursuing good works. Titus 2:14.

That the communication of thy faith may be made evident in the acknowledgment of every good work that is in you in Christ Jesus. Philem. 6.

God is not unjust, that he should forget your work, and the love which you have shown in his name, you who have ministered and do minister to the saints. And we desire that every one of you show forth the same carefulness to the accomplishing of hope unto the end. Heb. 6:10 f.

Let us consider one another to provoke unto charity and to good works. Heb. 10:24.

Walk worthy of God, in all things pleasing: being fruitful in every good work, and increasing in the knowledge of God. Col. 1:10.

A doer of the work: this man shall be blessed in his deed. Jas. 1:25.

Do you see that by works a man is justified, and not by faith only? Jas. 2:24.

To him, therefore, who knoweth to do good, and doeth it not, to him it is sin. Jas. 4:17.

Brethren, labor the more, that by good works you may make sure your vocation and election. For doing these things, you shall not sin at any time. 2 Pet. 1:10.

Now the axe is laid to the root of the trees. Every tree, therefore, that doth not yield good fruit shall be cut down, and cast into the fire. Mat. 3:10.

Every branch in me that beareth not fruit he will take away; and every one that beareth fruit he will purge it, that it may bring forth more fruit. John 15:2.

It is a faithful saying, and these things I will have thee affirm constantly, that they who believe in God may be careful to excel in good works. These things are good and profitable to men. Titus 3:8.

What shall it profit, my brethren, if a man say he hath faith, but have not works? shall faith be able to save him? Jas. 2:14.

If a brother or sister be naked and want daily food, and one of you say to them: Go in peace, be ye warmed and filled, yet give them not those things that are necessary for the body, what shall it profit? So faith also, if it have not works, is dead in itself. Jas. 2:15-17.

4. PURITY OF HEART AND PIETY TO BE UNITED TO EXTERIOR GOODNESS

To what purpose do you offer me the multitude of your victims? saith the Lord. I am full, I desire not holocausts of rams, and fat of fatlings, and blood of calves, and lambs and buck goats. Wash yourselves, be clean, take away the evil of your devices from my eyes; cease to do perversely, learn to do well: seek judgment, relieve the oppressed, judge for the fatherless, defend the widow. Is. 1:11, 16 f.

To whom shall I have respect, but to him that is poor and little, and of a contrite spirit, and that trembleth at my words? Is. 66:2.

What shall I offer to the Lord that is worthy? wherewith shall I kneel before the high God? Shall I offer holocausts unto him, and calves of a year old? Mich. 6:6.

May the Lord be appeased with thousands of rams, or with many thousands of fat he-goats? Shall I give my first-born for my wickedness, the fruit of my body for the sin of my soul? Mich. 6:7.

I will show thee, O man, what is good, and what the Lord requireth of thee. Verily to do judgment, and to love mercy, and to walk solicitous with thy God. Mich. 6:8.

Speak to all the people of the land, and to the priests saying: When you fasted and mourned in the fifth and the seventh month for these seventy years, did you keep a fast unto me? Zach. 7:5.

And when you did eat and drink, did you not eat for yourselves and drink for yourselves? Zach. 7:6.

Thus saith the Lord of hosts, saying: Judge ye true judgment, and show ye mercy and compassion every man to his brother. And oppress not the widow, and the fatherless, and the stranger, and the poor; and let not a man devise evil in his heart against his brother. Zach. 7:9 f.

Religion clean and undefiled before God and the Father is this: tc visit the fatherless and widows in their tribulation, and to keep one's self unspotted from this world. Jas. 1:27.

5. OF THOSE WHO NEGLECT DUTIES AND BOAST OF RELIGION

I am filled with the strength of the Spirit of the Lord, with judgment and power, to declare unto Jacob his wickedness, and to Israel his sin. Mich. 3:8.

Hear this, ye princes of the house of Jacob, and ye judges of the house of Israel, you that abhor judgment, and pervert all that is right. You shall build up Sion with blood, and Jerusalem with iniquity. The princes have judged for bribes, and her priests have taught for hire, and her prophets divined for money; and they leaned upon the Lord, saying: Is not the Lord in the midst of us? No evil shall come upon us. Therefore, because of you, Sion shall be plowed as a field, and Jerusalem shall be as a heap of stones, and the mountain of the temple as the high places of the forests. Mich.3:9-12.

Make your ways and your doings good, and I will dwell with you in this place. Jer. 7:3.

Trust not lying words, saying: The temple of the Lord, the temple of the Lord, it is the temple of the Lord. Jer. 7:4.

For if you will order well your ways and your doings, if you will execute judgment between a man and his neighbor, I will dwell with you in this place, in the land which I gave to your fathers from the beginning and for evermore. Jer. 7:5, 7.

Behold, you put your trust in lying words which shall not profit you. To steal, to murder, to commit adultery, to swear falsely, to offer to Baalim, and to go after strange gods which you know not. And you have come and stood before me in this house, in which my name is called upon, and have said: We are delivered, because we have done these abominations. Jer. 7:8-10.

Bring forth fruit worthy of penance. And think not to say within yourselves: We have Abraham for our father. Mat. 3:8 f.

Hear ye these things, O house of Jacob, you that are called by the name of Israel, and are come forth out of the waters of Juda, you who swear by the name of the Lord, and make mention of the God of Israel, but not in truth nor in justice. For they are called of the Holy City, and are established upon the God of Israel: the Lord of hosts is his name. Is. 48:1 f.

6. OPPORTUNITY FOR DOING GOOD

Seek ye the Lord while he may be found: call upon him while he is near. Is. 55:6.

If any man thirst, let him come to me and drink. John 7:37.

My sons, be not negligent. The Lord hath chosen you to stand before him, and to minister to him, and to worship him. 2 Par. 29:11.

In the morning sow thy seed, and in the evening let not thy hand cease, for thou knowest not which may rather spring up, this or that; and if both together, it shall be better. Eccles. 11:6.

Work your work before the time, and he will give you your reward in his time. Ecclus. 51:38.

The night cometh, when no man can work. John 9:4.

Trade till I come. Luke 19:13.

Yet a little while the light is among you. Walk whilst you have the light, that the darkness overtake you not. And he that walketh in darkness knoweth not whither he goeth. John 12:36 f.

See, brethren, how you walk circumspectly; not as unwise, but as wise; redeeming the time, because the days are evil. Eph. 5:15 f.

Behold, I stand at the gate and knock. If any man shall hear my voice, and open to me the door, I will come in to him, and will sup with him, and he with me. Apoc. 3:20.

Understand, ye senseless among the people; and you fools, be wise at last. Ps. 93:8.

Today, if you shall hear his voice, harden not your hearts. Ps. 94:8.

I called, and you refused: I stretched out my hand, and there was none that regarded. Prov. 1:24.

There is a time and opportunity for every business, and great affliction for man. Eccles. 8:6.

All things have their season, and in their time all things pass under heaven. Eccles. 3:1.

I gave her [Jezebel] a time that she might do penance, and she will not repent of her fornication. Apoc. 2:21.

7. FRUITS OF GOOD AND EVIL DEEDS

I am the Lord, who search the heart and prove the reins: who give to every one according to his way, and according to the fruit of his devices. Jer. 17:10.

I will bring upon them the things they feared, because they have done evil in my eyes, and have chosen the things that displease me. Is. 66:4.

The wicked maketh an unsteady work; but to him that soweth justice there is a faithful reward Prov. 11:18.

If you be willing, and will hearken to me, you shall eat the good things of the land. But if you will not, and will provoke me to wrath, the sword shall devour you. Is. 1:19 f.

Say to the just man that it is well, for he shall eat the fruit of his doings. Is. 3:10.

He will render to a man his work, and according to the ways of every one he will reward them. Job 34:11.

He will render to every man according to his works. To them indeed who, according to patience in good work, seek glory, and honor, and incorruption, eternal life. But to them that are contentious and obey not the truth, but give credit to iniquity, wrath and indignation. Rom. 2:6-8.

Tribulation and anguish upon every soul of man that worketh evil, of the Jew first, and also of the Greek. But glory, and honor, and peace to every one that worketh good, to the Jew first, and also to the Greek. For there is no respect of persons with God. Rom. 2:9-11.

8. ALL RIGHT ACTIONS TO BE DONE WITH A VIEW TO THE GLORY OF GOD

If any man speak, let him speak as the words of God. If any man minister, let him do it as of the power which God administereth; that in all things God may be honored through Jesus Christ; to whom is glory and empire forever and ever. Amen. 1 Pet. 4:11.

Whether you eat or drink, or whatsoever else you do, do all to the glory of God. 1 C. 10:31.

All whatsoever else you do in word or in work, do all in the name of the Lord Jesus Christ, giving thanks to God and the Father by him. Col. 3:17.

The light of thy body is thy eye. If thy eye be single, thy whole body shall be lightsome. But if thy eye be evil, thy whole body shall be darksome. If then the light that is in thee be darkness, the darkness itself how great shall it be! Mat. 6:22 f.

There was nothing in the temple that was not covered with gold. 3 K. 6:22.

Give praise to the Lord, for he is good; for his mercy endureth forever. Ps. 117:1.

Labor not for the meat which perisheth, but for that which endureth unto life everlasting, which the Son of man will give you. John 6:27.

He that doeth truth cometh to the light, that his works may be made manifest, because they are done in God. John 3:21.

Take heed that you do not your justice before men, that you may be seen by them: otherwise you shall not have a reward from your Father who is in heaven. And when thou dost alms, let not thy left hand know what thy right hand doth. But thou when thou shalt pray, enter into thy chamber, and having shut the door, pray to thy Father in secret; and thy Father, who seeth in secret, will repay thee. Mat. 6:1, 3, 6.

9. PURITY OF INTENTION ACCEPTABLE TO GOD

Fear the Lord, and serve him with a perfect and a most sincere heart. Jos. 24:14.

Let our hearts be perfect with the Lord our God, that we may walk in his statutes and keep his commandments. 3 K. 8:61.

The simplicity of the just shall guide them. Prov. 11:3

Thou shalt be perfect and without spot before the Lord thy God. Deut. 18:13.

Give your hearts and your souls to seek the Lord your God. 1 Par. 22:19.

With all watchfulness keep thy heart, because life issueth out from it. Prov. 4:23.

My son, attend to my wisdom, and incline thy ear to my prudence. That thou mayst keep thoughts, and thy lips may preserve instruction. Prov. 5:1 f.

A wicked word shall change the heart, out of which four manner of things arise, good and evil, life and death; and the tongue is continually the ruler of them. Ecclus. 37:21.

My son, give me thy heart; and let thy eyes keep my ways. Prov. 23:26.

Evil thoughts are an abomination to the Lord; and pure words most beautiful shall be confirmed by him. Prov. 15:26.

Purge out the old leaven, that you may be a new paste, as you are unleavened. For Christ our Pasch is sacrificed. Therefore let us feast not with the leaven of malice and wickedness, but with the unleavened bread of sincerity and truth. 1 C. 5:7 f.

At all times let thy garments be white, and let not oil depart from thy hand. Eccles. 9:8.

Thou hast a few names in Sardis which have not defiled their garments; and they shall walk with me in white, because they are worthy. Apoc. 3:4.

10. AN EVIL INTENTION DISPLEASING TO GOD

Cain offered, of the fruits of the earth, gifts to the Lord. Abel also offered of the firstlings of his flock and of their fat: and the Lord had respect to Abel and to his offerings. But to Cain and his offerings he had no respect. Gen. 4:3-5.

When you stretch forth your hands I will turn away my eyes from you: and when you multiply prayer I will not hear, for your hands are full of blood. Is. 1:15.

Woe to the sinner that goeth on the earth two ways! Ecclus. 2:14.

They shall not offer wine to the Lord, neither shall they please him: their sacrifices shall be like the bread of mourners; all that shall eat it shall be defiled; for their bread is life for their soul, it shall not enter into the house of the Lord. Osee 9:4.

They shall sow wind, and reap a whirlwind. Osee 8:7.

When thou dost an almsdeed sound not a trumpet before thee, as the hypocrites do in the synagogues and in the streets, that they may be honored by men. Mat. 6:2.

The unjust shall be caught in their own snares. Prov. 11:6.

The bud shall yield no meal; and if it should yield, strangers shall eat it. Osee 8:7.

Amen, amen I say to you, you seek me not because you have seen miracles, but because you did eat of the loaves and were filled. John 6:26.

11. ACTS OF HYPOCRISY

Thou art near, O Lord, in their mouth, and far from their reins. Jer. 12:2.

The vessels of the deceitful are most wicked; for he hath framed devices to destroy the meek with lying words, when the poor man speaketh judgment. Is. 32:7.

They have sharpened their tongues like a serpent; the venom of asps is under their lips. Ps. 139:4.

You have deceived your own souls; for you sent me to the Lord our God, saying: Pray for us to the Lord our God, and according to all that the Lord our God shall say to thee so declare unto us, and we will do it. And now I have declared it to you this day, and you have not obeyed the voice of the Lord your God. Jer. 42:20 f.

They spoke indeed peaceably to me; and speaking in the anger of the earth, they devised guile. And they opened their mouth wide against me: they said: Well done, well done; our eyes have seen it. Ps. 34:20 f.

Their throat is an open sepulcher; with their tongues they acted deceitfully; the poison of asps is under their lips. Ps. 13:3.

Let every man take heed of his neighbor, and let him not trust in any brother of his: for every brother will utterly supplant, and every friend will walk deceitfully. Jer. 9:4.

Their tongue is a piercing arrow, it hath spoken deceit: with his mouth one speaketh peace with his friend, and secretly lieth in wait for him. Jer. 9:8.

There is none to comfort her among all them that were dear to her: all her friends have despised her, and are become her enemies. Lam. 1:2.

They that eat with thee shall lay snares under thee. Abd. 7.

They say, and do not. For they bind heavy and insupportable burdens, and lay them on men's shoulders, and with a finger of their own they will not move them. Mat. 23:3 f.

All their works they do for to be seen of men. For they make their phylacteries broad, and enlarge their fringes. Mat. 23:5.

Woe to you scribes and Pharisees, hypocrites! because you shut the kingdom of heaven against men: for you yourselves do not enter in, and those that are going in you suffer not to enter. Woe to you scribes and Pharisees, hypocrites! because you devour the houses of widows, praying long prayers: for this you shall receive the greater judgment. Mat. 23:13 f.

Woe to you scribes and Pharisees, hypocrites! because you tithe mint and anise and cummin, and have left the weightier things of the law: judgment and mercy and faith. These things you ought to have done, and not leave those undone. Blind guides, who strain out a gnat and swallow a camel! Mat. 23:23 f.

Woe to you scribes and Pharisees, hypocrites! because you make clean the outside of the cup and of the dish, but within you are full of rapine and uncleanness. Thou blind Pharisee, first make clean the inside of the cup and of the dish, that the outside may become clean. Mat. 23:25 f.

There is a generation that are pure in their own eyes, and yet are not washed from their filthiness. Prov. 30:12.

There is one that humbleth himself wickedly, and his interior is full of deceit. Ecclus. 19:23.

There is one that submitteth himself exceedingly with a great lowliness; and there is one that casteth down his countenance, and maketh as if he did not see that which is unknown. Ecclus. 19:24.

And if he be hindered from sinning for want of power, if he shall find opportunity to do evil, he will do it. Ecclus. 19:25.

Lying lips hide hatred. Prov. 10:18.

12. EFFECTS OF HYPOCRISY

He that winketh with the eye shall cause sorrow. Prov. 10:10.

Their tongue is a piercing arrow, it hath spoken deceit; with his mouth one speaketh peace with his friend, and secretly he lieth in wait for him. Shall I not visit them for these things? saith the Lord; or shall not my soul be revenged on such a nation? Jer. 9:8 f.

He shall separate him, and appoint his portion with the hypocrites. There shall be weeping and gnashing of teeth. Mat. 24:51.

A deceitful tongue loveth not truth, and a slippery mouth worketh ruin. Prov. 26:28.

A heart that goeth two ways shall not have success, and the perverse of heart shall be scandalized therein. Ecclus. 3:28.

He that seeketh the law shall be filled with it; and he that dealeth deceitfully shall meet with a stumbling-block therein. Ecclus. 32:19.

The hope of the hypocrite shall perish. His folly shall not please him, and his trust shall be like the spider's web. He shall lean upon his house, and it shall not stand; he shall prop it up, and it shall not rise Job 8:13-15.

The congregation of the hypocrite is barren. Job 15:34.

This I know from the beginning, since man was placed upon the earth: that the praise of the wicked is short, and the joy of the hypocrite but for a moment. If his pride mount up even to heaven, and his head touch the clouds, in the end he shall be destroyed like a dunghill, and they that had seen him shall say: Where is he? As a dream that fleeth away, he shall not be found; he shall pass as a vision of the night. Job 20:4-8.

Deceitful souls go astray in sins. Prov. 13:13.

What is the hope of the hypocrite, if through covetousness he take by violence, and God deliver not his soul? Will God hear his cry when distress shall come upon him? Or can he delight himself with the Almighty, and call upon God at all times? Job 27:8-10.

13. HYPOCRISY SOONER OR LATER DETECTED

Nothing is covered that shall not be revealed, nor hid that shall not be known. Mat. 10:26.

He that covereth hatred deceitfully, his malice shall be laid open to the public assembly. Prov. 26:26.

The riches which he hath swallowed he shall vomit up, and God shall draw them out of his belly. Job 20:15.

He that walketh sincerely walketh confidently; but he that perverteth his ways shall be manifest. Prov. 10:9.

A man is known by his look; and a wise man, when thou meetest him, is known by his countenance. The attire of the body, and the laughter of the teeth, and the gait of the man show what he is. Ecclus. 19:26 f.

14. HYPOCRITES HATED BY GOD

A perverse heart is abominable to the Lord, and his will is in them that walk sincerely. Prov. 11:20.

Why call you me Lord, Lord, and do not the things which I say? Luke 6:46.

The Holy Spirit of discipline will fly from the deceitful. Wis. 1:5.

No hypocrite shall come before his presence. Job 13:16.

Dissemblers and crafty men prove the wrath of God; neither shall they cry out when they are bound. Job 36:13.

You are they who justify yourselves before men, but God knoweth your hearts; for that which is high to men is an abomination before God. Luke 16:15.

God is a Spirit, and they that adore him must adore him in spirit and in truth. John 4:24.

Forasmuch as this people draw near me with their mouth, and with their lips glorify me, but their heart is far from me, and they have feared me with the commandment and doctrines of men: therefore, behold I will proceed to cause an admiration in this people by a great and wonderful miracle; for wisdom shall depart from their wise men, and the understanding of their prudent men shall be hid. Is. 29:13 f.

15. HYPOCRISY CONDEMNED

Laying away all malice, and all guile, and dissimulations, and envies, and all destractions, as new-born babes desire the rational milk without guile. 1 Pet. 2:1.

Cleanse your hands, ye sinners; and purify your hearts, ye double-minded. Jas. 4:8.

Be not incredulous to the fear of the Lord; and come not to him with a double heart. Ecclus. 1:36.

Be not a hypocrite in the sight of men, and let not thy lips be a stumbling block to them. Ecclus. 1:37.

Watch over them, lest thou fall and bring dishonor upon thy soul, and God discover thy secrets, and cast thee down in the midst of the congregation. Because thou camest to the Lord wickedly, and thy heart is full of guile and deceit. Ecclus. 1:38-40.

Think of the Lord in goodness, and seek him in simplicity of heart. Wis. 1:1.

Fear the Lord, and serve him with a perfect and most sincere heart. Jos. 24:14.

Blessed is the man in whose spirit there is no guile. Ps. 31:2.

He that walketh sincerely walketh confidently. Prov. 10:9.

A perverse heart is abominable to the Lord: and his will is in them that walk sincerely. Prov. 11:20.

Let us feast, not with the old leaven, nor with the leaven of malice and wickedness, but with the unleavened bread of sincerety and truth. 1 C. 5:3.

Our glory is this, the testimony of our conscience, that in simplicity of heart and sincerity of God, and not in carnal wisdom, but in the grace of God, we have conversed in this world. 2 C. 1:12.

From a sincere heart love one another earnestly. 1 Pet. 1:22.

That you may be blameless, and sincere children of God, without reproof, in the midst of a crooked and perverse generation: among whom you shine as lights in the world. Phil. 2:15.

16. HUMAN ACTIONS, WHETHER GOOD OR EVIL, DO NOT INTRINSICALLY AFFECT GOD

If thou be wise, thou shalt be so to thyself; and if a scorner, thou alone shalt bear the evil. Prov. 9:12.

If thou sin, what shalt thou hurt him? and if thy iniquities be multiplied, what shalt thou do against him? Job 35:6.

If thou do justly, what shalt thou give him, or what shall he receive at thy hand? Job 35:7.

Thy wickedness may hurt a man that is like thee; and thy justice may help the son of man. By reason of the multitude of oppressors they shall cry out, and shall wail for the violence of the arm of tyrants. Job 35:8 f.

What is man, and what is his grace? and what is his good, or what is his evil? Ecclus. 18:7.

What doth it profit God if thou be just? or what dost thou give him if thy way be unspotted? Job 22:3.

When you shall have done all these things which are commanded you, say: We are unprofitable servants; we have done that which we ought to do. Luke 17:10.

Who hath first given to him, and recompense shall be made him? Rom. 11:35.

Whose helper art thou? Is it of him that is weak? and dost thou hold up the arm of him that has no strength? To whom hast thou given counsel? perhaps to him that hath no wisdom, and thou hast shown thy very great prudence. Job 26:2 f.

17. GOD CAN MAKE USE OF ONE MAN INSTEAD OF ANOTHER

Think not to say within yourselves: We have Abraham for our father. For I tell you that God is able of these stones to raise up children to Abraham. Mat. 3:9.

The number of the children of Israel shall be as the sand of the sea, that is without number, and shall not be numbered. And it shall be in the place where it shall be said to them: You are not my people; it shall be said to them: Ye are the sons of the living God. Osee 1:10.

The children of Juda and the children of Israel shall be gathered together; and they shall appoint themselves one head, and shall come up out of the land; for great is the day of Jezrahel. Osee 1:11.

The kingdom of God shall be taken from you, and shall be given to a nation yielding the fruits thereof. Mat. 21:43.

He saith to his servants: The marriage indeed is ready, but they that were invited were not worthy. Go ye therefore into the highways, and as many as you shall find, call to the marriage. Mat. 22:8 f.

Hold fast that which thou hast, that no man take thy crown. Apoc. 3:11.

He shall break in pieces many and innumerable, and shall make others to stand in their stead. Job 34:24.

III

EXTERNAL AND INTERNAL LAW

1. GOD THE SUPREME LAWGIVER

The Lord gave to Moses two stone tables of testimony, written with the finger of God. Ex. 31:18.

The Lord said to Moses: Write thee these words, by which I have made a covenant both with thee and with Israel. And he was there with the Lord forty days and forty nights: he neither ate bread nor drank water; and he wrote upon the tables the ten words of the covenant. Ex. 34:27 f.

The Lord gave me two tables of stone, written with the finger of God, and containing all the words that he spoke to you in the mount from the midst of the fire, when the people were assembled together. Deut. 9:10.

I shall write to them my manifold laws. Osee 8:12.

Thou camest down to Mount Sinai, and didst speak with them from heaven; and thou gavest them right judgments, and the law of truth, ceremonies and good precepts. 2 Es. 9:13.

The Lord is our Judge, the Lord is our Lawgiver, the Lord is our King: he will save us. Is. 33:22.

The Lord shall give unto him [Christ our Savior] the throne of David his father, and he shall reign in the house of Jacob forever. Luke 1:32.

Let every soul be subject to higher powers: for there is no power but from God; and those that are, are ordained of God. Rom. 13:1.

Therefore he that resisteth the power resisteth the ordinance of God. And they that resist purchase to themselves damnation. Rom. 13:2.

For princes are not a terror to the good work, but to the evil. Wilt thou not be afraid of the power? Do that which is good, and thou shalt have praise from the same. Rom. 13:3.

Wherefore be subject of necessity, not only for wrath, but also for conscience' sake. Rom. 13:5.

I have given to them my statutes, and I showed them my judgments, which if a man do, he shall live in them. Ez. 20:11.

Remember the law of Moses my servant, which I commanded him in Horeb for all Israel, the precepts and judgments. Mal. 4:4.

He set up a testimony in Jacob, and made a law in Israel. How great things he commanded our fathers, that they should make the same known to their children! Ps. 87:5.

2. COMPENDIUM AND END OF THE LAW

All things whatsoever you would that men should do to you, do you also to them. For this is the law and the prophets. Mat. 7:12.

The love of our neighbor worketh no evil. Love, therefore, is the fulfilling of the law. Rom. 13:10.

All the law is fulfilled in one word: Thou shalt love thy neighbor as thyself. Gal. 5:14.

Bear ye one another's burdens, and so you shall fulfil the law of Christ. Gal. 6:2.

The end of the commandment is charity from a pure heart, and a good conscience, and an unfeigned faith. 1 Tim. 1:5.

The law of the wise is a fountain of life, that he may decline from the ruin of death. Prov. 13:14.

If thou wilt enter into life, keep the commandments. Mat. 19:17.

By this shall all men know that you are my disciples, if you have love one for another. John 13:35.

Let us all hear together the conclusion of the discourse: Fear God and keep his commandments: for this is all man. Eccles. 12:13.

3. THE LAW OF GOD IS SWEET AND EASY

My yoke is sweet and my burden light. Mat. 11:30.

This is the charity of God, that we keep his commandments: and his commandments are not heavy. 1 John 5:3.

The word of the law shall be fulfilled without a lie, and wisdom shall be made plain in the mouth of the faithful. Ecclus. 34:8.

The commandment is a lamp, and the law a light, and reproofs of instruction are the way of life. Prov. 6:23.

The declaration of thy words giveth light: and giveth understanding to little ones. Ps. 118:130.

He that keepeth the law is a wise son. Prov. 28:7.

You shall observe and fulfil them in practice. For this is your wisdom and understanding in the sight of nations, that hearing all these precepts, they may say: Behold a wise and understanding people, a great nation. Deut. 4:6.

4. FRUITS OF FAITHFUL OBSERVANCE OF THE LAW

Good instruction shall give grace: in the way of scorners is a deep pit. Prov. 13:15.

If thou wilt keep the commandments and perform acceptable fidelity forever, they shall preserve thee. Ecclus. 15:16.

He that feareth the Lord will receive his discipline; and they that will seek him early shall find a blessing. He that seeketh the law shall be filled with it; and he that dealeth deceitfully shall meet with a stumbling block therein. Ecclus. 32:18 f.

A man of understanding is faithful to the law of God, and the law is faithful to him. Ecclus. 33:3.

He that keepeth the fig tree shall eat the fruit thereof; and he that is the keeper of his master shall be glorified. Prov. 27:18.

The son that keepeth the word shall be free from destruction. Prov. 29:27.

The keeping of her laws is the firm foundation of incorruption; and incorruption bringeth near to God. Wis. 6:19 f.

Take up my yoke upon you, and learn of me, because I am meek and humble of heart: and you shall find rest to your souls. Mat. 11:29.

They that remain shall know there is nothing better than the fear of God: and that there is nothing sweeter than to have regard to the commandments of the Lord. Ecclus. 23:37.

It is great glory to follow the Lord, for length of days shall be received from him. Ecclus. 23:38.

He that keepeth justice shall get the understanding thereof. The perfection of the fear of God is wisdom and understanding. Ecclus. 21:12 f.

He that keepeth the law multiplieth offerings. Ecclus. 35:1.

It is a wholesome sacrifice to take heed to the commandments, and to depart from all iniquity. And to depart from injustice is to offer a propitiatory sacrifice for injustices, and a begging of pardon for sins. Ecclus. 35:2 f.

5. EXHORTATIONS TO HEAR AND TO MEDITATE UPON GOD'S LAW

Incline thine ear, and hear the words of the wise, and apply thy heart to my doctrine: Which shall be beautiful for thee, if thou keep it in thy bowels, and it shall flow in thy lips. Prov. 22:17 f.

Let thy heart apply itself to instruction, and thy ears to words of knowledge. Prov. 23:12.

Let thy thoughts be upon the precepts of God, and meditate continually on his commandments: and he will give thee a heart, and the desire of wisdom shall be given to thee. Ecclus. 6:37.

These words which I command thee this day shall be in thy heart. Deut. 6:6.

Thou shalt bind them as a sign on thy hand, and they shall be and shall move between thy eyes. And thou shalt write them in the entry and on the doors of thy house. Deut. 6:8 f.

Lay up these my words in your hearts and minds, and hang them for a sign on your hands, and place them between your eyes. Thou shalt write them upon the posts and the doors of thy house. Deut. 11:18, 20.

Thou shalt tell them to thy children. Deut. 6:7.

Teach your children that they meditate on them, when thou sittest in thy house, and when thou walkest on the way, and when thou liest down and risest up. Deut. 11:19.

6. REWARDS PROMISED TO THE DOER OF THE LAW

My son, forget not my law, and let thy heart keep my commandments. For they shall add to thee length of days, and years of life and peace. Prov. 3:1 f.

Let not mercy and truth leave thee put them about thy neck, and write them in the tables of thy heart. And thou shalt find grace and good understanding before God and men. Prov. 3:3 f.

My son, let not these things depart from thy eyes: keep the law and counsel: and there shall be life to thy soul and grace to thy mouth. Then shalt thou walk confidently in thy way, and thy foot shall not stumble: if thou sleep thou shalt rest, and thy sleep shall be sweet. Be not afraid of sudden fear, nor of the power of the wicked falling upon thee. For the Lord will be at thy side, and will keep thy foot that thou be not taken. Prov. 3:21-26.

Hear, ye children, the instruction of a father, and attend that you may know prudence. Prov. 4:1.

I will give you a good gift, forsake not my law. For I also was my father's son, tender and as an only son in the sight of my mother. And he taught me, and said: Let thy heart receive my words, keep my commandments, and thou shalt live. Prov. 4:2-4.

Get wisdom, get prudence; forget not, neither decline from the words of my mouth. Forsake her not, and she shall keep thee: love her, and she shall preserve thee. Prov. 4:5 f.

My son, hearken to my words, and incline thy ear to my sayings. Let them not depart from thy eyes, keep them in the midst of thy heart; for they are life to those that find them, and health to all flesh. Prov. 4:20-22.

My son, keep the commandments of thy father, and forsake not the law of thy mother. Bind them in thy heart continually, and put them about thy neck. When thou walkest, let them go with thee: when thou sleepest, let them keep thee: and when thou awakest, talk with them. Prov.6:20-22.

My son, keep my words, and lay up my precepts with thee. Son, keep my commandments, and thou shalt live: and my law, as the apple of thy eye. Bind it upon thy fingers, write it upon the tables of thy heart. Prov. 7:1-3.

O my sons, be ye zealous for the law, and give your lives for the covenant of your fathers. And call to remembrance the works of the fathers, which they have done in their generations: and you shall receive great glory and an everlasting name. 1 Mac. 2:50 f.

My sons, take courage, and behave manfully in the law: for by it you shall be glorious. 1 Mac. 2:64.

Submit thyself then to him, and be at peace: and thereby thou shalt have the best fruits. Receive the law of his mouth, and lay up his words in thy heart. Job 22:21 f.

Hearken diligently to me, and eat that which is good, and your soul shall be delighted in fatness. Incline your ear and come to me: hear and your soul shall live, and I will make an everlasting covenant with you, the faithful mercies of David. Is. 55:2 f.

O that thou hadst hearkened to my commandments! thy peace had been as a river, and thy justice as the waves of the sea. Is. 48:18.

If thou wilt enter into life, keep the commandments. Mat. 19:17.

This is my beloved Son in whom I am well pleased: hear ye him. Mat. 17:5.

Be ye doers of the word; and not hearers only, deceiving your own selves. For if a man be a hearer of the word and not a doer, he shall be compared to a man beholding his natural countenance in a glass. For he beheld himself, and went his way, and presently forgot what manner of man he was. But he that hath looked into the perfect law of liberty, and hath continued therein, not becoming a forgetful hearer, but a doer of the work: this man shall be blessed in his deed. Jas. 1:22-25.

7. NEGLECT OF THE LAW BRINGING RUIN AND ETERNAL PUNISHMENT

Every one that heareth these my words and doth them not shall be like a foolish man that built his house upon the sand: and the rain fell, and the floods came, and the winds blew, and they beat upon that house; and it fell, and great was the fall thereof. Mat. 7:26 f.

Let us have pity on the wicked, but he will not learn justice: in the land of the saints he hath done wicked things, and he shall not see the glory of the Lord. Is. 26:10.

God hath given him place for penance, and he abuseth it unto pride: but his eyes are upon his ways. Job 24:23.

The heavens shall reveal his iniquity, and the earth shall rise up against him. The offspring of his house shall be exposed, he shall be pulled down in the day of God's wrath. This is the portion of a wicked man from God, and the inheritance of his doings from the Lord. Job 20:27-29.

He that soweth iniquity shall reap evils, and with the rod of his anger he shall be consumed. Prov. 22:8.

As a tempest that passeth, so the wicked shall be no more. Prov. 10:25.

The death of the wicked is very evil: and they that hate the just shall be guilty. Ps. 33:22.

When the wicked man is dead, there shall be no hope any more. Prov. 11:7.

They shall fall after this without honor, and be a reproach among the dead forever: for he shall burst them puffed up and speechless, and shall shake them from the foundations, and they shall be utterly laid waste: they shall be in sorrow, and their memory shall perish. They shall come with fear at the thought of their sins, and their iniquities shall stand against them to convict them. Wis. 4:19 f.

Then shall the just stand with great constancy against those that have afflicted them, and taken away their labors. These seeing it shall be troubled with terrible fear, saying within themselves, repenting, and groaning for anguish of spirit: These are they whom we had some time in derision, and for a parable of reproach. We fools esteemed their life madness, and their end without honor. Behold how they are numbered among the children of God, and their lot is among the saints. Therefore we have erred from the way of truth, and the light of justice hath not shined unto us, and the sun of understanding hath not risen upon us. We wearied ourselves in the way of iniquity and destruction, and have walked through hard ways, but the way of the Lord we have not known. What hath pride profited us? or what advantage hath the boasting of riches brought us? All those things are passed away like a shadow, and like a post that runneth on. So we also being born, forthwith ceased to be, and have been able to show no mark of virtue; but are consumed in our wickedness. Such things as these the sinners said in hell: for the hope of the wicked is as dust, which is blown away with the wind, and as a thin froth which is dispersed by the storm, and a smoke that is scattered abroad by the wind, and as the remembrance of a guest of one day that passeth by. Wis. 5:1-15.

Woe to the wicked unto evil, for the reward of his hands shall be given him! Is. 3:11.

Woe to them that desire the day of the Lord! to what end is it for you? The day of the Lord is darkness, and not light. Shall not the day of the Lord be darkness, and not light: and obscurity, and no brightness in it? Amos 5:18, 20.

Acting wickedly against the laws of God doth not pass unpunished. 2 Mac. 4:17.

Thy pride is brought down to hell, thy carcass is fallen down: under thee shall the moth be strewed, and worms shall be thy covering. Is. 14:11.

Depart from me, you cursed, into everlasting fire which was prepared for the devil and his angels. And these shall go into everlasting punishment. Mat. 25:41,46.

So shall it be at the end of the world. The angels shall go out, and shall separate the wicked from among the just. And shall cast them into the furnace of fire: there shall be weeping and gnashing of teeth. Mat. 13:49 f.

The kingdom of this world is become our Lord's and his Christ's, and he shall reign forever and ever. And thy wrath is come, and the time of the dead, that they should be judged, and that thou shouldest destroy them that have corrupted the earth. Apoc. 11:15, 18.

The fearful, and unbelieving, and the abominable, and murderers, and whoremongers, and sorcerers, and idolaters, and all liars, they shall have their portion in the pool burning with fire and brimstone, which is the second death. Apoc. 21:8.

Unless thou hold thyself diligently in the fear of the Lord, thy house shall quickly be overthrown. Ecclus. 27:4.

The earth is infected by the inhabitants thereof: because they have transgressed the laws, they have changed the ordinance, they have broken the everlasting covenant. Therefore shall a curse devour the earth, and the inhabitants thereof shall sin: and therefore they that dwell therein shall be mad, and few men shall be left. Is. 24:5 f.

The Lord Jesus shall be revealed from heaven with the angels of his power, in a flame of fire yielding vengeance to them who know not God, and who obey not the gospel of our Lord Jesus Christ. 2 Thess. 1:7 f.

8. FORCE OF HABIT FOR GOOD OR EVIL

Cleave ye unto the Lord your God, as you have done until this day. And then no man shall be able to resist you. Jos. 23:8 f.

Being confident of this very thing, that he who hath begun a good work in you will perfect it unto the day of Jesus Christ. Phil. 1:6.

If the Ethiopian can change his skin, or the leopard his spots, you also may do well when you have learned evil. Jer. 13:23.

It is a proverb: A young man according to his way, even when he is old he will not depart from it. Prov. 22:6.

It is good for a man when he hath borne the yoke from his youth. He shall sit solitary and hold his peace, because he hath taken it up upon himself. Lam. 3:27 f.

His bones shall be filled with the vices of his youth, and they shall sleep with him in the dust. Job 20:11.

Despairing, they have given themselves up to lasciviousness, unto the working of all uncleanness, unto covetousness. Eph. 4:19.

Woe to you that draw iniquity with cords of vanity, and sin as the rope of a cart! Is. 5:18.

9. STRENGTH OF CONSCIENCE FOR GOOD OR EVIL

The spirit of a man is the lamp of the Lord, which searches all the hidden things of the bowels. Prov. 20:27.

When the Gentiles, who have not the law, do by nature those things that are of the law; these having not the law, are a law to themselves: who show the work of the law written in their hearts, their conscience bearing witness to them, and their thoughts between themselves accusing or also defending one another. Rom. 2:14 f.

To him that esteemeth anything to be unclean, to him it is unclean. Rom. 14:14.

All things are clean to the clean; but to them that are defiled and to unbelievers nothing is clean, but both their mind and their consciences are defiled. Titus 1:15.

If our hearts do not reprehend us, we have confidence towards God: And whatsoever we shall ask, we shall receive of him, because we keep his commandments, and do those things which are pleasing in his sight. 1 John 3:21 f.

All the days of the poor are evil: a secure mind is like a continual feast. Prov. 15:15.

Our glory is this, the testimony of our conscience, that in simplicity of heart and sincerity of God, and not in carnal wisdom, but in the grace of God, we have conversed in this world, and more abundantly towards you. 2 C. 1:12.

In every work of thine regard thy soul in faith: for this is the keeping of the commandments. Ecclus. 32:27.

Day and night thy hand was heavy upon me: I am turned in my anguish whilst the thorn is fastened. Ps. 31:4.

Whereas wickedness is fearful, it beareth witness of its condemnation: for a troubled conscience always forecasteth grievous things. Wis. 17:10.

Over them [the Egyptians] only was spread a heavy night, an image of that darkness which was to come upon them. But they were to themselves more grievous than the darkness. Wis. 17:20.

The wicked man, when he is come into the depth of sins, contemneth: but ignominy and reproach follow him. Prov. 18:3.

By what things a man sinneth, by the same also he is tormented. Wis. 11:17.

I will make Babylon a possession for the ericius. Is. 14:23.

The wicked are like the raging sea, which cannot rest. Is. 57:20.

10. POWER OF THE PASSIONS

The heart of a man changeth his countenance either for good or for evil. Ecclus. 13:31.

A glad heart maketh a cheerful countenance; but by grief of mind the spirit is cast down. Prov. 15:13.

The wickedness of a woman changeth her face: and she darkeneth her countenance as a bear, and showeth it like sackcloth. Ecclus. 25:24.

The wicked man impudently hardeneth his face: but he that is righteous correcteth his way. Prov. 21:29.

As a city that lieth open and is not compassed with walls, so is a man that cannot restrain his own spirit in speaking. Prov. 25:28.

A hot soul is a burning fire: it will never be quenched till it devour something. Ecclus. 23:22.

Soundness of heart is the life of the flesh: but envy is the rottenness of the bones. Ps. 14:30.

11. ASPIRATIONS OF ONE WHO RESOLVES TO KEEP GOD'S LAW

O that my ways may be directed to keep thy justifications! Ps. 118:5.

I will keep thy justifications; O, do not thou utterly forsake me! Let me not stray from thy commandments. Ps. 118:8.

In thy words I have hoped exceedingly; so shall I always keep thy law, forever and ever. Ps. 118:44.

I have said, I would keep thy law. Ps. 118:57.

Thy justifications I will never forget, for by them thou hast given me life. Ps. 118:93.

I have sworn and am determined to keep the judgments of thy justice. Ps. 118:106.

I am ready and am not troubled: that I may keep thy commandments. Ps. 118:60.

If I have found favor in thy sight, show me thy face, that I may know thee, and may find grace before thy eyes Ex. 33:13.

If I have erred, teach thou me. Job 34:32.

With my whole heart have I sought after thee: let me not stray from thy commandments. Ps. 118:10.

Blessed art thou, O Lord: teach me thy justifications. Ps. 118:12.

Lead me into the path of thy commandments; for this same I have desired. Incline my heart unto thy testimonies, and not to covetousness. Ps. 118:35 f.

Show, O Lord, thy ways to me, and teach me my paths. Direct me in thy truth and teach me; for thou art God my Savior, and on thee have I waited all the day. Ps. 24:4 f.

Send forth thy light and thy truth: they have conducted me and brought me unto thy holy hill and into thy tabernacle. Ps. 42:3.

Lead me into the eternal way. Ps. 138:24.

Cause me to hear thy mercy in the morning, for in thee have I hoped. Make the way known to me wherein I should walk, for I have lifted up my soul to thee. Ps. 142:8.

Teach me to do thy will, for thou art my God. Thy good Spirit shall lead me into the right land, for thy name's sake. Ps. 142:10.

O Lord, make me know my end, and what is the number of my days, that I may know what is wanting to me. Ps. 38:5.

Conduct me, O Lord, in thy way, and I will walk in thy truth. Let my heart rejoice that it may fear thy name. Ps. 85:11.

Let my heart be undefiled in thy justifications, that I may not be confounded. Ps. 118:80.

Open thou my eyes, and I will consider the wondrous things of thy law. Ps. 118:18.

I am a sojourner on the earth: hide not thy commandments from me. Ps. 118:19.

I am thy servant: give me understanding, that I may know thy testimonies. Ps. 118:125.

Thy testimonies are justice forever: give me understanding, and I shall live. Ps. 118:144.

Make me to understand the way of thy justifications, and I shall be exercised in thy wondrous works. Ps. 118:27.

Give me understanding, and I will search thy law; and I will keep it with my whole heart. Ps. 118:34.

Thy hands have made me and formed me: give me understanding, and I will learn thy commandments. Ps. 118:73.

Make thy face to shine upon thy servant, and teach me thy justifications. Ps. 118:135.

Establish thy word to thy servant, in thy fear. Ps. 118:38.

Set before me for a law the way of thy justifications, O Lord, and I will always seek after it. Ps. 118: 33.

Direct my steps according to thy word, and let no iniquity have dominion over me. Ps. 118: 133.

Enlighten my eyes that I may never sleep in death; lest at any time my enemy say: I have prevailed against him. Ps. 12: 5.

My soul hath coveted to long for thy justifications at all times. Ps. 118: 20.

A fainting hath taken hold of me, because of the wicked that forsake thy law. Ps. 118: 53.

My eyes have sent forth springs of water, because they have not kept thy law. Ps. 118: 136.

My zeal hath made me pine away, because my enemies forgot thy words. Ps. 118: 139.

I beheld the transgressors, and I pined away, because they kept not thy word. Ps. 118: 158.

Thus saith the Lord God: Strike with thy hand and stamp with thy foot, and say: Alas for all the abominations of the evils of the house of Israel! Ez. 6: 11.

How long, O Lord, shall the enemy approach! Is the adversary to provoke thy name forever? Ps. 73: 10.

Thy justifications were the subject of my song in the place of my pilgrimage. Ps. 118: 54.

How sweet are thy words to my palate! More than honey to my mouth! Ps. 118: 103.

I have purchased thy testimonies for an inheritance forever, because they are the joy of my heart. Ps. 118: 111.

The law of thy mouth is good to me, above thousands of gold and silver. Ps. 118: 72.

I have been delighted in the way of thy testimonies, as in all riches. Ps. 118: 14.

They have dissipated thy law; therefore have I loved thy commandments above gold and the topaz. Ps. 118: 126 f.

O how have I loved thy law, O Lord! It is my meditation all the day. Ps. 118: 97.

Thy words were found, and I did eat them, and thy word was to me a joy and gladness of my heart. Jer. 15: 16.

My soul is continually in my hands, and I have not forgotten thy law. Ps. 118: 109.

The cords of the wicked have encompassed me: but I have not forgotten thy law. Ps. 118: 61.

The proud did iniquitously altogether: but I declined not from thy law. Ps. 118: 51.

The wicked have waited for me to destroy me: but I have understood thy testimonies. Ps. 118: 95.

Sinners have laid a snare for me: but I have not erred from thy precepts. Ps. 118: 110.

I beseech thee, O Lord, remember how I have walked before thee in truth and with a perfect heart, and have done that which is pleasing before thee. 4 K. 20: 3.

Remember me, O my God, for good, according to all that I have done for this people. 2 Es. 5: 19.

Remember me, O my God, for this thing, and wipe not out my kindnesses, which I have done relating to the house of my God and his ceremonies. 2 Es. 13: 14.

I spoke also to the Levites that they should be purified, and should come to keep the gates, and to sanctify the Sabbath day; for this also remember me, O my God, and spare me according to the multitude of thy tender mercies. 2 Es. 13: 22.

O Lord, thou knowest, remember me, and visit me, and defend me from them that persecute me: know that for thy sake I have suffered reproach. Jer. 15: 15.

IV

ACTUAL AND HABITUAL GRACE

1. SUFFICIENT GRACE TO ALL

He hath delivered us and called us by his holy calling; not according to our works, but according to his own purpose and grace, which was given us in Christ Jesus before the times of the world. 2 Tim. 1:9.

Behold, I stand at the gate, and knock. If any man shall hear my voice, and open to me the door, I will come in to him, and will sup with him, and he with me. Apoc. 3:20.

The Spirit helpeth our infirmity. For we know not what we should pray for as we ought: but the Spirit himself asketh for us with unspeakable groanings. Rom. 8:26.

Whosoever are led by the Spirit of God, they are the sons of God. Rom. 8:14.

His mercy shall prevent me. Ps. 58:11.

The Lord loveth mercy and truth: the Lord will give grace and glory. Ps. 83:12.

Of his fulness we all have received, and grace for grace. John 1:16.

To the meek he will give grace. Prov. 3:34.

God giveth grace to the humble. Jas. 4:8.

It is God who worketh in you both to will and to accomplish, according to his good will. And do ye all things without murmurings and hesitations. Phil. 2:13.

What hast thou that thou hast not received? 1 C. 4:7.

No man can come to me, except the Father, who hath sent me, draw him. John 6:44.

Lord, what wilt thou have me to do? Acts 9:6.

I was found by them that did not seek me: I appeared openly to them that asked not after me. Rom. 10:20.

All do not obey the gospel. For Isaias saith: Lord, who hath believed our report? Rom. 10:16.

The wicked have spoken false things. Their madness is according to the likeness of a serpent: like the deaf asp that stoppeth her ears: which will not hear the voice of the charmers, nor of the wizard that charmeth wisely. Ps. 57:5 f.

Turn ye to me, saith the Lord of hosts, and I will turn to you, saith the Lord of hosts. Zach. 1:3.

The Lord waiteth that he may have mercy on you. Is. 30:18.

If you be willing and will hearken to me, you shall eat the good things of the land. Is. 1:19.

If any man love me, he will keep my word, and my Father will love him; and we will come to him, and will make our abode with him. John 14:23.

Upon whom shall not his light arise? Job 25:3.

The Lord will be at thy side, and will keep thy foot, that thou be not taken. Prov. 3:26.

The number of the days of men, at the most, are a hundred years: as a drop of water of the sea are they esteemed: and as a pebble of the sand, so are a few years compared to eternity. Therefore God is patient in them, and poureth forth his mercy upon them. He hath seen the presumption of their heart that it is wicked, and hath known their end that it is evil. Therefore hath he filled up his mercy in their favor, and hath shown them the way of justice. Ecclus. 18:8-11.

That was the true light, which enlighteneth every man that cometh into this world. John 1:9.

We labor and are reviled, because we hope in the living God, who is the Savior of all men, especially of the faithful. 1 Tim. 4:10.

In times past he suffered all nations to walk in their own ways. Nevertheless he left not himself without testimony, doing good from heaven, giving rains and fruitful seasons, filling our hearts with food and gladness. Acts 14:15 f.

The invisible things of him, from the creation of the world, are clearly seen, being understood by the things that are made: his eternal power also and divinity: so that they are inexcusable. Because that, when they knew God, they have not glorified him as God, or given thanks: but became vain in thoughts, and their foolish heart was darkened. Rom. 1:20 f.

He will have all men to be saved, and to come to the knowledge of the truth. For there is one God, and one Mediator of God and men, the man Christ Jesus, who gave himself a redemption for all. 1 Tim. 2:4-6.

Sion said: The Lord hath forsaken me, and the Lord hath forgotten me. Can a woman forget her infant, so as not to have pity on the son of her womb? and if she should forget, yet will not I forget thee. Is. 49:14 f.

Thou, O son of man, say to the house of Israel: Thus you have spoken, saying: Our iniquities and our sins are upon us, and we pine away in them: how then can we live? Say to them: As I live, saith the Lord God, I desire not the death of the wicked, but that the wicked turn from his way, and live. Ez. 33:10 f.

Come to me, all you that labor and are burdened, and I will refresh you. Mat. 11:28.

The Lord delayeth not his promise, as some imagine, but dealeth patiently for your sake, not willing that any should perish, but that all should return to penance. 2 Pet. 3:9.

Despisest thou the riches of his goodness, and patience, and longsuffering? Knowest thou not that the benignity of God leadeth thee to penance? Rom. 2:4.

This every one is sure of that worshippeth thee, that his life, if it be under trial, shall be crowned: and if it be under tribulation, it shall be delivered: and if it be under correction, it shall be allowed to come to thy mercy. For thou art not delighted in our being lost: because after a storm thou makest a calm, and after tears and weeping thou pourest in joyfulness. Tob. 3:21 f.

Take heed, brethren, lest perhaps there be in any of you an evil heart of unbelief, to depart from the living God. But exhort one another every day, whilst it is called today, that none of you be hardened through the deceitfulness of sin. Heb. 3:12 f.

Return as you had deeply revolted, O children of Israel. Is. 31:6.

He hath not done in like manner to every nation, and his judgments he hath not made manifest to them. Ps. 147:20.

If in Tyre and Sidon had been wrought the miracles that have been wrought in you, they had long ago done penance in sackcloth and ashes. Mat. 11:21.

I confess to thee, O Father, Lord of heaven and earth, because thou hast hid these things from the wise and prudent, and hast revealed them to little ones. Yea, Father, for so hath it seemed good in thy sight. Mat. 11:25 f.

To you it is given to know the mysteries of the kingdom of heaven: but to them it is not given. Mat. 13:11.

He hath mercy on whom he will: and whom he will, he hardeneth. Rom. 9:18.

He that is good shall draw grace from the Lord. Prov. 12:2.

All you that thirst, come to the waters; and you that have no money, make haste, buy and eat; come ye, buy wine and milk without money, and without any price. Is. 55:1.

2. NECESSITY OF GRACE

No man can say, The Lord Jesus, but by the Holy Ghost. 1 C. 12:3.

Not that we are sufficient to think anything of ourselves as of ourselves; but our sufficiency is from God. 2 C. 3:5.

Blessed art thou, Simon Bar-Jona: because flesh and blood hath not revealed it to thee, but my Father, who is in heaven. Mat. 16:17.

No one knoweth the Son, but the Father; neither doth any one know the Father, but the Son, and he to whom it shall please the Son to reveal him. Mat. 11:27.

By grace you are saved through faith, and that not of yourselves; for it is the gift of God, not of works, that no man may glory. Eph. 2:8 f.

This is the work of God, that you believe in him whom he hath sent. John 6:29.

No man can come to me, unless it be given him by my Father. John 6:66.

God hath given to the Gentiles repentance unto life. Acts 11:18.

Knowest thou not that the benignity of God leadeth thee to penance? Rom. 2:4.

Charity is of God. 1 John 4:7.

The charity of God is poured forth in our hearts by the Holy Ghost, who is given to us. Rom. 5:5.

The fruit of the Spirit is charity. Gal. 5:22.

O God of hosts, convert us, and show us thy face, and we shall be saved. Ps. 49:8.

Convert us, O Lord, to thee, and we shall be converted. Lam. 5:21.

Convert me, and I shall be converted, for thou art the Lord my God. After thou didst convert me, I did penance; and after thou didst show unto me, I struck my thigh. Jer. 31:18 f.

No man can come to me, except the Father, who hath sent me, draw him. John 6:44.

It is God who worketh in you, both to will and to accomplish according to his good will. Phil. 2:13.

There is no man who sinneth not. 3 K. 8:46.

A just man shall fall seven times, and shall rise again. Prov. 24:16.

There is no just man upon earth that doth good, and sinneth not. Eccles. 7:21.

Then came Peter unto him, and said: Lord, how often shall my brother offend against me, and I forgive him? till seven times? Jesus saith to him: I say not to thee till seven times, but till seventy times seven times. Mat. 18:21 f.

Follow not in thy strength the desires of thy heart. Ecclus. 5:2.

The good which I will I do not; but the evil which I will not, that I do. Rom. 7:19.

If we say that we have no sin, we deceive ourselves, and the truth is not in us. 1 John 1:8.

In many things we all offend. Jas. 3:2.

I see another law in my members, fighting against the law of my mind, and captivating me in the law of sin. Rom. 7:23.

Who shall rise up for me against the evil-doers? or who shall stand with me against the workers of iniquity? Unless the Lord had been my helper, my soul had almost dwelt in hell. If I said: My foot is moved, thy mercy, O Lord, assisted me. Ps. 93:16-18.

Unless the Lord build the house, they labor in vain that build it. Ps. 126:1.

Unless the Lord keep the city, he

watcheth in vain that keepeth it. Ps. 126:1.

Be thou my helper, forsake me not; do not thou despise me, O God my Savior. Ps. 26:9.

Who is this that cometh up from the desert, flowing with delights, leaning upon her beloved? Cant. 8:5.

I know, O Lord, that the way of man is not his: neither is it in a man to walk and to direct his steps. Jer. 10:23.

Watch ye, and pray that ye enter not into temptation. Mat. 26:41.

Thus shall you pray: Lead us not into temptation, but deliver us from evil. Amen. Mat. 6:9, 13.

Holy Father, keep them in thy name whom thou hast given me: that they may be one, as we also are. I pray not that thou shouldst take them out of the world, but that thou shouldst keep them from evil. John 17:11, 15.

Simon, Simon, behold Satan hath desired to have you, that he may sift you as wheat. But I have prayed for thee, that thy faith fail not: and thou being once converted, confirm thy brethren. Luke 10:31 f.

We have this treasure in earthen vessels, that the excellency may be of the power of God and not of us. 2 C. 4:7.

3. COOPERATING GRACE

I will give you a new heart, and put a new spirit within you: and I will take away the stony heart out of your flesh, and will give you a heart of flesh. And I will put my Spirit in the midst of you: and I will cause you to walk in my commandments, and to keep my judgments and do them. Ez. 36:26 f.

Without me you can do nothing. John 15:5.

By the works of the law no flesh shall be justified before him. For by the law is the knowledge of sin. Rom. 3:20.

If thou wilt keep the commandments, and perform acceptable fidelity forever, they shall preserve thee. He hath set water and fire before thee: stretch forth thy hand to which thou wilt. Before man is life and death, good and evil: that which he shall choose shall be given him. Ecclus. 15:16-18.

This commandment, that I command thee this day, is not above thee, nor far off from thee: Nor is it in heaven, that thou shouldst say: Which of us can go up to heaven to bring it unto us, and we may hear and fulfil it in work? But the word is very nigh unto thee, in thy mouth and in thy heart, that thou mayst do it. Deut. 30:11, 12, 14.

If you love me, keep my commandments. John 14:15.

He that hath my commandments, and keepeth them, he it is that loveth me. John 14:21.

This is the charity of God, that we keep his commandments; and his commandments are not heavy. 1 John 5:3.

4. GRACE OF FINAL PERSEVERANCE

Abide in me, and I in you. As the branch cannot bear fruit of itself, unless it abide in the vine, so neither can you, unless you abide in me. John 15:4.

Abide in my love. If you keep my commandments, you shall abide in my love; as I also have kept my Father's commandments, and do abide in his love. John 15:9 f.

See the goodness and the severity of God: towards them indeed that are fallen, the severity; but towards thee, the goodness of God, if thou abide in goodness; otherwise thou also shalt be cut off. Rom. 11:22.

Be thou faithful unto death, and I will give thee the crown of life. Apoc. 2:10.

Stand fast in the faith. 1 C. 16:13.

Whosoever is born of God committeth not sin; for his seed abideth in him, and he cannot sin, because he is born of God. 1 John 3:9.

5. GOD THE EFFICIENT CAUSE OF GRACE

The Lord will give grace and glory. Ps. 83:12.

By the grace of God I am what I am. 1 C. 15:10.

He that is good shall draw grace from the Lord. Prov. 12:2.

Grace to you and peace from God our Father, and from the Lord Jesus Christ. Rom. 1:7.

He giveth grace to the humble. Jas. 4:6.

The God of all grace, who hath called us unto his eternal glory in Christ Jesus, after you have suffered a little, will himself perfect you, and confirm you, and establish you. 1 Pet. 5:10.

To him that believeth in him that justifieth the ungodly, his faith is reputed to justice according to the purpose of the grace of God. Rom. 4:5.

He is near that justifieth me: who will contend with me? Is. 50:8.

Who can make him clean that is conceived of unclean seed? Is it not thou who only art? Job 14:4.

I am, I am he that blot out thy iniquities for my own sake, and I will not remember thy sins. Is. 43:25.

Our God is the God of salvation: and of the Lord, of the Lord are the issues from death. Ps. 67:21.

Salvation is of the Lord. Ps. 3:9.

I am, I am the Lord: and there is no Savior besides me. Is. 43:11.

I am the Lord thy God: and thou shalt know no God but me, and there is no Savior besides me. Osee 13:4.

6. CHRIST THE MERITORIOUS CAUSE OF GRACE

He had predestinated us unto the adoption of children through Jesus Christ unto himself, according to the purpose of his will: unto the praise of the glory of his grace, in which he had graced us in his beloved Son. Eph. 1:5 f.

You were signed with the Holy Spirit of promise, who is the pledge of our inheritance unto the redemption of acquisition, unto the praise of his glory. Eph. 1:13 f.

He hath blessed us with all spiritual blessings in heavenly places in Christ. Eph. 1:3.

Of his fulness we have all received, and grace for grace. For the law was given by Moses; grace and truth came by Jesus Christ. John 1:16 f.

If by one man's offense death reigned through one, much more they who receive abundance of grace, and of the gift, and of justice, shall reign in life through one, Jesus Christ. Rom. 5:17.

Full of the glory of the Lord is his work. Ecclus. 42:16.

He that confirmeth us with you in Christ, and that hath anointed us, is God: who also hath sealed us, and given the pledge of the Spirit in our hearts. 2 C. 1:21 f.

7. ACTS OF FAITH, HOPE, AND CHARITY THE PREDISPOSING CAUSE OF SANCTIFYING GRACE

All have sinned, and do need the glory of God. Rom. 3:23.

Being justified freely by his grace, through the redemption which is in Christ Jesus, whom God hath proposed to be a propitiation through faith in his blood. Rom. 3:23-25.

Without faith it is impossible to please God. Heb. 11:6.

We are saved by hope. Rom. 8:24.

We know that when he shall appear, we shall be like to him, because we shall see him as he is. Every one that hath this hope in him sanctifieth himself, as he also is holy. 1 John 3:2 f.

The fear of the Lord driveth out sin: for he that is without fear cannot be justified. Ecclus. 1:27 f.

If the wicked do penance for all his sins which he hath committed, and keep all my commandments, and do judgment and justice, living he shall live, and shall not die. Ez. 18:21.

Unless you shall do penance, you shall all likewise perish. Luke 13:3.

He that loveth me shall be loved by my Father. John 14:21.

The Father himself loveth you, because you have loved me, and have believed that I came out from God. John 16:27.

We know that we have passed from death to life, because we love the brethren. He that loveth not abideth in death. 1 John 3:14.

8. GRACE NOT EQUAL IN ALL

The Lord said to Satan: Hast thou considered my servant Job, that there is none like him in the earth, a simple and upright man, fearing God, and avoiding evil?? Job 1:8.

Amen I say to you, there hath not risen among them that are born of women a greater than John the Baptist; yet he that is the lesser in the kingdom of heaven is greater than he. Mat. 11:11.

There was not among the children of Israel a goodlier person than he. 1 K. 9:2.

Ourselves also, who have the first-fruits of the Spirit, even we ourselves groan within ourselves, waiting for the adoption of the sons of God, the redemption of our body. Rom. 8:23.

To every one of us is given grace according to the measure of the giving of Christ. Eph. 4:7.

I gave you milk to drink, not meat; for you were not able as yet. But neither indeed are you now able; for you are yet carnal. 1 C. 3:2.

In a great house there are not only vessels of gold and of silver, but also of wood and of earth; and some indeed unto honor, but some unto dishonor. 2 Tim. 2:20.

I have labored more abundantly than all they; yet not I, but the grace of God with me. 1 C. 15:10.

9. UNCERTAINTY WHETHER WE ARE IN A STATE OF GRACE

If he come to me, I shall not see him; if he depart, I shall not understand. If I would justify myself, my own mouth shall condemn me; if I would show myself innocent, he shall prove me wicked. Although I should be simple, even this my soul shall be ignorant of, and I shall be weary of my life. Job 9:11, 20 f.

Who can understand sins? From my secret sins cleanse me, O Lord; and from those of others spare thy servant. Ps. 18:13.

The uncertain and unhidden things of thy wisdom thou hast made manifest to me. Ps. 50:8.

There are just men and wise men, and their works are in the hand of God; and yet man knoweth not whether he be worthy of love or hatred. But all things are kept uncertain for the time to come, because all things equally happen to the just and to the wicked, to the good and to the evil, to the clean and to the unclean, to him that offereth victims and to him that despiseth sacrifices. As the good is, so also is the sinner: as the perjured, so he also that sweareth truth. Ecclus. 9:1 f.

Be not without fear about sin forgiven, and add not sin upon sin. Ecclus. 5:5.

The heart is perverse above all things, and unsearchable. Who can know it? I am the Lord who search the heart and prove the reins: who give to every one according to his way, and according to the fruit of his devices. Jer. 17:9 f.

O king, let my counsel be acceptable to thee, and redeem thou thy sins with alms, and thy iniquities with works of mercy to the poor: perhaps he will forgive thy offenses. Dan. 4:24.

Neither do I judge my own self. For I am not conscious to myself of anything; yet am I not hereby justified: but he that judgeth me is the Lord. Therefore judge not before the time; until the Lord come, who both will bring to light the hidden things of darkness, and will make manifest the counsels of the hearts: and then shall every man have praise from God. 1 C. 4:3-5.

There is a way which seemeth just to a man; but the ends thereof lead to death. Prov. 14:12.

Every way of a man seemeth right to himself: but the Lord weigheth the hearts. Prov. 21:2.

I bear them witness that they have a zeal of God, but not according to knowledge. Rom. 10:2.

If any man think himself to be something, whereas he is nothing, he deceiveth himself. Gal. 6:3.

Wherefore hath the Lord pronounced against us all this great evil? What is our iniquity? And what is our sin that we have sinned against the Lord our God? Jer. 16:10.

10. POSSIBILITY OF KNOWING THAT WE ARE FRIENDS OF GOD

If our hearts do not reprehend us, we have confidence towards God. 1 John 3:21.

It is good for me to adhere to my God, to put my hope in the Lord God. Ps. 72:28.

The Lord will reward me according to my justice, and will repay me according to the cleanness of my hands: because I have kept the ways of the Lord, and have not done wickedly against my God. Ps. 17:21 f.

The voice of rejoicing and of salvation is in the tabernacles of the just. Ps. 117:15.

Either forgive them this trespass, or if thou do not, strike me out of the book that thou hast written. Ex. 32:31 f.

Although he should kill me, I will trust in him. Job 13:15.

The work of justice shall be peace, and the service of justice quietness and security forever. Is. 32:17.

The fruit of the Spirit is charity, joy, peace. Gal. 5:22.

In Christ Jesus neither circumcision availeth anything, nor uncircumcision, but a new creature. And whosoever shall follow this rule, peace on them and mercy, and upon the Israel of God. Gal. 6:15 f.

Fear is not charity; but perfect charity casteth out fear, because fear hath pain. And he that feareth is not perfected in charity. 1 John 4:12.

To him that overcometh I will give the hidden manna, and will give him a white counter, and in the counter a new name written, which no man knoweth but he that receiveth it. Apoc. 2:17.

As many as received him he gave them power to be made the sons of God, to them that believe in his name. Who are born, not of blood, nor of the will of the flesh, nor of the will of man, but of God. John 1:12 f.

Whosoever are led by the Spirit of God, they are the sons of God. For you have not received the spirit of bondage again in fear; but you have received the spirit of adoption of sons, whereby we cry, Abba (Father). For the Spirit himself giveth testimony to our spirit that we are the sons of God. Rom. 8:14-16.

If any man love me, my Father will love him. John 14:23.

He gave himself for us, that he might redeem us from all iniquity, and might cleanse to himself a people acceptable, a pursuer of good works. Titus 2:4.

11. EFFECTS OF GRACE

He hath given us most great and precious promises; that by these you may be made partakers of the divine nature, flying the corruption of that concupiscence which is in the world. 2 Pet. 4:1.

If any be in Christ a new creature, the old things are passed away; behold, all things are made new. 2 C. 5:17.

According to his mercy he saved us, by the laver of regeneration, and renovation of the Holy Ghost; whom he hath poured forth upon us abundantly, through Jesus Christ our Savior: that being justified by his grace, we may be heirs, according to hope of life everlasting. Titus 3:5-7.

If any man love me he will keep my word, and my Father will love him; and we will come to him, and will make our abode with him. John 14:23.

He that keepeth his commandments abideth in him, and he in him. And in this we know that he abideth in us by the Spirit which he hath given us.

God is charity; and he that abideth in charity abideth in God, and God in him. 1 John 4:16.

Know you not that your members are the temple of the Holy Ghost, who is in you, whom you have from God, and you are not your own? 1 C. 6:19.

Reckon that you are dead indeed to sin, but alive unto God, in Christ Jesus our Lord. Rom. 6:11.

Present yourselves to God as those that are alive from the dead. Rom. 6:13.

Incline your ear, and come to me; hear, and your soul shall live. Is. 55:3.

You shall know that I am the Lord when I shall have opened your sepulchers, and shall have brought you out of your graves, O my people; and shall have put my Spirit in you, and you shall live. Ex. 37:13 f.

My soul shall live, and shall praise thee. Ps. 118:175.

As the Father raiseth up the dead, and giveth life, so the Son also giveth life to whom he will. Amen, amen I say unto you, that the hour cometh, and now is, when the dead shall hear the voice of the Son of God; and they that hear shall live. John 5:21, 25.

The first man Adam was made into a living soul: the last Adam into a quickening Spirit. Yet that was not first which is spiritual, but that which is natural; afterwards that which is spiritual. Such as is the earthly, such also are the earthly; and such as is the heavenly, such also are they that are heavenly. 1 C. 15:45 f., 48.

Rise thou that sleepest, and arise from the dead, and Christ shall enlighten thee. Eph. 5:14.

If we live in the Spirit, let us also walk in the Spirit. Gal. 5:25.

God hath sent his only begotten Son into the world, that we may live by him. 1 John 4:9.

We are the circumcision, who serve God in spirit, and glory in Christ Jesus, not having confidence in the flesh. Phil. 3:3.

You, when you were dead in your sins and the uncircumcision of your flesh, he hath quickened together with him, forgiving you all offences. Col. 2:13.

The breath of our mouth, Christ the Lord, is taken in our sins; to whom we said: Under thy shadow we shall live among the Gentiles. Jas. 4:20.

They shall teach no more every man his neighbor and every man his brethren, saying: Know the Lord; for all shall know me, from the least of them even to the greatest, saith the Lord; for I will forgive their iniquity, and I will remember their sin no more. Jer. 31:34.

I will cleanse them from all their iniquity, whereby they have sinned against me; and I will forgive all their iniquities, whereby they have sinned against me and despised me. Jer. 33:8.

I have blotted out thy iniquities as a cloud, and thy sins as a mist. Return to me; for I have redeemed thee. Is. 44:22.

Wash yourselves, be clean, take away the evil of your devices from my eyes. If your sins be as scarlet, they shall be made as white as snow; and if they be red as crimson, they shall be white as wool. Is. 1:16, 18.

He will turn again, and have mercy on us. He will put away our iniquities, and he will cast all our sins into the bottom of the sea. Mich. 7:19.

According to the multitude of thy tender mercies, blot out my iniquity. Ps. 50:3.

There is now no condemnation to them that are in Christ Jesus, who walk according to the flesh. Rom. 8:1.

Neither fornicators, nor covetous, nor drunkards shall possess the kingdom of God. And such some of you were; but you are washed, but you are sanctified, but you are justified in the name of our Lord Jesus Christ, and in the Spirit of our God. 1 C. 6:10 f.

I will save you from all your uncleannesses. Ez. 36:29.

Jesus answered him: If I wash thee not, thou shalt have no part with me. John 13:8.

God himself will come and save you. Then shall the eyes of the blind be opened, and the ears of the deaf shall be unstopped; then shall the lame man leap as a hart, and the tongue of the dumb shall be free: for waters are broken out in the desert, and streams in the wilderness. Is. 35:5 f.

I am, I am he that blot out thy iniquities for my own sake, and I will not remember thy sins. Is. 43:25.

He appeared to take away our sins. 1 John 3:5.

I will turn my hand to thee, and I will clean purge away thy dross. Is. 1:25.

I said: O Lord, be thou merciful to me: heal my soul, for I have sinned against thee. Ps. 40:5.

Heal me, O Lord, and I shall be healed: save me, and I shall be saved: for thou art my praise. Jer. 17:14.

They that are in health need not a physician, but they that are ill. I am not come to call the just, but sinners. Mat. 9:12 f.

Are you angry at me because I have healed the whole man on the Sabbath day? John 7:23.

Blind the heart of this people, and make their ears heavy, and shut their eyes: lest they see with their eyes, and hear with their ears, and understand with their heart, and be converted, and I heal them. Is. 6:10.

12. GRACE THE PLEDGE OF GLORY, THE PRINCIPLE AND CAUSE OF MERIT

The grace of God [is] life everlasting in Christ Jesus our Lord. Rom. 6:23.

Now our Lord Jesus Christ himself, and God and our Father who hath loved us, and hath given us everlasting consolation and good hope in grace, exhort your hearts, and confirm you in every good work and word. 2 Thess. 2:15 f.

That as sin hath reigned unto death, so also grace might reign by justice unto life everlasting, through Jesus Christ our Lord. Rom. 5:21.

Being justified by his grace, we may be heirs according to hope of life everlasting. Titus 3:7.

The Spirit himself giveth testimony to our spirit that we are the sons of God; and if sons, heirs also: heirs indeed of God, and joint heirs with Christ. Rom. 8:16 f.

Now he is no more a servant, but a son. And if a son, an heir also through God. Gal. 4:7.

Being consummated, he became to all that obey him the cause of eternal salvation. Heb. 5:9.

All things of his divine power which appertain to life and godliness are given us through the knowledge of him who hath called us by his own proper glory and virtue. 2 Pet. 1:3.

If I should distribute all my goods to feed the poor, and if I should deliver my body to be burned, and have not charity, it profiteth me nothing. 1 C. 13:3.

Abide in me, and I in you. As the branch cannot bear fruit of itself, unless it abide in the vine, so neither can you, unless you abide in me. I am the vine; you the branches. He that abideth in me, and I in him, the same beareth much fruit: for without me you can do nothing. John 15:4 f.

The water that I will give him shall become in him a fountain of water, springing up into life everlasting. John 4:14.

13. EXHORTATIONS TO GROW IN GRACE

We helping do exhort you, that you receive not the grace of God in vain. 2 C. 6:1.

Being justified by faith, let us have peace with God, through our Lord Jesus Christ. Rom. 5:1.

Stand fast, and be not held again under the yoke of bondage. Gal. 5:1.

It is best that the heart be established with grace, not with meats: which have not profited those that walk in them. Heb. 13:9.

Health of the soul in holiness of justice is better than all gold and silver: and a sound body than immense revenues. Ecclus. 30:15.

Blessed are they that wash their robes: that they may have a right to the tree of life, and may enter in by the gates into the city. Apoc. 22:14.

Blessed is he that watcheth, and keepeth his garments, lest he walk naked, and they see his shame. Apoc. 16:15.

Blessed are the dead who die in the Lord. From henceforth now, saith the Spirit, that they may rest from their labors: for their works follow them. Apoc. 14:13.

Blessed are those servants whom the Lord, when he cometh, shall find watching. And if he shall come in the second watch, or if he shall come in the third watch, and find them so, blessed are those servants. Luke 12:37 f.

He that is just, let him be justified still; and he that is holy, let him be sanctified still. Apoc. 22:11.

Be not afraid to be justified even to death: for the reward of God continueth forever. Ecclus. 18:22.

The path of the just, as a shining light, goeth forwards, and increaseth even to perfect day. Prov. 4:18.

Blessed is the man whose help is from thee: in his heart he hath disposed to ascend by steps in the vale of tears, in the place which he hath set. Ps. 83:6 f.

Brethren, I do not count myself to have apprehended. But one thing I do: forgetting the things that are behind, and stretching forth myself to those that are before, I press towards the mark, to the prize of the supernal vocation of God in Christ Jesus. Phil. 3:13.

But doing the truth in charity, may we in all things grow up in him who is the head, even Christ. Eph. 4:15.

As new-born babes, desire the rational milk without guile, that thereby you may grow unto salvation. 1 Pet. 2:2.

Grow in grace, and in the knowledge of our Lord and Savior Jesus Christ. To him be glory, both now and unto the day of eternity. Amen. 2 Pet. 3:18.

As Christ is risen from the dead by the glory of the Father, so we also may walk in newness of life. Rom. 6:4.

I, a prisoner in the Lord, beseech you that you walk worthy of the vocation in which you are called. Eph. 4:1.

Walk in love. Eph. 5:2.

I will be as the dew, Israel shall spring as the lily, and his root shall shoot forth as that of Libanus. His branches shall spread, and his glory shall be as the olive tree. Osee 14:6 f.

V

VIRTUE AND SIN

1. PRAISE OF VIRTUE

Learn where is wisdom, where is strength, where is understanding, that thou mayst know also where is length of days and life, where is the light of the eyes and peace. Bar. 3:14.
1 John 3:24.

He that shall hear me shall rest without terror, and shall enjoy abundance without fear of evils. Prov. 1:33.

Now being made free from sin, and become servants to God, you have your first fruits unto sanctification, and the end life everlasting. For the wages of sin is death, but the grace of God life everlasting, in Christ Jesus our Lord. Rom. 6:22 f.

Amen, amen I say to you, if any man keep my word, he shall not see death forever. John 8:51.

If any man minister to me, let him follow me: and where I am, there also shall my minister be. If any man minister to me, him will my Father honor. John 12:26.

They shall go from virtue to virtue: the God of gods shall be seen in Sion. Ps. 83:8.

His power, when it is tried, reproveth the unwise. Wis. 1:3.

We fools have been able to show no mark of virtue, but are consumed in our wickedness. Such things as these the sinners said in hell. Wis. 5:13 f.

Rich men in virtue, lovers of beautifulness, living at peace in their houses: all these have gained glory in their generations, and were praised in their days. Ecclus. 44:6 f.

Give and take and justify thy soul. Before thy death work justice, for in hell there is no finding food. Ecclus. 14:16 f.

Get wisdom, because it is better than gold: and purchase prudence, for it is more precious than silver. Prov. 16:16.

Labor not for the meat which perisheth, but for that which endureth unto life everlasting, which the Son of man will give you. John 6:27.

Whatsoever things are true, whatsoever modest, whatsoever just, whatsoever holy, whatsoever lovely, whatsoever of good fame, if there be any virtue, if any praise of discipline, think on these things. Phil. 4:8.

Be ye all of one mind, having compassion one of another, being lovers of the brotherhood, merciful, modest, humble. 1 Pet. 3:8.

You, employing all care, minister in your faith, virtue: and in virtue, knowledge: and in knowledge, abstinence: and in abstinence, patience: and in patience, godliness: and in godliness, love of the brotherhood: and in love of the brotherhood, charity. 2 Pet. 1:5-7.

Decline not to the right nor to the left. Prov. 4:27.

Eat honey, my son, because it is good, and the honeycomb most sweet to thy throat. So also is the doctrine of wisdom to thy soul: which when thou hast found, thou shalt have hope in the end, and thy hope shall not perish. Prov. 24:13 f.

A good life hath its number of days, but a good name shall continue forever. Ecclus. 41:16.

Serve the Lord in truth, and seek to do the things that please him: and command your children that they do justice and almsdeeds, and that they be mindful of God, and bless him at all times in truth, and with all their power. Tob. 14:10 f.

He that keepeth his word, in him in very deed the charity of God is perfected: and by this we know that we are in him. 1 John 2:5.

If we love one another, God abideth in us, and his charity is perfected in us. 1 John 4:12.

In this is the charity of God perfected with us, that we may have confidence in the day of judgment: because as he is, so also are we in this world. 1 John 4:17.

One man among a thousand I have found. Eccles. 7:29.

Not as though I had already attained, or were already perfect: but I follow after, if I may by any means apprehend, and wherein I am also apprehended by Christ Jesus. Brethren, I do not count myself to have apprehended. But one thing I do: forgetting the things that are behind, and stretching forth myself to those that are before, I press towards the mark, to the prize of the supernal vocation of God in Christ Jesus. Phil. 3:12-14.

Fear is not charity: but perfect charity casteth out fear, because fear hath pain. And he that feareth is not perfected in charity. 1 John 4:18.

2. COUNSELS OF PERFECTION

Walk before me, and be perfect. Gen. 17:1.

Thou shalt be perfect, and without spot before the Lord thy God. Deut. 18:13.

Fear the Lord, and serve him with a perfect and most sincere heart. Jos. 24:14.

Be you therefore perfect, as also your heavenly Father is perfect. Mat. 5:48.

Let us also go, that we may die with him. John 11:16.

Behold, we have left all things, and have followed thee. Luke 18:28.

He that taketh not up his cross, and followeth me, is not worthy of me. Mat. 10:38.

For whosoever will save his life shall lose it: and he that shall lose his life for my sake shall find it. Mat. 18:25.

The kingdom of heaven is like unto a treasure hidden in a field: which when a man hath found, he hideth, and for joy thereof goeth and selleth all that he hath, and buyeth that field. Again, the kingdom of heaven is like to a merchant seeking good pearls: who, when he had found one pearl of great price, went his way, and sold all that he had, and bought it. Mat. 13:44-46.

If any man come to me, and hate not his father and mother, and wife and children, and brethren and sisters, yea and his own life also, he cannot be my disciple. And whosoever doth not carry his cross and come after me cannot be my disciple. So likewise every one of you that doth not renounce all that he possesseth cannot be my disciple. Luke 14:26 f., 33.

Let no man seek his own, but that which is for the welfare of another. All things are lawful to me, but all things do not edify. 1 C. 10:23 f.

For none of us liveth to himself, and no man dieth to himself. For whether we live, we live to the Lord; or whether we die, we die to the Lord. Therefore, whether we live or whether we die, we are the Lord's Rom. 14:7 f.

With Christ I am nailed to the cross. And I live: now not I, but Christ liveth in me. And that I live now in the flesh, I live in the faith of the Son of God, who loved me, and delivered himself for me Gal. 2:19 f.

3. THE FEAR OF THE LORD

The fear of the Lord is the beginning of wisdom, and was created with the faithful in the womb: it walketh with chosen women, and is known with the just and faithful. To fear God is the fulness of wisdom, and fulness is from the fruits thereof. Ecclus. 1:16, 20.

The root of wisdom is to fear the Lord: and the branches thereof are long-lived. In the treasures of wisdom is understanding, and religiousness of knowledge: but to sinners wisdom is an abomination. Ecclus. 1:25 f.

Give place to the fear of the Most High: for the fear of God is all wisdom, and therein is to fear God, and the disposition of the law is in all wisdom. Ecclus. 19:18.

Will not you then fear me? saith the Lord: and will you not repent at my presence? I have set the sand a bound for the sea, an everlasting ordinance which it shall not pass over. Jer. 5:22.

The fear of the Lord is the beginning of wisdom. Prov. 1:7.

I will give them one heart and one way, that they may fear me all days, and that it may be well with them and with their children after them. Jer. 32:39.

The fear of the Lord is the lesson of wisdom. Prov. 15:33.

I will give my fear in their heart, that they may not revolt from me. Jer. 32:40.

Be thou in the fear of the Lord all the day long: because thou shalt have hope in the latter end, and thy expectation shall not be taken away. Prov. 23:17 f.

Serve ye the Lord with fear. Ps. 2:11.

In the fear of the Lord is confidence of strength, and there shall be hope for his children. Prov. 14:26.

The fear of the Lord is honor, and glory, and gladness, and a crown of joy. The fear of the Lord shall delight the heart, and shall give joy and gladness, and length of days. The fear of the Lord driveth out sin. Ecclus. 1:11, 12, 27.

They that fear the Lord will not be incredulous to his word, and they that love him will keep his way. They that fear the Lord will seek after the things that are well pleasing to him: and they that love him shall be filled with his law. They that fear the Lord will prepare their hearts, and in his sight will sanctify their souls. They that fear the Lord keep his commandments, and will have patience even until his visitation. Ecclus. 2:18-21.

He that feareth the Lord shall tremble at nothing, and shall not be afraid: for he is his hope. Ecclus. 34:16.

The fear of the Lord is like a paradise of blessing, and they have covered it above all glory. Ecclus. 40:28.

They that remain shall know that there is nothing better than the fear of God: and that there is nothing sweeter than to have regard to the commandments of the Lord. Ecclus. 23:37.

The fear of the Lord is the beginning of his love: and the beginning of faith is to be fast joined unto it. Ecclus. 25:16.

Let us all hear together the conclusion of the discourse. Fear God and keep his commandments: for this is all man. Eccles. 12:13.

With him that feareth the Lord it shall be well in the latter end, and in the day of his death he shall be blessed. To fear God is the fulness of wisdom, and fulness is from the fruits thereof. She shall fill all her house with her increase, and the storehouses with her treasures. Ecclus. 1:13, 20 f.

No evils shall happen to him that feareth the Lord: but in temptation God will keep him, and deliver him from evils. Ecclus. 33:1.

The spirit of those that fear God is sought after, and by his regard shall be blessed. For their hope is on him that saveth them, and the eyes of God are upon them that love him. Ecclus. 34:14 f.

There is no want in the fear of the Lord, and it needeth not to seek for help. Ecclus. 40:27.

Fear the Lord, all ye his saints: for there is no want to them that fear him. Ps. 33:10.

Blessed is the man to whom it is given to have the fear of God: he that holdeth it, to whom shall he be likened? Ecclus. 25:15.

The fear of the Lord is a fountain of life, to decline from the ruin of death. Prov. 14:27.

Blessed is the man that is always fearful: but he that is hardened in mind shall fall into evil. Prov. 28:14.

Blessed is the man that feareth the Lord: he shall delight exceedingly in his commandments. His seed shall be mighty upon earth. Ps. 111:1.

The mercy of the Lord is from eternity and unto eternity, upon them that fear him. Ps. 102:17.

The angel of the Lord shall encamp round about them that fear him, and shall deliver them. Ps. 33:8.

He hath strengthened his mercy towards them that fear him. Ps. 102:11.

They that fear thee shall be great with thee in all things. Jdth. 16:19.

Glory and wealth shall be in his house: and his justice remaineth forever and ever. Ps. 111:3.

How great is he that findeth wisdom and knowledge! but there is none above him that feareth the Lord. The fear of God hath set itself above all things. Ecclus. 25:13 f.

The fruit of humility is the fear of the Lord, riches and glory and life. Prov. 22:4.

As the father hath compassion on his children, so hath the Lord compassion on them that fear him. Ps. 102:13.

Who is there among you that feareth the Lord? Let him hope in the name of the Lord, and lean upon his God. Is. 50:10.

His seed shall be mighty upon earth; the generation of the righteous shall be blessed. Ps. 111:2.

The fear of the Lord is his treasure. Is. 33:6.

Unless thou hold thyself diligently in the fear of the Lord thy house shall quickly be overthrown. Ecclus. 27:4.

These are the precepts, that thou mayst fear the Lord thy God, and keep all his commandments and precepts which I command thee and thy sons and thy grandsons, all the days of thy life, that thy days may be prolonged. Deut. 6:1 f.

4. EVEN THE JUST MAN MUST TAKE HEED LEST HE FALL

He that thinketh himself to stand, let him take heed lest he fall. 1 C. 10:12.

He that contemneth small things shall fall by little and little. Ecclus. 19:1.

Thou standest by faith. Be not highminded, but fear. Rom. 11:20.

A wise man will fear in everything, and in the days of sins will beware of sloth. Ecclus. 18:27.

I have always feared God as waves swelling over me, and his weight I was not able to bear. John 31:23.

Fear ye not them that kill the body, and are not able to kill the soul; but rather fear him that can destroy both soul and body into hell. Mat. 10:28.

Who shall not fear thee, O King of nations? For thine is the glory: among all the wise men of the nations, and in all their kingdoms, there is none like unto thee. Jer. 10:7.

If the just man shall scarcely be saved, where shall the ungodly and the sinner appear? 1 Pet. 4:18.

5. DESTRUCTION OF SIN

His bones shall be filled with the vices of his youth, and they shall sleep with him in the dust. Job 20:11.

Woe to the sinful nation, a people laden with iniquity, a wicked seed, ungracious children! they have forsaken the Lord, they have blasphemed the holy one of Israel, they are gone away backwards. Is. 1:4.

Thus saith the Lord: Thy bruise is incurable, thy wound is very grievous. Jer. 30:12.

There is none that doth penance for his sin, saying: What have I done? They are all turned to their own course, as a horse rushing to the battle. Jer. 8:6.

They that are Christ's have crucified their flesh, with the vices and concupiscences. Gal. 5:24.

I speak a human thing, because of the infirmity of your flesh. For as you have yielded your members to serve uncleanness and iniquity unto iniquity, so now yield your members to serve justice unto sanctification. For when you were servants of sin you were free men to justice. Rom. 6:19 f.

Mortify your members which are upon the earth, fornication, uncleanness, lust, evil concupiscence, and covetousness, which is the service of idols. Col. 3:5.

I beseech you therefore, brethren, by the mercy of God, that you present your bodies a living sacrifice, holy, pleasing unto God, your reasonable service. Rom. 12:1.

I came not to send peace but the sword. Mat. 10:34.

I chastise my body, and bring it into subjection; lest perhaps, when I have preached to others, I myself should become a castaway. 1 C. 9:27.

We are cast down, but we perish not: always bearing about in our body the mortification of Jesus, that the life also of Jesus may be made manifest in our bodies. 2 C. 4:9 f.

6. EXHORTATIONS TO ROOT UP VICE AND TO CONQUER PASSIONS

Go not after thy lusts, but turn away from thy own will. If thou give to thy soul her desires, she will make thee a joy to thy enemies. Ecclus. 18:30 f.

Circumcise the foreskin of your heart, and stiffen your neck no more. Deut. 10:16.

Be circumcised to the Lord, and take away the foreskin of your hearts, ye men of Juda, and ye inhabitants of Jerusalem, lest my indignation come forth like fire, and burn, and there be none that can quench it; because of the wickedness of your thoughts. Jer. 4:4.

If thy right eye scandalize thee, pluck it out and cast it from thee. For it is expedient for thee that one of thy members should perish, rather than thy whole body be cast into hell. Mat. 5:29.

Amen, amen I say to you, unless the grain of wheat falling into the ground die, itself remaineth alone. But if it die, it bringeth forth much fruit. He that loveth his life shall lose it; and he that hateth his life in this world keepeth it unto life eternal. John 12:24 f.

A faithful saying. For if we be dead with him, we shall live also with him. If we suffer, we shall also reign with him. If we deny him, he will also deny us. 2 Tim. 2:11 f.

He that nourisheth his servant delicately from his childhood, afterwards shall find him stubborn. Prov. 29:21.

Loose the bands of wickedness, undo the bundles that oppress, let them that are broken go free, and break asunder every burden. Is. 58:6.

If thou wilt take away the chain out of the midst of thee, and cease to stretch out the finger and to speak that which profiteth not, then shall thy light rise up in darkness, and thy darkness shall be as the noonday. Is. 58:9 f.

7. SIN IS THE TURNING FROM GOD TO CREATURES

What iniquity have your fathers found in me, that they have gone far from me, and have walked after vanity, and are become vain? Jer. 2:5.

They have forsaken me, the fountain of living water, and have digged to themselves cisterns, broken cisterns, that can hold no water. Jer. 2:5.

You have rejoiced in a thing of naught. Amos 6:14.

Without him was made nothing that was made. John 1:3.

They trust in a mere nothing, and speak vanities. Is. 59:4.

They violated me among my people, for a handful of barley and a piece of bread, to kill souls which should not die, and to save souls alive which should not live, telling lies to my people that believe lies. Ez. 13:19.

Such a man for a morsel of bread forsaketh the truth. Prov. 28:21.

You were sold gratis, and you shall be redeemed without money. Is. 52:3.

They have turned their back to me, and not their face; and in the time of their affliction they will say: Arise, and deliver us. Jer. 2:27.

Why will you contend with me in judgment? you have all forsaken me, saith the Lord. In vain have I struck your children. Jer. 2:29 f.

8. THE UNCLEANNESS OF SIN

Ephraim is under oppression and broken in judgment, because he began to go after filthiness. Osee 5:11.

They have sinned against him, and are none of his children in their filth. Deut. 32:5.

For that uncleanness of the land it shall be corrupted with a grievous corruption. Mich. 2:10.

Jesus [the high priest, who bore as it were the sins of all the people] was clothed with filthy garments. Zach. 3:3.

Behold, the hand of the Lord is not shortened that it cannot save, neither is his ear heavy that it cannot hear. But your iniquities have divided between you and your God, and your sins have hid his face from you that he should not hear. For your hands are defiled with blood, and your fingers with iniquity: your lips have spoken lies, and your tongue uttereth iniquity. And truth hath been forgotten: and he that departed from evil lay open to be a prey; and the Lord saw, and it appeared evil in his eyes, because there is no judgment. Is. 59:1-3, 15.

They did spit in his face, and buffet him, and others struck his face with the palms of their hands. Mat. 26:67.

Every one that shall be left in Sion and that shall remain in Jerusalem shall be called holy, if the Lord shall wash away the filth of the daughters of Sion, and shall wash away the blood of Jerusalem out of the midst thereof by the spirit of judgment and by the spirit of burning. Is. 4:3 f.

The night is past, and the day is at hand. Let us therefore cast off the works of darkness, and put on the armor of light. Rom. 13:12.

You were heretofore darkness, but now light in the Lord. Eph. 5:8.

Have no fellowship with the unfruitful works of darkness, but rather reprove them. Eph. 5:1.

If we say that we have fellowship with him, and walk in darkness, we lie, and do not the truth. 1 John 1:6.

Return to the Lord, and turn away from thy injustice, and greatly hate abomination. Ecclus. 17:23.

For their cursing and lying they shall be talked of when they are consumed: when they are consumed by thy wrath, and they shall be no more. Ps. 58:14.

When thou art come into the land which the Lord thy God shall give thee, beware lest thou have a mind to imitate the abominations of those nations. Deut. 32:10.

The eyes of the wicked shall decay, and the way to escape shall fail them, and their hope the abomination of the soul. Job 11:20.

Flee from sins as from the face of a serpent. The teeth thereof are the teeth of a lion killing the souls of men. All iniquity is like a two-edged sword: there is no remedy for the wound thereof. Ecclus. 21:2-4.

9. SIN DISASTROUS TO BODY AND SOUL

They have conceived labor, and brought forth iniquity. They have broken the eggs of asps, and have woven the webs of spiders: he that shall eat of their eggs shall die; and that which is brought out shall be hatched. Is. 59:4 f.

Behold, O Lord, for I am in distress, my bowels are troubled: my heart is turned within me, for I am full of bitterness: abroad the sword destroyeth, and at home there is death alike. Lam. 1:20.

They have labored to commit iniquity. Jer. 9:5.

Evil pursueth sinners. Prov. 13:21.

He that soweth iniquity shall reap evils, and with the rod of his anger he shall be consumed. Prov. 22:8.

Thy own wickedness shall reprove thee, and thy apostasy shall rebuke thee. Know thou and see that it is an evil and a bitter thing for thee to have left the Lord thy God, and that my fear is not with thee, saith the Lord the God of hosts. Jer. 2:19.

I have wounded thee with the wound of an enemy, with a cruel chastisement: by reason of the multitude of thy iniquities, thy sins are hardened. Jer. 30:14.

Do no evils, and no evils shall lay hold of thee: depart from the unjust, and evils shall depart from thee. My son, sow not evils in the furrows of injustice, and thou shalt not reap them sevenfold. Ecclus. 7:1-3.

Because he hath done more than he could, therefore they have perished. Jer. 48:36.

He that is perverse in his ways shall fall at once. Prov. 28:18.

Transgressors shall pine away in the end. Ecclus. 40:14.

Upon sinners are sevenfold more. Moreover death and bloodshed, strife and sword, oppressions, famine, and affliction, and scourges. Ecclus. 40:8 f.

A wicked soul shall destroy him that hath it, and maketh him to be a joy to his enemies, and shall lead him into the lot of the wicked. Ecclus. 6:4.

We have wearied ourselves in the way of iniquity and destruction, and have walked through hard ways, but the way of the Lord we have not known. What hath pride profited us? Wis. 5:7.

Nothing upon earth is done without a cause, and sorrow doth not spring out of the ground. Job 5:6.

I remember the evils that I have done in Jerusalem, from whence also I took away all the spoils of gold and of silver that were in it, and I sent to destroy the inhabitants of Juda without cause. I know therefore that for this cause these evils have found me: and behold, I perish with great grief in a strange land. 1 Mac. 6:12 f.

The wicked man diggeth evil, and in his lips is a burning fire. Prov. 16:27.

10. PUNISHMENT OF SIN

Transgressors shall all of them be plucked up as thorns, which are not taken away with hands. And if a man will touch them, he must be armed with iron and with the staff of a lance: but they shall be set on fire and burnt to nothing. 2 K. 23:6 f.

Behold, the day shall come kindled as a furnace, and all the proud and all that do wickedly shall be stubble: and the day that cometh shall set them on fire, saith the Lord of hosts: it shall not leave them root nor branch. Mal. 4:1.

Woe to you, ungodly men, who have forsaken the law of the most high Lord! And if you be born, you shall be born in malediction: and if you die, malediction shall be your portion. Ecclus. 41:11 f.

What things a man shall sow, those also shall he reap. For he that soweth in his flesh, of the flesh also shall reap corruption. But he that soweth in the spirit, of the spirit shall reap life everlasting. Gal. 6:8.

If any one abide not in me, he shall be cast forth as a branch, and shall wither: and they shall gather him up, and cast him into the fire, and he burneth. John 15:6.

Sin when it is completed, begetteth death. Jas. 1:15.

The fearful and unbelieving, and the abominable, and murderers, and whoremongers, and sorcerers, and idolaters, and all liars, they shall have their portion in the pool burning with fire and brimstone, which is the second death. Apoc. 21:8.

They shall eat the fruit of their own way, and shall be filled with their own devices. Prov. 1:31.

A man that shall wander out of the way of doctrine shall abide in the company of the giants. Prov. 21:16.

11. SIN ROBS THE SOUL OF SUPERNATURAL GIFTS

A certain man went down from Jerusalem to Jericho, and fell among robbers, who also stripped him and having wounded him went away, leaving him half-dead. Luke 10:30.

Is it a small thing to you that you sinned with Beelphegor, and the stain of that crime remaineth in us to this day? And many of the people perished. Jos. 22:17.

Christ loved the Church and delivered himself up for it, that he might sanctify it, cleansing it by the laver of water in the word of life; that he might present it to himself a glorious Church, not having spot or wrinkle, or any such thing, but that it should be holy and without blemish. Eph. 5:25-27.

His own iniquities catch the wicked, and he is fast bound with the ropes of his own sins. Prov. 5:22.

We shall sleep in our confusion, and our shame shall cover us, because we have sinned against the Lord our God. Jer. 3:25.

The lion always lieth in wait for prey: so do sins for them that work iniquities. Ecclus. 27:11.

He shall rain snares upon sinners: fire and brimstone and storms of winds shall be the portion of their cup. Ps. 10:7.

If the just man turn himself away from his justice, and do iniquity according to all the abominations which the wicked man useth to work, shall he live? All his justices which he had done shall not be remembered. Ez. 8:24.

I will put it in the hand of them that have oppressed thee, and have said to thy soul: Bow down, that we may go over: and thou hast laid thy body as the ground, and as a way to them that went over. Is. 51:23.

They may recover themselves from the snares of the devil, by whom they are held captive at his will. 2 Tim. 2:26.

You are of your father the devil, and the desires of your father you will do. John 8:44.

Depart from me, you cursed, into everlasting fire. Mat. 25:14.

O full of all guile and of all deceit, child of the devil! Acts 13:10.

They that commit sin and iniquity are enemies to their own soul. Tob. 12:10.

I know thy works, that thou hast the name of being alive: and thou art dead. Apoc. 3:1.

All that hate me love death. Prov. 8:36.

12. SIN CAUSES IGNORANCE IN THE UNDERSTANDING

Hearing hear, and understand not: and see the vision, and know it not. Blind the heart of this people, and make their ears heavy, and shut their eyes: lest they see with their eyes, and hear with their ears, and understand with their heart, and be converted, and I heal them. Is. 6:9 f.

Hear, ye deaf; and ye blind, behold, that you may see. Who is blind but my servant? or deaf, but he to whom I have sent my messengers? Who is blind, but he that is sold? or who is blind, but the servant of the Lord? Is. 42:18 f.

We have groped for the wall, and like the blind we have groped as if we had no eyes: we have stumbled at noonday as in darkness: we are in dark places, as dead men. Is. 59:10.

My foolish people have not known me: they are foolish and senseless children: they are wise to do evils, but to do good they have no knowledge. Jer. 4:22.

Bring forth the people that are blind, and have eyes: that are deaf, and have ears. Is. 43:8.

Hear, O foolish people, and without understanding: who have eyes, and see not; and ears, and hear not. Jer. 5:21.

They shall walk like blind men, because they have sinned against the Lord. Soph. 1:17.

They became vain in their thoughts, and their foolish heart was darkened. For professing themselves to be wise, they became fools. And they changed the glory of the incorruptible God into the likeness of the image of a corruptible man, and of birds, and of four-footed beasts, and of creeping things. Rom. 1:21-23.

As they liked not to have God in their knowledge, God delivered them up to a reprobate sense, to do those things which are not convenient. Rom. 1:28.

He who saith that he knoweth him, and keepeth not his commandments, is a liar, and the truth is not in him. 1 John 2:4.

Whosoever abideth in him sinneth not; and whosoever sinneth hath not seen him nor known him. 1 John 3:6.

There is a way which seemeth just to a man: but the ends thereof lead to death. Prov. 14:12.

The childish shall possess folly, and the prudent shall look for knowledge. Prov. 14:18.

These things they thought, and were deceived: for their own malice blinded them, and they knew not the secrets of God, nor hoped for the wages of justice, nor esteemed the honor of holy souls. Wis. 2:21 f.

They shall grope as in the dark, and not in the light, and he shall make them stagger like men that are drunk. Job 12:25.

Is this the return thou makest to the Lord, O foolish and senseless people? Is not he thy Father, that hath possessed thee, and made thee, and created thee? Deut. 32:6.

We fools esteemed their life madness, and their end without honor. Wis. 5:4.

13. SIN TURNS AWAY THE WILL FROM THE SUPREME GOOD

The Lord loveth the children of Israel, and they love the husks of grapes. Osee 3:1.

O children how long will you love childishness? and fools covet those things which are hurtful to themselves, and the unwise hate knowledge? Prov. 1:22.

And hearing the commandments of the Lord, they did all things contrary. Judg. 2:17.

Yield yourselves to the Lord, and come to his sanctuary, which he hath sanctified forever: serve the Lord the God of your fathers, and the wrath of his indignation shall be turned away from you. 2 Par. 30:8.

My people heard not my voice, and Israel hearkened not to me. So I let them go according to the desires of their heart: they shall walk in their own inventions. Ps. 70:12 f.

The man that with a stiff neck despiseth him that reproveth him shall suddenly be destroyed, and health shall not follow him. Prov. 29:1.

Be not as your fathers, to whom the former prophets have cried, saying: Thus saith the Lord of hosts: Turn ye from your evil ways and from your wicked thoughts; but they did not give ear, neither did they hearken to me, saith the Lord. Zach. 1:4.

They would not hearken, and they turned away the shoulder to depart; and they stopped their ears, not to hear. Zach. 7:11.

The Lord knoweth how to reserve the unjust unto the day of judgment, to be tormented; and especially them who walk after the flesh in the lust of uncleanness, and despise government: audacious, self-willed, they fear not to bring in sects, blaspheming. 2 Pet. 2:9 f.

You stiff-necked and uncircumcised in heart and ears, you always resist the Holy Ghost. As your fathers did, so do you also. Acts 7:51.

14. SIN BEGETS FEAR AND PERPLEXITY

The strength of the upright is the way of the Lord, and fear to them that work evil. Prov. 10:29.

It is joy to the just to do judgment, and death to them that work iniquity. Prov. 21:15.

The wicked man fleeth when no man pursueth; but the just, bold as a lion, shall be without dread. Prov. 28:1.

Whereas wickedness is fearful, it beareth witness to its condemnation; for a troubled conscience always forecasteth grievous things. Wis. 17:10.

Fear shall terrify him on every side, and shall entangle his feet. Job 18:11.

The sound of dread is always in his ears; and when there is peace, he always suspecteth treason. Job 15:21.

I will send fear in their hearts in the countries of their enemies; the sound of a flying leaf shall terrify, and they shall flee as it were from the sword; they shall fall when no man pursueth them. Lev. 26:36.

Tribulation shall terrify him, and distress shall surround him, as a king that is prepared for the battle. Job 15:24.

They have not called upon the Lord; there have they trembled for fear where there was no fear. Ps. 13:5.

15. SIN BRINGS WITH IT SHAME AND SHAMELESSNESS

What fruit had you then in those things, of which you are now ashamed? for the end of them is death. Rom. 6:21.

The wicked confoundeth, and shall be confounded. Prov. 13:5.

As the thief is confounded when he is taken, so is the house of Israel confounded, they and their kings, their princes and their priests, and their prophets. Jer. 2:26.

They shall be confounded for the idols to which they have sacrificed; and you shall be ashamed of the gardens which you have chosen; when you shall be as an oak with leaves falling off, and as a garden without water. Is. 1:29.

The wicked man impudently hardeneth his face; but he that is righteous correcteth his way. Prov. 21:29.

They were confounded because they committed abomination; yea, rather they were not confounded with confusion, and they knew not how to blush. Wherefore they shall fall among them that fall; in the time of their visitation they shall fall down, saith the Lord. Jer. 6:15.

16. SADNESS AND DESPAIR THE END OF SIN

Why have I hated instruction, and my heart consented not to reproof? And have not heard the voice of them that taught me, and have not inclined my ear to masters? Prov. 5:12 f.

What hath pride profited us? or what advantage hath the boasting of riches brought us? All those things have passed away like a shadow, and like a post that runneth on. Wis. 5:8 f.

Tribulation and anguish upon every soul of man that worketh evil. Rom. 2:9.

The mirth of timbrels hath ceased, the noise of them that rejoice is ended, the melody of the harp is silent. They shall not drink wine with a song; the drink shall be bitter to them that drink it. Is. 24:8 f.

My iniquity is greater than that I may deserve pardon. Gen. 4:13.

17. GOD EXHORTS SINNERS TO ABANDON SIN

Wash yourselves, be clean, take away the evil of your devices from my eyes: cease to do perversely, learn to do well: seek judgment, relieve the oppressed, judge for the fatherless, defend the widow. Is. 1:16 f.

Wash thy heart from wickedness, O Jerusalem, that thou mayst be saved. How long shall hurtful thoughts abide in thee? Jer. 4:14.

Thou shalt detest it as dung, and shalt utterly abhor it as uncleanness and filth, because it is an anathema. Deut. 7:26.

Thou hast forsaken me, saith the Lord, thou art gone backward; and I will stretch out my hand against thee, and I will destroy thee; I am weary of entreating thee. Jer. 15:6.

Return, as you had deeply revolted, O children of Israel. Is. 31:6.

O children, how long will you love childishness; and fools covet those things which are hurtful to themselves, and the unwise hate knowledge? Turn ye at my reproof. Behold, I will utter my spirit to you, and will show you my words. Prov. 1:22 f.

Be converted, and do penance for all your iniquities, and iniquity shall not be your ruin. Cast away from you all your transgressions by which you have transgressed, and make to yourselves a new heart and a new spirit; and why will you die, O house of Israel? For I desire not the death of him that dieth, saith the Lord God. Return ye, and live. Ez. 18:30-32.

Come to me, all you that labor and are burdened, and I will refresh you. Mat. 11:28.

Take up my yoke upon you: for my yoke is sweet, and my burden light. Mat. 11:29 f.

18. GOD PROMISES MERCY AND GRACE TO THOSE WHO REPENT

In that day I will make a covenant with them, with the beasts of the field, and with the fowls of the air, and with the creeping things of the earth; and I will destroy the bow, and the sword, and war out of the land; and I will make them sleep secure. And I will espouse thee to me forever; and I will espouse thee to me in justice, and judgment, and in mercy, and in commiserations. And I will espouse thee to me in faith; and thou shalt know that I am the Lord. Osee 2:18-20.

The bruised reed he shall not break, and the smoking flax he shall not quench. He shall bring forth judgment unto truth. Is. 42:3.

19. EXHORTATIONS TO THOROUGH CONVERSION

Delay not to be converted to the Lord, and defer it not from day to day. For his wrath shall come on a sudden, and in the time of vengeance he will destroy thee. Ecclus. 5:8 f.

Say not: I have sinned, and what harm hath befallen me? for the Most High is a patient rewarder. Add not sin upon sin: and say not: The mercy of the Lord is great, he will have mercy on the multitude of my sins. For mercy and wrath quickly come from him, and his wrath looketh upon sinners. Ecclus. 5:4-7.

It is now the hour for us to rise from sleep. For now our salvation is nearer than when we believed. The night is passed, and the day is at hand. Let us therefore cast off the works of darkness, and put on the armor of light. Let us walk honestly, as in the day: not in rioting and drunkenness, not in chambering and impurities, not in contention and envy. But put ye on the Lord Jesus Christ, and make not provision for the flesh in its concupiscences. Rom. 13:11-14.

Let us search our ways, and seek, and return to the Lord. Lam. 3:40.

Turn away from evil and do good: seek after peace and pursue it. Ps. 33:15.

To depart from iniquity is that which pleaseth the Lord, and to depart from injustice is an entreaty for sins. Ecclus. 35:5.

Be converted to me, and you shall be saved, all ye ends of the earth: for I am God, and there is no other. Jer. 45:22.

Be converted, and depart from your idols, and turn away your faces from all your abominations. Ez. 14:6.

Let the wicked forsake his way, and the unjust man his thoughts, and let him return to the Lord, and he will have mercy on him: and to our God, for he is bountiful to forgive. Is. 56:7.

And I will give them a heart to know me, that I am the Lord: and they shall be my people, and I will be their God: because they shall return to me with their whole heart. Jer. 24:7.

Is it my will that a sinner should die, saith the Lord God, and not that he should be converted from his ways and live? When the wicked turneth himself away from his wickedness which he hath wrought, and doeth judgment and justice, he shall save his soul alive. Cast away from you all your transgressions, by which you have transgressed, and make to yourselves a new heart and a new spirit: and why will you die, O house of Israel? For I desire not the death of him that dieth, saith the Lord God: return ye, and live. Ez. 18:23, 27, 31 f.

Be converted to me with all your heart, in fasting, and in weeping, and in mourning. And rend your hearts, and not your garments, and turn to the Lord your God: for he is gracious and merciful, patient and rich in mercy, and ready to repent of the evil. Who knoweth but he will return, and forgive, and leave a blessing behind him? Joel 2:12-14.

Therefore turn thou to thy God: keep mercy and judgment, and hope in thy God always. Osee 12:5.

Return, O Israel, to the Lord thy God: for thou hast fallen down by thy iniquity. Osee 14:2.

Hate evil, and love good, and establish judgment in the gate. Amos 5:15.

Return to me, and I will return to you, saith the Lord of hosts. Mal. 3:7.

Amen I say to you, unless you be converted, and become as little children, you shall not enter into the kingdom of heaven. Mat. 18:3.

The heart of this people is grown gross, and with their ears they have been dull of hearing, and their eyes they have shut: lest at any time they should see with their eyes, and hear with their ears, and understand with their hearts, and be converted, and I should heal them. Mat. 13:15.

To you first God, raising up his Son, hath sent him to bless you: that every one may convert himself from his wickedness. Be penitent, therefore, and be converted, that your sins may be blotted out. Acts 3:19, 26.

Draw nigh to God, and he will draw nigh to you. Cleanse your hands, ye sinners: and purify your hearts, ye double-minded. Jas. 4:8.

You were as sheep going astray: but you are now converted to the Shepherd and Bishop of your souls. 1 Pet. 2:25.

God indeed was in Christ, reconciling the world to himself, not imputing to them their sins: and he hath placed in us the word of reconciliation. 2 C. 5:19 f.

Having these promises, dearly beloved, let us cleanse ourselves from all defilement of the flesh and of the spirit, perfecting sanctification in the fear of God. 2 C. 7:1.

Rise, thou that sleepest, and arise from the dead: and Christ shall enlighten thee. Eph. 5:1.

Turn to the Lord and forsake thy sins: make thy prayer before the face of the Lord, and offend less. Return to the Lord and turn away from thy injustice, and greatly hate abomination. Ecclus. 17:21-23.

This then I say and testify in the Lord: that henceforward you walk not as also the Gentiles walk in the vanity of their mind, having their understanding darkened, being alienated from the life of God through the ignorance that is in them, because of the blindness of their hearts. Who despairing, have given themselves up to lasciviousness, unto the working of all uncleanness, unto covetousness. Eph. 4:17-19.

Do penance from this thy wickedness: and pray to God, if perhaps this thought of thy heart may be forgiven thee Acts 8:22.

Make your ways and your doings good: and I will dwell with you in this place. Jer. 7:3.

He shall pray to God, and he will be gracious to him: and he shall see his face with joy, and he will render to man his justice. Job 33:28.

20. WORDS OF THE SINNER WHO PURPOSES TO RETURN TO GOD

Returning to himself, he said: How many hired servants in my father's house abound with bread, and I here perish with hunger? I will arise, and will go to my father, and say to him: Father, I have sinned against heaven and before thee: I am not worthy to be called thy son: make me as one of thy hired servants. Luke 15:17-19.

I have sinned very much in what I have done: but I pray thee, O Lord, to take away the iniquity of thy servant, because I have done exceeding foolishly. 2 K. 24:10.

My God, I am confounded and ashamed to lift up my face to thee: for our iniquities are multiplied over our heads, and our sins are grown up even unto heaven. 1 Es. 9:6.

I have sinned, and indeed I have offended: and I have not received what I have deserved. Job 33:27.

I know my iniqity, and my sin is always before me. Ps. 50:5.

We have sinned with our fathers: we have acted unjustly, we have wrought iniquity. Ps. 105:6.

Your iniquities have divided between you and your God, and your sins have hid his face from you, that he should not hear: for your hands are defiled with blood, and your fingers with iniquity: your lips have spoken lies, and your tongue uttereth iniquity. Is. 59:2 f.

Our iniquities are multiplied before thee, and our sins have testified against us: for our wicked doings are with us, and we have known our iniquities. In sinning and lying against the Lord; and we have turned away so that we went not after our God, but spoke calumny and transgression: we have conceived and uttered from the heart words of falsehood. Is. 59:12 f.

I have sinned against the Lord. And Nathan said to David: The Lord also hath taken away thy sin. 2 K. 12:13.

Impute not to me, my Lord, the iniquity, nor remember the injuries of thy servant. For I thy servant acknowledge my sin. 2 K. 19:19 f.

I beseech thee, O Lord God of heaven, strong, great, and terrible, who keepest covenant and mercy with those that love thee, and keep thy commandments: let thy ears be attentive, and thy eyes open. to hear the prayer of thy servant, which I pray before thee now, night and day, for the children of Israel thy servants: and I confess the sins of the children of Israel, by which they have sinned against thee. 2 Es. 1:5 f.

And thou art just in all things that have come upon us: because thou hast done truth, but we have done wickedly. 2 Es. 9:33.

Evils without number have surrounded me; my iniquities have overtaken me, and I was not able to see. They are multiplied above the hairs of my head: and my heart hath forsaken me. Be pleased, O Lord, to deliver me: look down, O Lord, to help me. Ps. 39:13 f.

Have mercy on me, O God, according to thy great mercy. And according to the multitude of thy tender mercies blot out my iniquity: wash me yet more from my iniquity, and cleanse me from my sin. For I know my iniquity, and my sin is always before me. Ps. 50:3-5.

If I would justify myself, my own mouth shall condemn me: if I should show myself innocent, he shall reprove me wicked. Job 9:20.

How many are my iniquities and sins? Make me know my crimes and offences. Job 13:23.

With the hearing of the ear I have heard thee, but now my eye seeth thee. Therefore I reprehend myself, and do penance in dust and ashes. Job 42:5 f.

O God, thou knowest my foolishness: and my offences are not hidden from thee. Ps. 63:6.

PART III

THE THEOLOGICAL AND CARDINAL VIRTUES AND THEIR CONTRARY VICES

I

DIVINE FAITH AND CONTRARY VICES

1. FAITH RESTS ON DIVINE AUTHORITY

My speech and my preaching was not in the persuasive words of human wisdom, but in the showing of the Spirit and power. 1 C. 2:4.

I give you to understand that the gospel which was preached by me is not according to man: for neither did I receive it of man, nor did I learn it but by the revelation of Jesus Christ. Gal. 1:11 f.

We give thanks to God without ceasing: because that when you had received of us the word of the hearing of God, you received it not as the word of men, but (as it is indeed) the word of God. 1 Thess. 2:13.

If we receive the testimony of men, the testimony of God is greater. For this is the testimony of God, which is greater, because he hath testified of his Son. 1 John 5:9.

He that believeth in the Son of God hath the testimony of God in himself. He that hath the Son hath life. 1 John 5:10 f.

Blessed art thou, Simon Bar-Jona: because flesh and blood hath not revealed it to thee, but my Father who is in heaven. Mat. 16:17.

He that believeth in me doth not believe in me, but in him that sent me. John 12:44.

My doctrine is not mine, but his that sent me. John 7:16.

If any man will do the will of him, he shall know of the doctrine, whether it be of God, or whether I speak of myself. John 16:17.

Many other signs also did Jesus in the sight of his disciples which are not written in this book. But these are written that you may believe that Jesus is the Christ the Son of God: and that believing, you may have life in his name. John 20:30 f.

Believe in the Lord your God, and you shall be secure: believe the prophets, and all things shall succeed well. 2 Par. 20:20.

2. REVELATION

Go ye into the whole world, and preach the gospel to every creature. Mark 16:15.

Your faith is spoken of in the whole world. Rom. 1:8.

Penance and the remission of sins must be preached in his name unto all nations. Luke 24:47.

Abraham believed God, and it was reputed to him unto justice. Gen. 15:6.

You shall be witnesses unto me in Jerusalem, and in all Judea, and Samaria. Acts 1:8.

We see now through a glass in dark manner, but then face to face. 1 C. 13:12.

He enlighteneth every man that cometh into this world. John 1:9.

God will have all men to be saved, and to come to the knowledge of the truth. 1 Tim. 2:4.

3. GOD AS THE FIRST TRUTH

God is true: and every man a liar. Rom. 3:4.

God interposed an oath, that by two immutable things, in which it is impossible for God to lie, we may have the strongest comfort, who have fled for refuge to hold fast the hope set before us. Heb. 6:18.

God is faithful and without any iniquity. He is just and right. Deut. 32:4.

Heaven and earth shall pass away, but my words shall not pass away. Mat. 24:35.

May God give unto you the Spirit of wisdom, and of revelation in the knowledge of him: the eyes of your heart enlightened, that you may know what the hope is of his calling, and what are the riches of the glory of his inheritance in the saints: and what is the exceeding greatness of his power towards us, who believe according to the operation of the might of his power. Eph. 1:17-19.

4. THE NATURE OF FAITH

Faith is the substance of things to be hoped for, the evidence of things that appear not. Heb. 11:1.

This voice we heard brought from heaven, when we were with him in the holy mount. We have the more firm prophetical word: whereunto you do well to attend, as to a light that shineth in a dark place, until the day dawn and the day-star arise in your hearts. 2 Pet. 1:18 f.

Though we, or an angel from heaven, preach a gospel to you besides that which we have preached to you, let him be anathema. As we said before, so now I say again: If any one preach to you a gospel besides that which you have received, let him be anathema. Gal. 1:8 f.

No man hath seen God at any time: the only begotten Son, who is in the bosom of the Father, he hath declared him. John 1:18.

Thy testimonies are become exceedingly credible. Ps. 92:5.

How shall we escape if we neglect so great salvation? which having begun to be declared by the Lord, was confirmed unto us by them that heard him: God also bearing them witness by signs, and wonders, and divers miracles, and distributions of the Holy Ghost according to his own will. Heb. 2:3 f.

By grace you are saved through faith: and that not of yourselves, for it is the gift of God. Eph. 2:3.

5. THE UNITY AND NECESSITY OF FAITH

One Lord, one faith, one baptism. One God and Father of all, who is above all, and through all, and in us all. Eph. 4:5 f.

In Christ Jesus neither circumcision availeth anything, nor uncircumcision: but faith that worketh by charity. Gal. 5:6.

Without faith it is impossible to please God. For he that cometh to God must believe that he is, and is a Rewarder to them that seek him. Heb. 11:6.

This [Jesus] is the stone which was rejected by you the builders, which is become the head of the corner. Neither is there salvation in any other. For there is no other name under heaven given to men whereby we must be saved. Acts 4:11 f.

I cease not to give thanks for you, making commemoration of you in my prayers, that you may know what is the exceeding greatness of his power towards us who believe. Eph. 1:16, 19.

We are happy, O Israel: because the things that are pleasing to God are made known to us Bar. 4:4.

Praise the Lord, who declareth his justices and judgments to Israel. He hath not done in like manner to every nation: and his judgments he hath not made manifest to them. Alleluia. Ps. 147:19 f.

You are no more strangers and foreigners: but you are fellow citizens with the saints and the domestics of God. Eph. 2:19.

We cease not to pray for you, giving thanks to God the Father, who hath made us worthy to be partakers of the lot of the saints in light. Who hath delivered us from the power of darkness, and hath translated us into the kingdom of the Son of his love, in whom we have redemption through his blood, the remission of sins. Col. 1:12-14.

The things that were gain to me, the same I have counted loss for Christ. I count all things to be but loss, for the excellent knowledge of Jesus Christ my Lord: for whom I have suffered the loss of all things, and count them but as dung, that I may gain Christ. Phil. 3:7 f.

If you have faith as a grain of mustard seed, you shall say to this mountain: Remove from hence thither, and it shall remove. Mat. 17:19.

6. LIVING FAITH AND DEAD FAITH

The just shall live in his faith. Heb. 2:4.

Being justified by faith, let us have peace with God through our Lord Jesus Christ. Rom. 5:1.

Without the law the justice of God is made manifest, being witnessed by the law and the prophets: even the justice of God by faith of Jesus Christ, unto all and upon all them that believe in him: for there is no distinction. Rom. 3:21 f.

To him all the prophets give testimony, that through his name all receive remission of sins who believe in him. Acts 10:43.

He that believeth and is baptized shall be saved: but he that believeth not shall be condemned. Mark 16:16.

As many as received him, he gave them power to be made the sons of God, to them that believe in his name. John 1:12.

God so loved the world as to give his only begotten Son: that whosoever believeth in him may not perish, but may have life everlasting. John 3:16.

I am the bread of life: he that cometh to me shall not hunger; and he that believeth in me shall never thirst. John 6:35.

Amen, amen I say unto you, he that believeth in me hath everlasting life. John 6:47.

Amen, amen I say unto you, that he who heareth my word, and believeth him who sent me, hath life everlasting, and cometh not into judgment, but is passed from death to life. John 5:24.

He that believeth God taketh heed to the commandments: and he that trusteth in him shall fare never the worse. Ecclus. 32:28.

Some man will say: Thou hast faith, and I have works; show me thy faith without works, and I will show thee by works my faith. Jas. 2:18.

What shall it profit, my brethren, if a man say he hath faith, but hath not works? Shall faith be able to save him? And if a brother or sister be naked, and want daily food, and one of you say to them: Go in peace, be you warmed and filled, yet give them not those things that are necessary for the body, what shall it profit? So faith also, if it have not works, is dead in itself. Jas. 2:14-17.

Many of the chief men believed in him: but because of the Pharisees they did not confess him, that they might not be cast out of the synagogue. For they loved the glory of men more than the glory of God. John 12:42 f.

If thou wilt enter into life, keep the commandments. Mat. 19:17.

7. EXHORTATIONS TO LIVE A LIFE WORTHY OF FAITH

I therefore, a prisoner in the Lord, beseech you that you walk worthy of the vocation in which you are called. Eph. 4:1.

Let your conversation be worthy of the gospel of Christ: that whether I come and see you, or being absent may hear of you, that you stand fast in one spirit with one mind, laboring together for the faith of the gospel. Phil. 1:27.

We cease not to pray for you, and to beg that you may walk worthy of God in all things pleasing, and increasing in the knowledge of God. Col. 1:10.

Stand fast in the faith. 1 C. 16:13.

Thus saith the Lord: Stand ye on the ways, and see, and ask for the old paths, which is the good way, and walk ye in it: and you shall find refreshment for your souls. Jer. 6:16.

O senseless Galatians, who hath bewitched you that you should not obey the truth, before whose eyes Jesus Christ hath been set forth crucified among you? Gal. 3:1.

Stand fast, and be not held again under the yoke of bondage. Gal. 5:1.

You did run well: who hath hindered you, that you should not obey the truth? Gal. 5:7.

He gave some apostles, and some prophets, and other some evangelists, and other some pastors and doctors: that henceforth we be no more children tossed to and fro, and carried about with every wind of doctrine by the wickedness of men, by cunning and craftiness, by which they lie in wait to deceive. Eph. 4:11, 14.

Be not led away with various and strange doctrines. Heb. 13:9.

Labor the more, that by good works you may make sure your calling and election. 2 Pet. 1:10.

8. PROFESSION OF FAITH

He that shall be ashamed of me and of my words, of him the Son of man shall be ashamed when he shall come in his majesty, and that of his Father and of the holy angels. Luke 9:26.

With the heart we believe unto justice; but with the mouth confession is made unto salvation. Rom. 10:10.

These things his parents said, because they feared the Jews. For the Jews had already agreed among themselves, that if any man should confess him to be Christ, he should be put out of the synagogue. John 9:22.

We are the children of saints, and look for that life which God will give to those that never change their faith from him. Job 2:13.

By our Lord Jesus Christ we have received grace and apostleship for obedience to the faith in all nations for his name. Rom. 1:5.

We walk by faith. 2 C. 5:7.

Your faith groweth exceedingly, and the charity of every one of you towards each other aboundeth. 2 Thess. 1:3.

Take unto you the armor of God, that you may be able to resist in the evil day. In all things taking the shield of faith, wherewith you may be able to extinguish all the fiery darts of the most wicked one. Eph. 6:13, 16.

Every one that shall confess me before men, I will also confess him before my Father who is in heaven. Mat. 10:32.

We ought to obey God rather than men. Acts 5:29.

9. EXAMPLES OF HEROIC FAITH

Abraham believed God, and it was reputed to him unto justice. Gen. 15:6.

Entering into the house, they found the Child with Mary his mother, and falling down they adored him; and opening their treasures, they offered him gifts: gold, frankincense, and myrrh. Mat. 2:11.

She said within herself: If I shall touch only his garment, I shall be healed. Mat. 9:21.

Jesus saith to them: Do you believe that I can do this unto you? They say to him: Yea, Lord. Then he touched their eyes, saying: According to your faith be it done unto you. And their eyes were opened: and Jesus strictly charged them, saying: See that no man know this. Mat. 9:28-30.

They besought him that they might touch but the hem of his garment. And as many as touched were made whole. Mat. 14:36.

O woman, great is thy faith: be it done to thee as thou wilt. And her daughter was cured from that hour. Mat. 15:28.

Blessed art thou that hast believed, because those things shall be accomplished that were spoken to thee by the Lord. Luke 1:45.

Jesus, seeing their faith, said to the man sick of the palsy: Be of good heart, son: thy sins are forgiven thee. Mat. 9:2.

Thy faith hath made thee safe: go in peace. Luke 7:50.

10. UNBELIEF

He that is unbelieving, his soul shall not be right in himself; but the just shall live in his faith. Haba. 2:4.

He that doth not believe is already judged, because he believeth not in the name of the only begotten Son of God. John 3:18.

He that believeth in the Son hath life everlasting; but he that believeth not the Son shall not see life, but the wrath of God abideth on him. John 3:36.

If you believe not that I am he, you shall die in your sin. John 8:24.

Thou sayest: What doth God know? and he judgeth as it were through a mist. The clouds are his covert, and he doth not consider our things, and he walketh about the poles of heaven. Job 22:13 f.

Who is the Almighty that we should serve him? and what doth it profit us if we pray to him? Job 21:15.

The fool hath said in his heart: There is no God. They are corrupt, and are become abominable in their ways; there is none that doth good, no, not one. Ps. 13:1.

Say not before the angel: There is no Providence, lest God be angry at thy words, and destroy all the works of thy hands. Eccles. 5:5.

Woe to them that are fainthearted, who believe not God, and therefore shall not be protected by him! Ecclus. 2:15.

If you will not believe, you shall not continue. Is. 7:9.

I have spread forth my hands all the day to an unbelieving people, who walk in a way that is not good, after their own thoughts. Is. 65:2.

When the Son of man cometh, shall he find, think you, faith on earth? Luke 18:8.

He that believeth not shall be condemned. Mark 16:16.

If they hear not Moses and the prophets, neither will they believe if one rise again from the dead. Luke 16:31.

He upbraided them with their incredulity and hardness of heart, because they did not believe them who had seen him after he was risen again. Mark 16:14.

O foolish and slow of heart to believe in all things which the prophets have spoken! Luke 24:25.

Jesus Christ [is] a stone of stumbling and a rock of scandal to them that stumble at the word, neither do believe, whereunto also they are set. 1 Pet. 2:8.

If our gospel be also hid, it is hid to them that are lost: in whom the god of this world hath blinded the minds of unbelievers, that the light of the gospel of the glory of Christ, who is the image of God, should not shine unto them. 2 C. 4:3 f.

To whom did he swear that they should not enter into his rest, but to them that were incredulous? And we see that they could not enter in, because of unbelief. Heb. 3:18 f.

See that you refuse not him that speaketh. For if they escaped not who refused him that spoke upon earth, much more shall not we, that turn away from him that speaketh to us from heaven. Heb. 12:25.

In the last days there shall come deceitful scoffers, walking after their own lusts, saying: Where is his promise, or his coming? For since the time that the fathers slept all things continue as they were from the beginning of the creation. But of this one thing be not ignorant, my beloved: that one day with the Lord is as a thousand years, and a thousand years as one day. 2 Pet. 3:3 f., 8.

My doctrine is not mine, but his that sent me. If any man will do the will of him, he shall know of the doctrine, whether it be from God, or whether I speak of myself. John 7:16 f.

He that believeth in the Son hath life everlasting; but he that believeth not the Son shall not see life, but the wrath of God abideth in him. John 3:36.

He that is of God heareth the words of God. Therefore you hear them not, because you are not of God. John 8:47.

He that hateth me hateth my Father also. John 15:23.

He that despiseth me, and receiveth not my words, hath one that judgeth him: the word that I have spoken the same shall judge him in the last day. John 12:48.

He that loveth me not keepeth not my words; and the word which you have heard is not mine, but the Father's, who sent me. John 14:24.

Be not faithless, but believing. John 20:27.

The word of the cross to them indeed that perish is foolishness; but to them that are saved, that is, to us, it is the power of God. We preach Christ crucified, unto the Jews indeed a stumbling-block, and unto the Gentiles foolishness. 1 C. 1:18, 23.

These men blaspheme whatsoever things they know not; and what things soever they naturally know, like dumb beasts, in these they are corrupted. Jude 10.

The wrath of God is revealed from heaven against all ungodliness and injustice of these men that detain the truth of God in injustice; because that which is known of God is manifest in them; for God hath manifested it unto them. For the invisible things of him, from the creation of the world, are clearly seen, being understood by the things that are made: his eternal power also and divinity; so that they are inexcusable. Because that, when they knew God, they have not glorified him as God, or given thanks; but became vain in their thoughts, and their foolish heart was darkened. Rom. 1:18-21.

Certain men are secretly entered in (who were written of long ago unto this judgment), ungodly men, turning the grace of God into riotousness, and denying the only sovereign Ruler and our Lord Jesus Christ. Jude 4.

Whosoever denieth the Son, the same hath not the Father. 1 John 2:23.

11. OBSTACLES AND HELPS TO FAITH

How can you believe who receive glory one from another, and the glory which is from God alone you do not seek? John 5:44.

It is best that the heart be established with grace, not with meats, which have not profited those that walk in them. Heb. 13:9.

To the King of ages be honor and glory forever and ever. Amen. This precept I commend to thee, O son Timothy, according to the prophecies going before on thee, that thou war in them a good warfare. Having faith and a good conscience, which some rejecting have made shipwreck concerning the faith. 1 Tim. 1:17-19.

Because of unbelief they were broken off. But thou standest by faith; be not high-minded, but fear. For if God hath not spared the natural branches, fear lest perhaps he also spare not thee. See then the goodness and the severity of God: towards them indeed that are fallen the severity, but towards thee the goodness of God, if thou abide in goodness, otherwise thou shalt be cut off. Rom. 11:20-22.

12. EXAMPLES OF UNBELIEF

Eliseus said: Fine flour shall be sold for a stater, and two bushels of barley for a stater, in the gate of Samaria. Then one of the lords said: If the Lord should make floodgates in heaven, can that possibly be which thou sayest? And he said: Thou shalt see it with thy eyes, but shalt not eat thereof. 4 K. 7:1 f.

Zachary said to the angel: Whereby shall I know this? for I am an old man, and my wife is advanced in years. And the angel answering, said to him: And behold, thou shalt be dumb, and shalt not be able to speak until the day wherein these things shall come to pass, because thou hast not believed my words, which shall be fulfilled in their time. Luke 1:18-20.

He wrought not many miracles there, because of their unbelief. Mat. 13:58.

Immediately Jesus stretching forth his hand took hold of him, and said to him: O thou of little faith, why didst thou doubt? Mat. 14:31.

Put in thy finger hither, and see my hands; and bring hither thy hand, and put it into my side, and be not faithless but believing. Thomas answered, and said to him: My Lord and my God! John 20:27 f.

13. APOSTASY FROM THE FAITH

As a bird that wandereth from her nest, so is a man that leaveth his place. Prov. 27:8.

These are wandering stars, to whom the storm of darkness is reserved forever. Jude 13.

Save thy life: look not back, neither stay thou in all the country about: but save thyself in the mountain, lest thou be also consumed. Gen. 19:17.

His wife, looking behind her, was turned into a statue of salt. Gen. 19:26.

Be mindful from whence thou art fallen: and do penance, and do the first works. Or else I come to thee, and will move thy candlestick out of its place, except thou do penance. Apoc. 2:5.

It is impossible for those who were once illuminated, have tasted also the heavenly gift, and were made partakers of the Holy Ghost, have moreover tasted the good word of God, and the power of the world to come, and are fallen away, to be renewed again to penance, crucifying again to themselves the Son of God, and making him a mockery. Heb. 6:4-6.

If we sin wilfully after having received the knowledge of the truth, there is now left no sacrifice for sins, but a certain dreadful expectation of judgment. Heb. 10:26 f.

He forsook God who made him, and departed from God his Savior. Deut. 32:15.

The Lord was angry with Solomon, because his mind was turned away from the Lord the God of Israel, who had appeared to him twice. 3 K. 11:9.

O Lord, the hope of Israel, all that forsake thee shall be confounded: they that depart from thee shall be written in the earth: because they have forsaken the Lord, the vein of living waters. Jer. 17:13.

If you forsake him, he will forsake you. 2 Par. 15:2.

Thy own wickedness shall reprove thee, and thy apostasy shall rebuke thee. Know thou, and see that it is an evil and a bitter thing for thee to have left the Lord thy God, and that my fear is not with thee, saith the Lord the God of hosts. My people have done two evils. They have forsaken me, the fountain of living waters, and have digged to themselves cisterns, broken cisterns, that can hold no water. Jer. 2:19-23.

Thou hast forgotten the law of thy God: I also will forget thy children. Osee 4:6.

Because iniquity hath abounded, the charity of many shall grow cold. Mat. 24:12.

Take heed, brethren, lest perhaps there be in any of you an evil heart of unbelief, to depart from the living God. Heb. 3:12.

It had been better for them not to have known the way of justice, than after they have known it, to turn back from that holy commandment which was delivered to them. 2 Pet. 2:21.

Take heed lest being led aside by the error of the unwise, you fall from your own steadfastness. 2 Pet. 3:17.

14. HERESIES GENERATED BY A VICIOUS LIFE

As Jannes and Mambres resisted Moses, so these also resist the truth: men corrupted in mind, reprobate concerning the faith. 2 Tim. 3:8.

They went out from us, but they were not of us: for if they had been of us, they would no doubt have remained with us: but that they may be manifest that they are not all of us. 1 John 2:19.

In the last times some shall depart from the faith. 1 Tim. 4:1.

There must be also heresies, that they also who are approved may be made manifest among you. 1 C. 11:19.

They are of the world: therefore of the world they speak, and the world heareth them. 1 John 4:5.

15. IGNORANCE, PRIDE, AND OBSTINACY OF HERETICS

If any man teach otherwise, and consent not to the sound words of our Lord Jesus Christ, and to that doctrine which is according to godliness, he is proud, knowing nothing, but sick about questions and strifes of words: from which arise envies, contentions, blasphemies, evil suspicions, conflicts of men corrupted in mind, and who are destitute of the truth, supposing gain to be godliness. 1 Tim. 6:3-5.

Know also this, that in the last days shall come on dangerous times. Men shall be lovers of themselves, covetous, haughty, proud, blasphemers, disobedient to parents, ungrateful, wicked, without affection, without peace, slanderers, incontinent, unmerciful, without kindness, traitors, stubborn. puffed up, and lovers of pleasures more than of God: having an appearance indeed of godliness, but denying the power thereof. 2 Tim. 3:1-5.

Such false apostles are deceitful workmen, transforming themselves into the apostles of Christ. And no wonder: for Satan himself transformeth himself into an angel of light. Therefore it is no great thing if his ministers be transformed as the ministers of justice: whose end shall be according to their works. 2 C. 11:13-15.

They that are such serve not Christ our Lord, but their own belly: and by pleasing speeches, and good words, seduce the hearts of the innocent. Rom. 16:18.

Of this sort are they who creep into houses, and lead captive silly women loaded with sins, who are led away with divers desires. 2 Tim. 3:6.

Through covetousness shall they with feigned words make merchandise of you, whose judgment now of a long time lingereth not, and their perdition slumbereth not. 2 Pet. 2:3.

If God spared not the angels that sinned, but delivered them unto torments, [nevertheless] the Lord knoweth how to deliver the godly from temptation, but to reserve the unjust unto the day of judgment, to be tormented. 2 Pet. 2:4, 9.

16. HERETICS TO BE SHUNNED

The prophet who being corrupted with pride shall speak in my name things that I did not command him to say, or in the name of strange gods, shall be slain. Deut. 18:20.

A man that is a heretic after the first and second admonition, avoid: knowing that he that is such a one is subverted, and sinneth, being condemned by his own judgment. Titus 3:10 f.

Beware of false pophets, who come to you in the clothing of sheep, but inwardly they are ravening wolves. Mat. 7:15.

I beseech you, brethren, to mark them who cause dissensions and offences contrary to the doctrine which you have learned, and to avoid them. Rom. 16:17.

If any man come to you, and bring not this doctrine, receive him not into the house, nor say to him God speed you. For he that saith unto him, God speed you, communicateth with his wicked works. 2 John 10:11.

Beware of dogs, beware of evil workers, beware of the concision. Phil. 3:2.

17. PRESENCE OF HERETICS FROM APOSTOLIC TIMES

This precept I commend to thee, O son Timothy: according to the prophecies going before on thee, that thou war in them a good warfare, having faith and a good conscience, which some rejecting have made shipwreck concerning the faith: of whom is Hymeneus and Alexander, whom I have delivered up to Satan, that they may learn not to blaspheme. 1 Tim. 1:18-20.

Shun profane and vain babblings, for they grow much towards ungodliness. And their speech spreadeth like a canker: of whom are Hymeneus and Philetus; who have erred from the truth, saying that the resurrection is past already, and have subverted the faith of some. 2 Tim. 2:16-18.

Little children, it is the last hour, and as you have heard that Antichrist cometh, even now there are become many Antichrists, whereby we know that it is the last hour. 1 John 2:18.

I know that after my departure ravening wolves will enter in among you, not sparing the flock. And of your own selves shall arise men speaking perverse things to draw away disciples after them. Therefore watch, keeping in memory that for three years I ceased not with tears to admonish every one of you night and day. Acts 20:29-31.

There are false prophets among the people, even as there shall be among you lying teachers, who shall bring in sects of perdition, and deny the Lord who bought them, bringing upon themselves swift destruction. 2 Pet. 2:1.

Take heed that no man seduce you; for many will come in my name, saying: I am Christ, and they will seduce many. Mat. 24:4 f.

Many seducers are gone out into the world, who confess not that Jesus Christ is come in the flesh; this is a seducer and an Antichrist. Look to yourselves that you lose not the things which you have wrought; but that you may receive a full reward. 2 John 1:7 f.

II

THEOLOGICAL HOPE AND THE CONTRARY VICES

1. HOPE AND ITS KINDS

Now what is my hope? Is it not the Lord? Ps. 38:8.

Thou art my hope, O Lord, from my youth. Ps. 70:5.

The Lord shall be the hope of his people. Joel 3:16.

The hope that is laid up for you in heaven. Col. 1:5.

We glory in the hope of the glory of the sons of God. Rom. 5:2.

Now there remain, faith, hope, and charity. 1 C. 13:13.

This my hope is laid up in my bosom. Job 19:27.

In God is my salvation and my glory: he is the God of my glory: he is the God of my help, and my hope is in God. Ps. 61:8.

We are saved by hope. Rom. 8:24.

The grace of God our Savior hath appeared to all men, instructing us that we should live godly in this world. Looking for the blessed hope, and coming of the glory of the great God, and our Savior Jesus Christ. Titus 2:11, 13.

Hope that is seen is not hope. For what a man seeth, why doth he hope for? Rom. 8:24.

2. FRUITS OF HOPE IN GOD

My children, behold the generations of men: and know ye that no one hath hoped in the Lord, and hath been confounded. Who hath continued in his commandment, and hath been forsaken? or who hath called upon him, and he despised him? God is compassionate and merciful, and will forgive sins in the day of tribulation: and he is a protector to all that seek him in truth. Ecclus. 2:11-13.

Trust in the Lord, and do good, and thou shalt be fed with its riches. Ps. 36:3.

They that hope in the Lord shall renew their strength, they shall take wings as eagles, they shall run and not be weary, they shall walk and not faint. Is. 40:31.

When thou shalt cry let thy companions deliver thee, but the wind shall carry them all off, a breeze shall take them away, but he who putteth his trust in me shall inherit the land and shall possess my holy mount. Is. 57:13.

Blessed be the man that trusteth in the Lord, and the Lord shall be his confidence. He shall be as a tree that is planted by the waters, that spreadeth out its roots towards moisture: and it shall not fear when the heat cometh. Jer. 17:7.

Delivering, I will deliver thee, and thou shalt not fall by the sword: but thy life shall be saved for thee, because thou hast put thy trust in me, saith the Lord. Jer. 39:18.

He that feareth man shall quickly fall: he that trusteth in the Lord shall be set on high. Prov. 29:25.

He that believeth God taketh heed to the commandments: and he that trusteth in him shall fare never the worse. Ecclus. 32:28.

Thus consider through all generations: that none that trust in him fail in strength. 1 Mac. 2:61.

They who trust in him shall understand the truth, and they that are faithful in love shall rest in him, for grace and peace is to his elect. Wis. 3:9.

They that trust in the Lord shall be as Mount Sion: he shall not be moved forever. Ps. 124:1.

The expectation of the just is joy. Prov. 10:28.

I have trusted in thy mercy. My heart shall rejoice in thy salvation: I will sing to the Lord, who giveth me good things: yea, I will sing to the name of the Lord the Most High. Ps. 12:6.

In thee have our fathers hoped; they have hoped, and thou hast delivered them. They cried to thee, and they were saved; they trusted in thee, and were not confounded. Ps. 21:5 f.

Let them trust in thee who know thy name, for thou hast not forsaken them that seek thee, O Lord. Ps. 9:11.

To thee, O Lord, have I lifted up my soul. In thee, O my God, I put my trust: let me not be ashamed. Neither let my enemies laugh at me: for none of them that wait on thee shall be confounded. Ps. 24:1-3.

Blessed is the man whose trust is in the name of the Lord: and who hath not had regard to vanities and lying follies. Ps. 39:5.

3. EXHORTATIONS TO FIX OUR HOPE IN GOD

Who is there among you that feareth the Lord, that heareth the voice of his servant, that hath walked in darkness, and hath no light? Let him hope in the name of the Lord, and lean upon his God. Is. 50:10.

Have confidence in the Lord with all thy heart, and lean not upon thy own prudence. Prov. 3:5.

Believe God, and he will recover thee: and direct thy way, and trust in him. Keep his fear, and grow old therein. Ye that fear the Lord, wait for his mercy: and go not aside from him, lest ye fall. Ye that fear the Lord, believe him: and your reward shall not be made void. Ye that fear the Lord, hope in him: and mercy shall come to you for your delight. Ye that fear the Lord, love him, and your hearts shall be enlightened. Ecclus. 2:6-10.

Behave like men, and take courage, be not afraid nor dismayed for the king of the Assyrans, nor for all the multitude that is with him: for there are many more with us than with him. With him is an arm of flesh: with us the Lord our God, who is our helper, and fighteth for us. And the people were encouraged with these words of Ezechias king of Juda. 2 Par. 32:7 f.

Having the loins of your mind girt up, being sober, trust perfectly in the grace which is offered you in the revelation of Jesus Christ. 1 Pet. 1:13.

Trust in him, all ye congregation of people; pour out your hearts before him: God is our helper forever. Ps. 61:9.

Be you humbled under the mighty hand of God, that he may exalt you in the day of visitation. Casting all your care upon him, for he hath care of you. 1 Pet. 5:6 f.

Blessed are all they that trust in him. Ps. 2:13.

Blessed is the man whose trust is in the name of the Lord, and who hath not had regard to vanities and lying follies. Ps. 39:5.

He that trusteth in the Lord is blessed. Prov. 16:20.

There is no confusion to them that trust in thee. Dan. 3:40.

Be not solicitous therefore, saying: What shall we eat, or what shall we drink, or wherewith shall we be clothed? For all these things do the heathen seek. For your Father knoweth that you have need of all these things. Seek ye therefore first the kingdom of God and his justice, and all these things shall be added unto you. Be not therefore solicitous for tomorrow; for the morrow will be solicitous for itself. Sufficient for the day is the evil thereof. Mat. 6:31-34.

When they shall bring you into the synagogues, and to magistrates and powers, be not solicitous how or what you shall answer, or what you shall say. For the Holy Ghost shall teach you in the same hour what you must say. Luke 12:1 f.

4. STEADFAST HOPE OF THE JUST, VAIN SELF-RELIANCE OF THE WICKED

The expectation of the just is joy; but the hope of the wicked shall perish. Prov. 10:28.

The desire of the just is all good: the expectation of the wicked is indignation. Prov. 11:23.

The hope of the wicked is as dust which is blown away with the wind, and as a thin froth which is dispersed by the storm, and a smoke that is scattered abroad by the wind, and as a remembrance of a guest of one day that passeth by. Wis. 5:15.

Can the rush be green without moisture? or a sedgebush grow without water? When it is yet in flower, and is not plucked up with the hand, it withereth before all herbs. Even so are the ways of all that forget God, and the hope of the hypocrite shall perish: his folly shall not please him, and his trust shall be like the spider's web. He shall lean upon his house, and it shall not stand: he shall prop it up, and it shall not rise. Job 8:11-15.

The hopes of a man that is void of understanding are vain and deceitful; and dreams lift up fools. Ecclus. 34:1.

5. WARNINGS AGAINST SELF-CONFIDENCE

Cursed be the man that trusteth in man, and maketh flesh his arm, and whose heart departeth from the Lord. For he shall be like tamaric in the desert, and he shall not see when good shall come: but he shall dwell in dryness in the desert in a salt land, and not inhabited. Jer. 17:5 f.

Hanani the prophet came to Asa, king of Juda, and said to him: Because thou hast had confidence in the king of Syria, and not in the Lord thy God, therefore hath the army of the king of Syria escaped out of thy hand. Were not the Ethiopians and the Libyans much more numerous in chariots, and horsemen, and an exceeding great multitude? Yet because thou trustedst in the Lord, he delivered them into thy hand. The eyes of the Lord behold all the earth, and give strength to those who with a perfect heart trust in him. Wherefore thou hast done foolishly, and for this cause from this time wars shall arise against thee. 2 Par. 16:7-9.

O, grant us help from trouble: for vain is the help of man. Ps. 107:13.

Put not your trust in princes: in the children of men, in whom there is no salvation. Ps. 145:2.

He that trusteth in his own heart is a fool. Ps. 28:26.

Woe to you, apostate children, saith the Lord, that you would take counsel, and not of me: and would begin a web, and not by my Spirit, that you might add sin upon sin! Who walk to go down into Egypt, and have not asked my mouth, hoping for help in the strength of Pharao, and trusting in the shadow of Egypt. And the strength of Pharao shall be to your confusion, and the confidence of the shadow of Egypt to your shame. For thy princes were in Tanis, and thy messengers came even to Hanes. They were all confounded at a people that could not profit them: they were no help, nor to any profit, but to confusion and to reproach. Is. 30:1-5.

A thousand men shall flee for fear of one: and for fear of five shall you flee, till you be left as the mast of a ship on the top of a mountain, and as an ensign upon a hill. Is. 30:17.

Israel hath forgotten his Maker, and hath built temples: and Juda hath built many fenced cities: and I will send fire upon his cities, and it shall devour the houses thereof. Osee 8:14.

Woe to you that are wealthy in Sion, and to you that have confidence in the mountain of Samaria: ye great men, heads of the people, that go in with state into the house of Israel! Amos 6:1.

He that is good shall draw grace from the Lord: but he that trusteth in his own devices doth wickedly. Prov. 12:2.

Follow not in thy strength the desires of thy heart: and say not: How mighty am I! and who shall bring me under for my deeds? for God will surely take revenge. Ecclus. 5:2 f.

Put not your trust in princes, in the children of men, in whom there is no salvation. Ps. 145:2 f.

Blessed is he who hath the God of Jacob for his helper, whose hope is in the Lord his God: who made heaven and earth, the sea, and all the things that are in them. Ps. 145:5 f.

6. EXAMPLES OF HOPE AND CONFIDENCE IN GOD

Fear not, stand and see the great wonders of the Lord, which he will do this day: for the Egyptians, whom you see now, you shall see no more forever. Ex. 14:13.

Although he should kill me, I will trust in him. Job 13:15.

Be not rebellious against the Lord: and fear ye not the people of this land, for we are able to eat them up as bread. All aid is gone from them: the Lord is with us, fear ye not. Num. 14:9.

David said: The Lord who delivered me out of the paw of the lion, and out of the paw of the bear, he will deliver me out of the hand of this Philistine. 1 K. 17:37.

David said to the Philistine: Thou comest to me with a sword, and with a spear, and with a shield: but I come to thee in the name of the Lord of hosts, the God of the armies of Israel, which thou hast defied this day: and the Lord will deliver thee into my hand, and I will slay thee; that all the earth may know that there is a God in Israel. 1 K. 17:45 f.

Machabeus ever trusted with all hope that God would help them. And he exhorted his people not to fear the coming of the nations but to remember the help they had before received from heaven, and now to hope for victory from the Almighty. 2 Mac. 15:7 f.

I will deliver thee in that day, saith the Lord, and thou shalt not be given into the hands of the men whom thou fearest. But delivering, I will deliver thee, and thou shalt not fall by the sword; but thy life shall be saved for thee, because thou hast put thy trust in me, saith the Lord. Jer. 39:17 f.

7. EJACULATIONS OF A HOPEFUL SOUL

The Lord is with me as a strong warrior; therefore they that persecute me shall fall, and shall be weak: they shall be greatly confounded. Jer. 20:11.

The Lord is my portion, said my soul; therefore will I wait for him. The Lord is good to them that hope in him, to the soul that seeketh him. It is good to wait in silence for the salvation of God, for he will not cast off forever. Lam. 3:24-26

Though I should walk in the midst of the shadow of death, I will fear no evils, for thou art with me. Ps. 22:4.

Many say to my soul: There is no salvation for him in his God. But thou, O Lord, art my protector, my glory and the lifter up of my head. Ps. 3:3 f.

I will not fear thousands of the people surrounding me. Arise, O Lord; save me, O my God. Ps. 3:7.

Hope in God, for I will still give praise to him, the salvation of my countenance and my God. Ps. 41:6 f.

The Lord is my helper: I will not fear what man can do unto me. The Lord is my helper: and I will look over my enemies. It is good to confide in the Lord, rather than to have confidence in man. It is good to trust in the Lord, rather than to trust in princes. Ps. 117:6-9.

In thee, O Lord, I have hoped: let me never be put to confusion. Deliver me in thy justice. Ps. 70:1 f.

The God of hope fill you with all joy and peace in believing; that you may abide in hope, and in the Holy Ghost. Rom. 15:13.

8. THE BITTER FRUITS OF DESPAIR

We have no hopes; for we will go after our own thoughts, and we will do every one according to the perverseness of his evil heart. Jer. 18:12.

Despairing, they have given themselves up to lasciviousness, unto the working of all uncleanness, unto covetousness. Eph. 4:19.

The sound of a flying leaf shall terrify them, and they shall flee as it were from the sword: they shall fall when no man pursueth them. Lev. 26:36.

If thou lose hope, being weary in the day of distress, thy strength shall be diminished. Prov. 24:10.

III

CHARITY AND THE CONTRARY VICES

1. THE PERFECTION AND EXCELLENCE OF CHARITY IN GENERAL

The end of the commandment is charity from a pure heart, and a good conscience, and an unfeigned faith. 1 Thess. 1:5.

All the law is fulfilled in one word: Thou shalt love thy neighbor as thyself. Gal. 5:14.

He that loveth his neighbor hath fulfilled the law. For thou shalt not commit adultery; thou shalt not kill; thou shalt not steal; thou shalt not bear false witness; thou shalt not covet; and if there be any other commandment, it is comprised in this word: Thou shalt love thy neighbor as thyself. The love of our neighbor worketh no evil; love, therefore, is the fulfilling of the law. Rom. 13:8-10.

Charity is patient, is kind; charity envieth not, dealeth not perversely; is not puffed up; is not ambitious; seeketh not her own; is not provoked to anger; thinketh no evil; rejoiceth not in iniquity, but rejoiceth with the truth; beareth all things, believeth all things, hopeth all things, endureth all things. 1 C. 13:4-7.

Love is strong as death; jealousy as hard as hell. Many waters cannot quench charity, neither can the floods drown it. Cant. 8:6 f.

If I speak with the tongues of men and of angels, and have not charity, I am become as sounding brass or a tinkling cymbal. And if I should have prophecy, and should know all mysteries and all knowledge, and if I should have all faith, so that I could remove mountains, and have not charity, I am nothing. And if I should distribute all my goods to feed the poor, and if I should deliver my body to be burned, and have not charity, it profiteth me nothing. 1 C. 13:1-3.

Charity never falleth away, whether prophecies shall be made void, or tongues shall cease, or knowledge shall be destroyed. 1 C. 13:8.

In Christ Jesus neither circumcision availeth anything nor uncircumcision, but faith that worketh by charity. Gal. 5:6.

Above all these things have charity, which is the bond of perfection. Col. 3:14.

2. THE VALUE OF CHARITY

I am come to cast fire on the earth; and what will I but that it be kindled? Luke 12:49.

If a man should give all the substance of his house for love, he shall despise it as nothing. Cant. 8:7.

Blessed is the man that findeth wisdom. Length of days is in her right hand, and in her left hand riches and glory. Her ways are beautiful ways, and all her paths are peaceable. She is a tree of life to them that lay hold on her, and he that shall retain her is blessed. Prov. 3:13, 16-18.

The purchasing of wisdom is better than the merchandise of silver, and her fruit than the chiefest and purest gold. She is more precious than all riches, and all the things that are desired are not to be compared with her. Prov. 3:14 f.

3. THE KEEPING OF GOD'S COMMANDMENTS THE PROOF OF OUR LOVE FOR HIM

He that keepeth his word, in him in very deed the charity of God is perfected; and by this we know that we are in him. 1 John 2:5.

God is charity; and he that abideth in charity abideth in God, and God in him. 1 John 4:16.

If you love me, keep my commandments. John 14:15.

This is the charity of God, that we keep his commandments; and his commandments are not heavy. 1 John 5:3.

This is charity, that we walk according to his commandments. 2 John 6.

They that love God will keep his way. Ecclus. 2:18.

You that love the Lord, hate evil. Ps. 96:10.

4. FRUITS AND REWARDS OF CHARITY

He that abideth in me, and I in him, the same beareth much fruit: for without me you can do nothing. John 15:6.

He that hath my commandments, and keepeth them, he it is that loveth me; he that loveth me shall be loved of my Father: and I will love him, and will manifest myself to him. John 14:21.

If any one love me, he will keep my word, and my Father will love him: and we will come to him, and will make our abode with him. John 14:23.

I love them that love me; and they that in the morning early watch for me shall find me. Prov. 8:17.

They that love God shall be filled with his law. Ecclus. 2:19.

The love of God is honorable wisdom. Ecclus. 1:14.

The eyes of God are upon them that love him. Ecclus. 34:15.

He that loveth God shall obtain pardon for his sins by prayer, and shall refrain himself from them, and shall be heard in the prayer of days. Ecclus. 3:4.

He loved God that made him, and he gave him power over his enemies; and he will not utterly take away the seed of him that loveth the Lord. Ecclus. 47:10, 24.

5. PRECEPTS OF CHARITY; PUNISHMENT OF SINNING AGAINST CHARITY

Jesus said to him: Thou shalt love the Lord thy God with thy whole heart, and with thy whole soul, and with thy whole mind. This is the greatest and the first commandment. Mat. 22:37 f.

With all thy strength love him that made thee, and forsake not his ministers. Ecclus. 7:32.

Love God all thy life, and call upon him for thy salvation. Ecclus. 13:18.

If any man love not our Lord Jesus Christ, let him be anathema, Maranatha. 1 C. 16:22.

If any one abide not in me, he shall be cast forth as a branch, and shall wither: and they shall gather him up, and cast him into the fire, and he burneth. John 15:6.

6. CHARITY TOWARD OUR NEIGHBOR

Before all things have a constant mutual charity among yourselves: for charity covereth a multitude of sins. 1 Pet. 4:8.

We know that we have passed from death to life, because we love the brethren. He that loveth not, abideth in death. 1 John 3:14.

Every one that loveth is born of God, and knoweth God. 1 John 4:7.

If we love one another, God abideth in us, and his charity is perfected in us. 1 John 4:12.

By this shall all men know that you are my disciples, if you have love one for another. Jas. 13:35.

He that loveth his brother abideth in the light, and there is no scandal in him. 1 John 2:10.

Let us not love in word nor in tongue, but in deed and in truth. In this we know that we are in the truth, and in his sight shall persuade our hearts. 1 John 3:18 f.

To love one's neighbor as oneself is a greater thing than all holocausts and sacrifices. Mark 12:33.

Say not: I will do to him as he hath done to me; I will render to every one according to his work. Prov. 24:29.

Remember not any injury done thee by thy neighbor, and do thou nothing by deeds of injury. Ecclus. 10:6.

Forgive thy neighbor if he hath hurt thee; and then shall thy sins be forgiven thee when thou prayest. Ecclus. 28:2.

Hast thou heard a word against thy neighbor? let it die within thee. Ecclus. 19:10.

Love thy neighbor, and be joined to him with fidelity. Ecclus. 27:18.

Thou shalt love thy neighbor as thyself. Mat. 22:39.

As you would that men should do to you, do you also to them in like manner. And if you love them that love you, what thanks are to you? for sinners also love those that love them. And if you do good to them who do good to you, what thanks are to you? for sinners also do this. And if you lend to them of whom you hope to receive, what thanks are to you? for sinners also lend to sinners, for to receive as much. But love ye your enemies; do good, and lend, hoping for nothing thereby: and your reward shall be great, and you shall be the sons of the Highest; for he is kind to the unthankful and to the evil. Luke 6:31-35.

He said to them: Take heed what you hear. In what measure you shall mete, it shall be measured to you again, and more shall be given to you. Mark 4:24.

A new commandment I give unto you: That you love one another, as I have loved you, that you also love one another. John 13:34.

These things I command you, that you love one another. John 15:17.

Concerning fraternal charity we have no need to write to you; for yourselves have learned of God to love one another. We entreat you, brethren, that you abound more. 1 Thess. 4:9 f.

Loving one another with brotherly love; in honor preventing one another. Rom. 12:10.

The love of the neighbor worketh no evil. Love, therefore, is the fulfilling of the law. Rom. 13:10.

See thou never do to another what thou wouldst hate to have done to thee by another. Tob. 4:16.

Charity covereth all sins. Prov. 10:12.

By charity of the Spirit serve one another. For all the law is fulfilled in one sentence: Thou shalt love thy neighbor as thyself. Gal. 5:13 f.

May the Lord multiply you, and make you abound in charity towards one another and towards all men. 1 Thess. 3:12.

Let fraternal charity abide in you. Heb. 13:1.

If you fulfil the royal law, according to the Scriptures: Thou shalt love thy neighbor as thyself, you do well. Jas. 2:8.

Greater love than this no man hath, that a man lay down his life for his friends. John 15:13.

In this we have known the charity of God, because he hath laid down his life for us: and we ought to lay down our lives for the brethren. 1 John 3:16.

7. DUTY OF PRACTICING CHARITY

Show ye mercy and compassion every man to his brother. Zach. 7:9.

Let love be without dissimulation: loving one another with the charity of brotherhood, with honor preventing one another. Rom. 12:9 f.

Bear ye one another's burdens; and so you shall fulfil the law of Christ. Gal. 6:2.

I, a prisoner in the Lord, beseech you that you walk worthy of the vocation in which you are called, with all humility and mildness, with patience, supporting one another in charity. Eph. 4:1 f.

Be ye followers of God, as most dear children: and walk in love, as Christ also hath loved us, and hath delivered himself for us, an oblation and a sacrifice to God, for an odor of sweetness. Eph. 5:1 f.

If thou meet thy enemy's ox or ass going astray, bring it back to him. If thou see the ass of him that hateth thee lie underneath his burden, thou shalt not pass by, but shalt lift him up with him. Ex. 23:4 f.

Thou shalt not molest a stranger, nor afflict him: for yourselves also were strangers in the land of Egypt. Ex. 22:21.

Thou shalt not pass by, if thou seest thy brother's ox or his sheep go astray, but thou shalt bring them back to thy brother. Deut. 22:1.

When thou hast besieged a city a long time, and hath compassed it with bulwarks to take it, thou shalt not cut down the trees that may be eaten of, neither shalt thou spoil the country round about with axes. Deut. 20:19.

When thou hast reaped the corn in thy field, and hast forgot and left a sheaf, thou shalt not return to take it away; but thou shalt suffer the stranger and the fatherless and the widow to take it away: that the Lord thy God may bless thee in all the works of thy hands. Deut. 24:19.

If thy brother be impoverished and weak of hand, and thou receive him as a stranger and sojourner, and he live with thee, take not usury of him, nor more than thou gavest: fear thy God, that thy brother may live with thee. Lev. 25:35 f.

If thou lend money to any of my people that is poor that dwelleth with thee, thou shalt not be hard upon them as an extortioner, nor oppress them with usuries. Ex. 22:25.

Be not wanting in comforting them that weep, and walk with them that mourn. Be not slow to visit the sick: for by these things thou shalt be confirmed in love. Ecclus. 7:38 f.

All things, therefore, whatsoever you would that men should do to you, do you also to them: for this is the law and the prophets. Mat. 7:12.

I say to you: Love your enemies; do good to them that hate you, and pray for them that persecute and calumniate you. For if you love those that love you, what reward shall you have? do not even the publicans this? Mat. 5:44-46.

Fulfil ye my joy, that you be of one mind, having the same charity, being of one accord, agreeing in sentiment. Phil. 2:2.

With all humility and mildness, with patience, supporting one another in charity. Eph. 4:2.

Be ye all of one mind, having compassion one of another, being lovers of the brotherhood. 1 Pet. 3:8.

Above all these things have charity, which is the bond of perfection. Col. 3:14.

Let us consider one another to provoke unto charity and to good works. Heb. 10:24.

Let the charity of the brotherhood abide in you. Heb. 13:1.

Purifying your souls in the obedience of charity, with a brotherly love, from a sincere heart love one another earnestly: being born again, not of corruptible seed, but incorruptible, by the word of God, who liveth and remaineth forever. 1 Pet. 1:22 f.

Love the brotherhood. 1 Pet. 2:17.

As every man hath received grace, ministering the same one to another, as good stewards of the manifold grace of God. 1 Pet. 4:10.

This is the declaration, which you have heard from the beginning, that you should love one another. 1 John 3:11.

We that are stronger ought to bear the infirmities of the weak, and not to please ourselves. Let every one of you please his neighbor unto good to edification. For Christ did not please himself. Wherefore receive one another, as Christ also hath received you unto the honor of God. Rom. 15:1-3, 7.

Let all your things be done in charity. 1 C. 16:14.

As touching the charity of brotherhood we have no need to write you; for you yourselves have learned of God to love one another. For indeed you do it towards all the brethren in all Mecedonia. But we entreat you, brethren, that you abound more. 1 Thess. 4:9 f.

This is my commandment, that you love one another, as I have loved you. These things I command you, that you love one another. John 15:12, 17.

A new commandment I give unto you: that you love one another; as I have loved you, that you also love one another. John 13:34.

I wept for him that was afflicted, and my soul had compassion on the poor. Job 30:25.

We rejoice that we are weak and you are strong. 1 C. 13:8.

8. WHY WE SHOULD LOVE OUR NEIGHBOR

We being many are one body in Christ, and every one members one of another. Rom. 13:5.

We being many are one bread, one body, all that partake of one bread. 1 C. 10:17.

In one Spirit were we all baptized into one body, whether Jews or Gentiles, whether bond or free; and in one Spirit we have all been made to drink. 1 C. 12:13.

There is neither Jew nor Greek: there is neither bond nor free: there is neither male nor female; for you are all one in Christ Jesus. Gal. 3:28.

One body and one Spirit, as you are called in one hope of your calling. Eph. 4:4.

Owe no man anything, but to love one another. Rom. 13:8.

9. LOVE OF OUR NEIGHBOR IMPOSSIBLE WITHOUT THE LOVE OF GOD

If any man say, I love God, and hateth his brother, he is a liar. For he that loveth not his brother, whom he seeth, how can he love God, whom he seeth not? And this commandment we have from God: that he who loveth God love also his brother. 1 John 4:20 f.

He that loveth not abideth in death. Whosoever hateth his brother is a murderer. 1 John 3:14 f.

Whosoever is not just is not of God, nor he that loveth not his brother. 1 John 3:10.

He that hateth his brother is in darkness, and walketh in darkness, and knoweth not whither he goeth, because the darkness hath blinded his eyes. 1 John 2:11.

Friend, how camest thou in hither, not having on a wedding garment? But he was silent. Then the king said to the waiters: Bind his hands and feet, and cast him into the exterior darkness; there shall be weeping and gnashing of teeth. Mat. 22:12 f.

At last came also the other virgins, saying: Lord, Lord, open to us. But he answering, said: Amen I say to you, I know you not. Mat. 25:11 f.

10. EXAMPLES OF CHARITY TOWARD GOD AND CHRIST OUR LORD

Paul answered and said: What do you mean weeping and afflicting my heart? For I am ready not only to be bound, but to die also in Jerusalem, for the name of the Lord Jesus. Acts 21:13.

Simon, son of John, lovest thou me more than these? He saith to him: Yea, Lord, thou knowest that I love thee. He saith to him: Feed my lambs. John 21:15.

Who shall separate us from the love of Christ? Shall tribulation? or distress? or famine? or nakedness? or danger? or persecution? or the sword? As it is written: For thy sake we are put to death all the day long. We are accounted as sheep for the slaughter. But in all these things we overcome, because of him that hath loved us. For I am sure that neither death, nor life, nor angels, nor principalities, nor powers, nor things present, nor things to come, nor might, nor height, nor depth, nor any other creature shall be able to separate us from the love of God, which is in Christ Jesus our Lord. Rom. 8:35-39.

I judged not myself to know anything among you but Jesus Christ, and him crucified. 1 C. 2:2.

The things that were gain to me, the same I have counted loss for Christ. Furthermore, I count all things to be but loss, for the excellent knowledge of Jesus Christ my Lord; for whom I have suffered the loss of all things, and count them but as dung, that I may gain Christ. Phil. 3:7 f.

11. EXAMPLES OF CHARITY TOWARD OUR NEIGHBOR

Either forgive them this trespass, or if thou do not, strike me out of the book thou hast written. Ex. 32:31 f.

Why [asked Moses] hast thou emulation for me? O that all the people might prophesy, and that the Lord would give them his Spirit! Num. 11:29.

David said to the Lord, when he saw the angel striking the people: It is I, I am he that have sinned; I have done wickedly. These that are the sheep, what have they done? Let thy hand, I beseech thee, be turned against me, and against my father's house. 2 K. 24:17.

Thou knowest all things, and thou knowest that it was not out of pride and contempt, or any desire of glory, that I refused to worship the proud Aman; for I would willingly and readily, for the salvation of Israel, have kissed even the steps of his feet. Esth. 13:12 f.

You know what great battles I and my brethren, and the house of my father, have fought for the laws and the sanctuary, and the distress that we have seen: by reason whereof all my brethren have lost their lives for Israel's sake, and I am left alone. And now far be it from me to spare my life in any time of trouble: for I am not better than my brethren: I will avenge then my nation and the sanctuary, and our children and wives; for all the heathens are gathered together to destroy us out of mere malice. 1 Mac. 13:3-6.

I wished myself to be an anathema from Christ, for my brethren, who are my kinsmen according to the flesh. Rom. 9:3.

You know I have kept back nothing that was profitable to you, but have preached it to you, and taught you publicly and from house to house. Acts 20:20.

With desire I have desired to eat this Pasch with you before I suffer. Luke 22:15.

As the Father hath loved me, I also have loved you. John 15:9.

I long to see you, that I may impart unto you some spiritual grace, to strengthen you: that is to say, that I may be comforted together in you by that which is common to us both, your faith and mine. Rom. 1:11 f.

And I would not have you ignorant, brethren, that I have often purposed to come unto you, and have been hindered hitherto, that I might have some fruit among you also, even as among other Gentiles. Rom. 1:13.

To the Greeks and to the barbarians, to the wise and to the unwise, I am a debtor. So (as much as is in me) I am ready to preach the gospel to you also that are at Rome. Rom. 1:14 f.

Whereas I was free as to all, I made myself the servant of all, that I might gain the more. And I became to the Jews a Jew, that I might gain the Jews. To them that are under the law, as if I were under the law (whereas myself was not under the law), that I might gain them that were under the law. To them that were without the law, as if I were without the law (whereas I was not without the law of Christ), that I might gain them that were without the law. To the weak I became weak, that I might gain the weak. I became all things to all men, that I might save all. And I do all things for the gospel's sake, that I may be made partaker thereof. 1 C. 9:19-23.

12. EJACULATORY PRAYERS TO EXCITE IN OUR HEARTS THE LOVE OF GOD AND OF OUR NEIGHBOR

Lord, Thou knowest all things: thou knowest that I love thee. John 21:17.

I will love thee, O Lord, my strength. The Lord is my firmament, my refuge, and my deliverer. Ps. 17:1.

What have I in heaven? and besides thee what do I desire upon earth? Ps. 72:25.

Turn, O my soul, into thy rest: for the Lord hath been bountiful to thee. For he hath delivered my soul from death; my eyes from tears; my feet from falling. I will please the Lord in the land of the living. Ps. 114:7-9.

As the hart panteth after the fountains of water, so my soul panteth after thee, O my God. Ps. 41:1.

Thou hast delivered my soul that it should not perish, thou hast cast all my sins behind thy back. For hell shall not confess to thee, neither shall death praise thee: nor shall they that go down into the pit look for thy truth. The living, the living, he shall give praise to thee, as I do this day. Is. 38:17-19.

Hear my prayer, O Lord, and my supplication: give ear to my tears. Be not silent: for I am a stranger with thee, and a sojourner, as all my fathers were. O forgive me, that I may be refreshed before I go hence, and be no more. Ps. 38:13-15.

13. ACTS AND EFFECTS OF LOVE, OF WHICH SPIRITUAL JOY IS ONE OF THE FIRST

The fruit of the Spirit is charity, joy. Gal. 5:22.

The kingdom of God is not meat and drink, but justice, and peace, and joy in the Holy Ghost. Rom. 14:17.

The joy of the Lord is our strength. 2 Es. 8:10.

My soul refused to be comforted. I remembered God, and was delighted, and was exercised, and my spirit swooned away. Ps. 76:3.

There is no riches above the riches of the health of the body: and there is no pleasure above the joy of the heart. The joyfulness of the heart is the life of a man, and a never-failing treasure of holiness: and the joy of a man is length of life. A cheerful and good heart is always feasting: for his banquets are prepared with diligence. Ecclus. 30:16, 23, 27.

I will greatly rejoice in the Lord, and my soul shall be joyful in my God: for he hath clothed me with the garments of salvation, and with the robe of justice he hath covered me, as a bridegroom decked with a crown, and as a bride adorned with her jewels. Is. 61:10.

The voice of rejoicing and of salvation is in the tabernacles of the just. Ps. 117:15.

I will bring them into my holy mount, and will make them joyful in my house of prayer. Is. 56:7.

The light of thy countenance, O Lord, is signed upon us: thou hast given gladness in my heart. Ps. 4:7.

I will be glad and rejoice in thee: I will sing to thy name, O thou Most High. I will rejoice in thy salvation. Ps. 9:3, 16.

Thou hast made known to me the ways of life, thou shalt fill me with joy with thy countenance: at thy right hand are delights even to the end. Ps. 15:11.

Thou art my refuge from the trouble which hath encompassed me: my joy, deliver me from them that surround me. Be glad in the Lord, and rejoice, ye just; and glory, all ye right of heart. Ps. 31:7, 11.

For in him our hearts shall rejoice: and in his holy name we have trusted. Ps. 32:21.

Delight in the Lord, and he will give thee the requests of thy heart. Ps. 36:4.

My soul shall rejoice in the Lord, and shall be delighted in his salvation. Ps. 34:9.

Let my heart rejoice, that it may fear thy name. Ps. 85:11.

We are filled in the morning with thy mercy: and we have rejoiced, and are delighted all our days. We have rejoiced for the days in which thou hast humbled us: for the years in which we have seen evils. Ps. 89:14 f.

Whatsoever shall befall the just man, it shall not make him sad. Prov. 12:21.

It is joy to the just to do judgment. Prov. 21:15.

14. INCITEMENTS TO ASPIRE AFTER THIS TRUE JOY

These things I have spoken to you, that my joy may be in you, and your joy may be filled. John 15:11.

Let the just feast and rejoice before God, and be delighted with gladness. Ps. 67:4.

They shall rejoice before thee as they that rejoice in the harvest, as conquerors rejoice after taking a prey when they divide the spoils. Is. 9:3.

Let Israel rejoice in him that made him, and let the children of Sion be joyful in their King. Ps. 149:2.

Delight in the Lord, and he will give thee the requests of thy heart. Ps. 36:4.

Rejoice in the Lord, ye just: praise becometh the upright . Ps. 32:1.

Always rejoice. 1 Thess. 5:16.

The meek shall increase their joy in the Lord, and the poor men shall rejoice in the Holy One of Israel. Is. 29:19.

The kingdom of heaven is like unto a treasure hidden in a field, which a man having found hideth, and for joy thereof goeth and selleth all that he hath, and buyeth that field. Mat. 13:44.

Rejoice in the Lord always; again I say rejoice. Phil. 4:4.

The Eight Beatitudes (Mat. 5:3-10)

Blessed are the poor in spirit; for theirs is the kingdom of heaven.

Blessed are the meek; for they shall possess the land.

Blessed are they that mourn, for they shall be comforted.

Blessed are they that hunger and thirst after justice; for they shall be filled.

Blessed are the merciful; for they shall obtain mercy.

Blessed are the clean of heart; for they shall see God.

Blessed are the peacemakers; for they shall be called the children of God.

Blessed are they that suffer persecution for justice' sake; for theirs is the kingdom of heaven.

15. THE JOY OF THE WICKED VAIN AND FALSE

Many are the scourges of the sinner. Ps. 31:10.

Know thou, and see that it is an evil and a bitter thing for thee to have left the Lord thy God, and that my fear is not with thee, saith the Lord the God of hosts. Jer. 2:19.

This is thy wickedness, because it is bitter, because it hath touched thy heart. Is. 4:18.

Woe to you that call evil good and good evil: that put darkness for light and light for darkness: that put bitter for sweet and sweet for bitter! Is. 5:20.

Laughter I counted error, and to mirth I said: Why art thou vainly deceived? Ecclus. 2:2.

They are glad when they have done evil, and rejoice in most wicked things. Prov. 2:14.

Be afflicted, and mourn, and weep: let your laughter be turned into mourning, and your joy into sorrow. Jas 4:9.

The sinners in Sion are afraid, trembling hath seized upon the hypocrites. Which of you can dwell with devouring fire? Which of you shall dwell with everlasting burnings? Is. 33:14.

Evil pursueth sinners. Prov. 13:21.

Folly is joy to the fool. Prov. 15:24.

16. THE CONSOLATION OF TRUE JOY FLOWING FROM GOD

Blessed be the God and Father of our Lord Jesus Christ, the Father of mercies, and the God of all comfort. 2 C. 1:3.

God, who comforteth the humble, comforted us by the coming of Titus. 2 C. 7:6.

According to the multitude of my sorrows in my heart, thy comforts have given joy to my soul. Ps. 93:19.

You shall draw waters with joy out of the Savior's fountains. Is. 12:3.

My spirit hath rejoiced in God my Savior. Luke 1:47.

Ask, and you shall receive: that your joy may be full. John 16:24.

These things I have spoken to you, that my joy may be in you, and your joy may be filled. John 15:11.

Thou hast made known to me the ways of life: thou shalt make me full of joy with thy countenance. Acts 2:28.

If you partake of the suffering of Christ, rejoice; that when his glory shall be revealed, you may also be glad with exceeding joy 1 Pet. 4:13.

May the trial of your faith be found unto the praise and glory at the appearing of Jesus Christ, whom having not seen you love: in whom also now, though you see him not, you believe, and believing shall rejoice with joy unspeakable and glorified. 1 Pet. 1:8.

Rejoice in the Lord, O ye just: praise becometh the upright. Ps. 32:1.

They being dismissed went down to Antioch: and gathering together the multitude delivered the epistle, which when they had read they rejoiced for the consolation. Acts 15:30 f.

Rejoice in the Lord always; again I say rejoice. Phil. 4:4.

My heart and my flesh have rejoiced in the living God. Ps. 83:3.

What have I in heaven? and besides thee what do I desire upon earth? For thee my flesh and my heart fainted away. Thou art the God of my heart, and the God that is my portion forever. Ps. 72:25.

My soul doth magnify the Lord, and my spirit hath rejoiced in God my Savior. Luke 1:46 f.

Thou hast turned for me my mourning into joy: thou hast cut my sackcloth, and hast compassed me with gladness. Ps. 29:12.

Blessed are they that mourn; for they shall be comforted. Mat. 5:5.

O Lord, thou art my God: I will exalt thee, and give glory to thy name; for thou hast done wonderful things. Thou hast been a strength to the poor, a strength to the needy in his distress: a refuge from the whirlwind, a shadow from the heat. Is. 25:1, 4.

17. HUMAN CONSOLATION VAIN AND UNSTABLE

You are all troublesome comforters. Job 16:2.

I said in my heart: I will go and abound with delights, and enjoy good things And I saw that this also was vanity. Eccles. 2:1.

Give us help from trouble: for vain is the salvation of man. Ps. 59:13.

I looked for one that would grieve together with me, but there was none: and for one that would comfort, and I found none. Ps. 68:21.

All things have their seasons: a time to weep and a time to laugh, a time to mourn and a time to dance. Eccles. 3:4.

Laughter shall be mingled with sorrow, and mourning taketh hold of the end of joy. Prov. 14:13.

18. PEACE AND THE AUTHOR OF PEACE

A Child is born to us, and his name shall be called the Prince of peace. Is. 9:6.

Being justified therefore by faith, let us have peace with God. Rom. 5:1.

He is our peace, who hath made both one, and breaking down the middle wall of partition, the enmities in his flesh, that he might make the two in himself into one new man, making peace. Eph. 2:14.

The work of justice shall be peace, and the service of justice quietness, and security forever. And my people shall sit in the beauty of peace, and in the tabernacles of confidence, and in wealthy rest. Is. 32:17 f.

Much peace have they that love thy law; and to them there is no stumbling block. Ps. 118:165.

Grace be unto you and peace from him that is. Apoc. 1:4.

In his days shall justice spring up, and abundance of peace. Ps. 71:7.

The Lord turn his countenance to thee, and give thee peace. Num. 6:26.

When he granteth peace, who is there that can condemn? Job 34:29.

The Lord will bless his people with peace. Ps. 28:10.

When the ways of man shall please the Lord, he will convert even his enemies to peace. Prov. 16:7.

The work of justice shall be peace, and the service of justice quietness, and security forever. Is. 32:17.

Blessed are the peacemakers; for they shall be called the children of God. Mat. 5:9.

Have peace among you. Mark 9:49.

The peace of God, which surpasseth all understanding, keep your hearts and minds in Christ Jesus. Phil. 4:7.

The Lord of peace himself give you everlasting peace in every place. The Lord be with you all. 2 Thess. 3:16.

Follow peace with all men, and holiness; without which no man shall see God. Heb. 12:14.

The fruit of justice is sown in peace, to them that make peace. Jas. 3:18.

The God of patience and of comfort grant you to be of one mind one towards another, according to Jesus Christ. Rom. 15:5.

Grace be with you, mercy, and peace from God the Father, and from Christ Jesus, the Son of the Father, in truth and charity. 2 John 3.

These things I have spoken to you, that in me you may have peace. In the world you shall have distress; but have confidence, I have overcome the world. John 16:33.

Peace I leave with you, my peace I give unto you: not as the world giveth do I give unto you. Let not your heart be troubled, nor let it be afraid. John 14:27.

Glory be to God in the highest, and on earth peace to men of good will. Luke 2:14.

Peace be to you: it is I, fear not. Luke 24:36.

I will give peace in your coasts: you shall sleep, and there shall be none to make you afraid. I will take away evil beasts; and the sword shall not pass through your quarters. I will look on you and make you increase. Lev. 26:6, 9.

Holy Father, keep them in thy name whom thou hast given me: that they may be one, as we also are. And not for them only to I pray, but for them also who through their word shall believe in me: that they also may be one in us, that the world may believe that thou hast sent me. John 17:11, 20 f.

If it be possible, as much as is in you [have] peace with all men. Rom. 12:18.

The fruit of justice is sown in peace to them that make peace. Jas. 3:18.

The kingdom of God is not meat and drink; but justice and peace, and joy in the Holy Ghost. Rom. 14:17.

Let us follow after the things that are of peace, and keep the things that are of edification one towards another. Rom. 14:19.

God is not the God of dissension, but of peace: as also I teach in all the churches of the saints. 1 C. 14:33.

I beseech you [to be] careful to keep the unity of the Spirit in the bond of peace. Eph. 4:5.

Follow peace with all men, and holiness: without which no man shall see God. Heb. 12:14.

He that will love life and see good days, let him refrain his tongue from evil, and his lips that they speak no guile. Let him decline from evil, and do good: let him seek after peace and pursue it. 1 Pet. 3:10 f.

Have salt in you, and have peace among you. Mark 9:49.

I beseech of you, brethren, by the name of our Lord Jesus Christ, that you all speak the same thing, and that there be no schisms among you: but that you be perfect in the same mind and in the same judgment. 1 C. 1:10.

If there be any consolation in Christ, if any comfort of charity, if any society of the Spirit, if any bowels of commiseration, fulfil ye my joy, that you be of one mind, having the same charity, being of one accord, agreeing in sentiment. Let nothing be done through contention. Phil. 2:1-3.

Behold how good and how pleasant it is for brethren to dwell together in unity. Ps. 132:1.

19. PEACE COMMENDED BY THE APOSTLES

The peace of God, which surpasseth all understanding, keep your hearts and minds in Christ Jesus. Phil. 4:7.

Be of one mind one towards another. Rom. 12:16.

The God of patience and of comfort grant you to be of one mind one towards another, according to Jesus Christ: that with one mind and with one mouth you may glorify God and the Father of our Lord Jesus Christ. Rom. 15:5 f.

If you partake of the suffering of Christ, rejoice that when his glory shall be revealed you may also be glad with exceeding joy. 1 Pet. 4:13.

I beseech you, brethren, by the name of our Lord Jesus Christ, that you all speak the same thing, and that there be no schisms among you; but that you be perfect in the same mind and in the same judgment. 1 C. 1:10.

Let the peace of Christ rejoice in your hearts, wherein also you are called in one body. Col. 3:15.

Let your conversation be worthy of the gospel of Christ: that whether I come and see you, or being absent may hear of you, that you stand fast in one spirit, with one mind laboring together for the faith of the gospel. Phil. 1:27.

Glory, and honor, and peace to every one that worketh good: to the Jew first and also to the Greek. Rom. 2:10.

That we be of the same mind, let us continue in the same rule. Phil. 3:16.

The kingdom of God is not meat and drink; but justice and peace, and joy in the Holy Ghost. Rom. 14:17.

20. EXAMPLES OF CONCORD

All they that believed were together, and had all things in common. Acts 2:44.

The multitude of believers had but one heart and one soul; neither did any one say that aught of the things which he possessed was his own, but all things were common unto them. Acts 4:32.

They were all with one accord in Solomon's porch. Acts 5:12.

The seventh month was come, and the children of Israel were in their cities, and the people gathered themselves together as one man to Jerusalem. 1 Es. 2:1.

They [the Apostles] were persevering with one mind in prayer with the women, and Mary the mother of Jesus, and with his brethren. Acts 1:14.

21. REWARDS OF MERCY

I desired mercy and not sacrifice, and the knowledge of God more than holocausts. Osee 6:6.

I will show thee, O man, what is good, and what the Lord requireth of thee: verily to do judgment, and to love mercy, and to walk solicitous with thy God. Mich. 6:8.

Blessed are the merciful; for they shall obtain mercy. Mat. 5:7.

Acceptable is the man that showeth mercy and lendeth: he shall order his words with judgment, because he shall not be moved forever. Ps. 111:5.

Brethren are a help in the time of trouble; but mercy shall deliver more than they. Ecclus. 40:24.

But love ye your enemies: do good, and lend, hoping for nothing thereby: and your reward shall be great, and you shall be the sons of the Highest; for he is kind to the unthankful and to the evil. Be ye therefore merciful, as your Father also is merciful. Luke 6:35 f.

Judge not, and you shall not be judged. Condemn not, and you shall not be condemned. Forgive, and you shall be forgiven. Give, and it shall be given to you: good measure and pressed down and shaken together and running over shall they give into your bosom. For with the same measure that you shall mete withal it shall be measured to you again. Luke 6:37 f.

God is not unjust, that he should forget your work, and the love you have shown in his name, you who have ministered and do minister to the saints. Heb. 6:10.

22. WORKS OF MERCY

Thus saith the Lord of hosts: Judge ye true judgment, and show ye mercy and compassion every man to his brother. Zach. 7:9.

Shouldst not thou then have had compassion on thy fellow servant, even as I had compassion on thee? Mat. 18:33.

Remember them that are in bands, as if you were bound with them; and them that labor, as being yourselves also in the body. Heb. 13:3.

Be not slow to visit the sick; for by these things thou shalt be confirmed in love. Ecclus. 7:39.

Be not wanting in comforting them that weep, and walk with them that mourn. Ecclus. 7:38.

Deliver him that suffereth wrong out of the hand of the proud, and be not fainthearted in thy soul. Ecclus. 4:9.

Recover thy neighbor according to thy power, and take heed to thyself that thou fall not. Ecclus. 29:26.

Examples of Hospitality

1. Jesus entertains 5,000 in the desert. Mat. 14:14.
2. The 4,000 in the desert. Mat. 15:32.
3. His disciples on the shores of the Lake of Galilee. John 21:12.
4. Two disciples entertain Jesus at Emmaus. Luke 24:29.
5. Zacheus entertains our Lord "with joy." Luke 19:5.
6. Simon the tanner entertains St. Peter. Acts 10:6.
7. Lydia entertains St. Paul. Acts 16:14.
8. Publius "courteously" entertains St. Paul in the island of Melita for three days. Acts 28:7.
9. Gaius praised for his charity to strangers. 3 John 5.
10. Melchisedech entertains Abram. Gen. 14:18.
11. Abraham entertains angels. Gen. 18:3.
12. Laban entertains Abram's steward. Gen. 24:31.
13. Jethro entertains Moses when fleeing into Madian. Ex. 2:20.
14. Job, "whose door was open to the traveler." Job 31:32.
15. The widow woman of Sarepta entertains Elias. 3 K. 17:10.
16. The Sunamitess entertains Eliseus. 4 K. 4:8.
17. Eliseus entertains the Syrian robbers. 4 K. 6:22.
18. The Israelites entertain David fleeing from Saul. 1 Par. 12:38.

Judgment without mercy to him that hath not done mercy. And mercy exalteth itself above judgment. Jas. 2:13.

Shouldst not thou then have had compassion on thy fellow servant, even as I had compassion on thee? And his lord being angry delivered him to the torturers until he paid all the debt. Mat. 18:33 f.

23. ALMSGIVING

Son, defraud not the poor of alms, and turn not away thy eyes from the poor. Ecclus. 4:1.

Bow down thy ear cheerfully to the poor, and pay what thou owest, and answer peaceable words with mildness. Ecclus. 4:8.

Do not forget to do good and to impart; for by such sacrifices God's favor is obtained. Heb. 13:16.

By charity serve one another. Gal. 5:13.

He who soweth sparingly shall also reap sparingly; and he that soweth in blessings shall also reap in blessings. 2 C. 9:6.

According to thy ability be merciful. If thou have much, give abundantly; if thou have little, take care even so to bestow willingly a little. Tob. 4:8 f.

Amen I say to you, this poor widow hath cast in more than all they who have cast into the treasury. For all they did cast in of their abundance; but she of her want cast in all she had, even her whole living. Mark 12:43 f.

Give alms out of thy substance, and turn not away thy face from any poor person; for so it shall come to pass that the face of the Lord shall not be turned from thee. Tob. 4:7.

Eat thy bread with the hungry and the needy, and with thy garments cover the naked. Tob. 4:17.

When thou dost an almsdeed, sound not a trumpet before thee, as the hypocrites do in the synagogues and in the streets, that they may be honored by men. Amen I say to you, they have received their reward. But when thou dost alms, let not thy left hand know what thy right hand doth, that thy alms may be in secret; and thy Father, who seeth in secret, will repay thee. Mat. 6:2-4.

Every one as he hath determined in his heart, [let him give] not with sadness or of necessity: for God loveth a cheerful giver. 2 C. 9:7.

My son, in thy good deeds make no complaint: and when thou givest anything, add not grief by an evil word. Shall not the dew assuage the heat? so also the good word is better than the gift. So is not a word better than a gift? but both are with a justified man. Ecclus. 18:15-18.

Make thyself affable to the congregation of the poor. Ecclus. 4:7.

Afflict not the heart of the needy, and defer not to give to him that is in distress. Reject not the petition of the afflicted, and turn not way thy face from the needy. Ecclus. 4:3 f.

Say not to thy friend: Go and come again, and tomorrow I will give to thee, when thou canst give at present. Prov. 3:28.

As your mind is forward to be willing, so it may be also to perform out of that which you have. For if the will be forward, it is accepted according to that which a man hath, not according to that which he hath not. 2 C. 8:11 f.

Do good to thy friend before thou die, and according to thy ability stretch out thy hand, and give to the poor. Before thy death work justice; for in hell there is no finding food. Ecclus. 14:13, 17.

In the morning sow thy seed, and in the evening let not thy hand cease; for thou knowest not which may rather spring up, this or that: and if both together, it shall be the better. Eccles. 11:6.

In doing good let us not fail; for in due time we shall reap, not failing. Therefore whilst we have time let us work good to all men, but especially to those who are of the household of the faith. Gal. 6:9 f.

But you, brethren, be not weary in well-doing. 2 Thess. 3:13.

Sell what you possess, and give alms; make to yourselves bags which grow not old, a treasure in heaven that faileth not, where no thief approacheth, nor moth corrupteth. Luke 12:33.

Make unto you friends of the mammon of iniquity, that when you shall fail they may receive you into everlasting dwellings. Luke 16:9.

Do not withhold him from doing good who is able: if thou art able, do good thyself also. Prov. 3:27.

Let thy fountains be conveyed abroad, and in the streets divide thy waters. Prov. 5:16.

Let not thy hand be stretched out to receive, and shut when thou shouldst give. Ecclus. 4:36.

As in all things you abound in faith, and the word, and knowledge, and all carefulness: moreover also in your charity towards us, so in this grace may you also abound. I speak not as commanding, but by the carefulness of others, approving also the good disposition of your charity. For you know the grace of our Lord Jesus Christ, that being rich he became poor, for your sakes; that through his poverty you might be rich. 2 C. 8:7-9.

24. FRUITS OF ALMSGIVING

The lips of many shall bless him that is liberal of his bread, and the testimony of his truth is faithful. Ecclus. 31:28.

He that is inclined to mercy shall be blessed; for of his bread he hath given to the poor. Prov. 22:9.

Let my counsel be acceptable to thee, and redeem thou thy sins with alms, and thy iniquities with works of mercy to the poor: perhaps he will forgive thy offences. Dan. 4:24.

In this present time let your abundance supply their want, that their abundance also may supply your want. 2 C. 8:14.

He that showeth mercy to the poor shall be blessed. Prov. 14:21.

Whosoever shall give to drink to one of these little ones a cup of cold water only, in the name of a disciple, amen I say to you, he shall not lose his reward. Mat. 10:42.

Water quencheth a flaming fire, and alms resisteth sins: and God provideth for him that showeth favor. He remembereth him afterwards, and in the time of his fall he shall find a sure stay. Ecclus. 3:33 f.

Blessed is he that understandeth concerning the needy and the poor: the Lord will deliver him in the evil day. The Lord preserve him and give him life, and make him blessed upon earth, and deliver him not up to the will of his enemies. Ps. 40:1 f.

Help the poor because of the commandment: and send him not away empty-handed because of his poverty. Lose thy money for thy brother and thy friend, and hide it not under a stone to be lost. Place thy treasures in the commandments of the Most High, and it shall bring thee more profit than gold. Shut up alms in the heart of the poor, and it shall obtain help for thee against all evil. Better than the shield of the mighty, and better than the spear; it shall fight for thee against thy enemy. Ecclus. 29:12-17.

Prayer is good with fasting and alms, more than to lay up treasures of gold; for alms delivereth from death: and the same is that which purgeth away sins, and maketh to find mercy and life everlasting. Tob. 12:8 f.

Give alms: and behold all things are clean unto you. Luke 11:41.

The ransom of a man's life are his riches: but he that is poor beareth not reprehension. Prov. 13:8.

The relieving of thy father shall not be forgotten; for good shall be repaid to thee for the sin of thy mother. And in justice thou shalt be built up, and in the day of affliction thou shalt be remembered: and thy sins shall melt away as the ice in the fair warm weather. Ecclus. 3:15-17.

Stretch out thy hand to the poor, that thy expiation and thy blessing may be perfected. Ecclus. 7:36.

He that ministereth seed to the sower will both give you bread to eat, and will multiply your seed, and increase the growth of your fruits of justice. That being enriched in all things, you may abound unto all simplicity, which worketh through us thanksgiving to God. 2 C. 9:10 f.

Honor the Lord with thy substance, and give him the first of all thy fruits; and thy barns shall be filled with abundance, and thy presses shall run over with wine. Prov. 3:9 f.

I know thy charity. Apoc. 2:19.

Some distribute their own goods, and grow richer; others take away what is not their own, and are always in want. The soul which blesseth shall be made fat; and he that inebriateth shall be inebriated also himself. Prov. 11:24 f.

He that giveth to the poor shall not want; he that despiseth his entreaty shall suffer indigence. Prov. 28:27.

These were men of mercy, whose godly deeds have not failed. Ecclus. 44:10.

He that oppresseth the poor upbraideth his Maker; but he that hath pity on the poor honoreth him. Prov. 14:31.

25. EXAMPLES OF ALMSGIVING

Tobias daily went among all his kindred, and comforted them, and distributed to every one as he was able out of his goods. Tob. 1:19.

After the Sabbath they divided the spoils to the feeble and the orphans and the widows, and the rest they took for themselves. 2 Mac. 8:28.

In Joppe there was a certain disciple named Tabitha, which by interpretation is called Dorcas. This woman was full of good works and almsdeeds which she did. Acts 9:36.

There was a certain man in Caesarea named Cornelius, a centurion of that which is called the Italian band: a religious man, and fearing God with all his house, giving much alms to the people. Acts 10:1 f.

The disciples, every man according to his ability, purposed to send relief to the brethren who dwelt in Judea: which also they did, sending it to the ancients by the hands of Barnabas and Saul. Acts 11:29 f.

Zacheus, standing, said to the Lord: Behold, Lord, the half of my goods I give to the poor; and if I have wronged any man of anything, I restore him fourfold. Jesus said to him: This day is salvation come to this house, because he also is a son of Abraham. Luke 19:8 f.

God is not unjust that he should forget your work, and the love which you have shown in his name, you who have ministered and do minister to the saints. Heb. 6:10.

26. THE SIN AND PUNISHMENT OF SELFISHNESS

He that despiseth his neighbor sinneth, but he that showeth mercy to the poor shall be blessed. Prov. 14:21.

If a brother or sister be naked, and want daily food, and one of you say to them: Go in peace, be you warmed and filled, yet give them not those things that are necessary for the body, what shall it profit? Jas. 2:15 f.

He that hath the substance of this world, and shall see his brother in need, and shall shut up his bowels from him, how doth the charity of God abide in him? 1 John 3:17.

The bread of the needy is the life of the poor: he that defraudeth them thereof is a man of blood. He that taketh away bread begotten by sweat is like him that killeth his neighbor. Ecclus. 34:25 f.

Turn not away thy eyes from the poor, for fear of anger; and leave not to them that ask thee to curse thee behind thy back. For the prayer of him that curseth in the bitterness of his soul shall be heard; for he that made him will hear him. Ecclus. 4:5 f.

He that stoppeth his ear against the cry of the poor shall also cry himself, and shall not be heard. Prov. 21:13.

He that offereth sacrifice of the goods of the poor is as one that sacrificeth the son in presence of the father. Ecclus. 34:24.

Am I my brother's keeper? Gen. 4:9.

All have turned aside into their own way, every one after his own gain, from the first even to the last. Is. 56:11.

Who is there among you that will shut the doors, and will kindle the fire on my altar gratis? I have no pleasure in you, saith the Lord of hosts; and I will not receive a gift of your hands. Mal. 1:10.

He that loveth his life shall lose it. John 12:25.

In the last days shall come dangerous times. Men shall be lovers of themselves. 2 Tim. 3:1 f.

All seek the things that are their own, not the things that are Jesus Christ's. Phil. 2:21.

27. FRATERNAL CORRECTION

If thy brother shall offend against thee, go and rebuke him between thee and him alone. If he shall hear thee, thou shalt gain thy brother. If he will not hear thee, take with thee one or two more, that in the mouth of one or two witnesses every word may stand; and if he will not hear them, tell the Church. And if he will not hear the Church, let him be to thee as the heathen and publican. Mat. 18:15-17.

Thou shalt not hate thy brother in thy heart, but reprove him openly, lest thou incur sin through him. Lev. 19:17.

Reproofs of instruction are the way of life. Prov. 6:23.

The just man shall correct me in mercy, and shall reprove me. Ps. 140:5.

He that rebuketh a man shall afterwards find favor with him more than he that by a flattering tongue deceiveth him. Prov. 28:23.

He that loveth correction loveth knowledge: but he that hateth reproof is foolish. Prov. 12:1.

It is better to be rebuked by a wise man than to be deceived by the flattery of fools. Ecclus. 7:6.

A man that is prudent and well instructed will not murmur when he is reproved. Ecclus. 10:28.

Before thou inquire, blame no man: when thou hast inquired, reprove justly. Ecclus. 11:7.

I myself, my brethren, am assured of you, that you also are full of love, replenished with all knowledge, so that you are able to admonish one another. Rom. 15:14.

We beseech you, brethren, rebuke the unquiet. 1 Thess. 5:14.

Have no fellowship with the unfruitful works of darkness, but rather reprove them. Eph. 5:11.

Exhort one another every day, whilst it is called today, lest any of you be hardened by the deceitfulness of sin. Heb. 3:13.

Them that sin reprove before all, that the rest also may have fear. 1 Tim. 5:20.

Reverence not thy neighbor in his fall: and refrain not to speak in the time of salvation. Ecclus. 4:27.

Be not ashamed to inform the unwise and foolish, and the aged that are judged by young men: and thou shalt be well instructed in all things, and well approved in the sight of all men living. Ecclus. 42:8.

The wicked man impudently hardeneth his face: but he that is righteous correcteth his way. Prov. 21:29.

An ancient man rebuke not: but entreat him as a father: young men as brethren, young women as sisters, in all chastity. 1 Tim. 5:1 f.

Kindle not the coals of sinners by rebuking them, lest thou be burnt with the flame of the fire of their sins. Ecclus. 8:13.

The just man shall correct me in mercy, and shall reprove me: but let not the oil of the sinner fatten my head. Ps. 140:5.

With modesty admonish them that resist truth: if peradventure God may give them repentance to know the truth, and they may recover themselves from the snares of the devil, by whom they are held captive at his will. 2 Tim. 2:25 f.

Do not esteem him as an enemy,

but admonish him as a brother. 2 Tim. 3:15.

If a man be overtaken in any fault, you, who are spiritual, instruct such a one in the spirit of meekness, considering thyself, lest thou also be tempted. Gal. 6:1.

Reprove a friend, lest he may not have understood, and say: I did it not; or if he did it, that he may do it no more. Reprove thy neighbor, for it may be he hath not said it: and if he hath said it. that he may not say it again. Admonish thy friend; for there is often a fault committed. And believe not every word. Ecclus. 19:13-16.

Reprove, entreat, rebuke in all patience and doctrine. Titus 4:2.

Rebuke them sharply, that they may be sound in the faith. Titus 1:13.

These things speak, and exhort, and rebuke with all authority. Let no man despise thee. Titus 2:15.

Some indeed reprove, being judged. Jude 22.

We beseech you, brethren, rebuke the unquiet. 1 Thess. 3:14.

How much better it is to reprove than to be angry, and not to hinder him that confesseth in prayer! Ecclus. 20:1.

Admonish thy neighbor before thou threaten him, and give place to the fear of the Most High. Ecclus. 19:17 f.

He that teacheth a scorner doth an injury to himself: and he that rebuketh a wicked man getteth himself a blot. Rebuke not a scorner, lest he hate thee. Rebuke a wise man, and he will love thee. Give an occasion to a wise man, and wisdom shall be added to him. Teach a just man, and he shall make haste to receive it. Prov. 9:7-9.

A wise son heareth the doctrine of his father: but he that is a scorner heareth not when he is reproved. Prov. 13:1.

Why seest thou the mote that is in thy brother's eye, and seest not the beam that is in thy own eye? Or how sayest thou to thy brother: Let me cast the mote out of thy eye; and behold a beam is in thy own eye? Thou hypocrite! cast out first the beam out of thy own eye, and then thou shalt see to cast out the mote out of thy brother's eye. Mat. 7:3-5.

Am I then become your enemy, because I tell you the truth? Gal. 4:16.

A reproof availeth more with a wise man than a hundred stripes with a fool. Prov. 17:10.

The perverse are hard to be corrected, and the number of fools is infinite. Eccles. 1:15.

Consider the works of God, that no man can correct whom he hath despised. Ecclus. 7:14.

He that hateth to be reproved walketh in the trace of a sinner: and he that feareth God will turn to his own heart. Ecclus. 21:7.

Persevere under discipline. Heb. 12:7.

How good is it, when thou art reproved, to show repentance! for so thou shalt escape wilful sin. Ecclus. 20:4.

A man that is prudent and well instructed will not murmur when he is reproved. Ecclus. 10:28.

Poverty and shame to him that refuseth instruction: but he that yieldeth to reproof shall be glorified. Prov. 13:18.

A fool laugheth at the instruction of his father; but he that regardeth reproof shall become more prudent. Prov. 15:5.

The ear that heareth the reproofs of life shall abide in the midst of the wise. Prov. 15:31.

He that rejecteth instruction despiseth his own soul: but he that yieldeth to reproof possesseth understanding. Prov. 15:32.

The man that with a stiff neck despiseth him that reproveth him shall suddenly be destroyed, and health shall not follow him. Prov. 29:1.

The way of life to him that observeth correction: but he that forsaketh reproofs goeth astray. Prov. 10:17.

He that hateth chastisement shall have less life. Ecclus. 19:5.

Instruction is grievous to him that forsaketh the way of life: he that hateth reproof shall die. Prov. 15:10.

A sinful man will flee reproof, and will find an excuse according to his will. Ecclus. 32:21.

As an earring of gold and a bright pearl, so is he that reproveth the wise, and the obedient ear. Prov. 25:12.

It is better to be rebuked by a wise man than to be deceived with the flattery of fools; for as the crackling of thorns burning under a pot, so is the laughter of a fool: now this also is vanity. Eccles. 7:6 f.

Better are the wounds of a friend than the deceitful kisses of an enemy. Prov. 27:6.

Going out the next day, he [Moses] saw two Hebrews quarrelling; and he said to him that did the wrong: Why strikest thou thy neighbor? But he answered: Who hath appointed thee prince and judge over us? Wilt thou kill me, as thou didst yesterday kill the Egyptian? Ex. 2:13 f.

They [the Israelites] sent messengers to all the tribes of Benjamin, to say to them: Why hath so great an abomination been found among you? Deliver up the men of Gabaa that have committed this heinous crime, that they may die, and the evil may be taken out of Israel. Judg. 20:12 f.

And Elias coming to all the people, said: How long do you halt between two sides? If the Lord be God, follow him; but if Baal, then follow him. And the people did not answer him a word. 3 K. 18:21.

Tobias rebuked them, saying: Speak not so; for we are the children of saints, and look for that life which God will give to those that never change their faith from him. Tob. 2:17 f.

Thus saith all the people of the Lord: What meaneth this transgression? Why have you forsaken the Lord the God of Israel, building a sacrilegious altar, and revolting from the worship of him? Jos. 22:16.

I was exceedingly angry when I heard their cry, and my heart thought with myself: and I rebuked the nobles and magistrates, and said to them: Do you every one exact usury of your brethren? And I gathered together a great assembly against them. 2 Es. 5:6 f.

I pleaded the matter against the magistrates, and said: Why have we forsaken the house of God? 2 Es. 13:11.

O generation of vipers, how can you speak good things, whereas you are evil? for out of the abundance of the heart the mouth speaketh. Mat. 12:34.

Herod had apprehended John, and bound him, and put him in prison, because of Herodias, his brother's wife; for John said to him: It is not lawful for thee to have her. Mat. 14:3 f.

I have told you before, and foretell, as present and now absent, to them that sinned before, and to all the rest, that if I come again I will not spare. Do you seek a proof of Christ who speaketh in me, who towards you is not weak, but is mighty in you? 2 C. 13:2 f.

The other [thief] answering, rebuked him, saying: Neither dost thou fear God, seeing thou art under the same condemnation? And we indeed justly; for we receive the due reward of our deeds, but this man hath done no evil. Luke 23:40 f.

28. HATRED OF GOD AND OF OUR NEIGHBOR

All that hate me love death. Prov. 8:36.

Have I not hated them, O Lord, that hated thee, and pined away because of thy enemies? Prov. 138:21.

Esau always hated Jacob for the blessing wherewith his father had blessed him; and he said in his heart: The days will come of the mourning for my father, and I will kill my brother Jacob. Gen. 27:41.

They have hated him that rebuketh

in the gate; and have abhorred him that speaketh perfectly. Amos 5:10.

You shall be hated by all nations for my name's sake. Mat. 24:9.

If the world hate you, know ye that it hath hated me before you. John 15:18.

They hated me without cause. John 15:25.

He that loveth not abideth in death. Whosoever hateth his brother is a murderer. And you know that no murderer hath eternal life abiding in himself. 1 John 3:14 f.

He that saith he is in the light, and hateth his brother, is in darkness even until now. He that loveth his brother abideth in the light, and there is no scandal in him. But he that hateth his brother is in darkness, and walketh in darkness, and knoweth not whither he goeth, because the darkness hath blinded his eyes. 1 John 2:9-11.

By slothfulness a building shall be brought down, and through the weakness of hands the house shall drop through. Eccles. 10:18.

The sluggard is pelted with a dirty stone, and all men will speak of his disgrace. The sluggard is pelted with the dung of oxen, and every one that toucheth him will shake his hands. Ecclus. 22:1 f.

The fool foldeth his hands together, and eateth his own flesh, saying: Better is a handful with rest than both hands full with labor and vexation of mind. Eccles. 4:5 f.

His watchmen are all blind, they are all ignorant; dumb dogs, not able to bark; seeing vain things, sleeping and loving dreams. Is. 56:10.

All the Athenians and strangers that were there employed themselves in nothing else but either in telling or in hearing some new thing. Acts 17:21.

Slothfulness casteth into a deep sleep, and an idle soul shall suffer hunger. Prov. 19:15.

The sluggard willeth and willeth not. Prov. 13:4.

Hast thou seen a man swift in his work? he shall stand before kings, and shall not be before those that are obscure. Prov. 22:29.

29. ENVY

By the envy of the devil death came into the world: and they follow him that are of his side. Wis. 2:24 f.

Envy slayeth the little one. Job 5:2.

Neither will I go with consuming envy; for such a man shall not be partaker of wisdom. Wis. 6:25.

If you have bitter zeal, and there be contentions in your hearts, glory not, and be not liars against the truth. For this is not wisdom descending from above; but earthly, sensual, devilish. For where envy and contention is, there is inconstancy and every evil work. Jas. 3:14-16.

If you bite and devour one another, take heed you be not consumed one of another. Gal. 5:15.

Soundness of heart is the life of the flesh; but envy is the rottenness of the bones. Prov. 14:30.

A man that maketh haste to be rich, and envieth others, is ignorant that poverty shall come upon him. Prov. 28:22.

Be not emulous of evildoers; nor envy them that work iniquity. Envy not the man who prospereth in his way, the man who doth unjust things. Have no emulation to do evil. Ps. 36:1, 7 f.

Let not thy heart envy sinners; but be thou in the fear of the Lord all the day long. Prov. 23:17.

Instead of a friend become not an enemy to thy neighbor; for an evil man shall inherit reproach and shame: so shall every sinner that is envious and double-tongued. Ecclus. 6:1.

The eye of the envious is wicked; and he turneth away his face, and despiseth his own soul. Ecclus. 14:8.

To envy doth the spirit covet which dwelleth in you. Jas. 4:5.

Whereas there is among you envying and contention, are you not carnal, and walk according to man? 1 C. 3:3.

Charity envieth not. 1 C. 13:4.

Let us walk honestly, as in the day; not in contention and envy. Rom. 13:13.

The works of the flesh are manifest, which are: contentions, emulations, dissensions, sects, envies, and suchlike. Of the which I foretell you, as I have foretold to you, that they who do such things shall not obtain the kingdom of God. Gal. 5:19-21.

Let us not be made desirous of vainglory, provoking one another, envying one another. Gal. 5:26.

Laying away all malice and envies. 1 Pet. 2:1.

I considered all the labors of men, and I remarked that their industries are exposed to the envy of their neighbor: so in this also there is vanity and fruitless care. Eccles. 4:4.

Envy not the glory and riches of a sinner; for thou knowest not what his ruin shall be. Ecclus. 9:16.

Envy not the unjust man, and do not follow his ways. Prov. 3:31.

30. STRIFE

When the wood faileth, the fire shall go out; and when the talebearer is taken away, contentions shall cease. As coals are to burning coals, and wood to fire, so an angry man stirreth up strife. Prov. 26:20 f.

Whereas there is among you envying and contention, are you not carnal, and walk according to man? 1 C. 3:3.

Six things there are which the Lord hateth, and the seventh his soul detesteth. A deceitful witness that uttereth lies, and him that soweth discord among brethren. Prov. 6:16,19.

There arose a strife between the herdsmen of Abram and of Lot. Gen. 13:7.

If a wise man contend with a fool, whether he be angry or laugh, he shall find no rest. Prov. 29:9.

Strive not with a powerful man, lest thou fall into his hands. Contend not with a rich man, lest he bring an action against thee. For gold and silver hath destroyed many, and hath reached even to the heart of kings, and perverted them. Strive not with a man that is full of tongue, and heap not wood upon his fire. Ecclus. 8:1-4.

A passionate man kindleth strife, and a sinful man will trouble his friends, and bring in debate in the midst of them that are at peace. Ecclus. 28:11.

It is an honor for a man to separate himself from quarrels; but all fools are meddling with reproaches. Prov. 20:3.

Refrain from strife, and thou shalt diminish thy sins. Ecclus. 28:10.

If a man will contend with thee in judgment, and take away thy coat, let go thy cloak also unto him. Mat. 5:40.

Cast out the scoffer, and contention shall go out with him, and quarrels and reproaches shall cease. Prov. 22:10.

He that boasteth and puffeth up himself stirreth up quarrels. Prov. 28:25.

An evil man always seeketh quarrels; but a cruel angel shall be sent against him. Prov. 17:11.

The lips of a fool intermeddle with strife, and his mouth provoketh quarrels. Prov. 18:6.

Where envying and contention is, there is inconstancy and every evil work. Jas. 3:16.

A hasty contention kindleth a fire: and a hasty quarrel sheddeth blood: and a tongue that beareth witness bringeth death. Ecclus. 28:13.

Better is a dry morsel with joy than a house full of victims with strife. Prov. 17:1.

A man that is an apostate walketh with a perverse mouth. At all times he soweth discord; to such a one his destruction shall presently come, and he shall suddenly be destroyed, and shall no longer have any remedy. Prov. 6:12, 14 f.

Let nothing be done through contention, neither by vainglory. Phil. 2:3.

Contend not in words, for it is to no profit, but to the subverting of the hearers. 2 Tim. 2:14.

Avoid foolish and unlearned questions, knowing that they beget strifes: but the servant of the Lord must not wrangle. 2 Tim. 2:23 f.

If any man seem to be contentious, we have no such custom, nor the Church of God. 1 C. 11:16.

Brother goeth to law with brother, and that before unbelievers. Already indeed there is plainly fault among you, that you have lawsuits one with another. Why do you not rather take wrong? Why do you not rather suffer yourselves to be defrauded? But you do wrong, and defraud: and that to your brethren. 1 C. 6:6-8.

A passionate man provoketh quarrels: and he that is easily stirred up to wrath shall be more prone to sin. Prov. 29:22.

Quarrel not with a passionate man, and go not into the desert with a bold man; for blood is as nothing in his sight, and where there is no help he will overthrow thee. Ecclus. 8:19.

In the quarrels of the proud is the shedding of blood, and their cursing is a grievous hearing. Ecclus. 27:16.

As he that taketh a dog by the ears, so is he that passeth by in anger, and meddleth with another man's quarrel. Prov. 26:17.

31. WAR

Scatter thou the nations that delight in wars. Ps. 67:31.

From whence are wars and contentions among you? Are they not hence, from your concupiscences, which war in your members? Jas. 4:1.

Be of good comfort, O people of God, the memorial of Israel: you have been sold to the Gentiles, not for your destruction; but because you provoked God to wrath, you are delivered to your adversaries. For you have provoked him who made you. Bar. 4:5-7.

O you that of your own good will offered yourselves to danger, bless the Lord. The remnants of the people are saved, the Lord hath fought among the valiant ones. Judg. 5:9, 13.

Designs are strengthened by counsels, and wars are to be managed by governments. Prov. 20:19.

Because war is managed by due ordering: and there shall be safety where there are many counsels. Prov. 24:6.

If thou go to war against thy enemies, and see horsemen and chariots and the numbers of the enemy's army greater than thine, thou shalt not fear them, because the Lord thy God is with thee. And when the battle is now at hand, the priest shall stand before the army, and shall speak to the people in this manner: Hear, O Israel, you join battle this day against your enemies: let not your heart be dismayed, be not afraid, do not give back, fear ye them not: because the Lord your God is in the midst of you, and will fight for you against your enemies, to deliver you from danger. Deut. 20:1-4.

Do manfully, and be of good heart, fear not, nor be ye dismayed at their sight; for the Lord thy God he himself is thy Leader, and will not leave thee nor forsake thee. And the Lord, who is your Leader, he himself will be with thee: he will not leave thee, nor forsake thee: fear not, neither be dismayed. Deut. 31:6, 8.

Cleave ye unto the Lord your God, as you have done unto this day: and then the Lord God will take away before your eyes nations that are great and very strong, and no man shall be able to resist you; one of you shall chase a thousand men of the enemies: because the Lord your God himself will fight for you, as he hath promised: this only take care of with all diligence, that you love the Lord your God. Jos. 23:8, 11.

David said to the messenger: Thus shalt thou say to Joab: Let not this thing discourage thee; for various is the event of war: and sometimes one, sometimes another, is consumed by the sword: encourage thy warriors against the city, and exhort them, that thou mayest overthrow it. 2 K. 11:25.

Behave like men, and take courage: be not afraid or dismayed for the king of the Assyrians, nor for all the multitude that is with him; for there are many more with us than with him. For with him is an arm of flesh: with us the Lord our God, who is our helper, and fighteth for us. 2 Par. 32:7 f.

Thus saith the Lord to you: Fear ye not, and be not dismayed at this multitude; for the battle is not yours, but God's. 2 Par. 20:15.

Be not afraid of them. Remember the Lord, who is great and terrible, and fight for your brethren, your sons, and your daughters, and your wives, and your houses. In what place soever you shall hear the sound of the trumpet, run all thither unto us: our God will fight for us. 2 Es. 4:14, 20.

When they saw the army coming to meet them, they said to Judas: How shall we, being few, be able to fight against so great a multitude, and so strong, and we are ready to faint with fasting today? And Judas said: It is an easy matter for many to be shut up in the hands of a few: and there is no difference in the sight of the God of heaven to deliver with a great multitude or with a small company. For the success of war is not in the multitude of the army, but strength cometh from heaven. They come against us with an insolent multitude and with pride to destroy us, and our wives, and our children, and to take our spoils: but we will fight for our lives and our laws, and the Lord himself will overthrow them before our face: but as for you, fear them not. 1 Mac. 3:17-22.

Judas said: Gird yourselves, and be valiant men, and be ready against the morning, that you may fight with these nations that are assembled against us to destroy us and and our sanctuary: for it is better for us to die in battle than to see the evils of our nation and of the holies: nevertheless as it shall be the will of God in heaven, so be it done. 1 Mac. 3:58-60.

Judas said to the men that were with him: Fear ye not their multitude, neither be ye afraid of their assault. Remember in what manner our fathers were saved in the Red Sea, when Pharao pursued them with a great army. And now let us cry to heaven: and the Lord will have mercy on us, and will remember the covenant of our fathers, and will destroy this army before our face this day: and all nations shall know that there is One that redeemeth and delivereth Israel. 1 Mac. 4:8-11.

32 PRAYERS FOR VICTORY IN WAR

Lord, there is no difference with thee, whether thou help with few or with many: help us, O Lord our God; for with confidence in thee, and in thy name, we are come against this multitude. 2 Par. 14:11.

We have sinned with our fathers, we have done unjustly, we have committed iniquity. Have thou mercy on us, because thou art good, or punish our iniquities by chastising us thyself: and deliver not them that trust in thee to a people that knoweth not thee, that they may not say among the Gentiles: Where is their God? Jdth. 7:19-21.

Thou art our God, who destroyest wars from the beginning, and the Lord is thy name. Lift up thy arm as from the beginning, and crush their power with thy power: let their power fall in their wrath, who promise themselves to violate thy sanctuary. Jdth. 9:10 f.

And now, O Lord, O King, O God of Abraham, have mercy on thy people, because our enemies resolve to destroy us, and extinguish thy inheritance. Despise not thy portion, which thou hast redeemed for thyself. Esth. 13:15 f.

My Lord God, what shall I say, seeing Israel turning their backs to their enemies? And what wilt thou do to thy great name? Jos. 7:8 f.

Bless, O Lord, his strength, and receive the works of his hands. Strike the backs of his enemies, and let not them that hate him rise. Deut. 33:11.

O Lord God of heaven and earth, behold their pride, and look on our low condition, and have regard to the face of thy saints, and show that thou forsakest not them that trust on thee, and that thou humblest them that presume of themselves, and glory in their own strength. Jdth. 6:15.

Scatter them by thy power, and bring them down, O Lord my Protector. Ps. 58:12.

O my God, make them like a wheel, and as stubble before the wind. Ps. 82:14.

Let fear and dread fall upon them in the greatness of thy arm. Who is like to thee among the strong, O Lord? Ex. 15:11, 16.

33. THE BLESSINGS OF PEACE

The Lord will give strength to his people: the Lord will bless his people with peace. Ps. 28:11.

Come ye, and behold ye the works of the Lord: what wonders he hath done upon earth, making wars to cease even to the end of the earth. Ps. 45:9.

He shall destroy the bow, and break the weapons: and the shields he shall burn in the fire. Ps. 45:10.

When the ways of man shall please the Lord, he will convert even his enemies to peace. Prov. 16:7.

He shall judge the Gentiles and rebuke many people: and they shall turn their swords into plowshares, and their spears into sickles; nation shall not lift up sword against nation, neither shall they be exercised any more to war. Is. 2:4.

The fear of the Lord fell upon all the kingdoms of the lands when they heard that the Lord had fought against the enemies of Israel. And the kingdom of Josaphat was quiet, and God gave him peace round about. 2 Par. 20:29 f.

34. SCANDAL

Because thou hast given occasion to the enemies of the Lord to blaspheme, for this thing the child that is born to thee shall surely die. 2 K. 12:14.

He that shall scandalize one of these little ones that believe in me, it were better for him that a millstone should be hanged about his neck, and that he should be drowned in the depth of the sea. Woe to the world because of scandals! For it must needs be that scandals come: but nevertheless woe to that man by whom the scandal cometh! Mat. 18:6 f.

That we may not scandalize them, go to the sea, and cast in a hook: and that fish which shall first come up, take; and when thou hast opened its mouth, thou shalt find a stater: take that, and give it to them for me and thee. Mat. 17:26.

If meat scandalize my brother, I will never eat flesh, lest I should scandalize my brother. 1 C. 8:13.

Avoiding this, lest any man should blame us in this abundance which is administered by us. For we forecast what may be good not only before God, but also before men. 2 C. 8:20 f.

It doth not become our age, said he, to dissemble: whereby many young persons might think that Eleazar, at the age of fourscore and ten years, was gone over to the life of the heathens: and so they, through my dissimulation, and for a little time of a corruptible life, should be deceived, and hereby I should bring a stain and a curse upon my old age. 2 Mac. 6:24 f.

Who will give me in the wilderness a lodgingplace of wayfaring men, and I will leave my people, and depart from them? because they are all adulterers, an assembly of transgressors. Jer. 9:2.

Do not so, my sons; for it is no good report that I hear, that you make the people of the Lord to transgress. 1 K. 2:24.

Take away the stumbling blocks out of the way of my people. Is. 57:14.

The Son of man shall send his angels, and they shall gather out of his kingdom all scandals, and them that work iniquity. Mat. 13:41.

Let not him that eateth despise him that eateth not; and he that eateth not, let him not judge him that eateth. Destroy not the work of God for meat. All things, indeed, are clean: but it is evil for that man who eateth with offence. It is good not to eat flesh, and not to drink wine, nor anything whereby thy brother is offended, or scandalized, or made weak. Rom. 14:3, 20 f.

Be not delighted in the paths of the wicked, neither let the way of evil men please thee. Flee from it, pass not by it: go aside, and forsake it. Prov. 4:14 f.

Let us not judge one another any more. But judge this rather, that you put not a stumbling block or a scandal in your brother's way. For if, because of thy meat, thy brother be grieved, thou walkest not now according to charity. Destroy not him with thy meat for whom Christ died. Rom. 14:13-15.

Take heed lest perhaps this your liberty become a stumbling block to the weak. 1 C. 8:9.

If any man say: This has been sacrificed to idols, do not eat of it, for his sake that told it, and for conscience' sake. Conscience, I say: not thy own, but the other's. Be without offence to the Jews, and to the Gentiles, and to the Church of God. As I also in all things please all men, not seeking that which is profitable to myself, but to many, that they may be saved. 1 C. 10:28 f., 32 f.

From all appearance of evil refrain yourselves. 1 Thess. 5:22.

I beseech you, brethren, to mark them who make dissensions and offences contrary to the doctrines which you have learnt, and to avoid them. Rom. 16:17.

Beware thou never join in friendship with the inhabitants of that land, which may be thy ruin. Ex. 34:12.

His disciples came, and aid to him: Dost thou know that the Pharisees, when they heard this word, were scandalized? Mat. 15:12.

The Pharisees said to his disciples: Why doth your Master eat with publicans and sinners? But Jesus hearing it, said: They that are in health need not a physician, but they that are ill. Mat. 9:11 f.

The Pharisees said to him: Behold, thy disciples do that which is not lawful on the Sabbath days. But he said to them: Have you not read what David did when he was hungry, and they that were with him? How he entered into the house of God, and did eat the loaves of proposition, which it was not lawful for him to eat, nor for them that were with him, but for the priests only? Mat. 12:2-4.

Let them alone: they are blind, and leaders of the blind. And if the blind lead the blind, both fall into the pit. Mat. 15:14.

35. THE GIFT OF WISDOM

You shall know the truth, and the truth shall make you free. John 8:32.

The love of God is honorable wisdom. Ecclus. 1:14.

To fear God is the fulness of wisdom. Ecclus. 1:20.

The perfection of the fear of God is wisdom and understanding. Ecclus. 21:13.

Behold, the fear of the Lord, that is wisdom: and to depart from evil is understanding. Job 28:28.

The fear of the Lord is the beginning of wisdom. Ecclus. 1:16.

I will give you a mouth and wisdom, which all your adversaries shall not be able to resist and gainsay. Luke 21:15.

I will lead the blind into the way which they know not, and in the paths which they were ignorant of I will make them walk: I will make darkness light before them, and crooked things straight. Is. 42:16.

The word of God on high is the fountain of wisdom, and her ways are everlasting commandments. Ecclus. 1:5.

God hath given to me to speak as I would, and to conceive thoughts worthy of those things that are given me: because he is the Guide of wisdom, and the Director of the wise; for in his hand are both we, and our words, and all wisdom, and the knowledge and skill of works. Wis. 7:15 f.

The fear of the Lord is a crown of wisdom, filling up peace and the fruit of salvation; but both are the gifts of God. Ecclus. 1:22 f.

I hoped that greater age would speak, and that a multitude of years would teach wisdom. But, as I see, there is a spirit in men, and the inspiration of the Almighty giveth understanding. Job 32:7 f.

In [him] are hid all the treasures of wisdom and knowledge. Col. 2:3.

The wisdom, that is from above, first indeed is chaste, then peaceable, modest, easy to be persuaded, consenting to the good, full of mercy and good fruits, without judging, without dissimulation. Jas. 3:17.

The spirit of wisdom is benevolent. Wis. 1:6.

Where is wisdom to be found, and where is the place of understanding? The depth saith: It is not in me; and the sea saith: It is not with me. Job 28:12, 14.

The wisdom of doctrine is according to her name, and she is not manifest unto many; but with them to whom she is known she continueth even to the sight of God. Ecclus. 6:23.

I Wisdom dwell in counsel, and am present in learned thoughts. The fear of the Lord hateth evil: I hate arrogance, and pride, and every wicked way, and a mouth with a double tongue. Counsel and equity is mine, prudence is mine, strength is mine. By me kings reign, and lawgivers decree just things. I love them that love me: and they that in the morning early watch for me shall find me. Prov. 8:12-17.

Blessed are they that keep my ways. Hear instruction and be wise, and refuse it not. Blessed is the man that heareth me, and that watcheth daily at my gates, and waiteth at the posts of my doors. He that shall find me shall find life, and shall have salvation from the Lord: But he that shall sin against me shall hurt his own soul. All that hate me love death. Prov. 8:32-34.

My son, from thy youth up receive instruction, and even to thy gray hairs thou shalt find wisdom. Ecclus. 6:18.

Covet ye my words, and love them, and you shall have instruction. Wisdom is glorious, and never fadeth away, and is easily seen by them that love her, and is found by them that seek her. She preventeth them that covet her, so that she first showeth herself unto them. Wis. 6:12-14.

Wisdom will not enter into a malicious soul, nor dwell in a body subject to sins. For the Holy Spirit of discipline will flee from the deceitful, and will withdraw himself from thoughts that are without understanding, and he shall not abide when iniquity cometh in. Wis. 1:4 f.

I wished, and understanding was given me; and I called upon God, and the Spirit of wisdom came upon me. Wis. 7:7.

As I knew that I could not otherwise be continent except God gave it (and this also was a point of wisdom to know whose gift it was), I went to the Lord, and besought him, and [prayed for her] with my whole heart. Wis. 8:21.

The wise man will seek out the wisdom of all the ancients, and will be occupied in the prophets. He will give his heart to resort early to the Lord that made him, and he will pray in the sight of the Most High. He will open his mouth in prayer, and will make supplication for his sins. Ecclus. 39:1, 6 f.

I have determined to follow her: I have had a zeal for good, and shall not be confounded. My soul hath wrestled for her, and in doing it I have been confirmed. Ecclus. 51:24 f.

The fear of the Lord is the beginning of wisdom, a good understanding to all that do it. Ps. 110:10 f.

Son, if thou desire wisdom, keep justice, and God will give her to thee. Ecclus. 1:33.

Let thy thoughts be upon the precepts of God, and meditate continually on his commandments: and he will give thee a heart, and the desire of wisdom shall be given to thee. Ecclus. 6:37.

The wisdom of a scribe cometh by his time of leisure; and he that is less in action shall receive wisdom. Ecclus. 38:25.

If any man will do the will of him, he shall know of the doctrine, whether it be of God, or whether I speak of myself. John 7:17.

I will give them a heart to know me, that I am the Lord. Jer. 24:7.

He that rejecteth wisdom and discipline is unhappy; and their hope is vain, and their labors without fruit, and their works unprofitable. Their wives are foolish and their children wicked; their offspring is cursed. Wis. 3:11-13.

They to whom she shall show herself love her by the sigh' and by the knowledge of her great works. Ecclus. 1:15.

Wisdom shall perish from their wise men, and the understanding of their prudent men shall be hid. Is. 29:14.

He catcheth the wise in their craftiness, and disappointeth the counsel of the wicked. They shall meet with darkness in the day, and grope at noonday as in the night. Job 5:13 f.

The wisdom of this world is foolishness with God; for it is written: I will catch the wise in their own craftiness. 1 C. 3:19.

There is wisdom that aboundeth in evils. Ecclus. 21:15.

The wise men are confounded, they are dismayed and taken: for they have cast away the word of the Lord, and there is no wisdom in them. Jer. 8:9.

Professing themselves to be wise they became fools. And they changed the glory of the incorruptible God into the likeness of the image of a corruptible man. Rom. 1:22 f.

Beware lest any man cheat you by philosophy and vain deceit, according to the tradition of men, according to the elements of the world, and not according to Christ. Col. 2:8.

36. BLESSINGS OF WISDOM

Wisdom inspireth life into her children, and protecteth them that seek after her, and will go before them in the way of justice. They that hold her fast shall inherit life; and whithersoever she entereth, God will give a blessing. Ecclus. 4:12, 14.

If thou be wise, thou shalt be so to thyself; and if a scorner, thou alone shalt bear the evil. Prov. 9:12.

She reacheth from end to end mightily, and ordereth all things sweetly. Wis. 8:1.

If thou shalt call for wisdom, and incline thy heart to prudence, then shalt thou understand justice, and judgment, and equity, and every good path. If wisdom shall enter into thy heart, and knowledge please thy soul, counsel shall keep thee, and prudence shall preserve thee; that thou mayest be delivered from the evil way, and from the man that speaketh perverse things. Prov. 2:3, 9-12.

With thee is the fountain of life; and in thy light we shall see light. Ps. 35:10.

To the righteous a light is risen up in darkness. Ps. 111:4.

The Lord will fill thy soul with brightness, and deliver thy bones: and thou shalt be like a watered garden, and like a fountain of water whose waters shall not fail. Is. 58:11.

To you it is given to know the mysteries of the kingdom of heaven. Mat. 13:11.

You have the unction from the Holy One, and know all things. 1 John 2:20.

I directed my soul to her, and in knowledge I found her: I possessed my heart with her from the beginning; therefore I shall not be forsaken. Ecclus. 51:27 f.

If a man love justice, her labors have great virtues; for she teacheth temperance, and prudence, and justice, and fortitude, which are such things as men can have nothing more profitable in life. Wis. 8:7.

Her ways are beautiful ways, and all her paths are peaceable. She is a tree of life to them that lay hold on her; and he that shall retain her is blessed. Prov. 3:17 f.

She will disclose her secrets to him, and will heap upon him treasures of knowledge and understanding of justice. Eccles. 4:21.

There is great delight in her friendship. Wis. 8:18.

I purposed to take her to me to live with me; knowing that she will communicate to me of her good things, and will be a comfort in my care and grief. Wis. 8:9.

I saw that wisdom excelled folly as much as light differeth from darkness. Eccles. 2:13.

They that are free shall serve a servant that is wise. Ecclus. 10:28.

A man shall be known by his learning: but he that is vain and foolish shall be exposed to contempt. Prov. 12:8.

A wise man shall be filled with blessings, and they that see shall praise him. A wise man shall inherit honor among his people, and his name shall live forever. Ecclus. 37:27, 29.

They that serve her shall be servants to the Holy One: and God loveth them that love her. He that hearkeneth to her shall judge nations: and he that looketh upon her shall remain secure. Ecclus. 4:15 f.

Wisdom conducted the just through the right ways, and showed him the kingdom of God, and gave him the knowledge of the holy things, made him honorable in his labors, and accomplished his labors. Wis. 10:10.

Wisdom is better than all the most precious things: and whatsoever may be desired cannot be compared to it. Prov. 8:11.

She is an infinite treasure to men. Wis. 7:14.

If riches be desired in life, what is richer than wisdom, which maketh all things? Wis. 8:5.

Inexhaustible riches is in the works of her hands. Wis. 8:18.

By wisdom the house shall be built, and by prudence it shall be strengthened. By instruction the storerooms shall be filled with all precious and most beautiful wealth. Prov. 24:3 f.

With me are riches and glory, glorious riches and justice, that I may enrich them that love me, and may fill their treasures. Prov. 8:18, 21.

Knowledge is a fountain of life to him that possesseth it. Prov. 16:22.

The wise in heart shall be called prudent: and he that is sweet in words shall attain to greater things. Prov. 16:21.

The words of the wise are heard in silence, more than the cry of a prince among fools. Ecclus. 9:17.

A wise man instructeth his own people, and the fruits of his understanding are faithful. Ecclus. 37:26.

If it should please the great Lord, he will fill him with the Spirit of understanding: and he will pour forth the words of his wisdom as showers, and in his prayer he will confess to the Lord. He shall show forth the discipline he hath learned, and shall glory in the law of the covenant of the Lord. Ecclus. 39:8 f., 11.

The multitude of the wise is the welfare of the whole world: and a wise king is the upholding of the people. Wis. 6:28.

Learning to the prudent is an ornament of gold, and like a bracelet upon his right arm. Ecclus. 21:24.

Blessed is the man whom thou shalt instruct, O Lord: and shalt teach him out of thy law. Ps. 93:12.

The wisdom of a discreet man is to understand his way: and the imprudence of fools erreth. Prov. 14:8.

Folly is joy to the fool: and the wise man maketh straight his steps. Prov. 15:21.

The prudent man saw the evil, and hid himself: the simple passed on, and suffered loss. Prov. 22:3.

I saw that wisdom excelled folly as much as light differeth from darkness. The eyes of a wise man are in his head: the fool walketh in darkness. Eccles. 2:13 f.

The wisdom of the flesh is death: but the wisdom of the spirit is life and peace. Because the wisdom of the flesh is an enemy to God: for it is not subject to the law of God, neither can it be. Rom. 8:6 f.

37. EXHORTATIONS TO WISDOM

O that they would be wise and would understand, and would provide for their last end! Deut. 32:29.

O ye men, to you I call, and my voice is to the sons of men. O little ones, understand subtlety; and ye unwise, take notice. Receive my instruction, and not money; choose knowledge rather than gold. For wisdom is better than all the most precious things: and whatsoever may be desired cannot be compared to it. Prov. 8:4 f., 10 f.

Say to Wisdom: Thou art my sister: and call Prudence thy friend: that she may keep thee from the woman that is not thine, and from the stranger who sweeteneth her words. Prov. 7:4-5.

Get wisdom, because it is better than gold: and purchase prudence, for it is more precious than silver. Prov. 16:16.

Buy truth, and do not sell wisdom, and instruction, and understanding. Prov. 23:23.

You were heretofore darkness, but now light in the Lord. Walk ye as children of the light. Eph. 5:8.

Study wisdom, my son, and make my heart joyful, that thou mayst give an answer to him that reproacheth. Prov. 27:11.

O Lord, give me wisdom, that sitteth by thy throne, and cast me not off from among thy children. Wis. 9:4.

Send wisdom out of thy holy heaven, and from the throne of thy majesty, that she may be with me, and may labor with me, that I may know what is acceptable with thee. Wis. 9:10.

Who shall know thy thought, O Lord, except thou give wisdom, and send thy holy Spirit from above: And so the ways of them that are upon the earth may be corrected, and men may learn the things that please thee? For by wisdom they were healed, whosoever have pleased thee, O Lord, from the beginning. Wis. 9:17-19.

Conduct me, O Lord, in thy justice because of my enemies: direct my way in thy sight. Ps. 5:9.

Show, O Lord, thy ways to me, and teach me thy paths. Ps. 24:4.

Direct me in thy truth, and teach me: for thou art God my Savior, and on thee I have waited all the day. Ps. 24:5.

O Lord, make me know my end, and what is the number of my days, that I may know what is wanting to me. Ps. 38:5.

Send forth thy light and thy truth. They have conducted me and brought me unto thy holy hill and into thy tabernacle. Ps. 42:3.

Conduct me, O Lord, in thy way, and I will walk in thy truth: let my heart rejoice that it may fear thy name. Ps. 85:11.

Lead me in the eternal way. Ps. 138:24.

Cause me to hear thy mercy in the morning: for in thee have I hoped. Make the way known to me wherein I should walk: for I have lifted up my soul to thee. Deliver me from my enemies, O Lord, to thee have I fled: teach me to do thy will, for thou art my God. Thy good Spirit shall lead me into the right land: for thy name's sake, O Lord, thou wilt quicken me in thy justice. Ps. 142:8-11.

O Lord, Father, and sovereign Ruler of my life, leave me not to the counsel of my lips, nor suffer me to fall by them. Who will set scourges over my thoughts and the discipline of wisdom over my heart, that they spare not in their ignorances and that their sins may not appear: lest my ignorance increase, and my offences be multiplied, and my sins abound, and I fall before my adversaries, and my enemy rejoice over me? O Lord, Father, and God of my life, leave me not to their devices. Give me not haughtiness of my eyes, and turn away from me all coveting. Take from me greediness, and let not the lusts of the flesh take hold of me, and give me not over to a shameless and foolish mind. Ecclus. 23:1-6.

IV

PRUDENCE AND THE CONTRARY VICES

1. TRUE PRUDENCE COMMENDED

Give not that which is holy to dogs: neither cast ye your pearls before swine, lest perhaps they trample them under their feet, and turning upon you, tear you. Mat. 7:6.

Be ye wise as serpents and simple as doves. Mat. 10:16.

Walk with wisdom towards them that are without, redeeming the time. Col. 4:5.

I would have you to be wise in good and simple in evil. Rom. 16:19.

In the good day enjoy good things, and beware beforehand of the evil day. Eccles. 7:15.

Let not our good be evil spoken of. Rom. 14:16.

Be prudent, and watch in prayers. 1 Pet. 4:7.

The wise in heart shall be called prudent. Prov. 16:21.

The ear trieth words, and the mouth discerneth meats by the taste. Job 34:3.

Let us choose to us judgment, and let us see among ourselves what is the best. Job 34:4.

He shall order his words with judgment. Ps. 111:5.

The prudent man saw the evil, and hid himself: the simple passed on, and suffered loss. Prov. 22:3.

A net is spread in vain before the eyes of them that have wings. Prov. 1:17.

As the faces of them that look therein shine in the water, so the hearts of men are laid open to the wise. Prov. 27:19.

2. PRUDENCE OF THE WICKED CONDEMNED

The learning of wickedness is not wisdom: and the device of sinners is not prudence. Ecclus. 19:19.

A fool uttereth all his mind: a wise man deferreth, and keepeth it till afterwards. Prov. 29:11.

Dying flies spoil the sweetness of the ointment. Eccles. 10:1.

My foolish people have not known me: they are foolish and senseless children: they are wise to do evils, but to do good they have no knowledge. Jer. 4:22.

The wisdom of this world is foolishness with God. For it is written: I will catch the wise in their own craftiness. And again: The Lord knoweth the thoughts of the wise, that they are vain. 1 C. 3:19 f.

It is written: I will destroy the wisdom of the wise, and the prudence of the prudent I will reject. Where is the wise? Where is the scribe? Where is the disputer of this world? Hath not God made foolish the wisdom of this world? 1 C. 1:19 f.

They that are according to the flesh mind the things that are of the flesh: but they that are according to the Spirit mind the things that are of the Spirit. For the wisdom of the flesh is death: but the wisdom of the Spirit is life and peace. Because the wisdom of the flesh is an enemy to God: for it is not subject to the law of God, neither can it be. And they who are in the flesh cannot please God. Rom. 8:5-8.

Thou hast trusted in thy wickedness, and hast said: There is none that seeth me. Thy wisdom and thy knowledge, this hath deceived thee. Evil shall come upon thee, and thou shalt not know the rising thereof. Is. 47:10 f.

3. EXAMPLES OF PRUDENCE

David behaved wisely in all his ways, and the Lord was with him. And Saul saw that he was exceeding prudent, and began to beware of him. 1 K. 18:14 f.

From the beginning of their going forth, David behaved himself more wisely than all the servants of Saul, and his name became very famous. 1 K. 18:30.

4. THE OFFICE OF PRUDENCE

I Wisdom dwell in counsel, and am present in learned thoughts. Counsel and equity is mine, prudence is mine. Prov. 8:12, 14.

A skilful man hath taught many, and is sweet to his own soul. There is a wise man that is wise to his own soul: and the fruit of his understanding is commendable. Ecclus. 37:22, 26.

The way of a fool is right in his own eyes: but he that is wise hearkeneth unto counsels. Prov. 12:15.

They that do all things with counsel are ruled by wisdom. The prudent man doth all things with counsel: but he that is a fool layeth open his folly. Prov. 13:10, 16.

Designs are brought to nothing where there is no counsel: but where there are many counsellors they are established. Prov. 15:22.

My son, do thou nothing without counsel, and thou shalt not repent when thou hast done. Ecclus. 32:24.

A wise man feareth and declineth from evil: the fool leapeth over and is confident. Prov. 14:16.

The childish shall possess folly, and the prudent shall look for knowledge. Prov. 14:18.

In all thy works let the true word go before thee, and steady counsel before every action. Ecclus. 37:20.

There is safety where there is much counsel. Prov. 11:14.

Ointment and perfumes rejoice the heart: and the good counsels of a friend are sweet to the soul. Prov. 27:9.

The knowledge of a wise man shall abound like a flood, and his counsel continueth like a fountain of life. Ecclus. 21:16.

Be continually with ı holy man, whomsoever thou shalt know to observe the fear of God. Whose soul is according to thy own soul: and who, when thou shalt stumble in the dark, will be sorry for thee. Ecclus. 37:15 f.

According to thy power beware of thy neighbor, and treat with the wise and prudent. Ecclus. 9:21.

Seek counsel always of a wise man. Job 4:19.

Establish within thyself a heart of good counsel: for there is no other thing of more worth to thee than it. The soul of a holy man discovereth sometimes true things, more than seven watchmen that sit in a high place to watch. Ecclus. 37:17 f.

Above all these things pray to the Most High, that he may direct thy way in truth. A wise man instructeth his own people. Ecclus. 37:19, 26.

Advise not with fools, for they cannot love but such things as please them. Before a stranger do no matter of counsel, for thou knowest not what he will bring forth. Open not thy heart to every man: lest he repay thee with an evil turn, and speak reproachfully to thee. Ecclus. 8:20-22.

Be in peace with many, but let one of a thousand be thy counsellor. Ecclus. 6:6.

They have broken the eggs of asps, and have woven the webs of spiders: he that shall eat of their eggs shall die; and that which is brought out shall be hatched into a basilisk. Their webs shall not be for clothing, neither shall they cover themselves with their works: their works are unprofitable works, and the work of iniquity is in their hands. Is. 59:5 f.

A wicked word shall change the heart out of which four manner of things arise: good and evil, life and death. Ecclus. 37:21.

The counsels of the wicked are deceitful. Prov. 12:5.

My son, if sinners shall entice thee, consent not to them. Prov. 1:10.

He that deceiveth the just in a wicked way shall fall in his destruction: and the upright shall possess his goods. Prov. 28:10.

5. THE COUNSEL OF THE WICKED

He bringeth to naught the designs of the malignant, so that their hands cannot accomplish what they had begun. He catcheth the wise in their craftiness, and disappointeth the counsel of the wicked: they shall meet with darkness in the day, and grope at noonday as in the night. Job 5:12-14.

There is no wisdom, there is no prudence, there is no counsel against the Lord. Prov. 21:30.

6. THE WORD OF GOD SHALL ABIDE FOREVER

The Lord of hosts hath sworn, saying: Surely as I have thought, so shall it be: and as I have purposed. This is the counsel that I have purposed upon all the earth, and this is the hand that is stretched out upon all nations. For the Lord of hosts hath decreed, and who can disannul it? and his hand is stretched out, and who shall turn it away? Is. 14:24, 26 f.

From the beginning I am the same, and there is none that can deliver out of my hand: I will work, and who shall turn it away? Is. 43:13.

My counsel shall stand, and all my will shall be done. Is. 46:10.

I say to you, refrain from these men, and let them alone: for if this counsel or this work be of men, it will come to naught. But if it be of God, you cannot overthrow it: lest perhaps you be found to fight against God. And they consented to him. Acts 5:38 f.

The Lord bringeth to naught the counsels of nations; and he rejecteth the decrees of people, and casteth away the counsels of princes. But the counsel of the Lord standeth forever: the thoughts of his heart to all generations. Ps. 32:10 f.

7. FRUITS OF IMPRUDENCE

An unwise king shall be the ruin of his people: and cities shall be inhabited through the prudence of the rulers. Ecclus. 10:3.

A fool uttereth all his mind: a wise man deferreth and keepeth it till afterwards. Prov. 29:11.

The labor of fools shall afflict them that know not how to go to the city. Eccles. 10:15.

By three things the earth is disturbed: and the fourth it cannot bear: by a slave when he reigneth: by a fool when he is filled with meat. Prov. 30:21 f.

What is heavier than lead? and what other name hath he but fool? Sand and salt and a mass of iron is easier to bear than a man without sense, that is both foolish and wicked. Ecclus. 22:17 f.

He that answereth before he heareth showeth himself to be a fool, and worthy of confusion. Prov. 18:13.

Even a fool, if he will hold his peace, shall be counted wise: and if he close his lips, a man of understanding. Prov. 17:28.

Answer not a fool according to his folly, lest thou be made like him. Answer a fool according to his folly, lest he imagine himself to be wise. Prov. 26:4 f.

Judgment determineth causes: and he that putteth a fool to silence appeaseth anger. Prov. 26:10.

He that teacheth a fool is like one that glueth a potsherd together. He that telleth a word to him that heareth not is like one that waketh a man out of a deep sleep. He speaketh with one that is asleep who uttereth wisdom to a fool: and in the end of the discourse he saith: Who is this? Ecclus. 22:7-9.

I have seen those who work iniquity and sow sorrows reap the same. Job 4:8.

The Gentiles have stuck fast in the destruction which they prepared: their foot hath been taken in the very snare which they hid. Ps. 9:16.

They shall sow wind and reap the whirlwind. Osee 8:7.

Every man that shall eat the sour grape, his teeth shall be set on edge. Jer. 31:30.

He will render them their iniquity: and in their malice he will destroy them. Ps. 93:23.

The wicked shall fall in his net. Ps. 140:10.

They shall eat the fruit of their own way, and shall be filled with their own devices. Prov. 1:31.

The promotion of fools is disgrace. Prov. 3:35.

His own iniquities catch the wicked, and he is fast bound with the ropes of his own sins. He shall die, because he hath not received instruction, and in the multitude of his folly he shall be deceived. Prov. 5:22 f.

V

JUSTICE AND THE CONTRARY VICES

1. PRAISE OF JUSTICE

If thou followest justice, thou shalt obtain her: and shalt put her on as a long robe of honor, and thou shalt dwell with her: and she shall protect thee forever, and in the day of acknowledgment thou shalt find a strong foundation. Birds resort unto their like: so truth will return to them that practise her. Eccles. 27:9 f.

Judge ye true judgment. Zach. 7:9.

The just shall live for evermore: and their reward is with the Lord, and the care of them with the Most High. Therefore shall they receive a kingdom of glory and a crown of beauty at the hand of the Lord: for with his right hand he will cover them, and with his holy arm he will defend them. Wis. 5:16 f.

As to the rest, there is laid up for me a crown of justice, which the Lord the just Judge will render to me in that day: and not only to me, but to them also that love his coming. 2 Tim. 4:8.

He that followeth justice and mercy shall find life, justice, and glory. Prov. 21:21.

The wicked man fleeth when no man pursueth: but the just, bold as a lion, shall be without dread. Prov. 28:1.

In abundant justice there is the greatest strength: but the devices of the wicked shall be rooted out. The house of the just is very much strength: and in the fruits of the wicked is trouble. Prov. 15:5 f.

The just shall be in everlasting remembrance: he shall not fear the evil hearing. Ps. 111:7.

I will show thee, O man, what the Lord requireth of thee: verily to do judgment, and to love mercy, and to walk solicitous with thy God. Mich. 6:8.

As you would that men should do to you, do you also to them in like manner. Luke 6:31.

The eyes of the Lord are upon the just, and his ears unto their prayers. The just cried, and the Lord heard them, and delivered them out of all their troubles. Ps. 33:16, 18.

Keep ye judgment and do justice. Is. 56:1.

2. CONTRASTS BETWEEN THE JUST AND THE UNJUST

The blessing of the Lord is upon the head of the just: but iniquity covereth the mouth of the wicked. The memory of the just is with praises: and the name of the wicked shall rot. The wise of heart receiveth precepts: a fool is beaten with lips. He that walketh sincerely walketh confidently: but he that perverteth his ways shall be manifest. The mouth of the just is a vein of life: and the mouth of the wicked covereth iniquity. Prov. 10:6-9, 11.

When it goeth well with the just the city shall rejoice; and when the wicked perish there shall be praise. By the blessing of the just the city shall be exalted: and by the mouth of the wicked it shall be overthrown. The desire of the just is all good: the expectation of the wicked is indignation. Prov. 11:10 f., 23.

Man shall not be strengthened by wickedness, and the root of the just shall not be moved. The thoughts of the just are judgments, and the counsels of the wicked are deceitful. The words of the wicked lie in wait for blood: the mouth of the just shall deliver them. Turn the wicked, and they shall not be: but the house of the just shall stand firm. Prov. 12:3, 5-7.

The light of the just giveth joy, but the lamp of the wicked shall be put out. The just eateth and filleth his soul: but the belly of the wicked is never to be filled. Prov. 13:9, 25.

The house of the wicked shall be destroyed: but the tabernacles of the just shall flourish. Prov. 14:11.

The Lord is far from the wicked: and he will hear the prayers of the just. Prov. 15:29.

To do mercy and judgment pleaseth the Lord more than victims. Prov. 21:3.

3. INJUSTICE FORBIDDEN

Do not any unjust thing in judgment, in rule, in weight, or in measure. Lev. 19:35.

Thou shalt not have divers weights in thy bag, a greater and a less: neither shall there be in thy house a greater bushel and a less. Thou shalt have a just and a true weight, and thy bushel shall be equal and true: that thou mayst live a long time upon the land which the Lord thy God shall give thee. For the Lord thy God abhorreth him that doth these things, and he hateth all injustice. Deut. 25:13-16.

Thou shalt not calumniate thy neighbor, nor oppress him by violence. The wages of him that hath been hired by thee shall not abide with thee until the morning. Lev. 19:13.

It is no good thing to do hurt to the just. Prov. 17:26.

Be not pleased with the wrong done by the unjust, knowing that even to hell the wicked shall not please. Ecclus. 9:17.

Cursed be he that removeth his neighbor's landmarks: and all the people shall say: Amen. Deut. 27:17.

Oppress not the widow, and the fatherless, and the stranger, and the poor; and let not a man devise evil in his heart against his brother. Zach. 7:10.

4. INJUSTICE PUNISHED BY GOD

If thou shalt see the oppressions of the poor, and violent judgments, and justice perverted in the province, wonder not at this matter: for he that is high hath another higher, and there are others still higher than these. Moreover there is the king, that reigneth over all the land subject to him. Eccles. 5:7 f.

Every violent taking of spoils, with tumult, and garment mingled with blood, shall be burnt, and be fuel for the fire. Is. 9:5.

Fire shall devour their tabernacles who love to take bribes. Job 15:34.

A kingdom is translated from one people to another, because of injustices, and wrongs, and injuries, and divers deceits. Ecclus. 10:8.

He that buildeth his house at other men's charges is as he that gathereth himself stones to build in the winter. Ecclus. 21:9.

If thou do well, shalt thou not receive? but if ill, shall not sin forthwith be present at the door? Gen. 4:7.

I am the Lord, who search the heart and prove the reins: who give to every one according to his way, and according to the fruit of his devices. Jer. 17:10.

Thine eyes are open upon all the ways of the children of Adam, to render unto every one according to his ways, and according to the fruit of his devices. Jer. 32:18.

I will judge thee according to thy

ways: and I will set all thy abominations against thee. Ezech. 7:3.

Woe to thee that spoilest! Shalt not thou be spoiled? And thou that despiseth, shalt not thyself also be despised? When thou shalt have made an end of spoiling, thou shalt be spoiled: when, being wearied, thou shalt cease to despise, thou shalt be despised. Is. 33:1.

They shall serve them four hundred years. But I will judge the nation which they shall serve. Gen. 15:13 f.

5. JUST JUDGES

A wise judge shall judge his people, and the government of a prudent man shall be steady. Ecclus. 10:1.

The king that judgeth the poor in truth, his throne shall be established forever. Prov. 29:14.

As the judge of the people is himself, so also are his ministers: and what manner of man the ruler of a city is, such also are they that dwell therein. Ecclus. 10:2.

He that hath not taken bribes against the innocent, he that doth these things, shall not be moved forever. Ps. 14:5.

Judge not against a judge: for he judgeth according to that which is just. Ecclus. 8:17.

6. UNJUST JUDGES

Thy princes are faithless, companions of thieves: they all love bribes, they run after rewards. They judge not for the fatherless: and the widow's cause cometh not in to them. Therefore saith the Lord the God of hosts, the Mighty One of Israel: Ah! I will comfort myself over my adversaries; and I will be revenged of my enemies. Is. 1:23 f.

The Lord will enter into judgment with the ancients of his people, and its princes; for you have devoured the vineyard, and the spoil of the poor is in your house. Why do you consume my people, and grind the faces of the poor? saith the Lord the God of hosts. Is. 3:14 f.

O thou that art grown old in evil days, now are thy sins come out, which thou hast committed before: the judging unjust judgments, oppressing the innocent, and letting the guilty to go free; whereas the Lord saith: The innocent and the just thou shalt not kill. Dan. 13:52 f.

You that turn judgment into wormwood, and forsake justice in the land, seek him that turneth darkness into morning. Amos 5:7 f.

Can horses run upon the rocks, or can anyone plow with buffles? for you have turned judgment into bitterness, and the fruit of justice into wormwood. Amos 6:13.

How long will you judge unjustly, and accept the persons of the wicked? Judge for the needy and fatherless: do justice to the humble and the poor. Rescue the poor, and deliver the needy out of the hand of the sinner. Ps. 81:2-4.

For three crimes of Israel, and for four, I will not convert him, because he hath sold the just man for silver, and the poor man for a pair of shoes. They bruise the heads of the poor upon the dust of the earth, and turn aside the way of the humble to profane my holy name. Amos 2:6 f.

Thou shalt not accept person nor gifts; for gifts blind the eyes of the wise, and change the words of the just. Deut. 16:19.

The wicked man taketh gifts out of the bosom, that he may pervert the paths of judgment. Prov. 17:23.

He that hath respect to a person in judgment doth not well. Such a man even for a morsel of bread forsaketh the truth. Prov. 28:21.

7. PUNISHMENT OF UNJUST JUDGES

Cursed be he that perverteth the judgment of the stranger, of the fatherless, and the widow; and all the people shall say: Amen. Deut. 27:19.

Judge ye judgment in the morning, and deliver him that is oppressed by violence out of the hand of the oppressor: lest my indignation go forth like a fire, and be kindled, and there be none to quench it, because of the evil of your ways. Jer. 21:12.

They that say to the wicked man: Thou art just, shall be cursed by the people, and the tribes shall abhor them. Prov. 24:24.

He that justified the wicked, and he that condemneth the just, both are abominable before God. Prov. 17:5.

Give ear, you that rule the people, and that please yourselves in multitudes of nations. For power is given you by the Lord, and strength by the Most High, who will examine your works, and search out your thoughts. Because being ministers of his kingdom you have not judged rightly, nor kept the law of justice, nor walked according to the will of God, horribly and speedily will he appear to you; for a most severe judgment shall be for them that bear rule. For to him that is little, mercy is granted, but the mighty shall be mightily tormented. For God will not except any man's person, neither will he stand in awe of any man's greatness: for he made the little and the great, and he hath equally care of all. But a greater punishment is ready for the more mighty Wis. 6:3-9.

Thus saith the Lord: You have not hearkened to me, in proclaiming liberty every man to his neighbor and every man to his friend. Behold, I proclaim a liberty for you, saith the Lord, to the sword, to the pestilence, and to the famine; and I will cause you to be removed to all the kingdoms of the earth. Jer. 34:17.

To crush under his feet all the prisoners of the land; to turn aside the judgment of a man before the face of the Most High; to destroy a man wrongfully in his judgment, the Lord hath not approved. Who is he that commanded a thing to be done when the Lord commandeth it not? Shall not both evil and good proceed out of the mouth of the Highest? Lam. 3:34-38.

8. VIRTUES NECESSARY FOR A JUDGE

He shall not judge according to the sight of the eyes, nor reprove according to the hearing of the ears; but he shall judge the poor with justice, and shall reprove with equity for the meek of the earth: and he shall strike the earth with the rod of his mouth, and with the breath of his lips he shall slay the wicked: and justice shall be the girdle of his loins, and faith the girdle of his reins. Is. 11:3-5.

He shall bring forth judgment to the Gentiles. He shall not cry, nor have respect to persons, neither shall his voice be heard abroad. The bruised reed he shall not break, and smoking flax he shall not quench: he shall bring forth judgment unto truth. He shall not be sad nor troublesome till he set judgment in the earth; and the islands shall wait for his law. Is. 42:1-4.

Provide out of all the people able men, such as fear God, in whom there is truth, and that hate avarice, and appoint of them rulers of thousands, and of hundreds, and of fifties, and of tens. Ex. 18:21.

I was clad with justice; and I clothed myself with my judgment, as with a robe and a diadem. I was an eye to the blind, and a foot to the lame. I was the father of the poor, and the cause which I knew not I searched out most diligently. I broke the jaws of the wicked man, and out of his teeth I took away the prey. Job 29:14-17.

In the morning I put to death all the wicked of the land, that I might cut off all the workers of iniquity from the city of the Lord. Ps. 100:8.

I have given thee a wise and understanding heart, insomuch that there hath been no one like thee before thee, nor shall arise after thee. 3 K. 3:12.

Thou, being master of power, judgest with tranquillity, and with great favor disposest of us; for thy power is at hand when thou wilt. Wis. 12:18.

Then [there were] all the judges, every one by name, whose heart was not corrupted: who turned not away from the Lord, that their memory might be blessed. Ecclus. 46:13 f.

The just taketh notice of the cause of the poor: the wicked is void of knowledge. Prov. 29:7.

O ye kings, understand; receive instruction, you that judge the earth. Serve ye the Lord with fear, and rejoice unto him with trembling. Embrace discipline, lest at any time the Lord be angry, and you perish from the just way. Ps. 2:10-12.

Let the king provide a wise and industrious man, and make him ruler over the land of Egypt. Gen. 41:33.

Love justice, you that are judges of the earth. Think of the Lord in goodness, and seek him in simplicity of heart. Wis. 1:1.

9. JUDICIAL ACTS TO BE CARRIED OUT

Deliver them that are led to death; and those that are drawn to death forbear not to deliver. If thou say: I have not strength enough, he that seeth into the heart he understandeth, and nothing deceiveth the Keeper of thy soul; and he shall render to a man according to his works. Prov. 24:11 f.

If thou perceive that there be among you a hard and doubtful matter in judgment between blood and blood, cause and cause, leprosy and leprosy, and thou see that the words of the judges within the gates do vary, arise, and go up to the place which the Lord thy God shall choose. Deut. 17:8.

When after most diligent inquisition they shall find that the false witness hath told a lie against his brother, they shall render to him as he meant to do to his brother, and thou shalt take away the evil out of the midst of thee. Deut. 19:18 f.

Execute judgment and justice, and deliver him who is oppressed out of the hand of the oppressor; and afflict not the stranger, the fatherless, and the widow, nor oppress them unjustly. Jer. 22:3.

I charge thee before God, and Christ Jesus, and the elect angels, that thou observe these things without prejudice, doing nothing by declining to either side. 1 Tim. 5:21.

10. ADVICE TO JUDGES

Thou shalt not follow the multitude to do evil, neither shalt thou yield in judgment to the opinion of the most part, to stray from the truth. Neither shalt thou favor a poor man in judgment. Thou shalt not go aside in the poor man's judgment. Ex.23:2 f., 6.

Thou shalt not do that which is unjust, nor judge unjustly. Respect not the person of the poor, nor honor the countenance of the mighty. But judge thy neighbor according to justice. Lev. 19:15.

If there be a controversy between men, and they call upon judges, they shall give the prize of justice to him whom they perceive to be just: and him whom they find to be wicked they shall condemn of wickedness. Deut. 25:1.

Judge ye true judgment, and show ye mercy and compassion every man to his brother. Zach. 7:9.

Speak ye truth every one to his neighbor: judge ye truth and judgment of peace in your gates. Zach. 8:16.

Seek judgment, relieve the oppressed, judge for the fatherless, defend the widow. Is. 1:17.

In judging be merciful to the fatherless as a father, and as a husband to their mother. And thou shalt be as the obedient son of the Most High, and he will have mercy on thee more than a mother. Ecclus. 4:10 f.

Open thy mouth for the dumb, and for the causes of all the children that pass. Open thy mouth, decree that which is just, and do justice to the needy and poor. Prov. 31:8 f.

Judge not according to the appearance, but judge just judgment. John 7:24.

Take heed what you do; for you exercise not the judgment of man, but of the Lord; and whatsoever you judge, it shall redound to you. Let the fear of the Lord be with you, and do all things with diligence: for there is no iniquity with the Lord our God, nor respect of persons, nor desire of gifts. 2 Par. 19:6 f.

11. EXAMPLES OF GOOD AND EVIL JUDGES

Moses, being very angry, said to the Lord: Respect not their sacrifices: Thou knowest that I have not taken of them so much as a young ass at any time, nor have injured any of them. Num. 16:15.

Samuel judged Israel all the days of his life. And he went every year about to Bethel and to Galgal and to Masphath, and he judged Israel in the aforesaid places. 1 K. 7:15 f.

Speak of me before the Lord, and before his anointed, whether I have taken any man's ox or ass: if I have wronged any man, if I have oppressed any man, if I have taken a bribe at any man's hand, and I will despise it this day, and will restore it to you. And they said: Thou hast not wronged us, nor oppressed us, nor taken aught at any man's hand. And he said to them: The Lord is witness against you, and his anointed is witness this day, that you have not found anything in my hand. 1 K. 12:3-5.

There were two of the ancients of the people appointed judges that year, of whom the Lord said: Iniquity came out from Babylon from the ancient judges, that seemed to govern the people. Dan. 13:5.

12. EJACULATIONS OF THE SOUL IMPLORING THE DIVINE JUDGMENT

Judge me, O Lord, according to my justice. Ps. 7:9.

Judge me, O God, and distinguish my cause from the nation that is not holy: deliver me from the unjust and deceitful man. Ps. 42:1.

Judge me, O Lord, for I have walked in my innocence: and I have put my trust in the Lord and shall not be weakened. Ps. 25:1.

Enter not into judgment with thy servant: for in thy sight no man living shall be justified. Ps. 142:2.

Arise, O God, judge thou the earth, for thou shalt inherit among all the nations. Ps. 81:8.

O earth, let not my cry find a hiding-place in thee. For behold, my witness is in heaven, and he that knoweth my conscience is on high. Job 16:19 f

13. UNDUE PARTIALITY

A deceitful balance is an abomination before the Lord, and a just weight is his will. Prov. 11:1.

Judge not according to the appearance, but judge just judgment. John 7:24.

My brethren, have not the faith of our Lord Jesus Christ of glory with respect of persons. For if there come into your assembly a man having a golden ring, in fine apparel; and there shall come in also a poor man in mean attire, and you have respect to him that is clothed with the fine apparel, and shall say to him: Sit thou here well; but say to the poor man: Stand thou there, or sit under my footstool: do you not judge within yourselves, and are become judges of unjust thoughts? Jas. 2:1-4.

If you have respect to persons, you commit sin, being reproved by the law as transgressors. Jas. 2:9.

Respect not the person of the poor, nor honor the countenance of the mighty. But judge thy neighbor according to justice. Lev. 19:15.

In very deed I perceive that God is not a respecter of persons. But in every nation, he that feareth him, and worketh justice, is acceptable to him. Acts 10:34 f

14. MURDER

When they were in the field, Cain rose up against his brother Abel, and slew him. Gen. 4:8.

What hast thou done? The voice of thy brother's blood crieth to me from the earth. Gen. 4:10.

Cursed shalt thou be upon the earth, which hath opened her mouth and received the blood of thy brother at thy hand. When thou shalt till it, it shall not yield to thee its fruit: a fugitive and a vagabond shalt thou be upon the earth. Gen. 4:11 f.

Whosoever shall shed man's blood, his blood shall be shed. Gen. 9:6.

He that shall kill by the sword, must be killed by the sword. Apoc. 13:10.

Put up again thy sword into its place; for all that take the sword shall perish with the sword. Mat. 26:52.

If any man strike with iron, and he die that was struck, he shall be guilty of murder, and he himself shall die. If he throw a stone, and he that was struck die, he shall be punished in the same manner. If he that is struck with wood die, he shall be revenged by the blood of him that struck him. Num. 35:16-18.

You shall not take money of him that is guilty of blood, but he shall die forthwith. Num. 35:31.

15. ADULTERY

Thou shalt not commit adultery. Ex. 20:14.

The fault is not so great when a man hath stolen; for he stealeth to fill his hungry soul. And if he be taken, he shall restore sevenfold, and shall give up all the substance of his house. But he that is an adulterer, for the folly of his heart shall destroy his own soul. Prov. 6:30-32.

Every man that passeth beyond his own bed shall be in disgrace with all men, because he understood not the law of the Lord. So every woman also that leaveth her husband, and bringeth in an heir by another: for first, she hath been unfaithful to the law of the Most High; and secondly, she hath offended against her husband; thirdly, she hath fornicated in adultery, and hath gotten her children of another man. Ecclus. 23:25, 31-33.

The eye of the adulterer observeth darkness, saying: No eye shall see me; and he will cover his face. He diggeth through houses in the dark, as in the day they had appointed for themselves, and they have not known the light. If the morning suddenly appear, it is to them the shadow of death; and they walk in darkness as if it were in light. Job 24:15-17.

Have no fellowship with the unfruitful works of darkness, but rather reprove them. For the things that are done by them in secret it is a shame even to speak of. Eph. 5:11 f.

Every man that passeth beyond his own bed, despising his own soul, and saying: Who seeth me? Darkness compasseth me about, and the walls cover me, and no man seeth me. Whom do I fear? The Most High will not remember my sins: this man shall be punished. Ecclus. 23:25 f., 30.

Take heed to keep thyself, my son, from all fornication, and beside thy wife never endure to know a crime. Job 4:13.

They have committed adultery with the wives of their friends: I am the Judge and the Witness, saith the Lord. Jer. 29:23.

16. PUNISHMENT OF ADULTERY

Can a man hide fire in his bosom, and his garments not burn? Or can he walk upon hot coals, and his feet not be burnt? So he that goeth in to his neighbor's wife shall not be clean when he shall touch her. Prov.6:27-29.

Do not err: neither adulterers shall possess the kingdom of God. 1 C. 6:9.

The mouth of a strange woman is a deep pit: he whom the Lord is angry with shall fall into it. Prov. 22:14.

This is a heinous crime, and a most grievous iniquity. It is a fire that devoureth even to destruction, and rooteth up all things that spring. Job 31:11 f.

Fornicators and adulterers God will judge. Heb. 13:4.

The eye of the adulterer observeth darkness. Cursed be his portion on the earth: let him not walk by the way of the vineyards. Let him pass from the snow waters to excessive heat, and his sin even to hell. Let mercy forget him: may worms be his sweetness: let him be remembered no more, but be broken in pieces as an unfruitful tree. Job 24:15, 18-20.

This man shall be punished in the streets of the city, and he shall be chased as a colt: and where he suspected not he shall be taken. Ecclus. 23:30.

Let us not commit fornication, as some of them committed fornication, and there fell in one day three-and-twenty thousand. 1 C. 10:8.

He that is an adulterer gathereth to himself shame and dishonor, and his reproach shall not be blotted out. Prov. 6:33.

Because thou hast given occasion to the enemies of the Lord to blaspheme, for this thing the child that is born to thee shall surely die. 2 K. 12:14.

If any man violate the temple of God, him shall God destroy. For the temple of God is holy, which you are. 1 C. 3:17.

Lo, thou shalt die for the woman thou hast taken: for she hath a husband. Gen. 20:3.

The children that are born of unlawful beds are witnesses of wickedness against their parents in their trial. Wis. 4:6.

I will kill her children [Jezabel's] with death. Apoc. 2:23.

17. THEFT

Thou shalt not steal. Ex. 20:15.

He that stole, let him now steal no more: but rather let him labor, working with his hands the thing which is good, that he may have something to give to him that suffereth need. Eph. 4:28.

He that is partaker with a thief hateth his own soul: he heareth one putting him to his oath, and discovereth not. Prov. 29:24.

He that stealeth anything from his father, or from his mother, and saith, this is no sin, is the partner of a murderer. Prov. 28:24.

Thou shalt not take nor remove thy neighbor's landmark. Deut. 19:14.

Thou shalt not have divers weights in thy bag, a greater and a less. Neither shall there be in thy house a greater bushel and a less. Thou shalt have a just and a true weight, and thy bushel shall be equal and true: that thou mayest live a long time upon the land which the Lord thy God shall give thee. For the Lord thy God abhorreth him that doth these things, and he hateth all injustice. Deut. 25:13-16.

Diverse weights and diverse measures both are abominable before God. Prov. 20:10.

The robberies of the wicked shall be their downfall, because they would not do judgment. Prov. 21:7.

Be not anxious for goods unjustly gotten, for they shall not profit thee in the day of calamity and revenge. For confusion and repentance is upon a thief. Eccles. 5:10, 17.

As the partridge hath hatched eggs which she did not lay, so is he that hath gathered riches, and not by right: in the midst of his days he shall leave them, and in his latter end he shall be a fool. Jer. 17:10.

You shall have just balances, and a just ephi, and a just bate. Ezech. 45:10.

Woe to him that heapeth together that which is not his own! How long also doth he load himself with thick clay? Hab. 2:6.

Do not steal, do no fraud. Mark 10:19.

He that is unjust in that which is little is unjust also in that which is greater. If you have not been faithful in that which is another's, who will give you that which is your own? Luke 16:10. 12.

Why was not this ointment sold for three hundred pence, and given to the poor? Now he said this, not because he cared for the poor, but because he was a thief, and having the purse, carried the things that were put therein. John 12:5 f.

Thou shalt not steal. Rom. 13:9.

You do wrong and defraud: and that to your brethren. Know you not that the unjust shall not possess the kingdom of God? Nor thieves, nor covetous, nor drunkards, nor railers, nor extortioners shall possess the kingdom of God. 1 C. 6, 8-10.

He that doeth an injury shall receive for that which he hath done unjustly. Col. 3:25.

[Let] no man overreach nor circumvent his brother in business: because the Lord is the avenger of all these things, as we have told you before, and have testified. He therefore that despiseth these things despiseth not man, but God. 1 Thess. 4:6, 8.

Do not err: neither fornicators, nor thieves, nor extortioners shall possess the kingdom of God. 1 C. 6:9 f.

The rest of the men did not do penance from the works of their hands that they should not adore devils. Neither did they penance from their murders, nor from their sorceries, nor from their fornication, nor from their thefts. Apoc. 9:20 f.

This is the curse that goeth forth over the face of the earth: for every thief shall be judged as is there written; and every one that sweareth in like manner shall be judged by it. I will bring it forth, saith the Lord of hosts: and it shall come to the house of the thief, and to the house of him that sweareth falsely by my name: and it shall remain in the midst of his house, and shall consume it, with the timber thereof and the stones thereof. Zach. 5:3 f.

Some distribute their own goods, and grow richer: others take away what is not their own, and are always in want. Prov. 11:24.

18. OFFERINGS OF STOLEN GOODS

You brought in of rapine the lame and the sick, and brought in an offering: shall I accept it at your hands? saith the Lord. Cursed is the deceitful man that hath in his flock a male, and making a vow offereth in sacrifice that which is feeble to the Lord. Mal. 1:13 f.

The offering of him that sacrificeth of a thing wrongfully gotten is stained, and the mockeries of the unjust are not acceptable. The Most High approveth not the gifts of the wicked: neither hath he respect to the oblations of the unjust, nor will he be pacified for sins by the multitude of their sacrifices. He that offereth sacrifice of the goods of the poor is as one that sacrificeth the son in the presence of his father. Eccles. 34:21.

Do not offer wicked gifts, for such he will not receive. And look not upon an unjust sacrifice, for the Lord is judge, and there is not with him respect of persons. Ecclus. 35:14 f.

19. EXAMPLES OF THEFT

I saw among the spoils a scarlet garment exceeding good, and two hundred sicles of silver, and a golden rule of fifty sicles: and I coveted them, and I took them away, and hid them in the ground in the midst of my tent, and the silver I covered with the earth I dug up. Jos. 7:21.

Josue took Achan, the son of Zare, and the silver, and the garment, and the golden rule, his sons also, and his daughters, his oxen, and asses, and sheep, the tent also, and all the goods, and brought them to the valley of Achor. Where Josue said: Because thou hast troubled us, the Lord trouble thee this day. And all Israel stoned him, and all things that were his were consumed with fire. Jos. 7:24 f.

It came to pass that she [Anna] received a young kid, and brought it home. And when her husband heard it bleating, he said: Take heed, lest perhaps it be stolen: restore ye it to its owners, for it is not lawful for us either to eat or to touch anything that cometh by theft. Tob. 2:20 f.

20. DECEIT AND FRAUD

From within out of the heart of men proceed evil thoughts, adulteries, deceit. All these evil things defile a man. Mark 7:21 f.

Thy habitation is in the midst of deceit: through deceit they have refused to know me, saith the Lord. Jer. 9:6.

In his sight he hath done deceitfully, that his iniquity may be found unto hatred. The words of his mouth are iniquity and guile: he would not understand that he might do well. He hath devised iniquity on his bed, he hath set himself on every way that is not good: but evil he hath not hated. Ps. 35:3-5.

You are of your father the devil; and the desires of your father you will do. He stood not in the truth, because truth is not in him. When he speaketh a lie, he speaketh of his own: for he is a liar, and the father thereof. John 8:44.

Wherefore, putting away lying, speak ye the truth every man with his neighbor: for we are members one of another. Eph. 4:25.

He that will love life, and see good days, let him refrain his tongue from evil, and his lips that they speak no guile. 1 Pet. 3:10.

Wherefore laying aside all malice, and all guile, and dissimulations. 1 Pet. 2:1.

Lie not one to another. Col. 3:9.

All liars shall have their portion in the pool burning with fire and brimstone: which is the second death. Apoc. 21:8.

Who is a liar but he who denieth that Jesus is the Christ? 1 John 2:22.

You shall not lie, neither shall any man deceive his neighbor. Lev. 19:11.

Thou shalt fly lying. Ex. 23:7.

The wicked are alienated from the womb, they have gone astray from the womb, they have spoken false things. Ps. 57:4.

He that trusteth to lies feedeth the winds. Prov. 10:4.

The dissembler with his mouth deceiveth his friend. He that walketh deceitfully revealeth secrets: but he that is faithful concealeth the thing committed to him by his friend. Prov. 11:9, 13.

A hasty witness frameth a lying tongue. Prov. 12:19.

Deceitful souls go astray in sins. The crafty man is hateful. Prov. 13:13, 17.

The double-dealer uttereth lies. Prov. 14:17.

The evil man obeyeth an unjust tongue, and the deceitful hearkeneth to lying lips. Prov. 17:4.

A false witness shall not be unpunished, and he that speaketh lies shall not escape. Prov. 19:5.

The bread of lying is sweet to a man: but afterwards his mouth shall be filled with gravel. Prov. 20:17.

Deceive not any man with thy lips. Prov. 24:28.

A deceitful tongue loveth not truth, and a slippery mouth worketh ruin. Prov. 26:28.

The Holy Spirit of discipline will flee from the deceitful. Wis. 1:5.

In no wise speak against the truth, but be ashamed of the lie of thy ignorance. Ecclus. 4:30.

Be not willing to make any manner of lie; for the custom thereof is not good. Ecclus. 7:14.

Winnow not with every wind, and go not into every way: for so is every sinner proved by a double tongue. Ecclus. 5:11.

A lie is a foul blot in a man, and yet it will be continually in the mouth of men without discipline. A thief is better than a man that is always lying: but both of them shall inherit destruction. The manners of lying men are without honor, and their confusion is with them without ceasing. Ecclus. 20:26-28.

Thou shalt not bear false witness. Ex. 20:16.

21. PUNISHMENT OF DECEIT

He that diggeth a pit shall fall into it: and he that rolleth a stone, it shall return to him. Prov. 26:27.

Their foot hath been taken in the very snare which they hid. Ps. 9:16.

He hath opened a pit and dug it, and he is fallen into the hole he made. Ps. 7:16.

He that deceiveth the just in a wicked way shall fall in his own destruction, and the upright shall possess his goods. Prov. 28:10.

A man that speaketh to his friend with flattering and dissembling words spreadeth a net for his feet. Prov. 29:5.

He that breaketh a hedge, a serpent shall bite him. He that removeth stones shall be hurt by them, and he that cutteth trees shall be wounded by them. Eccles. 10:8 f.

If one cast a stone on high, it will fall upon his own head: and the deceitful stroke will wound the deceitful. And he that setteth a stone for his neighbor shall stumble upon it, and he that layeth a snare for another shall perish in it. A mischievous counsel shall be rolled back upon the author, and he shall not know from whence it cometh to him. Ecclus. 27:28-30.

His sorrow shall be turned on his own head, and his iniquity shall come down upon his crown. Ps. 7:17.

They speak peace with their neighbor, but evils are in their hearts. Give them according to their works, and according to the wickedness of their inventions. According to the works of their hands give thou to them: render to them their reward. Ps. 27:3 f.

The deceitful man shall not find gain: but the substance of a just man shall be precious gold. Prov. 12:27.

A kingdom is translated from one people to another, because of injustices, and wrongs, and injuries, and divers deceits. Ecclus. 10:8.

Bloody and deceitful men shall not live out half their days: but I will trust in thee, O Lord. Ps. 54:24.

The bloody and the deceitful man the Lord will abhor. Ps. 5:7.

A deceitful balance is an abomination before the Lord, and a just weight is his will. Prov. 11:1.

Cursed is the deceitful man, that hath in his flock a male, and making a vow, offereth in sacrifice that which is feeble to the Lord. Mal. 1:14.

The crafty man is hateful. Prov. 14:17.

22. DETRACTION

If a serpent bite in silence, he is nothing better that backbiteth secretly. Eccles. 10:11.

In his lips is a burning fire. Prov. 16:27.

Their throat is an open sepulcher: with their tongues they acted deceitfully; the poison of asps is under their lips. Ps. 13:3.

They have whetted their tongues like a sword: they have bent their bow a bitter thing, to shoot in secret the undefiled. Ps. 63:4 f.

Whosoever speaketh ill of anything bindeth himself for the time to come: but he that feareth the commandment shall dwell in peace. Prov. 13:13.

His mouth is full of cursing, and of bitterness, and of deceit: under his tongue are labor and sorrow. Ps. 9:28.

The detractor is the abomination of men. Prov. 24:9.

A fool is beaten with lips. Prov. 10:8.

The spirit of wisdom is benevolent, and will not acquit the evil speaker from his lips: for God is witness of his reins, and he is a true searcher of his heart, and a hearer of his tongue. Therefore he that speaketh unjust things cannot be hid, neither shall the chastising judgment pass him by. Wis. 1:6, 8.

Refrain your tongue from detraction, for an obscure speech shall not go for naught. Wis. 1:11.

My son, fear the Lord and the king, and have nothing to do with detractors. For their destruction shall rise suddenly: and who knoweth the ruin of both? Prov. 24:21 f.

Neither fornicators, nor adulterers, nor railers shall possess the kingdom of God. 1 C. 6:9.

Remove from thee a froward mouth, and let detracting lips be far from thee. Prov. 4:24.

Detract not one another, my brethren. He that detracteth his brother, or he that judgeth his brother, detracteth the law and judgeth the law. But if thou judge the law, thou art not a doer of the law, but a judge. Jas. 4:11.

Laying away all malice and all detractions, as newborn babes desire the rational milk. 1 Pet. 2:1 f.

I fear lest contentions and detractions be among you. 2 C. 12:20.

Thou shalt not speak ill of the gods, and the prince of thy people thou shalt not curse. Ex. 22:28.

Why then were you not afraid to speak ill of my servant Moses? Num. 12:8.

Detract not the king, no, not in thy thought: and speak not evil of the rich man in thy private chamber: because even the birds of the air will carry thy voice, and he that hath wings will tell what thou hast said. Eccles. 10:20.

Accept no person against thy own person, nor against thy soul a lie. Ecclus. 4:66.

Thou hast loved malice more than goodness, and iniquity rather than to speak righteousness. Thou hast loved all the words of ruin, O deceitful tongue. Therefore will God destroy thee forever: he will pluck thee out, and remove thee from thy dwelling-place, and thy root out of the land of the living. Ps. 51:5-7.

Thy mouth hath abounded with evil, and thy tongue framed deceits. Sitting thou didst speak against thy brother, and didst lay a scandal against thy mother's son: these things hast thou done, and I was silent. Thou thoughtest unjustly that I shall be like to thee: but I will reprove thee, and set before thy face. Ps. 49:19-21.

Thou shalt not be a detractor nor a whisperer among the people. Lev. 19:16.

Lie not in wait, nor seek after wickedness in the house of the just, nor spoil his rest. For a just man shall fall seven times, and shall rise again: but the wicked shall fall down into evil. My son, fear the Lord and the king, and have nothing to do with detractors. Prov. 24:15 f., 21.

Do not apply thy heart to all words that are spoken, lest perhaps thou hear thy servant reviling thee. For thy conscience knoweth that thou also hast often spoken evil of others. Eccles. 7:22 f.

The whisperer and the double-tongued is accursed: for he hath troubled many that were at peace. Ecclus. 28:15.

An evil man out of the evil treasure [of his heart] bringeth forth that which is evil. For out of the abundance of the heart the mouth speaketh. Luke 6:45.

If I speak with the tongues of men and of angels, and have not charity, I am become as sounding brass or a tinkling cymbal. 1 C. 13:1.

Speak evil of no man. Titus 3:2.

If you bite and devour one another, take heed you be not consumed one of another. Gal. 5:15.

Render not evil for evil. 1 Pet. 3:9.

Pray for them that persecute and calumniate you. Mat. 5:44.

Instead of making me a return of love, they detracted me: but I gave myself to prayer. Ps. 108:4.

Blessed are ye when they shall speak all that is evil against you. Mat. 5:11.

Bless them that persecute you. Rom. 12:14.

We are reviled, and we bless: we

are persecuted, and we suffer it. 1 C. 4:12.

Hedge in thy ears with thorns, hear not a wicked tongue, and make doors and bars to thy mouth. Ecclus. 28:28.

The man that in private detracted his neighbor, him did I persecute. Ps. 100:5.

He that rejoiceth in iniquity shall be censured, and he that hateth chastisement shall have less life, and he that hateth babbling extinguisheth evil. He that sinneth against his own soul shall repent, and he that is delighted with wickedness shall be condemned. Ecclus. 19:5 f.

The north wind driveth away rain, as doth a sad countenance a backbiting tongue. Prov. 25:23.

Anger is better than laughter: because by the sadness of the countenance the mind of the offender is corrected. Eccles. 7:4.

Rehearse not again a wicked and harsh word, and thou shalt not fare the worse. Tell not thy mind to friend or foe: and if there be a sin with thee, disclose it not. For he will hearken to thee, and will watch thee, and as it were defending thy sin he will hate thee, and so will he be with thee always. Hast thou heard a word against thy neighbor? Let it die within thee, trusting that it will not burst thee. At the hearing of a word the fool is in travail, as a woman groaning in the bringing forth a child. As an arrow that sticketh in a man's thigh, so is a word in the heart of a fool. Ecclus. 19:7-12.

23. CALUMNY

Thou shalt not calumniate thy neighbor. Lev. 19:13.

Thou shalt not receive the voice of a lie; neither shalt thou join thy hand to bear false witness for a wicked person. Ex. 23:1.

Devise not a lie against thy brother, neither do the like against thy friend. Eccles. 7:13.

Be not witness without cause against thy neighbor; and deceive not any man with thy lips. Say not: I will do to him as he hath done to me: I will render to every one according to his work. Prov. 24:28 f.

Do violence to no man. Neither calumniate any man. Luke 3:14.

As a bird flying to other places, and a sparrow going here or there, so a curse uttered without cause shall come upon a man. Prov. 26:2.

Accept no person against thy own person, nor against thy soul a lie. Ecclus. 4:26.

Oppression troubleth the wise, and shall destroy the strength of his heart. Eccles. 7:8.

Of three things my heart hath been afraid. The accusation of a city, and the gathering together of the people, and a false calumny all are more grievous than death. Ecclus. 26:5-7.

Blessed is he that is defended from a wicked tongue, that hath not passed into the wrath thereof, and that hath not drawn the yoke thereof, and hath not been bound in its bands: for its yoke is a yoke of iron, and its bands are bands of brass. The death thereof is a most evil death, and hell is preferable to it. Ecclus. 28:23-25.

Its continuance shall not be for a long time, but it shall possess the ways of the unjust: and the just shall not be burnt with its flame. They that forsake God shall fall into it, and it shall burn in them, and shall not be quenched: and it shall be sent upon them as a lion, and as a leopard it shall tear them. Ecclus. 28:26 f.

He shall save the children of the poor: and he shall humble the oppressor. Ps. 71:4.

A man that beareth false witness against his neighbor is like a dart, and a sword, and a sharp arrow. Prov. 25:18.

If a lying witness stand against a man, accusing him of transgression, both of them between whom the controversy is shall stand before the Lord, in the sight of the priests and the judges that shall be in those days.

and when, after most diligent inquisition, they shall find that the false witness hath told a lie against his brother, they shall render to him as he meant to do to his brother, and thou shalt take away the evil out of the midst of thee: that others hearing may fear, and may not dare to do such things. Thou shalt not pity him, but shalt require life for life, eye for eye, tooth for tooth, hand for hand, foot for foot. Deut. 19:16-21.

A false witness shall not be unpunished, and he that speaketh lies shall not escape. Prov. 19:5.

If they have called the goodman of the house Beelzebub, how much more them of his household? Mat. 10:25.

This man casteth not out devils but by Beelzebub, the prince of the devils. Mat. 12:24.

How came this man by this wisdom and miracles? Is not this the carpenter's son? Is not his mother called Mary, and his brethren James and Joseph and Simon and Jude? And his sisters, are they not all with us? Whence therefore hath he all these things? And they were scandalized in his regard. Mat. 13:54-57.

The chief priests and the whole council sought false witness against Jesus, that they might put him to death. And they found not, whereas many false witnesses had come in. Mat. 26:59 f.

I have done judgment and justice: give me not up to them that slander me. Uphold thy servant unto good. Ps. 118:121.

Redeem me from the calumnies of men, that I may keep thy commandments. Ps. 118:134.

I beg, O Lord, that thou loose me from the band of this reproach, or else take me away from the earth. Job 3:15.

How long shall sinners, O Lord, how long shall sinners glory? Shall they utter and speak iniquity? shall all speak who work iniquity? Ps. 93:3 f.

24. EVIL-SPEAKING

Cast out the scoffer, and contention shall go out with him, and quarrels and reproaches shall cease. Prov. 22:10.

Lying lips hide hatred: he that uttereth reproach is foolish. Prov. 10:18.

The man that is accustomed to opprobrious words will never be corrected all the days of his life. Ecclus. 23:20.

The tongue is a fire. Jas. 3:6.

Injuries and wrongs will waste riches. Ecclus. 21:5.

As the vapor of a chimney and the smoke of the fire goeth up before the fire, so also injurious words and reproaches and threats before blood. Ecclus. 22:30.

Mockery and reproach are of the proud, and vengeance as a lion shall lie in wait for him. Ecclus. 27:31.

A wise man will be grieved with the disgrace. Ecclus. 21:27.

He that pricketh the eye bringeth out tears; and he that pricketh the heart bringeth forth resentment. Ecclus. 22:24.

He that flingeth a stone at birds shall drive them away; so he that upbraideth his friend breaketh friendship. Ecclus. 22:25.

Stand not against the face of an injurious person, lest he sit as a spy to entrap thee in thy words. Ecclus. 8:14.

25. RAILING

Whosoever shall say to his brother, Raca, shall be in danger of the council; and whosoever shall say, Thou fool, shall be in danger of hell fire. Mat. 5:22.

Be ye all of one mind: not rendering evil for evil, nor railing for railing; but contrariwise, blessing: for unto this are you called, that you may inherit a blessing. 1 Pet. 3:8 f.

The things which thy eyes have seen utter not hastily in a quarrel; lest afterwards thou mayest not be able to make amends, when thou hast dishonored thy friend. Prov. 25:8.

If thou offer thy gift at the altar, and there thou remember that thy brother hath anything against thee, leave there thy offering before the altar, and go first to be reconciled to thy brother; and then coming, thou shalt offer thy gift. Mat. 5:23 f.

The wicked man when he is come into the depths of sins contemneth; but ignominy and reproach follow him. Prov. 18:3.

Every mocker is an abomination to the Lord. Prov. 3:32.

He that despiseth his friend is mean of heart. Prov. 11:12.

The foolish man despiseth his mother. Prov. 15:20.

In the way of scorners is a deep pit. Prov. 13:15.

He that despiseth his neighbor sinneth. Prov. 14:21.

No man can correct whom he hath despised. Eccles. 7:14.

Laugh no man to scorn in the bitterness of his soul: for there is One who humbleth and exalteth, God who seeth all. Ecclus. 7:12.

He shall scorn the scorners. Prov. 3:34.

Despise not a just man that is poor, and do not magnify a sinful man that is rich. Ecclus. 10:26.

Despise not a man that turneth away from sin, nor reproach him therewith: remember that we are all worthy of reproof. Despise not a man in his old age; for we shall also become old. Ecclus. 8:6 f.

God hath showed to me to call no man common or unclean. Acts 10:28.

You, my dearly beloved, be mindful of the words which have been spoken before by the apostles of our Lord Jesus Christ; who told you that in the last time there should come mockers, walking according to their own desires in ungodliness. Jude 17 f.

I said: I will take heed to my ways, that I sin not with my tongue. I have set a guard to my mouth when the sinner stood against me. I was dumb, and was humbled, and kept silence from good things, and my sorrow was renewed. I was dumb, and I opened not my mouth, because thou hast done it. Remove thy scourges from me. Ps. 38:1-3, 10 f.

Owe no man anything. Rom. 13:8.

26. TALEBEARING

The words of a talebearer are as it were simple, but they reach to the innermost parts of the belly. Prov. 26:22.

The whisperer and the double-tongued is accursed: for he hath troubled many that were at peace. The tongue of a third person hath disquieted many, and scattered them from nation to nation. It hath destroyed the strong cities of the rich, and hath overthrown the houses of great men. It hath cut in pieces the forces of people, and undone strong nations. The tongue of a third person hath cast out valiant women, and deprived them of their labors. He that hearkeneth to it shall never have rest, neither shall he have a friend in whom he may repose. Ecclus. 28:15-20.

The stroke of a whip maketh a blue mark: but the stroke of the tongue will break the bones. Many have fallen by the edge of the sword, but not so many as have perished by their own tongue. Ecclus. 28, 21 f.

The talebearer shall defile his own soul, and be hated by all: and he that shall abide with him shall be hateful: the silent and wise man shall be honored. Ecclus. 21:31.

I attended and hearkened: no man speaketh what is good. Jer. 8:6.

In many words shall be found folly. Eccles. 5:2.

I heard the reproaches of many, and terror on every side: Persecute him, and let us persecute him. Jer. 20:10.

Being idle they learn to go about from house to house, and are not only idle but tattlers also, and busybodies, speaking things which they ought not. 1 Tim. 5:13.

Admonish them to speak evil of no man. Titus 3:2.

Let none of you suffer as a railer. 1 Pet. 4:15.

Be not called a whisperer, and be not taken in thy tongue, and confounded. For confusion and repentance is upon a thief, and an evil mark of disgrace upon the double-tongued: but to the whisperer, hatred, and enmity, and reproach. Ecclus. 5:16 f.

Detract not one another. Jas. 4:11.

Every idle word that men shall speak they shall render an account for it in the day of judgment. Mat. 12:36.

VI

VIRTUES AND VICES CONNECTED WITH JUSTICE

1. EXHORTATION TO PRAY

Old Testament Texts

We shall say much, and yet shall want words: but the sum of our words is, He is all. What shall we be able to do to glorify him? For the Almighty himself is above all his works. The Lord is terrible and exceeding great, and his power is admirable. Glorify the Lord as much as ever you can, for he will yet far exceed, and his magnificence is wonderful. Blessing the Lord, exalt him as much as you can: for he is above all praise. When you exalt him, put forth all your strength, and be not weary: for you can never go far enough. Ecclus. 43:29-34.

You shall call upon me, and you shall go: and you shall pray to me, and I will hear you. You shall seek me, and shall find me, when you shall seek me with all your heart. Is. 29:12 f.

Cry to me, and I will hear thee; and I will show thee great things, and sure things which thou knowest not. Jer. 33:3.

Seek ye the Lord and his power, seek ye his face evermore. And say ye: Save us, O God our Savior: and gather us together, and deliver us from the nations, that we may give glory to thy holy name. 1 Par. 16:11, 35.

Ask what thou wilt that I should give thee. 3 K. 3:5.

Seek ye the Lord while he may be found: call upon him while he is near. Is. 55:6.

Let us lift up our hearts with our hands to the Lord in the heavens. Lam. 3:41.

Let nothing hinder thee from praying always. Ecclus. 18:22.

Pray to the Lord for the city. Jer. 29:7.

Love God all thy life, and call upon him for thy salvation. Ecclus. 13:18.

Lay open thy works to the Lord, and thy thoughts shall be directed. Prov. 16:3.

Commit thy way to the Lord, and trust in him, and he will do it. Ps. 36:5.

Desire of him to direct thy ways, and that all thy counsels may abide in him. Job 4:20.

I will restore to the people a chosen lip, that all may call upon the name of the Lord, and may serve him with one shoulder. Soph. 3:9.

I will pour out upon the house of David, and upon the inhabitants of Jerusalem, the spirit of grace and of prayers. Zach. 12:10.

New Testament Texts

Love your enemies: do good to them that hate you: and pray for them that persecute and calumniate you. Mat. 5:44.

The Lord's Prayer. Mat. 6:7-15. (Cf. Mark 11:25 f.; Luke 11:1-4.)

Pray ye therefore the Lord of the harvest, that he send forth laborers into his harvest. Mat. 9:38.

Watch ye: and pray that ye enter not into temptation. The spirit indeed is willing, but the flesh is weak. Mat. 26:41.

Take ye heed, watch and pray. For ye know not when the time is. Mark 13:33.

Bless them that curse you and pray for them that calumniate you. Luke 6:28.

When he was come to the place, he said to them: Pray, lest ye enter into temptation. Luke 22:40.

I beseech you therefore, brethren, through our Lord Jesus Christ and by the charity of the Holy Ghost, that you help me in your prayers to God, that I may be delivered from the unbelievers that are in Judea and that the oblation of my service may be acceptable in Jerusalem to the saints. Rom. 15:30 f.

By all prayer and supplication praying at all times in the spirit: and in the same watching with all instance and supplication for all the saints. Eph. 6:18 f.

Be nothing solicitous: but in everything, by prayer and supplication, with thanksgiving, let your petitions be made known to God. Phil. 4:6.

Be instant in prayer: watching in it with thanksgiving. Praying withal for us also, that God may open unto us a door of speech to speak the mystery of Christ (for which also I am bound): that I may make it manifest as I ought to speak. Col. 4:3 f.

Pray for us that the word of God may run and may be glorified, even as among you: and that we may be delivered from importunate and evil men: for all men have not faith. 2 Thess. 3:1 f.

I desire therefore, first of all, that supplication, prayers, intercessions and thanksgivings be made for all men: for kings and for all that are in high station: that we may lead a quiet and a peaceable life in all piety and chastity. 1 Tim. 2:1-3.

Let us go therefore with confidence to the throne of grace: that we may obtain mercy and find grace in seasonable aid. Heb. 4:16.

If any of you want wisdom, let him ask of God who giveth to all men abundantly and upbraideth not. And it shall be given him. Jas. 1:5 f.

Is any of you sad? Let him pray. Is he cheerful in mind? Let him sing. Jas. 5:13.

Is any man sick among you? Let him bring in the priests of the church and let them pray over him, anointing him with oil in the name of the Lord. Jas. 5:14.

Pray one for another, that you may be saved. For the continual prayer of a just man availeth much. Jas. 5:16.

2. QUALITIES OF PRAYER

Old Testament Texts

Before prayer prepare thy soul, and be not as a man that tempteth God. Ecclus. 18:33.

Thou hast hardened thy heart, and hast spread thy hands to him. If thou wilt put away from thee the iniquity that is in thy hand, let not injustice remain in thy tabernacle: then mayst thou lift up thy face without spot, and thou shalt be steadfast and shalt not fear. Job 11:13-15.

He that turneth away his ears from hearing the law, his prayer shall be an abomination. Prov. 28:9.

He that adoreth God with joy shall be accepted, and his prayer shall approach even to the clouds. Ecclus. 35:20.

If I have looked at iniquity in my heart, the Lord will not hear me. Ps. 65:18.

Think of the Lord in goodness, and seek him in simplicity of heart: for he is found by them who tempt him not: and he showeth himself to them that have faith in him. Wis. 1:1 f.

Nor from the beginning have the proud been acceptable to thee: but the prayer of the humble and the meek hath always pleased thee. Jdth. 9:16.

The prayer of him that humbleth himself shall pierce the clouds: and till it come nigh he will not be comforted: and he will not depart till the Most High behold. Ecclus. 35:21.

Then shall they call upon me, and I will not hear: they shall rise in the morning and shall not find me: because they have hated instruction, and received not the fear of the Lord. Prov. 1:28 f.

He that stoppeth his ear against the cry of the poor shall also cry himself, and shall not be heard. Prov. 21:13.

He that turneth away his ears from hearing the law, his prayer shall be an abomination. Prov. 28:9.

Then this wicked man [Antiochus] prayed to the Lord, of whom he was not to obtain mercy. 2 Mac. 9:13.

You shall cry out in that day from the face of the king whom you have chosen to yourselves: and the Lord will not hear you in that day, because you desired unto yourselves a king. 1 K. 8:18.

Then shall they cry to the Lord, and he will not hear them: and he will hide his face from them at that time, as they have behaved wickedly in their devices. Mich. 3:4.

Prayer is good with fasting and alms, more than to lay up treasures of gold. For alms delivereth from death, and the same is that which purgeth away sins, and maketh to find mercy and life everlasting. Job 12:8 f.

The prayer of the humble and the meek hath always pleased thee. O God of the heavens, Creator of the waters, and Lord of the whole creation, hear me a poor wretch making supplication to thee and presuming on thy mercy. Jdth. 9:16.

New Testament Texts

When ye pray, ye shall not be as the hypocrites that love to stand and pray in the synagogues and corners of the streets, that they may be seen by men. Amen I say to you, they have received their reward. But when thou shalt pray, enter into thy chamber and, having shut the door, pray to thy Father in secret: and thy Father who seeth in secret will repay thee. Mat. 6:5 f.

When you are praying, speak not much, as the heathens. For they think that in their much speaking they may be heard. Mat. 6:7.

This people honoreth me with their lips: but their heart is far from me. Mat. 15:8.

Woe to you scribes and Pharisees, hypocrites, because you devour the houses of widows, praying long prayers. Mat. 23:14.

When you shall stand to pray, forgive, if you have aught against any man: that your Father also, who is in heaven, may forgive you your sins. Mark 11:25.

Parable of the Pharisee and the publican. Luke 18:10-14.

God is a spirit: and they that adore him must adore him in spirit and in truth. John 4:24.

The Spirit also helpeth our infirmity. For we know not what we should pray for as we ought: but the Spirit himself asketh for us with unspeakable groanings. Rom. 8:26.

I will pray with the spirit, I will pray also with the understanding. 1 C. 14:15.

Let him ask in faith, nothing wavering. Jas. 1:6.

You ask and receive not: because you ask amiss. Jas. 4:3.

This is the confidence which we have towards him: that, whatsoever we shall ask according to his will, he heareth us. And we know that he heareth whatsoever we ask: we know that we have the petitions which we request of him. 1 John 5:14 f.

Parable of the importunate friend. Luke 11:5-8.

Parable of the unjust judge. Luke 18:1-8.

3. EFFICACY OF PRAYER

Old Testament Texts

The Lord is far from the wicked, and he will hear the prayers of the just. Prov. 15:29.

He will do the will of them that fear him: and he will hear their prayer. Ps. 144:19.

In thee, O Lord, have I hoped: thou wilt hear me, O Lord my God. Ps. 37:16.

Know ye that the Lord will hear your prayers, if you continue with fastings and prayers in the sight of the Lord. Jdth. 4:11.

Call upon me in the day of trouble. I will deliver thee, and thou shalt glorify me. Ps. 49:15.

Cry to me, and I will hear thee: and I will show thee great things, and sure things which thou knowest not. Jer. 33:3.

Weeping thou shalt not weep. He will surely have pity on thee at the voice of thy cry: as soon as he shall hear, he will answer thee. Is. 30:19.

It shall come to pass that before they call I will hear: as they are yet speaking I will hear. Is. 65:24.

Neither is there any other nation so great, that hath gods so nigh them, as our God is present to all our petitions. Deut. 4:7.

Who hath continued in his commandment, and hath been forsaken? or who hath called upon him, and he despised him? Ecclus. 2:12.

My people, being converted, shall make supplication to me, and seek out my face, and do penance from their most wicked ways: then I will hear from heaven, and will forgive their sins, and will heal their land. 2 Par. 7:14.

New Testament Texts

Ask, and it shall be given you, seek, and you shall find: knock, and it shall be opened to you. Mat. 7:7.

If you then being evil, know how to give good gifts to your children: how much more will your Father who is in heaven give good things to them that ask him? Mat. 7:11.

If two of you shall consent upon earth concerning anything whatsoever they shall ask, it shall be done to them by my Father who is in heaven. Mat. 18:19.

All things whatsoever you shall ask in prayer believing, you shall receive. Mat. 21:22.

When he was come into the house, his disciples secretly asked him: Why could not we cast him out? And he said to them: This kind can go out by nothing, but by prayer and fasting. Mark 9:27 f.

All things, whatsoever you ask when ye pray, believe that you shall receive: and they shall come unto you. Mark 11:24.

Fear not, Zachary, for thy prayer is heard. Luke 1:13.

We know that God doth not hear sinners: but if a man be a server of God and doth his will, him he heareth. John 9:31.

Whatsoever you shall ask the Father in my name, that will I do: that the Father may be glorified in the Son. If you shall ask me anything in my name, that I will do. John 14:13 f.

If you abide in me and my words abide in you, you shall ask whatever you will: and it shall be done unto you. John 15:7.

In that day you shall not ask me anything. Amen, amen I say to you: if you ask the Father anything in my name, he will give it you. Hitherto you have not asked anything in my name. Ask, and you shall receive; that your joy may be full. John 16:23 f.

Whosoever shall call upon the name of the Lord shall be saved. Rom. 10:13.

Let him bring in the priests of the church and let them pray over him, anointing him with oil in the name of the Lord. And the prayer of faith shall save the sick man. And the Lord shall raise him up: and if he be in sins, they shall be forgiven him. Jas. 5:15.

Pray one for another, that you may be saved. For the continual prayer of a just man availeth much. Jas. 5:16.

If our heart do not reprehend us, we have confidence towards God. And whatsoever we shall ask, we shall receive of him: because we keep his commandments and do those things which are pleasing in his sight. 1 John 3:21 f.

This is the confidence which we have towards him: that, whatsoever we shall ask according to his will, he heareth us. 1 John 5:14.

4. TIMES OF PRAYER

Old Testament Texts

We ought to prevent the sun to bless thee, and adore thee at the dawning of the light. Wis. 16:28.

In the morning I will stand before thee, and will see, because thou art not a God that willest iniquity. Ps. 5:5.

Arise, give praise in the night; in the beginning of the watches pour out thy heart like water before the face of the Lord. Lam. 2:19.

O God, my God, to thee do I watch at break of day. For thee my soul hath thirsted; for thee my flesh, O how many ways! Ps. 62:1 f.

If I have remembered thee upon my bed, I will meditate on thee in the morning, because thou hast been my helper. Ps. 62:7 f.

I rose at midnight to give praise to thee, for the judgments of thy justification. Ps. 118:62.

Seven times a day I have given praise to thee, for the judgments of thy justice. Ps. 118:164.

When Daniel knew this, that is to say, that the law was made, he went into his house: and opening the window in his upper chamber towards Jerusalem, he knelt down three times a day, and adored, and gave thanks before his God, as he had been accustomed to do before. Dan. 6:10.

Let tears run down like a torrent day and night: give thyself no rest, and let not the apple of thy eye cease. Arise, give praise in the night, in the beginning of the watches: pour out thy heart like water before the face of the Lord, lift up thy hands to him. Lam. 2:18 f.

New Testament Texts

Watch ye, therefore, praying at all times. Luke 21:36.

Peter and John went up into the temple at the ninth hour of prayer. Acts 3:1.

Peter went up to the highest parts of the house to pray about the sixth hour. Acts 10:9.

At midnight, Paul and Silas praying, praised God. And they that were in prison heard them. Acts 16:25.

When he had said these things, kneeling down, he prayed with them all. And there was much weeping among them all. And falling on the neck of Paul, they kissed him, being grieved most of all for the word which he had said, that they should see his face no more. And they brought him on his way to the ship. Acts 20:36-38.

Take unto you the helmet of salvation and the sword of the Spirit (which is the word of God). By all prayer and supplication praying at all times in the spirit: and in the same watching with all instance and supplication for all the saints. Eph. 6:17 f.

5. PLACES OF PRAYER

Old Testament Texts

That thou mayest hearken to the prayer, which thy servant prayeth in this place to thee. 3 K. 8:29.

If heaven shall be shut up, and there shall be no rain, because of their sins, and they, praying in this place, shall do penance to thy name and shall be converted from their sins, by occasion of their affliction: then hear thou them in heaven. 3 K. 8:35 f.

That thou mayest open thy eyes upon this house, day and night, upon the place wherein thou hast promised that thy name should be called upon, and that thou wouldst hear the prayer which thy servant prayeth in it. . . Whosoever shall pray in this place, hear thou from thy dwelling place, that is, from heaven. 2 Par. 6:20 f.

But yet the people sacrificed in the high places: for there was no temple built to the name of the Lord until that day. 3 K. 3:2.

New Testament Texts

Thou, when thou shal. pray, enter into thy chamber and, having shut the door, pray to thy Father in secret: and thy Father who seeth in secret will repay thee. Mat. 6:6.

It is written: My house shall be called the house of prayer. Mat. 21:13.

Our fathers adored on this mountain: and you say that at Jerusalem is the place where men must adore. Jesus saith to her: Woman, believe me that the hour cometh, when you shall neither on this mountain nor in Jerusalem adore the Father. John 4:20 f.

All these were persevering with one mind in prayer, with the women and Mary the mother of Jesus, and with his brethren. Acts 1:14.

Continuing daily with one accord in the temple and breaking bread from house to house, they took their meat with gladness and simplicity of heart, praising God. Acts 2:46 f.

Upon the Sabbath day, we went forth without the gate by a river side, where it seemed that there was prayer. Acts 16:13.

Departing we went forward, they all bringing us on our way, with their wives and children, till we were out of the city. And we kneeled down on the shore: and we prayed. Acts 21:5.

I will therefore that men pray in every place, lifting up pure hands, without anger and contention. 1 Tim. 2:8.

6. EXAMPLES OF PRAYER

By Christ

Having dismissed the multitudes, he went into a mountain alone to pray.

Rising very early, going out, he went into a desert place: and there he prayed. Mark 1:35.

When he had dismissed them, he went up to the mountain to pray. Mark 6:46.

It came to pass, when all the people were baptized, that Jesus also being baptized and praying, heaven was opened. Luke 3:21.

He retired into the desert and prayed. Luke 5:16.

He went out into a mountain to pray: and he passed the whole night in the prayer of God. Luke 6:12.

It came to pass, as he was alone praying, his disciples also were with him: and he asked them, saying: Whom do the people say that I am? Luke 9:18.

It came to pass, about eight days after these words, that he took Peter and James and John and went up into a mountain to pray. And whilst he prayed, the shape of his countenance was altered and his raiment became white and glittering. Luke 9:28 f.

As he was in a certain place praying, when he ceased, one of his disciples said to him: Lord, teach us to pray, as John also taught his disciples. And he said to them: When you pray, say: Father, hallowed be thy name. Luke 11:1 f.

I have prayed for thee, that thy faith fail not: and thou, being once converted, confirm thy brethren. Luke 22:32.

Going a little further, he fell upon his face, praying and saying: My Father, if it be possible, let this chalice pass from me. Nevertheless, not as I will but as thou wilt. . . . Again the second time, he went and prayed, saying: My Father, if this chalice may not pass, but I must drink it, thy will be done. And he cometh again and findeth them sleeping: for their eyes were heavy. And leaving them, he went again: and he prayed the third time, saying the selfsame word. Mat. 26:39, 42-44.

Jesus said: Father, forgive them, for they know not what they do. Luke 23:34.

Jesus crying with a loud voice, said: Father, into thy hands I commend my spirit. Luke 23:46.

Jesus lifting up his eyes, said: Father, I give thee thanks that thou hast heard me. And I knew that thou hearest me always; but because of the people who stand about have I said it, that they may believe that thou hast sent me. When he had said these things, he cried with a loud voice: Lazarus, come forth. John 11:41-43.

Christ's prayer after the Last Supper. John 17:1-26.

Prayer to Christ

A leper came and adored him, saying: Lord, if thou wilt, thou canst make me clean. And Jesus stretching forth his hand, touched him, saying: I will. Be thou made clean. And forthwith his leprosy was cleansed. Mat. 8:2 f.

A great tempest arose in the sea, so that the boat was covered with waves, but he was asleep. And they came to him and awaked him, saying: Lord, save us, we perish. Mat. 8:24 f.

As Jesus passed from thence, there followed him two blind men crying out and saying: Have mercy on us, O Son of David. Mat. 9:27.

Peter making answer, said: Lord, if it be thou, bid me to come to thee upon the waters. And he said: Come. And Peter going down out of the boat walked upon the water to come to Jesus. But seeing the wind strong, he was afraid: and when he began to sink, he cried out, saying: Lord, save me. Mat. 14:28 30.

Behold a woman of Canaan, who came out of those coasts, crying out, said to him: Have mercy on me, O Lord, thou Son of David: my daughter is grievously troubled by a devil. Mat. 15:22.

Two blind men sitting by the wayside heard that Jesus passed by. And they cried out, saying: O Lord, thou Son of David, have mercy on us. . . . And Jesus stood and called them and said: What will ye that I do to you? They say to him: Lord, that our eyes be opened. And Jesus having compassion on them, touched their eyes. And immediately they saw and followed him. Mat. 20:30-34.

They bring to him one deaf and dumb: and they besought him that he would lay his hand upon him. Mark 7:32.

They came to Bethsaida: and they bring to him a blind man. And they besought him that he would touch him. Mark 8:22.

One of the multitude, answering, said: Master, I have brought my son to thee, having a dumb spirit. . . . Oftentimes hath he cast him into the fire and into the waters to destroy him. But if thou canst do anything, help us, having compassion on us. And Jesus saith to him: If thou canst believe, all things are possible to him that believeth. And immediately the father of the boy crying out, with tears said: I do believe, Lord. Help my unbelief. Mark 9:16, 21-23.

Jesus answering, said to him: What wilt thou that I should do to thee? And the blind man said to him: Rabboni, that I may see. Mark 10:51.

Jesus rising up out of the synagogue, went into Simon's house. And Simon's wife's mother was taken with a great fever: and they besought him for her. And standing over her, he commanded the fever: and it left her. Luke 4:38-40.

As he entered into a certain town, there met him ten men that were lepers, who stood afar off and lifted up their voice, saying: Jesus, Master, have mercy on us. Luke 17:12 f.

He said to Jesus: Lord, remember me when thou shalt come into thy kingdom. And Jesus said to him: Amen I say to thee: This day thou shalt be with me in paradise. Luke 23:42 f.

He having heard that Jesus was come from Judea into Galilee, went to him and prayed him to come down and heal his son: for he was at the point of death. Jesus therefore said to him: Unless you see signs and wonders you believe not. The ruler saith to him: Lord, come down before that my son die. John 4:47-49.

When he had entered into Capharnaum, there came to him a centurion, beseeching him, and saying: Lord, my servant is grievously tormented. And Jesus saith to him: I will come and heal him. Mat. 8:5-7.

Other Prayers

Old Testament Texts

When thou didst pray with tears, and didst bury the dead, and didst leave thy dinner, and hide the dead by day in thy house, and bury them by night, I offered thy prayer to the Lord. And now the Lord hath sent me to heal thee, and to deliver Sara thy son's wife from the devil. Tob. 12:12, 14.

Isaac besought the Lord for his wife, because she was barren: and he heard him, and made Rebecca to conceive. Gen. 25:21.

When the Jews heard of Nicanor's coming, and that the nations were assembled against them, they cast earth upon their heads, and made supplication to him, who chose his people, to keep them forever, and who protected his portion by evident signs. 2 Mac. 14:15.

Judas and they that were with him, encountered them, calling upon God by prayers. So fighting with their hands, but praying to the Lord with their hearts, they slew no less than five and thirty thousand, being greatly cheered with the presence of God. 2 Mac. 15:26 f.

Blot out, O Lord, my iniquities as a cloud, and as a mist my sins. Is. 44:22.

Have mercy on us, O Lord, and put away our iniquities, and cast all our sins into the bottom of the sea. Mich. 7:19.

See my abjection and my labor: and forgive me all my sins. Ps. 24:18.

If thou, O Lord, wilt mark iniquities; Lord, who shall stand it? Ps. 129:3.

And now, O Lord, think of me, and take not revenge of my sins, neither remember my offences, nor those of my parents. Job 3:3.

Turn to me, O Lord, and deliver my soul: O save me for thy mercy's sake. Ps. 6:5.

O forgive me, that I may be refreshed before I go hence and be no more. Ps. 38:14.

Evils without number have surrounded me; my iniquities have overtaken me, and I was not able to see. They are multiplied above the hairs of my head; and my heart hath forsaken me. Be pleased, O Lord, to deliver me: look down, O Lord, to help me. Ps. 39:13 f.

Heal me, O Lord, and I shall be healed: save me, and I shall be saved. Jer. 17:14.

And now, O Lord, thou art our Father, and we are clay: and thou art our Maker, and we all are the works of thy hands. Be not very angry, O Lord, and remember no longer our iniquity: behold, see we are all thy people. Is. 64:8 f.

In the multitude of thy mercy hear me. Draw me out of the mire, that I may not stick fast: deliver me from them that hate me, and out of the deep waters. Let not the tempest of water drown me, nor the deep swallow me up: and let not the pit shut her mouth upon me. Ps. 68:14-16.

Bow down thy ear to me: make haste to deliver me. Be thou unto me a God, a protector, and a house of refuge to save me. Ps. 33:3.

Turn not away thy face from me: in the day when I am in trouble, incline thy ear to me. In what day soever I shall call upon thee, hear me speedily. Ps. 101:3.

Hear us, O God our Savior, who art the hope of all the ends of the earth, and in the sea afar off. Ps. 64:6.

New Testament Texts

She was a widow until fourscore and four years: who departed not from the temple, by fastings and prayers serving night and day. Luke 2:37.

They said to him: Why do the disciples of John fast often and make prayers, and the disciples of the Pharisees in like manner: but thine eat and drink? Luke 5:33.

All these were persevering with one mind in prayer, with the women and Mary the mother of Jesus, and with his brethren. Acts 1:14.

And they were persevering in the doctrine of the apostles and in the communication of the breaking of bread and in prayers. Acts 2:42.

When they had prayed, the place was moved wherein they were assembled: and they were all filled with the Holy Ghost. Acts 4:31.

This man saw in a vision manifestly, about the ninth hour of the day, an angel of God coming in unto him and saying to him: Cornelius. And he, beholding him, being seized with fear, said: What is it, Lord? And he said to him: Thy prayers and thy alms are ascended for a memorial in the sight of God. Acts 10:3 f.

Peter therefore was kept in prison. But prayer was made without ceasing by the church unto God for him. Acts 12:5.

When they had ordained to them priests in every church and had prayed with fasting, they commended them to the Lord, in whom they believed. Acts 14:22.

The father of Publius lay sick of a fever and of a bloody flux. To whom Paul entered in: and when he had prayed and laid his hands on him, he healed him. Acts 28:8.

God is my witness, whom I serve in my spirit in the gospel of his Son, that without ceasing I make a commemoration of you: always in my prayers making request, if by any means now at length I may have a prosperous journey, by the will of God, to come unto you. Rom. 1:9 f.

Wherefore, I also, hearing of your faith that is in the Lord Jesus and of your love towards all the saints, cease not to give thanks for you, making commemoration of you in my prayers. Eph. 1:15 f.

I give thanks to my God in every remembrance of you: always in all my prayers making supplication for you all with joy. Phil. 1:3 f.

Therefore we also, from the day that we heard it, cease not to pray for you and to beg that you may be filled with the knowledge of his will, in all wisdom and spiritual understanding. Col. 1:9 f.

Epaphras saluteth you, who is one of you, a servant of Christ Jesus, who is always solicitous for you in prayers, that you may stand perfect and full in all the will of God. Col. 4:12.

We give thanks to God always for you all: making a remembrance of you in our prayers without ceasing. 1 Thess. 1:2.

We pray always for you: that our God would make you worthy of his vocation and fulfil all the good pleasure of his goodness and the work of faith in power: that the name of our Lord Jesus may be glorified in you, and you in him, according to the grace of the Lord Jesus Christ. 2 Thess. 1:11 f.

I give thanks to God, whom I serve from my forefathers, with a pure conscience, that without ceasing I have a remembrance of thee in my prayers night and day. 2 Tim. 1:3.

Concerning all things, I make it my prayer that thou mayest proceed prosperously and fare well as thy soul doth prosperously. 3 John 2.

I give thanks to my God, always making a remembrance of thee in my prayers. Philem. 4.

The Magnificat. Luke 1:46 ff.

The Benedictus. Luke 1:68 ff.

The Nunc dimittis. Luke 2:29 ff.

Suddenly there was with the angel a multitude of the heavenly army, praising God and saying: Glory to God in the highest: and on earth peace to men of good will. Luke 2:13 f.

They stoned Stephen, invoking and saying: Lord Jesus, receive my spirit. And falling on his knees, he cried with a loud voice, saying: Lord, lay not this sin to their charge. Acts 7:58 f.

The peace of God, which surpasseth all understanding, keep your hearts and minds in Christ Jesus. Phil. 4:7.

7. CONTEMPLATION OF THE WONDERFUL WORKS OF GOD

Mine eyes have looked unto thee before the morning, that I might think upon thy words. Ps. 118:148.

How have I loved thy law, O Lord! it is my meditation all the day long. Ps. 118:97.

I have lifted up mine eyes unto the hills, from whence my help shall come. Ps. 120:1.

That which is at present momentary and light of our tribulation worketh for us above measure exceedingly an eternal weight of glory: while we look not at the things which are seen, but at the things which are not seen. For the things which are seen are temporal: but the things which are not seen are eternal. 2 C. 4:17 f.

Consider the works of God, that no man can correct whom he hath despised. Eccles. 7:14.

Thou hast given me, O Lord, delight in thy doings: and in the works of thy hands shall I rejoice. Ps. 91:5.

The things that God hath commanded thee, think on them always. Ecclus. 3:22.

Let thy thoughts be upon the precepts of God, and meditate continually on his commandments; and he will give thee a heart, and the desire of wisdom shall be given to thee. Ecclus. 6:37.

The corruptible body is a load upon the soul, and the earthly habitation presseth down the mind that museth upon many things. Wis. 9:15.

Thus saith the Lord of hosts: Set your hearts to consider your ways. Agge. 1:5.

Blessed is the man that shall continue in wisdom and shall meditate in his justice, and in his mind shall think of the all-seeing eye of God. Ecclus. 14:22.

Thou shalt love the Lord thy God with thy whole heart, and with thy whole soul, and with thy whole strength. And these words that I command thee this day shall be in thy heart. And thou shalt tell them to thy children, and thou shalt meditate upon them sitting in thy house, and walking on thy journey, sleeping and rising. Deut. 6:5-7.

The Lord also said to Moses: Speak to the children of Israel, and thou shalt tell them to make to themselves fringes in the corners of their garments, putting in them ribbons of blue. That when they shall see them they may remember all the commandments of the Lord, and not follow their own thoughts and eyes, going astray after divers things. Num. 15:37-39.

I thought upon the days of old: and I had in my mind the eternal years. Ps. 76:6.

I meditated on thy commandments, which I loved. Ps. 118:47.

In all thy works remember thy last end, and thou shalt never sin. Ecclus. 7:40.

Remember the wrath that shall be at the last day, and the time of repaying when he shall turn away his face. Ecclus. 18:24.

For the rest, brethren, whatsoever things are true, whatsoever things are modest, whatsoever just, whatsoever holy, whatsoever lovely, whatsoever of good fame, if there be any virtue, if any praise of discipline, think on these things. Phil. 4:8.

Trouble and anguish have found me; thy commandments are my meditation. Ps. 118:143.

In all thy ways think on him, and he will direct thy steps. Prov. 3:6.

Evil men think not on judgment: but they that seek after the Lord take notice of all things. Prov. 28:5.

I remember the works of the Lord for I will be mindful of thy wonders from the beginning. And I will meditate on all thy works, and will be employed in thy doings. Ps. 76:12 f.

Let us run by patience to the fight proposed to us; looking on Jesus, the author and finisher of faith, who, having joy set before him, endured the cross, despising the shame, and now sitteth on the right hand of the throne of God. For think diligently upon him that endured such opposition from sinners against himself: that you be not wearied, fainting in your minds. Heb. 12:2 f.

They were always in the temple, praising and blessing God. Luke 24:53.

All they that believed were together, and continuing daily with one accord in the temple. Acts 2:46.

At the same time Isaac was walking along the way to the well which is called Of the living and the seeing: for he dwelt in the south country. And he was gone forth to meditate in the field, the day being now well spent. Gen. 24:62 f.

Teach your children that they meditate on them [the commandments] when thou sittest in thy house, and when thou walkest on the way, and when thou liest down and risest up: thou shalt write them upon the posts and doors of thy house. Deut. 11:19 f.

In a desert land, and where there is no way and no water, so in the sanctuary have I come before thee, to see thy power and thy glory. Ps. 62:3.

Upon the Sabbath day we went forth without the gate by a riverside, where it seemed that there was prayer. Acts 16:13.

Evening and morning and at noon I will speak and declare: and he shall hear my voice. Ps. 54:18.

My eyes shall be open, and my ears to the prayer of him that shall pray in this place. For I have chosen and have sanctified this place, that my name may be there forever, and my eyes and my heart may remain there perpetually. 2 Par. 7:15 f.

Solomon stood before the altar of the Lord in the sight of the assembly of Israel, and spread forth his hands to heaven. 3 K. 8:22.

I will rejoice under the covert of thy wings, my soul hath stuck close to thee: thy right hand hath received me. Ps. 62:8 f.

Rising very early, going out, he went into a desert place: and there he prayed. Mark 1:35.

I will meditate on thy commandments, and I will consider thy ways. I will think upon thine ordinances: I will not forget thy words. Ps. 118:15 f.

Princes did sit and speak against me: but thy servant was occupied in thy statutes. Ps. 118:23.

Thy testimonies are my meditation, and thine ordinances are my counsel. Ps. 118:24.

I meditated on thy commandments, which I loved. And I lifted up my hands unto thy commandments, which I have loved: and I meditated on thine ordinances. Ps. 118:47 f.

Because I have not known learning, I will go in to the powers of the Lord: O Lord, I will be mindful of thy justice alone. Ps. 70:16.

Thou hast taught me, O God, from my youth: and till now I will declare thy wondrous works, and unto old age and gray hairs. O God, forsake me not, until I show forth thine arm to all the generation that is to come. Ps. 70:17 f.

8. OATHS

Thou shalt swear: As the Lord liveth, in truth, and in judgment, and in justice: and the Gentiles shall bless him, and shall praise him. Jer. 4:2.

Men swear by one greater than themselves: and an oath for confirmation is the end of all their controversy. Heb. 6:16.

Let not thy mouth be accustomed to swearing: for in it there are many falls. And let not the naming of God be usual in thy mouth, and meddle not with the names of saints, for thou shalt not escape free from them. For as a slave daily put to the question is never without a blue mark, so every one that sweareth, and nameth, shall not be wholly pure from sin. A man that sweareth much shall be filled with iniquity, and a scourge shall not depart from his house. Ecclus. 23:9-12.

A man that beareth false witness against his neighbor is like a dart and a sword and a sharp sword Prov. 25:18.

A faithful witness will not lie, but a deceitful witness uttereth a lie. Prov. 14:5.

I say to you not to swear at all: neither by heaven, for it is the throne of God: nor by the earth, for it is his footstool: nor by Jerusalem, for it is the city of the great King: neither shalt thou swear by thy head, because thou canst not make one hair white or black. But let your speech be: Yea, yea: No, no: and that which is over and above these is of evil. Mat. 5:34-37.

He that sweareth by the altar sweareth by it, and by all things that are upon it: and whosoever shall swear by the temple sweareth by it, and by him that dwelleth in it: and he that sweareth by heaven sweareth by the throne of God, and by him that sitteth thereon. Mat. 23:20-22.

Above all things, my brethren, swear not: neither by heaven, nor by the earth, nor by any other oath. But let your speech be: Yea, yea: No, no: that you fall not under judgment. Jas. 5:12.

From the heart come forth false testimonies. Mat. 15:19.

9. PERJURY

Thou shalt not bear false witness against thy neighbor. Deut. 5:20.

Thou shalt not receive the voice of a lie: neither shalt thou join thy hand to bear false witness for a wicked person. Ex. 33:1.

A false witness shall not be unpunished: and he that speaketh lies shall perish. Prov. 19:9.

Thou shalt not take the name of the Lord thy God in vain: for the Lord will not hold him guiltless that shall take the name of the Lord his God in vain. Ex. 20:7.

The person that sweareth, and uttereth with his lips, that he would do either evil or good, and bindeth the same with an oath and his word, and having forgotten it afterwards, understandeth his offence, let him do penance for his sin. Lev. 5:4 f.

Thou shalt not swear falsely by my name, nor profane the name of thy God. I am the Lord. Lev. 19:12.

He that sweareth to his neighbor, and deceiveth not, shall dwell in thy tabernacle. Ps. 14:5.

Who shall ascend into the mountain of the Lord? or who shall stand in his holy place? He that hath clean hands and a pure heart: who hath not taken his soul in vain, nor sworn deceitfully to his neighbor. Ps. 23:3 f.

Let none of you imagine evil in your hearts against his friend, and love not a false oath: for all these are the things that I hate, saith the Lord. Zach. 8:17.

He said to me: This is the curse that goeth forth over the face of the earth: for every thief shall be judged as is there written: and every one that sweareth in like manner shall be judged by it. Zach. 5:3.

I will be a speedy witness against false swearers. Mal. 3:5.

10. VOWS

When thou hast made a vow to the Lord thy God, thou shalt not delay to pay it, because the Lord thy God will require it. And if thou delay, it shall be imputed to thee for a sin. If thou wilt not promise, thou shalt be without sin. But that which is once gone out of thy lips thou shalt observe, and shalt do as thou hast promised to the Lord thy God, and hast spoken with thy own will and with thy own mouth. Deut. 23:21-23.

If thou hast vowed anything to God, defer not to pay it; for unfaithful and foolish promise displeaseth him: but whatsoever thou hast vowed, pay it: and it is much better not to vow, than after a vow not to perform the things promised. Ecclus. 5:3 f.

It is ruin to a man to devour holy ones, and after vows to retract. Prov. 20:25.

Jacob made a vow, saying: If God shall be with me, and shall keep me in the way by which I walk, and shall give me bread to eat and raiment to put on, and I shall return prosperously to my father's house, the Lord shall be my God: and this stone, which I have set up for a title, shall be called the house of God: and of all things that thou shalt give to me, I will offer tithes to thee. Gen. 28:20-22.

Israel, binding himself by vow to the Lord, said: If thou wilt deliver this people into my hand, I will utterly destroy their cities. And the Lord heard the prayers of Israel, and delivered up the Chanaanite. Num. 21:2 f.

The things which his father had vowed, and he himself had vowed, he brought into the house of the Lord, gold and silver, and vessels of divers uses. 2 Par. 15:18.

The people rejoiced when they promised their offerings willingly, because they offered them to the Lord with all their heart: and David the king rejoiced also with a great joy. 1 Par. 29:9.

The children of Israel and Juda, that dwelt in the cities of Juda, brought in the tithes of oxen and sheep, and the tithes of holy things, which they had vowed to the Lord their God: and carrying them all, made many heaps. 2 Par. 31:6.

So Heliodorus after he had offered a sacrifice to God, and made great vows to him, that had granted him life, and given thanks to Onias, taking his troops with him, returned to the king. 2 Mac. 3:35.

11. TITHES

Tithes of the land, whether of corn or of the fruits of trees, are the Lord's, and are sanctified to him. Lev. 27:30.

All the things that you shall offer of the tithes, and shall separate for the gifts of the Lord, shall be the best and choicest things. Num. 18:29.

Woe to you, scribes and Pharisees, hypocrites! because you tithe mint, and anise, and cummin, and have left the weightier things of the law. Mat. 23:23.

Of all things that thou shalt give to me, I will offer tithes to thee. Gen. 28:22.

12. FEAST DAYS

Remember that thou keep holy the Sabbath day. Ex. 20:8.

Six days shall ye do work: the seventh day, because it is the rest of the Sabbath, shall be called holy. You shall do no work on that day: it is the Sabbath of the Lord in all your habitations. Lev. 23:3.

If thou turn away thy foot from the Sabbath, from doing thy own will in my holy day, and call the Sabbath delightful, and the holy of the Lord glorious, and glorify him, while thou dost not thy own ways, and thy own will is not found to speak a word: then shalt thou be delighted in the Lord, and I will lift thee up above the high places of the earth, and will feed thee with the inheritance of Jacob thy father. For the mouth of the Lord hath spoken it. Is. 58:13 f.

Take heed to your souls, and carry no burdens on the Sabbath day: and bring them not in by the gates of Jerusalem: if you will hearken to me, saith the Lord, to bring in no burdens by the gates of this city on the Sabbath day, and if you will sanctify the Sabbath day, to do no work therein. Jer. 17:21, 24.

Nehemias said to them: Go, eat fat meats, and drink sweet wine, and send portions to them that have not prepared for themselves: because it is the holy day of the Lord, and be not sad: for the joy of the Lord is our strength. 2 Es. 8:10.

When there was a festival of the Lord, and a good dinner was prepared in Tobias's house, he said to his son: Go, and bring some of our tribe that fear God, to feast with us. Tob. 2:1 f.

Jewish Feasts and Their Figurative Meaning

Daily

The perpetual sacrifice of a lamb slain morning and evening, figuring the perpetuity of Christ's presence in the Church. Lev. 23:35. (Heb. 13:8.)

Weekly

The solemnity of the Sabbath, figuring our spiritual rest through Christ. Lev. 23:36. (Heb. 4:4.)

Monthly

Feast of the new moon, figuring the illumination of the early Church through Christ's ministry. Num. 28:1.

Yearly

Feast of the Pasch, figuring the death of Christ for the redemption of the world. Ex. 12:3. (1 C. 5:7.)

Feast of Pentecost, figuring the descent of the Holy Ghost. Deut. 16:9.

Feast of Trumpets, figuring the preaching of the apostles. Lev. 23:24.

Feast of Expiation, figuring the cleansing of the Christian people from sin. Lev. 16:30.

Feast of Tabernacles, figuring our journey through this life from virtue to virtue. Lev. 23:43.

Feast of Ingathering, figuring the gathering in of the faithful into our heavenly home. Deut. 16:13.

Other Feasts and Ceremonies

Feast of the Dedication of Solomon's Temple. 3 K. 8:65.

Feast of Lots. Esth. 9:31.

Reading of the law aloud to the people every seventh year. Deut. 31:11.

The covenant of circumcision, figuring the sacrament of baptism. Gen. 17:13. (1 C. 2:11.)

The eating of the Paschal lamb, figuring the sacrament of the Holy Eucharist. Ex. 12:8.

The purifications, figuring the sacrament of penance. Ex. 30:18.

Consecration of the priests, figuring the sacrament of holy orders. Ex. 28:41.

The covenant sacrifice offered once for all in the desert, figuring the sacrifice of the Cross. Ex. 24:8.

13. GOD TO BE GLORIFIED AND PRAISED

Magnify his name, and give glory to him with the voice of your lips, and with the canticles of your mouths, and with harps: and in praising him you shall say in this manner: All the works of the Lord are exceeding good. Ecclus. 39:20 f.

Give thanks whilst thou art living: whilst thou art alive and in health thou shalt give thanks, and shalt praise God, and shalt glory in his mercies. How great is the mercy of the Lord, and his forgiveness to them that turn to him! Ecclus. 17:27 f.

Be ye filled with the Holy Spirit; speaking to yourselves in psalms and hymns and spiritual canticles, singing and making melody in your hearts to the Lord. Eph. 5:18 f.

Let the word of Christ dwell in you abundantly, in all wisdom: teaching and admonishing one another in psalms, hymns, and spiritual canticles, singing in grace in your hearts to God. Col. 3:10.

By him let us offer the sacrifice of praise always to God; that is to say, the fruit of lips confessing to his name. Heb. 13:15.

Is any of you sad? let him pray. Is he cheerful in mind? let him sing. Jas. 5:13.

---

[1] See St. Thomas, *Summa theol.*, Ia, q. 102, a. 4.

The Lord is great, and exceedingly to be praised: he is to be feared above all gods. Ps. 95:4.

Who shall declare the powers of the Lord? who shall set forth all his praises? Ps. 105:2.

14. DIVINATIONS AND OTHER SUPERSTITIONS

Deceitful divinations, and lying omens, and the dreams of evildoers are vanity. And the heart fancieth as that of a woman in travail: except it be a vision sent forth from the Most High, set not thy heart upon them. Ecclus. 34:5 f.

Learn not according to the ways of the Gentiles; and be not afraid of the signs of heaven, which the heathens fear. Jer. 10:2.

Go not aside after wizards, neither ask anything of soothsayers, to be defiled by them: I am the Lord your God. Lev. 19:31.

Let there not be found among you any one that . . . consulteth soothsayers, or observeth dreams and omens; neither let there be any wizard, nor charmer, nor any one that consulteth pythonic spirits or fortune-tellers, or that seeketh the truth from the dead. For the Lord abhorreth all these things. Deut. 18:10-12.

Stand now with thy enchanters, and with the multitude of thy sorceries, in which thou hast labored from thy youth, if so be it may profit thee anything, or if thou mayest become stronger. Thou hast failed in the multitude of thy counsels: let now the astrologers stand and save thee, they that gazed at the stars and counted the months, that from them they might tell the things that shall come to thee. Behold, they are as stubble, fire hath burnt them. Is. 47:12 f.

I am the Lord, that make void the tokens of diviners, and make the soothsayers mad. Is. 44:25.

Wizards thou shalt not suffer to live. Ex. 22:18.

The soul that shall go aside after magicians and soothsayers, and shall commit fornication with them, I will set my face against that soul, and destroy it out of the midst of its people. Lev. 20:6.

Thou hast cast off thy people, the house of Jacob, because they are filled as in times past, and have had soothsayers, as the Philistines. Is. 2:6.

Sorcerers shall have their portion in the pool burning with fire and brimstone, which is the second death. Apoc. 21:8.

Many of them who had followed curious arts brought together their books, and burnt them before all; and counting the price of them, they found the money to be fifty thousand pieces of silver. Acts 19:19.

15. BLASPHEMY

Amen I say to you, that all sins shall be forgiven unto the sons of men, and the blasphemies wherewith they shall blaspheme: but he that shall blaspheme against the Holy Ghost shall never have forgiveness, but shall be guilty of an everlasting sin. Mark 3:28 f.

The man that curseth his God shall bear his sin; and he that blasphemeth the name of the Lord, dying let him die: all the multitude shall stone him, whether he be a native or a stranger. Lev. 24:15 f.

Lay you all away anger, indignation, malice, blasphemy. Col. 3:8.

16. HONOR DUE TO PARENTS

My son, hear the instruction of thy father, and forsake not the law of thy mother: that grace may be added to thy head, and a chain of gold to thy neck. Prov. 1:8 f.

Hearken to thy father that begot thee, and despise not thy mother when she is old. Prov. 23:22.

Honor thy father and mother, as the Lord thy God hath commanded thee, that thou mayest live a long time, and it may be well with thee in the land which the Lord thy God will give thee. Deut. 5:16.

Let every one fear his father and his mother. Lev. 19:3.

Thou shalt honor thy mother all the days of her life. Tob. 4:3.

Hear, ye children, the instruction of a father, and attend, that you may know prudence. Prov. 4:1.

A wise son maketh the father glad; but a foolish son is the sorrow of his mother. Prov. 10:1.

My son, keep my words, and lay up my precepts with thee. Prov. 7:1.

My son, forget not my law, and let thy heart keep my commandments. For they shall add to thee length of days, and years of life and peace. Prov. 3:1 f.

My son, keep the commandments of thy father, and forsake not the law of thy mother. Prov. 6:20.

A wise son maketh a father joyful; but the foolish man despiseth his mother. Prov. 15:20.

He that afflicteth his father, and chaseth away his mother, is infamous and unhappy. Prov. 19:26.

He that curseth his father and mother, his lamp shall be put out in the midst of darkness. Prov. 20:20.

No good shall come to the deceitful son. Prov. 14:15.

Children, hear the judgment of your father, and so do that you may be saved: for God hath made the father honorable to the children: and seeking the judgment of the mothers, hath confirmed it upon the children. Ecclus. 3:2 f.

Children, obey your parents in the Lord: for this is just. Eph. 6:1.

Honor thy father and thy mother, that thou mayest be long-lived upon the land which the Lord thy God will give thee. Ex. 20:12.

Honor thy father, and forget not the groanings of thy mother: remember that thou hadst not been born but through them: and make a return to them as they have done for thee. Ecclus. 7:29 f.

He that honoreth his mother is as one that layeth up a treasure. He that honoreth his father shall have joy in his own children, and in the day of his prayer he shall be heard. He that honoreth his father shall enjoy a long life: and he that obeyeth the father shall be a comfort to his mother. He that feareth the Lord honoreth his parents, and will serve them as his masters that brought him into the world. Honor thy father in word, and work, and all patience, that a blessing may come upon thee from him, and his blessing may remain in the latter end. The father's blessing establisheth the houses of the children: but the mother's curse rooteth up the foundation. Ecclus. 3:5-11.

Speak not so, for we are the children of saints, and look for that life which God will give to those that never change their faith from him. Tob. 2:17 f.

We are the children of saints, and we must not be joined together like heathens that know not God. Tob. 8:5.

A wise son heareth the doctrine of his father: but he that is a scorner heareth not when he is reproved. Prov. 13:1.

Glory not in the dishonor of thy father, for his shame is no glory to thee: for the glory of a man is from the honor of his father, and a father without honor is the disgrace of the son. Ecclus. 3:12 f.

Son, support the old age of thy father, and grieve him not in his life: and if his understanding fail, have patience with him, and despise him not when thou art in thy strength: for the relieving of the father shall not be forgotten. Ecclus. 3:14 f.

If a man have a stubborn and unruly son who will not hear the commandments of his father or mother, and being corrected slighteth obedience: they shall take him and bring him to the ancients of the city, and to the gate of judgment, and shall say to them: This our son is rebellious and stubborn, he slighteth hearing our admonitions, he giveth himself to revelling, and to debauchery and banquetings: the people of the city shall stone him: and he shall die, that you may take away the evil out of the midst of you, and all Israel hearing it may be afraid. Deut. 21:18-21.

Of what an evil fame is he that forsaketh his father! and he is cursed of God that angereth his mother. Ecclus. 3:18.

The eye that mocketh at his father and that despiseth the labor of his mother in bearing him, let the ravens of the brook pick it out, and the young eagles eat it. Prov. 30:17.

A son ill taught is the confusion of the father: and a foolish daughter shall be to his loss. A wise daughter shall bring an inheritance to her husband: but she that confoundeth becometh a disgrace to her father. She that is bold shameth both her father and her husband, and will not be inferior to the ungodly, and shall be disgraced by them both. Ecclus.22:3-5.

He that curseth his father or mother, dying let him die: he hath cursed his father and mother, let his blood be upon him. Lev. 20:9.

17. DUTIES OF PARENTS

You fathers, provoke not your children to anger: but bring them up in the discipline and correction of the Lord. Eph. 6:4.

Suffer the little children to come to me, and forbid them not: for of such is the kingdom of God. Mark 10:14.

Nine things that are not to be imagined by the heart have I magnified, and the tenth I will utter to men with my tongue: a man that hath joy of his children. Ecclus. 25:9 f.

Rejoice not in ungodly children, if they be multiplied: neither be delighted in them, if the fear of God be not with them. Trust not to their life, and respect not their labors. For better is one that feareth God than a thousand ungodly children. And it is better to die withhout children than to leave ungodly children. Ecclus. 16:1-4.

It is better that thy children should ask of thee, than that thou look toward the hands of thy children. Ecclus. 33:22.

18. BLESSING OF MEMBERSHIP IN THE CHURCH

Blessed be the God and Father of our Lord Jesus Christ, who blessed us with spiritual blessings in heavenly places, in Christ. Eph. 1:3.

We are his workmanship: for which cause be mindful that you being heretofore Gentiles in the flesh who are called uncircumcision by that which is called circumcision in the flesh made by hands, that you were at that time without Christ, being aliens from the conversation of Israel, and strangers to the testament, having no hope of the promise, and without God in this world. But now in Christ Jesus, you, who sometime were afar off, are made nigh by the blood of Christ. Eph. 2:10-13.

Now you are no more strangers and foreigners: but you are fellow citizens with the saints, and the domestics of God: built upon the foundation of the apostles and prophets, Jesus Christ himself being the chief cornerstone. Eph. 2:19 f.

You are a chosen generation, a kingly priesthood, a holy nation, a purchased people: that you may declare his virtues, who hath called you out of darkness into his marvellous light. Who in time past were not a people: but are now the people of God. Who had not obtained mercy: but now have obtained mercy. 1 Pet. 2:9 f.

God is faithful: by whom you are called unto the fellowship of his Son, Jesus Christ our Lord. 1 C. 1:9.

Give thanks to God the Father, who hath made us worthy to be partakers of the lot of the saints in light: who hath delivered us from the power of darkness, and hath translated us into the kingdom of the Son of his love. Col. 1:12 f.

19. OFFICES AND DUTIES OF RELIGIOUS LIFE

If any man will come after me, let him deny himself, and take up his cross and follow me. Mat. 16:24.

If any man think himself to be religious, not bridling his tongue, but deceiving his own heart, this man's religion is vain. Jas. 1:26.

Blessed are they that dwell in thy house, O Lord: they shall praise thee forever and ever. Ps. 83:5.

Blessed are thy men, and blessed are thy servants, who stand before thee always, and hear thy wisdom. 3 K. 10:8.

Better is one day in thy courts above thousands: I have chosen to be an abject in the house of my God, rather than to dwell in the tabernacles of sinners. Ps. 83:1.

I a prisoner in the Lord beseech you that you walk worthy of the vocation in which you are called. With all humility and mildness, with patience, supporting one another in charity. Eph. 4:1 f.

20. APOSTASY

Hath not this been done to thee because thou hast forsaken the Lord thy God at that time when he led thee by the way? Thy own wickedness shall reprove thee, and thy apostasy shall rebuke thee. Know thou and see that it is an evil and a bitter thing for thee to have left the Lord thy God, and that my fear is not with thee, saith the Lord the God of hosts. Jer. 2:17.

Ye children of Israel, turn again to the Lord, and he will return to the remnant of you. Harden not your necks, as your fathers did: yield yourselves to the Lord and come to his sanctuary: serve the Lord, and the wrath of his indignation shall be turned away from you. 2 Par. 30:6, 8.

Knowest thou not that the benignity of God leadeth thee to penance? Rom. 2:4.

Go not down into Egypt, but stay in the land that I shall tell thee. Gen. 26:2.

No man putting his hand to the plow, and looking back, is fit for the kingdom of God. Luke 9:62.

Little children, it is the last hour: and as you have heard that Antichrist cometh, even now there are become many Antichrists: whereby we know that it is the last hour. They went out from us; but they were not of us. For if they had been of us, they would no doubt have remained with us: but that they may be manifest that they are not all of us. 1 John 2:18 f.

21. EVANGELICAL POVERTY

Every one that hath left house, or brethren, or sisters, or father, or mother, or wife, or children, or lands, for my name's sake, shall receive an hundredfold, and shall possess life everlasting. Mat. 19:29. (See also Luke 18:29 f.)

It came to pass that the beggar died, and was carried by the angels into Abraham's bosom: and the rich man also died, and he was buried in hell. Luke 16:22.

Blessed are the poor in spirit: for theirs is the kingdom of heaven. Mat. 5:3.

The poor shall eat, and shall be filled: and they shall praise the Lord that seek him, their hearts shall live forever and ever. Ps. 21:27.

If thou wilt be perfect, go sell what thou hast, and give to the poor, and thou shalt have treasure in heaven: and come, follow me. Mat. 19:21.

Hath not God chosen the poor in this world, rich in faith, and heirs of the kingdom which God hath promised to them that love him? Jas. 2:5.

22. THE POOR IN SPIRIT

The foxes have holes, and the birds of the air nests: but the Son of man hath not where to lay his head. Mat. 8:20.

Do not possess gold, nor silver, nor money in your purses: nor scrip for your journey, nor two coats, nor shoes, nor a staff· for the workman is worthy of his meat. Mat. 10:9 f.

She brought forth her firstborn Son, and wrapped him up in swaddling clothes, and laid him in a manger, because there was no room for them in the inn. Luke 2:7.

They had all things common: their possessions and goods they sold, and divided them to all, according as every one had need. Acts 2:44 f.

Great grace was in them all. For neither was there any one needy among them. For as many as were owners of lands, or houses, sold them, and brought the price of the things they sold, and laid it down before the feet of the apostles. And distribution was made to every one according as he had need. Acts 4:33-35.

Silver and gold I have none. Acts 3:6.

I have not coveted any man's silver, gold, or apparel, as you yourselves know: for such things as were needful for me and them that are with me, these hands have furnished. Acts 20:33 f.

23. CHASTITY

In the resurrection they shall neither marry nor be married, but shall be as the angels of God in heaven. Mat. 22:30.

There are eunuchs who were born so from their mother's womb: and there are eunuchs who were made so by men: and there are eunuchs who have made themselves eunuchs for the kingdom of heaven. He that can take, let him take it. Mat. 19:12.

All things are clean to the clean: but to them that are defiled, and to unbelievers, nothing is clean: but both their mind and their conscience are defiled. Titus 1:15.

Dearly beloved, I beseech you as strangers and pilgrims to refrain yourselves from carnal desires, which war against the soul. 1 Pet. 2:11.

Never have I joined myself with them that play: neither have I made myself partaker with them that walk in lightness. Tob. 3:17.

Evil thoughts are an abomination to the Lord: and pure words most beautiful shall be confirmed by him. Prov. 15:26.

He that loveth cleanness of heart, for the grace of his lips shall have the king for his friend. Prov. 22:11.

Remove anger from thy heart, and put away evil from thy flesh. For youth and pleasure are vain. Eccles. 11:10.

No price is worthy of a continent soul. Ecclus. 26:20.

As I knew that I could not otherwise be continent except God gave it, I went to the Lord, and besought him. Wis. 8:21.

Blessed are the clean of heart: for they shall see God. Mat. 5:8.

I beseech you, brethren, by the mercy of God, that you present your bodies a living sacrifice, holy, pleasing to God, your reasonable service. Rom. 12:1.

Know you not that you are the temple of God, and that the Spirit of God dwelleth in you? But if any one violate the temple of God, him shall God destroy. For the temple of God is holy: which you are. 1 C. 3:16 f.

Or know you not that your members are the temple of the Holy Ghost, who is in you, whom you have from God; and you are not your own? For you are bought with a great price. Glorify and bear God in your body. 1 C. 6:19 f.

24. VIRGINITY

No man could say the canticle but those hundred forty-four thousand, who were purchased from the earth. These are they who were not defiled with women: for they are virgins. These follow the Lamb whithersoever he goeth. These were purchased from among men, the first fruits to God and to the Lamb. Apoc. 14:4 f.

I will give to them in my house, and within my walls, a place, and a name better than sons and daughters: I will give them an everlasting name, which shall never perish. Is. 56:5.

Happy is the barren, and the undefiled that hath not known bed in sin: she shall have fruit in the visitation of holy souls: and the eunuch that hath not wrought iniquity with his hands, nor thought wicked things against God: for the precious gift of faith shall be given to him, and a most acceptable lot in the temple of God. Wis. 3:13 f.

I would that all men were even as myself: but every one hath his proper gift from God, one after this manner, and another after that. But I say to the unmarried, and to the widows: it is good for them if they so continue, even as I. 1 C. 7:7 f.

Now concerning virgins I have no commandment of the Lord: but I give counsel, as having obtained mercy of the Lord to be faithful. I think therefore that this is good for the present necessity, that it is good for a man so to be. 1 C. 7:25 f.

25. OBEDIENCE

If it be just in the sight of God to hear you rather than God, judge ye: for we cannot but speak the things which we have seen and heard. Acts 4:19 f.

We ought to obey God rather than men. Acts 5:29.

Be subject to God: but resist the devil, and he will fly from you. Jas. 4:7.

This is my beloved Son, in whom I am well pleased: hear ye him. Mat. 17:5.

Obey your prelates, and be subject to them. For they watch as being to render an account of your souls: that they may do this with joy, and not with grief: for this is not expedient for you. Heb. 13:17.

The scribes and Pharisees have sitten on the chair of Moses. All things therefore whatsoever they shall say to you, observe and do: but according to their works do ye not: for they say, and do not. Mat. 23:2 f.

He that heareth you, heareth me: and he that despiseth you, despiseth me. And he that despiseth me, despiseth him that sent me. Luke 10:16.

Let every soul be subject to higher powers: for there is no power but from God: and those that are, are ordained of God. Therefore he that resisteth the power, resisteth the ordinance of God. And they that resist, purchase to themselves damnation. For princes are not a terror to the good work, but to the evil. Wilt thou then not be afraid of the power? Do that which is good: and thou shalt have praise from the same. Wherefore be subject of necessity, not only for wrath, but also for conscience' sake. Rom. 13:1-3, 5.

Admonish them to be subject to princes and powers, to obey at a word, to be ready to every good work. Titus 3:1.

Be ye subject to every human creature for God's sake: whether it be to the king as excelling: or to governors as sent by him for the punishment of evildoers, and for the praise of the good. For so is the will of God, that by doing well you may put to silence the ignorance of foolish men: as free, and not as making liberty a cloak for malice, but as the servants of God. Honor all men. Love the brotherhood. Fear God. Honor the king. 1 Pet. 2:13-17.

Servants, be subject to your masters with all fear, not only to the good and gentle, but also to the froward. 1 Pet. 2:18.

Servants, be obedient to them that are your lords according to the flesh, with fear and trembling, in the simplicity of your heart, as to Christ: not serving to the eye, as it were pleasing men, but, as the servants of Christ, doing the will of God from the heart, with a good will serving, as to the Lord, and not to men, knowing that whatsoever good thing any man shall do, the same shall he receive from the Lord, whether he be bond or free. Eph. 6:5-8.

Purify your souls in the obedience of charity, with a brotherly love, from a sincere heart love one another earnestly. 1 Pet. 1:22.

An obedient man shall speak of victory. Prov. 21:28.

Much better is obedience than the victims of fools, who know not what evil they do. Eccles. 4:17.

Doth the Lord desire holocausts and victims, and not rather that the voice of the Lord should be obeyed? For obedience is better than sacrifices, and to hearken rather than to offer the fat of rams. 1 K. 15:22.

Every one that is of the truth heareth my voice. John 15:37.

Man liveth not by bread alone, but by every word that proceedeth out of the mouth of God. Mat. 4:4.

Whosoever heareth these my words, and doeth them, shall be likened to a wise man, who built his house upon a rock: and the rain fell, and the floods came, and the winds blew, and they beat upon that house: and it fell not, for it was founded upon a rock. Mat. 7:24 f.

If you continue in my word, you shall be my disciples indeed: and you shall know the truth, and the truth shall make you free. Amen, amen I say to you: If any man keep my word, he shall not see death forever. John 8:31 f., 51.

My sheep hear my voice: and I know them, and they follow me. John 10:27.

He that despiseth me, and receiveth not my words, hath One that judgeth him: the word that I have spoken, the same shall judge him in the last day. John 12:48.

He that is of God heareth the words of God. John 8:47.

If any one love me, he will keep my word: and my Father will love him, and we will come to him, and will make our abode with him. John 14:23.

The word of the Lord endureth forever; and this is the word which by the gospel hath been preached unto you. 1 Pet. 1:25.

26. PUNISHMENT OF DISOBEDIENCE

Because thou hast eaten of the tree whereof I commanded thee that thou shouldst not eat, cursed is the earth in thy work. Gen. 3:17.

Because thou hast not been obedient to the Lord, thy dead body shall not be brought into the sepulcher of thy fathers. 3 K. 13:21.

By the disobedience of one man many were made sinners. Rom. 5:19.

Every disobedience received a just recompense of reward. Heb. 2:2.

It is like the sin of witchcraft to rebel; and like the crime of idolatry to refuse to obey. Forasmuch therefore as thou hast rejected the word of the Lord, the Lord hath also rejected thee from being king. 1 K. 15:23.

He that despiseth these things despiseth not man, but God, who also hath given his Holy Spirit in us. 1 Thess. 4:8.

Let not any man judge, and let not a man be rebuked: for the people are as they that contradict the priest. Osee 4:4.

Because I called, and you refused; I stretched out my hand, and there was none that regarded; you have despised all my counsel, and have neglected my reprehensions: I also will laugh in your destruction, and will mock when that shall come to you which you feared. Prov. 1:24-26.

Behold, I set forth in your sight this day a blessing and a curse: a blessing, if you obey the commandments of the

Lord your God, which I command you this day: a curse, if you obey not the commandments of the Lord your God, but revolt from the way which now I show you, and walk after strange gods which you know not. Deut. 11:26-28.

If you be willing, and will hearken to me, you shall eat the good things of the land. But if you will not, and will provoke me to wrath, the sword shall devour you, because the mouth of the Lord hath spoken it. Is. 1:19 f.

27. EXAMPLES OF OBEDIENCE

Go forth out of thy country. . . . So Abram went out, as the Lord had commanded him. Gen. 11:1, 4.

They made answer to Josue, and said: All that thou hast commanded us we will do; and whithersoever thou shalt send us we will go. As we obeyed Moses in all things, so will we obey thee also: only be the Lord thy God with thee, as he was with Moses. He that shall gainsay thy mouth, and not obey all thy words that thou shalt command him, let him die: only take thou courage, and do manfully. Jos. 1:16-18.

As the Lord had commanded Moses his servant, so did Moses command Josue, and he accomplished all: he left not one thing undone of all the commandments which the Lord had commanded Moses. Jos. 11:15.

The Lord called Samuel. And he answered: Here am I. 1 K. 3:5.

Heli called Samuel, and said: Samuel, my son. And he answered: Here am I. 1 K. 3:18.

Burnt offering and sin offering thou didst not require: then said I: Behold, I come. In the head of the book it is written of me that I should do thy will: O my God, I have desired it, and thy law in the midst of my heart. Ps. 29:8 f.

Joseph also went up from Galilee out of the city of Nazareth into Judea, to the city of David, which is called Bethlehem. because he was of the house and family of David, to be enrolled with Mary his espoused wife, who was with child. Luke 2:4 f.

He arose, and took the Child and his mother by night, and retired into Egypt. Mat. 2:14.

His parents went every year to Jerusalem, at the solemn day of the Pasch. And when he was twelve years old, they [went] up into Jerusalem, according to the custom of the feast. Luke 2:41 f.

He went down with them and came to Nazareth, and was subject to them. Luke 2:51.

I seek not my own will, but the will of him who sent me. John 5:30.

I have meat to eat which you know not. John 4:32.

My meat is to do the will of him who sent me. John 4:34.

Lord, what wilt thou have me to do? Acts 9:6.

Being bound in the spirit, I go to Jerusalem, not knowing the things which shall befall me there. Save that the Holy Ghost in every city witnesseth to me, saying that bands and afflictions wait for me at Jerusalem. Acts 20:22 f.

I fear none of these things, neither do I count my life more precious than myself, so that I may consummate my course, and the ministry of the word which I received from the Lord Jesus to testify the gospel of the grace of God. Acts 20:24.

Trusting in thy obedience, I have written to thee, knowing that thou wilt also do more than this. Philem. 21.

He humbled himself, becoming obedient unto death, even to the death of the cross. For which cause God also hath exalted him, and given him a name which is above all names: that in the name of Jesus every knee should bow, of those that are in heaven, on earth, and under the earth. Phil. 2:8-10.

28. LIBERALITY

A secret present quencheth anger; and a gift in the bosom the greatest wrath. Prov. 21:14.

He that hateth covetousness shall prolong his days. Prov. 28:16.

It is more blessed to give than to receive. Acts 20:35.

Thou shalt not appear empty in the sight of the Lord. . . . Give glory to God with a good heart: and diminish not the first fruits of thy hands. In every gift show a cheerful countenance, and sanctify thy tithes with joy. Give to the Most High according to what he hath given to thee; and with a good eye do according to the ability of thy hands. For the Lord maketh recompense, and will give thee seven times as much. Ecclus. 35:6-13.

Say not to thy friend: Go, and come again: and tomorrow I will give to thee: when thou canst give at present. Prov. 3:28.

Do not transgress against thy friend deferring money, nor despise thy dear brother for the sake of gold. Ecclus. 7:20.

Lose thy money for thy brother and thy friend: and hide it not under a stone to be lost. Ecclus. 29:13.

Some distribute their own goods, and grow richer: others take away what is not their own, and are always in want. Prov. 11:24.

The lips of many shall bless him that is liberal of his bread. Ecclus. 31:28.

God giveth to all men abundantly, and upbraideth not. Jas. 1:5.

For you know the grace of our Lord Jesus Christ, that being rich he become poor, for your sakes; that through his poverty you might be rich. 2 C. 8:9.

Charge the rich of this world not to trust in the uncertainty of riches, but in the living God, who giveth us abundantly all things to enjoy. 1 Thess. 6:17.

All the multitude of the children of Israel going out from the presence of Moses, offered first fruits to the Lord with a most ready and devout mind, to make the work of the tabernacle of the testimony. Ex. 35:20 f.

The workmen being constrained to come, said to Moses: The people offereth more than is necessary. Moses therefore commanded proclamation to be made by the crier's voice: Let neither man nor woman offer any more for the work of the sanctuary. And so they ceased from offering gifts: because the things that were offered did suffice, and were too much. Ex. 36:4-7.

He distributed to all the multitude of Israel, both men and women, to every one, a cake of bread, and a piece of roasted beef, and fine flour fried with oil: and all the people departed every one to his house. 2 K. 6:12.

When David was come to the camp, Sobi, the son of Naas of Rabbath of the children of Ammon, and Machir, the son of Lodabar, and Berzellai, the Galaadite of Rogelim, brought him beds, and tapestry, and earthen vessels, and wheat, and barley, and meal, and parched corn, and beans, and lentils, and fried pulse, and honey, and butter, and sheep, and fat calves, and they gave to David and the people that were with him: for they suspected that the people were faint with hunger and thirst in the wilderness. 2 K. 17:27-29.

29. AVARICE

Covetousness is the root of all evils. 1 Tim. 6:10.

Covetousness is the service of idols. Col. 3:5.

Nothing is more wicked than the covetous man. Ecclus. 10:9.

There is not a more wicked thing than to love money, for such a one setteth his soul at stake because, while he liveth, he hath cast away his bowels. Ecclus. 10:10.

All have turned aside into their own way, every one after his own gain, from the first even to the last. Is. 56:11.

From the least even to the greatest, all are given to covetousness: and from the prophet even to the priest, all are guilty of deceit. Jer. 6:13.

Surely man passeth as an image: yea, and he is disquieted in vain. He storeth up: and he knoweth not for whom he shall gather these things. Ps. 38:7.

Treasures of wickedness shall profit nothing: but justice shall deliver from death. Prov. 10:2.

Trust not in iniquity, and covet not robberies. Ps. 61:11.

He that gathereth treasures by a lying tongue, is vain and foolish, and shall stumble upon the snares of death. Prov. 21:6.

Lift not up thy eye to riches which thou canst not have. Prov. 23:5.

He that heapeth together riches by usury and loan, gathereth them for him that will be bountiful to the poor. Prov. 28:8.

Let not thy hand be stretched out to receive, and shut when thou shouldst give. Ecclus. 4:36.

Set not thy heart upon unjust possessions, and say not: I have enough to live on: for it shall be of no service in the time of vengeance and darkness. Ecclus. 5:1.

There is one that is enriched by living sparingly, and this is the portion of his reward. In that he saith: I have found me rest, and now I will eat of my goods alone: and he knoweth not what time shall pass, and that death approacheth, and that he must leave all to others, and shall die. Ecclus. 11:18-20.

The eye of the covetous man is insatiable in his portion of iniquity: he will not be satisfied till he consume his own soul, drying it up. Ecclus. 14:9.

He that loveth gold, shall not be justified; and he that followeth after corruption shall be filled with it. Many have been brought to fall for gold, and the beauty thereof hath been their ruin. Ecclus. 31:5 f.

For the iniquity of his covetousness I was angry, and I struck him: I hid my face from thee, and was angry: and he went away wandering in his own heart. Is. 57:17.

Woe to him that gathereth together an evil covetousness to his house, that his nest may be on high, and thinketh he may be delivered out of the hand of evil. Haba. 2:9.

Labor not to be rich: but set bounds to thy prudence. Prov. 23:4.

He that maketh haste to be rich shall not be innocent. A man that maketh haste to be rich, and envieth others, is ignorant that poverty shall come upon him. Prov. 28:20, 22.

Substance got in haste shall be diminished: but that which by little and little is gathered with the hand shall increase. Prov. 13:11.

Set not thy heart upon unjust possessions. Be not anxious for goods unjustly gotten: for they shall not profit thee in the day of calamity and revenge. Ecclus. 5:9 f.

He that loveth gold shall not be justified: and he that followeth after corruption, shall be filled with it. Gold is a stumbling block to them that sacrifice to it: woe to them that eagerly follow after it. Ecclus. 31:5, 7 f.

No man can serve two masters. For either he will hate the one, and love the other: or he will sustain the one, and despise the other. You cannot serve God and mammon. Mat. 6:24.

What doth it profit a man, if he gain the whole world, and lose his own soul? Mat. 16:26.

All seek the things that are their own; not the things that are Jesus Christ's. Phil. 2:21.

Lay not up for yourselves treasures on earth: where the rust and the moth consume, and where thieves dig through, and steal. But lay up for yourselves treasures in heaven: where neither the rust nor the moth doth consume, and where thieves do not dig through, nor steal. For where thy treasure is, there is thy heart also. Mat. 6:19-21.

Covetousness, let it not so much as be named among you, as it becometh saints; for know ye this and understand, that no covetous person (which is a serving of idols) hath an inheritance in the kingdom of Christ, and of God. Eph. 5:3-5.

Let your manners be without covetousness, contented with such things as you have: for he hath said: I will not leave thee, neither will I forsake thee. Heb. 13:5.

Fornication and all uncleanliness, or covetousness, let it not so much as be named among you, as it becometh saints. Eph. 5:3.

My son, if thou have anything, do good to thyself, and offer to God worthy offerings. Ecclus. 14:11.

Better it is to see what thou mayst desire, than to desire that which thou canst not know. But this also is vanity and presumption of spirit. Eccles. 6:9.

30. EFFECTS OF AVARICE

Woe to you that join house to house and lay field to field even to the end of the place: shall you alone dwell in the midst of the earth? Is. 5:8.

The ways of every covetous man destroy the souls of the possessor. Prov. 1:9.

Neither thieves, nor the covetous, nor drunkards, nor railers, nor extortioners shall possess the kingdom of God. 1 C. 6:10.

He that hideth up corn shall be cursed among the people: but a blessing upon the head of them that sell. Prov. 11:26.

What profit shall a man have of all his labor and vexation of spirit, with which he has been tormented under the sun? All his days are full of sorrows and miseries: even in the night he doth not rest in mind: and is not this vanity? Eccles. 2:22 f.

There is also another grievous evil which I have seen under the sun: riches kept to the hurt of the owner. For they are lost with very great affliction: he hath begotten a son who shall be in extremity of want. Eccles. 5:12 f.

They who would become rich fall into temptation and into the snare of the devil, and into many unprofitable and hurtful desires, which drown men in destruction and perdition. For covetousness is the root of all evils: which some desiring have erred from the faith, and have entangled themselves in many sorrows. 1 Tim. 6:9 f.

The eye of the covetous man is insatiable in his portion of iniquity; he will not be satisfied till he consume his own soul. Ecclus. 14:9.

The rich have wanted and have suffered hunger: but they that seek the Lord shall not be deprived of any good. Ps. 33:11.

All the labor of man is for his mouth: but his soul shall not be filled. Eccles. 6:7.

A covetous man shall not be satisfied with money. Eccles. 5:9.

Hell and destruction are never filled: so the eyes of men are never satisfied. Prov. 27:20.

He that loveth riches shall reap no fruit from them: so this also is vanity. Eccles. 5:9.

He that gathereth together by wronging his own soul gathereth for others: and another will squander away his goods in rioting. He that is evil to himself, to whom will he be good? and he shall not take pleasure in his goods. Ecclus. 14:4 f.

An evil eye is towards evil things, and he shall not have his fill of bread, but shall be needy and pensive at his own table. Ecclus. 14:10.

Watching for riches consumeth the flesh: and the thought thereof driveth away sleep. Ecclus. 31:1.

He that is greedy of gain troubleth his own house: but he that hates bribes shall live. Prov. 15:27.

God hath given to the sinner vexation and superfluous care, to heap up and to gather together, and to give to him that hath pleased God: but this also is vanity and a fruitless solicitude of the mind. Eccles. 2:26.

31. THE PUNISHMENT OF AVARICE

Woe to you, scribes and Pharisees, hypocrites; because you devour the houses of widows, making long prayers: therefore you shall receive the greater judgment. Mat. 23:14.

What will you give me, and I will deliver him unto you? Mat. 26:15.

The Pharisees, who were covetous, heard all these things and they derided him. Luke 16:14.

He spoke a similitude to them, saying: The land of a certain rich man brought forth plenty of fruit: and he thought within himself, saying: What shall I do, because I have not where to lay up together my fruits? And he said: This will I do: I will pull down my barns, and will build greater: and into them will I gather all things that are grown to me, and my goods: and I will say to my soul: Soul, thou hast much goods laid up for many years; take thy rest, eat, drink, make good cheer. But God said to him: Thou fool, this night do they require thy soul of thee: and whose shall those things be which thou hast provided? Luke 12:16-20.

The wicked have said, reasoning with themselves, but not right: The time of our life is short and tedious. Let us fill ourselves with costly wine and ointments: and let not the flower of the time pass by us. Wis. 2:7.

Woe to you rich, because you have your consolation. Woe to you that are filled: for you shall hunger. Woe to you that laugh now, for you shall mourn and weep. Luke 6:24 f.

32. GRATITUDE

In everything, by prayer and supplication, with thanksgiving, let your petitions be made known to God. Phil. 4:6.

All whatsoever you do in word or in work, do all in the name of the Lord Jesus Christ, giving thanks to God and the Father by him. Col. 3:17.

Walk ye in him, abounding in him in thanksgiving. Col. 2:6 f.

Be instant in prayer; watching in it with thanksgiving. Col. 4:2.

We ought to give thanks always to God for you, brethren, as it is meet, because your faith increaseth exceedingly; and the charity of every one of you towards each other aboundeth. 2 Thess. 1:3.

I desire, first of all, that supplications, prayers, intercessions, and thanksgivings be made for all men: for kings and all who are in high places. 1 Tim. 2:1.

Let the peace of Christ rejoice in your hearts wherein also you are called in one body; and be ye thankful. Col. 3:15.

Nothing is to be rejected that is received with thanksgiving. 1 Tim. 4:4.

Covetousness, let it not so much as be named among you, as it becometh saints: but rather giving thanks. Eph. 5:3 f.

Be ye filled with the Holy Ghost: speaking to yourselves in psalms and hymns, and spiritual canticles, and making melody in your hearts to the Lord: giving thanks always for all things in the house of our Lord Jesus Christ to God and the Father. Eph. 5:18-20.

Jesus, lifting up his eyes, said: Father, I give thee thanks that thou hast heard me. John 11:41.

When they [the Jews] came to Jesus, they besought him earnestly, saying to him: he is worthy that thou shouldst do this for him. For he loveth our nation and hath built us a synagogue. Luke 7:4 f.

I bear you witness, that if it could be done, you would have plucked out your own eyes, and would have given them to me. Gal. 4:15.

Daniel knelt down three times a day, and adored, and gave thanks before his God. Dan. 6:10.

Go into thy house to thy friends; and tell them how great things the Lord hath done for thee, and hath had mercy on thee. And he went his way and began to publish in Decapolis how great things Jesus had done for him: and all men wondered. Mark 5:19 f.

Jesus, lifting up his eyes, said: Father, I give thee thanks that thou hast heard me. John 11:41.

Thanks be to God, who hath given us the victory through our Lord Jesus Christ. 1 C. 15:57.

33. ACTS OF THANKSGIVING

Blessed be the God and Father of our Lord Jesus Christ, who hath blessed us with all spiritual blessings in heavenly places, in Christ. Eph. 1:3.

I bless the God of heaven and I give glory to him in the sight of all that live, because he hath shown his mercy to me. Tob. 12:6.

Thanks be to God for his unspeakable gift. 2 C. 9:15.

I will give praise to thee, O Lord, with my whole heart: I will narrate all thy wonders: I will be glad and rejoice in thee; I will sing to thy name, O thou, Most High. Ps. 9:1 f.

Thanks be to God, who hath given us the victory through our Lord Jesus Christ. 1 C. 15:57.

I will give thanks to thee, O Lord, for thou wast angry with me: thy wrath is turned away, and thou hast comforted me. Is. 12:1.

Let the people, O God, confess to thee; let all the people give praise to thee: the earth hath yielded her fruit. Ps. 66:6 f.

We give thanks to thee, our God, and we praise thy glorious name. 1 Par. 29:13.

Let us come before his presence with thanksgiving. Ps. 94:2.

Bless the Lord, O my soul, and never forget all he hath done for thee. Who forgiveth all thy iniquities: who healeth all thy diseases. Who redeemeth thy life from destruction: who crowneth thee with mercy and compassion. Ps. 102:2-4.

I will bless the Lord, who hath given me understanding. Ps. 15:7.

Thy mercy is better than life: thee my lips shall praise. Ps. 62:4.

I will give thanks to thee in a great Church. Ps. 34:18.

We give thanks to God. 1 Thess. 1:2.

34. INGRATITUDE

The hope of the unthankful shall melt away as the winter's ice, and shall run off as unprofitable water. Wis. 16:29.

He that rendereth evil for good, evil shall not depart from his house. Prov. 17:13.

They are inexcusable because that, when they had known God, they have not glorified him as God, nor gave thanks: but became vain in their thoughts; and their foolish heart was darkened: for professing themselves to be wise, they became fools. Rom. 1:21 f.

Know this, that in the last days, shall come dangerous times: men shall be lovers of themselves, covetous, haughty, proud, blasphemous, disobedient to parents, ungrateful, wicked. 2 Tim. 3:1 f.

The people, seeing that Moses delayed to come down from the mount, gathering together against Aaron, said: Arise, make us gods that may go before us; for, as to this Moses, the man that brought us out of the land of Egypt, we know not what has befallen him. And, rising in the morning, they offered holocausts and peace victims: and the people sat down to eat and drink, and they rose up to play. Ex. 32:1, 6.

He [Ezechias] did not render again according to the benefits he had received: for his heart was lifted up: and wrath was enkindled against him, and against Juda and Jerusalem. 2 Par. 32:25.

He falsified all whatsoever he had said, and alienated himself from Jonathan, and did not reward him according to the benefits he had received from him, but gave him great trouble. 1 Mac. 11:53.

35. FORGETFULNESS OF GOD'S BENEFITS

The son honoreth the father, and the servant his master: if then I be a Father, where is my honor? and if I be a Master, where is my fear? saith the Lord of hosts. Mal. 1:6.

Is this the return thou makest to the Lord, O foolish and senseless people? Is he not thy Father that hath possessed thee, and made thee, and created thee? Deut. 32:6.

Hear, O ye heavens, and give ear, O earth, for the Lord hath spoken: I have brought up children and exalted them: but they have despised me. The ox knoweth his owner, and the ass his master's crib: but Israel hath not known me, and my people hath not understood. Is. 1:2 f.

They remembered not his hand in the day that he redeemed them from the hand of him that afflicted them. Ps. 77:42.

They forgot God, who saved them, who had done great things in Egypt; wondrous works in the land of Cham, terrible things in the Red Sea. Ps. 105:21 f.

You have provoked him who made you, the eternal God, offering sacrifices to devils and not to God. For you have forgotten God who brought you up, and you have grieved Jerusalem who nursed you. Bar. 4:7 f.

You this day have rejected God, who only hath saved you out of all your evils and your tribulations. 1 K. 10:19.

What iniquity have your fathers found in me, that they are gone far from me, and have walked after vanity and are become vain? Jer. 2:5.

Were there not ten made clean? and where are the nine? There is no one found to return, and give glory to God, but this stranger. Luke 17:17 f.

Many good works I have shown to you from my Father: for which of those works do you stone me? John 10:32.

They shall say to him: What are these wounds in the midst of thy hands? And he shall say: With these I was wounded in the house of them that loved me. Zach. 13:6.

Jerusalem, Jerusalem, thou that killest the prophets, and stonest them that are sent unto thee, how often would I have gathered thy children, as the hen doth gather her chickens under her wings, and thou wouldest not! Mat. 23:37.

Because thou didst not serve the Lord thy God with joy and gladness of heart, for the abundance of all things: thou shalt serve thy enemy whom the Lord will send upon thee, in hunger, and thirst, and nakedness, and in want of all things: and he shall put an iron yoke upon thy neck, till he consume thee. Deut. 28:47 f.

36. THE RIGHT USE OF THE TONGUE

The fruit of the Spirit is charity, goodness, benignity. Gal. 5:22.

The spirit of wisdom is benevolent. Wis. 1:6.

In wisdom is the spirit of understanding, sweet, loving that which is good, beneficent. Wis. 7:22.

Shall not the dew assuage the heat? So also the good word is better than the gift. Ecclus. 18:16.

My son, in thy good deeds make no complaint, and when thou givest anything, add not grief by an evil word. Ecclus. 18:15.

Lo, is not a word better than a gift? But both are with a justified man. Ecclus. 18:17.

Put ye on, as the elect of God, holy and beloved, the bowels of mercy, benignity. Col. 3:12.

Be ye kind one to another, merciful. Eph. 4:32.

In many things we all offend. If any man offend not in word, the same is a perfect man. He is able also with a bridle to turn about the whole body. Jas. 3:2.

Blessed is the man that hath not slipt by a word out of his mouth, and is not pricked with the remorse of sin. Ecclus. 14:1.

Who is there that hath not offended with his tongue? Ecclus. 19:17.

Praise not a man before he speaketh; for this is the trial of men. Ecclus. 27:28.

As the dressing of a tree showeth the fruit thereof, so a word out of the thought of the heart of man. Ecclus. 27:7.

Out of the abundance of the heart, the mouth speaketh. A good man, out of a good treasure, bringeth forth good things: and an evil man, out of an evil treasure, bringeth forth evil things. Mat. 12:34 f.

Death and life are in the power of the tongue; they that love it shall eat the fruits thereof. Prov. 18:21.

Behold, how small a fire kindleth a great wood! And the tongue is a fire, a world of iniquity. The tongue is placed among our members, which defileth the whole body, and setteth on fire the wheel of our nativity, being set on fire by hell. Jas. 3:5 f.

Every kind of beast, and of birds, and of serpents, and of the rest is tamed and hath been tamed by mankind. But the tongue no man can tame: a restless evil, full of poison. Jas. 3:7 f.

Keep thy tongue from evil. Ps. 33:14.

Who is a wise man and endued with knowledge among you? Let him show by a good conversation his work in the meekness of wisdom. Jas. 3:13.

Speak thou that art elder: for it becometh thee to speak the first word with careful knowledge. Ecclus. 32:4.

Let the thought of God be in thy mind, and all thy discourse on the commandments of the Most High. Ecclus. 9:23.

Speak thou the things that become sound doctrine. The sound word that cannot be blamed: that he who is on the contrary part may be afraid, having no evil to say of us. Titus 2:1, 8.

Treat not with a man without religion concerning holiness; nor with an unjust man concerning justice; nor with a woman concerning her of whom she is jealous; nor with a coward concerning war; nor with a merchant concerning traffic; nor with a buyer of selling; nor with an envious man of giving thanks. Nor with the ungodly of piety; nor with the dishonest of honesty; nor with the field laborer of every work. Nor with an idle servant of much business. Give not heed to these in any matter of counsel. Ecclus. 37:12-14.

He that despiseth his friend is mean of heart: but the wise man will hold his peace. Prov. 11:12.

Speak not in the ears of fools: because they will despise the instruction of thy speech. Prov. 23:9.

In the midst of the unwise, keep in the word till it is time; but be continually among men that think. Ecclus. 27:13.

Where there is no hearing, pour not out words: and be not lifted up out of season with thy wisdom. Ecclus. 32:6.

If thou have understanding, answer thy neighbor; but, if not, let thy hand be upon thy mouth, lest thou be surprised in an unskilful word, and be confounded. Ecclus. 5:14.

Let your speech be always in grace, seasoned with salt, that you may know how you ought to answer any man. Col. 4:6.

The mind of the just studieth obedience: the mouth of the wicked overfloweth with evils. Prov. 15:28.

Make doors and bars to thy mouth. Melt down thy gold and silver, and make a balance for thy words, and a just bridle for thy mouth: and take heed lest thou slip with thy tongue and fall in the sight of thy enemies who lie in wait for thee, and thy fall be incurable unto death. Ecclus. 28:28-30.

In the multitude of words there shall not want sin: but he that refraineth his lips is most wise. Prov. 10:19.

Let every man be swift to hear: but slow to speak. Jas. 1:19.

Answer not a fool according to his folly, lest thou be made like him. Answer a fool according to his folly, lest he imagine himself to be wise. Prov. 26:4 f.

There is one that holdeth his peace, that is found wise: and there is another that is hateful, that is bold in speech. There is one that holdeth his peace, because he knoweth not what to say: and there is another that holdeth his peace, knowing the proper time. Ecclus. 20:5 f.

There is a time to keep silence, and a time to speak. Ecclus. 3:7.

A wise man will hold his peace till he see opportunity: but a babbler and a fool will regard no time. Ecclus. 10:7.

By the tongue wisdom is discerned: and understanding, and knowledge, and learning, by the word of the wise, and steadfastness in the works of justice. Ecclus. 4:29.

He that setteth bounds to his words is knowing and wise: and the man of understanding is of a precious spirit. Prov. 17:27.

A parable coming out of a fool's mouth shall be rejected, for he doth not speak it in due season. Ecclus. 20:22.

Even a fool, if he will hold his peace, shall be accounted wise: and if he close his lips, a man of understanding. Prov. 17:28.

Be not hasty in thy tongue. Ecclus. 4:34.

He that keepeth his mouth and his tongue, keepeth his soul from distress. Prov. 21:23.

If any man offend not in word, the same is a perfect man. He is able also, with a bridle, to turn about the whole body. For if we put bits into the mouths of horses that they may obey, we turn about their whole body. Jas. 3:2 f.

A man rejoiceth in the sentence of his mouth: and a word in due time is best. Prov. 15:23.

The lip of truth shall be steadfast forever: but he that is a hasty witness frameth a lying tongue. Prov. 12:19.

A wise man shall advance himself with his words: and a prudent one shall please the great ones. Ecclus. 20:29.

To speak a word in due time is like apples of gold on beds of silver. Prov. 25:11.

The words of the mouth of a wise man are grace: but the lips of a fool shall throw him down headlong. Eccles. 10:12.

By patience a prince shall be appeased, and a soft tongue shall break hardness. Prov. 25:15.

A sweet word multiplieth friends, and appeaseth enemies: and a gracious tongue in a good man aboundeth. Ecclus. 6:5.

The flute and the psaltery make a sweet melody: but a pleasant tongue is above them both. Ecclus. 40:21.

The tongue of the wise is health. Prov. 12:18.

He that hateth chastisement shall have less life: and he that hateth babbling extinguisheth evil. Ecclus. 19:5.

37. INDISCREET USE OF THE TONGUE

A fool uttereth all his mind: a wise man deferreth, and keepeth it till afterwards. Prov. 29:11.

A fool multiplieth words. Eccles. 10:14.

He that useth many words shall hurt his own soul. Ecclus. 20:8.

In many words shall be found folly. Eccles. 5:2.

Hast thou seen a man hasty to speak? folly is rather to be looked for than his amendment. Prov. 29:20.

A man full of tongue is terrible in his city: and he that is rash in his word shall be hateful. Ecclus. 9:25.

He is hateful, that is bold in speech. Ecclus. 20:5.

A parable coming out of a fool's mouth shall be rejected; for he doth not speak it in due season. Ecclus. 20:22.

In the multitude of words there shall not want sin. Prov. 10:19.

A slippery mouth worketh ruin. Prov. 26:28.

The tongue is a fire. Jas. 3:6.

A man without grace is a vain fable: it shall be continually in the mouth of the unwise. Eccles. 20:21.

The mouth of the wicked overfloweth with evils. Prov. 15:28.

As a city that lieth open and is not compassed with walls, so is a man that cannot refrain his own spirit in speaking. Prov. 25:28.

The lips of a fool shall throw him down headlong. The beginning of his words is folly: and the end of his talk a mischievous error. Eccles. 10:12 f.

Many have fallen by the edge of the sword: but not so many as have perished by their own tongue. Ecclus. 28:22.

A man that speaketh to his friend with flattering and dissembling words, spreadeth a net for his feet. Prov. 29:5.

A tale out of time, is like music in mourning. Ecclus. 22:6.

The discourse of sinners is hateful: and their laughter is at the pleasure of sin. Ecclus. 27:14.

The tongue of a third person hath disquieted many, and scattered them from nation to nation. It hath destroyed the strong cities of the rich, and hath overthrown the houses of great men. It hath cut in pieces the forces of people and undone nations. The tongue of a third person hath cast out valiant women, and deprived them of their labors. He that hearkeneth to it shall never have rest: neither shall he have a friend in whom he may repose. The stroke of a whip maketh a blue mark: but the stroke of the tongue will break the bones. Ecclus. 28:16-21.

Blessed is he that is defended from a wicked tongue, that hath not passed into the wrath thereof, and that hath not drawn the yoke thereof, and hath not been bound in its bands. Ecclus. 28:23.

They spoke vain things. Ps. 37:13.

Let no evil speech proceed from your mouth: but that which is good, to the edification of faith, that it may afford grace to the hearers. Eph. 4:29.

He that will love life and see good days, let him refrain his tongue from evil, and his lips, that they speak no guile. 1 Pet. 3:10.

Let not thy mouth be accustomed to indiscreet speech: for therein is the word of sin. Ecclus. 23:17.

If any man think himself to be religious, not bridling his tongue, but deceiving his own heart, this man's religion is vain. Jas. 1:26.

Speak not anything rashly, and let not thy heart be hasty to utter a word before God. For God is in heaven, and thou upon earth: therefore let thy words be few. Dreams follow many cares, and in many words shall be found folly. Eccles. 5:1 f.

Be not full of words in a multitude of ancients, and repeat not the word in thy prayer. Ecclus. 7:15.

Be not hasty in thy tongue: and slack and remiss in thy works. Ecclus. 4:34.

The tongue no man can tame. By it we bless God and the Father; and by it we curse men who are made after the likeness of God. Out of the same mouth proceedeth blessing and cursing. My brethren, these things ought not so to be. Doth a fountain send forth through the same passage sweet and bitter water? Can the fig tree, my brethren, bear grapes; or the vine, figs? So neither can the salt water yield sweet. Jas. 3:8-12.

38. WORDS OF THE WISE AND OF THE FOOLISH MAN

Honor and glory is the word of the wise; but the tongue of the fool is his ruin. Ecclus. 5:15.

A wise man will hold his peace till he see opportunity, but a babbler and a fool will regard no time. A man, wise in words, shall make himself beloved, but the graces of fools shall be poured out. Ecclus. 20:7, 13.

The talking of the fool is like a burden in the way: but in the lips of the wise grace shall be found. The mouth of the prudent is sought after in the church: and they will think upon his words in their hearts. As a house that is destroyed, so is wisdom to a fool, and the knowledge of the unwise is as words without sense. Ecclus. 21:19-21.

The lips of the unwise will be telling foolish things, but the words of the wise shall be weighed in a balance. The heart of fools is in their mouth, and the mouth of wise men is in their heart. Ecclus. 21:28 f.

Of the fruit of his own mouth shall a man be filled with good things; but the soul of transgressors is wicked. He that keepeth his mouth, keepeth his soul; but he that hath no guard on his speech shall meet with evils. Prov. 13:2 f.

In the mouth of a fool is the rod of pride; but the lips of the wise preserve them. Prov. 14:3.

A mild answer breaketh wrath; but a harsh word stirreth up fury. The tongue of the wise adorneth knowledge; but the mouth of fools babbleth out folly. Prov. 15:1 f.

A peaceable tongue is a tree of life, but that which is immoderate shall crush the spirit. The lips of the wise shall disperse knowledge: the heart of fools shall be unlike. Prov. 15:4, 7.

39. EXAMPLES OF WISE SPEECH

I said, I will take heed to my ways, that I sin not with my tongue. Ps. 38:1.

I have set a guard to my mouth, when the sinner stood against me: I was dumb and was humbled, and kept silence from good things. Ps. 38:2.

With my lips I have pronounced all the judgments of my mouth. Ps.118:13.

I spoke of thy testimonies before kings, and I was not ashamed. Ps. 118:46.

With great power did the apostles give testimony of the resurrection of Jesus Christ, our Lord: and great grace was in them all. Acts 4:33.

40. PRAYERS FOR WISDOM IN SPEECH

Set a watch, O Lord, before my mouth; and a door round about my lips: incline not my heart to evil words, to make excuses in sins. Ps. 140:3 f.

Who will set a guard before my mouth, and a sure seal upon my lips, that I fall not by them, and that my tongue destroy me not? Ecclus. 22:33.

O Lord, deliver my soul from wicked lips, and a deceitful tongue. What shall be given to thee, or what shall be added to thee, to a deceitful tongue? Ps. 119:2 f.

O Lord, thou wilt open my lips, and my mouth shall declare thy praise. Ps. 50:17.

41. LYING

Lying lips are an abomination to the Lord: but they that deal faithfully please him. Prov. 12:22.

A deceitful witness that uttereth lies, the Lord detesteth. Prov. 6:19.

Three sorts my soul hateth, and I am greatly grieved at their life: a poor man that is proud; a rich man that is a liar; an old man that is a fool and doting. Ecclus. 25:3 f.

A thief is better than a man that is always lying: but both of them shall inherit destruction. Ecclus. 20:27.

You are of your father, the devil, and the desires of your father you will do: he was a murderer from the beginning, and he stood not in the truth, because truth is not in him. When he speaketh a lie, he speaketh of his own; for he is a liar and the father thereof. John 8:44.

The crafty man is hateful. Prov. 14:17.

The bread of lying is sweet to a man; but afterwards his mouth shall be filled with gravel. Prov. 20:17.

The just shall hate a lying word; but the wicked confoundeth and shall be confounded. Prov. 13:5.

A lying witness shall perish. Prov. 21:28.

The mouth that belieth, killeth the soul. Wis. 1:11.

The slipping of a false tongue is as one that falleth on the pavement: so the fall of the wicked shall come speedily. Ecclus. 20:20.

A lie is a foul blot on a man, and yet it will be continually in the mouth of men without discipline. The manners of lying men are without honor: and their confusion is with them without ceasing. Ecclus. 20:26-28.

Putting away lying, speak ye the truth, every man to his neighbor: for we are members one of another. Eph. 4:25.

Lie not one to another, stripping yourselves of the old man with his deeds. Col. 3:9.

Be not willing to make any manner of lie. Ecclus. 7:14.

You shall not lie, neither shall any man deceive his neighbor. Lev. 19:11.

He that trusteth to lies feedeth the winds: and the same runneth after birds that fly away. Prov. 10:4.

In no wise speak against the truth, but be ashamed of the lie of thy ignorance. Be not ashamed to confess thy sins; but submit not thyself to every man for sin. Ecclus. 4:30 f.

Just lips are the delight of kings: he that speaketh right things shall be loved. Prov. 16:13.

Love ye truth. Zach. 8:19.

I shall not be foolish: for I will say the truth. 2 C. 12:6.

Be not liars against the truth. Jas. 3:14.

I say the truth in Christ: I lie not. Rom. 8:1.

42. THE JUSTICE OF GOD

The wicked man is reserved to the day of destruction, and he shall be brought to the day of wrath. Job 21:30.

Acting wickedly against the laws of God doth not pass unpunished. 2 Mac. 4:17.

The congregation of sinners is like tow heaped together; and the end of them is a flame of fire. Ecclus. 21:10.

Whithersoever they meant to go, the hand of the Lord was upon them, as he had said, and as he had sworn to them: and they were greatly distressed. Judg. 2:15.

Though for the present time, I should be delivered from the punishments of men, yet should I not escape the hand of the Almighty, neither alive nor dead. 2 Mac. 6:26.

Do not think that thou shalt escape unpunished, for that thou hast attempted to fight against God. 2 Mac. 7:49.

O how good and sweet is thy Spirit, O Lord in all things! And therefore thou chastisest them that err, by little and little, and admonishest them. and speakest to them concerning the things wherein they offend; that, leaving their wickedness, they may believe in thee, O Lord. Wis. 12:1 f.

Follow not in thy strength the desires of thy heart. And say not: How mighty am I! and who shall bring me under for my deeds? For God will surely take revenge. Say not: I have sinned, and what harm hath befallen me? for the Most High is a patient rewarder. Ecclus. 5:2-4.

It is a token of great goodness when sinners are not suffered to go on in their ways for a long time, but are presently punished. For, not as with other nations, whom the Lord patiently expecteth, that when the day of judgment shall come he may punish them in the fulness of their sins, doth he also deal with us, so as to suffer our sins to come to their height, and then take vengeance on us. And therefore he never withdraweth his mercy from us: but though he chastiseth his people with adversity, he forsaketh them not. 2 Mac. 6:13-16.

The soul that sinneth, the same shall die: the son shall not bear the iniquity of the father, and the father shall not bear the iniquity of the son: the justice of the just shall be upon him, and the wickedness of the wicked shall be upon him. Ez. 18:20.

He that hath sinned against me, him will I strike out of my book. Ex. 32:33.

Far be it from thee to do this thing and to slay the just with the wicked, and for the just to be in like case with the wicked; this is not beseeming thee: thou who judgest all the earth, wilt not make this judgment. Gen. 18:25.

For so much then as thou art just, thou orderest all things justly: thinking it not agreeable to thy power, to condemn him who deserveth not to be punished. Wis. 12:15.

He shall be punished for all that he did, and yet shall not be consumed: according to the multitude of his devices, so also shall he suffer. Job 20:18.

Esteeming these very punishments to be less than our sins deserve, let us believe that these scourges of the Lord, with which like servants we are chastised, have happened for our amendment, and not for our destruction. Jdth. 8:27.

When they were tried, and chastised with mercy, they knew how the wicked were judged with wrath and tormented. For thou didst admonish and try them as a father: but the others, as a severe king, thou didst examine and condemn. Wis. 11:10 f.

I will visit their iniquities with a rod, and their sins with stripes. But my mercy I will not take away from him, nor will I suffer my truth to fail. Ps. 88:33 f.

43. PUNISHMENT OF SINNERS

By what things a man sinneth, by the same also he is tormented. Wis. 11:17.

Thou hast greatly tormented them who in their life have lived foolishly and unjustly, by the same things which they worshipped. Wis. 12:23.

A thousand men shall flee for fear of one; and for fear of five shall you flee, till you be left as the mast of a ship on the top of a mountain, and as an ensign upon a hill. Is. 30:17.

If thou didst punish the enemies of thy servants, and that deserved to die, with so great deliberation, giving them time and place, whereby they might be changed from their wickedness: with what circumspection hast thou judged thy own children, to whose parents thou hast sworn, and made covenants of good promises? Therefore, whereas thou chastisest us, thou scourgest our enemies very many ways, to the end that when we judge, we may think on thy goodness: and when we are judged, we may hope for thy mercy. Wis. 12:20-22.

The Lord is a consuming fire. Deut. 4:24.

They that remain shall know that there is nothing better than the fear of God, and that there is nothing sweeter than to have regard to the commandments of the Lord. Ecclus. 23:37.

The wicked man being scourged, the fool shall be wiser; but if thou rebuke a wise man, he will understand discipline. Prov. 19:25.

When a pestilent man is punished, the little one will be wiser; and if he follow the wise, he will receive knowledge. Prov. 21:11.

Because sentence is not speedily pronounced against the evil, the children of men commit evils without any fear. Eccles. 8:11.

Thou hast taught thy people by such works that they must be just and humane, and hast made thy children to be of good hope: because in judging thou givest place for repentance for sins. Wis. 12:19.

Be not over just: and be not more wise than is necessary, lest thou become stupid. Eccles. 7:17.

Persevere under discipline. Heb. 12:7.

He [the wicked Jason] that had driven many out of their country, perished in a strange land, going to Lacedemon, as if for kindred sake, he should have refuge there. But he that had cast out many unburied, was himself cast forth unlamented and unburied, neither having foreign burial, nor being partaker of the sepulcher of his fathers. 2 Mac. 5:9 f.

The murderer and blasphemer [Antiochus] being grievously struck, as himself had treated others, died a miserable death, in a strange country, among the mountains. 2 Mac. 9:28.

So Aman was hanged on the gibbet which he had prepared for Mardochai: and the king's wrath ceased. Esth. 7:10.

Thou wicked servant, I forgave thee all the debt because thou besoughtest me. Shouldst not thou then have had compassion also on thy fellow servant, even as I had compassion on thee? And his lord, being angry, delivered him to the torturers until he should pay all the debt. Mat. 18:32-34.

VII

TEMPERANCE AND INTEMPERANCE

1. TEMPERANCE

The chief thing for man's life is water and bread and clothing, and a house to cover shame. Ecclus. 29:27.

The principal things necessary for the life of men are water, fire and iron, salt, milk, and bread of flour, and honey, and the cluster of the grape, and oil, and clothing. Ecclus. 39:31.

Daniel purposed in his heart that he would not be defiled with the king's table, nor with the wine which he drank: and he requested the master of the eunuchs that he might not be defiled. Dan. 1:8.

How sufficient is a little wine for a man well taught, and in sleeping thou shalt not be uneasy with it, and thou shalt feel no pain. Watching, and choler, and gripes, are with an intemperate man. Ecclus. 31:22 f.

Wine drunken with excess raiseth quarrels, and wrath, and many ruins. Wine drunken with excess is bitterness of the soul. Ecclus. 31:38 f.

Better is the poor man's fare under a roof of boards, than sumptuous cheer abroad in another man's house. Ecclus. 29:28.

It is better to be invited to herbs with love, than to a fatted calf with hatred. Prov. 15:17.

I thought in my heart, to withdraw my flesh from wine, that I might avoid folly, till I might see what was profitable for the children of men; and what they ought to do under the sun all the days of their life. Eccles. 2:3.

Blessed is the land, whose king is noble, and whose princes eat in due season for refreshments, and not for riotousness. Eccles. 10:17.

He that is temperate shall prolong life. Ecclus. 37:34.

Sound and wholesome sleep is with a moderate man; he shall sleep till morning, and his soul shall be delighted with him. Ecclus. 31:24.

2. INTEMPERANCE

Many walk, of whom I have told you often (and now tell you weeping), that they are enemies of the cross of Christ; whose end is destruction, whose god is their belly, and whose glory is in their shame: who mind earthly things. Phil. 3:18 f.

When they have eaten, and are full and fat, they will turn away after strange gods, and will serve them; and will despise me, and make void my covenant. Deut. 31:20.

Woe to you that are filled: for you shall hunger. Luke 6:25.

Take heed to yourselves, lest perhaps your hearts be overcharged with surfeiting and drunkenness and the cares of this life; and that day come upon you suddenly. Luke 21:24.

Be not greedy in any feasting, and pour not out thyself upon any meat: for in many meats there will be sickness, and greediness will then turn to choler. By surfeiting many have perished; but he that is temperate shall prolong life. Ecclus. 37:32-34.

He that loveth good cheer, shall be in want: he that loveth wine, and fat things, shall not be rich. Prov. 21:17.

Be not in the feasts of great drinkers, nor in their revelings, who contribute flesh to eat: because they that give themselves to drinking, and that club together, shall be consumed. Prov. 23:20 f.

A workman that is a drunkard shall not be rich: and he that contemneth small things shall fall by little and little. Ecclus. 19:1.

He that is delighted in passing his time over wine, leaveth a reproach in his strongholds. Prov. 12:11.

These also have been ignorant through wine, and through drunkenness, have erred: the priest and the prophet have been ignorant through drunkenness, they are swallowed up with wine, they have gone astray in drunkenness, they have not known him that seeth, they have been ignorant of judgment. Is. 28:7.

Fornication, and wine, and drunkenness take away the understanding. Osee 4:11.

Fire trieth hard iron: so wine drunk to excess shall rebuke the hearts of the proud. Ecclus. 31:31.

Wine is a luxurious thing, and drunkenness riotous: whosoever is delighted therewith shall not be wise. Prov. 20:1.

Who hath woe? Whose father hath woe? Who hath contentions? Who falls into pits? Who hath wounds without cause? Who hath redness of eyes? Surely they that pass their time in wine, and study to drink off their cups. Prov. 23:29 f.

Wine hath destroyed very many. Ecclus. 31:30.

Noe drinking of the wine was made drunk. Gen. 9:21.

Baltassar the king made a great feast for a thousand of his nobles, and every one drank according to his age. And being now drunk he commanded that they should bring the vessels of gold and silver which Nabuchodonosor his father had brought away out of the temple, that was in Jerusalem, that the king, and his nobles, and his wives, and his concubines, might drink in them. Dan. 5:1 f.

3. DRUNKENNESS AND GLUTTONY

Let us walk honestly, as in the day, not in rioting and drunkenness. But put ye on the Lord Jesus Christ, and make not provision for the flesh in its concupiscences. Rom. 13:13 f.

Woe to you that rise up early in the morning to follow drunkenness, and to drink to the evening, to be inflamed with wine. The harp, and the lyre, and the timbrel, and the pipe, and wine are in your feasts: and the work of the Lord you regard not, nor do you consider the works of his hands. Is. 5:11 f.

Be not drunk with wine, wherein is luxury. Eph. 5:18.

Meat for the belly, and the belly for the meats: but God shall destroy both it and them: but the body is not for fornication, but for the Lord, and the Lord for the body. 1 C. 6:13.

Give not to kings, O Samuel, give not wine to kings: because there is no secret where drunkenness reigneth: and lest they drink, and forget judgments, and pervert the cause of the children of the poor. Prov. 31:4 f.

A drunken woman is a great wrath: and her reproach and shame shall not be hid. Ecclus. 26:11.

Neither fornicators, nor adulterers, nor drunkards shall possess the kingdom of God. 1 C. 6:9 f.

Look not upon the wine when it is yellow, when the color thereof shineth in the glass: it goeth in pleasantly. But in the end, it will bite like a snake, and will spread abroad poison like a basilisk. Prov. 23:31 f.

Woe to the crown of pride, to the drunkards of Ephraim, and to the fading flower, the glory of his joy, who were on the head of the fat valley, staggering with wine. Is. 28:1.

Eat not with an envious man, and

desire not his meats, because, like a soothsayer and diviner, he thinketh that which he knoweth not. Eat and drink, will he say to thee: and his mind is not with thee. The meat which thou hadst eaten, thou shalt vomit up: and shalt lose thy beautiful words. Prov. 23:6-8.

4. CONDUCT AT TABLE

Let just men be thy guests, and let thy glory be in the fear of God. Ecclus. 9:22.

Be not in the feasts of great drinkers. Prov. 23:20.

When thou art invited to a wedding, sit not down in the first place, lest perhaps one more honorable than thou be invited by him; and he that invited thee and him, come and say to thee, Give this man place: and then thou begin with shame to take the lowest place. But when thou art invited, go, sit down in the lowest place: that when he who invited thee cometh, he may say to thee: Friend, go up higher. Then shalt thou have glory before them that sit at table with thee. Luke 14:8-10.

Challenge not them that love wine: for wine hath destroyed very many. Ecclus. 31:30.

Art thou set at a great table? be not the first to open thy mouth upon it. Say not: There are many things which are upon it. Ecclus. 31:12 f.

Stretch not out thy hand first, lest being disgraced with envy thou be put to confusion. Be not hasty in a feast. Judge of the disposition of thy neighbor by thyself. Use as a frugal man the things that are set before thee; lest if thou eatest much, thou be hated. Leave off first, for manners' sake: and exceed not, lest thou offend. Ecclus. 31:16-20.

Rebuke not thy neighbor in a banquet of wine: and despise him not in his mirth. Speak not to him words of reproach: and press him not in demanding again. Ecclus. 41:42.

A concert of music in a banquet of wine is as a carbuncle set in gold. As a signet of an emerald in a work of gold: so is the melody of music with pleasant and moderate wine. Hear in silence, and for thy reverence, good grace shall come to thee. Ecclus. 32:7-9.

And he said to him also: When thou makest a dinner or a supper, call not thy friends, nor thy brethren, nor thy kinsmen, nor thy neighbors who are rich: lest perhaps they also invite thee again and a recompense be made to thee. But when thou makest a feast, call the poor, the maimed, the lame, and the blind. And thou shalt be blessed, because they have not wherewith to make thee recompense: for recompense shall be made thee at the resurrection of the just. Luke 14:12-14.

Be not greedy in any feasting, and pour not out yourself upon any meat. Ecclus. 27:32.

Take heed to yourselves, lest perhaps your hearts be overcharged with surfeiting and drunkenness and the cares of this life, and that day come upon you suddenly. Luke 21:34.

5. ADVANTAGES AND EXAMPLES OF FASTING

Prayer is good with fasting and alms, more than to lay up treasures of gold: for alms delivereth from death, and the same is that which purgeth away sins, and maketh to find mercy and life everlasting. Tob. 12:8 f.

Be converted to me with all your heart, in fasting, and in weeping, and in mourning. Joel 2:12.

Let us exhibit ourselves as the ministers of God, in much patience, in fastings. 2 C. 6:4.

When you fast, be not as the hypocrites, sad, for they disfigure their faces, that they may appear unto men to fast. Amen I say to you, they have received their reward. But thou, when thou fastest, anoint thy head and wash thy face. That thou appear not to men to fast, but to thy Father who is in secret: and thy Father who seeth in secret will repay thee. Mat. 6:16-18.

As they were ministering to the Lord, and fasting, the Holy Ghost said to them: Separate me Saul and Barnabas, for the work whereunto I have taken them. Then they, fasting and praying, and imposing their hands upon them, sent them away. Acts 13:2 f.

When they had ordained to them priests in every church, and had prayed with fasting, they commended them to the Lord, in whom they believed. Acts 14:22.

This kind is not cast out but by prayer and fasting.' Mat. 17:20.

Christ fasted forty days and forty nights. Mat. 4:2.

She [Anna] was a widow until fourscore and four years; who departed not from the temple, by fastings and prayers serving night and day. Luke 2:37.

6. TOTAL ABSTINENCE

The Lord also said to Aaron: You shall not drink wine, nor anything that may make drunk, thou nor thy sons, when you enter into the tabernacle of the testimony, lest you die, because it is an everlasting precept through your generations. Lev. 10:8 f.

Moses, saying: Speak to the children of Israel, and thou shalt say to them: When a man or woman shall make a vow to be sanctified, and will consecrate themselves to the Lord: They shall abstain from wine, and from everything that may make a man drunk. They shall not drink vinegar of wine, or of any other drink, nor anything that is pressed out of the grape; nor shall they eat grapes either fresh or dried. Num. 6:1-3.

You have not eaten bread, nor have you drunk wine or strong drink: that you might know that I am the Lord thy God. Deut. 29:6.

But he answered thus: Behold, thou shalt conceive and bear a son: beware thou drink no wine, nor strong drink, nor eat any unclean thing: for the child shall be a Nazarite of God from his infancy, from his mother's womb until the day of his death. Judg. 13-7.

For he shall be great before the Lord: and shall drink no wine nor strong drink: and he shall be filled with the Holy Ghost even from his mother' womb. Luke 1:15.

Afterwards, Jesus knowing that all things were now accomplished, that the Scripture might be fulfilled, said: I thirst. Now there was a vessel set there full of vinegar. And they putting a sponge full of vinegar about hyssop, put it to his mouth. Jesus therefore when he had taken the vinegar, said: It is consummated. And bowing his head, he gave up the ghost. John 19:28-30.

It is good not to eat flesh, and not to drink wine, nor anything whereby thy brother is offended, or scandalised, or made weak. Rom. 14:21.

7. EXAMPLES OF CONTINENCE AND CHASTITY

Behold, my master [Pharao] hath delivered all things to me [Joseph]. Neither is there anything which is not in my power, or that he hath not delivered to me, but thee, who art his wife: how then can I do this wicked thing, and sin against my God? Gen. 39:8 f.

Thou hast done manfully, and thy heart has been strengthened, because thou hast loved chastity, and after thy husband hast not know any other: therefore also the hand of the Lord hath strengthened thee, and therefore thou shalt be blessed forever. Jdth. 15:11.

Thou knowest, O Lord [said Sara, the wife of young Tobias], that I never coveted a husband, and have kept my soul clean from all lust. Tob. 3:16.

As I knew that I could not otherwise be continent, except God gave it, and this also was a point of wisdom, to know whose gift it was: I went to the Lord, and besought him, and said with my whole heart: Give me wisdom. Wis. 8:21; 9:4.

I made a covenant with my eyes, that I would not so much as think upon a virgin. Job 31:1.

As for him that is pure, his work is right. Prov. 21:8.

8. SINS OF LUST

This is the will of God, your sanctification: that you should abstain from fornication. That every one of you should know how to possess his vessel in sanctification and honor. Not in the passion of lust, like the Gentiles that know not God. 1 Thess. 4:3-5.

Marriage honorable in all, and the bed undefiled. For fornicators and adulterers God will judge. Heb. 13:4.

The body is not for fornication, but for the Lord, and the Lord for the body. 1 C. 6:13.

Know you not that your bodies are the members of Christ? Shall I then take the members of Christ, and make them the members of a harlot? God forbid. Or know you not, that he who is joined to a harlot is made one body? For they shall be, saith he, two in one flesh. But he who is joined to the Lord, is one spirit. Fly fornication. Every sin that a man doth, is without the body: but he that committeth fornication, sinneth against his own body. Or know you not, that your members are the temple of the Holy Ghost, who is in you, whom you have from God, and you are not your own? For you are bought with a great price. Glorify and bear God in your body. 1 C. 15-20.

Why art thou seduced, my son, by a strange woman, and art cherished in the bosom of another? Prov. 5:20.

Thou shalt not commit adultery. Ex. 20:14.

Neither shalt thou desire his wife. Ex. 20:17.

Whosoever shall look on a woman to lust after her, hath already committed adultery with her in his heart. Mat. 5:28.

How long shall hurtful thoughts abide in thee? Jer. 4:14.

I looked out of the window of my house through the lattice, and I see little ones, I behold a foolish young man, who passeth through the street by the corner, and goeth nigh the way of her house, in the dark, when it grows late, in the darkness and obscurity of the night. Prov. 7:6-9.

She entangled him with many words, and drew him away with the flattery of her lips. Immediately he followeth her as an ox led to be a victim, and as a lamb playing the wanton, and not knowing he is drawn like a fool to bonds. Till the arrow pierce his liver: as if a bird should make haste to the snare, and knoweth not that his life is in danger. Prov. 7:21-23.

9. CONSEQUENCES OF LUST

Know you not that the unjust shall not possess the kingdom of God? Do not err. Neither fornicators, nor idolators, nor adulterers, nor the effeminate, nor liers with mankind, nor thieves, nor covetous, nor drunkards, nor railers, nor extortioners shall possess the kingdom of God. 1 C. 6:9 f.

Know ye this and understand that no fornicator, nor unclean, nor covetous person (which is a serving of idols) hath inheritance in the kingdom of Christ and of God. Eph. 5:5.

Her house inclineth unto death, and her paths to hell. Prov. 2:18.

Give not thy substance to women, and thy riches to destroy kings. Prov. 31:3.

I made a covenant with my eyes, that I would not so much as think upon a virgin. For what part should God from above have in me, and what inheritance the almighty from on High? Is not destruction to the wicked and aversion to them that work iniquity? Job 31:1-3.

Mind not the deceit of a woman. For the lips of a harlot are like a honeycomb dropping, and her throat is smoother than oil. But her end is bitter as wormwood, and sharp as a two-edged sword. Her feet go down into death, and her steps go in as far as hell. They walk not by the path of life, her steps are wandering, and unaccountable. Prov. 5:2-6.

Let not thy mind be drawn away in her ways; neither be thou deceived with her paths. For she hath cast down many wounded, and the strongest have been slain by her. Her house is the way to hell, reaching even to the inner chambers of death. Prov. 7:25-27.

For a harlot is a deep ditch: and a strange woman is a narrow pit. She lieth in wait in the way as a robber, and him whom she shall see unwary, she will kill. Prov. 23:27 f.

The woman catcheth the precious soul of a man. Prov. 6:26.

Dearly beloved, I beseech you as strangers and pilgrims, to refrain yourselves from carnal desires which war against the soul. 1 Pet. 2:11.

Flee youthful desires. 2 Tim. 2:22.

They will not set their thoughts to return to their God: for the spirit of fornication is in the midst of them, and they have not known the Lord. Osee 5:4.

None that go in unto her shall return again, neither shall they take hold of the paths of life. Prov. 2:19.

The price of a harlot is scarce one loaf. Prov. 6:26.

To a man that is a fornicator all bread is sweet; he will not be weary of sinning unto the end. Ecclus. 23:24.

Wine and women make wise men fall off, and shall rebuke the prudent. Ecclus. 19:2.

A man of sense will praise every wise word he shall hear, and will apply it to himself: the luxurious man hath heard it, and it shall displease him, and he will cast it behind his back. Ecclus. 21:18.

Woe to you that are wanton on your couches: and are not concerned for the affliction of Joseph. Amos 6:4-6.

He that joineth himself to harlots, will be wicked. Rottenness and worms shall inherit him, and he shall be lifted up for a greater example, and his soul shall be taken away out of the number. Ecclus 19:3.

Behold, I will cast her into a bed; and they that commit adultery with her shall be in very great tribulation, except they do penance for their deeds: and I will kill her children with death. Apoc. 2:22 f.

If what he charged her with be true, and virginity be not found in the damsel: they shall cast her out of the doors of her father's house, and the men of the city shall stone her to death, and she shall die: because she that done a wicked thing in Israel, to play the whore in her father's house; and thou shalt take away the evil out of the midst of thee. Deut. 22:20 f.

He that maintaineth harlots, shall squander away his substance. Prov. 29:3.

Give not thy soul to harlots in any point: lest thou destroy thyself and thy inheritance. Ecclus. 9:6.

The younger son gathering all together, went abroad into a far country, and there wasted his substance, living riotously. Luke 15:13.

Be ashamed of fornication before father and mother. Ecclus. 41:21.

Give not thy honor to strangers, and thy years to the cruel. Lest strangers be filled with thy strength, and thy labors be in another man's house, and thou mourn at the last, when thou shalt have spent thy flesh and thy body. Prov. 5:9-11.

Every woman that is a harlot shall be trodden upon as dung in the way. Ecclus. 9:10.

Many walk that are enemies of the cross of Christ: whose end is destruction: whose god is their belly: and whose glory is in their shame. Phil. 3:18 f.

By thy body thou wast brought under subjection. Thou hast stained thy glory. Ecclus. 47:21 f.

10. PUNISHMENTS OF THE SINS OF LUST

The Lord rained upon Sodom and Gomorrha brimstone and fire from the Lord out of heaven. And he destroyed these cities, and all the country about, all the inhabitants of the cities, and all the things that spring from the earth. Gen. 19:24 f.

Behold, one of the children of Israel went in before his brethren to a harlot of Madian, in the sight of Moses, and of all the children of Israel, who were weeping before the door of the tabernacle. And when Phinees, the son of Eleazar, the son of Aaron the priest, saw it, he rose up from the midst of the multitude, and, taking a dagger, went in after the Israelite into the brothel-house, and thrust both of them through together, to wit, the man and the woman, and the scourge ceased from the children of Israel. And there were slain four-and-twenty thousand men. Num. 25:6-9.

Jacob called his sons, and said to them: Ruben, my firstborn, thou art my strength, and the beginning of my sorrow, excelling in gifts, greater in command. Thou art poured out as water, grow thou not: because thou wentest up to thy father's bed, and didst defile his couch. Gen. 49:3 f.

11. TRUE AND FALSE SHAME

For thy soul be not ashamed to say the truth. For there is a shame that bringeth sin, and there is a shame that bringeth glory and grace. Ecclus. 4:24 f.

Have a shame of these things I am now going to speak of. For it is not good to keep all shamefacedness: and all things do not please all men in opinion. Ecclus. 41:19 f.

Accept no person against thy own person, nor against thy soul a lie. Reverence not thy neighbor in his fall: and refrain not to speak in the time of salvation. Hide not thy wisdom in her beauty. For by the tongue wisdom is discerned: and understanding, and knowledge, and learning by the word of the wise, and steadfastness in the works of justice. In no wise speak against the truth, but be ashamed of the lie of thy ignorance. Be not ashamed to confess thy sins, but submit not thyself to every man for sin. Resist not against the face of the mighty, and do not strive against the stream of the river. Strive for justice for thy soul, and even unto death fight for justice, and God will overthrow thy enemies for thee. Ecclus. 4:26-33.

There is that will destroy his own soul through shamefacedness, and by occasion of an unwise person he will destroy it: and by respect of person he will destroy himself. Ecclus. 20:24.

There is that for bashfulness promiseth to his friend, and maketh him his enemy for nothing. Ecclus. 20:25.

12. HUMILITY

I am a worm, and no man: the reproach of men, and the outcast of the people. Ps. 21:7.

I will both play and make myself meaner than I have done: and I will be little in my own eyes; and with the handmaids of whom thou speakest I shall appear more glorious. 2 K. 6:22.

Seeing I have once begun, I will speak to my Lord, whereas I am dust and ashes. Gen. 18:27.

He that shall come after me is mightier than I, whose shoe I am not worthy to bear. Mat. 3:11.

Lord, I am not worthy that thou shouldst enter under my roof: but only say the word, and my servant shall be healed. Mat. 8:8.

Tell ye the daughter of Sion: Behold, thy king cometh to thee, meek, and sitting upon an ass, and a colt, the foal of her that is used to the yoke. Mat. 21:5.

The four-and-twenty ancients fell down before him that sitteth on the throne, and adored him that liveth forever and ever, and cast their crowns before the throne. Apoc. 4:10.

Father, I have sinned against heaven, and before thee: I am now not worthy to be called thy son: make me as one of thy hired servants. Luke 15:18 f.

Last of all, he was seen also by me, as by one born out of due time. For I am the least of the apostles, who am not worthy to be called an apostle, because I persecuted the church of God. But by the grace of God, I am what I am: and his grace in me hath not been void, but I have labored more abundantly than all they; yet not I, but the grace of God with me. 1 C. 15:8-10.

Would to God you could bear with some little of my folly: but do bear with me. 2 C. 11:1.

We are fools for Christ's sake, but you are wise in Christ: we are weak, but you are strong; you are honorable, but we without honor. 1 C. 4:10.

We are made as the refuse of this world, the off-scouring of all even until now. 1 C. 4:13.

To me, the least of all the saints, is given this grace. Eph. 3:8.

Blessed are the poor in spirit, for theirs is the kingdom of heaven. Mat. 5:3.

I will be little in my own eyes. 2 K. 6:22.

Thou wilt save the humble people; but wilt bring down the eyes of the proud. Ps. 17:22.

He that hath been humbled shall be in glory: and he that shall bow down his eyes, he shall be saved. Job 22:29.

Whosoever is a little one, let him come to me. Prov. 9:4.

The Lord is the keeper of little ones: I was humbled, and he delivered me. Ps. 114:6.

He hath had regard to the prayer of the humble: and he hath not despised their petition. Ps. 101:18.

Where humility is, there also is wisdom. Prov. 11:2.

Seek not of the Lord a preeminence, nor of the king the seat of honor. Ecclus. 7:4.

The greater thou art, the more humble thyself in all things, and thou shalt find grace before God. For great is the power of God alone, and he is honored by the humble. Ecclus. 3:20 f.

Amen I say to you, whosoever shall not receive the kingdom of God as a little child, shall not enter into it. Mark 10:15.

He that is the lesser among you all, he is the greater. Luke 9:48.

In that same hour he rejoiced in the Holy Ghost, and said: I confess to thee, O Father, Lord of heaven and earth, that thou hast hid these things from the wise and prudent, and hast revealed them to little ones. Yea, Father, for so it hath seemed good in thy sight. Luke 10:21.

He said to them: The kings of the Gentiles lord it over them; and they that have power over them are called beneficent. But you not so; but he that is the greater among you, let him be as the younger: and he that is the leader, as he that serveth. I am in the midst of you, as he that serveth. Luke 22:25-27.

Charity is not ambitious. 1 C. 13:5.

The fire never saith: It is enough. Prov. 30:16.

How can you believe, who receive glory one from another: and the glory which is from God alone, you do not seek? John 5:44.

Because of the Pharisees they did not confess him, that they might not be cast out of the synagogue. For they loved the glory of men, more than the glory of God. John 12:42 f.

Seek not to be made a judge, unless thou have strength enough to extirpate iniquities: lest thou fear the person of the powerful, and lay a stumbling block for thy integrity. Ecclus. 7:6.

Neither doth any man take the honor to himself, but he that is called by God, as Aaron was. Heb. 5:4.

Whosoever will be the greater among you, let him be your minister. And he that will be first among you, shall be your servant. Mat. 20:26 f.

If his pride mount up even to heaven, and his head touch the clouds: in the end he shall be destroyed like a dunghill, and they that had seen him, shall say: Where is he? As a dream that fleeth away he shall not be found, he shall pass as a vision of the night. Job 20:6-8.

13. EFFECTS OF HUMILITY

The prayer of the humble and the meek hath always pleased thee. Jdth. 9:16.

Thus saith the high and the eminent, that inhabiteth eternity: and his name is holy, who dwelleth in the high and holy place, and with a contrite and humble spirit, to revive the spirit of the humble, and to revive the heart of the contrite. Is. 57:15.

Blessed are the poor in spirit; for theirs is the kingdom of heaven. Mat. 5:3.

Amen I say to you, unless you be converted, and become as little children, you shall not enter the kingdom of heaven. Mat. 12:3.

He will save the humble of spirit. Ps. 33:19.

To whom shall I have respect but to him that is poor and little, and of a contrite heart, and that trembleth at my words? Is. 66:2.

Who is as the Lord our God, who dwelleth on high, and looketh down on the low things in heaven and on earth? Ps. 112:5.

The Lord is high, and looketh on the low, and the high he knoweth afar off. Ps. 137:6.

God resisteth the proud, but to the humble he giveth grace. 1 Pet. 5:5.

Be you humbled under the mighty hand of God, that he may exalt you in the time of visitation. 1 Pet. 5:6.

Humility goeth before glory. Prov. 15:33.

Glory shall uphold the humble of spirit. Prov. 29:23.

He that hath been humbled shall be in glory: and he that shall bow down his eyes, he shall be saved. Job 22:23.

He raiseth up the needy from the dust, and lifteth up the poor from the dunghill: that he may sit with princes, and hold the throne of glory. 1 K. 2:8.

God hath overturned the thrones of proud princes, and hath set up the meek in their stead. Ecclus. 10:17.

The wisdom of the humble shall exalt his head, and shall make him sit in the midst of great men. Ecclus. 11:1.

He hath regarded the humility of his handmaid: for behold from henceforth all generations shall call me blessed. Luke 1:48.

Whosoever, therefore, shall humble himself as this little child, he is the greater in the kingdom of heaven. Mat. 18:4.

He hath put down the mighty from their seat, and hath exalted the humble. Luke 1:52.

Where humility is, there also is wisdom. Prov. 11:2.

The declaration of thy words giveth light: and giveth understanding to little ones. Ps. 118:130.

I confess to thee, O Father, Lord of heaven and earth, because thou hast hid these things from the wise and prudent, and hast revealed them to little ones. Yea, Father, for so hath it seemed good in thy sight. Mat. 11:25, 28.

The fruit of humility is the fear of the Lord, riches and glory and life. Prov. 22:4.

John stayed him, saying: I ought to be baptized by thee, and comest thou to me? And Jesus answering, said to him: Suffer it to be so now, for so it becometh us to fulfil all justice. Mat. 3:14 f.

14. EXHORTATIONS TO HUMILITY

Let no man deceive himself: if any man among you seem to be wise in this world, let him become a fool that he may be wise. For the wisdom of this world is foolishness with God. 1 C. 3:18 f.

Let nothing be done through contention, neither by vainglory: but in humility, let each esteem others better than themselves. Phil. 2:3.

Let the brother of low condition glory in his exaltation. Jas. 1:9.

Be humbled in the sight of the Lord, and he will exalt you. Jas. 4:10.

Be subject to God. Draw nigh to God, and he will draw nigh to you. Jas. 4:7 f.

Ye young men, be subject to the ancients. And do you all insinuate humility one to another, for God resisteth the proud, but to the humble he giveth grace. 1 Pet. 5:5.

Learn of me, because I am meek, and humble of heart, and you shall find rest to your souls. Mat. 11:29.

Not minding high things, but consenting to the humble. Be not wise in your own conceits. Rom. 12:16.

Let this mind be in you, which was also in Christ Jesus: who being in the form of God, thought it not robbery to be equal with God: but debased himself, taking the form of a servant. Phil. 2:5 f.

Humble thy spirit very much: for the vengeance on the flesh of the ungodly is fire and worms. Ecclus. 7:19.

Humble thyself to God, and wait for his hands. Beware that thou be not deceived into folly, and be humbled. Ecclus. 13:9.

The greater thou art, the more humble thyself in all things, and thou shalt find grace before God: for great is the power of God alone, and he is honored by the humble. Ecclus. 3:20 f.

When thou art invited, go, sit down in the lowest place: that when he who invited thee cometh, he may say to thee: Friend, go up higher. Then shalt thou have glory before them that sit at table with thee. Luke 14:10.

Thou standest by faith: be not highminded, but fear. Rom. 11:20.

Put ye on, as the elect of God, holy, and beloved, the bowels of mercy, humility. Col. 3:12.

15. INSTANCES OF HUMILITY; PRAYERS FOR THE SAME

O God, I am not worthy of the least of all thy mercies, and of thy truth which thou hast fulfilled to thy servant. Gen. 32:10.

Moses said to God: Who am I that I should go to Pharao, and should bring forth the children of Israel out of Egypt? Ex. 3:11.

I beseech thee, Lord, I am not eloquent from yesterday and the day before: and since thou hast spoken to thy servant, I have more impediment and slowness of tongue. Ex. 4:10.

David said to Saul: Who am I, or what is my life, or my father's family in Israel, that I should be son-in-law of the king? And David said: Doth it seem to you a small matter to be the king's son-in-law? But I am a poor man, and of small ability. 1 K. 18:18, 23.

David bowing himself down again to the ground, worshipped. After whom dost thou come out, O king of Israel? After whom dost thou pursue? after a dead dog, after a flea? 1 K. 24:9, 15.

David said: Wherefore doth my Lord persecute his servant? What have I done? or what evil is there in my hand? 1 K. 26:18.

He would not have the ark of the Lord brought in to himself in the city of David: but he caused it to be carried into the house of Obededom the Gethite. 2 K. 6:10.

David went in, and sat before the Lord, and said: Who am I, O Lord God, and what is my house, that thou hast brought me thus far? But yet this hath seemed little in thy sight, O Lord God, unless thou didst also speak of the house of thy servant for a long time to come. 2 K. 7:18 f.

It is not good to take the bread of the children, and cast it to the dogs. But she said: Yea, Lord, for the whelps also eat of the crumbs that fall from the table of their masters. Mat. 15:26 f.

O Lord, for I am thy servant: I am thy servant, and the son of thy handmaid. Ps. 115:16.

16. PRIDE

Pride is hateful before God and men: and all iniquity of nations is execrable. Ecclus. 10:7.

Three sorts my soul hateth, and I am greatly grieved at their life: a poor man that is proud. Ecclus. 25:3 f.

We have heard of the pride of Moab; he is exceeding proud: his pride and his arrogance, and his indignation is more than his strength. Is. 16:6.

Never suffer pride to reign in thy mind or in thy words: for from it all perdition took its beginning. Job 4:14.

Be not wise in thy own conceit: fear God, and depart from evil. Prov. 3:7.

Not minding high things, but consenting to the humble. Rom. 12:16.

I hate arrogance and pride. Prov. 8:13.

Thou wilt say then: The branches were broken off, that I might be grafted in. Well, because of unbelief, they were broken off. But thou standest by faith: be not high-minded, but fear. For if God hath not spared the natural branches: fear, lest perhaps he also spare not thee. Rom. 11:19-21.

I say, through the grace that is given me, to all that are among you, not to be more wise than it behoveth to be wise, but to be wise unto sobriety, and according as God hath divided to every one the measure of faith. Rom. 12:3.

Who distinguisheth thee? Or what hast thou that thou hast not received? And if thou hast received: why dost thou glory, as if thou hadst not received it? 1 C. 4:7.

If any man thinketh himself to be something, whereas he is nothing, he deceiveth himself. But let every one prove his own work, and so he shall have glory in himself only, and not in another. Gal. 6:3 f.

Let not the wise man glory in his wisdom, and let not the strong man glory in his strength, and let not the rich man glory in his riches: but let him that glorieth glory in this, that he understandeth and knoweth me. For I am the Lord that exercise mercy, and judgment, and justice in the earth: for these things please me, saith the Lord. Jer. 9:23 f.

Praise not a man for his beauty, neither despise a man for his look. The bee is small among flying things, but her fruit hath the chiefest sweetness. Ecclus. 11:2 f.

Glory not in apparel at any time, and be not exalted in the day of thy honor: for the works of the Highest only are wonderful, and his works are glorious, and secret, and hidden. Many tyrants have sat on the throne, and he whom no man could think on, hath worn the crown. Many mighty men have been greatly brought down, and the glorious have been delivered into the hand of others. Ecclus. 11:4-6.

Shall the axe boast itself against him that cutteth with it? or shall the saw exalt itself against him by whom it is drawn? as if a rod should lift itself up against him that lifteth it up, and a staff exalt itself, which is but wood? Is. 10:15.

Why is earth and ashes proud? When a man shall die, he shall inherit serpents, and beasts, and worms. Ecclus. 10:9, 13.

17. EFFECTS OF PRIDE

Woe to you that are wealthy in Sion, and to you that have confidence in the mountain of Samaria: ye great men, heads of the people, that go in with state into the house of Israel. Amos 6:1.

Every proud man is an abomination to the Lord: though hand should be joined to hand, he is not innocent. Prov. 16:5.

The congregation of the proud shall not be healed: for the plant of wickedness shall take root in them, and it shall not be perceived. Ecclus. 3:30.

Extol not thyself in the thoughts of thy soul like a bull: lest thy strength be quashed by folly, and it eat up thy leaves, and destroy thy fruit, and thou be left as a dry tree in the wilderness. Ecclus. 6:2 f.

Woe to you that are wise in your own eyes, and prudent in your own conceits. Is. 5:21.

Thy heart is lifted up with thy strength. Therefore, thus saith the Lord God: Because thy heart is lifted up as the heart of God: therefore, behold, I will bring upon thee strangers, the strongest of the nations: and they shall draw their swords against the beauty of thy wisdom, and they shall defile thy beauty. They shall kill thee, and bring thee down: and thou shalt die the death of them that are slain in the heart of the sea. Ez. 28:5-8.

Thou hast said: There is none that seeth me. Thy wisdom, and thy knowledge, this hath deceived thee. And thou hast said in thy heart: I am, and besides me there is no other. Is. 47:10.

When they knew God, they have not glorified him as God, or given thanks: but became vain in their thoughts, and their foolish heart was darkened. For professing themselves to be wise, they became fools. Rom. 1:21 f.

Thy heart was lifted up with thy beauty: thou hast lost thy wisdom in thy beauty. I have cast thee to the ground: I have set thee before the face of kings, that they might behold thee. Ex. 28:17.

For judgment I am come into this world; that they who see not, may see: and they who see, may become blind. John 9:39.

Hast thou seen a man wise in his own conceit? there shall be more hope of a fool than of him. Prov. 26:12.

How can you believe, who receive glory one from another; and the glory which is from God alone you do not seek? John 5:44.

Many of the chief men also believed in him: but because of the Pharisees they did not confess him, that they might not be cast out of the synagogue. John 12:42.

The beginning of the pride of man, is to fall off from God: because his heart is departed from him that made him: for pride is the beginning of all sin: he that holdeth it shall be filled with maledictions, and it shall ruin him in the end. Ecclus. 10:14 f.

Where pride is, there also shall be reproach: but where humility is, there also is wisdom. Prov. 11:2.

Among the proud there are always contentions: but they that do all things with counsel, are ruled by wisdom. Prov. 13:10.

Haughtiness of the eyes is the enlarging of the heart: the lamp of the wicked is sin. Prov. 21:4.

He is proud knowing nothing. 1 Tim. 6:4.

The lofty eyes of man are humbled, and the haughtiness of men shall be made to stoop: and the Lord alone shall be exalted in that day. Because the day of the Lord of hosts shall be upon every one that is proud and high-minded, and upon every one that is arrogant, and he shall be humbled. Is. 2:11 f.

Behold the sovereign Lord of hosts shall break the earthen vessel with terror, and the tall of stature shall be cut down, and the lofty shall be humbled. And the thickets of the forest shall be cut down with iron, and Libanus with its high ones shall fall. Is. 10:33 f.

The Lord of hosts hath designed it to pull down the pride of all glory, and bring to disgrace all the glorious ones of the earth. Is. 23:9.

He shall bring down them that dwell on high, the high city he shall lay low. Is. 26:5.

Thus saith the Lord God: Because he was exalted in height, and shot up his top green and thick, and his heart was lifted up in his height: I have delivered him into the hands of the mighty one of the nations. He shall deal with him: I have cast him out according to his wickedness. Ez. 31:10 f.

Scatter the proud in thy indignation, and behold every arrogant man, and humble him. Look on all that are proud, and confound them, and crush the wicked in their place. Hide them in the dust together, and plunge their faces into the pit. Job 40:6-8.

They are lifted up for a little while, and shall not stand, and shall be brought down as all things, and shall be taken away, and as the tops of the ears of corn they shall be broken. Job 24:24.

God hath abolished the memory of the proud: and hath preserved the memory of them that are humble in mind. Ecclus. 10:21.

He hath put down the mighty from their seat, and hath exalted the humble. Luke 1:52.

The pride of thy heart hath lifted thee up, who dwellest in the clefts of the rocks, and settest up thy throne on high: who sayest in thy heart: Who shall bring me down to the ground Though thou be exalted as an eagle, and though thou set thy nest among the stars: thence will I bring thee down, saith the Lord. Abd. 3 f.

The proud and the arrogant is called ignorant, who in anger worketh pride. Prov. 21:24.

Whosoever shall exalt himself, shall be humbled: and he that shall humble himself, shall be exalted. Mat. 23:12.

The proud one shall fall. Jer. 50:32.

That Babylon, glorious among the kingdoms, the famous pride of the Chaldeans, shall be even as the Lord destroyed Sodom and Gomorrha. Is. 13:19.

The Lord will destroy the house of the proud: and will strengthen the borders of the widow. Prov. 15:25.

Hear these things thou that art delicate, and dwellest confidently, that sayest in thy heart: I am, and there is none else besides me: I shall not sit as a widow, and I shall not know barrenness. These two things shall come upon thee suddenly in one day, barrenness and widowhood. Is. 47:49.

God resisteth the proud. Jas. 4:6.

18. PUNISHMENT OF PRIDE

The serpent said to the woman: God doth know that in what day soever you shall eat thereof [the tree of knowledge], your eyes shall be opened, and you shall be as gods, knowing good and evil. Gen. 3:5.

Pharao answered: Who is the Lord, that I should hear his voice, and let Israel go? I know not the Lord, neither will I let Israel go. Ex. 5:2.

When Antiochus had taken away out of the temple a thousand and eight hundred talents, he went back in all haste to Antioch, thinking, through pride, that he might now make the land navigable, and the sea passable on foot: such was the haughtines of his mind. 2 Mach. 5:21.

Each one said to his neighbor: Come, let us make brick, and bake them with fire. And they had brick instead of stones, and slime instead of mortar. And they said: Come, let us make a city, and a tower, the top whereof may reach to heaven: and let us make our name famous before we be scattered abroad into all lands. Gen. 11:3 f.

He did not render again according to the benefits which he had received, for his heart was lifted up, and wrath was enkindled against him, and against Juda and Jerusalem. And he humbled himself afterwards, because his heart had been lifted up, both he and the inhabitants of Jerusalem: and therefore the wrath of the Lord came not upon them in the days of Ezechias. 2 Par. 32:25 f.

Upon a day appointed, Herod, being arrayed in kingly apparel, sat in the judgment seat, and made an oration to them. And the people made acclamation, saying: It is the voice of a god, and not of a man. And forthwith an angel of the Lord struck him, because he had not given the honor to God; and being eaten up by worms, he gave up the ghost. Acts 12:21-23.

19. BOASTING AND PRESUMPTION

He that boasteth, and puffeth up himself, stirreth up quarrels: but he that trusteth in the Lord, shall be healed. Prov. 28:25.

May the Lord destroy all deceitful lips, and the tongue that speaketh proud things. Ps. 11:4.

I will take away out of the midst of thee thy proud boasters, and thou shalt no more be lifted up because of my holy mountain. Soph. 3:11.

Professing themselves to be wise, they became fools. Rom. 1:22.

Do not multiply to speak lofty things, boasting: let old matters depart from your mouth. 1 K. 2:3.

Let another praise thee, and not thy own mouth: a stranger, and not thy own lips. Prov. 27:2.

The Pharisee standing, prayed thus with himself: O God, I give thee thanks that I am not as the rest of men, extortioners, unjust, adulterers, as also is this publican. I fast twice in the week; I give tithes of all that I possess. Luke 18:11 f.

I say to you, this man went down into his house justified rather than the other. Luke 18:14.

Say not, how mighty am I? Ecclus. 5:3.

20. MEEKNESS

Brethren, if a man be overtaken in any fault, you, who are spiritual, instruct such a one in the spirit of meekness, considering thyself, lest thou also be tempted. Gal. 6:1.

Blessed are the meek, for they shall possess the land. Mat. 5:4.

A mild answer breaketh wrath: but a harsh word stirreth up fury. Prov. 15:1.

Learn of me, for I am meek, and humble of heart, and you shall find rest to your souls. Mat. 11:29.

Casting away all uncleanness, and abundance of naughtiness, with meekness receive the ingrafted word, which is able to save your souls. Jas. 1:21.

Admonish them not to be litigious, but gentle: showing all mildness to all men. Titus 3:2.

The servant of the Lord must not wrangle: but be mild towards all men, apt to teach, patient. 2 Tim. 2:24.

I, a prisoner in the Lord, beseech you, that you walk worthy of the vocation in which you are called, with all humility and meekness. Eph. 4:1.

My son, do thy works in meekness, and thou shalt be beloved above the glory of men. Ecclus. 3:19.

My son, keep thy soul in meekness, and give it honor according to its desert. Who will justify him that sinneth against his own soul? and who will honor him that dishonoreth his own soul? Ecclus. 10:31 f.

To the meek he will give grace. Prov. 3:34.

It is better to be humbled with the meek, than to divide the spoils with the proud. Prov. 16:19.

Seek the Lord, all ye meek of the earth, you that have wrought his judgment: seek the just, seek the meek: if by any means you may be hid in the day of the Lord's indignation. Soph. 2:3.

When God arose in judgment, to save all the meek of the earth. Ps. 75:10.

The meek shall increase their joy in the Lord, and the poor men shall rejoice in the holy one of Israel. Is. 29:19.

Now I Paul myself beseech you, by the meekness and gentleness of Christ. 2 C. 10:1.

He will exalt the meek. Ps. 149:4.

Fear not: can we resist the will of God? You thought evil against me [Joseph]: but God turned it into good, that he might exalt me, as at present you see, and might save many people. Fear not, I will feed you and your children. Gen. 50:19-21.

Moses was a man exceeding meek above all men that dwelt on earth. Num. 12:3.

The publicans and sinners drew near unto him to hear him. And the Pharisees and the scribes murmured, saying: This man receiveth sinners and eateth with them. Luke 15:1 f.

Behold, thy king cometh to thee, meek. Mat. 21:5.

21. SIN OF ANGER

Pride was not made for men, nor wrath for the race of women. Ecclus. 10:22.

Anger and fury are both of them abominable, and the sinful man shall be subject to them. Ecclus. 27:33.

As the wood of the forest is, so the fire burneth; and as a man's strength is, so shall his anger be, and according to his riches he shall increase his anger. Ecclus. 28:12.

A peaceable tongue is a tree of life: but that which is immoderate, shall crush the spirit. Prov. 15:4.

A spirit that is easily angered, who can bear? Prov. 18:14.

He that is impatient shall suffer damage. Prov. 19:19.

It is better to dwell in a wilderness, than with a quarrelsome and passionate woman. Prov. 21:19.

Man to man reserveth anger, and doth he seek remedy of God? He hath no mercy on a man like himself, and doth he entreat for his own sins? He that is but flesh, nourisheth anger, and doth he ask forgiveness of God? Who shall obtain pardon for his sins? Remember thy last things, and let enmity cease. Ecclus. 28:3-6.

Be not as a lion in thy house, terrifying them of thy household, and oppressing them that are under thee. Ecclus. 4:35.

A hot soul is a burning fire, it will never be quenched, till it devour something. Ecclus. 23:22.

He that provoketh wrath, bringeth forth strife. Prov. 30:33.

Hast thou seen a man hasty to speak? folly is rather to be looked for than his amendment. A passionate man provoketh quarrels. Prov. 29:20, 22.

Cease from anger, and leave rage. Ps. 36:8.

He that is impatient, exalteth his folly. Prov. 14:29.

If thou blow the spark, it shall burn as a fire: and if thou spit upon it, it shall be quenched: both come out of the mouth. Ecclus. 28:14.

A stone is heavy, and sand weighty; but the anger of a fool is heavier than them both. Anger hath no mercy, nor fury when it breaketh forth: and who can bear the violence of one provoked? Prov. 27:3 f.

A fool immediately showeth his anger: but he that dissembleth injuries is wise. Prov. 12:16.

A fool uttereth all his mind: a wise man deferreth, and keepeth it till afterwards. Prov. 29:11.

The wrath of high spirits is his ruin. Ecclus. 1:28.

He that is easily stirred up to wrath, shall be more prone to sin. Prov. 29:22.

Envy and anger shorten a man's days, and pensiveness will bring old age before the time. Ecclus. 30:26.

Anger indeed killeth the foolish. Job 5:2.

A passionate man kindleth strife, and a sinful man will trouble his friends, and bring in debate in the midst of them that are at peace. Ecclus. 28:11.

A passionate man stirreth up strifes: he that is patient appeaseth those that are stirred up. Prov. 15:18.

As coals are to burning coals, and wood to fire, so an angry man stirreth up strife. Prov. 26:21.

Whosoever is angry with his brother, shall be in danger of the judgment. Mat. 5:22.

Let all bitterness, and anger, and indignation, and clamor, and blasphemy be put away from you, with all malice. Eph. 4:31.

Remove anger from thy heart, and

put away evil from thy flesh. Eccles. 11:10.

Let every man be slow to speak and slow to anger. For the anger of man worketh not the justice of God. Jas. 1:19 f.

Be angry, and sin not. Let not the sun go down upon your anger. Eph. 4:26.

Remember the fear of God, and be not angry with thy neighbor. Remember the covenant of the most High, and overlook the ignorance of thy neighbor. Ecclus. 28:8 f.

22. ZEAL FOR THE HONOR OF GOD

Behold, I give Phinees the peace of my covenant. And the covenant of the priesthood forever shall be both to him, and his seed, because he hath been zealous for his God, and hath made atonement for the wickedness of the children of Israel. Num. 25:12 f.

When he came nigh to the camp, he saw the calf, and the dances: and being very angry, he threw the tables out of his hand, and broke them at the foot of the mount. And laying hold of the calf which they had made, he burnt it, and beat it to powder, which he strowed into water, and gave thereof to the children of Israel to drink. Ex. 32:19 f.

Standing in the gate of the camp, he said: If any man be on the Lord's side, let him join with me. And all the sons of Levi gathered themselves together unto him. Ex. 32:26.

Elias said to them: Take the prophets of Baal, and let not one of them escape. And when they had taken them, Elias brought them down to the torrent Cison, and killed them there. 3 K. 18:40.

With zeal have I been zealous for the Lord of hosts: because the children of Israel have forsaken thy covenant: They have destroyed thy altars, they have slain thy prophets with the sword, and I alone am left, and they seek my life to take it away. 3 K. 19:14.

When I had heard this word I rent my mantle and my coat, and plucked off the hairs of my head and my beard, and I sat down mourning. And at the evening sacrifice I rose up from my affliction, and having rent my mantle and my garment, I fell upon my knees, and spread out my hands to the Lord my God. 1 Es. 9:3, 5.

Jesus went into the temple of God, and cast out all them that sold and bought in the temple, and overthrew the tables of the money-changers, and the chairs of them that sold doves: and he said to them: It is written: My house shall be called a house of prayer, but you have made it a den of thieves. Mat. 21:12 f.

When his disciples James and John had seen this, they said: Lord, wilt thou that we command fire to come down from heaven and consume them? And turning, he rebuked them, saying: You know not of what spirit you are. The Son of man came not to destroy souls, but to save. Luke 9:54-56.

Who is he that can hurt you, if you be zealous of good? 1 Pet. 3:13.

I endure all things for the sake of the elect, that they also may obtain the salvation which is in Christ Jesus with heavenly glory. 2 Tim. 2:10.

I have a baptism wherewith I am to be baptized: and how am I straitened until it be accomplished? Luke 12:50.

If you have bitter zeal, and there be contentions in your hearts: glory not, and be not liars against the truth. For this is not wisdom, descending from above; but is earthly, sensual, diabolical. Jas. 3:14 f.

I know thy works, that thou art neither cold, nor hot. I would thou wert cold, or hot: but because thou art lukewarm, and neither cold, nor hot, I will begin to vomit thee out of my mouth. Those whom I love, I rebuke and chastise. Be zealous therefore, and do penance. Apoc. 3:15 f., 19.

Be zealous for that which is good in a good thing always. Gal. 4:18.

Whereas I was free as to all, I

made myself the servant of all: that I might gain the more. And I became to the Jews a Jew, that I might gain the Jews. To the weak I became weak, that I might gain the weak. I became all things to all men, that I might save all. And I do all things for the gospel's sake: that I may be made partaker thereof. Know you not that they that run in the race all run indeed, but one receiveth the prize? So run that you may obtain. 1 C. 9:19 f., 22-24.

The pasch of the Jews was at hand, and Jesus went up to Jerusalem: and he found in the temple those that sold oxen and sheep and doves, and the changers of money sitting. And when he had made as it were a scourge of little cords, he drove them all out of the temple, the sheep also and the oxen, and he poured out the changers' money: and the tables he overthrew. And he said to them that sold doves: Take these things hence: and make not the house of my Father a house of traffic. And his disciples remembered that it was written: The zeal of thy house hath eaten me up. John 2:13-17.

23. EXAMPLES OF INDISCREET ZEAL

Then were little children presented to him, that he should impose hands on them and pray. And the disciples rebuked them. But Jesus said to them: Suffer the little children, and forbid them not to come to me: for the kingdom of heaven is for such. Mat. 19:13 f.

The disciples seeing [the pouring of so much ointment on the head of Christ], had indignation, saying: To what purpose is this waste? For this might have been sold for much, and given to the poor. Mat. 26:8 f.

John answering, said: Master, we saw a certain man casting out devils in thy name, and we forbade him, because he followeth not with us. And Jesus said to him: Forbid him not: for he that is not against you is for you. Luke 9:49 f.

There came together to Jerusalem a multitude out of the neighboring cities, bringing sick persons, and such as were troubled with unclean spirits, who were all healed. Then the high priest rising up, and all they that were with him, were filled with envy: and they laid hands on the apostles, and put them in the common prison. Acts 5:16-18.

The next Sabbath day the whole city almost came together to hear the word of God. And the Jews, seeing the multitudes, were filled with envy, and contradicted those things which were said by Paul, blaspheming. Acts 13:44 f.

24. MODESTY

Let your modesty be known to all men. Phil. 4:5.

A man is known by his look, and a wise man when thou meetest him is known by his countenance. The attire of the body, and the laughter of the teeth, and the gait of the man show what he is. Ecclus. 19:26 f.

The fruit of modesty is the fear of the Lord, riches, and glory, and life. Prov. 22:4.

Wisdom shinneth in the face of the wise: the eyes of fools are in the ends of the earth. Prov. 17:24.

A fool will peep through the window into the house, but he that is well taught will stand without. Ecclus. 21:26.

Look not round about thee in the ways of the city, nor wander up and down in the streets thereof. Turn away thy face from a woman dressed up, and gaze not upon another's beauty. Ecclus. 9:7 f.

Let another praise thee, and not thy own mouth: a stranger, and not thy own lips. Prov. 27:2.

There is a shame that bringeth glory and grace. Ecclus. 4:25.

A holy and shame-faced woman is grace upon grace. Ecclus. 26:19.

It is the folly of a man to hearken at the door, and a wise man will be grieved with the disgrace. Ecclus. 21:26.

Because the daughters of Sion are haughty and have walked with stretched-out necks, and wanton glances of their eyes, and made a noise as they walked with their feet, and moved in a set pace, the Lord will make bald the crown of the head of the daughter of Sion, and the Lord will discover their hair. Is. 3:16 f.

Behold, they that are clothed in soft garments are in the houses of kings. Mat. 11:8.

There was a certain rich man who was clothed in purple and fine linen: and feasted sumptuously every day. The rich man died, and he was buried in hell. Luke 16:19, 22.

They have turned the ornament of their jewels into pride, and have made of it the images of their abominations and idols: therefore I have made it an uncleanness to them. And I will give it into the hands of strangers for spoil, and to the wicked of the earth for a prey, and they shall defile it. Ez. 7:20 f.

VIII

FORTITUDE AND THE CONTRARY VICES

1. EXAMPLES OF FORTITUDE

Behold our God, whom we worship, is able to save us from the furnace of burning fire, and to deliver us out of thy hands, O king. But if he will not, be it known to thee, O king, that we will not worship thy gods, nor adore the golden statue which thou hast set up. Dan. 3:17 f.

It is better for me to fall into your hands without doing it than to sin in the sight of the Lord. Dan. 13:23.

They dissuaded him, saying: We shall not be able, but let us save our lives now, and return to our brethren, and then we will fight against them; for we are but few. Then Judas said: God forbid we should do this thing, and flee away from them: but if our time be come, let us die manfully for our brethren, and let us not stain our glory. 1 Mac. 9:9 f.

Then they all together blessed the merciful Lord, and took great courage, being ready to break through not only men, but also the fiercest beasts, and walls of iron. So they went on courageously, having a helper from heaven, and the Lord who showed mercy to them. And rushing violently upon the enemy, like lions, they slew of them eleven thousand footmen and one thousand six hundred horsemen. 2 Mac. 11:9-11.

Joseph of Arimathea, a noble counsellor, who was also himself looking for the kingdom of God, came and went in boldly to Pilate, and begged the body of Jesus. Mark 15:43.

Behold, I am in your hands: do with me what is good and right in your eyes: But know ye, and understand, that if ye put me to death, you will shed innocent blood against your own selves and against this city, and the inhabitants thereof. For in truth the Lord sent me to you, to speak all these words in your hearing. Jer. 26:14 f.

I saw under the altar the souls of them that were slain for the word of God, and for the testimony which they held. And they cried with a loud voice, saying: How long, O Lord (holy and true), dost thou not judge and revenge our blood on them that dwell on the earth? Apoc. 6:9 f.

Whosoever shall confess me before men, him shall the Son of man also confess before the angels of God. But he that shall deny me before men, shall be denied before the angels of God. Luke 12:8 f.

Amen, amen, I say to you, unless the grain of wheat falling into the ground, die, itself remaineth alone. But if it die, it bringeth forth much fruit. He that loveth his life shall lose it; and he that hateth his life in this world, keepeth it unto life eternal. John 12:24 f.

Though in the sight of men they suffered torments, their hope is full of immortality. Afflicted in few things, in many they shall be well rewarded. Wis. 3:4 f.

These are they who are come out of great tribulation, and have washed their robes, and have made them white in the blood of the Lamb. Apoc. 7:14.

2. WORDS OF THE SEVEN MACHABEAN BROTHERS AND OF THEIR MOTHER (2 Mac., chap. 7)

1. What wouldst thou ask or learn of us? We are ready to die rather than to transgress the laws of God received from our fathers. The Lord God will look upon the truth, and will take pleasure in us, as Moses declared in the profession of the canticle: and in his servants he will take pleasure.

2. I will not do it. Thou indeed, O most wicked man, destroyest us out of this present life: but the King of the world will raise us up, who die for his laws, in the resurrection of eternal life.

3. These [tongue and hands] I have from heaven, but for the laws of God I now despise them: because I hope to receive them again from him.

4. It is better being put to death by men, to look for hope from God, to be raised up again by him: for as to thee, thou shalt have no resurrection unto life.

5. Whereas thou hast power among men, though thou art corruptible, thou dost what thou wilt: but think not that our nation is forsaken by God. But stay patiently a while, and thou shalt see his great power, in what manner he will torment thee and thy seed.

6. Be not deceived without cause: for we suffer these things for ourselves, having sinned against our God, and things worthy of admiration are done to us. But do not think that thou shalt escape unpunished, for that thou hast attempted to fight against God.

7. For whom do you stay? I will not obey the commandment of the king, but the commandment of the law, which was given us by Moses. But thou that hast been the author of all mischief against the Hebrews shalt not escape the hand of God. For we suffer thus for our sins. And though the Lord our God is angry with us a little while for our chastisement and correction: yet he will be reconciled again to his servants. For my brethren, having undergone a short pain, are under the covenant of eternal life: but thou by the judgment of God shalt receive just punishment for thy pride. But I, like my brethren, offer up my life and my body for the laws of our fathers, calling upon God to be speedily merciful to our nation, and that thou by torments and stripes mayst confess that he alone is God.

8. Their mother.

Her Words to Her Seven Sons

I know not how you were formed in my womb, for I neither gave you breath, nor soul, nor life, neither did I frame the limbs of every one of you. But the Creator of the world, that formed the nativity of man, and that found out the origin of all, he will restore to you again his mercy, both breath and life, as now you despise yourselves for the sake of his laws.

Her Words to Her Youngest Son

My son, have pity upon me, that bore thee nine months in my womb, and gave thee suck three years, and nourished thee, and brought thee up unto this age. I beseech thee, my son, look upon heaven and earth, and all that is in them: and consider that God made them out of nothing, and mankind also: so thou shalt not fear this tormentor, but being made a worthy partner with thy brethren, receive death, that in that mercy I may receive thee again with thy brethren.

3. FORTITUDE AND CHARITY

The patient man is better than the valiant: and he that ruleth his spirit, than he that taketh cities. Prov. 16:32.

Charity is patient. 1 C. 13:4.

[Know] that the trying of your faith worketh patience. Jas. 1:3.

Tribulation worketh patience. Rom. 5:3.

No man should be moved in these tribulations: for yourselves know that we are appointed thereunto. 1 Thess. 3:3.

All that will live godly in Christ Jesus, shall suffer persecution. 2 Tim. 3:12.

Dearly beloved, think not strange the burning heat which is to try you, as if some new thing happened to you. 1 Pet. 4:12.

If you partake of the sufferings of Christ, rejoice that when his glory shall be revealed, you may also be glad with exceeding joy. If you be reproached for the name of Christ, you shall be blessed: for that which is of the honor, glory, and power of God, and that which is his Spirit, resteth upon you. But let none of you suffer as a murderer, or a thief, or a railer, or a coveter of other men's things. But if as a Christian, let him not be ashamed; but let him glorify God in that name. 1 Pet. 4:13-16.

Show thyself a man. 3 K. 2:3.

4. TO SUFFER FOR CHRIST A GREAT HAPPINESS

This is thankworthy, if for conscience towards God, a man endure sorrows, suffering wrongfully. For what glory is it, if committing sin, and being buffeted for it, you endure? But if doing well you suffer patiently; this is thankworthy before God. For unto this are you called: because Christ also suffered for us, leaving you an example that you should follow his steps. 1 Pet. 2:19-21.

Unto you it is given for Christ, not only to believe in him, but also to suffer for him. Having the same conflict as that which you have seen in me, and now have heard of me. Phil. 1:29 f.

If you suffer anything for justice' sake, blessed are ye. 1 Pet. 3:14.

Blessed are they that suffer persecution for justice' sake; for theirs is the kingdom of heaven. Blessed are ye when they shall revile you, and persecute you, and speak all that is evil against you, untruly, for my sake: be glad and rejoice, for your reward is very great in heaven; for so they persecuted the prophets that were before you. Mat. 5:10-12.

By faith Moses, when he was grown up, denied himself to be the son of Pharao's daughter; rather choosing to be afflicted with the people of God, than to have the pleasure of sin for a time, esteeming the reproach of Christ greater riches than the treasure of the Egyptians. For he looked unto the reward. Heb. 11:24-26.

If the world hate you, know ye that it hath hated me before you. If you had been of the world, the world would love its own; but because you are not of the world, but I have chosen you out of the world, therefore the world hateth you. Remember my word that I said to you: The servant is not greater than his master. If they have persecuted me, they will also persecute you: if they have kept my word they will keep yours also. But all these things they will do to you for my name's sake: because they know not him that sent me. John 15:18-21.

Christ having suffered in the flesh, be you also armed with the same thought: for he that hath suffered in the flesh, hath ceased from sins. 1 Pet. 4:1.

5. THE REWARDS OF PATIENCE

Patience is necessary for you: that doing the will of God, you may receive the promise. Heb. 10:36.

We are the sons of God. And if sons, heirs also: heirs indeed of God, and joint heirs with Christ: yet so, if we suffer with him, that we may be also glorified with him. Rom. 8:16 f.

The patience of the poor shall not perish forever. Ps. 9:19.

A patient man shall bear for a time, and afterwards joy shall be restored to him. Ecclus. 1:29.

Because thou hast kept the word of my patience, I will also keep thee from the hour of temptation, which shall come upon the whole world to try them that dwell upon the earth. Apoc. 3:10.

That on the good ground are they who, in a good and perfect heart, hearing the word, keep it, and bring forth fruit in patience. Luke 8:15.

In your patience you shall possess your souls. Luke 21:19.

Patience hath a perfect work: that you may be perfect and entire, failing in nothing. Jas. 1:4.

God hath regenerated us unto an inheritance incorruptible, Wherein you shall greatly rejoice, if now you must be for a little time made sorrowful in divers temptations: that the trial of your faith [much more precious than gold, which is tried by the fire] may be found unto praise, and glory, and honor, at the appearing of Jesus Christ.

Patience [worketh] trial, and trial hope: and hope confoundeth not. Rom. 5:4 f.

The Lord gave Job twice as much as he had before. Job 42:10.

A passionate man stirreth up strifes: he that is patient appeaseth those that are stirred up. Prov. 15:18.

By patience a prince shall be appeased, and a soft tongue shall break hardness. Prov. 25:15.

The learning of a man is known by patience: and his glory is to pass over wrongs. Prov. 19:11.

The fruit of the Spirit is charity, joy, peace, patience. Gal. 5:22.

6. EXHORTATIONS TO PATIENCE

Humble thy heart and endure: incline thine ear, and receive the words of understanding: and make not haste in the time of clouds. Wait on God with patience: join thyself to God, and endure, that thy life may be increased in the latter end. Take all that shall be brought upon thee: and in thy sorrow endure, and in thy humiliation keep patience: for gold and silver are tried in the fire, but acceptable men in the furnace of humiliation. Ecclus. 2:2-5.

My son, reject not the correction of the Lord: and do not faint when thou art chastised by him. For whom the Lord loveth, he chastiseth: and as a father in the son he pleaseth himself. Prov. 3:11 f.

I say to you not to resist evil: but if one strike thee on thy right cheek, turn to him also the other. Mat. 5:39.

Rejoicing in hope. Patient in tribulation. Instant in prayer. Rom. 12:12.

I beseech you, that you walk worthy of the vocation in which you are called, with all humility and mildness, with patience, supporting one another in charity. Eph. 4:1 f.

We beseech you, brethren, be patient towards all men. 1 Thess. 5:14.

What things soever were written, were written for our learning: that through patience and the comfort of the Scriptures, we might have hope. Rom. 15:4.

Take, my brethren, for an example of suffering evil, of labor and patience, the prophets, who spoke in the name of the Lord. Behold, we count them blessed who have endured. You have heard of the patience of Job, and you have seen the end of the Lord, that the Lord is merciful and compassionate. Jas. 5:10 f.

Here is the patience of the saints, who keep the commandments of God and the faith of Jesus. Apoc. 14:12.

I know thy works, and thy labor, and thy patience, and how thou canst not bear them that are evil: and thou hast patience, and hast endured for my name, and hast not fainted. Apoc. 2:2 f.

7. PERSEVERANCE

A holy man continueth in wisdom as the sun: but a fool changed as the moon. Ecclus. 27:12.

He that shall persevere unto the end, he shall be saved. Mat. 10:22.

No man putting his hand to the

plow, and looking back, it fit for the kingdom of God. Luke 9:62.

Abide in my love. If you keep my commandments, you shall abide in my love: as I also have kept my Father's commandments, and do abide in his love. John 15:9 f.

My beloved brethren, be ye steadfast and unmovable: always abounding in the work of the Lord, knowing that your labor is not vain in the Lord. 1 C. 15:58.

In doing good, let us not fail For in due time we shall reap, not failing. Therefore whilst we have time, let us work good to all men, but especially to those who are of the household of the faith. Gal. 6:9 f.

My dearly beloved brethren, and most desired, my joy and my crown; so stand fast in the Lord, my dearly beloved. Phil. 4:1.

Be thou faithful until death, and I will give thee the crown of life. Apoc. 2:10.

Behold I come quickly: hold fast that which thou hast, that no man take thy crown. Apoc. 3:11.

Brethren, be not weary in well-doing. 2 Thess. 3:13.

We desire that every one of you show forth the same carefulness to the accomplishing of hope unto the end: that you become not slothful, but followers of them, who through faith and patience shall inherit the promises. Heb. 6:11 f.

Be steadfast in thy covenant, and be conversant therein, and grow old in the work of thy commandments. Abide not in the works of sinners, but trust in God, and stay in thy place. Ecclus. 11:21 f.

Henceforth let us be no more children, tossed to and fro, and carried about with every wind of doctrine by the wickedness of men, by cunning craftiness, by which they lie in wait to deceive. Eph. 4:14.

Jesus Christ, yesterday and today: and the same forever. Be not led away with various and strange doctrines. For it is best that the heart be established with grace, not with meats: which have not profited those that walk in them. Heb. 13:8 f.

You brethren, knowing these things before, take heed, lest being led aside by the error of the unwise, you fall from your own steadfastness. 2 Pet. 3:17.

Look to yourselves, that you lose not the things which you have wrought: but that you may receive a full reward. Whosoever revolteth, and continueth not in the doctrine of Christ, hath not God. He that continueth in the doctrine, the same hath both the Father and the Son. 2 John 8 f.

The just man shall hold on his way, and he that hath clean hands shall be stronger and stronger. Job 17:9.

Be steadfast in the way of the Lord and in the truth of thy judgment, and in knowledge, and let the word of peace and justice keep with thee. Ecclus. 5:12.

If you continue in my word, you shall be my disciples indeed. John 8:31.

Being confident of this very thing, that he who hath begun a good work in you, will perfect it unto the day of Christ Jesus. Phil. 1:6.

Persevere under chastisement. God dealeth with you as with his sons. Heb. 12:7.

He that shall overcome, shall thus be clothed in white garments, and I will not blot out his name out of the book of life, and I will confess his name before my Father, and before his angels. Apoc. 3:5.

8. INCONSTANCY

The inhabitants of them were weak of hand, they trembled, and were confounded: they became like the grass of the field, and the herb of the pasture, and like the grass of the housetops, which withered before it was ripe. Is. 37:27.

This man began to build, and was not able to finish. Luke 14:30.

Waters wear away the stones, and with inundation the ground by little and little is washed away. Job 14:19.

The heart of a fool is as a wheel of a cart: and his thoughts are like a rolling axle-tree. Ecclus. 33:5.

A holy man continueth in wisdom as the sun: but the fool is changed as the moon. Ecclus. 27:12.

As a bird that wandereth from her nest, so is a man that leaveth his place. Prov. 27:8.

The wicked are like the raging sea, which cannot rest, and the waves thereof cast up dirt and mire. Is. 57:20.

Your mercy is as a morning cloud, and as the dew that goeth away in the morning. Osee 6:4.

What went you out into the desert to see? a reed shaken with the wind? Mat. 11:7.

Behold they that serve him are not steadfast, and in his angels he found wickedness. Job 4:18.

A double minded man is inconstant in all his ways. Jas. 1:8.

Winnow not with every wind, and go not into every way: for so is every sinner proved by a double tongue. Be steadfast in the way of the Lord, and in the truth of thy judgment, and in knowledge, and let the word of peace and justice keep with thee. Ecclus. 5:11 f.

9. TRIBULATION

I will chastise thee in judgment that thou mayst not seem to thyself innocent. Jer. 30:11.

Good things and evil, life and death, poverty and riches, are from God. Ecclus. 11:14.

As it was your mind to go astray from God, so when you return again you shall seek him ten times as much. For he that hath brought evils upon you, shall bring you everlasting joy again with your salvation. Bar. 4:28 f.

In the good day enjoy good things, and beware beforehand of the evil day: for God hath made both the one and the other, that man may not find against him any just complaint. Eccles. 7:15.

Rabbi, who hath sinned, this man, or his parents, that he should be born blind? Jesus answered: Neither hath this man sinned, nor his parents: but that the works of God should be made manifest in him. John 9:2 f.

Tribulation worketh patience, and patience trial. Rom. 5:3 f.

Behold, the devil will cast some of you into prison, that you may be tried. Apoc. 2:10.

The furnace trieth the potter's vessels, and the trial of affliction just men. Ecclus. 27:6.

As silver is tried by fire, and gold in the furnace, so the Lord trieth the hearts. Prov. 17:3.

Thou hast chastised me, and I was instructed as a young bullock unaccustomed to the yoke. Jer. 31:18.

Because thou wast acceptable to God, it was necessary that temptation should prove thee. Tob. 12:13.

Our fathers were tempted that they might be proved, whether they worshipped their God truly. Jdth. 8:21.

Thus saith the Lord: Let thy voice cease from weeping, and thine eyes from fears, for there is a reward for thy work. Jer. 31:16.

I beseech those that shall read this book that they be not shocked at these calamities, but that they consider the things that happened not as being for the destruction of our nation. For it is a token of great goodness when sinners are not suffered to go on in their ways for a long time, but are presently punished. For, not as with other nations (whom the Lord patiently expecteth, that when the day of judgment shall come he may punish them in the fulness of their sins), doth he also deal with us, so as to suffer our sins to come to their height, and then take vengeance on us. And therefore he never withdraweth his mercy from us: but though he chastise his people with adversity, he forsaketh them not. 2 Mac. 6:12-16.

Whatsoever shall befall the just man, it shall not make him sad: but the wicked shall be filled with mischief. Prov. 12:21.

They must remember how our father Abraham was tempted, and being proved by many tribulations was made the friend of God. So Isaac, so Jacob, so Moses, and all that have pleased God, passed through many tribulations, remaining faithful. Jdth. 8:22 f.

All that will live godly in Christ Jesus shall suffer persecution. 2 Tim. 3:12.

Gold and silver are tried in the fire, but acceptable men in the furnace of humiliation. Ecclus. 2:5.

The Lord will not cast off forever. For if he hath cast off, he will also have mercy, according to the multitude of his mercies. Lam. 3:31 f.

The mercy of God is beautiful in the time of affliction, as a cloud of rain in the time of drought. Ecclus. 35:36.

This sickness is not unto death, but for the glory of God: that the Son of God may be glorified by it. John 11:4.

Amen I say to you, there is no man who hath left house, or brethren, or sisters, or father, or mother, or children, or land for my sake and for the gospel, who shall not receive an hundred times as much, now in this time; houses, and brethren, and sisters, and mothers, and children, and lands with persecutions: and in the world to come life everlasting. Mark 10:29 f.

Correct me, O Lord, but yet with judgment: and not in thy fury, lest thou bring me to nothing. Jer. 10:24.

Afflicted in few things, in many they shall be well rewarded: because God hath tried them, and found them worthy of himself. Wis. 3:5.

The God of all grace, who hath called us unto his eternal glory in Christ Jesus, after you have suffered a little, will himself perfect you, and confirm you and establish you. To him be glory and empire forever and ever. 1 Pet. 5:10.

I reckon that the sufferings of this time are not worthy to be compared with the glory to come, that shall be revealed in us. Rom. 8:18.

That which is at present momentary and light of our tribulation, worketh for us above measure exceedingly an eternal weight of glory. While we look not at the things which are seen, but at the things which are not seen. 2 C. 4:17 f.

10. FRUITS OF TRIBULATION

They that sow in tears shall reap in joy. Going they went and wept, casting their seeds. But coming they shall come with joyfulness, carrying their sheaves. Ps. 125:5-7.

Blessed is the man whom God correcteth: refuse not therefore the chastising of the Lord. Job 5:17.

We know that to them that love God, all things work together unto good, to such as, according to his purpose, are called to be saints. Rom. 8:28.

Blessed is the man that endureth temptation; for when he hath been proved, he shall receive the crown of life, which God hath promised to them that love him. Jas. 1:12.

Blessed are they that suffer persecution for justice' sake: for theirs is the kingdom of heaven. Mat. 5:10.

Paul and Barnabas returned to Antioch, confirming the souls of the disciples, and exhorting them to continue in the faith: and that through many tribulations we must enter into the kingdom of God. Acts 14:21.

Now all chastisement for the present indeed seemeth not to bring with it joy, but sorrow: but afterwards it will yield, to them that are exercised by it, the most peaceable fruit of justice. Heb. 12:11.

He that taketh not up his cross and followeth me, is not worthy of me. Mat. 10:38.

As the sufferings of Christ abound

in us, so also by Christ doth our comfort abound. That our hope for you may be steadfast: knowing that as you are partakers of the sufferings, so shall you be also of the consolation. 2 C. 1:5, 7.

I am filled with comfort: I exceedingly abound with joy in all our tribulation. 2 C. 7:4.

In all things we suffer tribulation, but are not distressed: we are straitened, but are not destitute: we suffer persecution, but are not forsaken: we are cast down, but we perish not. For which cause we faint not: but though our outward man is corrupted, yet the inward man is renewed day by day. 2 C. 4:8 f., 16.

He saith to me: My grace is sufficient for thee: for power is made perfect in infirmity. Gladly therefore will I glory in my infirmities, that the power of Christ may dwell in me. 2 C. 12:9.

He said to them: O foolish and slow of heart to believe in all things which the prophets have spoken. Ought not Christ to have suffered these things, and so to enter into his glory? Luke 24:25 f.

He humbled himself, becoming obedient unto death, even the death of the cross. For which cause God also hath exalted him, and hath given him a name. Phil. 2:8 f.

When he slew them, then they sought him: and they returned and came to him early in the morning. Ps. 77:34.

Fill their faces with shame: and they shall seek thy name, O Lord. Ps. 82:17.

Whom the Lord loveth, he chastiseth; and he scourgeth every son whom he receiveth. Persevere under discipline. God dealeth with you as with his sons; for what son is there, whom the father doth not correct? But if you be without chastisement, whereof all are made partakers, then are you bastards, and not sons. Heb. 12:6-8.

Whom the Lord loveth, he chastiseth; and as a father in the son he pleaseth himself. Prov. 3:12.

Such as I love, I rebuke and chastise. Apoc. 3:19.

He that loveth correction, loveth knowledge: but he that hateth reproof is foolish. Prov. 12:1.

In the day of evils be not unmindful of good things: for it is easy before God in the day of death to reward every one according to his ways. Ecclus. 11:27 f.

My brethren count it all joy, when you shall fall into divers temptations; knowing that the trying of your faith worketh patience. Jas. 1:2 f.

If I must needs glory, I will glory of the things that concern my infirmity. 2 C. 11:30.

Gladly will I glory in my infirmities, that the power of Christ may dwell in me. 2 C. 12:9.

We glory in tribulations. Rom. 5:3.

The just cried, and the Lord heard them: and delivered them out of all their troubles. The Lord is nigh unto them that are of a contrite heart: and he will save the humble of spirit. Many are the afflictions of the just: but out of them all will the Lord deliver them. Ps. 33:18-20.

We would not have you ignorant, brethren, of our tribulation, which came to us in Asia, that we were pressed out of measure above our strength, so that we were weary even of life. But we had within ourselves the answer of death, that we should not trust in ourselves, but in God who raiseth the dead. 2 C. 1:8 f.

Call to mind the former days, wherein, being illuminated, you endured a great fight of afflictions. And on the one hand indeed, by reproaches and tribulations were made a gazing stock; and on the other, became companions of them that were used in such sort. For you both had compassion on them that were in bands, and took with joy the being stripped of your own goods, knowing that you have a better and a lasting substance. Heb. 10:32-34.

In the time of their tribulation, they cried to thee, and thou heardst from heaven, and according to the multitude of thy tender mercies, thou gavest them saviors, to save them from the hands of their enemies. 2 Es. 9:27.

I know thy tribulation, and thy poverty, but thou art blasphemed by them that say they are Jews and are not, but are the synagogue of Satan. Fear none of those things which thou shalt suffer. Behold, the devil will cast some of you into prison that you may be tried. Be thou faithful unto death: and I will give thee the crown of life. Apoc. 9 f.

Surely he hath borne our infirmities, and carried our sorrows: and we have thought him as it were a leper, and as one struck by God and afflicted. But he was wounded for our iniquities, He was bruised for our sins: the chastisement of our peace was upon him, and by his bruises we are healed. All we like sheep have gone astray, every one hath turned aside into his own way: and the Lord hath laid on him the iniquity of us all. Is. 53:4-6.

If we have received good things at the hand of God, why should we not receive evil? Job 2:10.

The Lord gave, and the Lord hath taken away: as it hath pleased the Lord so is it done. Blessed be the name of the Lord. Job 1:22.

It is the Lord: let him do what is good in his sight. 1 K. 3:18.

PART IV

THE WORD OF GOD

I

THE WORD OF GOD

1. THE WORD OF GOD IN GENERAL

Not in bread alone doth man live, but in every word that proceedeth from the mouth of God. Deut. 8:3.

The word of God is living and effectual, and more piercing than any two-edged sword: and reaching unto the division of the soul and the marrow, and is a discerner of the thoughts and intents of the heart. Heb. 4:12.

Are not my words as a fire? saith the Lord; and as a hammer that breaketh the rock in pieces? Jer. 23:29.

As the rain and the snow come down from heaven, and return no more thither, but soak the earth, and water it, and make it to spring, and give seed to the sower, and bread to the eater: so shall my word be, which shall go forth from my mouth. Is. 55:10 f.

I have manifested thy name to the men whom thou hast given me out of the world. Thine they were, and to me thou gavest them. And they have kept thy word. I have given them thy word. Sanctify them in truth. Thy word is truth. John 17:6, 14, 17.

Be strengthened in the Lord and in the might of his power, in all things taking the shield of faith, wherewith you may be able to extinguish all the fiery darts of the most wicked one. And take unto you the helmet of salvation, and the sword of the Spirit, which is the word of God. Eph. 6:10, 16 f.

Faith cometh by hearing, and hearing by the word of Christ. Rom. 10:17.

Thy word is truth. Ps. 118:160.

2. THE UNWRITTEN WORD OF GOD

Hold the form of sound words which thou hast heard of me in faith and in the love which is in Christ Jesus. Keep the good thing committed to thy trust by the Holy Ghost, who dwelleth in us. 2 Tim. 1:13 f.

I have received of the Lord that which also I delivered unto you, that the Lord Jesus, the same night in which he was betrayed, took bread. 1 C. 11:23.

[Pray] withal for us also that God may open unto us a door to speak the mystery of Christ, for which also I am bound, that I may make it manifest, as I ought to speak. Col. 4:3 f.

Going, teach ye all nations. Mat. 20:19.

Go ye into the whole world, and preach the gospel to every creature. Mark 15:16.

Brethren, stand fast: and hold the traditions which you have learned, whether by word or by our epistle. 2 Thess. 2:14.

Now I praise you, brethren, that in all things you are mindful of me: and keep my ordinances as I have delivered them unto you. 1 C. 11:2.

If any man seem to be contentious: we have no such custom, nor the church of God. 1 C. 11:16.

Remember you not that when I was yet with you I told you these things? And now you know what withholdeth, that he may be revealed in his name. 2 Thess. 2:5 f.

O Timothy, keep that which is committed to thy trust, avoiding the profane novelties of words, and oppositions of knowledge falsely so called. 1 Tim. 6:20.

The things which thou hast heard of me by many witnesses, the same commend to faithful men, who shall be fit to teach others also. 2 Tim. 2:2.

Blessed are they who hear the word of God and keep it. Luke 11:28.

Whatsoever you shall bind upon earth, shall be bound also in heaven: and whatsoever you shall loose upon earth, shall be loosed also in heaven. Mat. 18:18.

He that heareth you heareth me: and he that despiseth you despiseth me. Luke 10:16.

It is not you that speak, but the Spirit of your Father that speaketh in you. Mat. 10:20.

Some coming down from Judea [to Antioch] taught the brethren: that except you be circumcised after the manner of Moses you cannot be saved. Then it pleased the apostles and ancients with the whole church to choose men of their own company, and to send them to Antioch with Paul and Barnabas. Writing by their hands: It hath seemed good to the Holy Ghost and to us, to lay no further burden upon you than these necessary things: that you abstain from things strangled and from fornication. And he [Paul] went through Syria and Cilicia, confirming the churches, commanding them to keep the precepts of the apostles and the ancients. Acts 15:1, 22 f., 28 f., 41.

I have yet many things to say to you; but you cannot bear them now. But when he, the Spirit of truth, is come, he will teach you all truth. John 16:12 f.

3. THE WRITTEN WORD OF GOD

The Lord said to Moses: Come up to me into the mount and be there; and I will give thee tables of stone, and the law and the commandments which I have written: that thou mayst teach them. Ex. 24:12.

The Lord said to Moses: Write this for a memorial in a book, and deliver it to the ears of Josue. Ex. 17:14.

The Lord said to Moses: Write thee these words, by which I have made a covenant, both with thee and with Israel. Ex. 34:27.

Taking the copy of the law from the priests of the Levitical tribe, he [the king] shall have it with him, and shall read it all the days of his life, that he may learn to fear the Lord and keep his words and ceremonies that are commanded in the law. Deut. 17:18.

Jeremias wrote in one book all the evil that was to come upon Babylon: all these words that were written against Babylon. And Jeremias said to Saraias: When thou shalt come into Babylon and shalt see and shalt read all these words thou shalt say. . . . Jer. 51:60 f.

The word that Jeremias the prophet spoke to Baruch, the son of Nerias, when he had written these words in a book, out of the mouth of Jeremias, in the fourth year of Joakim, the son of Josias, king of Juda, saying. . . . Jer. 43:1.

Go in, and write for them upon box, and write it diligently in a book, and it shall be in the latter days for a testimony forever. Is. 30:8.

After Moses had wrote the words of this law in a volume, and finished it: he commanded the Levites, who carried the ark of the covenant of the Lord, saying: Take this book and put it in the side of the ark of the covenant of the Lord your God, that it may be there for a testimony against thee. For I know thy obstinacy and thy most stiff neck. While I am yet living, and going in with you, you have always been rebellious against the Lord: how much more when I shall be dead? Deut. 31:24-27.

4. HOLY SCRIPTURES DIVINELY INSPIRED

I was with you in weakness, and in fear, and in much trembling: and my speech and my preaching was not in the persuasive words of human wisdom, but in the showing of the Spirit and power: that your faith might not stand on the wisdom of men, but on the power of God. Which things also we speak, not in the learned words of human wisdom: but in the doctrine of the Spirit, comparing spiritual things with spiritual. 1 C. 2: 3-5, 13.

Or did the word of God come out from you? or came it only unto you? If any seem to be a prophet, or spiritual, let him know the things that I write to you, that they are the commandments of the Lord. 1 C. 14: 36 f.

I give you to understand, brethren, that the gospel which was preached by me is not according to man. For neither did I receive it of man, nor did I learn it: but by the revelation of Jesus Christ. Gal. 1: 11 f.

We give thanks to God without ceasing: because that when you had received of us the word of the hearing of God, you received it not as the word of men, but (as it is indeed) the word of God, who worketh in you that have believed. 1 Thess. 2: 13.

Of which salvation the prophets have inquired and diligently searched, who prophesied of the grace to come in you. Searching what or what manner of time the Spirit of Christ in them did signify: when it foretold those sufferings that are in Christ, and the glories that should follow: to whom it was revealed, that not to themselves, but to you they ministered those things which are now declared to you by them that have preached the gospel to you, the Holy Ghost being sent down from heaven, on whom the angels desire to look. 1 Pet. 1: 10-12.

Thou camest down also to Mount Sinai, and didst speak with them from heaven, and thou gavest them right judgments, and the law of truth, ceremonies, and good precepts. Thou madest known to them thy holy Sabbath, and didst prescribe to them commandments, and ceremonies, and the law by the hand of Moses thy servant. 2 Es. 9: 13 f.

Now these are David's last words. David the son of Isai said: The man to whom it was appointed concerning the Christ of the God of Jacob, the excellent psalmist of Israel said: The Spirit of the Lord hath spoken by me and his word by my tongue. 2 K. 23: 1 f.

God is not as man, that he should lie. Num. 23: 19.

Heaven and earth shall pass away, but my words shall not pass. Mat. 24: 35.

The Scripture cannot be broken. John 10: 35.

This is the book of the commandments of God and the law that is forever: all they that keep it shall come to life, but they that have forsaken it to death. Bar. 4: 1.

Every word of God is fire-tried. Prov. 30: 5.

Prophecy came not by the will of man at any time: but the holy men of God spoke, inspired by the Holy Ghost. 2 Pet. 1: 21.

To one indeed, by the Spirit, is given the word of wisdom: to another, the word of knowledge: to another, interpretation of speeches. 1 C. 12: 8-10.

They made their heart as the adamant stone, lest they should hear the law, and the words which the Lord of hosts sent in his Spirit by the hand of the former prophets. Zach. 7: 12.

Do not think that I am come to destroy the law, or the prophets. I am not come to destroy, but to fulfil. For amen I say unto you, till heaven and earth pass, one jot, or one tittle shall not pass of the law, till all be fulfilled. Mat. 5: 17 f.

The law and the prophets were until John; from that time the kingdom of God is preached, and every one useth violence towards it. And it is easier for heaven and earth to pass than one tittle of the law to fall. Luke 16: 16 f.

The Scriptures must needs be fulfilled which the Holy Ghost spoke before by the mouth of David. Acts 1:16.

Well did the Holy Ghost speak to our fathers by Isaias the prophet. Acts 28:25.

Wherefore, as the Holy Ghost saith: Today if you shall hear his voice. Heb. 3:7.

The Holy Ghost signifying this, that the way into the holies was not yet made manifest. Heb. 9:8.

The revelation of Jesus Christ, which God gave unto him to make known to his servants the things which must shortly come to pass: and signified, sending by his angel to his servant John. Who hath given testimony to the word of God, and the testimony of Jesus Christ, what things soever he hath seen. Write therefore the things which thou hast seen, and which are, and which must be done hereafter. Apoc. 1:1 f., 19.

Secret things to the Lord our God: things that are manifest, to us and to our children forever, that we may do all the words of this law. Deut. 29:29.

The word of the Lord endureth forever, and this is the word which hath been preached unto you. 1 Pet. 1:25.

5. THE CHURCH THE DIVINE INTERPRETER OF HOLY SCRIPTURE

If thou perceive that there be among you a hard and doubtful matter in judgment between blood and blood, cause and cause, leprosy and leprosy: and that thou see that the words of the judges within thy gates do vary: arise, and go up to the place which the Lord thy God shall choose. Deut. 17:8.

Assembling together all the chief priests and the scribes of the people, he inquired of them where Christ should be born. Mat. 2:4.

If he will not hear the church, let him be to thee as the heathen and publican. Mat. 18:17.

When there shall be a controversy the priests shall stand in my judgments and shall judge. They shall keep my law and my ordinances in all my solemnities and sanctify my Sabbaths. Ez. 44:24.

Thou shalt do whatsoever they shall say, that preside in the place, which the Lord shall choose, and what they shall teach thee, according to his law: and thou shalt follow their sentence: neither shalt thou decline to the right hand nor to the left hand. But he that will be proud, and refuse to obey the commandment of the priest, who ministereth at that time to the Lord thy God, and the decree of the judge, that man shall die. Deut. 17:10-12.

The scribes and the Pharisees have sitten on the chair of Moses. All things therefore whatsoever they shall say to you, observe and do: but according to their works do ye not: for they say and do not. Mat. 23:2 f.

He that knoweth God, heareth us. He that is not of God, heareth us not. By this we know the Spirit of truth, and the spirit of error. 1 John 4:6.

Then he opened their understanding that they might understand the Scriptures. Luke 24:45.

I saw in the right hand of him that sat on the throne a book written within and without, sealed with seven seals. Apoc. 5:1.

Woe to you lawyers, for you have taken away the key of knowledge: you yourselves have not entered in, and those that were entering in you have hindered. Luke 11:52.

Beginning at Moses and all the prophets, he expounded to them in all the Sriptures the things that were concerning him. Luke 24:27.

An angel of the Lord spoke to Philip, saying: Arise, go towards the south. And rising up he went. And behold a man of Ethiopia, an eunuch, had come to Jerusalem to adore. And he was returning sitting in his chariot, and reading Isaias the prophet. And the Spirit said to Philip: Go near and join thyself to this chariot. And

Philip, running thither, heard him reading the prophet Isaias, and he said: Thinkest thou that thou understandest what thou readest? Who said: And how can I unless some man show me? And he desired Philip that he would come up and sit with him. And the place of the Scripture which he was reading was this: He was led like a sheep to the slaughter. And the eunuch said: I beseech thee of whom doth the prophet speak this? Then Philip, opening his mouth and beginning at this Scripture, preached unto him Jesus. Acts 8:26-32, 34 f.

I charge thee before God and Jesus Christ, who shall judge the living and the dead, by his coming and his kingdom: Preach the word: be instant in season, out of season: reprove, entreat, rebuke in all patience and doctrine. Do the work of an evangelist. 2 Tim. 4:1 f., 5.

6. THE STUDY OF SCRIPTURE

All Scripture, inspired of God, is profitable to teach, to reprove, to correct, to instruct in justice. That the man of God may be perfect furnished to every good work. 2 Tim. 3:16 f.

Search ye diligently in the book of the Lord and read. Is. 34:16.

They taught the people in Juda, having with them the book of the law of the Lord. 2 Par. 17:9.

He read all the words of the book of the covenant. 4 K. 23:2.

They have Moses and the prophets, let them hear them. Luke 16:29.

He that is of God, heareth the words of God. John 8:47.

Blessed are they who hear the word of God, and keep it. Luke 11:28.

Not the hearers of the law are just before God: but the doers of the law shall be justified. Rom. 2:13.

It had been better for them not to have known the way of justifce, than after they have known it to turn back from that holy commandment which was delivered to them. For, that of the true proverb has happened to them. The dog is returned to his vomit: and, the sow that was washed to her wallowing in the mire. 2 Pet. 2:21 f.

Be ye doers of the word, and not hearers only, deceiving your own selves. For if a man be a hearer of the word and not a doer: he shall be compared to a man beholding his own countenance in a glass. For he beheld himself, and went his way and presently forgot what manner of man he was. Jas. 1:22-24.

The Lord answered me, and said: Write the vision, and make it plain upon tables: that he that readeth it may run over it. Haba. 2:2.

These words which I command thee this day, shall be in thy heart: and thou shalt tell them to thy children, and thou shalt meditate upon them sitting in thy house, and walking on thy journey, sleeping, and rising. And thou shalt bind them as a sign on thy hand, and they shall be and shall move between thy eyes. And thou shalt write them in the entry, and on the doors of thy house. Deut. 6:6-9.

This commandment, that I command thee this day is not above thee, nor far off from thee: nor is it in heaven that thou shouldst say: Which of us can go up to heaven to bring it unto us, and we may hear and fulfil it in work? Nor is it beyond the sea: that thou mayst excuse thyself, and say: Which of us can cross the sea, and bring it unto us: that we may hear, and do that which is commanded? But the word is very nigh unto thee, in thy mouth and in thy heart, that thou mayst do it. Deut. 30:11-14.

After he is raised to the throne of his kingdom, he shall copy out to himself the Deuteronomy of this law in a volume, taking the copy of the priests of the Levitical tribe. And he shall have it with him, and shall read it all the days of his life, that he may learn to fear the Lord his God, and keep his words and ceremonies, that are commanded in the law. Deut. 17:18 f.

Take courage, and be very valiant that thou mayst observe and do all the law, which Moses my servant hath commanded thee; turn not from it to the right hand or to the left, that thou mayst understand all things which thou dost. Let not the book of this law depart from thy mouth: but thou shalt meditate on it day and night, that thou mayst observe and do all things that are written in it: then thou shalt direct thy way, and understand it. Jer. 1:7 f.

Bind them in thy heart continually, and put them about thy neck. When thou walkest, let them go with thee: when thou sleepest, let them keep thee, and when thou awakest talk with them. Because the commandment is a lamp, and the law a light, and reproofs of instruction are the way of life. Prov. 6:21-23.

Moses spoke, in the hearing of the whole assembly of Israel, the words of this canticle, and finished it even to the end. Deut. 31:30.

Set your hearts on all the words which I testify to you this day: which you shall command your children to observe and to do, and to fulfil all that is written in the law. For they are not commanded you in vain, but that every one should live in them. Deut. 32:46 f.

Remember forever his covenant: the word which he commanded to a thousand generations. 1 Par. 16:15.

Receive the law of his mouth, and lay up his words in thy heart. Job 22:22.

Go thou in, and read out of the volume which thou hast written from my mouth, the words of the Lord in the hearing of all the people in the house of the Lord on the fasting day. Jer. 36:6.

I charge you by the Lord that this epistle be read to all the holy brethren. 1 Thess. 5:27.

Blessed is he, that readeth and heareth the words of this prophecy: and keepeth those things which are written in it. For the time is at hand. Apoc. 1:3.

He that hath an ear, let him hear what the Spirit saith to the churches. Apoc. 2:29.

Let not the book of the law depart from thy mouth, but thou shalt meditate upon it day and night that thou mayst observe, and do all things that are written in it: then shalt thou direct thy way and understand it. Jas. 1:8.

Be meek to hear the word that thou mayst understand and return a true answer with wisdom. Ecclus. 5:13.

Search the Scriptures, for you think in them to have life everlasting, and the same are they that give testimony of me. John 5:39.

My son, hearken to my words, and incline thy ear to my sayings. Let them not depart from thy eyes, keep them in the midst of thy heart. For they are life to those that find them, and health to all flesh. Prov. 4:20-22.

Moses called all Israel, and said to them: Hear, O Israel, the ceremonies and judgments which I speak in your ears this day: learn them, and fulfil them in work. Deut. 5:1.

I have not departed from the commandments of his lips, and the words of his mouth I have hid in my bosom. Job 23:12.

I meditated also on thy commandments, which I loved. And I lifted up my hands to thy commandments, which I loved: and I was exercised in thy justification. Ps. 118:47 f.

7. EXCELLENCE OF HOLY SCRIPTURE

These are written that you may believe that Jesus is the Christ the Son of God: and believing you may have life in his name. John 20:31.

Thy words were found, and I did eat them, and thy word was to me a joy and gladness of my heart. Jer. 15:18.

My little children, these things I write to you that you may not sin. 1 John 2:1.

Thy words have I hidden in my heart that I may not sin against thee. Ps. 118:11.

Thy word is a lamp to my feet, and a light to my paths. Ps. 118:105.

I will rejoice at thy words as one that hath found great spoil. Ps. 118:162.

The declaration of thy words giveth light; and giveth understanding to little ones. Ps. 118:130.

Eat honey, my son, because it is good, and the honeycomb most sweet to thy throat. So is the doctrine of wisdom to thy soul. Prov. 24:13 f.

How sweet are thy words to my palate, more than honey to my mouth. Ps. 118:103.

What things soever were written, were written for our learning, that through patience and the comfort of the Scriptures we may have hope. Rom. 15:4.

Continue thou in those things which thou hast learned, and which have been committed to thee: knowing of whom thou hast learned them. And because from thy infancy thou hast known the holy Scriptures, which can instruct thee to salvation through the faith which is in Christ Jesus. All Scripture inspired of God is profitable to teach, to reprove, to correct, to instruct in justice. That the man of God may be perfect, furnished to every good work. 2 Tim. 3:15 f.

The words of the Lord are pure words: as silver tried by the fire, purged from the earth, refined seven times. Ps. 11:7.

Every one that heareth these my words, and doth them, shall be likened to a wise man that built his house upon a rock. And the rain fell, and the floods came, and the winds blew, and they beat upon that house, and it fell not, for it was founded on a rock. Mat. 7:24 f.

These things we write to you that you may rejoice, and your joy may be full. 1 John 1:4.

These things I write to you that you may know that you have eternal life, you who believe in the name of the Son of God. 1 John 5:13.

These words are most faithful and true. Apoc. 22:6.

Jesus said to those Jews who believed him: If you continue in my word, you shall be my disciples indeed. And you shall know the truth, and the truth shall make you free. John 8:31 f.

Hear, O ye heavens, the things I speak, let the earth give ear to the words of my mouth. Let my doctrine gather as the rain, let my speech distil as the dew, as a shower upon the herb, and as drops upon the grass. Deut. 32:1 f.

The law of the Lord is unspotted, converting souls: the testimony of the Lord is faithful, giving wisdom to little ones. The justices of the Lord are right, rejoicing hearts: the commandment of the Lord is lightsome, enlightening the eyes, more to be desired than gold and many precious stones: and sweeter than honey and the honeycomb. For thy servant keepeth them, and in keeping them there is a great reward. Ps. 18:8 f., 11 f.

Incline thy ear, and hear the words of the wise: and apply thy heart to my doctrine: which shall be beautiful for thee if thou keep it in thy bowels, and it shall flow in thy lips: that thy trust may be in the Lord. wherefore I have also shown it to thee this day. Behold, I have described it to thee three manner of ways, in thoughts and knowledge. That I might show thee the certainty, and the words of truth, to answer out of these to them that sent thee. Prov. 22:17-21.

They being dismissed went down to Antioch: and gathering together the multitude, delivered the epistle: which when they had read, they rejoiced for the consolation. Acts 15:30 f.

Behold, this second epistle I write to you, my dearly beloved, in which I stir up by way of admonition your sincere mind. That you may be mindful of those words which I told you before from the holy prophets, and of your apostles, of the precepts of the Lord and Savior. 2 Pet. 3:1 f.

Understanding this first, that no prophecy of Scripture is made by private interpretation. For prophecy came not by the will of man at any time: but the holy men of God spoke, inspired by the Holy Ghost. 2 Pet. 1:20 f.

You shall not add to the word that I speak to you, neither shall you take away from it: keep the commandments of the Lord your God which I command you. Deut. 12:32.

Add not anything to his words, lest thou be reproved and found a liar. Prov. 30:6.

And when they had heard all the words, they looked upon one another with astonishment, and they said to Baruch: We must tell the king all these words. Jer. 36:16.

And they went in to the king into the court: but they laid up the volumes in the chamber of Elisama the scribe: and they told all the words in the hearing of the king. Jer. 36:20.

Account the long-suffering of our Lord, salvation, as also our most dear brother Paul, according to the wisdom given him, hath written to you: as also in all his epistles, speaking in them of these things: in which are certain things hard to be understood, which the unlearned and unstable wrest, as they do also the other Scriptures, to their own destruction. 2 Pet. 3:15 f.

I testify to every one that heareth the words of the prophecy of this book. If any man shall add to these things, God shall add unto him the plagues written in this book. And if any man shall take away from the words of the book of this prophecy, God shall take away his part out of the book of life, and out of the holy city, and from these things that are written in this book. Apoc. 22:18 f.

Every one that heareth these my words, and doth them not, shall be like a foolish man that built his house upon the sand. And the rain fell, and the floods came, and the winds blew, and they beat upon that house, and it fell, and great was the fall thereof. Mat. 7:26 f.

There shall be a time, when they will not endure sound doctrine: but according to their own desires they will heap to themselves teachers, having itching ears, and will indeed turn away their hearing from the truth, but will be turned unto fables. 2 Tim. 4:3 f.

To whom shall I speak? and to whom shall I testify, that he may hear? Behold, their ears are uncircumcised, and they cannot hear: behold the word of the Lord is become unto them a reproach: and they will not receive it. Jer. 6:10.

8. THE UNDERSTANDING OF SCRIPTURE

Open thou my eyes, and I will consider the wondrous things of thy law. Ps. 118:18.

I am a sojourner on the earth: hide not thy commandments from me. Ps. 118:19.

I am thy servant: give me understanding that I may know thy testimonies. Ps. 118:125.

Thy testimonies are justice forever: give me understanding, and I shall live. Ps. 118:144.

Give me understanding, and I will search thy law: and I will keep it with my whole heart. Ps. 118:34.

Direct my steps according to thy word, and let no iniquity have dominion over me. Ps. 118:133.

The Protestant Bible omits the following books:

Tobias
Judith
Wisdom
Ecclesiasticus
Baruch
1 Machabees
2 Machabees
and portions of Daniel and Esther.

II

THE CHURCH

1. CHRIST, THE HEAD OF THE CHURCH

You are God's building. 1 C. 3:9.

Other foundation no man can lay but that which is laid, which is Christ Jesus. 1 C. 3:11.

The stone which the builders rejected the same is become the head of the corner. Ps. 117:22.

They drank of the spiritual rock that followed them, and the rock was Christ. 1 C. 10:4.

I am the vine, you the branches. John 15:5.

What shall be answered to the messengers of the nations? That the Lord hath founded Sion. Is. 14:32.

The Highest himself hath founded her. Ps. 86:5.

[The flood] could not shake it, for it was founded on a rock. Luke 6:49.

A Son is given to us, and the government is upon his shoulders. Is. 9:6.

O poor little one, tossed with tempest, without all comfort, behold I will lay thy stones in order, and will lay thy foundations with sapphires. And I will make thy bulwarks of jasper: and thy gates of graven stones, and all thy borders of desirable stones. Is. 54:11 f.

Mountains are about Jerusalem, so the Lord is round about his people, from henceforth, now, and forever. Ps. 124:2.

In his first-born may he lay the foundation thereof. Jos. 6:26.

He hath made him head over all the church, which is his body. Eph. 1:22 f.

Doing the truth in charity, we may in all things grow up in him who is the head, even Christ. Eph. 4:15.

From whom the whole body, being compacted, and fitly joined together, by what every joint supplieth, according to the operation in the measure of every part, maketh increase of the body unto the edifying of itself in charity. Eph. 4:16.

The husband is the head of the wife, as Christ is the head of the church. He is the Savior of his body. Eph. 5:23.

You are the body of Christ, and members of member. 1 C. 12:27.

I saw the holy city, the new Jerusalem, coming down out of heaven from God, prepared as a bride adorned for her husband. Apoc. 21:2.

2. CHRIST BUILDS HIS CHURCH UPON THE FOUNDATION OF THE APOSTLES

Having called his twelve disciples together, he gave them power over unclean spirits, to cast them out, and to heal all manner of diseases, and all manner of infirmities. And the names of the twelve apostles are these: the first, Simon who is called Peter, and Andrew his brother. James the son of Zebedee, and John his brother, Philip and Bartholomew, Thomas and Matthew the publican, and James the son of Alpheus, and Thaddeus, Simon the Cananean, and Judas Iscariot, who also betrayed him. Mat. 10:1-3.

Going up into a mountain, he called unto him whom he would himself. And they came to him. And he made that twelve should be with him and that he might send them to preach. . . . And to Simon he gave the name Peter. And James the son of Zebedee. And John the brother of James; and he named them Boanerges, which is, the sons of thunder. And Andrew and Philip, and Bartholomew and Matthew, and Thomas and James of Alpheus, and Thaddeus and Simon the Cananean. And Judas Iscariot, who also betrayed him. Mark 3:13-19.

It came to pass in those days, that he went out into a mountain to pray, and he passed the whole night in the prayer of God. And when day was come, he called unto him his disciples: and he chose twelve of them (whom also he named apostles): Simon whom he surnamed Peter, and Andrew his brother, James and John, Philip and Bartholomew, Matthew and Thomas, James the son of Alpheus, and Simon who is called Zelotes, and Jude the brother of James, and Judas Iscariot, who was the traitor. Luke 6:12-16.

They returned to Jerusalem from the mount that is called Olivet, which is nigh Jerusalem, within a Sabbath day's journey. And when they were come in, they went up into an upper room, where abode Peter and John, James and Andrew, Philip and Thomas, Bartholomew and Matthew, James of Alpheus and Simon Zelotes, and Jude the brother of James. Acts 1:12 f.

And they appointed two, Joseph, called Barsabas, who was surnamed Justus, and Matthias. And praying they said: Thou, Lord, who knowest the hearts of all men, show whether of these two thou hast chosen, to take the place of this ministry and apostleship from which Judas hath by transgression fallen, that he might go to his own place. And they gave them lots, and the lot fell upon Matthias, and he was numbered with the eleven apostles. Acts 1:23-26.

Jesus answered them: Have not I chosen you twelve? John 6:71.

3. CHRIST'S COMMANDS TO HIS TWELVE APOSTLES

These twelve Jesus sent: commanding them, saying: Go ye not into the way of the Gentiles, and into the cities of the Samaritans enter ye not. But go ye rather to the lost sheep of the house of Israel. And going, preach, saying: The kingdom of heaven is at hand. Heal the sick, raise the dead, cleanse the lepers, cast out devils: freely have you received, freely give. Do not possess gold, nor silver, nor money in your purses: nor scrip for your journey, nor two coats, nor shoes, nor a staff: for the workman is worthy of his meat. Mat. 10:5-10.

If he will not hear them: tell the church. And if he will not hear the church, let him be to thee as the heathen and publican. Amen I say to you, whatsoever you shall bind upon earth, shall be bound also in heaven: and whatsoever you shall loose upon earth, shall be loosed also in heaven. Again I say to you, that if two of you shall consent upon earth, concerning anything whatsoever they shall ask, it shall be done to them by my Father who is in heaven. For where there are two or three gathered together in my name, there am I in the midst of them. Mat. 18:17-20.

Jesus coming spoke to them, saying: All power is given to me in heaven and in earth. Going therefore teach ye all nations: baptizing them in the name of the Father, and of the Son, and of the Holy Ghost, teaching them to observe all things whatsoever I have commanded you: and behold I am with you all days, even to the consummation of the world. Mat. 28:18-20.

He called the twelve and began to send them two and two, and gave them power over unclean spirits. And he commanded them that they should take nothing for the way, but a staff only: no scrip, no bread, nor money in their purse. But to be shod with sandals, and that they should not put on two coats. And he said to them: Wheresoever you shall enter into a house, there abide till you depart from that place. And whosoever shall not receive you, nor hear you, going forth from thence, shake off the dust from your feet for a testimony to them. Mark 6:7-11.

He said to them: Go ye into the whole world and preach the gospel to every creature. He that believeth and is baptized, shall be saved: but he that believeth not, shall be condemned. And these signs shall follow them that believe: in my name they shall cast out devils: they shall speak with new tongues, they shall take up serpents: and if they shall drink any deadly thing, it shall not hurt them: they shall lay their hands upon the sick, and they shall recover. And the Lord Jesus, after he had spoken to them, was taken up into heaven, and sitteth on the right hand of God. But they going forth preached everywhere: the Lord working withal, and confirming the word with signs that followed. Mark 16:15-20.

Do this for a commemoration of me. Luke 22:19.

Calling together the twelve apostles, he gave them power and authority over all devils, and to cure diseases. And he sent them to preach the kingdom of God and to heal the sick. And he said to them: Take nothing for your journey, neither staff, nor scrip, nor bread, nor money, neither have two coats. And whatsoever house you shall enter into, abide there, and depart not from thence. And whosoever will not receive you, when ye go out of that city, shake off even the dust of your feet for a testimony against them. And going out they went about through the towns, preaching the gospel and healing everywhere. Luke 9:1-6.

Behold I have given you power to tread upon serpents and scorpions, and upon all the power of the enemy, and nothing shall hurt you. But yet rejoice not in this that spirits are subject unto you: but rejoice in this, that your names are written in heaven. Luke 10:19 f.

You are witnesses of these things. Luke 24:48.

He said therefore to them again: Peace be to you. As the Father hath sent me, I also send you. When he had said this, he breathed on them; and he said to them: Receive ye the Holy Ghost. Whose sins you shall forgive, they are forgiven them: and whose sins you shall retain they are retained. John 20:21-23.

Amen, amen, I say to you, he that receiveth whomsoever I send, receiveth me: and he that receiveth me, receiveth him that sent me. John 13:20.

You shall give testimony because you are with me from the beginning. John 15:27.

4. THE SEVENTY-TWO DISCIPLES

After these things the Lord appointed also other seventy-two: and he sent them two and two before his face into every city and place whither he himself was to come. And he said to them: The harvest indeed is great, but the laborers are few. Pray ye therefore the Lord of the harvest, that he send laborers into his harvest.

Go: Behold I send you as lambs among wolves. Carry neither purse nor scrip, nor shoes: and salute no man by the way. Into whatsoever house you enter, first say: Peace be to this house: and if the son of peace be there, your peace shall rest upon him: but if not, it shall return to you. And in the same house remain, eating and drinking such things as they have. For the laborer is worthy of his hire. Remove not from house to house. And into what city soever you enter, and they receive you, eat such things as are set before you: And heal the sick that are therein, and say to them: The kingdom of God is come nigh unto you. But into whatsoever city you enter, and they receive you not, going forth into the streets thereof, say: Even the very dust of your city that cleaveth to us we wipe off against you. Yet know this: that the kingdom of God is at hand. I say to you, it shall be more tolerable at that day for Sodom, than for that city.

Woe to thee, Corozain, woe to thee, Bethsaida. For if in Tyre and Sidon had been wrought the mighty works that have been wrought in you, they would have done penance long ago, sitting in sackcloth and ashes. But it shall be more tolerable for Tyre and Sidon at the judgment, than for you. And thou, Capharnaum, which art exalted unto heaven: thou shalt be thrust down to hell. He that heareth you, heareth me: and he that despiseth you, despiseth me. And he that despiseth me, despiseth him that sent me. Luke 10:1-16.

5. SPECIAL MENTION OF ST. PETER IN THE GOSPELS

First Meeting with Jesus

Andrew, the brother of Simon Peter, was one of the two who had heard of John, and followed him. He findeth first his brother Simon, and saith to him: We have found the Messias, which is, being interpreted, the Christ. And he brought him to Jesus. And Jesus looking upon him, said: Thou art Simon, the son of Jona: thou shalt be called Cephas, which is interpreted Peter. John 1:40-42.

Philip was of Bethsaida, the city of Andrew and Peter. John 1:44.

Curing of Peter's Mother-in-law

Jesus rising up out of the synagogue, went into Simon's house. And Simon's wife's mother was taken with a great fever, and they besought him for her. And standing over her, he commanded the fever, and it left her. And immediately rising, she ministered to them. Luke 4:38 f. (Cf. Mat. 8:14 f.; Mark 1:29-31.)

Jesus Leaves Capharnaum

Rising very early, going out he went into a desert place: and there he prayed. And Simon and they that were with him followed after him. And when they had found him, they said to him, All seek for thee. And he saith to them: Let us go into the neighboring towns and cities, that I may preach there also: for to this purpose am I come. Mark 1:35-38.

The Draught of Fishes

Going up into one of the ships that was Simon's, he desired him to draw back a little from the land. And sitting he taught the multitudes out of the ship.

Now when he had ceased to speak, he said to Simon: Launch out into the deep, and let down your nets for a draught. And Simon answering, said to him: Master, we have labored all the night, and have taken nothing; but at thy word I will let down the net.

And when they had done this, they enclosed a very great multitude of fishes, and their net broke. And they beckoned to their partners that were in the other ship, that they should come and help them. And they came, and filled both the ships, so that they were almost sinking.

Which when Simon Peter saw, he fell down at Jesus' knees, saying: Depart from me, for I am a sinful man, O Lord. For he was wholly astonished, and all that were with him, at the draught of the fishes which they had taken.

And so were also James and John, the sons of Zebedee, who were Simon's partners. And Jesus saith to Simon: Fear not: from henceforth thou shalt catch men. And having brought their ships to land, leaving all things, they followed him. Luke 5:3-11. (Cf. Mat. 4:18-22; Mark 1:16-20.)

Jesus Chooses His Twelve Apostles

When day was come, he called unto him his disciples; and he chose twelve of them (whom also he named apostles): Simon, whom he surnamed Peter, and Andrew his brother. . . . Luke 6:13 f. (Cf. Mat. 10:1 f.; Mark 3:13-16.)

In the House of Jairus

And Jesus said: Who is it that touched me? And all denying, Peter and they that were with him, said: Master, the multitudes throng and press thee, and dost thou say, Who touched me? . . . And when he was come to the house, he suffered not any man to go in with him, but Peter and James and John, and the father and mother of the maiden. Luke 8:45, 51. (Cf. Mark 5:37.)

Jesus Walks upon the Waters

Immediately Jesus spoke to them, saying: Be of good heart: it is I, fear ye not. And Peter making answer, said: Lord, if it be thou, bid me come to thee upon the waters. And he said: Come.

And Peter going down out of the boat, walked upon the water to come to Jesus. But seeing the wind strong, he was afraid: and when he began to sink, he cried out, saying: Lord, save me. And immediately Jesus stretching forth his hand took hold of him, and said to him: O thou of little faith, why didst thou doubt? Mat. 14:27-31.

Defection of Many Disciples

After this many of his disciples went back; and walked no more with him. Then Jesus said to the twelve: Will you also go away? And Simon Peter answered him: Lord, to whom shall we go? Thou hast the words of eternal life. And we have believed and have known that thou art the Christ, the Son of God. John 6:67-70.

Jesus' Teaching about Legal Defilement

Not that which goeth into the mouth defileth a man: but what cometh out of the mouth, this defileth a man. . . . And Peter answering, said to him: Expound to us this parable. But he said: Are you also yet without understanding? Mat. 15:11, 15 f.

The Promise of the Primacy

Jesus saith to them: But whom do you say that I am? Simon Peter answered and said: Thou art Christ the Son of the living God. And Jesus answering, said to him: Blessed art thou, Simon Bar-Jona: because flesh and blood hath not revealed it to thee, but my Father who is in heaven. And I say to thee: That thou art Peter; and upon this rock I will build my church, and the gates of hell shall not prevail against it. And I will give to thee the keys of the kingdom of heaven. And whatsoever thou shalt bind upon earth, it shall be bound also in heaven: and whatsoever thou shalt loose on earth, it shall be loosed also in heaven. Mat. 16:15-19. (Cf. Mark 8:29; Luke 9:20.)

Prediction of the Passion

Jesus began to show to his disciples, that he must go to Jerusalem, and suffer many things from the ancients and scribes and chief priests, and be put to death, and the third day rise again.

And Peter taking him, began to rebuke him, saying: Lord, be it far from thee, this shall not be unto thee. Who turning said to Peter: Go behind me, Satan, thou art a scandal unto me: because thou savorest not the things that are of God, but the things that are of men. Mat. 16:21-23. (Cf. Mark 8:31-33.)

The Transfiguration

It came to pass about eight days after these words, that he took Peter and James and John, and went up into a mountain to pray. . . . But Peter and they that were with him were heavy with sleep. And waking, they saw his glory, and the two men that stood with him. And it came to pass that as they were departing from him, Peter saith to Jesus: Master, it is good for us to be here; and let us make three tabernacles, one for thee, and one for Moses, and one for Elias: not knowing what he said. Luke 9:28, 32 f. (Cf. Mat. 17:1-4; Mark 9:1-5.)

Forgiveness of Injuries

Then came Peter unto him, and said: Lord, how often shall my brother offend against me, and I forgive him? Till seven times? Jesus saith to him: I say not to thee, till seven times; but till seventy times seven times. Mat. 18:21 f.

The Tribute Money

When they were come to Capharnaum, they that received the didrachmas, came to Peter, and said to him: Doth not your master pay the didrachma? He said: Yes. And when he was come into the house, Jesus prevented him, saying: What is thy opinion, Simon? The kings of the earth, of whom do they receive tribute or custom? of their own children, or of strangers? And he said: Of strangers. Jesus said to him: Then the children are free. But that we may not scandalize them, go to the sea, and cast in a hook: and that fish which shall first come up, take: and when thou hast opened its mouth, thou shalt find a stater: take that, and give it to them for me and thee. Mat.17:23-26.

The Need for Vigilance

Be you then also ready: for at what hour you think not, the Son of man will come. And Peter said to him: Lord, dost thou speak this parable to us, or likewise to all? Luke 12:40 f.

The Reward of the Followers of Christ

Then Peter said: Behold, we have left all things, and have followed thee. Who said to them: Amen, I say to you, there is no man that hath left house or parents or brethren or wife or children for the kingdom of God's sake, who shall not receive much more in this present time, and in the world to come life everlasting. Luke 18:28-30. (Cf. Mat. 19:27-29; Mark 10:28-30.)

The Withered Fig Tree

When they passed by in the morning, they saw the fig tree dried up from the roots. And Peter remembering, said to him: Rabbi, behold the fig tree which thou didst curse, is withered away. Mark 11:20 f.

The Time of the Destruction of Jerusalem

And as he sat on the mount of Olivet over against the temple, Peter and James and John and Andrew asked him apart: Tell us, when shall these things be? and what shall be the sign when all these things shall begin to be fulfilled? Mark 13:3 f.

Preparation for the Last Supper

The day of the unleavened bread came, on which it was necessary that the pasch should be killed. And he sent Peter and John, saying: Go and prepare for us the pasch, that we may eat. Luke 22:7 f.

Christ Washes Peter's Feet

After that, he putteth water into a basin and began to wash the feet of the disciples and to wipe them with the towel wherewith he was girded. He cometh therefore to Simon Peter. And Peter saith to him: Lord, doth thou wash my feet? Jesus answered and said to him: What I do, thou knowest not now; but thou shalt know hereafter. Peter saith to him: Thou shalt never wash my feet. Jesus answered him: If I wash thee not, thou shalt have no part with me. Simon Peter saith to him: Lord, not only my feet, but also my hands and my head. Jesus saith to him: He that is washed needeth not but to wash his feet, but is clean wholly. John 13:5-10.

Who Is the Traitor?

Now there was leaning on Jesus' bosom one of his disciples whom Jesus loved. Simon Peter therefore beckoned to him, and said to him: Who is it of whom he speaketh? John 13:23 f.

Peter Will Confirm His Brethren

The Lord said: Simon, Simon, behold Satan hath desired to have you that he may sift you as wheat. But I have prayed for thee that thy faith fail not: and thou being once converted, confirm thy brethren. Luke 22:31 f.

Peter's Denial Foretold

Simon Peter saith to him: Lord, whither goest thou? Jesus answered: Whither I go, thou canst not follow me now, but thou shalt follow hereafter: Peter saith to him: Why cannot I follow thee now? I will lay down my life for thee. John 13:36 f. (Cf. Mat. 26:33; Mark 14:29; Luke 22:33.)

And Jesus saith to him: Amen I say to thee, today even in this night, before the cock crow twice, thou shalt deny me thrice. But he spoke the more vehemently: Although I should die together with thee, I will not deny thee. And in like manner also said they all. Mark 14:30 f. (Cf. Mat. 26:34 f.; Luke 22:34; John 13:38.)

The Agony in the Garden of Gethsemani

And he taketh Peter and James and John with him; and he began to fear and to be heavy. And he saith to them: My soul is sorrowful even unto death; stay you here, and watch. . . . And he cometh and findeth them sleeping. And he saith to Peter: Simon, sleepest thou? Couldst thou not watch one hour? Watch ye, and pray that you enter not into temptation. The spirit indeed is willing, but the flesh is weak. Mark 14:33 f., 37 f. (Cf. Mat. 26:37 ff.)

Peter Cuts Off Malchus' Ear

Then Simon Peter having a sword, drew it; and struck the servant of the high priest, and cut off his right ear. And the name of the servant was Malchus. Jesus therefore said to Peter: Put up thy sword into the scabbard. The chalice which my Father hath given me, shall I not drink it? John 18:10 f. (Cf. Mat. 26:51 f.; Mark 14:47; Luke 22:50 f.)

Peter's Denials

Peter followed him afar off, even to the court of the high priest. And going in, he sat with the servants, that he might see the end. . . .

But Peter sat without in the court: and there came to him a servant maid, saying: Tou also wast with Jesus the Galilean. But he denied before them all, saying: I know not what thou sayest.

And as he went out of the gate, another maid saw him, and she saith to them that were there: This man also was with Jesus of Nazareth. And again he denied with an oath, I know not the man.

And after a little while they came that stood by, and said to Peter: Surely thou also art one of them; for even thy speech doth discover thee. Then he began to curse and to swear that he knew not the man.

And immediately the cock crew. And Peter remembered the word of Jesus which he had said: Before the cock crow, thou wilt deny me thrice. And going forth, he wept bitterly. Mat. 26:58, 69-75. (Cf. Mark 14:53 f., 66-72; Luke 22:54-62.)

The Angel's Message to the Holy Women

Entering into the sepulcher, they saw a young man sitting on the right side, clothed with a white robe: and they were astonished. Who saith to them: Be not affrighted; you seek Jesus of Nazareth, who was crucified: he is risen, he is not here, behold the place where they laid him. But go, tell his disciples and Peter, that he goeth before you into Galilee; there you shall see him, as he told you. Mark 16:5-7.

Peter and John at the Sepulcher

Peter therefore went out, and that other disciple, and they came to the sepulcher. And they both ran together, and that other disciple did outrun Peter, and came first to the sepulcher. And when he stooped down, he saw the linen cloths lying: but he went not in. Then cometh Simon Peter, following him, and went into the sepulcher, and saw the linen cloths lying. And the napkin that had been about his head, not lying with the linen cloths, but apart, wrapt up into one place. Then that other disciple also went in, who came first to the sepulcher: and he saw and believed. John 20:3-8. (Cf. Luke 24:12.)

The Two Disciples Report the Appearance of Christ on the Road to Emmaus

Rising up, the same hour, they went back to Jerusalem: and they found the eleven gathered together, and those that were with them, saying: The Lord is risen indeed, and hath appeared to Simon. Luke 24:31-34.

Appearance of Christ by the Sea of Tiberias

After this Jesus showed himself again to the disciples at the sea of Tiberias. And he showed himself after this manner. There were together Simon Peter, and Thomas who is called Didymus, and Nathanael, who was of Cana of Galilee, and the sons of Zebedee, and two others of his disciples.

Simon Peter saith to them: I go a-fishing. They say to him: We also come with thee. And they went forth and entered into the ship: and that night they caught nothing. But when morning was come, Jesus stood on the shore: yet the disciples knew not that it was Jesus.

Jesus therefore said to them: Children, have you any meat? They answered him: No. He saith to them: Cast the net on the right side of the ship; and you shall find. They cast therefore: and now they were not able to draw it for the multitude of fishes. That disciple therefore whom Jesus loved, said to Peter: It is the Lord.

Simon Peter, when he heard that it was the Lord, girt his coat about him (for he was naked) and cast himself into the sea. But the other disciples came in the ship (for they were not far from the land, but as it were two hundred cubits) dragging the net with fishes. . . . Simon Peter went up, and drew the net to land, full of great fishes, one hundred and fifty-three. And although there were so many, the net was not broken. . . .

When therefore they had dined, Jesus saith to Simon Peter: Simon son of John, lovest thou me more than these? He saith to him: Yea, Lord, thou knowest that I love thee. He saith to him: Feed my lambs. He saith to him again: Simon son of John, lovest thou me? He saith to him: Yea, Lord, thou knowest that I love thee. He saith to him: Feed my lambs. He said to him the third time: Simon son of John, lovest thou me? Peter was grieved, because he had said to him the third time, Lovest thou me? And he said to him: Lord, thou knowest all things: thou knowest that I love thee. He said to him: Feed my sheep.

Amen, amen, I say to thee: when thou wast younger, thou didst gird thyself, and didst walk where thou wouldst. But when thou shalt be old, thou shalt stretch forth thy hands, and another shall gird thee, and lead thee whither thou wouldst not. And this he said, signifying by what death he should glorify God. And when he had said this, he saith to him: Follow me.

Peter turning about, saw that disciple whom Jesus loved following, who also leaned on his breast at supper, and said: Lord, who is he that shall betray thee? Him therefore when Peter had seen, he saith to Jesus: Lord, and what shall this man do? Jesus saith to him: So I will have him to remain till I come, what is it to thee? John 21:1-8, 11, 15-22.

6. ST. PETER IN THE ACTS OF THE APOSTLES

The Ascension of Christ. 1:9 ff.

In the upper room after the Ascension. 1:13 f.

The election of Matthias. 1:15 ff.

Descent of the Holy Ghost. 2:1 ff.

Sermon on Pentecost. 2:14 ff.

Baptism of the first converts. 2:37 ff.

Cure of the lame man in the temple. 3:1 ff.

Sermon in the temple. 3:12 ff.

He is arrested. 4:1 ff.

Address to the Sanhedrin. 4:8 ff.

Deliberation of the Sanhedrin. 4:13 ff.

Reply to the Sanhedrin. 4:19 ff.

Ananias and Saphira. 5:1 ff.

Many sick persons brought to him. 5:15.

He is arrested again. 5:18.

He is delivered from prison. 5:19.

He is arrested again. 5:26 f.

Reply to the Sanhedrin. 5:29 ff.

He is scourged. 5:40.

He goes to Samaria with John. 8:14 ff.

Simon Magus. 8:18 ff.

Cure of Eneas at Lydia. 9:32 ff.

At Joppe he raises Tabitha (Dorcas) to life. 9:36 ff.

The vision of clean and unclean animals. 10:9 ff.

The baptism of Cornelius. 10:48.

At Jerusalem he explains the conversion of Cornelius. 11:1 ff.

He is imprisoned. 12:3 ff.

He is delivered by an angel. 12:7 ff.

The council of Jerusalem. 15:7 ff.

7. THE CHURCH THE MYSTICAL BODY OF CHRIST

He is the head of the body, the church. Col. 1:18.

Careful to keep the unity of the Spirit in the bond of peace. One body and one Spirit: as you are called in one hope of your calling. One Lord, one faith, one baptism. One God and Father of all, who is above all, and through all, and in us all. Eph. 4:3-6.

To every one of us is given grace according to the measure of the giving of Christ. Eph. 4:7.

He gave some apostles, and some prophets, and other some evangelists, and other some pastors and doctors: for the perfecting of the saints, for the work of the ministry, for the edifying of the body of Christ: until we all meet into the unity of faith, and of the knowledge of the Son of God, unto a perfect man, unto the measure of the age of the fulness of Christ: that henceforth we be no more children tossed to and fro, and carried about with every wind of doctrine by the wickedness of men, by cunning craftiness by which they lie in wait to deceive.

But doing the truth in charity, we may in all things grow up in him who is the head, even Christ: from whom the whole body being compacted and fitly joined together, by what every joint supplieth, according to the operation in the measure of every part, maketh increase of the body unto the edifying of itself in charity. Eph. 4:11-16.

We, being many, are one bread, one body, all that partake of one bread. 1 C. 10:17.

Let the peace of Christ rejoice in your hearts, wherein also you are called in one body. Col. 3:15.

There are diversities of graces, but the same Spirit; and there are diversities of ministries, but the same Lord. And there are diversities of operations, but the same God, who worketh all in all. But the manifestation of the Spirit is given to every man unto profit. 1 C. 12:4-7.

To one, indeed, by the Spirit is given the word of wisdom: and to another the word of knowledge, according to the same Spirit: to another, faith in the same spirit: to another, the grace of healing in one Spirit: to another, the working of miracles: to another, prophecy: to another, the discerning of spirits: to another, diverse kinds of tongues: to another, interpretation of speeches. 1 C. 12:8-10.

But all these things one and the same Spirit worketh, dividing to every one according as he will. For as the body is one, and hath many members; and all the members of the body, whereas they are many, yet are one body, so also is Christ.

For in one Spirit were we all baptized in one body, whether Jews or Gentiles, whether bond or free: and in one Spirit we have all been made to drink. 1 C. 12:11-13.

For the body also is not one member, but many. If the foot should say, because I am not the hand, I am not of the body: is it therefore not of the body? And if the ear should say, because I am not the eye, I am not of the body: is it therefore not of the body?

If the whole body were the eye, where would be the hearing? If the whole were hearing, where would be the smelling? But now God hath set the members, every one of them in the body as it hath pleased him. And if they all were one member, where would be the body? But now there are many members indeed, yet one body. And the eye cannot say to the hand: I need not thy help; nor again the head to the feet: I have no need of you. Yea, much more those that seem to be the more feeble members of the body, are more necessary. And such as we think to be the less honorable members of the body, about these we put more abundant honor: and those that are our uncomely parts, have more abundant comeliness. But our comely parts have no need: but God hath tempered the body together, giving to that which wanted the more abundant honor. That there might be no schism in the body, but the members might be mutually careful one for another. And if one member suffer anything, all the members suffer with it: or, if one member glory, all the members rejoice with it.

Now you are the body of Christ, and members of member. And God indeed hath set some in the church: first apostles, secondly prophets, thirdly doctors: after that miracles: then the graces of healings, helps, governments, kinds of tongues, interpretations of speeches. 1 C. 12:14-28.

Are all apostles? Are all prophets? Are all doctors? Are all workers of miracles? Have all the grace of healing? Do all speak with tongues? Do all interpret? But be zealous for the better gifts. And I show unto you a yet more excellent way. 1 C. 12:29-31.

I Paul . . . rejoice in my sufferings for you, and fill up those things that are wanting of the sufferings of Christ, in my flesh for his body, which is the church. Col. 1:24.

As in one body we have many members, but all the members have not the same office: so we being many, are one body in Christ, and every one members one of another. And having different gifts, according to the grace that is given us, whether prophecy, to be used according to the rule of faith; or ministry, in ministering: or he that teacheth, in doctrine, he that exhorteth in exhorting, he that giveth with simplicity, he that ruleth with carefulness, he that showeth mercy with cheerfulness. Rom. 12:4-8.

8. THE HOLY SPIRIT IN HIS RELATION TO THE CHURCH

Announced by the Prophets

They from the west shall fear the name of the Lord: and they from the rising of the sun, his glory: when he shall come as a violent stream, which the Spirit of the Lord driveth on: and there shall come a Redeemer to Sion, and to them that return from iniquity in Jacob, saith the Lord. This is my covenant with them, saith the Lord: My Spirit that is in thee, and my words that I have put in thy mouth shall not depart out of thy mouth, nor out of the mouth of thy seed, nor out of the mouth of thy seed's seed, saith the Lord, from henceforth and forever. Is. 59:12-21.

The house is forsaken, the multitude of the city is left, darkness and obscurity are come upon its dens forever. A joy of wild asses, the pastures of flocks, until the Spirit be poured upon us from on high: and the desert shall be as a charmel, and charmel shall be counted for a forest. And judgment shall dwell in the wilderness, and justice shall sit in charmel. And the work of justice shall be peace, and the service of justice quietness, and security forever. And my people shall sit in the beauty of peace, and in the tabernacles of confidence, and in wealthy rest. Is. 32:14-18.

Now, hear, O Jacob, my servant, and Israel whom I have chosen. Thus saith the Lord that made and formed thee, thy Helper from the womb: Fear not, O my servant Jacob, and thou most righteous whom I have chosen. For I will pour out waters upon the thirsty ground, and streams upon the dry land: I will pour out my Spirit upon thy seed, and my blessing upon thy stock. and they shall spring up among the herbs, as willows beside the running waters. Is. 44:1-4.

It shall come to pass after this, that I will pour out my Spirit upon all flesh: and your sons and your daughters shall prophesy: your old men shall dream dreams, and your young men shall see visions. Moreover upon my servants and handmaids in those days I will pour forth my Spirit. Joel 2:28 f.

I will pour out upon the house of David, and upon the inhabitants of Jerusalem, the Spirit of grace, and of prayers: and they shall look upon me, whom they have pierced. Zach. 12:10.

Promised by Our Lord

I will ask the Father, and he shall give you another Paraclete, that he may abide with you forever. The Spirit of truth, whom the world cannot receive, because it seeth him not, nor knoweth him: but you shall know him, because he shall abide with you, and shall be in you. John 14:16 f.

I tell you the truth: it is expedient to you that I go: for if I go not, the Paraclete will not come to you: but if I go, I will send him to you. And when he is come, he will convince the world of sin, and of justice, and of judgment. Of sin: because they believed not in me. And of justice: because I go to the Father; and you shall see me no longer. And of judgment: because the prince of this world is already judged.

I have yet many things to say to you: but you cannot bear them now. But when he, the Spirit of truth, is come, he will teach you all truth. For he shall not speak of himself: but what things soever he shall hear, he shall speak, and the things that are to come he shall show you. He shall glorify me: because he shall receive of mine, and shall show it to you. John 16:7-14.

When the Paraclete cometh whom I will send you from the Father, the Spirit of truth, who proceedeth from the Father, he shall give testimony of me. John 15:26 f.

On the last and great day of the festivity, Jesus stood and cried, saying: If any man thirst, let him come to me, and drink. He that believeth in me, as the Scripture saith, Out of his belly shall flow rivers of living water. Now this he said of the Spirit which they should receive who believed in him: for as yet the Spirit was not given, because Jesus was not yet glorified. John 7:37-39.

His Descent upon the Disciples

When the days of the Pentecost were accomplished, they were all together in one place: and suddenly there came a sound from heaven, as of a mighty wind coming, and it filled the whole house where they were sitting. And there appeared to them parted tongues as it were of fire, and it sat upon every one of them: and they were all filled with the Holy Ghost, and they began to speak with divers tongues, according as the Holy Ghost gave them to speak.

Now there were dwelling at Jerusalem Jews, devout men out of every nation under heaven. And when this was noised abroad, the multitude came together, and were confounded in mind, because that every man heard them speak in his own tongue. And they were all amazed and wondered, saying: Behold, are not all these, that speak, Galileans? And how have we heard, every man our own tongue wherein we were born? Parthians, and Medes, and Elamites, and inhabitants of Mesopotamia, Judea, and Cappadocia, Pontus and Asia, Phrygia, and Pamphilia, Egypt, and the parts of Libya about Cyrene, and strangers of Rome, Jews also, and proselytes, Cretes, and Arabians: we have heard them speak in our own tongues the wonderful works of God.

And they were all astonished, and wondered, saying one to another: What meaneth this? But others mocking said: These men are full of new wine.

But Peter standing up with the eleven, lifted up his voice, and spoke to them: Ye men of Judea, and all you that dwell in Jerusalem, be this known to you, and with your ears receive my words. For these are not drunk, as you suppose, seeing it is but the third hour of the day; but this is that which was spoken of by the prophet Joel:

> And it shall come to pass, in the last days (saith the Lord), I will pour out of my Spirit upon all flesh: and your sons and your daughters shall prophesy, and your young men shall see visions, and your old men shall dream dreams. And upon my servants indeed, and upon my handmaids will I pour out in those days of my Spirit, and they shall prophesy. Acts 2:1-18.

God hath not given us the Spirit of fear: but of power, and of love, and of sobriety. 2 Tim. 1:7.

Keep the good thing committed to thy trust by the Holy Ghost, who dwelleth in us. 2 Tim. 1.14.

For our gospel hath not been unto you in word only, but in power also, and in the Holy Ghost, and in much fulness, as you know what manner of men we have been among you for your sakes. And you became followers of us, and of the Lord: receiving the word in much tribulation, with joy of the Holy Ghost. 1 Thess. 1:5 f.

It is the Spirit which testifieth that Christ is the Truth. And there are three who give testimony in heaven, the Father, the Word, and the Holy Ghost. And these three are one. And there are three that give testimony on earth: the spirit, and the water, and the blood. And these three are one. 1 John 5:6 f.

The Holy Ghost is in you. 1 C.6:19.

9. ROME THE NEW JERUSALEM OF THE NEW LAW

Names of the Holy City

The king and all the men that were with him went to Jerusalem, to the Jebusites, the inhabitants of the land: and they said to David: Thou shalt not come in hither unless thou take away the blind and the lame that say: David shall not come in hither. But David took the castle of Sion, the same is the city of David. For David had offered that day a reward to whosoever should strike the Jebusites and get up to the gutters of the tops of the houses, and take away the blind and the lame that hated the soul of David: therefore it is said in the proverb: The blind and the lame shall not come into the temple. And David went into the castle, and called it, The city of David: and built round about from Mello and inwards. 2 K. 5:6-9.

The stream of the river maketh the city of God joyful; the Most High hath sanctified his own tabernacle. Ps. 45:5.

Look upon Sion, the city of our solemnity: thy eyes shall see Jerusalem, a rich habitation, a tabernacle that cannot be removed; neither shall the nails thereof be taken away forever, neither shall any of the cords thereof be broken. Is. 33:20.

The princes of the people dwelt at Jerusalem: but the rest of the people cast lots, to take one part in ten to dwell in Jerusalem, the holy city, and nine parts in the other cities. 2 Es. 11:1.

All the ancients of Israel, with the princes of the tribes and the heads of the families of the children of Isreal were assembled to king Solomon in Jerusalem, that they might carry the ark of the covenant of the Lord out of the city of David, that is, out of Sion. 3 K. 8:1.

With the joy of the whole earth is Mount Sion founded, on the sides of the north the city of the great king. Ps. 47:3.

In Judea God is known: his name is great in Israel. And his place is in peace: and his abode is in Sion. Ps. 75:2 f.

Chosen and Beloved by God

I will appoint a place for my people Israel, and I will plant them, and they shall dwell therein, and shall be disturbed no more: neither shall the children of iniquity afflict them any more as they did before. 2 K. 7:10.

From the day that I brought my people out of the land of Egypt, I chose no city among all the tribes of Israel, for a house to be built in it to my name: neither chose I any other man to be a ruler of my people Israel. But I chose Jerusalem, that my name might be there: and I chose David to set him over my people Israel. 2 Par. 6:5 f.

I will protect this city, and will save it for my own sake, and for David, my servant's sake. And it came to pass that night that an angel of the Lord came and slew in the camp of the Assyrians a hundred and eighty-five thousand. And when he arose early in the morning, he saw all the bodies of the dead. 4 K. 19:34 f.

Beloved by God's People

I rejoiced at the things that were said to me: We shall go into the house of the Lord. Our feet were standing in thy courts, O Jerusalem. Jerusalem, which is built as a city, which is compact together. For thither did the tribes go up, the tribes of the Lord: the testimony of Israel, to praise the name of the Lord. Because their seats have sat in judgment, seats upon the house of David. Pray ye for the things that are for the peace of Jerusalem: and abundance for them that love thee. Let peace be in thy strength: and abundance in thy towers. For the sake of my brethren and of my neighbors, I spoke peace of thee. Because of the house of the Lord our God, I have sought good things for thee. Ps. 121:1-9.

Upon the rivers of Babylon, there we sat and wept: when we remembered Sion. On the willows in the midst thereof we hung up our instruments. For there they that led us into captivity, required of us the words of songs. And they that carried us away said: Sing ye to us a hymn of the songs of Sion. How shall we sing the song of the Lord in a strange land? If I forget thee, O Jerusalem, let my right hand be forgotten. Let my tongue cleave to my jaws if I do not remember thee, if I make not Jerusalem the beginning of my joy. Ps. 136:1-6.

For Sion's sake I will not hold my peace, and for the sake of Jerusalem, I will not rest till her just one come forth as brightness, and her Savior be lighted as a lamp. And the Gentiles shall see thy just one and all kings thy glorious one: and thou shalt be called by a new name, which the mouth of the Lord shall name. And thou shalt be a crown of glory in the hand of the Lord and a royal diadem in the hand of thy God.

Thou shalt no more becalled Forsaken: and my land shall no more be called Desolate: but thou shalt be called My pleasure in her, and thy land Inhabited. Because the Lord hath been well pleased with thee; and thy land shall be inhabited. For the young man shall dwell with the virgin, and thy children shall dwell in thee. And the bridegroom shall rejoice over the bride, and thy God shall rejoice over thee.

Upon thy walls, O Jerusalem, I have appointed watchmen all the day, and all the night, they shall never hold their peace. You that are mindful of the Lord, hold not your peace. And give him no silence till he establish, and till he make Jerusalem a praise in the earth. Is. 62:1-7.

Beloved Even by the Heathen

Artaxerxes king of kings to Esdras the priest, the most learned scribe of the law of the God of heaven, greeting. It is decreed by me, that all they of the people of Israel, and of the priests, and of the Levites thereof in my realm, that are minded to go into Jerusalem, should go with thee. For thou art sent from before the king, and his seven counsellors to visit Judea and Jerusalem according to the law of thy God, which is in thy hand. And to carry the silver and gold, which the king and his counsellors have freely offered to the God of Israel, whose tabernacle is in Jerusalem. And all the silver and gold that thou shalt find in all the province of Babylon, and that the people is willing to offer, and that the priests shall offer of their own accord to the house of their God, which is in Jerusalem.

Take freely, and buy diligently with this money, calves, rams, lambs, with the sacrifices and libations of them, and offer them upon the altar of the temple of your God, that is in Jerusalem. And if it seem good to thee, and to thy brethren to do anything with the rest of the silver and gold, do it according to the will of your God. The vessels also, that are given thee for the service of the house of thy God, deliver thou in the sight of God in Jerusalem. And whatsoever more there shall be need of for the house of thy God, how much soever thou shalt have occasion to spend, it shall be given out of the treasury, and the king's exchequer, and by me.

I, Artaxerxes the king, have ordered and decreed to all the keepers of the public chest, that are beyond the river, that whatsoever Esdras the priest, the scribe of the law of the God of heaven, shall require of you, you give it without delay, unto a hundred talents of silver, and unto a hundred cores of wheat,and unto a hundred bates of wine, and unto a hundred bates of oil, and salt without measure. All that belongeth to the rites of the God of heaven, let it be given diligently in the house of the God of heaven: lest his wrath should be enkindled against the realm of the king, and of his sons.

We give you also to understand concerning all the priests, and the Levites, and the singers, and the porters, and the Nathinites, and ministers of the house of this God, that you have no authority to impose toll or tribute, or custom upon them.

And thou, Esdras, according to the wisdom of thy God, which is in thy hand, appoint judges and magistrates, that may judge all the people, that is beyond the river, that is, for them who know the law of thy God, yea, and the ignorant teach ye freely. And whosoever will not do the law of thy God, and the law of the king diligently, judgment shall be executed upon him, either unto death or unto banishment, or to the confiscation of goods, or at least to prison. Blessed be the Lord the God of our fathers, who hath put this in the king's heart, to glorify the house of the Lord, which is in Jerusalem. 1 Es. 7:12-28.

10. PAPAL INFALLIBILITY

The Lord said: Simon, Simon, behold Satan hath desired to have you that he may sift you as wheat. But I have prayed for thee that thy faith fail not: and thou being once converted, confirm thy brethren. Luke 22:31 f.

Jesus saith to them, But whom do you say that I am? Simon Peter answered and said: Thou art Christ, the Son of the living God. And Jesus answering, said to him:

Blessed art thou, Simon Bar-Jona: because flesh and blood hath not revealed it to thee, but my Father who is in heaven:

And I say to thee that thou art Peter [Rock];

And on this rock I will build my church;

And the gates of hell shall not prevail against it;

And to thee I will give the keys of the kingdom of heaven;

And whatsoever thou shalt bind upon earth, it shall be bound also in heaven: and whatsoever thou shalt loose on earth, it shall be loosed also in heaven. Mat. 16:15-19.

Jesus said to Simon Peter: Simon son of John, lovest thou me more than these? He saith to him: Yea, Lord, thou knowest that I love thee. He saith to him: Feed my lambs. He saith to him again: Simon son of John, lovest thou me? He saith to him: Yea, Lord, thou knowest that I love thee. He saith to him: Feed my lambs. He saith to him the third time: Simon son of John, lovest thou me? Peter was grieved, because he said to him the third time, Lovest thou me? And he said to him: Lord, thou knowest all things; thou knowest that I love thee. He said to him: Feed my sheep. John 21:15-17.

11. ECCLESIASTICAL HIERARCHY

Thus saith the Lord of hosts: Ask the priests of the law. Agge. 2:12.

The lips of the priest shall keep knowledge, and they shall seek the law at his mouth; because he is the angel of the Lord of hosts. Mal. 2:7.

If anything be to be done, Eleazar the priest shall consult the Lord for him. He, and all the children of Israel with him, and the rest of the multitude, shall go out and go in at his word. Num. 27:21.

It doth not belong to thee, Ozias, to burn incense to the Lord, but to the priests, that is, to the sons of Aaron, who are consecrated for this ministry. 2 Par. 28:18.

There are diversities of graces, but the same Spirit; and there are diversities of ministries, but the same Lord; and there are diversities of operations, but the same God who worketh all in all. 1 C. 12:4-6.

God indeed hath set some in the church: first apostles, secondly prophets, thirdly doctors; after that miracles; then the graces of healings, helps, governments, kinds of tongues, interpretations of speeches. 1 C. 12:28.

The names of the twelve apostles are these: the first, Simon who is called Peter Mat. 10:2.

I will give to thee the keys of the kingdom of heaven. Mat. 16:19.

Feed my lambs, feed my sheep. John 21:17.

Feed the flock of God which is among you, taking care of it not by constraint, but willingly, according to God: not for filthy lucre's sake, but voluntarily. Neither as lording it over the clergy, but being made a pattern of the flock from the heart. 1 Pet. 5:2 f.

When the Prince of pastors shall appear, you shall receive a never-fading crown of glory. 1 Pet. 5:4.

The church that is in Babylon elected together with you, saluteth you, and so doth my son Mark. 1 Pet. 5:13.

12. THE PASTORS OF THE CHURCH

I will give you pastors, according to my own heart, and they shall feed you with knowledge and doctrine. Jer. 3:15.

Pray ye the Lord of the harvest, that he send forth laborers into his harvest. Mat. 9:38.

My doctrine is not mine, but his that sent me. John 7:16.

All things are of God, who hath reconciled us to himself by Christ; and hath given to us the ministry of reconciliation. 2 C. 5:18.

For Christ we are ambassadors, God, as it were, exhorting by us. 2 C. 5:20.

Let a man so account of us as of the ministers of Christ, and the dispensers of the mysteries of God. Here now it is required among the dispensers, that a man be found faithful. 1 C. 4:1 f.

Woe is unto me if I preach not the gospel. 1 C. 9:16.

For this cause I left thee in Crete, that thou shouldest set in order the things that are wanting, and shouldest ordain priests in every city. Titus 1:5.

What I forgave, if I have forgiven anything, for your sakes have I done it in the person of Christ. 2 C. 2:10.

[You] received me as an angel of God, even as Christ Jesus. Gal. 4:14.

Blessed is he whom thou hast chosen and taken to thee: he shall dwell in thy courts. Ps. 64:5.

Blessed be he that cometh in the name of the Lord. Ps. 117:26.

How beautiful upon the mountains are the feet of him that bringeth good tidings, and that preacheth peace: of him that showeth forth good, that preacheth salvation, that saith to Sion: Thy God shall reign! The voice of thy watchmen: they have lifted up their voice, they shall praise together: for they shall see eye to eye when the Lord shall convert Sion. Is. 52:7 f.

Thou, O son of man, I have made thee a watchman to the house of Israel: therefore thou shalt hear the word from my mouth, and shalt tell it them from me. Ez. 33:7.

Jesus saith to them: Come ye after me, and I will make you to be fishers of men. Mat. 4:19.

To Levi he said: Thy perfection, and thy doctrine be to thy holy man, whom thou hast proved in the temptation, and judged at the waters of contradiction. Who hath said to his father, and to his mother: I do not know you; and to his brethren: I know you not, and their own children they have not known. These have kept thy word, and observed thy covenant. Deut. 33:8 f.

He that receiveth you, receiveth me: and he that receiveth me, receiveth him that sent me. Mat. 10:40.

They shall be holy to their God, and shall not profane his name: for they offer the burnt offering of the Lord, and the bread of their God, and therefore they shall be holy. The high priest, that is to say, the priest that is the greatest among his brethren, upon whose head the oil of unction hath been poured, and whose hands have been consecrated for the priesthood, and who hath been vested with the holy vestments, shall not uncover his head, he shall not rend his garments. Lev. 21:6,10.

He said [to his apostles]: Go ye into the whole world, and preach the gospel to every creature. Mark 16:15.

Go. Behold I send you as lambs among wolves. Into whatsoever house you enter, first say: Peace be to this house: and if the son of peace be there, your peace shall rest upon him: but if not, it shall return to you. He that heareth you, heareth me: and he that despiseth you, despiseth me. And he that despiseth me, despiseth him that sent me. Luke 10:3, 5 f., 16.

We will give ourselves continually to prayer, and to the ministry of the word. Acts 6:4.

We are God's coadjutors: you are God's husbandry, you are God's building. 1 C. 3:9.

As we were approved of God, that the gospel should be committed to us; even so we speak, not as pleasing men, but God, who proveth our hearts. 1 Thess. 2:4.

If also I should boast somewhat more of our power, which the Lord hath given us unto edification, and not for your destruction; I should not be ashamed. 2 C. 10:8.

The eleven disciples went into Galilee, unto the mountain where Jesus had appointed them. And Jesus coming, spoke to them, saying: All power is given to me in heaven and in earth. Going therefore, teach ye all nations; baptizing them in the name of the Father, and of the Son, and of the Holy Ghost. Teaching them to observe all things whatsoever I have commanded you; and behold, I am with you all days, even to the consummation of the world. Mat. 28:16, 18-20.

You shall receive the power of the Holy Ghost coming upon you, and you shall be witnesses unto me in Jerusalem, and in all Judea, and Samaria, and even to the uttermost parts of the earth. Acts 1:8.

13. LEGISLATIVE POWER

Obey your prelates, and be subject to them. For they watch, as being to render an account of your souls. Heb. 13:17.

As the Father hath sent me, so I also send you. John 20:21.

For it hath seemed good to the Holy Ghost and to us, to lay no further burden upon you than these necessary things. That you abstain from things sacrificed to idols, and from blood and from fornication. Acts 15:28 f.

He went through Syria and Cilicia, confirming the churches; commanding them to keep the precepts of the apostles and the ancients. Acts 15:41.

I write these things being absent, that, being present, I may not deal more severely, according to the power which the Lord hath given me unto edification, and not unto destruction. 2 C. 13:10.

What will you? shall I come to you with a rod, or in charity, and in the spirit of meekness? 1 C. 4:21.

I indeed absent in body, but present in spirit, have already judged as though I were present, him that hath so done. In the name of our Lord Jesus Christ, you being gathered together and my spirit, with the power of our Lord Jesus. To deliver such a one to Satan for the destruction of the flesh, that the spirit may be saved in the day of our Lord Jesus Christ. 1 C. 5:3-5.

14. THE CHURCH ONE

You are all one in Christ Jesus. Gal. 3:28.

Other sheep I have that are not of this fold: them also I must bring, and there shall be one fold and one Shepherd. John 10:16.

We being many are one body. 1 C. 10:17.

One body and one Spirit: as you are called in one hope of your calling. One Lord, one faith, one baptism. One God and Father of all. Eph. 4:4-6.

Not the God of dissension, but of peace. 1 C. 14:33.

Holy Father, keep them in thy name, whom thou hast given me: that they may be one, as we also are. John 17:11.

15. THE CHURCH HOLY

You are a chosen generation, a kingly priesthood, a holy nation, a purchased people. 1 Pet. 2:9.

Thou hast redeemed us to God, in thy blood, out of every tribe, and tongue, and people, and nation, and hast made us to our God a kingdom and priests. Apoc. 5:9 f.

Christ loved the church, and delivered himself up for it. That he might sanctify it, cleansing it by the laver of water in the word of life. That he might present it to himself a glorious church not having spot or wrinkle, or any such thing, but that it should be holy and without blemish. Eph. 5:25-27.

In the last time there should come mockers, walking according to their own desires in ungodliness. These are they who separate themselves, sensual men, having not the Spirit. But you, my beloved, building yourselves upon your most holy faith, praying in the Holy Ghost, keep yourselves in the love of God. Jude 18-21.

You are no more strangers and foreigners; but you are fellow citizens with the saints, and the domestics of God. Eph. 2:19.

You are come to Mount Sion, and to the city of the living God, the heavenly Jerusalem, and to the company of many thousands of angels, and to the church of the firstborn, who are written in the heavens. Heb. 12:22.

The wall of the city had twelve foundations, and in them, the twelve names of the twelve apostles of the Lamb. Apoc. 21:14.

Holiness becometh thy house, O Lord. Ps. 92:5.

That being delivered from the hand of our enemies, we may serve him without fear, in holiness and justice before him, all our days. Luk 1:74 f.

Sanctify them in truth. Thy word is truth. And for them do I sanctify myself: that they also may be sanctified in truth. John 17:17, 19.

He chose us in him before the foundation of the world, that we should be holy and unspotted in his sight in charity. Eph. 1:4.

In [Christ] all the building, being framed together, groweth up into a holy temple in the Lord. Eph. 2:21.

Christ gave himself for us, that he might redeem us from all iniquity, and might cleanse to himself a people acceptable, a pursuer of good works. Titus 2:14.

These signs shall follow them that believe: in my name they shall cast out devils: they shall speak with new tongues. They shall take up serpents: and if they shall drink any deadly thing, it shall not hurt them: they shall lay their hands on the sick, and they shall recover. Mark 16:17 f.

Amen, amen, I say to you, he that believeth in me, the works that I do, he also shall do, and greater than these shall he do. John 14:12.

To one indeed, by the Spirit, is given the word of wisdom: and to another, the word of knowledge, according to the same Spirit: to another, faith in the same Spirit: to another, the grace of healing in one spirit. To another, the working of miracles: to another, prophecy; to another, the discerning of spirits: to another, diverse kinds of tongues: to another, interpretations of speeches. But all these things one and the same Spirit worketh, dividing to every one according as he will. 1 C. 12:8-11.

By their fruits you shall know them Every good tree bringeth forth good fruit. Mat. 7:16 f.

I, John, saw the holy city, the new Jerusalem, coming down out of heaven from God, prepared as a bride adorned for her husband. Apoc. 21:2.

God is faithful: by whom you are called unto the fellowship of his Son Jesus Christ our Lord. 1 C. 1:9.

The house of our holiness. Is. 64:11.

16. THE CHURCH CATHOLIC

In the days of these kingdoms, the God of heaven will set up a kingdom that shall never be destroyed. Dan. 2:44.

Seventy weeks are shortened upon thy people, and upon the holy city, that transgression may be finished and sin may have an end, and iniquity may be abolished: and everlasting justice may be brought, and vision and prophecy may be fulfilled: and the Saint of saints may be anointed. Dan. 9:24.

My Spirit is in thee: and my words that I have put in thy mouth, shall not depart out of thy mouth, nor out of the mouth of thy seed, nor out of the mouth of thy seed's seed, saith the

Lord, from henceforth and forever. Is. 59:21.

I will make a perpetual covenant with them. Is. 61:8.

Thy gates shall be open continually: they shall not be shut day nor night, that the strength of the Gentiles may be brought to thee, and their kings may be brought. For the nation and the kingdom that will not serve thee shall perish. Is. 60:11 f.

With the joy of the whole earth is Mount Sion founded: on the sides of the north, the city of the great King. Ps. 47:3.

As we have heard, so have we seen in the city of the Lord of hosts, in the city of our God: God hath founded it forever. Ps. 47:9.

I have made a covenant with my elect: I have sworn to David my servant: Thy seed will I settle forever. And I will build up thy throne unto generation and generation. Ps. 88:4 f.

His empire shall be multiplied, and there shall be no end of peace: he shall sit upon the throne of David, and upon his kingdom: to establish it, to strengthen it with judgment, and with justice, from henceforth and forever: the zeal of the Lord of hosts will perform this. Is. 9:7.

In thy seed shall all the nations of the earth be blessed. Gen. 22:18. (Cf. Gal. 3:8.)

Ask of me, and I will give thee the Gentiles for thy inheritance: and the utmost parts of the earth for thy possession. Ps. 2:8.

All the ends of the earth shall remember, and shall be converted to the Lord. Ps. 21:28.

From the rising of the sun even to the going down, my name is great among the Gentiles, and in every place there is sacrifice, and there is offered to my name a clean oblation. Mal. 1:11.

This gospel of the kingdom shall be preached in the whole world. Mat. 24:14.

The gospel is come unto you, as also it is in the whole world. Col. 1:6.

Behold thou shalt conceive in thy womb, and shalt bring forth a Son; and thou shalt call his name Jesus. He shall be great, and shall be called the Son of the Most High; and the Lord God shall give unto him the throne of David his father: and he shall reign in the house of Jacob forever. And of his kingdom there shall be no end. Luke 1:31-33.

He hath on his garment and on his thigh written: King of kings, and Lord of lords. Apoc. 19:16.

All power is given to me in heaven and in earth. Going therefore, teach ye all nations; baptizing them in the name of the Father, and of the Son, and of the Holy Ghost. Mat. 28:18 f.

Their sound hath gone forth into all the earth, and their words unto the ends of the whole world. Rom. 10:13.

In the last days the mountain of the house of the Lord shall be prepared on the top of mountains, and it shall be exalted above the hills, and all nations shall flow unto it. Is. 2:2.

Come and let us go up to the mountain of the Lord, and to the house of the God of Jacob. Ps. 2:3.

The Lord will roar from Sion, and utter his voice from Jerusalem. Amos 1:2.

A city seated on a mountain cannot be hid. Mat. 5:14.

Neither do men light a candle and put it under a bushel, but upon a candlestick, that it may shine to all that are in the house. Mat. 5:15.

Be blameless without reproof in the midst of a crooked and perverse generation; among whom you shine as lights in the world, holding forth the word of life. Phil. 2:15 f.

They going forth preached everywhere; the Lord working withal, and confirming the word with signs that followed. Mark 16:20.

If he will not hear them: tell the church. Mat. 18:17.

So let your light shine before men, that they may see your good works, and glorify your Father who is in heaven. Mat. 5:16.

Look upon Sion the city of our solemnity: thy eyes shall see Jerusalem, a rich habitation, a tabernacle that cannot be removed: neither shall the nails thereof be taken away forever, neither shall any of the cords thereof be broken: because only there our Lord is magnificent: a place of rivers, very broad and spacious streams. Is. 33:20 f.

Arise, be enlightened, O Jerusalem, for thy light is come, and the glory of the Lord is risen upon thee. For behold darkness shall cover the earth, and a mist the people: but the Lord shall arise upon thee, and his glory shall be seen upon thee. And the Gentiles shall walk in thy light, and kings in the brightness of thy rising. Lift up thy eyes round about, and see: all these are gathered together, they are come to thee: thy sons shall come from afar, and thy daughters shall rise up at thy side. Then shalt thou see and abound, and thy heart shall wonder and be enlarged, when the multitude of the sea shall be converted to thee, the strength of the Gentiles shall come to thee. Is. 60:1-5.

They shall know their seed among the Gentiles, and their offspring in the midst of peoples: all that shall see them, shall know them, that these are the seed which the Lord hath blessed. I will greatly rejoice in the Lord, and my soul shall be joyful in my God: for he hath clothed me with the garments of salvation and with the robe of justice he hath covered me, as a bridegroom decked with a crown, and as a bride adorned with her jewels. For as the earth bringeth forth her bud, and as the garden causeth her seed to shoot forth: so shall the Lord God make justice to spring forth, and praise before all the nations. Is. 61:9-11.

He shall rule from sea to sea, and from the river unto the ends of the earth. Ps. 71:8.

Fear not, for I am with thee: I will bring thy seed from the east, and gather thee from the west. I will say to the north: Give up: and to the south: Keep not back: bring my sons from afar, and my daughters from the ends of the earth. Is. 43:3-6.

Behold I have given thee to be the light of the Gentiles, that thou mayest be my salvation even to the farthest part of the earth. Is. 49:6.

The earth shall be filled, that men may know the glory of the Lord, as waters covering the sea. Haba. 2:14.

Many peoples, and strong nations shall come to seek the Lord of hosts in Jerusalem, and to entreat the face of the Lord. Zach. 8:22.

I saw another angel flying through the midst of heaven, having the eternal gospel, to preach unto them that sit upon the earth. Apoc. 14:6.

17. THE CHURCH APOSTOLIC

Thou art Peter, and upon this rock I will build my church. Mat. 16:18.

You are fellow citizens with the saints, built upon the foundation of the apostles and prophets, Jesus Christ himself being the chief cornerstone. Eph. 2:19 f.

He gave some apostles and some prophets. For the perfecting of the saints, for the work of the ministry, for the edifying of the body of Christ: until we all meet into the unity of faith, and of the knowledge of the Son of God, unto a perfect man, unto the measure of the age of the fulness of Christ. That henceforth we be no more children tossed to and fro, and carried about with every wind of doctrine by the wickedness of men, by cunning craftiness by which they lie in wait to deceive. Eph. 4:11-14.

18. THE CHURCH INFALLIBLE

A path and a way shall be there, and it shall be called the holy way: the unclean shall not pass over it, and this shall be unto you a straight way, so that fools shall not err thereon. Is. 35:8.

O poor little one, tossed with tempest, without all comfort, behold I will lay thy stones in order, and will lay thy foundations with sapphires. And I will make thy bulwarks of jasper: and thy gates of graven stones, and all thy borders of desirable stones. All thy children shall be taught of the Lord: and great shall be the peace of thy children. And thou shalt be founded in justice. Is. 54:11-14.

His mercy is confirmed upon us: and the truth of the Lord remaineth forever. Ps. 116:2.

The heavens shall confess thy wonders, O Lord: and thy truth in the church of the saints. Ps. 88:6.

This is my covenant with them, saith the Lord: My Spirit that is in thee, and my words that I have put in thy mouth, shall not depart out of thy mouth, nor out of the mouth of thy seed, nor out of the mouth of thy seed's seed, saith the Lord, from henceforth and forever. Is. 59:21.

It shall be called the City of Truth. Zach. 8:3.

The gates of hell shall not prevail against it. Mat. 16:18.

If you continue in my word you shall be my disciples indeed. And you shall know the truth, and the truth shall make you free. John 8:31 f.

The sheep hear his voice, and the sheep follow him because they know his voice. But a stranger they follow not, but fly from him: because they know not the voice of strangers. John 10:4 f.

I will ask the Father and he shall give you another Paraclete that he may abide with you forever. The Spirit of truth, whom the world cannot receive, because it seeth him not. nor knoweth him: but you shall know him, because he shall abide with you, and shall be in you. John 14:16 f.

The Spirit of truth will teach you all truth. John 16:13.

The house of God, which is the church of the living God. the pillar and ground of the truth. 1 Tim. 3:15.

These things have I written to you concerning them that seduce you. And as for you, let the unction which you have received from him abide in you. And you have no need that any man teach you: but as his unction teacheth you of all things, and is truth, and is no lie. 1 John 2:26 f.

I pray also for them who through their word shall believe in me. That they all may be one as thou, Father, in me, and I in thee, that they also may be one in us that the world may believe that thou hast sent me. John 17:20 f.

Behold I am with you all days, even to the consummation of the world. Mat. 28:20.

Every one that heareth my words and doeth them, shall be likened to a wise man that built his house upon a rock. And the rain fell, and the floods came, and the winds blew, and they beat upon that house, and it fell not, for it was founded on a rock. Mat. 7:24 f.

We have the mind of Christ. 1 C. 2:16.

19. THE CHURCH IMPREGNABLE

Upon this rock I will build my church, and the gates of hell shall not prevail against it. Mat. 16:18.

The church of the living God [is] the pillar and ground of the truth. 1 Tim. 3:15.

Thou shalt no more be called forsaken: and thy land shall no more be called desolate. Is. 62:4.

The word of the Lord endureth forever. 1 Pet. 1:25.

I will ask the Father, and he shall give you another Paraclete, that he may abide with you forever. John 14:16.

When he, the Spirit of truth, is come, he will teach you all truth. John 16:13.

He gave some apostles, and some prophets, and other some evangelists, and other some pastors and doctors, for the perfecting of the saints, for the work of the ministry, for the edifying of the body of Christ: until we all meet into the unity of faith, and of the knowledge of the Son of God, unto a perfect man, unto the measure of the age of the fulness of Christ. Eph. 4:11-13.

20. NAMES AND CHARACTERISTICS OF THE CHURCH

I

Dearly beloved, we are now the sons of God: and it hath not yet appeared what we shall be. 1 John 3:2.

As many as received him, he gave them power to be made the sons of God, to them that believe in his name. John 1:12.

Whosoever are led by the Spirit of God, they are the sons of God. Rom. 8:14.

Do ye all things without murmurings and hesitations: that you may be blameless, and sincere children of God. Phil. 2:14 f.

God sent his Son, that he might redeem them who were under the law; that we might receive the adoption of sons. And because you are sons, God hath sent the Spirit of his Son into your hearts, crying: Abba, Father. Gal. 4:5 f.

It became him, for whom are all things, and by whom are all things, who had brought many children into glory, to perfect the Author of their salvation, by his Passion. Heb. 2:10.

Persevere under discipline. God dealeth with you as with his sons: for what son is there whom the father does not correct? But if you be without chastisement, whereof all are made partakers; then you are bastards, and not sons. Heb. 12:7 f.

I will be a Father to you: and you shall be my sons and daughters, saith the Lord Almighty. 2 C. 6:18.

Blessed are the peacemakers: for they shall be called the children of God. Mat. 5:9.

Being the high priest of that year, he [Caiphas] prophesied that Jesus should die for the nation. And not only for the nation, but to gather together in one the children of God, that were dispersed. John 11:51 f.

The expectation of the creature waiteth for the revelation of the sons of God. For the creature was made subject to vanity, not willingly, but by reason of him that made it subject, in hope; because the creature also itself shall be delivered from the servitude of corruption, into the liberty of the glory of the children of God. Rom. 8:19-21.

Whosoever is born of God, committeth not sin: for his seed abideth in him and he cannot sin, because he is born of God. In this the children of God are manifest, and the children of the devil. 1 John 3:9 f.

You are not in the flesh, but in the Spirit, if so be that the Spirit of God dwell in you. Now if any man have not the Spirit of Christ, he is none of his. Rom. 8:9.

It shall be, in the place where it was said unto them, you are not my people: there they shall be called sons of the living God. Rom. 9:26.

You are all children of God by faith, in Christ Jesus. Gal. 3:26.

Be ye followers of God, as most dear children. Eph. 5:1.

Trust perfectly in the grace which is offered you in the revelation of Jesus Christ, as children of obedience, not fashioned according to the former desires of your ignorance. 1 Pet. 1:13 f.

The Spirit himself giveth testimony to our spirit, that we are the sons of God. And if sons, heirs also; heirs indeed of God, and joint heirs with Christ. Rom. 8:16 f.

If you be Christ's, then are you the seed of Abraham, heirs according to the promise. Gal. 3:29.

Now he is not a servant, but a son. And if a son, an heir through God. Gal. 4:7.

Are the angels not all ministering spirits, sent to minister for them, who shall receive the inheritance of salvation? Heb. 1:14.

Grace to you and peace be accomplished in the knowledge of God, and of Christ Jesus our Lord: by whom he hath given us most great and precious promises: that by these you may be made partakers of the divine nature. 2 Pet. 1:2,4.

Whosoever believeth that Jesus is the Christ, is born of God. We know that whosoever is born of God, sinneth not: but the generation of God preserveth him, and the wicked one toucheth him not. 1 John 5:1, 18.

Blessed be the God and Father of our Lord Jesus Christ, who according to his great mercy hath regenerated us unto a lively hope, by the resurrection of Jesus Christ from the dead. 1 Pet. 1:3.

With a brotherly love, from a sincere heart love one another earnestly: being born again not of corruptible seed, but incorruptible, by the word of God who liveth and remaineth forever. 1 Pet. 1:22 f.

Amen, amen I say to thee, unless a man be born again of water and the Holy Ghost, he cannot enter into the kingdom of God. That which is born of the flesh, is flesh; and that which is born of the Spirit, is spirit. John 3:5 f.

As many as received him, he gave them power to be made the sons of God, to them that believe in his name. Who are born, not of blood, nor of the will of the flesh, nor of the will of man, but of God. John 1:12 f.

Dearly beloved, let us love one another: for charity is of God. And every one that loveth is born of God, and knoweth God. 1 John 4:7.

Whatsoever is born of God, overcometh the world. And this is the victory which overcometh the world, our faith. 1 John 5:4.

If you know that he is just; know ye, that every one also, who doth justice, is born of him. 1 John 2:29.

As new-born babes, desire the rational milk without guile, that thereby you may grow unto salvation. 1 Pet. 2:2.

Of him are you in Christ Jesus, who of God is made unto us wisdom, and justice, and sanctification, and redemption. 1 C. 1:30.

The man indeed ought not to cover his head, because he is the image and glory of God: but the woman is the glory of the man. 1 C. 11:7.

The Lord knoweth how to deliver the godly from temptation, but to reserve the unjust unto the day of judgment to be tormented. 2 Pet. 2:9.

I pray that they all may be one, as thou, Father, in me, and I in thee: that they also may be one in us: that the world may believe that thou hast sent me. John 17:21.

The glory which thou hast given me, I have given to them: that they may be one, as we also are one. John 17:22.

Father, I will, that where I am, they also whom thou hast given me may be with me: that they may see my glory which thou hast given me. John 17:24.

II

The marriage of the Lamb is come, and his wife hath prepared herself. And it is granted to her that she should clothe herself with fine linen, glittering and white. For the fine linen are the justifications of saints. Apoc. 19:7 f.

Him, that knew no sin, for us he hath made [himself a victim for] sin, that we might be made the justice of God in him. 2 C. 5:21.

They shall see his face: and his name shall be on their foreheads. Apoc. 22:4.

I beheld, and lo a Lamb stood upon Mount Sion, and with him an hundred forty-four thousand having his name, and the name of his Father written on their foreheads. Apoc. 14:1.

It was commanded them that they should not hurt the grass of the earth, nor any green thing, nor any tree; but only the men who have not the sign of God on their foreheads. Apoc. 9:4.

The Gentiles shall see thy just one, and all kings thy glorious one, and thou shalt be called by a new name, which the mouth of the Lord shall name. Is. 62:2.

They shall call them, The holy people, the redeemed of the Lord. But thou shalt be called: A city sought after, and not forsaken. Is. 62:12.

You shall leave your name for an execration to my elect: and the Lord God shall slay thee, and call his servants by another name. Is. 65:15.

They taught a great multitude, so that at Antioch the disciples were first named Christians. Acts 11:26.

Do not the rich oppress you by might? Do not they blaspheme the good name that is invoked upon you? Jas. 2:6 f.

After these things I will return, and will rebuild the tabernacle of David. That the residue of men may seek after the Lord, and all nations upon whom my name is invoked, saith the Lord who doth these things. Acts 15:16 f.

God will save Sion, and the cities of Juda shall be built up. And they shall dwell there, and acquire it by inheritance. And the seed of his servants shall possess it: and they that love his name shall dwell therein. Ps. 68:36 f.

In him were all things created in heaven, and on earth, visible and invisible, whether thrones, or dominations, or principalities, or powers: all things were created by him, and in him. Col. 1:16.

Thou art worthy, O Lord our God, to receive glory, and honor, and power: because thou hast created all things, and for thy will they were, and have been created. Apoc. 4:11.

The Spirit of God made me, and the breath of the Almighty gave me life. Job 33:4.

O bless our God, ye Gentiles: and make the voice of his praise to be heard. Who hath set my soul to live: and hath not suffered my feet to be moved. Ps. 65:8 f.

Fight the good fight of faith: lay hold on eternal life whereunto thou art called. 1 Tim. 6:12.

Behold how good and how pleasant it is for brethren to dwell together in unity: as the dew of Hermon, which descendeth upon Mount Sion. For there the Lord hath commanded blessing, and life for evermore. Ps. 132:1, 3.

We are his workmanship, created in Christ Jesus in good works, which God hath prepared that we should walk in them. Eph. 2:10.

Put on the new man, who according to God, is created in justice, and holiness of truth. Eph. 4:24.

Mortify your members which are upon the earth, stripping yourselves of the old man with his deeds. And putting on the new, him who is renewed unto knowledge, according to the image of him that created him. Col. 3:5, 9 f.

To me is given this grace, to enlighten all men: that they may see what is the dispensation of the mystery which hath been hidden from eternity in God, who created all things. Eph. 3:8 f.

If then any be in Christ a new creature: the old things are passed away, behold all things are made new. 2 C. 5:17.

In Christ Jesus neither circumcision availeth anything, nor uncircumcision, but a new creature. Gal. 6:15.

Our sufficiency is from God; who also hath made us fit ministers of the new testament, not in the letter, but in the Spirit. For the letter killeth: but the Spirit quickeneth. 2 C. 3:5 f.

Jesus answered: Amen, amen I say to thee, unless a man be born again of water and the Holy Ghost, he cannot enter into the kingdom of God. That which is born of the flesh, is flesh: and that which is born of the Spirit, is spirit. Wonder not that I said to thee, you must be born again. The Spirit breatheth where he will; and thou hearest his voice, but thou knowest not whence he cometh and whither he goeth: so is every one that is born of the Spirit. John 3:5-8.

Paul an apostle of Jesus Christ by the will of God, according to the promise of life, which is in Christ Jesus. 2 Tim. 1:1.

Always [bear] about in our body the mortification of Jesus, that the life also of Jesus may be made manifest in our bodies. 2 C. 4:10.

These things are written that you may believe that Jesus is the Christ, the Son of God: and that believing, you may have life in his name. John 20:31.

You are dead: and your life is hid with Christ in God. When Christ shall appear, who is your life: then you also shall appear with him in glory. Col. 3:3 f.

Let them be blotted out of the Book of the living; and with the just let them not be written. Ps. 68:29.

I live, now not I: but Christ liveth in me. And that I live now in the flesh: I live in the faith of the Son of God, who loved me, and delivered himself for me. Gal. 2:20.

Such as is the earthly, such also are the earthly: and such as is the heavenly, such also are they that are heavenly. Therefore as we have borne the image of the earthly, let us bear also the image of the heavenly. 1 C. 15:48 f.

III

From a sincere heart love one another earnestly: being born again not of corruptible seed, but incorruptible, by the Word of God who liveth and remaineth forever. 1 Pet. 1:22 f.

Of his own will hath he begotten us by the Word of truth, that we might be some beginning of his creature. Jas. 1:18.

This hath comforteth me in my humiliation: because thy word hath enlivened me. Ps. 118:50.

Amen, amen, I say to you that he who heareth my word, and believeth him that sent me, hath life everlasting; and cometh not into judgment, but is passed from death to life. John 5:24.

He afflicted thee with want, and gave thee manna for thy food, which neither thou nor thy fathers knew: to show that not in bread alone doth man live, but in every word that proceedeth from the mouth of God. Deut. 8:3.

Jesus answered him: It is written that man liveth not by bread alone, but by every word of God. Luke 4:4.

Husbands, love your wives; as Christ also loved the church, and delivered himself up for it: that he might sanctify it, cleansing it by the laver of water in the word of life. Eph. 5:25 f.

Now you are clean by reason of the word, which I have spoken to you. John 15:3.

Let him that is instructed in the word, communicate to him that instructeth him, in all good things. Gal. 6:6.

The Jews of Berea were more noble than those in Thessalonica, who received the word with all eagerness, daily searching the Scriptures, whether these things were so. Acts 17:11.

What saith the Scripture? The word is nigh thee, even in thy mouth, and in thy heart. This is the word of faith, which we preach. Rom. 10:8.

Jesus said to those Jews who believed him: If you continue in my word, you shall be my disciples indeed. John 8:31.

My mother and my brethren are they who hear the word of God and do it. Luke 8:21.

Be ye doers of the word, and not hearers only, deceiving your own selves. Jas. 1:22.

A bishop must be without crime. Embracing that faithful word which is according to doctrine, that he may be able to exhort in sound doctrine, and to convince the gainsayers. Titus 1:7, 9.

I have manifested thy name to the men whom thou hast given me out of the world. Thine they were, and to me thou gavest them: and they have kept thy word. John 17:6.

The multitude of men and women who believed in the Lord was more increased. Acts 5:14.

Let no man despise thy youth: but be thou an example of the faithful, in word, in conversation, in charity, in faith, in chastity. 1 Tim. 4:12.

Whom he foreknew, he also predestinated to be made conformable to the image of his Son: that he might be the firstborn amongst many brethren. Rom. 8:29.

I beseech you, brethren, by the mercy of God, that you present your bodies a living sacrifice, holy, pleasing unto God, your reasonable service. Rom. 12:1.

Both he that sanctifieth, and they who are sanctified, are all of one. For which cause he is not ashamed to call them brethren, saying: I will declare thy name to my brethren: in the midst of the church I will praise thee. Heb. 2:11 f.

It behoved him in all things to be made like unto his brethren, that he might become a merciful and faithful high priest before God, that he might be a propitiation for the sins of the people. Heb. 2:17.

We have this treasure in earthen vessels, that the excellency may be of the power of God, and not of us. 2 C. 4:7.

Because the children are partakers of flesh and blood, he also himself in like manner hath been partaker of the same: that through death he might destroy him who had the empire of death, that is to say, the devil. Heb. 2:14.

Lay you all away anger and indignation, stripping yourselves of the old man with his deeds, and putting on the new, him who is renewed unto knowledge, according to the image of him that created him. Col. 3:8-10.

He gave some apostles, and some prophets, until we all meet into the unity of faith, and of the knowledge of the Son of God, unto a perfect man, unto the measure of the age of the fulness of Christ. Eph. 4:11, 13.

Though our outward man is corrupted: yet the inward man is renewed day by day. 2 C. 4:16.

Our conversation is in heaven: from whence we look for the Savior, our Lord Jesus Christ. Who will reform the body of our lowness, made like to the body of his glory, according to the operation whereby also he is able to subdue all things unto himself. Phil. 3:20 f.

Dearly beloved, we are now the sons of God; and it hath not yet appeared what we shall be. We know that, when he shall appear, we shall be like to him: because we shall see him as he is. 1 John 3:2.

All these died according to faith not having received the promises, but beholding them afar off, and saluting them, and confessing that they are pilgrims and strangers on the earth. Heb. 11:13.

IV

He that is called in the Lord, being a bondman, is the freeman of the Lord. Likewise he that is called, being free, is the bondman of Christ. 1 C. 7:22.

Upon my servants indeed, and upon my handmaids will I pour out in those days of my Spirit, and they shall prophesy. Acts 2:18.

I will bring forth a seed out of Jacob, and out of Juda a possessor of my mountains: and my elect shall inherit it, and my servants shall dwell there. Is. 65:9.

Thus saith the Lord God: Behold my servants shall eat, and you shall be hungry: behold my servants shall drink, and you shall be thirsty. Behold my servants hall rejoice, and you shall be confounded: behold my servants shall praise for joyfulness of heart, and you shall cry for sorrow of heart, and shall howl for grief of spirit. Is. 65:13 f.

Jesus answered: My kingdom is not of this world. If my kingdom were of this world, my servants would certainly strive that I should not be delivered to the Jews: but now my kingdom is not from hence. John 18:36.

I have against thee a few things: because thou sufferest the woman Jezabel, who calleth herself a prophetess, to teach and to seduce my servants. Apoc. 2:20.

And now, Lord, behold their threatenings, and grant unto thy servants, that with all confidence they may speak thy word. Acts 4:29.

For so is the will of God, that by doing well you may put to silence the ignorance of foolish men: as free, and not making liberty a cloak for malice, but as the servants of God. 1 Pet. 2:15 f.

Hurt not the earth, nor the sea, nor the trees, till we sign the servants of our God in their foreheads. Apoc. 7:3.

Let them say always: The Lord be magnified, who delights in the peace of his servant. Ps. 34:27.

Serve ye the Lord Christ. Col. 3:24.

These men are the servants of the most high God, who preach unto you the way of salvation. Acts 16:17.

The Lord is well pleased with his people: he will exalt the meek unto salvation. Ps. 149:4.

The Spirit of the Lord is upon me, because the Lord hath anointed me: he hath sent me to preach to the meek, to heal the contrite of heart, and to preach a release to the captives, and deliverance to them that are shut up. Is. 61:1.

Blessed are the meek: for they shall possess the land. Mat. 5:4.

Blessed are the poor in spirit: for theirs is the kingdom of heaven. Mat. 5:3.

To whom shall I have respect, but to him that is poor and little, and of a contrite spirit, and that trembleth at my words? Is. 66:2.

If any man minister to me, him will my Father honor. John 12:26.

It is written in the prophets: And they shall all be taught of God. Every one that hath heard of the Father, and hath learned, cometh to me. John 6:45.

All thy children shall be taught of the Lord: and great shall be the peace of thy children. Is. 54:13.

As touching the charity of brotherhood, we have no need to write to you: for yourselves have learned of God to love one another. 1 Thess. 4:9.

As for you, let the unction, which you have received from him, abide in you. And you have no need that any man teach you: but as his unction teacheth you of all things, and is truth, and is no lie. And as it hath taught you, abide in him. 1 John 2:2.

Saul as yet breathing out threatenings and slaughter against the disciples of the Lord, went to the high priest. Acts 9:1.

When he was come into Jerusalem, he essayed to join himself to the disciples, and they were all afraid of him, not believing that he was a disciple. Acts 9:26.

They conversed there in the church a whole year; and they taught a great multitude, so that at Antioch the disciples were first named Christians. Acts 11:26.

It came to pass while Apollo was at Corinth, that Paul, having passed through the upper coasts, came to Ephesus, and found certain disciples. Acts 19:1.

When Paul would have entered in unto the people, the disciples suffered him not. Acts 19:30.

After the tumult was ceased, Paul, calling to him the disciples, and exhorting them, took his leave, and set forward to go into Macedonia. Acts 20:1.

God indeed hath set some in the church, first apostles, secondly prophets, thirdly doctors, after that miracles, then the graces of healing, helps, governments, kinds of tongues, interpretation of speeches. 1 C. 12:28.

He gave some apostles, and some prophets, and other some evangelists, and other some pastors and doctors. Eph. 4:11.

Touch ye not my anointed; and do no evil to my prophets. Ps. 104:15.

Rejoice over her, thou heaven, and ye holy apostles and prophets: for God hath judged your judgment on her. Apoc. 18:20.

Are not the angels ministering spirits, sent to minister for them, who shall receive the inheritance of salvation? Heb. 1:14.

He hath called you by our gospel, unto the purchasing of the glory of our Lord Jesus Christ. 2 Thess. 2:13.

God hath not appointed us unto the purchasing of salvation by our Lord Jesus Christ. 1 Thess. 5:9.

Every one that calleth upon my name I have created him for my glory, I have formed him, and made him. Is. 43:7.

Let all that seek thee be joyful and glad in thee; and let such as love thy salvation say always: The Lord be magnified. Ps. 39:17.

As for you, let the unction which you have received from him, abide in you. And you have no need that any man teach you; but as his unction teacheth you of all things, and is truth, and is no lie. And as it hath taught you, abide in him. 1 John 2:27.

He hath delivered us and called us by his holy calling, not according to our works, but according to his own purpose and grace which was given us in Christ Jesus before the times of the world. 2 Tim. 1:9.

I give thanks to my God always for you for the grace of God that is given you in Christ Jesus. 1 C. 1:4.

Not as the offence, so also the gift. For if by the offence of one many died; much more the grace of God, and the gift, by the grace of one man, Jesus Christ, hath abounded unto many. Rom. 5:15.

Not as though I had already attained, or were already perfect; but I follow after, if I may by any means apprehend wherein I am also apprehended by Jesus Christ. Brethren, I do not count myself to have apprehended. But one thing I do: forgetting the things that are behind, and stretching forth myself to those things that are before, I press towards the mark, to the prize of the supernal vocation of God in Christ Jesus. Phil. 3:12-14.

Christ died for all: that they also who live, may not now live to themselves, but unto him who died for them and rose again. 2 C. 5:15.

God indeed was in Christ, reconciling the world to himself, not imputing to them their sins, and he hath placed in us the word of reconciliation. 2 C. 5:19.

There is now no condemnation to those that are in Christ Jesus, who walk not according to the flesh. Rom. 8:1.

Be ye kind one to another: merciful, forgiving one another, even as God hath forgiven you in Christ. Eph. 4:32.

Know that man is not justified by the works of the law, but by the faith of Jesus Christ; we also believe in Christ Jesus, that we may be justified by the faith of Christ, and not by the works of the law, because by the works of the law no flesh shall be justified. Gal. 2:16.

Whosoever shall give you to drink a cup of water in my name, because you belong to Christ; amen I say to you, he shall not lose his reward. Mark 9:40.

You are Christ's, and Christ is God's. 1 C. 3:23.

My brethren, you are become dead to the law, by the body of Christ; that you may belong to another, who is risen from the dead, that we may bring forth fruit to God. Rom. 7:4.

You, brethren have been called unto liberty; only make not liberty an occasion to the flesh, but by charity of the Spirit serve one another. Gal. 5:13.

He that is called in the Lord, being

a bondman, is the freeman of the Lord. Likewise he that is called, being free, is the bondman of Christ. 1 C. 7:22.

To them that are beloved in God the Father, and preserved in Jesus Christ, and called, peace and charity be fulfilled. Jude 1 f.

He hath raised us up together, and hath made us sit together in the heavenly places, through Jesus Christ. Eph. 2:6.

I live, now not I; but Christ liveth in me. Gal. 2:20.

Know you not your own selves, that Christ Jesus is in you, unless, perhaps, you be reprobates? 2 C. 13:5.

The husband is the head of the wife, as Christ is the head of the church. He is the Savior of his body. Eph. 5:23.

Receive one another, as Christ also hath received you unto the honor of God. Rom. 15:9.

They that are of faith shall be blessed with faithful Abraham. Gal. 3:9.

If you be Christ's, then are you the seed of Abraham, heirs according to the promise. Gal. 3:29.

God commendeth his charity towards us: because when as yet we were sinners, according to the time, Christ died for us: much more therefore, being now justified by his blood, shall we be saved from wrath through him. Rom. 5:8 f.

V

There came one of the seven angels, who had the vials full of the seven last plagues, and spoke with me, saying: Come and I will show thee the bride, the wife of the Lamb. Apoc. 21:9.

Let us be glad and rejoice, and give glory to him; for the marriage of the Lamb is come, and his wife hath prepared herself. Apoc. 19:7.

He that hath the bride is the bridegroom; but the friend of the bridegroom, who standeth and heareth him, rejoiceth with joy because of the bridegroom's voice. This my joy therefore is fulfilled. John 3:29.

I, John, saw the holy city, the new Jerusalem, coming down out of heaven from God, prepared as a bride adorned for her husband. Apoc. 21:2.

I am jealous of you with the jealousy of God. For I have espoused you to one husband, that I may present you as a chaste virgin to Christ. 2 C. 11:2.

These are they who were not defiled with women; for they are virgins. These follow the Lamb whithersoever he goeth; these were purchased from among men, the first-fruits to God and to the Lamb. Apoc. 14:4.

They shall walk with me in white, because they are worthy. He that shall overcome shall thus be clothed in white garments, and I will not blot out his name out of the book of life, and I will confess his name before my Father, and before his angels. Apoc. 3:4 f.

These are they who are come out of great tribulation, and have washed their robes and have made them white in the blood of the Lamb. Apoc. 7:14.

Husbands, love your wives as Christ also loved the church, and delivered himself up for it. Eph. 5:25.

I live in the faith of the Son of God, who loved me, and delivered himself for me. Gal. 2:20.

No man ever hated his own flesh, but nourisheth and cherisheth it, as also Christ doth the church. Eph. 5:29.

As the church is subject to Christ, so also let the wives be to their husbands in all things. Eph. 5:24.

I fill up those things that are wanting of the sufferings of Christ, in my flesh, for his body, which is the church. Col. 1:24.

To all that are at Rome the beloved of God, called to be saints. Grace to you, and peace from God our Father, and from the Lord Jesus Christ. Rom. 1:7.

Thou hast given a warning to them that fear thee; that they may flee from before the bow: that thy beloved may be delivered. Ps. 59:6.

To the church of God that is at Corinth, to them that are sanctified in Christ Jesus, called to be saints, with all that invoke the name of our Lord Jesus Christ, in every place of theirs and ours. 1 C. 1:2.

Take heed to yourselves, and to the whole flock, wherein the Holy Ghost hath placed you bishops, to rule the church of God, which he hath purchased with his own blood. Acts 20:28.

That he might present it to himself a glorious church, not having spot or wrinkle or any such thing; but that it should be holy and without blemish. Eph. 5:27.

They shall call them: The holy people, the Redeemed of the Lord. But thou shalt be called, A city sought after, and not forsaken. Is. 62:12.

Thou shalt be called the City of the just, a faithful city. Is. 1:26.

Thus saith the Lord of hosts: I am returned to Sion, and I will dwell in the midst of Jerusalem; and Jerusalem shall be called the City of truth, and the Mountain of the Lord of hosts, the sanctified mountain. Zach. 8:3.

The name of the city from that day was, The Lord is there. Ez. 48:35.

He took me up in spirit to a great and high mountain; and he showed me the holy city Jerusalem coming down out of heaven from God. Apoc. 21:10.

You are come to Mount Sion, and to the city of the living God, the heavenly Jerusalem, and to the company of many thousands of angels. Heb. 12:22.

The city hath no need of the sun, nor of the moon, to shine in it. For the glory of God hath enlightened it, and the Lamb is the lamp thereof. Apoc. 21:23.

I saw a great multitude, which no man could number, of all nations, and tribes, and peoples, and tongues, standing before the throne, and in sight of the Lamb, clothed with white robes, and palms in their hands. Apoc. 7:9.

You are come to Mount Sion. And to the church of the first-born, who are written in the heavens, and to God the Judge of all, and to the spirits of the just made perfect. Heb. 12:23.

This is he that was in the church in the wilderness, with the angel who spoke to him on Mount Sina, and with our fathers; who received the words of life to give unto us. Acts 7:38.

Sing ye to the Lord a new canticle: let his praise be in the church of the saints. Ps. 149:1.

Let the peace of Christ rejoice in your hearts, wherein also you are called in one body; and be ye thankful. Col. 3:15.

Feed the flock of God, which is among you, taking care of it, not by constraint, but willingly, according to God; not for filthy lucre's sake, but voluntarily. Neither as lording it over the clergy, but being made a pattern of the flock from the heart. 1 Pet. 5:2 f.

I am the good shepherd, and I know mine, and mine know me. As the Father knoweth me, and I know the Father; and I lay down my life for my sheep. John 10:14 f.

Take heed to yourselves, and to the whole flock, wherein the Holy Ghost hath placed you bishops, to rule the church of God, which he hath purchased with his own blood. Acts 20:28.

The Lord their God will save them in that day, as the flock of his people; for holy stones shall be lifted up over his land. Zach. 9:16.

You my flocks, the flocks of my pasture are men; and I am the Lord your God, saith the Lord God. Ez. 34:31.

Fear not, little flock, for it hath pleased your Father to give you a kingdom. Luke 12:32.

You, by the power of God, are kept by faith unto salvation, ready to be revealed in the last time. 1 Pet. 1:5.

Thou hast conducted thy people like sheep, by the hand of Moses and Aaron. Ps. 76:21.

They skipped like lambs, praising thee, O Lord, who hadst delivered them. Wis. 19:6.

Give ear, O thou that rulest Israel, thou that leadest Joseph like a sheep. Ps. 79:1.

He took away his own people as sheep, and guided them in the wilderness like a flock. Ps. 77:52.

I am the good shepherd. The good shepherd giveth his life for his sheep. John 10:11.

O God, why hast thou cast us off unto the end; why is thy wrath enkindled against the sheep of thy pasture? Ps. 73:1.

We thy people, and the sheep of thy pasture, will give thanks to thee forever. Ps. 79:13.

Woe to the pastors that destroy and tear the sheep of my pasture, saith the Lord. Jer. 23:1.

Thus saith the Lord God: Behold I myself will seek my sheep, and will visit them. Ez. 34:11.

You do not believe because you are not my sheep. John 10:26.

Jesus saith to him again: Simon son of John, lovest thou me more than these? He saith to him: Yea, Lord, thou knowest that I love thee. He saith to him: Feed my lambs. He said to him the third time: Simon son of John, lovest thou me? Peter was grieved, because he had said to him the third time: lovest thou me? And he said to him: Lord, thou knowest all things; thou knowest that I love thee. He said to him: Feed my sheep. John 21:16 f.

I will strike the shepherd, and the sheep shall be dispersed. Mat. 26:31.

He shall set the sheep on his right hand, but the goats on his left. Mat. 25:33.

He that entereth in by the door is the shepherd of the sheep. John 10:2.

May the God of peace, who brought again from the dead the great Pastor of the sheep, our Lord Jesus Christ, in the blood of the everlasting testament, fit you in all goodness, that you may do his will. Heb. 13:20.

Go ye rather to the lost sheep of the house of Israel. Mat. 10:6.

Jesus answering said: I was not sent but to the sheep that are lost of the house of Israel. Mat. 15:24.

What man of you that hath an hundred sheep; and if he shall lose one of them, doth he not leave the ninety-nine in the desert, and go after that which was lost, until he find it? And coming home call together his friends and neighbors, saying to them: Rejoice with me because I have found my sheep that was lost? Luke 15:4, 6.

All we like sheep have gone astray, every one hath turned aside into his own way; and the Lord hath laid on him the iniquity of us all. Is. 53:6.

My people hath been a lost flock, their shepherds have caused them to go astray, and have made them wander in the mountains; they have gone from mountain to hill, they have forgotten their resting places. Jer. 50:6.

You were as sheep going astray; but you are now converted to the Shepherd and Bishop of your souls. 1 Pet. 2:25.

For thy sake we are killed all the day long; we are counted as sheep for the slaughter. Ps. 43:22.

Behold I send you as sheep in the midst of wolves. Be ye therefore wise as serpents and gentle as doves. Mat. 10:16.

He hath brought me up on the water of refreshment. He hath converted my soul. He hath led me on the paths of justice for his own name's sake. Ps. 22:2 f.

He hath set me in a place of pasture. Ps. 22:2.

He is the Lord our God; and we are the people of his pasture, and the sheep of his hand. Ps. 94:7.

Know ye that the Lord he is God; he made us, and not we ourselves. We are his people and the sheep of his pasture. Ps. 99:3.

He shall feed his flock like a shepherd; he shall gather together the lambs with his arm, and shall take them up in his bosom, and he himself shall carry them that are with young. Is. 40:11.

I will turn my hand to the little ones. Zach. 13:7.

VI

If the first-fruit be holy so is the lump also; and if the root be holy so are the branches. And if some of the branches be broken, and thou, being a wild olive, art ingrafted in them, and art made partaker of the root, and of the fatness of the olive tree, boast not against the branches. But if thou boast, thou bearest not the root, but the root thee. Rom. 11:16-18.

Thy people shall be all just, they shall inherit the land forever, the branch of my planting, the work of my hand to glorify me. Is. 60:21.

Every branch in me, that beareth not fruit, my Father will take away; and every one that beareth fruit, he will purge it, that it may bring forth more fruit. Abide in me, and I in you. As the branch cannot bear fruit of itself, unless it abide in the vine, so neither can you, unless you abide in me. If any one abide not in me, he shall be cast forth as a branch and shall wither, and they shall gather him up, and cast him into the fire, and he burneth. John 15:2, 4, 6.

We cease not to pray for you. That you may walk worthy of God, in all things pleasing; being fruitful in every good work, and increasing in the knowledge of God. Col. 1:9 f.

The fruit of the Spirit is charity, joy, peace, patience, benignity, goodness, longanimity, mildness, faith, modesty, continency, chastity. Against such there is no law. Gal. 5:22 f.

Of his own will hath he begotten us by the word of truth, that we might be some beginning of his creature. Jas. 1:18.

They that are planted in the house of the Lord shall flourish in the courts of the Lord. Ps. 91:14.

Turn again, O God of hosts, look down from heaven, and see, and visit this vineyard; and perfect the same which thy right hand hath planted. Ps. 79:15 f.

Every plant which my heavenly Father hath not planted, shall be rooted up. Mat. 15:13.

He shall be like a tree which is planted near the running waters, which shall bring forth its fruit in due season. Ps. 1:3.

He shall be as a tree that is planted by the waters, that spreadeth out its roots towards moisture, and it shall not fear when the heat cometh. And the leaf thereof shall be green, and in the time of drought it shall not be solicitous, neither shall it cease at any time to bring forth fruit. Jer. 17:8.

They that are planted in the house of the Lord shall flourish in the courts of the house of our God. Ps. 91:14.

If we have been planted together in the likeness of his death, we shall be also in the likeness of his resurrection. Rom. 6:5.

His fan is in his hand, and he will purge his floor, and will gather the wheat into his barn; but the chaff he will burn with unquenchable fire. Luke 3:17.

O my thrashing, and the children of my floor, that which I have heard of the Lord of hosts, the God of Israel, I have declared unto you. Is. 21:10.

We, being many, are one bread, one body, all that partake of one bread. 1 C. 10:17.

Our fathers did eat manna in the desert, as it is written: He gave them bread from heaven to eat John 6:31.

Whilst you have the light, believe in the light, that you may be the children of light. John 12:36.

You were heretofore darkness, but now light in the Lord. Walk then as children of the light. Eph. 5:8.

You are a chosen generation, a kingly priesthood, a holy nation, a purchased people; that you may declare his virtues, who hath called you out of darkness, into his marvellous light. 1 Pet. 2:9.

All you are children of the light, and children of the day: we are not of the night, nor of darkness. 1 Thess. 5:5.

A great sign appeared in heaven: a woman clothed with the sun, and the moon under her feet, and on her head a crown of twelve stars. Apoc. 12:1.

You are the light of the world. A city seated on a mountain cannot be hid. Mat. 5:14.

Do ye all things without hesitation, that you may be blameless and sincere children of God, without reproof, in the midst of a crooked and perverse generation; among whom you shine as lights in the world. Phil. 2:14 f.

So let your light shine before men, that they may see your good works, and glorify your Father who is in heaven. Mat. 5:16.

The path of the just, as a shining light, goeth forwards and increaseth even to perfect day. Prov. 4:18.

We all beholding the glory of the Lord, with open face, and transformed into the same image from glory to glory, as by the Spirit of the Lord. 2 C. 3:18.

He showed me the holy city Jerusalem coming down out of heaven from God; having the glory of God, and the light thereof was like a precious stone, as to the jasper stone, even as crystal. Apoc. 21:10 f.

The parable of the ten virgins. Mat. 25:1-12.

They that are learned shall shine as the brightness of the firmament; and they that instruct many to justice, as stars for all eternity. Dan. 12:3.

One is the glory of the sun, another the glory of the moon, and another the glory of the stars. For star differeth from star in glory. 1 C. 15:41.

The mystery which hath been hidden from ages and generations is now being made manifest to his saints. To whom God would make known the riches of the glory of this mystery among the Gentiles, which is Christ, in you the hope of glory. Col. 1:27.

The Holy Ghost, he hath poured forth upon us abundantly, through Jesus Christ our Savior. That being justified by his grace, we may be heirs, according to hope of life everlasting. Titus 3:27.

Blessed be the God and Father of our Lord Jesus Christ, who according to his great mercy hath regenerated us unto a lively hope by the resurrection of Jesus Christ from the dead. 1 Pet. 1:3.

One body, and one Spirit, as you are called in one hope of your calling. Eph. 4:4.

The creature also itself shall be delivered from the servitude of corruption, into the liberty of the glory of the children of God. Rom. 8:21.

Rejoicing in hope. Patient in tribulation. Instant in prayer. Rom. 12:12.

By him we have access through faith unto this grace, wherein we stand, and glory in the hope of the glory of the sons of God. Rom. 5:2.

Hope confoundeth not; because the charity of God is poured forth in our hearts, by the Holy Ghost, who is given to us. Rom. 5:5.

Blessed are they that dwell in thy house, O Lord; they shall praise thee forever and ever. Ps. 83:5.

Be strengthened in the Lord, and in the might of his power. Eph. 6:10.

Behold, God is my Savior, I will deal confidently, and will not fear: because the Lord is my strength, and my praise, and he is become my salvation. Is. 12:2.

As I live, saith the Lord: every knee shall bow to me, and every tongue shall confess to God. Is. 45:24.

The Lord is my strength and my praise, and he is become my salvation. Ps. 117:14.

I will love thee, O Lord, my strength. Ps. 17:2.

The Lord is my helper, and my protection: in him hath my heart confided, and I have been helped. Ps. 27:7.

God hath girded me with strength, and made my way perfect. 2 K. 22:33.

I write unto you, babes, because you have known the Father. I write unto you, young men, because you are strong, and the word of God abideth in you, and you have overcome the wicked one. 1 John 2:14.

He said to me: My grace is sufficient for thee: for power is made perfect in infirmity. Gladly therefore will I glory in my infirmities, that the power of Christ may dwell in me. For which cause I please myself in my infirmities, in reproaches, in necessities, in persecutions, in distresses, for Christ. For when I am weak, then I am powerful. 2 C. 12:9 f.

Time would fail me to tell of those who by faith have conquered kingdoms, wrought justice, obtained promises, stopped the mouths of lions, quenched the violence of fire, escaped the edge of the sword, recovered strength from weakness, became valiant in battle, put to flight the armies of foreigners. Heb. 11:33 f.

His shoe shall be iron and brass. As the days of thy youth, so also shall thy old age be. There is no other God like the God of the righteous: He that is mounted upon the heavens is thy helper. By his magnificence the clouds run hither and thither. His dwelling is above, and underneath are the everlasting arms; he shall cast out the enemy from before thee, and shall say: Be thou brought to nought. Deut. 33:25-27.

God interposed an oath, that by two immutable things, in which it is impossible for God to lie, we may have the strongest comfort, who have fled for refuge to hold fast the hope set before us. Heb. 6:17 f.

I am forgotten as one dead from the heart. But I have put my trust in thee, O Lord; I said: Thou art my God. Ps. 30:13, 15.

Our God is our refuge and strength, a helper in troubles, which have found us exceedingly. Ps. 45:1.

The Lord is my light and my salvation, whom shall I fear? Ps. 26:1.

Be thou, O my soul, subject to God; for from him is my patience. For he is my God and my Savior: He is my helper, I shall not be moved. In God is my salvation and my glory; he is the God of my help, and my hope is in him. Ps. 61:6-8.

VII

We are God's coadjutors; you are God's husbandry; you are God's building. 1 C. 3:9.

Built upon the foundation of the apostles and prophets, Jesus Christ himself being the chief cornerstone. Eph. 2:20.

In him all the building, being framed together, groweth up into an holy temple in the Lord. In him you are built together, into an habitation of God in the Spirit. Eph. 21:22.

Walk ye in him, rooted and built up in him, and confirmed in the faith, as also you have learned, abounding in him in thanksgiving. Col. 2:7.

Iniquity shall no more be heard in thy land, wasting nor destruction in thy borders, and salvation shall possess thy walls, and praise thy gates. Is. 60:18.

In that day shall this canticle be sung in the land of Juda. Sion the city of our strength a Savior, a wall and a bulwark shall be set therein. Is. 26:1.

It had a wall great and high, having twelve gates, and in the gates twelve angels, and names written thereon, which are the names of the twelve tribes of the children of Israel. Apoc. 21:12.

Be you as living stones built up, a spiritual house, a holy priesthood, to offer up spiritual sacrifices, acceptable to God by Jesus Christ. 1 Pet. 2:5.

Know how thou oughtest to behave thyself in the house of God, which is the church of the living God, the pillar and ground of truth. 1 Tim. 3:15.

You are no more strangers and foreigners; but you are fellow citizens with the saints, and domestics of God. Eph. 2:19.

Our conversation is in heaven, from whence also we look for the Savior, our Lord Jesus Christ, who will reform the body of our lowness, made like to the body of his glory, according to the operation whereby also he is able to subdue all things unto himself. Phil. 3:20 f.

If any man violate the temple of God, him will God destroy. For the temple of God is holy, which you are. 1 C. 3:17.

Know you not, that you are the temple of God, and that the Spirit of God dwelleth in you? 1 C. 3:16.

Know you not, that your members are the temple of the Holy Ghost, who is in you, whom you have from God; and you are not your own? 1 C. 6:19.

In him you are built together, into an habitation of God in the Spirit. Eph. 2:22.

Be you as living stones built up, a spiritual house, a holy priesthood, to offer up spiritual exercises, acceptable to God by Jesus Christ. 1 Pet. 2:5.

He hath made us a kingdom, and priests to God and his Father, to him be glory and empire forever. Amen. Apoc. 1:6.

Thou, O Lord, hath made us to our God a kingdom and priests, and we shall reign on the earth. Apoc. 5:10.

Blessed and holy is he that hath part in the first resurrection. In these the second death hath no power: but they shall be priests of God and of Christ, and shall reign with him a thousand years. Apoc. 20:6.

You are a chosen generation, a kingly priesthood, a holy nation, a purchased people; that you may declare his virtues, who hath called you out of darkness into his marvellous light. 2 Pet. 2:9.

The Lord's portion is his people, Jacob the lot of his inheritance. Deut. 32:9.

I cease not [to pray that the God of our Lord Jesus Christ, the Father of glory, may enlighten the eyes of your heart] that you may know what the hope is of his calling, and what are the riches of the glory of his inheritance in the saints. Eph. 1:18.

I beseech you, brethren, by the mercy of God, that you present your bodies a living sacrifice, holy, pleasing unto God, your reasonable service. Rom. 12:1.

The law having a shadow of the good things to come, not the very image of the things; by the selfsame sacrifices which they offer continually every year, can never make the comers thereunto perfect: for then they would have ceased to be offered; because the worshippers once cleansed should have no conscience of sin any longer. Heb. 10:1 f.

The hour cometh and now is when the true adorers shall adore the Father in spirit and in truth. For the Father seeketh such to adore him. John 4:23.

VIII

Unless those days had been shortened, no flesh should be saved; but for the sake of the elect those days shall be shortened. Mat. 24:22.

According to the foreknowledge of God the Father, unto the sanctification of the Spirit, unto obedience and sprinkling of the blood of Jesus Christ: grace unto you and peace be multiplied. 1 Pet. 1:2.

Unless the Lord had shortened the days, no flesh should be saved; but for the sake of the elect which he hath chosen, he hath shortened the days. Mark 13:20.

He shall send his angels, and shall gather together his elect from the four winds, from the uttermost part of the earth to the uttermost part of heaven. Mark 13:27.

For the sake of my servant Jacob, and Israel my elect, I have even called thee by thy name; I have made a likeness of thee, and thou hast not known me. Is. 45:4.

I will bring forth a seed out of Jacob, and out of Juda, a possessor of my mountains; and my elect shall inherit it, and my servants shall dwell there. Is. 65:9.

They shall not build, and another inhabit; they shall not plant, and another eat; for as the days of a tree, so shall be the days of my people, and the works of their hands shall be of long continuance. Is. 65:22.

Will not God revenge his elect, who cry to him day and night; and will he have patience in their regard? Luke 18:7.

If you had been of the world, the world would love its own; but because you are not of the world, but I have chosen you out of the world, therefore the world hateth you. John 15:19.

You are a chosen generation. 1 Pet. 2:9.

Now I am not in the world, and these are in the world, and I come to thee. Holy Father, keep them in thy name whom thou hast given me; that they may be one, as we also are. John 17:11.

While I was with them, I kept them in thy name. Those whom thou gavest me have I kept; and none of them is lost, but the son of perdition, that the Scripture may be fulfilled. John 17:12.

Who shall accuse against the elect of God? God that justifieth. Rom. 8:33.

Paul, a servant of God, and an apostle of Jesus Christ, according to the faith of the elect of God, and the acknowledging of the truth, which is according to godliness. Titus 1:1.

Put ye on as the elect of God, holy, and beloved, the bowels of mercy, benignity, humility, modesty, patience. Col. 3:12.

When the children were not yet born, nor had done any good or evil (that the purpose of God according to election might stand), it was said to her [Rebecca]: The elder shall serve the younger. Rom. 9:11 f.

Even so at this present time also, there is a remnant saved according to the election of grace. Rom. 11:5.

These shall fight with the Lamb, and the Lamb shall overcome them, because he is Lord of lords, and King of kings, and they that are with him are called, and elect, and faithful. Apoc. 17:14.

To all that are at Rome, the beloved of God, called to be saints. Grace to you, and peace from God our Father, and from the Lord Jesus Christ. Rom. 1:7.

To the church of God that is at Corinth, to them that are sanctified in Christ Jesus, called to be saints, with all that invoke the name of our Lord Jesus Christ, in every place of theirs and ours. Grace to you, and peace from God our Father and from the Lord Jesus Christ. 1 C. 1:2 f.

We know that to them that love God, all things work together unto good, to such as, according to his purpose, are called to be saints. Rom. 8:28.

All things of his divine power which appertain to life and godliness, are given us, through the knowledge of him who hath called us by his own proper glory and virtue. 2 Pet. 1:3.

The Lord delayeth not his promise, as some imagine, but dealeth patiently for your sake, not willing that any should perish, but that all should return to penance. 1 Pet. 3:9.

The Lord knoweth how to deliver the godly from temptation, but to reserve the unjust unto the day of judgment to be tormented. 1 Pet. 2:9.

You, brethren, have been called unto liberty: only make not liberty an occasion to the flesh, but by charity of the Spirit serve one another. Gal. 5:13.

God is faithful; by whom you are called unto the fellowship of his Son Jesus Christ our Lord. 1 C. 1:9.

By him we have received grace and apostleship for obedience to the faith in all nations for his name. Among whom are you also the called of Jesus Christ. Rom. 1:5 f.

He is faithful who hath called you, who also will do it. 1 Thess. 5:24.

Whom he predestinated, them he also called. And whom he called, them he also justified. And whom he justified, them he also glorified. Rom. 8:30.

Hearken to me, O Jacob, and thou Israel whom I call; I am he, I am the First, and I am the Last. Is. 48:12.

God hath not cast away his people, which he foreknew. Know you not what the Scripture saith of Elias, how he calleth on God against Israel? Rom. 11:2.

That which Israel sought, he hath not obtained; but the election hath obtained it; and the rest have been blinded. Rom. 11:7.

Blessed are they that dwell in thy house, O Lord: they shall praise thee forever and ever. Ps. 83:5.

Hast thou not dried up the sea, the water of the mighty deep, who madest the depth of the sea a way, that the delivered might pass through? And now they that are redeemed by the Lord shall return, and shall come into Sion, singing praises, and joy everlasting shall be upon their heads, they shall obtain joy and gladness, sorrow and mourning shall flee away. Is. 51:10 f.

Blessed are the poor in spirit: for theirs is the kingdom of heaven. Blessed are the meek: for they shall possess the land. Blessed are they that mourn: for they shall be comforted. Blessed are they that hunger and thirst after justice: for they shall have their fill. Blessed are the merciful: for they shall obtain mercy. Blessed are the clean of heart: for they shall see God. Blessed are the peacemakers: for they shall be called the children of God. Blessed are they that suffer persecution for justice' sake: for theirs is the kingdom of heaven. Blessed are ye when they shall revile you, and persecute you, and speak all that is evil against you, untruly, for my sake. Mat. 5:3-11.

Blessed be you of the Lord who made heaven and earth. Ps. 113:15.

Then shall the King say to them that shall be on his right hand: Come, ye blessed of my Father, possess you the kingdom prepared for you from the foundation of the world. Mat. 25:34.

Blessed are they whose iniquities are forgiven, and whose sins are covered. Blessed is the man to whom the Lord hath not imputed sin, and in whose spirit there is no guile. Ps. 31:1 f.

Blessed is he that shall not be scandalized in me. Mat. 11:6.

Jesus saith to him: Because thou hast seen me, Thomas, thou hast believed; blessed are they that have not seen, and have believed. John 20:29.

Blessed are they who hear the word of God, and keep it. Luke 11:28.

Blessed be the God and Father of our Lord Jesus Christ, who hath blessed us with spiritual blessings in heavenly places in Christ. Eph. 1:3.

When thou makest a feast, call the poor, the maimed, the lame, and the blind. And thou shalt be blessed, because they have not wherewith to make thee recompense; for recompense shall be made to thee at the resurrection of the just. When one of them that sat at table with him had heard these things, he said to him: Blessed is he that shall eat bread in the kingdom of God. Luke 14:13-15.

He that hath looked into the perfect law of liberty, and hath continued therein, not becoming a forgetful hearer, but a doer of the work; this man shall be blessed in his deed. Religion clean and undefiled before God and the Father, is this: to visit the fatherless and widows in their tribulation; and to keep ourself unspotted from this world. Jas. 1:25, 27.

Blessed is that servant, whom when his Lord shall come he shall find so doing. Mat. 24:46.

They that are of faith, shall be blessed with faithful Abraham. Gal. 3:9.

Blessed is the man that endureth temptation; for when he hath been proved, he shall receive the crown of life, which God hath promised to them that love him. Jas. 1:12.

I heard a voice from heaven, saying to me: Write; Blessed are the dead, who die in the Lord. From henceforth now, saith the Spirit, that they may rest from their labors, for their works follow them. Apoc. 14:13.

He said to me: Write: Blessed are they that are called to the marriage supper of the Lamb. And he saith to me: These words of God are true. Apoc. 19:9.

Blessed and holy is he that hath part in the first resurrection. In these the second death hath no power; but they shall be priests of God and of Christ; and shall reign with him a thousand years: Apoc. 20:6.

Thou hast begun to bless the house of thy servant that it may be always before thee; for seeing thou blessest it, O Lord, it shall be blessed forever. 1 Pet. 17:27.

IX

The Gentiles shall see thy just one, and all kings thy glorious one, and thou shalt be called by a new name, which the mouth of the Lord shall name. Is. 62:2.

Light is risen to the just, and joy to the right of heart. Ps. 96:11.

Do good, O Lord, to those that are good, and to the upright of heart. Ps. 124:4.

He that is mocked by his friends as I, shall call upon God and he will hear him, for the simplicity of the just man is laughed to scorn. Job 12:4.

My just man liveth by faith; but if he withdraw himself, he shall not please my soul. Heb. 10:38.

To the saints and faithful brethren in Christ Jesus who are at Colossae: Grace be to you and peace from God. Col. 1:2 f.

Paul, an apostle of Jesus Christ by the will of God, to the faithful in Christ Jesus. Grace be to you and peace. Eph. 1:1.

His Lord said to him: Well done, good and faithful servant, because thou hast been faithful over a few things, I will place thee over many things: enter thou into the joy of thy Lord. Mat. 25:21.

You are come to Mount Sion, and to the church of the first-born, who are written in the heavens, and to God the judge of all, and to the spirits of the just made perfect. Heb. 12:23.

X

I commend you to God and to the word of his grace, who is able to build up, and to give an inheritance among all the sanctified. Acts 20:32.

By one obligation he hath perfected forever them that are sanctified. Heb. 10:14.

Both he that sanctifieth, and they who are sanctified, are all of one. For which cause he is not ashamed to call them brethren. Heb. 2:11.

Then said I, Behold I come to do thy will, O God. In the which will we are sanctified by the oblation of the body of Jesus Christ once. Heb. 10:9 f.

Paul . . . to the church of God that is at Corinth, to them that are sanctified in Christ Jesus, called to be saints, with all that invoke the name of our Lord Jesus Christ, in every place of theirs and ours. 1 C. 1:2 f.

I have written to you, brethren, because of the grace which is given me from God: that I should be the minister of Christ Jesus among the Gentiles: sanctifying the gospel of God, that the oblation of the Gentiles may be made acceptable and sanctified in the Holy Ghost. Rom. 15:15 f.

To this end have I appeared to thee, that I may make thee a minister of those things which thou hast seen, delivering thee from the people, and from the nations to which I now send thee, to open their eyes, that they may be converted from darkness to light, and from the power of Satan to

God, that they may receive forgiveness of sins, and a lot among the saints by the faith that is in me. Acts 26: 16-18.

Jude the servant of Jesus Christ, and brother of James: to them that are beloved in God the Father, and preserved in Jesus Christ. Jude 1.

For them do I sanctify myself: that they also may be sanctified in truth. John 17: 19.

How much more do you think he deserveth worse punishments, who hath trodden under foot the Son of God, and hath esteemed the blood of the testament unclean, by which he was sanctified, and hath offered an affront to the Spirit of grace? Heb. 10: 29.

But you are washed, but you are sanctified, but you are justified in the name of our Lord Jesus Christ, and the Spirit of our God. 1 C. 8: 11.

If any man shall cleanse himself from these, he shall be a vessel unto honor, sanctified and profitable to the Lord, prepared unto every good work. 2 Tim. 2: 21.

He chose us in him before the foundation of the world, that we should be holy and unspotted in his sight in charity. Eph. 1: 4.

They shall call them: The holy people, the redeemed of the Lord. Is. 62: 12.

Brethren, if a man be overtaken in any fault, you, who are spiritual, instruct such a one in the spirit of meekness, considering thyself, lest thou also be tempted. Gal. 6: 1.

[Look] for the blessed hope and coming of the glory of the great God and our Savior Jesus Christ, who gave himself for us, that he might redeem us from all iniquity, and might cleanse to himself a people acceptable, a pursuer of good works. Titus 2: 13 f.

I have said to the Lord, Thou art my God, for thou hast no need of my goods. To the saints, who are in his land, he hath made wonderful all my desires in them. Ps. 15: 2 f.

Prophecy came not by the will of man at any time: but the holy men of God spoke, inspired by the Holy Ghost. 2 Pet. 1: 21.

Sing ye to the Lord a new canticle: let his praise be in the church of his saints. Ps. 149: 1.

Communicating to the necessities of the saints. Pursuing hospitality. Rom. 12: 13.

It hath pleased them of Macedonia and Achaia to make a contribution for the poor of the saints that are in Jerusalem. Rom. 15: 26.

I beseech you, brethren, that you help me in your prayers for me to God, that I may be delivered from the unbelievers that are in Judea, and that the oblation of my service may be acceptable in Jerusalem to the saints. Rom. 15: 30 f.

Paul an apostle of Jesus Christ. To the saints and faithful brethren in Christ Jesus who are at Colossa. Col. 1: 1 f.

I give thanks to my God, hearing of thy charity and faith which thou hast in the Lord Jesus, and towards all the saints. Philem. 4: 5.

There was given to him much incense, that he should offer of the prayers of all saints upon the golden altar, which is before the throne of God. Apoc. 8: 3.

To me, the least of all the saints, is given this grace, to preach among the Gentiles the unsearchable riches of Christ. Eph. 3: 8.

I pray that you may be able to comprehend, with all the saints, what is the breadth, and length, and height, and depth [of] the charity of Christ. Eph. 3: 18.

Fornication and all uncleanness, or covetousness, let it not so much as be named among you, as becometh saints. Eph. 5: 3.

Paul and Timothy, the servants of Jesus Christ; to all the saints in Christ Jesus, who are at Philippi, with the bishops and deacons. Phil. 1: 1.

The heavens shall confess thy wonder, O Lord; and thy truth in the church of the saints. Ps. 88:6.

God is glorified in the assembly of the saints: great and terrible above all them that are about him. Ps. 88:8.

The saints shall rejoice in glory: they shall be joyful in their beds. Ps. 149:5.

I beheld, and lo, that horn made war against the saints, and prevailed over them. Dan. 7:21.

The graves were opened: many bodies of the saints that had slept arose. Mat. 27:52.

It came to pass, that Peter, as he passed through visiting all, came to the saints who dwelt at Lydda. Acts 9:32.

Giving her [Tabitha] his hand, he lifted her up. And when he had called the saints and the widows, he presented her alive. Acts 9:41.

Indeed I did formerly think that I ought to do many things contrary to the name of Jesus of Nazareth. Which also I did at Jerusalem, and many of the saints did I shut up in prison. Acts 26:9 f.

We give thanks to God, hearing your faith in Christ Jesus, and the love which you have towards all the saints. Col. 1:3 f.

Let a widow be chosen, having testimony for her good works, if she have brought up children, if she have received to harbor, if she have washed the saints' feet. 1 Tim. 5:9 f.

I have had great joy and consolation in thy charity, because the bowels of the saints have been refreshed by thee, brother. Philem. 7.

God is not unjust, that he should forget your work and the love which you have shown in his name, you who have ministered, and do minister to the saints. Heb. 6:10.

I was under a necessity to write unto you: to beseech you to contend earnestly for the faith once delivered to the saints. Jude 3.

The smoke of the incense of the prayers of the saints ascended up before God, from the hand of the angel. Apoc. 8:4.

It was given unto him to make war with the saints, and to overcome them. Apoc. 13:7.

He that shall kill by the sword, must be killed by the sword. Here is the patience and the faith of the saints. Apoc. 13:10.

Here is the patience of the saints, who keep the commandments of God, and the faith of Jesus. Apoc. 14:13.

They have shed the blood of saints and prophets, and thou hast given them blood to drink: for they are worthy. Apoc. 16:6.

I saw the woman drunk with the blood of the saints, and with the blood of the martyrs of Jesus Apoc. 17:6.

In her was found the blood of saints, and of all that were slain upon the earth. Apoc. 18:24.

It is granted to her that she should clothe herself with fine linen glittering and white. For the fine linen are the justifications of saints. Apoc. 19:8.

They came upon the breadth of the earth, and encompassed the camp of the saints, and the beloved city. Apoc. 20:8.

Concerning the ministry, that is done towards the saints, it is superfluous for me to write unto you. 2 C. 9:1.

The administration of this office doth not only supply the wants of the saints, but aboundeth also by many thanksgivings in the Lord. 2 C. 9:12.

Salute one another with a holy kiss. All the saints salute you. 2 C. 13:12.

The brethren who are with me salute you. All the saints salute you: especially they that are of Caesar's household. Phil. 4:22.

Paul an apostle of Jesus Christ by the will of God, to all the saints who are at Ephesus, and to the faithful in Christ Jesus. Grace be to you and peace from God the Father, and from the Lord Jesus Christ. Eph. 1:1 f.

I also hearing of your faith that is in the Lord Jesus, and of your love towards all the saints; cease not to give thanks for you. Eph. 1:15.

You are no more strangers and foreigners: but you are fellow citizens with the saints and the domestics of God. Eph. 2:19.

He gave some apostles and other some pastors and doctors. For the perfecting of the saints, for the work of the ministry, for the edifying of the body of Christ. Eph. 4:11 f.

He that searcheth the hearts, knoweth what the Spirit desireth: because he asketh for the saints according to God. Rom. 8:27.

I shall go to Jerusalem, to minister unto the saints. Rom. 15:25.

Salute Philologus and Julia, Nereus and his sister, and Olympias; and all the saints that are with them. Rom. 16:15.

Salute all your prelates, and all the saints. Heb. 13:24.

Dare any of you, having a matter against another, go to be judged, before the unjust, and not before the saints? 1 C. 8:1.

Know you not that the saints shall judge this world? 1 C. 6:2.

Let thy priests, O Lord God, put on salvation, and thy saints rejoice in good things. 2 Par. 6:41.

I will wait on thy name, for it is good in the sight of thy saints. Ps. 15:11.

Let thy priests be clothed with justice: and let thy saints rejoice. Ps. 131:9.

Let all thy works, O Lord, praise thee: and let thy saints bless thee. Ps. 144:9.

Ananias answered: Lord, I have heard by many of this man, how much evil he hath done to thy saints in Jerusalem. Acts 9:13.

He will keep the feet of his saints, and the wicked shall be silent in darkness, because no man shall prevail by his own strength. 1 K. 2:9.

Behold among his saints none is unchangeable, and the heavens are not pure in his sight. Job 15:15.

O love the Lord, all ye his saints: for the Lord will require truth, and will repay them abundantly that act proudly. Ps. 30:24.

The Lord loveth judgment, and will not forsake his saints: they shall be preserved forever. Ps. 36:28.

You that love the Lord, hate evil: the Lord preserveth the souls of his saints. Ps. 96:10.

Precious in the sight of the Lord, is the death of his saints. Ps. 115:15.

A hymn to all his saints: to the children of Israel, a people approaching to him. Ps. 148:14.

This glory is to all his saints. Ps. 149:9.

The Lord will protect them that walk in simplicity. Keeping the paths of justice, and guarding the ways of saints. Prov. 2:7 f.

The mystery which hath been hidden from ages and generations, now is manifested to his saints. Col. 1:26.

May the Lord make you abound in charity towards one another, to confirm your hearts without blame, in holiness, before God and our Father, at the coming of our Lord Jesus Christ with all his saints. 1 Thess. 3:12 f.

To you who are troubled, rest with us when the Lord Jesus shall be revealed from heaven with the angels of his power, when he shall come to be glorified in his saints, and to be made wonderful in all them who have believed: because our testimony was believed upon you in that day. 2 Thess. 1:7, 10.

Enoch, the seventh from Adam, prophesied, saying: Behold the Lord cometh with thousands of his saints. Jude 14.

The saints of the most high God shall take the kingdom: and they shall possess the kingdom forever and ever. Dan. 7:18.

I beheld, and lo, that horn made war against the saints, and prevailed over them, till the Ancient of days came and gave judgment to the saints of the Most High, and the time came, and the saints obtained the kingdom. Dan. 7:21 f.

Another [king] shall rise up after them. And he shall speak words against the High One, and shall crush the saints of the Most High. Dan. 7:24 f.

Judgment shall sit, that his power may be taken away. And that the kingdom, and power, and the greatness of the kingdom, under the whole heaven, may be given to the people of the saints of the Most High: whose kingdom is an everlasting kingdom, and all kings shall serve him, and shall obey him. Dan. 7:26 f.

Gather ye together his saints to him: who set his covenant before sacrifices. Ps. 49:5.

Sing to the Lord, O you his saints: and give praise to the memory of his holiness. Ps. 29:5.

Giving thanks to God the Father, who hath made us worthy to be partakers of the lot of the saints in light. Col. 1:12.

To him who is able to preserve you without sin, and to present you spotless before the presence of his glory with exceeding joy in the coming of our Lord Jesus Christ, be glory and magnificence. Jude 24.

XI

You are come to Mount Sion. And to the church of the first-born, who are written in the heavens, and to God the Judge of all, and to the spirits of the just made perfect. Heb. 12:22 f.

I will declare thy name to my brethren: in the midst of the church I will praise thee. Heb. 2:12.

He answering him that told him, said: Who is my mother, and who are my brethren? And stretching forth his hand towards his disciples, he said: Behold my mother and my brethren. Mat. 12:48 f.

Answering them, he said: Who is my mother and my brethren? And looking round about on them who sat about him, he saith: Behold my mother and my brethren. Mark 3:33 f.

The King answering, shall say to them: Amen I say to you, as long as you did it to one of these my least brethren, you did it to me. Mat. 25:40.

Jesus saith to them: Fear not. Go, tell my brethren that they go into Galilee, there they shall see me. Mat. 28:10.

My mother and my brethren, are they who hear the word of God, and do it. Luke 8:21.

Jesus saith to her: Do not touch me, for I am not yet ascended to my Father: but go to my brethren, and say to them: I ascend to my Father and to your Father, to my God and to your God. John 20:17.

It behoved him in all things to be made like unto his brethren, that he might become a merciful and faithful high priest before God, that he might be a propitiation for the sins of the people. Heb. 2:17.

I bow my knees to the Father of our Lord Jesus Christ. Of whom all paternity in heaven and earth is named. Eph. 3:14 f.

Whosoever shall follow this rule, peace on them, and mercy, and upon the Israel of God. Gal. 6:16.

They are equal to the angels, and are the children of God, being the children of the resurrection. Luke 20:36.

Blessed be the God and Father of our Lord Jesus Christ, who according to his great mercy hath regenerated us unto a lively hope, by the resurrection of Jesus Christ from the dead. 1 Pet. 1:3.

He hath subjected all things under his feet: and hath made him head over all the church, which is his body, and the fulness of him, who is filled all in all. Eph. 1:22 f.

He gave some apostles and other some pastors and doctors: for the perfecting of the saints, for the work of the ministry, for the edifying of the body of Christ. Eph. 4:12.

I, Paul, am made a minister, who now rejoice in my sufferings for you. and fill up those things that are wanting of the sufferings of Christ, in my flesh for his body, which is the church. Col. 1:23 f.

You are the body of Christ, and members of member. 1 C. 12:27.

[Be] careful to keep the unity of the Spirit in the bond of peace. One body and one Spirit: as you are called in one hope of your calling. Eph. 4:4.

No man ever hated his own flesh: but nourisheth and cherisheth it, as also Christ doth the church: because we are members of his body, of his flesh, and of his bones. Eph. 5:29 f.

In one Spirit were we all baptized into one body, whether Jews, or Gentiles, whether bond, or free: and in one Spirit we have all been made to drink. 1 C. 12:13.

Know you not, that your bodies are the members of Christ? Shall I then take the members of Christ, and make them the members of an harlot? God forbid. 1 C. 6:15.

You are filled in him, who is the head of all principality and power. Col. 2:10.

Labor as a good soldier of Christ Jesus. 2 Tim. 2:3.

No man, being a soldier to God, entangleth himself with secular businesses: that he may please him to whom he hath engaged himself. 2 Tim. 2:4.

This precept I commend to thee, O son Timothy: according to the prophecies going on before thee, that thou war in them a good warfare. 1 Tim. 1:18.

Though we walk in the flesh, we do not war according to the flesh. 2 C. 10:3.

Fight the good fight of faith: lay hold on eternal life, whereunto thou art called, and hast confessed a good confession before many witnesses. 1 Tim. 6:12.

I say to you: Refrain from these men, and let them alone: for if this counsel or this work be of men, it will come to nought. But if it be of God, ye cannot overthrow it; lest perhaps you be found even to fight against God. Acts 5:38 f.

Some of the Pharisees rising up, strove, saying: We find no evil in this man. What if a spirit hath spoken to him, or an angel? Acts 23:9.

At that time shall Michael rise up, the great prince, who standeth for the children of thy people: and a time shall come such as never was from the time that nations began even until that time. And at that time shall thy people be saved, every one that shall be found written in the book. Dan. 12:1.

Put you on the armor of God, that you may be able to stand against the deceits of the devil. For our wrestling is not against flesh and blood: but against principalities and powers, against the rulers of the world of this darkness, against the spirits of wickedness in the high places. Therefore take unto you the armor of God, that you may be able to resist in the evil day, and to stand in all things perfect. Stand therefore, having your loins girt about with truth, and having on the breastplate of justice, and your feet shod with the preparation of the gospel of peace: in all things taking the shield of faith, wherewith you may be able to extinguish all the fiery darts of the most wicked one. And take unto you the helmet of salvation: and the sword of the Spirit (which is the word of God). Eph. 6:11-17.

Let us, who are of the day, be sober, having on the breastplate of faith and charity, and for a helmet, the hope of salvation. 1 Thess. 5:8.

Let us run by patience to the fight proposed to us: looking on Jesus, the Author and Finisher of faith, who having joy set before him, endured the cross, despising the shame, and now sitteth on the right hand of the throne of God. Heb. 12:1 f.

I so run, not as at an uncertainty; I so fight not as one beating the air: but I chastise my body, and bring it into subjection. 1 C. 9:26 f.

Jesus was led by the Spirit into

the desert, to be tempted by the devil. Mat. 4:1.

In all these things we overcome because of him that hath loved us. Rom. 8:37.

Thanks be to God, who hath given us the victory through our Lord Jesus Christ. 1 C. 15:57.

XII

Jesus Christ who is the faithful witness, who hath washed us from our sins in his own blood, and hath made us a kingdom and priests to God and his Father, to him be glory and empire forever and ever. Amen. Apoc. 1:5 f.

Thou hast made us to our God a kingdom and priests, and we shall reign on the earth. Apoc. 5:10.

We cease not to pray for you, giving thanks to God the Father, who hath delivered us from the power of darkness, and hath translated us into the kingdom of the Son of his love. Col. 1:9, 13.

The children of the kingdom shall be cast out into the exterior darkness; there shall be weeping and gnashing of teeth. Mat. 8:12.

The field is the world. And the good seed are the children of the kingdom. Mat. 13:38.

Fear not, little flock, for it hath pleased your Father to give you a kingdom. Luke 12:32.

Hearken, my dearest brethren: hath not God chosen the poor in this world, rich in faith, and heirs of the kingdom which God hath promised to them that love him? Jas. 2:5.

We ourselves also glory in you for your patience, and faith, and in all your persecutions, and tribulations which you endure, for an example of the just judgment of God, that you may be counted worthy of the kingdom of God, for which also you suffer. 2 Thess. 1:4 f.

We testified to every one of you that you would walk worthy of God, who hath called you unto his kingdom and glory. 1 Thess. 2:12.

It came to pass afterwards, that he travelled through the cities and towns, preaching and evangelizing the kingdom of God; and the twelve with him. Luke 8:1.

He sent them to preach the kingdom of God, and to heal the sick. Luke 9:2.

He said to them: To you it is given to know the mystery of the kingdom of God: but to them that are without, all things are done in parables. Mark 4:11.

Jesus answered and said to him: Amen, amen I say to thee, unless a man be born again, he cannot see the kingdom of God. Nicodemus saith to him: How can a man be born when he is old? can he enter a second time into his mother's womb, and be born again? Jesus answered: Amen, amen I say to thee, unless a man be born again of water and the Holy Ghost, he cannot enter into the kingdom of God. John 3:3-5.

Not every one that saith to me, Lord, Lord, shall enter into the kingdom of heaven: but he that doth the will of my Father who is in heaven, he shall enter into the kingdom of heaven. Mat. 7:21.

Grace to you, and peace from God our Father, and from the Lord Jesus Christ. 1 C. 1:3.

The peace of God which surpasseth all understanding, keep your hearts and minds in Christ Jesus. Phil. 4:7.

The God of hope fill you with all joy and peace in believing; that you may abound in hope, and in the power of the Holy Ghost. Rom. 15:13.

The God of peace be with you all. Amen. Rom. 15:33.

The fruit of the Spirit is charity, joy, peace, patience, benignity, goodness, longanimity, mildness, faith, modesty, continency, chastity. Against such there is no law. Gal. 5:22 f.

Grace be unto you and peace from him that is, and that was, and that is to come, and from the seven spirits which are before his throne. Apoc. 1:4.

Being justified by faith, let us have peace with God through our Lord Jesus Christ. Rom. 5:1.

These things I have spoken to you, that in me you may have peace. In the world you shall have distress: but have confidence, I have overcome the world. John 16:31.

Peace I leave with you, my peace I give unto you: not as the world giveth, do I give unto you. Let not your heart be troubled, nor let it be afraid. John 14:21.

If the unbeliever depart, let him depart. For a brother or sister is not under servitude in such cases. But God hath called us in peace. 1 C. 7:15.

The God of all grace, who hath called us unto his eternal glory in Christ Jesus, after you have suffered a little, will himself perfect you, and confirm you, and establish you. 1 Pet. 5:10.

The grace of God our Savior hath appeared to all men, instructing us that we should live godly in this world. Looking for the blessed hope and coming of the glory of the great God and our Savior Jesus Christ. Titus 2:11-13.

The Spirit himself giveth testimony to our spirit, that we are the sons of God. And if sons, heirs also: heirs indeed of God, and joint heirs with Christ: yet so if we suffer with him, that we may be also glorified with him. Rom. 8:16 f.

When Christ shall appear, who is your life: then you also shall appear with him in glory. Col. 3:4.

The mystery is Christ, in you the hope of glory. Col. 1:27.

He shall come to be glorified in his saints, and to be made wonderful in all them who have believed. 2 Thess. 1:10.

Whom he predestinated: them he also called. And whom he called: them he also justified. And whom he justified: them he also glorified. Rom. 8:30.

God loveth mercy and truth: the Lord will give grace and glory. Ps. 83:12.

Being justified by faith, let us have peace with God through our Lord Jesus Christ. By whom also we have access through faith into this grace, wherein we stand, and glory in the hope of the glory of the sons of God. Rom. 5:1 f.

I am myself also a witness of the sufferings of Christ: as also a partaker of that glory which is to be revealed in time to come. 1 Pet. 5:1.

To him be glory in the church and in Christ Jesus unto all generations, world without end. Amen. Eph. 3:21.

Know you not that the saints shall judge this world? And if the world shall be judged by you, are you unworthy to judge the smallest matters? Know you not that we shall judge angels? How much more things of this world? 1 C. 6:2 f.

Jesus said to them: Amen I say to you, that you who have followed me in the regeneration, when the Son of man shall sit on the seat of his majesty: you also shall sit on twelve seats, judging the twelve tribes of Israel. Mat. 19:28.

I dispose to you, as my Father hath disposed to me, a kingdom: that you may eat and drink at my table in my kingdom: and may sit upon thrones judging the twelve tribes of Israel. Luke 22:29 f.

But thou, why judgest thou thy brother? or thou, why dost thou despise thy brother? For we shall all stand before the judgment seat of Christ. Rom. 14:10.

We must all be manifested before the judgment seat of Christ, that every one may receive the proper things of the body, according as he hath done, whether it be good or evil. 2 C. 5:10.

To me it is a very small thing to be judged by you, or by man's day, but neither do I judge my own self. For I am not conscious to myself of anything, yet am I not hereby justified: but he that judgeth me is the Lord. Therefore judge not before the time: until the Lord come, who both will bring to light the hidden things of darkness, and will make manifest the counsels of the hearts: and then shall every man have praise from God. 1 C. 4:3-5.

21. MICHAEL THE ARCHANGEL

When Josue was in the field of the city of Jericho, he lifted up his eyes and saw a man standing over against him, holding a drawn sword, and he went to him, and said: Art thou one of ours, or of our adversaries? And he answered: No: but I am prince of the host of the Lord, and now I am come. Josue fell on his face to the ground. And worshipping, said: What saith my lord to his servant? Loose, saith he, thy shoes from off thy feet: for the place whereon thou standest is holy. And Josue did as was commanded him. Jos. 5:13-16.

At that time Michael shall rise up, the great prince, who standeth for the children of thy people; and a time shall come such as never was from the time that nations began even until that time. And at that time shall thy people be saved: every one that shall be found written in the book. Dan. 12:1.

Daniel's vision. Dan. 10:1-20.

When Michael the archangel, disputing with the devil, contended about the body of Moses, he durst not bring against him the judgment of reviling, but said: The Lord command thee. Jude 9.

There was a great battle in heaven, Michael and his angels fought with the dragon, and the dragon fought and his angels: and they prevailed not, neither was their place found any more in heaven. Apoc. 12:7 f.

God signified the things which must shortly come to pass, sending by his angel to his servant John, who hath given testimony to the word of God, and the testimony of Jesus Christ, what things soever he hath seen. Blessed is he that readeth and heareth the words of this prophecy: and keepeth those things which are written in it. For the time is at hand. John to the seven churches, which are in Asia. Grace be unto you and peace from him that is, and that was, and that is to come, and from the seven spirits which are before his throne, and from Jesus Christ, who is the faithful witness, the first begotten of the dead, and the prince of the kings of the earth, who hath loved us, and washed us from our sins, in his own blood. Apoc. 1:1-5.

22. DUTIES OF THE FAITHFUL TOWARD THEIR PASTORS

He that will be proud, and refuse to obey the commandment of the priest, who ministereth at that time to the Lord thy God, and the decree of the judge, that man shall die, and thou shalt take away the evil from Israel. Deut. 17:12.

He commanded the people that dwelt in Jerusalem, to give to the priests, and the Levites their portion, that they might attend to the law of the Lord. 2 Par. 31:4.

All the multitude of the children of Israel going out from the presence of Moses, offered first fruits to the Lord with a most ready and devout mind, to make the work of the tabernacle of the testimony. Whatsoever was necessary to the service, and to the holy vestments. Ex. 35:20 f.

The people rejoiced, when they promised their offerings willingly: because they offered them to the Lord with all their heart. Now, therefore, our God, we give thanks to thee, and we praise thy glorious name. All things are thine: and we have given thee what we received of thy hand. 1 Par. 29:9, 13 f.

The lips of the priest shall keep knowledge, and they shall seek the law at his mouth: because he is the angel of the Lord of hosts. Mal. 2:7.

With all thy soul fear the Lord, and reverence his priests. With all thy strength love him that made thee: and forsake not his ministers. Honor God with all thy soul, and give honor to the priests. Give them thy portion, as it is commanded thee. Ecclus. 7:31-34.

Give to the Most High according to what he hath given to thee, and with a good eye do according to the ability of thy hands. Ecclus. 35:12.

Keep thy foot, when thou goest into the house of God, and draw near to hear. For much better is obedience, than the victims of fools, who know not what evil they do. Eccles. 13:20.

Amen, amen, I say to you, he that receiveth whomsoever I send, receiveth me: and he that receiveth me, receiveth him that sent me. John 13:20.

The harvest, indeed, is great, but the laborers are few. Pray ye, therefore, the Lord of the harvest, that he send forth laborers into his harvest. Mat. 9:37 f.

Go, show yourselves to the priests. And it came to pass, that as they went, they were made clean. Luke 17:14.

If thy brother shall offend against thee, go and reprove him between thee and him alone. If he shall hear thee, thou shalt gain thy brother. But if he will not hear thee, take with thee one or two more, that in the mouth of two or three witnesses every word may stand. And if he will not hear them, tell the church. And if he will not hear the church, let him be to thee as the heathen and the publican. Mat. 18:15-17.

Let him who is instructed in the word, communicate to him, who instructeth him, in all good things. Gal. 6:6.

If we have shown unto you spiritual things, is it a great matter if we reap your carnal things? So also the Lord ordained that they who preach the gospel, should live by the gospel. 1 C. 9:11, 14.

You have done well, in communicating to my tribulation. Not that I seek the gift: but I seek the fruit that may abound to your account. The things you sent, an odor of sweetness, an acceptable sacrifice, pleasing to God. Phil. 4:14, 17 f.

We beseech you, brethren, to know them who labor among you, and are over you in the Lord, and admonish you: that you esteem them more abundantly in charity for their work's sake. Have peace with them. 1 Thess. 5:12 f.

That you also be subject to such, and to every one that worketh with us, and laboreth. 1 C. 16:16.

Let the priests who rule well be esteemed worthy of double honor: especially they who labor in the word and doctrine. 1 Thess. 5:17.

Be ye followers of me, as I also am of Christ. 1 C. 11:1.

Obey your prelates. Heb. 13:17.

23. INTERCESSION OF THE SAINTS

The angel that delivereth me from all evils, bless these boys. Gen. 48:16.

O Lord, think of me. Tob. 3:3.

Call now if there be any that will answer thee, and turn to some of the saints. Job 5:1.

If there shall be an angel speaking for him, one among thousands, to declare man's uprightness, he shall have mercy on him. Job 33:23 f.

They shall be as the angels of God. Mat. 22:30.

There shall be joy before the angels of God upon one sinner doing penance. Luke 15:10.

Cease not to cry to the Lord our God for us, that he may save us out of the hand of the Philistines.

I beseech you, brethren, that you help me in your prayers for me to God. Rom. 15:30.

Pray withal for us also, that God may open unto us a door of speech to speak the mysteries of Christ. Col. 4:3.

Charity never falleth away. 1 C. 13:8.

I will do my endeavor, that after my decease also, you may often have whereby you may keep a memory of these things. 2 Pet. 1:15.

Confess your sins one to another: and pray one for another, that you may be saved. For the continual prayer of a just man availeth much. Jas. 5:16.

Are they all ministering spirits, sent to minister for them, who shall receive the inheritance of salvation? Heb. 1:14.

Their angels in heaven always see the face of my Father who is in heaven. Mat. 18:10.

Behold I will send my angel, who shall go before thee, and keep thee in thy journey, and bring thee into the place that I have prepared. Ex. 23:20.

Two angels took Machabeus between them, and covered him on every side with their arms, and kept him safe: but cast darts and fire-balls against the enemy, so that they fell down, being both confounded with blindness and filled with trouble. 2 Mac. 10:30.

I am prince of the host of the Lord, and now I am come. Jos. 5:14.

Behold Michael, one of the chief princes, came to help me. Dan. 10:13.

If Moses and Samuel shall stand before me, my soul is not towards this people. Jer. 15:1.

If any man minister to me, him will my Father honor. John 12:26.

To me thy friends, O God, are made exceedingly honorable: their principality is exceedingly strengthened. Ps. 138:17.

In his sight the malignant are brought to nothing: but he glorifieth them that fear the Lord. Ps. 14:4.

The angel of the Lord answered and said: O Lord of hosts, how long wilt thou not have mercy on Jerusalem? Zach. 1:13.

When thou didst pray with tears, and didst bury the dead, I offered thy prayer to the Lord. Tob. 12:12.

When Moses lifted up his hands, Israel overcame, but if he let them down a little, Amalec overcame. Ex. 17:11.

We give thanks to God always for you all, making mention of you all in our prayers without ceasing. 1 Thess. 1:2.

Praying always with all prayer and supplication in the Spirit, and watching thereunto with all instance and supplication for all the saints: and for me, that speech may be given unto me. Eph. 6:18 f.

The Lord said to Moses: I see that this people is stiff-necked: let me alone, that my wrath may be kindled against them, and that I may destroy them, and I will make of thee a great nation. But Moses besought the Lord his God, saying: Why, O Lord, is thy indignation enkindled against thy people, whom thou hast brought out of the land of Egypt, with great power, and with a mighty hand? Let not the Egyptians say, I beseech thee: He craftily brought them out, that he might kill them in the mountains, and destroy them from the earth: let thy anger cease, and be appeased upon the wickedness of thy people. Remember Abraham, Isaac, and Israel, thy servants, to whom thou sworest by thy own self, saying: I will multiply your seed as the stars of heaven: and this whole land that I have spoken of, I will give to your seed, and you shall possess it forever. And the Lord was appeased from doing the evil which he had spoken against his people. Ex. 32:9-14.

The Lord said to Moses: Get ye out from the midst of this multitude. this moment will I destroy them. And as they were lying on the ground, Moses said to Aaron: Take the censer, and putting fire in it from the altar, put incense upon it, and go quickly to the people to pray for them: for already wrath is gone out from the Lord, and the plague rageth. When Aaron had done this, and had run to the midst of the multitude which the burning fire was now destroying, he offered the incense: and standing between the dead and the living, he prayed for the people, and the plague ceased. Num. 16:44-48.

Now the vision was in this manner: Onias, who had been high priest, a good and virtuous man, modest in his looks, gentle in his manners, and graceful in his speech, and who from a child was exercised in virtues, holding up his hands, prayed for all the people of the Jews: after this there appeared also another man, admirable for age, and glory, and environed with great beauty and majesty. Then Onias answering, said: This is a lover of his brethren, and of the people of Israel: this is he that prayeth much for the people, and for all the holy city, Jeremias the prophet of God. 2 Mac. 15:12-14.

I desire first of all that supplications, prayers, intercessions, and thanksgivings be made for all men: for kings, and for all that are in high stations: that we may lead a quiet and a peaceable life in all piety and chastity. For this is good and acceptable in the sight of God our Savior, who will have all men to be saved, and to come to the knowledge of the truth. For there is one God, and one Mediator of God and men, the man Christ Jesus. 1 Tim. 2:1-5.

John to the seven churches which are in Asia. Grace be unto you and peace from him that is, and that was, and that is to come, and from the seven spirits which are before his throne, and from Jesus Christ, who is the faithful witness, the first-begotten of the dead, and the prince of the kings of the earth, who hath loved us, and washed us from our sins, in his own blood. Apoc. 1:4 f.

When he had opened the book, the four living creatures, and the four-and-twenty ancients fell down before the Lamb, having every one of them harps, and golden vials full of odors, which are the prayers of saints. Apoc. 5:8.

When he had opened the fifth seal, I saw under the altar the souls of them that were slain for the word of God, and for the testimony which they held. And they cried with a loud voice, saying: How long, O Lord (holy and true), dost thou not judge and revenge our blood on them that dwell on the earth? And white robes were given to every one of them one: and it was said to them that they should rest yet for a little time, till their fellow servants, and their brethren, who are to be slain, even as they, should be filled up. Apoc. 6:9-11.

Another angel came, and stood before the altar, having a golden censer; and there was given to him much incense, that he should offer of the prayers of all saints upon the golden altar, which is before the throne of God. Apoc. 8:3.

We, being many, are one bread, one body: all that partake of one bread. 1 C. 10:17.

There is neither Jew, nor Greek: there is neither bond, nor free: there is neither male, nor female. For you are all one in Christ Jesus. Gal. 3:28.

And some, indeed, he gave to be apostles, and some prophets, and others evangelists, and others pastors and teachers. For the perfection of the saints, for the work of the ministry, unto the edification of the body of Christ: till we all meet in the unity of faith, and of the knowledge of the Son of God, unto a perfect man, unto the measure of the age of the fulness of Christ. From whom the whole body, compacted and fitly joined together by what every joint supplieth, according to the operation in the measure of every part, making increase of the body, unto the edifying of itself in charity. Eph. 4:11-13, 16.

You are come to Mount Sion, and to the city of the living God, the heavenly Jerusalem, and to the company of many thousands of angels. And to the church of the first-born, who are written in heaven, and to God the Judge of all, and to the spirits of the just made perfect, and to Jesus the Mediator of the new testament. Heb. 12:22-24.

That which we have seen and have heard, we declare unto you; that you also may have fellowship with us, and our fellowship may be with the Father, and with his Son Jesus Christ. 1 John 1:3.

Holy Father, keep them in thy name, whom thou hast given me: that they may be one, as we also are. That they all may be one, as thou, Father, in me, and I in thee: that they also may be one in us: that the world may believe that thou hast sent me. And the glory which thou hast given me, I have given to them: that they may be one, as we also are one. John 17:11, 21 f.

So we being many, are one body in Christ, and each one members one of another. Rom. 12:5.

For as the body is one, and hath many members: and all the members of the body, whereas they are many, yet are one body: so also is Christ. For in one Spirit were we all baptized into one body, whether Jews or Gentiles, whether bond or free: and in one Spirit we have all been made to drink. For the body also is not one member, but many. But now there are many members indeed, yet one body. And if one member suffer anything, all the members suffer with it: or if one member glory, all the members rejoice with it. Now you are the body of Christ, and members of member. 1 C. 12:12-14, 20, 26 f.

Help in prayer for us. 2 C. 1:11.

24. HOLY IMAGES AND RELICS

Thou shalt make two cherubim of beaten gold, on the two sides of the oracle. Let one cherub be on the one side, and the other on the other. Let them cover both sides of the propitiatory, spreading their wings, and covering the oracle, and let them look one towards the other, their faces being turned towards the propitiatory wherewith the ark is to be covered. Ex. 25:18-20.

The Lord said to him: Make a brazen serpent, and set it up for a sign: whosoever being struck shall look on it, shall live. Moses therefore made a brazen serpent, and set it up for a sign: which when they that were bitten looked upon, they were healed. Num. 21:8 f.

He made in the oracle two cherubims of olive tree, of ten cubits in height. 3 K. 6:23.

He overlaid the cherubim with gold. And all the walls of the temple round about he carved with divers figures and carvings: and he made in them cherubim and palm trees, and divers representations as it were standing out, and coming forth from the wall. 3 K. 6:28 f.

He made in the entrance of the temple posts of olive tree four-square: and two doors of fir tree, one of each side; and each door was double, and so opened with folding leaves. And he carved cherubim, and palm trees, and carved work standing very much out: and he overlaid all with gold plates in square work by rule. 3 K. 6:33-35.

God forbid that I should glory save in the cross of our Lord Jesus Christ; by whom the world is crucified to me, and I to the world. Gal. 6:14.

Come not nigh hither, put off thy shoes from thy feet: for the place whereon thou standest is holy ground. Ex. 3:5.

Josue rent his garments, and fell flat on the ground before the ark of the Lord until the evening, both he and all the ancients of Israel. Jos. 7:6.

His sepulcher shall be glorious. Is. 11:10.

If I shall touch only his garment, I shall be healed. And the woman was made whole from that hour. Mat. 9:21.

He struck the waters with the mantle of Elias, and they were divided hither and thither, and Eliseus passed over. 4 K. 2:14.

When it had touched the bones of Eliseus, the man came to life. 4 K. 13:21.

They brought forth the sick into the streets, and laid them on beds and couches, that when Peter came his shadow at the least might overshadow any of them, and they might be delivered from their infirmities. Acts 5:15.

God wrought by the hand of Paul more than common miracles. So that even there were brought from his body to the sick handkerchiefs and aprons, and the diseases departed from them, and the wicked spirits went out of them. Acts 19:11 f.

25. FALSE MISSION OF SECTARIAN TEACHERS

Beware of false prophets, who come to you in the clothing of sheep, but inwardly they are ravening wolves. Mat. 7:15.

How shall they preach unless they be sent? Rom. 10:15.

Neither doth any man take the honor to himself, but he hat is called by God, as Aaron was. Heb. 5:4.

He that entereth not by the door into the sheepfold, but climbeth up another way, the same is a thief and a robber. John 10:1.

By their fruits you shall know them. Do men gather grapes of thorns, or figs of thistles? Mat. 7:16.

He that speaketh of himself, seeketh his own glory: but he that seeketh the glory of him that sent him, he is true. John 7:18.

If I glorify myself, my glory is nothing. It is my Father that glorifieth me. John 8:54.

Thou givest testimony of thyself: thy testimony is not true. John 8:13.

I am come in the name of my Father, and you receive me not: if another shall come in his own name, him you shall receive. John 5:43.

I did not send prophets, yet they ran; I have not spoken to them, yet they prophesied. Jer. 23:21.

Behold I am against the prophets, saith the Lord: who use their tongues, and say: The Lord saith it. Behold I am against the prophets that have lying dreams, saith the Lord: and tell them, and cause my people to err by their lying, and by their wonders: when I sent them not, nor commanded them, who have not profited this people at all, saith the Lord: if therefore this people, or the prophet, or the priest, shall ask thee, saying: What is the burden of the Lord? thou shalt say to them: You are the burden: for I will cast you away, saith the Lord. Jer. 23:31-33.

The Lord said to me: The prophets prophesy falsely in my name: I sent them not, neither have I commanded them, nor have I spoken to them: they pophesy unto you a lying vision, and divination and deceit, and the seduction of their own heart. Jer. 14:14.

How do you say: We are wise, and the law of the Lord is with us? Indeed the lying pen of the scribes hath wrought falsehood. The wise men are confounded, they are dismayed, and taken: for they have cast away the word of the Lord, and there is no wisdom in them. Jer. 8:8 f.

There were false prophets among the people, even as there shall be among you lying teachers, who shall bring in sects of perdition, and deny the Lord who bought them: bringing upon themselves swift destruction. And many shall follow their luxuries, through whom the way of truth shall be evil spoken of. And through covetousness shall they with feigned words make merchandise of you. Whose judgment now of a long time lingereth not, and their perdition slumbereth not. 2 Pet. 2:1-3.

Such false apostles are deceitful workmen, transforming themselves into the apostles of Christ. And no wonder: for Satan himself transformeth himself into an angel of light.

Therefore it is no great thing if his ministers be transformed as the ministers of justice: whose end shall be according to their works. 2 C. 11:13-15.

Many false prophets shall rise, and shall seduce many. Mat. 24:11.

There will arise up false prophets, and they shall show signs and wonders, to seduce (if it were possible) even the elect. Take you heed therefore; behold I have foretold you all things. Mark 13:22 f.

26. PERSECUTION OF ANTICHRIST

Let no man deceive you by any means: for unless there come a revolt first, and the man of sin be revealed, the son of perdition, who opposeth, and is lifted up above all that is called God, or that is worshipped, so that he sitteth in the temple of God, showing himself as if he were God. Remember you not, that when I was yet with you, I told you these things? And now you know what withholdeth, that he may be revealed in his time. For the mystery of iniquity already worketh: only that he who now holdeth, do hold, until he be taken out of the way. And then that wicked one shall be revealed, whom the Lord Jesus shall kill with the Spirit of his mouth: and shall destroy with the brightness of his coming: him, whose coming is according to the working of Satan, in all power, and signs, and lying wonders. And in all seduction of iniquity to them that perish: because they received not the love of the truth that they might be saved. Therefore God shall send them the operation of error, to believe lying. 2 Thess. 2:3-10.

Who is a liar, but he who denieth that Jesus is Christ? 1 John 2:22.

Then shall many be scandalized: and shall betray one another: and shall hate one another. And many false prophets shall arise, and shall seduce many. And because iniquity hath abounded, the charity of many shall grow cold. Mat. 24:10-12.

There shall be then great tribulation, such as hath not been from the beginning of the world until now. Mat. 24:21.

It was given unto him to make war with the saints, and to overcome them. And power was given him over every tribe, and people, and tongue, and nation. And all that dwell upon the earth adored him, whose names are not written in the book of life. Apoc. 13:7 f.

It was given him to give life to the image of the beast and that the image of the beast should speak: and should cause, that whosoever will not adore the image of the beast, should be slain. Apoc. 13:15.

Immediately after the tribulation of those days, the sun shall be darkened. Mat. 24:29.

For the sake of the elect those days shall be shortened. Mat. 24:22.

I will give unto my two witnesses, and they shall prophesy a thousand two hundred sixty days, clothed in sackcloth. Apoc. 11:3.

How art thou fallen from heaven, O Lucifer, who didst rise in the morning? how art thou fallen to the earth, that didst wound the nations? And thou saidst in thy heart: I will ascend into heaven, I will exalt my throne above the stars of God, I will sit in the mountain of the covenant, in the sides of the north. I will ascend above the height of the clouds, I will be like the Most High. And yet thou shalt be brought down to hell, into the depth of the pit. Is. 14:12-15.

The word of the Lord came to me, saying: Son of man, say to the prince of Tyre: Thus saith the Lord God: Because thy heart is lifted up, and thou hast said: I am God, and I sit in the chair of God in the heart of the sea: whereas thou art a man, and not God: and hast set thy heart as if it were the heart of God. Behold thou art wiser than Daniel: no secret is hid from thee. In thy wisdom and thy understanding thou hast made thyself strong: and hast gotten gold, and silver into thy treasures. By the greatness of thy wisdom, and by thy traffic thou hast increased thy strength: and thy heart is lifted up with thy strength. Therefore, thus saith the Lord God: Because thy heart is lifted up as the heart of God: therefore behold, I will bring upon thee strangers the strongest of the nations: and they shall draw their swords against the beauty of thy wisdom, and they shall defile thy beauty. They shall kill thee, and bring thee down: and thou shalt die the death of them that are slain in the heart of the sea. Wilt thou yet say before them that slay thee: I am God; whereas thou art a man, and not God, in the hand of them that slay thee? Thou shalt die the death of the uncircumcised by the hand of strangers: for I have spoken it, saith the Lord God. Ex. 23:1-10.

When iniquity shall be grown up, there shall arise a king of a shameless face, and understanding dark sentences. And his power shall be strengthened, but not by his own force: and he shall lay all things waste, and shall prosper, and do more than can be believed. And he shall destroy the mighty and the people of the saints, according to his will, and craft shall be successful in his hand: and his heart shall be puffed up, and in the abundance of all things he shall kill many: and he shall rise up against the Prince of princes, and shall be broken without hand. Dan. 8:23-25.

27. FINAL TRIUMPH OF THE CHURCH

Now is come salvation and strength, and the kingdom of our God, and the power of his Christ. Apoc. 12:10.

Afterwards shall come the end, when he shall have delivered up the kingdom to God and the Father. 1 C. 15:24.

He that shall persevere to the end he shall be saved. Mat. 24:13.

His empire shall be multiplied, and there shall be no end of peace: he shall sit upon the throne of David, and upon his kingdom: to establish it and strengthen it with judgment and with justice, from henceforth and for ever: the zeal of the Lord of hosts will perform this. Is. 9:7.

I beheld therefore in the vision of the night, and lo, one like the Son of man came with the clouds of heaven, and he came even to the Ancient of days: and they presented him before him. And he gave him power, and glory, and a kingdom and all peoples, tribes, and tongues shall serve him; his power is an everlasting power that shall not be taken away: and his kingdom, that shall not be destroyed. Dan. 7:13 f.

The saints of the most high God shall take the kingdom: and they shall possess the kingdom forever and ever. Dan. 7:18.

Behold, I create new heavens, and a new earth: and the former things shall not be in remembrance, and they shall not come upon the heart. But you shall be glad and rejoice forever in these things which I create: for behold I create Jerusalem a rejoicing, and the people thereof joy. And I will rejoice in Jerusalem and joy in my people, and the voice of weeping shall no more be heard in her, nor the voice of crying. Is. 65:17-19.

All the ends of the earth shall remember, and shall be converted to the Lord: and all the kindreds of the Gentiles shall adore in his sight. For the kingdom is the Lord's: and he shall have dominion over the nations. All the fat ones of the earth have eaten and have adored: all they that go down to the earth shall fall before him. Ps. 21:28-30.

They shall speak of the glory of thy kingdom: and shall tell of thy power: to make thy might known to the sons of men: and the glory of the magnificence of thy kingdom. Thy kingdom is a kingdom of all ages: and thy dominion endureth throughout all generations. Ps. 44:11-13.

In the days of those kingdoms the God of heaven will set up a kingdom that shall never be destroyed, and his kingdom shall not be delivered up to another people, and it shall break in pieces and shall consume all these kingdoms, and itself shall stand forever. Dan. 2:44.

28. THE CHURCH SUFFERING IN PURGATORY

There shall not enter into it anything defiled. Apoc. 21:27.

Rejoice not, thou my enemy, over me, because I am fallen. I shall arise. When I sit in darkness, the Lord is my light. I will bear the wrath of the Lord, because I have sinned against him; until he judge my cause and execute judgment for me: he will bring me forth into the light, I shall behold his justice. Mich. 7:8 f.

He shall sit refining and cleansing the silver. Mal. 3:3.

Thou by the blood of thy testament hast sent forth thy prisoners out of the pit wherein is no water. Zach. 9:11.

In the name of Jesus, every knee should bow, of those that are in heaven, on earth, and under the earth. Phil. 2:10.

Restrain not grace from the dead. Ecclus. 7:37.

That servant who knew the will of his Lord, and hath not prepared, and did not according to his will, shall be beaten with many stripes. But he that knew not, and did things worthy of stripes, shall be beaten with few stripes. Luke 12:47 f.

Make an agreement with thy adversary quickly, whilst thou art in the way with him; lest, perhaps, the adversary deliver thee to the judge, and the judge deliver thee to the officer, and thou be cast into prison. Amen I say to thee, thou shalt not go out from thence, till thou pay the last farthing. Mat. 5:25 f.

I say unto you, that every idle word that men shall speak, they shall render an account for it in the Day of Judgment. He that shall speak against the Holy Ghost it shall not be forgiven him neither in this world, nor in the world to come. Mat. 12:32, 36.

Christ died once for our sins, the Just for the unjust; that he might offer us to God, being put to death indeed in the flesh, but enlivened in the Spirit. In which also coming he preached to those spirits who were in prison. 1 Pet. 3:18 f.

He that descended is the same also that ascended above all the heavens, that he might fill all things. Eph. 4:10.

As silver is tried by fire, and gold in the furnace: so the Lord trieth the heart. Prov. 17:3.

What shall they do that are baptized for the dead, if the dead rise not at all? Why are they then baptized for them? 1 C. 15:29.

The most valiant Judas exhorted the people to keep themselves from sin, forasmuch as they saw before their eyes what had happened, because of the sins of those that were slain. And making a gathering, he sent twelve thousand drachms of silver to Jerusalem for sacrifice to be offered for the sins of the dead, thinking well and religiously concerning the resurrection. (For if he had not hoped that they that were slain should rise again, it would have seemed superfluous and vain to pray for the dead.) And because he considered that they who had fallen asleep with godliness, had great grace laid up for them. It is therefore a holy and wholesome thought to pray for the dead, that they may be loosed from sins. 2 Mac. 12:42-46.

29. THE CHURCH TRIUMPHANT IN HEAVEN

Glorious things are said of thee, O City of God. Ps. 83:3.

We know, if our earthly house of this habitation be dissolved that we have a building of God, a house not made with hands, eternal in heaven. 2 C. 5:1.

Christ ascending on high, led captivity captive. He that descended is the same also that ascended above all the heavens. Eph. 4:8, 10.

While we are in the body, we are absent from the Lord. But we are confident, and have a good will to be absent rather from the body and to be present with the Lord. 2 C. 5:6-8.

I am straitened between two; having a desire to be dissolved and to be with Christ, a thing by far the better. But to abide still in the flesh, is needful for you. Phil. 1:23 f.

For to me to live is Christ; and to die is gain. Phil. 1:21.

These are they who are come out of great tribulation, and have washed their robes, and made them white in the blood of the Lamb. Therefore they are before the throne of God, and they serve him day and night. Apoc. 7:14 f.

I am the God of Abraham, and the God of Isaac, and the God of Jacob. He is not the God of the dead, but of the living. Mat. 22:23.

This day thou shalt be with me in paradise. Luke 23:43.

From the beginning of the world they have not heard, nor perceived with the ears: the eye hath not seen, O God, besides thee, what things thou hast prepared for them that wait for thee. Is. 54:4.

Thy kingdom is a kingdom of all ages: and thy dominion endureth throughout all generations. Ps. 144:13.

Lift up your eyes to heaven, and look down to the earth beneath: for the heavens shall vanish like smoke, and the earth shall be worn away like a garment, and the inhabitants thereof shall perish in like manner: but my salvation shall be forever, and my justice shall not fail. Is. 51:6.

The redeemed of the Lord shall return, and shall come into Sion with praise, and everlasting joy shall be upon their heads: they shall obtain joy and gladness, and sorrow and mourning shall flee away. Is. 35:10.

Behold, I create new heavens, and a new earth; and the former things shall not be in remembrance, and they shall not come upon the heart. But you shall be glad and rejoice forever in these things, which I create: for behold I create Jerusalem rejoicing, and the people thereof joy. And I will rejoice in Jerusalem, and joy in my people, and the voice of weeping shall no more be heard in her, nor the voice of crying. Is. 65:17-19.

Thou shalt no more have the sun for thy light by day, neither shall the brightness of the moon enlighten thee: but the Lord shall be unto thee for an everlasting light, and thy God for thy glory. Thy sun shall go down no more, and thy moon shall not decrease: for the Lord shall be unto thee for an everlasting light, and the days of thy mourning shall be ended. And thy people shall be all just, they shall inherit the land forever, the branch of my planting, the work of my hand to glorify me. The least shall become a thousand, and a little one a most strong nation: I the Lord will suddenly do this thing in its time. Is. 60:19-22.

Fear not, little flock, for it hath pleased your Father to give you a kingdom. Luke 12:32.

In my Father's house there are many mansions. If not, I would have told you, because I go to prepare a place for you. John 14:7.

30. A PRAYER FOR THE CHURCH OF GOD

Have mercy upon us, O God of all, and behold us, and show us the light of thy mercies.

And send thy fear upon the nations, that have not sought after thee: that they may know that there is no God beside thee, and that they may show forth thy wonders.

Lift up thy hand over the strange nations, that they may see thy power. For as thou hast been sanctified in us in their sight, so thou shalt be magnified among them in our presence, that they may know thee, as we also have known thee, that there is no God beside thee, O Lord.

Renew thy signs, and work new miracles.

Glorify thy hand, and thy right arm.

Raise up indignation, and pour out wrath.

Take away the adversary, and crush the enemy.

Hasten the time, and remember the end, that they may declare thy wonderful works.

Let him that escapeth be consumed by the rage of the fire: and let them perish that oppress thy people.

Crush the head of the princes of the enemies that say: There is no other beside us.

Gather together all the tribes of Jacob: that they may know that there is no God besides thee, and may declare thy great works: and thou shalt inherit them as from the beginning.

Have mercy on thy people, upon whom thy name is invoked; and upon Israel, whom thou hast raised up to be thy first-born.

Have mercy on Jerusalem, the city which thou hast sanctified, the city of thy rest.

Fill Simon with thy unspeakable words, and thy people with thy glory.

Give testimony to them that are thy creatures from the beginning, and raise up the prophesies which the former prophets spoke in thy name.

Reward them that patiently wait for thee, that thy prophets may be found faithful; and hear the prayers of thy servants,

According to the blessing of Aaron over thy people, and direct us into the way of justice, and let all know that dwell upon the earth, that thou art God the beholder of all ages. Ecclus. 36:1-19.

III

THE SACRAMENTS

1. SACRAMENTS IN GENERAL

Blessed be the God and Father of our Lord Jesus Christ, who hath blessed us with all spiritual blessings in heavenly places, in Christ. As he chose us in him before the foundation of the world, that we should be holy and unspotted in his sight in charity. Who had predestinated us unto the adoption of children through Jesus Christ unto himself: according to the purpose of his will. Unto the praise of the glory of his grace, in which he hath graced us in his beloved Son. In whom we have redemption through his blood, the remission of sins according to the riches of his grace, which hath superabounded in us in all wisdom and prudence, that he might make known unto us the mystery of his will, according to his good pleasure which he hath purposed in him, in the dispensation of the fulness of times, to re-establish all things in Christ, that are in heaven and on earth, in him. Eph. 1:3-10.

With me are riches and glory, glorious riches, and justice. For my fruit is better than gold and the precious stones, and my blossoms than choice silver. Prov. 8:18 f.

How great are thy works. O Lord! Thou hast made all things in wisdom. The earth is filled with thy riches. Ps. 103:24.

Glory and wealth shall be in his house, Ps, 111:3.

I will give thee hidden treasures, and the concealed riches of secret places: that thou mayst know that I am the Lord who call thee by thy name, the God of Israel. Is. 45:3.

O the depth of the riches of the wisdom and of the knowledge of God! Rom. 11.33.

2. BAPTISM

Going therefore teach ye all nations: baptizing them in the name of the Father, and of the Son, and of the Holy Ghost. Mat. 28:19.

Unless a man be born again of water and of the Holy Ghost, he cannot enter into the kingdom of God. John 3:5.

Can any man forbid water, that these should not be baptized who have received the Holy Ghost as well as we? And he commanded them to be baptized in the name of the Lord Jesus Christ. Acts 10:47 f.

Christ loved the Church, and delivered himself up for it, that he might sanctify it: cleansing it by the laver of water in the word of life. Eph. 5:25 f.

He that believeth and is baptized shall be saved. Mark 16:16.

[In the ark] eight souls were saved by water. Whereunto baptism being of the like form, now saveth you also: not the putting away of the filth of the flesh, but the examination of a good conscience towards God by the resurrection of Jesus Christ. 1 Pet. 3:20 f.

When they believed Philip preaching of the kingdom of God, in the name of Jesus Christ they were baptized both men and women. Acts 8:12.

He commanded the chariot to stand still; and they went down into the water, both Philip and the eunuch, and he baptized him. Acts 8:38.

Immediately there fell from his eyes as it were scales, and he received his sight; and rising up he was baptized. Acts 8:18.

Know you not that all we who are baptized in Christ Jesus are baptized in his death? Rom. 6:3.

In that day there shall be a fountain open to the house of David, and to the inhabitants of Jerusalem: for the washing of the sinner. Zach. 13:1.

I will pour upon you clean water, and you shall be cleansed from all your filthiness. Ez. 36:25.

Rise up and be baptized, and wash away thy sins. Acts 22:16.

Do penance, and be baptized every one of you, for the remission of your sins. Acts 2:38.

He saved us by the laver of regeneration and renovation of the Holy Ghost, whom he hath poured forth upon us abundantly. Titus 3:5.

He said to them: Have you received the Holy Ghost since ye believed? But they said to him: We have not so much as heard whether there be a Holy Ghost. And he said: In what then were you baptized: Who said: In John's baptism. Then Paul said: John baptized the people with the baptism of penance, saying: That they should believe in him who was to come after him, that is to say, in Jesus. Having heard these things they were baptized in the name of the Lord Jesus. Acts 19:2-5.

I would not have you ignorant, brethren, that our fathers were all under the cloud, and all passed through the sea. And all in Moses were baptized, in the cloud, and in the sea. 1 C. 10:1 f.

Now this I say, that every one of you saith: I indeed am of Paul: and I am of Apollo: and of Cephas: and I of Christ. Is Christ divided? Was Paul then crucified for you? or were you baptized in the name of Paul? I give God thanks, that I baptized none of you, but Crispus and Caius: lest any should say that you were baptized in my name. And I baptized also the household of Stephanas: besides, I know not whether I baptized any other. For Christ sent me not to baptize, but to preach the gospel. 1 C. 1:12-17.

There is one baptism. Eph. 4:5.

3. ST. PAUL ON THE VALUE OF CIRCUMCISION

Christ Jesus was minister of the circumcision for the truth of God, to confirm the promises made unto the fathers. Rom. 15:8.

Circumcision profiteth indeed, if thou keep the law: but if thou be a transgressor of the law, thy circumcision is made uncircumcision. If then the uncircumcised keep the justices of the law, shall not his uncircumcision be counted for circumcision? And shall not that which by nature is uncircumcision, if it fulfil the law, judge thee who by the letter and circumcision art a transgressor of the law? Rom. 2:25-27.

This blessedness then doth it abide in the circumcision only, or in the uncircumcision also? For we say that unto Abraham faith was reputed to justice. How then was it reputed? When he was in circumcision or uncircumcision? Not in circumcision, but in uncircumcision. And he received the sign of circumcision, a seal of the justice of the faith which he had being uncircumcised: that he might be the father of all them that believe being uncircumcised, that unto them also it may be reputed to justice: and he might be the father of circumcision, not to them only that are of the circumcision, but to them also that follow the steps of the faith that is in the uncircumcision of our father Abraham. Rom. 4:9-12.

Beware of dogs, beware of evil workers, beware of the concision. For we are the circumcision, who in spirit serve God: and glory in Christ Jesus, not having confidence in the flesh. Phil. 3:2 f.

It is not he is a Jew, that is so outwardly: nor is that circumcision which is outward in the flesh, but he is a Jew that is one inwardly: and the circumcision is that of the heart, in the spirit, not in the letter: whose praise is not of men, but of God. Rom. 2:28 f.

You are filled in him, who is the head of all principality and power; in whom also you are circumcised with circumcision not made by hand in the despoiling of the body of the flesh, but in the circumcision of Christ: buried with him in baptism, in whom also you are risen again by the faith of the operation of God, who hath raised him up from the dead. And you, when you were dead in your sins, and the uncircumcision of your flesh: he hath quickened together with him; forgiving you all offences. Col. 2:10-13.

4. THE BAPTISM OF ST. JOHN THE BAPTIST

John was in the desert baptizing and preaching the baptism of penance unto remission of sins. And there went out to him all the country of Judea, and all they of Jerusalem, and were baptized by him in the river of Jordan, confessing their sins. Mark 1:4 f.

This man was instructed in the way of the Lord: and being fervent in spirit spoke, and taught diligently the things that are of Jesus, knowing only the baptism of John. Acts 18:25.

After these things Jesus and his disciples came into the land of Judea: and there he abode with them, and baptized. And John also was baptizing in Ennon near Salim; because there was much water there, and they came and were baptized. John 3:22 f.

When Jesus understood that the Pharisees had heard that Jesus maketh more disciples, and baptized more than John (though Jesus himself did not baptize, but his disciples), he left Judea, and went again into Galilee. John 4:1 f.

John indeed baptized with water, but you shall be baptized with the Holy Ghost not many days hence. Acts 1:5.

Then went out to him Jerusalem and all Judea, and all the country about Jordan: and were baptized by him in the Jordan, confessing their sins. I indeed baptize you in water unto penance, but he that shall come after me, is mightier than I, whose shoes I am not worthy to bear; he shall baptize you in the Holy Ghost and fire. Whose fan is in his hand, and he will thoroughly cleanse his floor: and gather his wheat into the barn, but the chaff he will burn with unquenchable fire. Mat. 3:5 f., 11 f.

Then cometh Jesus from Galilee to the Jordan, unto John, to be baptized by him. But John stayed him, saying: I ought to be baptized by thee, and comest thou to me? And Jesus answering, said to him: Suffer it to be so now. For so it becometh us to fulfil all justice. Then he suffered him. And Jesus being baptized, forthwith came out of the water: and lo, the heavens were opened to him: and he saw the Spirit of God descending as a dove, and coming upon him. And behold a voice from heaven, saying: This is my beloved Son, in whom I am well pleased. Mat. 3:13-17.

And John preached, saying: I have baptized you with water: but he shall baptize you with the Holy Ghost. And it came to pass, in those days Jesus came from Nazareth of Galilee; and was baptized by John in the Jordan. And forthwith coming up out of the water, he saw the heavens opened, and the Spirit as a dove descending and remaining on him. And there came a voice from heaven: Thou art my beloved Son, in thee I am well pleased. Mark 1:8-11.

5. THE SPIRITUAL SIGNIFICANCE OF BAPTISM

As many as received him, he gave them power to be made the sons of God, to them that believe in his name. Who are born, not of blood, nor of the will of the flesh, nor of the will of man, but of God. John 1: 12 f.

Know you not that all we, who are baptized in Christ Jesus, are baptized in his death? For we are buried together with him by baptism unto death; that as Christ is risen from the dead by the glory of the Father, so we also may walk in newness of life. For if we have been planted together in the likeness of his death, we shall also be in the likeness of his resurrection. Knowing this, that our old man is crucified with him, that the body of sin may be destroyed, and that we may serve sin no longer. Rom. 6: 3-6.

In one Spirit were we all baptized into one body, whether Jews or Gentiles, whether bond or free: and in one Spirit we have all been made to drink. 1 C. 12 f.

You are all the children of God by faith, in Christ Jesus. For as many of you as have been baptized in Christ, have put on Christ. Gal. 3: 27.

[You are] buried with him in baptism, in whom also you are risen again by the faith of the operation of God, who hath raised him up from the dead. Col. 2: 12.

Christ died once for our sins, the Just for the unjust: that he might offer us to God, being put to death indeed in the flesh, but enlivened in the spirit. In which also coming he preached to those spirits that were in prison: which had been some time incredulous, when they had waited for the patience of God in the days of Noe, when the ark was a building: wherein a few, that is, eight souls, were saved by water. Whereunto baptism being of the like form, now saveth you also: not the putting away of the filth of the flesh, but the examination of a good conscience towards God by the resurrection of Jesus Christ. 1 Pet. 3: 18-21.

Being asked by the Pharisees when the kingdom of God should come, he answered them and said: The kingdom of God cometh not with observation: neither shall they say: Behold here, or behold there. For lo, the kingdom of God is within you. Luke 17: 20 f.

Call to mind the former days, wherein being illuminated, you endured a great fight of afflictions. Heb. 10: 32.

There are three that give testimony on earth: the spirit and the water and the blood. 1 John 5: 8.

Mind the things that are above, not the things that are upon the earth. For you are dead; and your life is hid with Christ in God. Col. 3: 2 f.

In this we know that we abide in him, and he in us; because he hath given us of his Spirit. 1 John 4: 13.

Jesus answered and said to him: Amen, amen I say to thee, unless a man be born again, he cannot see the kingdom of God. Amen, amen I say to thee, unless a man be born again of water and the Holy Ghost, he cannot enter the kingdom of God. That which is born of the flesh, is flesh: and that which is born of the Spirit, is spirit. Wonder not that I say to thee, You must be born again. John 3: 3, 5-7.

Not by the works of justice, which we have done, but according to his mercy he saved us, by the laver of regeneration, and renovation of the Holy Ghost. Whom he hath poured forth upon us abundantly through Jesus Christ our Savior. Titus 3: 5 f.

Every one that loveth is born of God, and knoweth God. 1 John 4: 7.

Being born again not of corruptible seed, but incorruptible, by the word of God, who liveth and remaineth forever. 1 Pet. 1: 23.

If you know that he is just; know ye, that every one also, who doth justice, is born of him. 1 John 2: 29.

He is a Jew that is one inwardly; and the circumcision is that of the heart, in the spirit, not in the letter: whose praise is not of men, but of God. Rom. 2:29.

For in Christ Jesus neither circumcision availeth anything, nor uncircumcision but a new creature. Gal. 6:15.

If then any be in Christ a new creature: the old things are passed away, behold all things are made new. 2 C. 5:17.

If so be that you have heard him, and have been taught in him, as the truth is in Jesus. To put off, according to former conversation, the old man, who is corrupted according to the desire of error. And be renewed in the spirit of your mind: and put on the new man, who according to God, is created in justice, and holiness of truth. Eph. 4:21-24.

The first man was of the earth, earthly: the second Man from heaven, heavenly. As we have borne the image of the earthly, let us bear also the image of the heavenly. 1 C. 15:47-49.

If you be risen with Christ, seek the things that are above; where Christ is sitting at the right hand of God: stripping yourselves of the old man with his deeds, and putting on the new, him who is renewed unto knowledge, according to the image of him that created him. Where there is neither Gentile nor Jew, circumcision nor uncircumcision, barbarian nor Scythian, bond nor free: but Christ is all, and in all. Col. 3:1, 9-11.

Yet a little while: and the world seeth me no more. But you see me: because I live, and you shall live. In that day you shall know that I am in my Father, and you in me and I in you. John 14:19 f.

There is now therefore no condemnation to them that are in Jesus Christ, who walk not according to the flesh. For the law of the Spirit of life, in Christ Jesus, hath delivered me from the law of sin and of death. Now if any man have not the Spirit of Christ, he is none of his. And if Christ be in you; the body indeed is dead because of sin, but the spirit liveth because of justification. Rom. 8:1 f., 9 f.

That I may live to God: with Christ I am nailed to the cross. And I live, now not I: but Christ liveth in me. And that I live now in the flesh: I live in the faith of the Son of God, who loved me, and delivered himself for me. Gal. 2:19 f.

Now if we be dead with Christ, we believe that we shall live also together with Christ. Rom. 6:8.

A faithful saying. For if we be dead with him, we shall live also with him. 2 Tim. 2:11.

As therefore you have received Jesus Christ the Lord, walk ye in him. Rooted and built up in him, and confirmed in the faith, as also you have learned abounding in him in thanksgiving. Col. 2:6 f.

He who is joined to the Lord is one spirit. 1 C. 6:17.

Know you not your own selves, that Jesus Christ is in you? unless perhaps you be reprobates. 2 C. 13:5.

The mystery, which hath been hidden from ages and generations, but now is made manifest to his saints, to whom God would make known the riches of the glory of this mystery among the Gentiles, which is Christ, in you the hope of glory. Col. 1:26 f.

When Christ shall appear, who is your life; then shall you also appear with him in glory. Col. 3:4.

Sanctify the Lord Christ in your hearts. 1 Pet. 3:15.

By this hath the charity of God appeared towards us, because God hath sent his only begotten Son into the world, that we may live by him. 1 John 4:9.

Whosoever keepeth his word, the charity of God is truly perfect in him; and by this we know that we are in him. He that saith he abideth in him ought himself also to walk, even as he walked. 1 John 2:5 f.

6. THE CEREMONIES OF BAPTISM

The Breathing

The Lord God formed man of the slime of the earth: and breathed into his face the breath of life, and man became a living soul. Gen. 2:7.

Say to the Spirit: Thus saith the Lord God: Come, Spirit, from the four winds, and blow upon these slain, and let them live again. Ezech. 37:9.

He breathed on them. John 20:22.

The Sign of the Cross

Mark Thau upon the foreheads. Ez. 9:4.

The sign of the living God. Apoc. 7:2.

God forbid that I should glory, save in the cross of our Lord Jesus Christ, by whom the world is crucified to me, and I to the world. Gal. 6:14.

The Salt

Whatsoever sacrifice thou offerest thou shalt season it with salt, neither shalt thou take away the salt of the covenant of thy God from thy sacrifice. In all thy oblations thou shalt offer salt. Lev. 2:13.

Exorcisms

He gave them power to cast out devils. Mark 3:15.

He gave them power over unclean spirits, to cast them out. Mat. 10:1.

He gave them power and authority over all devils. Luke 9:1.

They bring to him one deaf and dumb: and they besought him that he would lay his hand upon him. And taking him from the multitude apart, he put his fingers into his ears, and spitting, he touched his tongue. And looking up to heaven, he groaned, and said to him: Ephpheta, which is, Be thou opened. And immediately his ears were opened, and the string of his tongue was loosed, and he spoke right. Mark 7:32-35.

Holy Oil of Chrism

Thou shalt consecrate all with the oil of unction that they may be most holy. Lev. 40:11.

God anointed him with the Holy Ghost. Acts 10:38.

You have the unction from the Holy One, and know all things. 1 John 2:20.

The White Garment

At all times let thy garments be white. Eccles. 9:8.

Thou hast a few names in Sardis, which have not defiled their garments; and they shall walk with me in white, because they are worthy. He that shall overcome, shall thus be clothed in white garments, and I will not blot out his name out of the book of life, and I will confess his name before my Father, and before his angels. He that hath an ear, let him hear what the Spirit saith to the churches. Apoc. 3:4-6.

The king said to him: Friend, how camest thou in hither not having on a wedding garment? But he was silent. Then the king said to the waiters: Bind his hands and feet, and cast him into the exterior darkness: there shall be weeping and gnashing of teeth. Mat. 22:12 f.

The Lighted Candle

You are the light of the world. A city seated on a mountain cannot be hid. Neither do men light a candle and put it under a bushel, but upon a candlestick, that it may shine to all that are in the house. So let your light shine before men, that they may see your good works, and glorify your Father who is in heaven. Mat. 5:14-16.

Through the bowels of the mercy of our God, in which the Orient, from on high, hath visited us. To enlighten them that sit in darkness, and in the shadow of death: to direct their feet into the way of peace. Luke 1:78 f.

Jesus answered: Are there not twelve hours of the day? If a man walk in the day, he stumbleth not, because he seeth the light of this world: But if he walk in the night he stumbleth, because the light is not in him. John 11: 9 f.

Jesus spoke to them, saying: I am the light of the world: he that followeth me, walketh not in darkness, but shall have the light of life. John 8: 12.

Jesus said to them: Yet a little while, the light is among you. Walk whilst you have the light, that the darkness overtake you not. And he that walketh in darkness knoweth not whither he goeth. Whilst you have the light, believe in the light, that you may be the children of light. John 12: 35 f.

[He shall be] as the light of the morning when the sun riseth, shining in the morning without clouds. 2 K. 23: 4.

The light is sweet, and it is delightful for the eyes to see the sun. Eccles. 11: 7.

He was a burning and a shining light, and you were willing for a time to rejoice in his light. John 5: 35.

You are all the children of light, and children of the day: we are not of the night nor of darkness. 1 Thess. 5: 5.

I the Lord have called thee in justice, and taken thee by the hand, and preserved thee. And I have given thee for a covenant of the people, for a light of the Gentiles. That thou mightest open the eyes of the blind, and bring forth the prisoner out of prison, and them that sit in darkness out of the prison-house. Is. 42: 6 f.

God is light. 1 John 1: 5.

7. NAMES AND TITLES OF THE BAPTIZED

1. Christians. Acts 11: 26.
2. Christ-bearers. 2 C. 13: 5.
3. Brethren of Christ. Heb. 2: 11.
4. Partakers of Christ. Heb. 3: 14.
5. Members of the Body of Christ. Eph. 5: 30.
6. The Born of God. 1 John 5: 1.
7. Children of God. 1 John 3: 10.
8. Children of Light. 1 Thess. 5: 5.
9. Children of the Day. 1 Thess. 5: 5.
10. Children of Promise. Gal. 4: 28.
11. Sons of God. 1 John 3: 1.
12. Adopted Sons of God. Gal. 4: 5.
13. The New Man. Eph. 4: 24.
14. Partakers of the Divine Nature. 2 Pet. 1: 4.
15. Partakers of a Heavenly Vocation. Heb. 3: 1.
16. Heirs of Life Everlasting. 1 Pet. 3: 22.
17. Saints. Acts 9: 32.
18. Fellow-citizens with the Saints. Eph. 2: 19.
19. Domestics of God. Eph. 2: 19.
20. Living Stones. 1 Pet. 2: 5.
21. A New Creature. 2 C. 5: 17.
22. A Holy Priesthood. 1 Pet. 2: 5.
23. A Chosen Generation. 1 Pet. 2: 9.
24. A Kingly Priesthood. 1 Pet. 2: 9.
25. A Holy Nation. 1 Pet. 2: 9.
26. A Purchased People. 1 Pet. 2: 9.
27. A Spiritual House. 1 Pet. 2: 5.
28. The Habitation of God. Eph. 2: 22.
29. The Temple of God. 1 C. 3: 17.
30. The Temple of the Holy Ghost. 1 C. 6: 19.
31. The Temple of the Living God. 2 C. 6: 16.
32. My Sons and Daughters, saith the Lord Almighty. 2 C. 6: 18.
33. Children of the Kingdom. Mat. 13: 38.

8. CONFIRMATION

When the apostles, who were in Jerusalem, had heard that Samaria had received the word of God; they sent unto them Peter and John. Who when they were come, prayed for them that they might receive the Holy Ghost. For he was not yet come upon any of them: but they were only baptized in the name of the Lord Jesus. Then they laid their hands upon them, and they received the Holy Ghost. Acts 8: 14-17.

When Paul had imposed his hands on them, the Holy Ghost came upon them. Acts 19:6.

I will ask the Father, and he shall give you another Paraclete, that he may abide with you forever. John 14:16.

He that confirmeth us with you in Christ, and that hath anointed us, is God, who also hath given the pledge of the Spirit in our hearts. 2 C. 1:21 f.

Believing in Christ you were signed with the Holy Spirit of promise. Eph. 1:13.

I will pour out of my Spirit upon all flesh. Acts 2:17.

This he said of the Spirit which they should receive who believed in him. John 7:39.

Be you perfect as also your heavenly Father is perfect. Mat. 5:48.

Who shall know thy thought, except thou give wisdom, and send thy Holy Spirit from above? Wis. 9:17.

Your Father from heaven will give the good Spirit to them that ask him. Luke 11:13.

The Holy Spirit of wisdom will not enter into a malicious soul, nor dwell in a body subject to sins. Wis. 1:4.

Thou hast anointed my head with oil. Ps. 22:5.

God, thy God hath anointed thee with the oil of gladness. Ps. 44:8.

The Spirit of the Lord shall rest upon him.

The Spirit of wisdom,
and of understanding,
the Spirit of counsel,
and of fortitude,
the Spirit of knowledge,
and of godliness.

And the Spirit of the fear of the Lord. Is. 11:2 f.

The fruit of the Spirit is
charity,
joy,
peace,
patience,
benignity,
goodness,
longanimity,
mildness,
faith,
modesty,
continency,
chastity.

Against such there is no law. Gal. 5:22 f.

IV

THE HOLY EUCHARIST

1. THE INSTITUTION OF THE HOLY EUCHARIST

Whilst they were at supper, Jesus took bread, and blessed, and broke: and gave to his disciples, and said: Take ye, and eat: this is my body. And taking the chalice he gave thanks: and gave to them, saying: Drink ye all of this. For this is my blood of the new testament which shall be shed for many unto remission of sins. Mat. 26:26-28.

Whilst they were eating, Jesus took bread: and blessing broke, and gave to them, and said: Take ye, this is my body. And having taken the chalice, giving thanks he gave it to them. And they all drank of it. And he said to them: This is my blood of the new testament, which shall be shed for many. Mark 14:22-24.

Taking bread, he gave thanks, and brake, and gave to them, saying: This is my body which is given for you. Do this for a commemoration of me. In like manner the chalice also, after he had supped, saying: This is the chalice, the new testament in my blood, which shall be shed for you. Luke 22:19 f.

The Lord Jesus, the same night in which he was betrayed, took bread. And giving thanks, broke, and said: Take ye and eat: this is my body which shall be delivered for you: this do for the commemoration of me. In like manner also the chalice, after he had supped, saying: This chalice is the new testament in my blood: this do ye, as often as you shall drink, for the commemoration of me. For as often as you shall eat this bread, and drink the chalice, you shall show the death of the Lord until he come. 1 C. 11:23-26.

2. THE BLESSED SACRAMENT FORESHADOWED BY THE PROPHETS

The Lord God brought forth of the ground the tree of life in the midst of Paradise. Gen. 2:9.

Melchisedech the king of Salem, bringing forth bread and wine, for he was the priest of the most high God, blessed him and said: Blessed be Abram by the most high God, who created heaven and earth. Gen.14:18 f.

If the blood of goats and of oxen, and the ashes of an heifer being sprinkled, sanctify such as are defiled, to the cleansing of the flesh: how much more shall the blood of Christ, who by the Holy Ghost offered himself unspotted unto God, cleanse our conscience from dead works to serve the living God? Heb. 9:13 f.

In the morning a dew lay round about the camp. And when it had covered the face of the earth it appeared in the wilderness small, and as it were beaten with a pestle, like unto the hoar-frost on the ground. And when the children of Israel saw it, they said one to another: Manhu! which signifieth: What is this! for they knew not what it was. And Moses said to them: This is the bread which the Lord hath given you to eat. Ex. 16:13-15.

And Elias went forward one day's journey into the desert. And when he was there and sat under a juniper tree, he requested for his soul that he might die, and said: It is enough for me, Lord, take away my soul: and he cast himself down and slept in the shadow of the juniper tree: and behold an angel of the Lord touched him, and said to him: Arise and eat. He looked, and behold there was at his head a hearthcake, and a vessel of water: and he ate and drank and he fell asleep again. And the angel of the Lord came again the second time and touched him: Arise, eat, for thou hast yet a great way to go. And he arose, and ate, and drank, and walked in the strength of that food forty days and forty nights, unto the mount of God, Horeb. 3 K. 19:4-8.

All these things happened to them in figure. 1 C. 10:11.

They did all eat the same spiritual food. 1 C. 10:3.

Thou didst feed thy people with the food of angels, and gavest them bread from heaven prepared without labor; having in it all that is delicious, and the sweetness of every taste. Wis. 16:20.

Wisdom hath built herself a house, she hath hewn her out seven pillars. She hath slain her victims, mingled her wine, and set forth her table. Prov. 9:1 f.

Come, eat my bread, and drink the wine which I have mingled for you. Prov. 9:5.

Thou hast prepared a table before me, against them that afflict me. Ps. 22:5.

I will take the chalice of salvation; and I will call upon the name of the Lord. Ps. 115:13.

Verily thou art a hidden God, the God of Israel, the Savior. Is. 45:15.

I myself that spoke, behold I am here. Is. 52:6.

Seek ye the Lord while he may be found: call upon him while he is near. Is. 55:6.

A throne shall be prepared in mercy. And One shall sit upon it in truth in the tabernacle of David. Is. 16:5.

I am with thee, saith the Lord, to save thee. Jer. 30:11.

3. THE BLESSED SACRAMENT PROMISED BY OUR LORD

Amen, amen, I say to you, you seek me not because you have seen miracles, but because you did eat of the loaves, and were filled. Labor not for the meat which perisheth, but for that which endureth unto life everlasting, which the Son of man will give you. For him hath God, the Father, sealed. They said therefore unto him: What shall we do that we may work the works of God? Jesus answered, and said to them: This is the work of God, that you believe in him whom he hath sent. They said therefore to him: What sign therefore dost thou show that we may see, and may believe thee? what dost thou work? Our fathers did eat manna in the desert as it is written: He gave them bread from heaven to eat. Then Jesus said to them: Amen, amen, I say to you: Moses gave you not bread from heaven, but my Father giveth you the true bread from heaven. John 6:26-32.

For the bread of God is that which cometh down from heaven, and giveth life to the world. They said therefore unto him: Lord, give us always this bread. And Jesus said to them: I am the bread of life, he that cometh to me shall not hunger; and he that believeth in me, shall never thirst. But I said unto you, that you also have seen me, and you believe not. All that the Father giveth to me shall come to me; and him that cometh to me, I will not cast out: because I came down from heaven, not to do my own will, but the will of him that sent me. Now this is the will of the Father who sent me: that of all that he hath given me, I should lose nothing, but should raise it up again in the last day. John 6:33-39.

And this is the will of my Father that sent me: that every one who seeth the Son, and believeth in him, may have life everlasting, and I will raise him up in the last day. The Jews therefore murmured at him, because he had said, I am the living bread which came down from heaven. And they said: Is not this Jesus the son of Joseph, whose father and mother we know? How then saith he, I came down from heaven? Jesus therefore answered and said to them: Murmur not among yourselves. No man can come to me, except the Father, who hath sent me, draw him, and I will raise him up in the last day. It is written in the prophets: And they shall all be taught of God. Every one that hath heard of the Father, and hath learned, cometh to me. Not that any man hath seen the Father, but he who is of God, he hath seen the Father. John 6:40-46.

Amen, amen, I say unto you: He that believeth in me hath everlasting life. I am the bread of life. Your fathers did eat manna in the desert, and are dead. This is the bread which cometh down from heaven; that if any man eat of it, he may not die. I am the living bread, which came down from heaven. If any man eat of this bread, he shall live forever: and the bread that I will give, is my flesh for the life of the world. The Jews therefore strove among themselves, saying: How can this man give us his flesh to eat? John 6:47-53.

Then Jesus said to them: Amen, amen, I say unto you: Except you eat the flesh of the Son of man, and drink his blood, you shall not have life in you. He that eateth my flesh, and drinketh my blood, hath everlasting life: and I will raise him up in the last day. For my flesh is meat indeed: and my blood is drink indeed: he that eateth my flesh, and drinketh my blood, abideth in me, and I in him. As the living Father hath sent me, and I live by the Father: so he that eateth me, the same also shall live by me. This is the bread that came down from heaven. Not as your fathers did eat manna, and are dead. He that eateth this bread shall live forever. These things he said teaching in the synagogue, in Capharnaum. John 6:54-60.

Many therefore of his disciples hearing it, said: This saying is hard, and who can hear it? But Jesus knowing in himself, that his disciples murmured at this, said to them: Doth this scandalize you? If then you shall see the Son of man ascend up where he was before? It is the spirit that quickeneth; the flesh profiteth nothing. The words that I have spoken to you, are spirit and life. But there are some of you that believe not. For Jesus knew from the beginning who they were that did not believe, and who he was that would betray him. And he said: Therefore did I say to you, that no man can come to me, unles it be given him by my Father. After this many of his disciples went back; and walked no more with him. Then Jesus said to the twelve: Will you also go away? And Simon Peter answered him: Lord, to whom shall we go? Thou hast the words of eternal life. And we have believed and have known that thou art the Christ the Son of God. John 6:61-70.

Whosoever drinketh of this water shall thirst again: but he that shall drink of the water that I will give him, shall not thirst forever. John 4:13.

I have told you before it come to pass: that when it shall come to pass you may believe. John 14:29.

I will not leave you orphans: I will come to you. John 14:18.

I will come again and take you to myself, that where I am, you also may be. John 14:3.

4. THE HOLY EUCHARIST CELEBRATED BY THE APOSTLES

Whosoever shall eat this bread or drink the chalice of the Lord unworthily, shall be guilty of the body and of the blood of the Lord. 1 C. 11:27.

Let a man prove himself: and so let him eat of that bread and drink of the chalice. For he that eateth and drinketh unworthily, eateth and drinketh judgment to himself, not discerning the body of the Lord. Therefore there are many infirm and weak among you, and many sleep. But if we would judge ourselves we should not be judged by the Lord. 1 C. 11:28-31.

When he had said these things, taking bread he gave thanks to God in the sight of them all, and when he had broken it, he began to eat. Acts 27:35.

As often as you shall eat this bread, and drink the chalice you shall show the death of the Lord, until he come. 1 C. 11:28.

We, being many, are one bread, one body, all that partake of one bread. 1 C. 10:17.

The chalice of benediction which we bless, is it not the communion of the blood of Christ? 1 C. 10:16.

5. UNLEAVENED BREAD USED FOR CONSECRATION

You shall eat unleavened bread. Ex. 12:18.

They made hearth cakes unleavened. Ex. 12:39.

When thou offerest a sacrifice baked in the oven of flour, to wit, unleavened wafers, if thy oblation be without leaven, thou shalt divide it into little pieces. Lev. 2:4-6.

They shall offer unleavened wafers. Lev. 7:12.

Taking out of the basket of unleavened bread a loaf without leaven and a wafer, he [Moses] put them upon the right shoulder, delivering all to Aaron and to his sons: who having lifted them up before the Lord, he took them again from their hands, and burnt them upon the altar of holocaust, because it was the oblation of consecration, for a sweet odor of sacrifice to the Lord. Lev. 8:26-28.

It is the solemnity of the unleavened bread of the Lord. Lev. 23:8.

He shall take one unleavened cake out of the basket and one unleavened wafer. And he shall elevate them in the sight of the Lord. Num. 6:19 f.

Seven days shall they eat unleavened bread. Num. 28:17.

They ate unleavened bread of the corn of the land. And the manna ceased after they ate the corn of the land. Is. 5:11 f.

Purge out the old leaven, that you may be a new paste, as you are unleavened. For Christ our Pasch, is sacrificed. Therefore let us feast, not with the old leaven, nor with the leaven of malice and wickedness, but with the unleavened bread of sincerity and truth. 1 C. 5:7-9.

6. CHRIST WHOLE UNDER EITHER SPECIES

Knowing that Christ rising again from the dead, dieth now no more, death shall no more have dominion over him. For in that he died to sin, he died once: but is alive unto God in Christ Jesus our Lord. Rom. 6:9 f.

Every spirit that dissolveth Jesus, is not of God: and this is Antichrist. 1 John 4:3.

He that eateth my flesh, and drinketh my blood, abideth in me, and I in him. John 6:57.

He that eateth me, the same also shall live by me. I am the living bread, which came down from heaven. John 6:51, 58.

The bread that I will give, is my flesh for the life of the world. If any man eat of this bread he shall live forever. John 6:52.

This do ye, as often as you shall drink, for the commemoration of me. 1 C. 11:25.

They were persevering in the doctrine of the apostles, and in the communication of the breaking of bread. Acts 2:42.

We, being many, are one bread, one body, all that partake of one bread. 1 C. 10:17.

On the first day of the week, when we were assembled to break bread. Acts 20:7.

7. BENEFITS OF THE BLESSED SACRAMENT

They gathered, one more, another less. And they measured by the measure of a gomor: neither had he more that had gathered more: nor did he find less that had provided less: but every one had gathered, according to what they were able to eat. Ex. 16:17 f.

If any man eat of this bread, he shall live forever. John 6:52.

Not as your fathers did eat manna and are dead. He that eateth this bread shall live forever. John 6:59

Blessed are they that hunger and thirst after justice: for they shall have their fill. Mat. 5:6.

I am the bread of life. He that cometh to me shall not hunger; and he that believeth in me shall never thirst. John 6:35.

He hath made a remembrance of his wonderful works, being a merciful and gracious Lord: he hath given food to them that fear him. Ps. 110:4.

We, being many, are one bread, one body, all that partake of one bread. 1 C. 10:17.

The chalice of benediction which we bless, is it not the communion of the blood of Christ? 1 C. 10:16.

He walked in the strength of that food unto the mount of God. 3 K. 19:8.

O how great is the multitude of thy sweetness, O Lord, which thou hast hidden for them that fear thee. Ps. 30:20.

The Lord will give grace and glory. Ps. 83:12.

He touched my mouth and said: Thy iniquities shall be taken away. Is. 6:7.

Take this gift from God, wherewith thou shalt overthrow the adversaries. 2 Mac. 15:16.

Blessed is he that shall eat bread in the kingdom of God. Luke 14:15.

Was not our heart burning within us, whilst he spoke in the way? Luke 24:32.

He that shall drink of the water that I will give him, shall not thirst forever. John 4:13.

Labor not for the meat which perisheth, but for that which endureth unto life everlasting. John 6:27.

I will raise him up in the last day. John 6:55.

There is no condemnation to them that are in Christ. Rom. 8:1.

Come ye to him, and be enlightened. Ps. 33:6.

O taste and see that the Lord is sweet. Ps. 33:9.

Thou hast prepared a table before me against them that afflict me. Ps. 22:5.

Thou didst feed thy people with the food of angels, and gavest them bread from heaven prepared without labor; having in it all that is delicious, and the sweetness of every taste. For thy sustenance showed thy sweetness to thy children and serving every man's will, it was turned to what every man liked. Wis. 16:20 f.

8. SUPREME WORSHIP DUE TO OUR LORD IN THE BLESSED SACRAMENT

The Lord thy God shalt thou adore, and him only shalt thou serve. Mat. 4:10.

When he bringeth in the first begotten into the world, he saith: And let all the angels of God adore him. Heb. 1:6.

Falling down they adored him. Mat. 2:11.

Falling down he adored him. John 8:38.

Behold Jesus met them, saying: All hail. But they came up and took hold of his feet, and adored him. Mat. 28:9.

All the ends of the earth shall remember, and shall be converted to the Lord; and all the kindreds of the Gentiles shall adore in his sight. Ps. 28:17 f.

The Lamb that was slain is worthy to receive power, and divinity, and wisdom, and strength, and honor, and glory, and benediction. Apoc. 5:12.

9. THE SACRIFICE OF CHRIST UPON THE CROSS

Christ also hath loved us, and hath delivered himself for us, an oblation and a sacrifice to God for an odor of sweetness. Eph. 5:2.

Called by God a high priest according to the order of Melchisedech. Heb. 5:10.

For them do I sanctify myself: that they also may be sanctified in truth. John 17:19.

Therefore doth the Father love me: because I lay down my life, that I may take it again. No man taketh it away from me; but I lay it down of myself. John 10:17 f.

Looking on Jesus, the author and finisher of faith, who having joy set before him, endured the cross, despising the shame. Heb. 12:2.

[Christ] in the days of his flesh with a strong cry and tears, offering up prayers and supplications to him that was able to save him from death, was heard for his reverence. Heb. 5:7.

He became to all who obey him, the cause of eternal salvation. Heb. 5:9.

10. THE PERPETUITY OF THE SACRIFICE DECLARED IN PROPHECY

I have no pleasure in you, saith the Lord of hosts: and I will not receive a gift of your hand. For from the rising of the sun even to the going down, my name is great among the Gentiles, and in every place there is sacrifice, and there is offered to my name a clean oblation: for my name is great among the Gentiles, saith the Lord of hosts. Mal. 1:10 f.

In that day there shall be an altar of the Lord in the midst of the land of Egypt. And the Egyptians shall know the Lord in that day. Is. 19:19, 21.

You shall be called the priests of the Lord: to you it shall be said: Ye ministers of our God. Is. 61:6.

I will take of them to be priests, and Levites, saith the Lord. For as the new heavens and the new earth, which I will make to stand before me, saith the Lord; so shall your seed stand, and your name. Is. 66:21 f.

They shall defile the sanctuary of strength, and shall take away the continual sacrifice, and they shall place there the abomination unto desolation. Dan. 11:31.

In those days and at that time, I will make the bud of justice to spring forth unto David, and he shall do judgment and justice in the earth. In those days shall Juda be saved, and Jerusalem shall dwell securely: and this is the name that they shall call him, The Lord our just one. For thus saith the Lord: There shall not be cut off from David a man to sit upon the throne of the house of Israel. Neither shall there be cut off from the priests and Levites a man before my face to offer holocausts, and to burn sacrifice, and to kill victims continually. Jer. 33:15-18.

Thus saith the Lord: If my covenant with the day can be made void, and my covenant with the night, that there should not be day and night in their season: also my covenant with David my servant may be made void, that he should not have a son to reign upon his throne, and with the Levites and priests my ministers. As the stars of heaven cannot be numbered, nor the sand of the sea be measured: so will I multiply the seed of David my servant, and the Levites my ministers. Jer. 33:20-22.

The Lord hath sworn, and he will not repent: Thou art a priest forever according to the order of Melchisedech. Ps. 109:4.

It is yet far more evident: if according to the similitude of Melchisedech there ariseth another priest. Heb. 7:15.

Melchisedech the king of Salem, bringing forth bread and wine, for he was the priest of the most high God, blessed him, and said: Blessed be Abram by the most high God, who created heaven and earth. And blessed be the most high God, by whose protection the enemies are in thy hands. Gen. 14:18-20.

He shall offer a male without blemish, at the door of the testimony, to make the Lord favorable to him: and he shall put his hand upon the head of the victim, and it shall be acceptable, and help to its expiation. Lev. 1:3-4.

Aaron shall offer a calf for sin, and a ram for a holocaust. Lev. 16:3.

11. SCRIPTURE OF HOLY MASS [1]

1. *The Beginning of Mass to the Offertory*

In the name of the Father, and of the Son, and of the Holy Ghost. Mat. 28:19.

Amen. Apoc. 5:14.

Antiphon

P. I will go in to the altar of God. Ps. 42:4.

R. To God who giveth joy to my youth. Ps. 42:4.

Psalm

P. Judge me, O God, and distinguish my cause from the nation that is not holy, deliver me from the unjust and deceitful man.

R. For thou art God my strength: why hast thou cast me off? and why do I go sorrowful whilst the enemy afflicteth me?

P. Send forth thy light and thy truth: they have conducted me, and brought me unto thy holy hill, and into thy tabernacles.

R. And I will go in to the altar of God: to God who giveth joy to my youth.

P. To thee, O God my God, I will give praise upon the harp: why art thou sad, O my soul? and why dost thou disquiet me?

R. Hope in God, for I will still give praise to him: the salvation of my countenance, and my God. Ps. 42:1-6.

P. Our help is in the name of the Lord. Ps. 123:8.

R. Who made heaven and earth. Ps. 123:8.

Confiteor

General confession made to

1. Almighty God. Apoc. 4:8.
2. Blessed Mary ever a virgin. Luke 1:27.
3. Blessed Michael the Archangel. Dan. 10:13.
4. Blessed John the Baptist. John 1:6.
5. St. Peter. John 21:15.
6. St. Paul. Acts 9:1.
7. All the saints. Apoc. 7:9.
8. To one another. Jas. 5:16.

P. Thou wilt turn, O God, and bring us to life. Ps. 84:7.

R. And thy people shall rejoice in thee. Ps. 84:7.

P. Show us. O Lord, thy mercy. Ps. 84:8.

R. And grant us thy salvation. Ps. 84:8.

P. Hear, O Lord, my prayer. Ps. 101:1.

R. And let my cry come to thee. Ps. 101:1.

P. The Lord be with you. 2 Tim. 3:16.

R. And with thy spirit. 2 Tim. 4:22.

Oremus

Texts probably alluded to

I pray thee, O Lord, to take away the iniquity of thy servant. 2 K. 24:10.

Every one that shall touch the altar shall be holy. Ex. 29:37.

The saints whose relics are under the altar are invoked. Apoc. 6:9.

[1] The proper being taken from the Mass of the Blessed Trinity.

Introit

Give glory to him because he hath shown his mercy to you. Tob. 12:6.

O Lord, our Lord, how admirable is thy name in all the earth! Ps. 8:10.

The Kyrie Eleison

P. Lord, have mercy on us. Mat. 20:31.

The Angelic Song

Glory to God in the highest: and on earth peace to men of good will. Luke 2:14.

Epistle

O the depth of the riches of the wisdom and of the knowledge of God! How incomprehensible are his judgments, and how unsearchable his ways! For who hath known the mind of the Lord? Or who hath been his counsellor? Or who hath first given to him, and recompense shall be made him? For of him, and by him, and in him, are all things: to him be glory forever. Amen. Rom. 11:33-36.

R. Thanks be to God. 2 C. 9:15.

Gradual

Blessed art thou, O Lord, that beholdest the depths, and sittest upon the cherubim. Blessed art thou, O Lord, in the firmament of heaven; and worthy of praise forever. Dan. 3:55 f.

Alleluia, Alleluia. Apoc. 19:1.

Blessed art thou, O Lord, the God of our fathers, worthy to be praised forever. Dan. 3:52.

Prayer before the Gospel

An allusion to this passage in Isaias.

One of the seraphim flew to me, and in his hand was a live coal, which he had taken with the tongs off the altar. And he touched my mouth and said: Behold, this hath touched thy lips, and thy iniquities shall be taken away, and thy sin shall be cleansed. Is. 6:6 f.

P. The Lord be with you. 2 Tim. 3:16.

R. And with thy spirit. 2 Tim. 4:22.

The Holy Gospel

Jesus spoke to them saying: All power is given to me in heaven and in earth. Going therefore teach ye all nations: baptizing them in the name of the Father, and of the Son, and of the Holy Ghost, teaching them to observe all things whatsoever I have commanded you: and behold I am with you all days, even to the consummation of the world. Mat. 28:18-20.

The Nicene Creed

I believe in one God (Heb. 11:6),
the Father (1 C. 8:6)
almighty (Apoc. 1:8),
Maker of heaven and earth (Ex. 20:11),
and of all things visible and invisible. (Jer. 32:17).
And in one Lord (Acts 10:36)
Jesus (Mat. 1:21)
Christ (John 4:25),
the only-begotten Son of God (John 1:14),
born of the Father, before all ages (1 John 4:9):
God of God, light of light (John 1:4),
true God of true God (John 5:18);
begotten, not made (John 8:58);
consubstantial with the Father (John 10:30);
by whom all things were made (John 1:3).
Who for us men and for our salvation (Mat. 1:21)
came down from heaven (John 3:31),
and was incarnate by the Holy Ghost (Luke 1:35)
of the Virgin Mary (Luke 2:6 f.);
and was made man (John 1:14).
He was crucified also for us (Mark 15:25);
suffered under Pontius Pilate (Mat. 27:26),
and was buried (Mat. 27:60).
And the third day he rose again (Mat. 28:6)
according to the Scriptures (1 Cor. 15:4);

and ascended into heaven (Luke 24:51).
He sitteth at the right hand of the Father (Mark 16:19);
and he shall come again with glory (Mat. 25:31)
to judge the living and the dead (2 Tim. 4:1);
of whose kingdom there shall be no end (Luke 1:33).
And in the Holy Ghost (John 14:26),
the Lord (cf. Is. 6:8; Acts 28:25),
and Giver of life (Rom. 8:2),
who proceedeth from the Father (John 15:26)
and the Son (Rom. 8:9),
who, together with the Father and the Son, is adored and glorified (Apoc. 4:8);
who spoke by the prophets (2 Pet. 1:21).
And one (John 10:16)
holy (Eph. 5:26)
Catholic and (Rom. 10:18)
apostolic church (Eph. 2:20).
I confess one baptism (Eph. 4:5)
for the remission of sins (Acts 2:38).
And I look for the resurrection of the dead (Rom. 6:5),
and the life of the world to come (Mat. 25:34).

2. *The Offertory to the Canon*

Offertory

(By allusion)

He hath given us most great and precious promises: that by these you may be made partakers of the divine nature. 2 Pet. 1:3.

An odor of sweetness, an acceptable sacrifice, pleasing God. Phil. 4:18.

Prayer

while incensing the altar

Let my prayer be directed as incense in thy sight: the lifting up of my hands, as evening sacrifice. Set a watch, O Lord, before my mouth: and a door round about my lips. Incline not my heart to evil words; to make excuses in sins. Ps. 140:2-4.

The Lavabo

I will wash my hands among the innocent: and will compass thy altar, O Lord.

That I may hear the voice of thy praise: and tell of all thy wondrous works.

I have loved, O Lord, the beauty of thy house: and the place where thy glory dwelleth.

Take not away my soul, O God, with the wicked: nor my life with bloody men.

In whose hands are iniquities: their right hand is filled with gifts.

But as for me, I have walked in my innocence: redeem me, and have mercy on me.

My foot hath stood in the direct way: in the churches I will bless thee, O Lord. Ps. 25:6-10.

The Suscipe

Reference made to

1. The passion of our Lord. Mat. 27:1.
2. His resurrection. Mat. 28:1.
3. His ascension. Luke 24:51.

Preface

Holy, holy, holy, Lord God of hosts. Heaven and earth are full of thy glory. Is. 6:3.

Hosanna in the highest. Mat. 21:9.

Blessed is he that cometh in the name of the Lord. Hosanna in the highest. Mat. 21:9.

3. *The Canon to the Communion*

Canon

(Saints invoked)

1. The Blessed Virgin. Luke 1:27.
2. St. Peter. Mat. 4:18.
3. St. Paul. Rom. 1:1.
4. St. Andrew. Mat. 10:2.
5. St. James. Mat. 10:3.
6. St. John. *Ibid.*
7. St. Thomas. *Ibid.*

8. St. James. *Ibid.*
9. St. Philip. *Ibid.*
10. St. Bartholomew. *Ibid.*
11. St. Matthew. *Ibid.*
12. St. Simon. Mat. 10:4.
13. St. Thaddeus. Mat. 10:3.
14. St. Linus. 2 Tim. 4:21.
15. St. Clement. Phil. 4:3.

Consecration

He took bread, and blessed and broke: and gave to his disciples, and said: Take ye, and eat: this is my body. Mat. 26:26.

In like manner also after he had supped (Luke 22:20),

Taking the chalice he gave thanks: and gave to them, saying: Drink ye all of this. For this is my blood of the new testament; the mystery of faith (1 Tim. 3:9): which shall be shed for many unto remission of sins. Mat. 26:27 f.

After the Consecration

Reference made to the sacrifice of

1. Abel. Gen. 4:4.
2. Abraham. Gen. 22:1.
3. Melchisedech. Gen. 14:18.

Nobis Quoque Peccatoribus

In which are mentioned

1. St. John. Apoc. 1:1.
2. St. Stephen. Acts 6:8.
3. St. Matthias. Acts 1:26.
4. St. Barnabas. Acts 13:2.

By reference.

Of him, and by him, and in him are all things: to him be glory forever. Amen. Rom. 11:36.

The Pater Noster

Our Father, who art in heaven, hallowed be thy name: thy kingdom come; thy will be done on earth as it is in heaven. Give us this day our daily bread: and forgive us our trespasses, as we forgive them that trespass against us. And lead us not into temptation. But deliver us from evil. Amen. Mat. 6:9-13.

P. The peace of God be with you. Rom. 15:33.

R. And with thy spirit. 2 Tim. 4:22.

Prayer

While putting the particle into the chalice

(By allusion)

He that eateth my flesh and drinketh my blood hath everlasting life; and I will raise him up in the last day. John 5:55.

Agnus Dei

Lamb of God who takest away the sins of the world (John 1:29),

Have mercy on us. Is. 33:2.

Peace I leave with you, my peace I give unto you. John 15:27.

4. *The Communion to the end*

Holy Communion

Lord, I am not worthy that thou shouldst enter under my roof: but only say the word, and my [soul] shall be healed. Mat. 8:8.

What shall I render to the Lord for all the things that he hath rendered to me? I will take the chalice of salvation, and I will call upon the name of the Lord. Ps. 115:12 f.

Postcommunion

Bless the God of heaven. Give glory to him in the sight of all that live, because he hath shown his mercy to you. Tob. 12:6.

P. The Lord be with you. 2 Tim. 3:16.

R. And with thy spirit. 2 Tim. 4:22.

The Last Gospel

In the beginning was the Word, and the Word was with God, and the Word was God. The same was in the beginning with God. All things were made by him: and without him was made nothing that was made. In him was life, and the life was the light of men: and the light shineth in darkness, and the darkness did not comprehend it.

There was a man sent from God, whose name was John. This man came for a witness, to give testimony of the light, that all men might believe through him. He was not the light, but was to give testimony of the light.

That was the true light, which enlighteneth every man that cometh into this world. He was in the world, and the world was made by him, and the world knew him not. He came unto his own, and his own received him not. But as many as received him, he gave them power to be made the sons of God, to them that believe in his name. Who are born, not of blood, nor of the will of the flesh, nor of the will of man, but of God.

And the Word was made flesh and dwelt among us (and we saw his glory as it were of the only-begotten of the Father) full of grace and truth. John 1:1-14.

R. Thanks be to God. 2 C. 9:15.

12. THE RESERVATION OF THE BLESSED SACRAMENT

This is the perpetual fire which shall never go out on the altar. Lev. 6:13.

Moses said to Aaron: Take a vessel and put manna into it, as much as a gomor can hold: and lay it up before the Lord to keep unto your generations, as the Lord commanded Moses. And Aaron put it in the tabernacle to be kept. Ex. 16:33 f.

Thou shalt set upon the table loaves of proposition in my sight always. Ex. 25:30.

The loaves shall be always on the table of proposition. Num. 4:7.

As thou didst with David so do with me, that I may build a house to the name of the Lord, and for the continual setting forth of bread. 2 Par. 2:4.

I am always with thee. Ps. 72:23.

I have chosen and have sanctified this place that my name may be there forever, and my eyes and my heart may remain there perpetually. 2 Par. 7:16.

He had promised to give a lamp to him and to his sons forever. 2 Par. 21:7.

The Lord shall sit King forever. Ps. 28:10.

In thy tabernacle I shall dwell forever. Ps. 60:5.

There the Lord shall dwell unto the end. Ps. 67:17.

Here will I dwell, for I have chosen it. Ps. 131:14.

We have heard out of the law that Christ abideth forever. John 12:34.

I set the Lord always in my sight: for he is at my right hand, that I be not moved. Ps. 15:8.

I foresaw the Lord before my face always. Acts 2:25.

Behold I am with you all days, even to the consummation of the world. Mat. 28:20.

The Lord is in his holy temple: let all the earth keep silence before him. Haba. 2:20.

Let all flesh be silent at the presence of the Lord. Zach. 2:13.

Assemble yourselves, and let us enter into the fenced cities, and let us be silent there. Jer. 8:14.

He shall sit solitary and hold his peace, because he hath taken it upon himself. Lam. 3:28.

Hold your peace a little while that I may speak whatsoever my mind shall suggest to me. Job 13:13.

He will be silent in his love. Soph. 3:17.

13. THE TABERNACLE

They shall make me a sanctuary, and I will dwell in the midst of them. Ex. 25:8.

The altar shall be sanctified by my glory. Ex. 29:43.

I will sanctify also the tabernacle of the testimony with the altar. And I will dwell in the midst of the children of Israel, and will be their God: and they shall know that I am the Lord their God, who have brought them out of the land of Egypt, that I might abide among them, I the Lord their God. Ex. 29:44-46.

I will set my tabernacle in the midst of you, and my soul shall not cast you off. I will walk among you, and will be your God, and you shall be my people. Lev. 26:11 f.

The word of the Lord came to Solomon, saying: This house, which thou buildest, if thou wilt walk in my statutes, and execute my judgments, and keep all my commandments, walking in them, I will fulfil my word to thee which I spoke to David thy father. And I will dwell in the midst of the children of Israel, and will not forsake my people Israel. 3 K. 6:11-13.

Building, I have built a house for thy dwelling, to be thy most firm throne forever. 3 K. 8:13.

I have built a house to his name, that he might dwell there forever. 2 Par. 6:2.

A throne shall be prepared in mercy, and one shall sit upon it in truth in the tabernacle of David. Is. 16:5.

I John saw the holy city the new Jerusalem coming down out of heaven from God, prepared as a bride adorned for her husband. And I heard a great voice from the throne, saying: Behold the tabernacle of God with men, and he will dwell with them. And they shall be his people: and God himself with them shall be their God. Apoc. 21:2 f.

My face shall go before thee, and I will give thee rest. Ex. 33:14.

Moses did all that the Lord had commanded. So in the first month of the second year, the first day of the month, the tabernacle was set up, and Moses reared it up, and placed the boards, and the sockets and the bars, and set up the pillars, and spread the roof over the tabernacle, putting over it a cover, as the Lord had commanded. And he put the testimony in the ark, thrusting bars underneath, and the oracle above. And when he had brought the ark into the tabernacle, he drew the veil before it to fulfil the commandment of the Lord. Ex. 40:14-19.

And he set the table in the tabernacle of the testimony at the north side without the veil, setting there in order the loaves of proposition, as the Lord had commanded Moses. He set the candlestick also in the tabernacle of the testimony, over against the table on the south side, placing the lamps in order, according to the precept of the Lord. He set also the altar of gold under the roof of the testimony over against the veil, and burnt upon it the incense of spices, as the Lord had commanded Moses. And he put also the hanging in the entry of the tabernacle of the testimony, and the altar of holocaust of the entry of the testimony, offering the holocaust, and the sacrifices upon it, as the Lord had commanded. And he set the laver between the tabernacle of the testimony and the altar, filling it with water. And Moses and Aaron, and his sons washed their hands and feet, when they went into the tabernacle of the covenant, and went to the altar, as the Lord had commanded Moses. Ex. 40:20-30.

He set up also the court round about the tabernacle and the altar, drawing the hanging in the entry thereof. After all things were perfected, the cloud covered the tabernacle of the testimony, and the glory of the Lord filled it. Neither could Moses go into the tabernacle of the covenant, the cloud covering all things and the majesty of the Lord shining, for the cloud had covered all. If at any time the cloud removed from the tabernacle, the children of Israel went forward by their troops: If it hung over, they remained in the same place. For the cloud of the Lord hung over the tabernacle by day, and a fire by night, in the sight of all the children of Israel throughout all their mansions. Ex. 40:31-36.

14. THE LAMP OF THE SANCTUARY

Command the children of Israel that they bring thee the purest oil of the olives, and beaten with a pestle: that a lamp may burn always in the tabernacle of the testimony, without the veil that hangs before the testimony. And Aaron and his sons shall order it, that it may give light before the Lord until the morning. It shall be a perpetual observance throughout their successions among the children of Israel. Ex. 27:20 f.

These are the things you must take, oil to make lights. Ex. 25:6.

The Lord spoke to Moses, saying: Command the children of Israel, that they bring unto thee the finest and clearest oil of olives, to furnish the lamps continually, without the veil of the testimony in the tabernacle of the covenant. And Aaron shall set them from evening until morning before the Lord, by a perpetual service and rite in your generations. They shall be set upon the most pure candlestick before the Lord continually. Lev. 24:1-4.

The Lord spoke to Moses, saying: Speak to Aaron, and thou shalt say to him: When thou shalt place the seven lamps, let the candlestick be set up on the south side. Give orders therefore that the lamps look over against the north, towards the table of the loaves of proposition, over against that part shall they give light, towards which the candlestick looketh. And Aaron did so, and he put the lamps upon the candlestick, as the Lord had commanded Moses. Now this was the work of the candlestick, it was of beaten gold, both the shaft in the middle, and all that came out of both sides of the branches: according to the pattern which the Lord had shown to Moses, so he made the candlestick. Num. 8:1-4.

Thou art my lamp, O Lord: and thou, O Lord, wilt enlighten my darkness. 2 K. 22:29.

I have prepared a lamp for my anointed. Ps. 131:17.

Thou lightest my lamp, O Lord. Ps. 17:29.

The Lamb is the lamp thereof, and the nations shall walk in the light of it. Apoc. 21:23 f.

Behold a candlestick all of gold, and its lamp upon the top of it. Zach. 4:2.

15. BENEDICTION OF THE BLESSED SACRAMENT

Jesus led them as far as Bethania: and lifting up his hands he blessed them. Luke 26:50.

The king turned his face, and blessed all the multitude of Israel. 2 Par. 6:3.

Moses blessed the children of Israel. Deut. 33:1.

May the Lord out of Sion bless thee, he that made heaven and earth. Ps. 133:3.

The blessing of the Lord maketh men rich. Prov. 10:22.

I will make them a blessing round about my hill. There shall be showers of blessings. Ez. 34:26.

The Almighty shall bless thee with the blessings of heaven above. Gen. 49:25.

I will bless thee. Gen. 12:2.

The Lord bless thee and keep thee. Num. 6:24.

The Lord show his face to thee, and have mercy on thee. Num. 6:25.

The Lord turn his countenance to thee, and give thee peace. Num. 6:26.

They shall invoke my name, and I will bless them. Num. 6:27.

Now, O Lord God, bless the house of thy servant, that it may endure forever before thee: because thou, O Lord God, hast spoken it, and with thy blessing let the house of thy servant be blessed forever. 2 K. 7:29.

16. PERPETUAL ADORATION OF THE BLESSED SACRAMENT

Happy are thy men, and happy are thy servants who stand always before thee and hear thy wisdom. 2 Par. 9:7.

The Levites shall pitch their tents round about the tabernacle, and they shall keep watch and guard the tabernacle of the testimony. Num. 1:53.

They keep the watches of the Lord. Num. 9:23.

I will take delight in the Lord. Ps. 103:34.

Blessed is he whom thou hast chosen, and taken to thee: he shall dwell in thy courts. We shall be filled with the good things of thy house. Ps. 64:5.

They abode in their watches round about the temple of the Lord. 1 Par. 9:27.

They dwelt in the chambers by the temple, that they might serve continually day and night in their ministry. 1 Par. 9:33.

They shall be converted that sit under his shadow: they shall live upon wheat, and they shall blossom as a vine. Osee 14:8.

Blessed are thy men, and blessed are thy servants who stand before thee always. 3 K. 10:8.

Some of them he hath sanctified, and set near himself. Ecclus. 33:12.

My sons, be not negligent: the Lord hath chosen you to stand before him, and to minister to him, and to worship him, and to burn incense to him. 2 Par. 29:11.

Thus saith the Lord: Whosoever shall glorify me, him will I glorify: but they that despise me shall be despised. 1 K. 2:30.

Thy God, whom thou always servest, he will deliver thee. Dan. 6:16.

How lovely are thy tabernacles, O Lord of hosts! My soul longeth and fainteth for the courts of the Lord. My heart and my flesh have rejoiced in the living God. For the sparrow hath found herself a house, and the turtle a nest for herself where she may lay her young ones: thy altars, O Lord of hosts, my King and my God. Blessed are they that dwell in thy house, O Lord: they shall praise thee forever and ever. Ps. 83:2-5.

Be continually with a holy man. Ecclus. 37:15.

Behold, O God our Protector: and look on the face of thy Christ. For better is one day in thy courts above thousands. I have chosen to be an abject in the house of my God, rather than to dwell in the tabernacles of sinners. Ps. 83:10 f.

Before the tabernacle of the covenant shall Moses and Aaron camp, with their sons, having the custody of the sanctuary, in the midst of the children of Israel. What stranger soever cometh unto it, shall be put to death. Num. 3:38.

All that were in distress and under affliction of mind gathered themselves together unto him: and he became their prince. 1 K. 22:2.

She departed not from the temple, by fastings and prayers serving night and day. Luke 2:37.

They were always in the temple, praising and blessing God. Luke 24:53.

Day and night shall you remain in the tabernacle, observing the watches of the Lord. Lev. 8:35.

17. NOCTURNAL ADORATION

In the nights lift up your hands to the holy places, and bless ye the Lord. May the Lord out of Sion bless thee, he that made heaven and earth. Ps. 133:3 f.

One of the ancients said to me: These that are clothed in white robes, who are they? and whence came they? And I said to him: My lord, thou knowest. And he said to me: These are they who are come out of great tribulation, and have washed their robes, and have made them white in the blood of the Lamb. Therefore they are before the throne of God, and they serve him day and night in his temple. Apoc. 7:13-15.

Jesus went up into a mountain to pray, and he passed the whole night in the prayer of God. Luke 6:12.

I rose at midnight to give praise to thee. Ps. 118:62.

By night I sought him whom my soul loveth. Cant. 3:1.

Nicodemus came to Jesus by night. John 3:2.

In the night I have remembered thy name, O Lord. Ps. 118:55.

In the day of my trouble I sought God, with my hand lifted up to him in the night, and I was not deceived. Ps. 76:3.

Weeping she hath wept in the night, and her tears are on her cheeks. Lam. 1:2.

Arise, give praise in the night, in the beginning of the watches: pour out thy heart like water before the face of the Lord. Lam. 2:19.

My soul hath desired thee in the night: yea, and with my spirit within me in the morning early I will watch to thee. Is. 26:9.

Samuel cried unto the Lord all night. 1 K. 15:11.

As a lion he cried out, I am upon the watchtower of the Lord, standing continually by day: and I am upon my ward, standing whole nights. Is. 21:8.

In the daytime, he was teaching in the temple: but at night, going out, he abode in the mount that is called Olivet. Luke 21:37.

There shall be no night there. Apoc. 21:25.

I was in many watchings. 2 C. 11:27.

18. TEXTS FOR MEDITATION BEFORE THE BLESSED SACRAMENT

God is with us. Is. 8:10.

Juda gathered themselves together to pray to the Lord, and all came out of their cities to make supplication to him. 2 Par. 20:4.

As we know not what to do, we can only turn our eyes to thee. 2 Par. 20:12.

Rejoice, and praise, O thou inhabitant of Sion: for great is he that is in the midst of thee, the Holy One of Israel. Is. 12:6.

Behold I am alive for evermore. Apoc. 1:18.

Say to the cities of Juda: Behold thy God. Is. 40:9.

The Lord is with us, fear ye not. Num. 14:9.

Behold I am with you all days, even to the consummation of the world. Mat. 28:20.

He had opened the doors of heaven, and had rained down manna upon them to eat, and had given them the bread of heaven. Man ate the bread of angels; he sent them provisions in abundance. Ps. 77:24 f.

He fed them with the fat of wheat. Ps. 80:17.

Behold he is set for a sign which shall be contradicted. Luke 2:34.

When Moses entered into the tabernacle of the covenant, to consult the oracle, he heard the voice of one speaking to him from the propitiatory. Num. 7:89.

What hast thou that thou hast not received? 1 C. 4:7.

Let us fetch unto us the ark of the covenant of the Lord from Silo, and let it come in the midst of us, that it may save us from the hand of our enemies. 1 K. 4:3.

Thou shalt eat bread at my table always. 2 K. 11:7.

Let all the earth adore Thee. Ps. 65:4.

Let the just feast, and rejoice before God. Ps. 67:4.

Rejoice ye before him, but the wicked shall be troubled at his presence. Ps. 67:5.

With the holy, thou wilt be holy, and with the innocent man thou wilt be innocent. Ps. 17:26.

No one shall appear with his hands empty before the Lord. Deut. 16:16.

All the kindreds of the Gentiles shall adore in his sight. Ps. 21:28.

They that were ready went in. Mat. 25:10.

Send forth thy light and thy truth: they have conducted me, and brought me unto thy holy hill and into thy tabernacles, and I will go in to the altar of God: to God who giveth joy to my youth. Ps. 42:3 f.

To thee, O God my God, I will give praise upon the harp: why art thou sad, O my soul? and why dost thou disquiet me? Hope in God, for I will still give praise to him: the salvation of my countenance and my God. Ps. 42:5 f.

Give us this day our daily bread. Luke 11:3.

The Most High hath sanctified his own tabernacle. God is in the midst thereof. Ps. 45:5 f.

I am God thy God. Ps. 49:7.

Thou art my refuge in the day of my trouble. Ps. 58:17.

Thou shalt be perfect and without spot before the Lord thy God. Deut. 18:13.

In thy tabernacle I shall dwell forever. I shall be protected under the covert of thy wings. Ps. 60:5.

The boat in the midst of the sea was tossed by the waves. Mat. 14:24.

All nations shall serve him. Ps. 71:11.

I am always with thee. Ps. 72:23.

I am come to cast fire on the earth. Luke 12:49.

I will compass thy altar, O Lord, that I may hear the voice of thy praise. Ps. 25:6 f.

I have loved, O Lord, the beauty of thy house, and the place where thy glory dwelleth. Ps. 25:8.

With desire I have desired to eat this Pasch with you. Luke 22:15.

In the churches I will bless thee, O Lord. Ps. 25:12.

For thy name's sake thou wilt nourish me. Ps. 30:4.

O how great is the multitude of thy sweetness, O Lord, which thou hast hidden for them that fear thee! Ps. 30:20.

Thou hast multiplied thy wonderful works, O Lord my God: in thy thoughts there is no one like to thee. Ps. 39:6.

O foolish and slow of heart to believe! Luke 24:25.

As the hart panteth after the fountains of water: so my soul panteth after thee, O God. Ps. 41:2.

My soul hath thirsted after the strong living God: when shall I come and appear before the face of God? Ps. 41:3.

Of his fulness we have all received. John 1:16.

I will come unto thy house, I will worship towards thy holy temple, in thy fear. Ps. 5:8.

The Lord is in his holy temple. Ps. 10:6.

The Lord is the portion of my inheritance. Ps. 15:5.

I set the Lord always in my sight. Ps. 15:8.

I am come in the name of my Father. John 5:43.

Trust in him, all ye congregation of people; pour out your hearts before him: God is our helper forever.

In the sanctuary have I come before thee to see thy power and thy glory. Ps. 61:9.

The woman saith to him: I know that the Messias cometh. Jesus saith to her: I am he who am speaking with thee. John 4:25 f.

Keep not far from him, lest thou be forgotten. Ecclus. 13:13.

Come over to me all ye that desire me, and be filled with my fruits. Ecclus. 24:26.

Thou shalt not appear empty in the sight of the Lord. Ecclus. 35:6.

God so loved the world as to give his only begotten Son. John 3:16.

They that approach to his feet shall receive of his doctrine. Deut. 33:3.

Go to him early in the morning, and let thy foot wear the steps of his doors. Ecclus. 6:36.

A faithful friend is a strong defence, and he that hath found him hath found a treasure. Ecclus. 6:14.

If any man thirst, let him come to me and drink. John 7:37.

All the nations thou hast made shall come and adore before thee, O Lord: and they shall glorify thy name. Ps. 85:9.

Loose thy shoes from off thy feet: for the place whereon thou standest is holy. Jos. 5:16.

I am come that you may have life. John 10:10.

The Lord will be at thy side, and will keep thy foot that thou be not taken. Prov. 3:26.

I love them that love me. Prov. 8:17.

I am God, the Holy One in the midst of thee. Osee 11:9.

He loved them unto the end. John 13:1.

I am thy portion and inheritance in the midst of the children of Israel. Num. 18:20.

I, if I be lifted up from the earth, will draw all things to myself. John 12:32.

Be not afraid: for I am with thee to deliver thee, saith the Lord. Jer. 1:8.

I will dwell in the midst of the children of Israel and will be their God. Ez. 29:45.

I am with thee, saith the Lord, to save thee. Jer. 30:11.

You call me Master, and Lord: and you say well, for so I am. John 13:13.

They shall know that I the Lord their God am with them, and that they are my people, the house of Israel: saith the Lord. Ez. 34:30.

I am the vine. John 15:5.

The altar shall be sanctified by my glory. Ex. 29:43.

I will set my tabernacle in the midst of you. Lev. 26:9.

I will set my sanctuary in the midst of them forever. And my tabernacle shall be with them: and I will be their God, and they shall be my people. Ez. 37:26 f.

As the branch cannot bear fruit of itself unless it abide in the vine, so neither can you unless you abide in me. John 15:4.

Seek ye the Lord while he may be found: call upon him while he is near. Is. 55:6.

Incline your ear and come to me; hear and your soul shall live, and I will make an everlasting covenant with you, the faithful mercies of David. Is. 55:3.

Jesus said, I thirst. John 19:28.

Fear not, for I am with thee. Is. 43:5.

My Just One is near at hand. Is. 51:5.

O expectation of Israel, the Savior thereof in time of trouble: why wilt thou be as a stranger in the land, and as a wayfaring man turning in to lodge? Why wilt thou be as a wandering man, as a mighty man that cannot save? But thou, O Lord, art among us, and thy name is called upon us, forsake us not. Jer. 14:8 f.

The end of the law is Christ. Rom. 10:4.

I am with thee, to save thee, and to deliver thee, saith the Lord. Jer. 15:20.

He humbled himself. Phil. 2:7.

He shall feed his flock like a shepherd. Is. 40:11.

Fear not, I am with thee. Is. 41:10.

I am the Lord thy God, the Holy One of Israel, thy Savior. Is. 43:3.

Verily thou art a hidden God, the God of Israel, the Savior. Is. 45:15.

Come ye near unto me. Is. 48:16.

Christ liveth in me. Gal. 2:20.

He that cometh to me shall not hunger. John 6:35.

Behold the Lamb of God. Behold him who taketh away the sin of the world. John 1:29.

The name of the city from that day was: The Lord is there. Ez. 48:35.

Why dost thou not adore Bel? And he answered, and said to him: Because I do not worship idols made with hands, but the living God that created heaven and earth, and hath power over all flesh. Dan. 14:4.

In him dwelleth all the fulness of the Godhead corporally. Col. 2:9.

My eyes shall be open, and my ears attentive to the prayer of him that shall pray in this place. For I have chosen and have sanctified this place, that my name may be there forever, and my eyes and my heart may remain there perpetually. 2 Par. 7:15 f.

Hold the mystery of faith in a pure conscience. 1 Tim. 3:9.

I will dwell in the midst of thee. Zach. 2:11.

Receive the ingrafted word which is able to save your souls. Jas. 1:21.

We [have] all things together in thee alone. Tob. 10:5.

Thou shalt not fear them because the Lord thy God is in the midst of thee, a God mighty. Deut. 7:21.

They that go far from thee shall perish. Ps. 72:27.

To him that thirsteth I will give of the fountain of the water of life, gratis. Apoc. 21:6.

The King of Israel the Lord is in the midst of thee, thou shalt fear evil no more. In that day it shall be said to Jerusalem: Fear not: to Sion: Let not thy hands be weakened. The Lord thy God in the midst of thee is mighty, he will save: he will rejoice over thee with gladness, he will be silent in his love, he will be joyful over thee in praise. Soph. 3:15-17.

The throne of God and of the Lamb shall be in it, and his servants shall serve him. Apoc. 22:3.

In that day man shall bow down himself to his Maker, and his eyes shall look to the Holy One of Israel. Is. 17:7.

He is near that justifieth me. Is. 50:8.

I, I myself will comfort you. Is. 51:12.

My people shall know my name in that day: for I myself that spoke, behold I am here. Is. 52:6.

He that thirsteth, let him come: and he that will, let him take the water of life, gratis. Apoc. 22:17.

19. SACRAMENTALS

Holy Water

They shall pour living waters . . . into a vessel. And a man that is clean shall dip hyssop in them, and shall sprinkle therewith all the tent and all the furniture, and the men that are defiled by touching the corpse of a man, or his bone, or his grave. Num. 19:17 f.

Let them be sprinkled with the water of purification. Num. 8:7.

Wash me yet more from my iniquity, and cleanse me from my sin. Ps. 50:4.

Thou shalt sprinkle me with hyssop, and I shall be cleansed. Ps. 50:7.

Incense

Thou shalt make an altar to burn incense. Ex. 30:1.

When he shall place them in the evening, he shall burn an everlasting incense before the Lord throughout your generations. Ex. 30:8.

Let my prayer be directed as incense in thy sight. Ps. 140:2.

Taking the censer, which he hath filled with the burning coals of the altar, and taking up with his hand the compounded perfume for incense, he shall go in within the veil into the holy place: that when the perfumes are put upon the fire, the cloud and vapor thereof may cover the oracle, which is over the testimony, and he may not die. Lev. 16:12 f.

These are the things you must take . . . spices for sweet smelling incense. Ex. 25:6.

The oil of unction and the incense of spices in the sanctuary, all things which I have commanded thee shall they make. Ex. 31:11.

All the multitude of the people was praying without, at the hour of incense. Luke 1:10.

Another angel came, and stood before the altar, having a golden censer: and there was given to him much incense, that he should offer of the prayers of all saints upon the golden altar, which is before the throne of God. And the smoke of the incense of the prayers of the saints ascended up before God, from the hand of the angel. Apoc. 8:3 f.

The Angelus

The angel of the Lord declared unto Mary. Luke 1:26.

And she conceived of the Holy Ghost. Luke 1:31.

Hail, Mary. Luke 1:28.

Behold the handmaid of the Lord. Luke 1:38.

Be it done to me according to thy word. Luke 1:38.

The Word was made flesh. John 1:14.

And dwelt amongst us. John 1:14.

Ashes

In the sweat of thy face shalt thou eat bread till thou return to the earth, out of which thou wast taken: for dust thou art, and unto dust thou shalt return. Gen. 3:19.

Abraham answered, and said: Seeing I have once begun, I will speak to my Lord, whereas I am dust and ashes. Gen. 18:27.

Mardochai put on sackcloth, strewing ashes on his head. Esth. 4:1.

I reprehend myself, and do penance in dust and ashes. Job 42:6.

He hath fed me with ashes. Lam. 3:16.

Woe to thee, Corozain, woe thee, Bethsaida: for if in Tyre and Sidon had been wrought the miracles that had been wrought in you, they had long ago done penance in sackcloth and ashes. Mat. 11:21.

Palm Branches

On the next day a great multitude, that was come to the festival day, when they had heard that Jesus was coming to Jerusalem, took branches of palm trees, and went forth to meet him, and cried: Hosanna, blessed is he that cometh in the name of the Lord, the King of Israel. John 12:12 f.

The just shall flourish like the palm tree. Ps. 91:13.

All the walls of the temple round about he carved with divers figures and carvings: and he made in them cherubim and palm trees, and divers representations as it were standing out, and coming forth from the wall. 3 K. 6:29.

After this, I saw a great multitude, which no man could number, of all nations, and tribes, and peoples, and tongues: standing before the throne, and in sight of the Lamb, clothed with white robes, and palms in their hands. Apoc. 7:9.

Grace at Table (1 C. 10:31)

Before Meals

V. The eyes of all

R. Hope in thee, O Lord: and thou givest them meat in due season. Thou openest thy hand, and fillest with blessing every living creature. Ps. 144:15 f.

O Lord, have mercy on us. Mat. 20:31.

Our Father. Mat. 6:9.

P. And lead us not into temptation. Mat. 6:13.

R. But deliver us from evil. Amen. Mat. 6:13.

After Meals

P. O Lord, have mercy on us. Mat. 20:31.

R. Thanks be to God. 2 C. 9:15.

P. Let all thy works, O Lord, praise thee.

R. And let thy saints bless thee. Ps. 144:10.

Miserere psalm. Ps. 50:2-21.

O Lord have mercy on us. Mat. 20:31.

Our Father. Mat. 6:9.

P. And lead us not into temptation,

R. But deliver us from evil. Amen. Mat. 6:13.

P. He hath distributed, he hath given to the poor.

R. His justice remaineth forever and ever. Ps. 111:9.

P. I will bless the Lord at all times.

R. His praise shall always be in my mouth.

P. In the Lord shall my soul be praised.

R. Let the meek hear and rejoice.

P. O magnify the Lord with me.

R. And let us extol his name together. Ps. 33:2-4.

Our Father. Mat. 6:9.

20. IDOLATRY

Finding out a device, he made two golden calves, and said to them: Go ye up no more to Jerusalem: behold thy gods, O Israel, who brought thee out of the land of Egypt. And he set the one in Bethel, and the other in Dan: and this thing became an occasion of sin: for the people went to adore the calf as far as Dan. 3 K. 12:28-30.

He commanded altars to be built, and temples, and idols, to the end that they should forget the law, and should change all the justifications of God. 1 Mac. 1:50.

They provoked him with their inventions. Ps. 105:29.

They went disloyally after their own inventions. Ps. 105:39.

Their idols have caused them to err. Amos 2:4.

The idols have spoken what was unprofitable, and the diviners have seen a lie, and the dreamers have spoken vanity: therefore they were led away as a flock: they shall be afflicted, because they have no shepherd. Zach. 10:2.

According to the plenty of his land he hath abounded with idols. Osee 10:1.

If we have spread forth our hands to a strange God: shall not God search out these things? Ps. 43:21 f.

Who hath formed a god and made a graven thing that is profitable for nothing? Behold all the partakers thereof shall be confounded. Is. 44:10 f.

They have provoked me with that which was no god, and have angered me with their vanities: and I will provoke them with that which is no people, and will vex them with a foolish nation. Deut. 32:21.

Their gods themselves have no sense. Bar. 6:41.

Thou shalt not have strange gods before me. Ex. 20:3.

Thou shalt not make to thyself a graven thing, nor the likeness of any things that are in heaven above or that are in the earth beneath or that abide in the waters under the earth. Thou shalt not adore them, and thou shalt not serve them. Deut. 5:8 f.

You shall not make to yourselves any idol to adore it. Lev. 26:1.

Let them all be confounded that adore graven things and that glory in their idols. Ps. 96:7.

The Spirit brought me near the inner gate, where was set the idol of jealousy to provoke to jealousy. Ez. 8:3.

Their land is full of idols: they have adored the work of their own hands which their own fingers have made. Is. 2:8.

They have wandered from me after their idols. Ez. 44:10.

Daniel said: I adore the Lord my God: for he is the living God: but that is no living god. Dan. 14:24.

The idol that is made by hands, is cursed, as well it, as he that made it: he because he made it; and it because, being frail, it is called a god. Wis. 14:6.

They have set their idols in the house, in which my name is called upon, to defile it. Jer. 32:34.

They burnt sweet-smelling frankincense to all their idols. Ez. 7:13.

They light candles to them, and in great number, of which they cannot see one. Bar. 6:18.

He set up the abominable idol of desolation upon the altar of God, and they built altars throughout all the cities of Juda round about. And they burnt incense. 1 Mac. 1:57 f.

I have become rich, I have found me an idol. Osee 12:8.

He shall make no account of the God of his fathers. But he shall worship the god Maozim in his place: and a god whom his fathers knew not, he shall worship with gold and silver and precious stones and things of great price. Dan. 11:37 f.

They bear him on their shoulders and carry him, and set him in his place, and he shall stand, and shall not stir out of his place. Yea, when they shall cry also unto him, he shall not hear: he shall not save them from tribulation. Is. 46:7.

21. THE BOOK OF WISDOM ON THE GROWTH OF IDOLATRY

A father being afflicted with bitter grief made to himself the image of his son who was quickly taken away: and him who then had died as a man, he began now to worship as a god, and appointed him rites and sacrifices among his servants.

Then in process of time, wicked custom prevailing, this error was kept as a law, and statues were worshipped by the commandment of tyrants.

And those whom men could not honor in presence, because they dwelt far off, they brought their resemblance from afar, and made express image of the king whom they had a mind to honor: that by this their diligence, they might honor as present, him that was absent.

And to the worshipping of these, the singular diligence also of the artificer helped to set forward the ignorant.

For he being willing to please him that employed him, labored with all his art to make the resemblance in the best manner.

And the multitude of the men, carried away by the beauty of the work, took him now for a god that a little while before was but honored as a man. 14:15-20.

22. FALSE PRIESTS

You have cast out the priests of the Lord, the sons of Aaron, and the Levites: and you have made you priests, like all the nations of the earth. . . . But the Lord is our God, whom we forsake not, and the priests who minister to the Lord are the sons of Aaron, and the Levites are in their order. 2 Par. 13:9 f.

He withstood the king, and said: It doth not belong to thee, Ozias, to burn incense to the Lord, but to the priests, that is, to the sons of Aaron, who are consecrated for this ministry: go out of the sanctuary, do not despise: for this thing shall not be accounted to thy glory by the Lord God. 2 Par. 26:18.

Thou hast no healing medicines. Jer. 30:13.

Cursed be he that maketh the blind to wander out of the way: and all the people shall say: Amen. Deut. 27:18.

Your hands are defiled with blood, and your fingers with iniquity: your lips have spoken lies, and your tongue uttereth iniquity. Is. 59:3.

I will visit in that day upon every one that entereth arrogantly over the threshold: them that fill the house of the Lord their God with iniquity and deceit. Soph. 1:9.

The sin of the young men was exceeding great before the Lord: because they withdrew from the sacrifice of the Lord. 1 K. 2:17.

In vain dost thou multiply medicines, there shall be no cure for thee. Jer. 46:11.

You have eaten the fruit of lying. Osee 10:13.

They design to extinguish the glory of thy temple and altar. Esth. 14:9.

Thou hast set up altars of confusion. Jer. 11:13.

23. FALSE PROPHETS

They see vain things, and they foretell lies, saying: The Lord saith: whereas the Lord hath not sent them; and they have persisted to confirm what they have said. Ez. 13:6.

Thou hast forgotten me, and hast trusted in falsehood. Jer. 13:25.

My people have done two evils. They have forsaken me, the fountain of living water, and have digged to themselves cisterns, broken cisterns, that can hold no water. Jer. 2:13.

They healed the breach of the daughter of my people disgracefully, saying: Peace, peace: and there was no peace. Jer. 6:14.

O ye sons of men, how long will you be dull of heart? Why do you love vanity and seek after lying? Ps. 4:3.

There were false prophets among the people, even as there shall be among you lying teachers who shall bring in sects of perdition. 2 Pet. 2:1.

There shall arise false christs and false prophets, and shall show great signs and wonders, insomuch as to deceive, if possible, even the elect. Mat. 24:24.

24. MEN VICTIMS OF THEIR OWN DECEITS

As for the word which thou hast spoken to us in the name of the Lord, we will not hearken to thee: but we will certainly do every word that shall proceed out of our own mouth: and we were filled with bread, and it was well with us, and we saw no evil. Jer. 44:16 f.

Counsel has perished from her children: their wisdom is become unprofitable. Jer. 49:7.

Every man has become foolish by his knowledge, for what he hath cast is a lie. Jer. 51:17.

If one cast a stone on high, it will fall upon his own head: and the deceitful stroke will wound the deceitful. Ecclus. 27:28.

He that diggeth a pit, shall fall into it: and he that setteth a stone for his neighbor, shall stumble upon it: and he that layeth a snare for another, shall perish in it. Ecclus. 27:29.

A mischievous counsel shall be rolled back upon the author, and he shall not know from whence it cometh to him. Ecclus. 27:30.

Their foot hath been taken in the very snare which they hid. The sinner hath been caught in the works of his own hands. Ps. 9:16 f.

They are caught in the counsels which they devise. Ps. 9:23.

Let them be confounded that act unjust things. Ps. 24:4.

My people heard not my voice: and Israel hearkened not to me. So I let them go according to the desires of their heart: they shall walk in their own inventions. Ps. 80:12 f.

You have eaten the fruit of lying because thou hast trusted in thy ways, in the multitude of thy strong ones. Osee 10:13.

For the sin of their mouth let them be taken in their pride. Ps. 58:13.

Let their table become as a snare before them, and a recompense and a stumblingblock. Ps. 68:23.

O wicked presumption, whence camest thou to cover the earth with thy malice and deceitfulness? Ecclus. 37:3.

Cursed be the man that trusteth in man, and maketh flesh his arm. Jer. 17:5.

We will magnify our tongue: our lips are our own. Ps. 11:5.

25. ADMONITIONS TO AVOID IDOLATRY

Depart not from the Lord, and from our society, by building an altar beside the altar of the Lord our God. Jos. 22:19.

Why have you forsaken the Lord the God of Israel, building a sacrilegious altar, and revolting from the worship of him? Is it a small thing to you? Jos. 22:16 f.

Ltitle children, keep yourselves from idols. 1 John 5:21.

If thy brother, the son of thy mother, or thy son, or daughter, or thy wife that is in thy bosom, or thy friend, whom thou lovest as thy own soul, would persuade thee secretly saying: Let us go, and serve strange gods, which thou knowest not, nor thy fathers, of all the nations round about, that are near or afar off, from one end of the earth to the other, consent not to him, hear him not, neither let thy eye spare him to pity and conceal him. Deut. 13:6-8.

Thy prophets have seen false and foolish things for thee: and they have not laid open thy iniquity, to excite thee to penance: but they have seen for thee false revelations and banishments. Lam. 2:14.

Fight not against the Lord the God of your fathers, for it is not good for you. 2 Par. 13:12.

Harden not your necks, as your fathers did: yield yourselves to the Lord, and come to his sanctuary, which he hath sanctified forever: serve the Lord the God of your fathers, and the wrath of his indignation shall be turned away from you. 2 Par. 30:8.

All that belongeth to the rites of the God of heaven, let it be given diligently in the house of the God of heaven: lest his wrath should be enkindled against the realm of the king, and of his sons. 1 Es. 7:23.

All the men of thy confederacy have deceived thee: the men of thy peace have prevailed against thee: they that eat with thee shall lay snares under thee: there is no wisdom in him. Abd. 7.

Thus saith the Lord to the house of Israel: Seek ye me, and you shall live. But seek not Bethel, and go not into Galgal, neither shall you pass over into Bersabee: for Galgal shall go into captivity, and Bethel shall be unprofitable. Seek ye the Lord, and live: lest the house of Joseph be burnt with fire, and it shall devour, and there shall be none to quench Bethel. Amos 5:4-6.

Dost thou trust a staff of a broken reed, upon which if a man lean, it will break and go into his hand, and pierce it? 4 K. 18:21.

Put not your trust in princes: in the children of men, in whom there is no salvation. His spirit shall go forth, and he shall return into his earth: in that day all their thoughts shall perish. Ps. 145:2-4.

Be not desirous of his meats, in which is the bread of deceit. Prov. 23:3.

Hast thou seen a man wise in his own conceit? There shall be more hope of a fool than of him. Prov. 26:12.

Woe to you that are wise in your own eyes, and prudent in your own conceits. Is. 5:21.

Woe to you, apostate children, saith the Lord, that you would take counsel, and not of me: and would begin a web, and not by my Spirit, that you might add sin upon sin. Is. 30:1.

Thou sayest: I am rich and made wealthy, and have need of nothing: and knowest not that thou art wretched, and miserable, and poor, and blind, and naked. Apoc. 3:17.

You have forgotten the name of our God, and if we have spread forth our hands to a strange god, shall not God search out these things? Ps. 43:21 f.

God keep us from any such wickedness that we should revolt from the Lord, and leave off following his steps, by building an altar to offer holocausts, and sacrifices, and victims, beside the altar of the Lord our God, which is erected before his tabernacle. Jer. 22:29.

26. GOD'S PUNISHMENT OF THE GUILTY

The Lord is patient, and great in power, and will not cleanse and acquit the guilty. Nah. 1:3.

Who can stand before the face of his indignation? and who shall resist in the fierceness of his anger? His indignation is poured out like fire: and the rocks are melted by him. Nah. 1:6.

The Lord is good and giveth strength in the day of trouble: and knoweth them that hope in him. Nah. 1:7.

But with a flood that passeth by, he will make an utter end of the place thereof: and darkness shall pursue his enemies. Nah. 1:8.

They have provoked me with that which was no god, and have angered me with their vanities: and I will provoke them with that which is no people, and will vex them with a foolish nation. A fire is kindled in my wrath, and shall burn even to the lowest hell: and shall devour the earth with her increase, and shall burn the foundations of the mountains. Deut. 32:21 f.

Revenge is mine, and I will repay them in due time, that their foot may slide: the day of destruction is at hand: and the time makes haste to come. Deut. 31:35.

Behold the day shall come kindled as a furnace: and all the proud, and all that do wickedly shall be stubble: and the day that cometh shall set them on fire, saith the Lord of hosts, it shall not leave them root nor branch. Mal. 4:1.

I will pour out upon thee my indignation: in the fire of my rage will I blow upon thee, and will give thee into the hands of men that are brutish and contrive thy destruction. Thou shalt be fuel for the fire, thy blood shall be in the midst of the land, thou shalt be forgotten: for I the Lord have spoken it. Ez. 21:31 f.

Behold I will bring an affliction upon this place, so that whosoever shall hear it, his ears shall tingle. Because they have forsaken me, and have profaned this place. Jer. 19:3 f.

Be circumcised to the Lord, and take away the foreskins of your hearts, ye men of Juda, and ye inhabitants of Jerusalem: lest my indignation come forth like fire, and burn, and there be none that can quench it: because of the wickedness of your thoughts. Jer. 4:4.

It shall be at an instant suddenly. A visitation shall come from the Lord of hosts in thunder, and with earthquake, and with a great noise of whirlwind and tempest, and with the flame of devouring fire. Is. 29:6.

He shall destroy the wicked, and the sinners together: and they that have forsaken the Lord, shall be consumed. For they shall be confounded for the idols, to which they have sacrificed: and you shall be ashamed of the gardens which you had chosen. Is. 1:28 f.

Thou hast trusted in thy wickedness, and hast said: There is none that seeth me. Thy wisdom, and thy knowledge, this hath deceived thee. And thou hast said in thy heart: I am, and beside me there is no other. Evil shall come upon thee, and thou shalt not know the rising thereof: and calamity shall fall violently upon thee, which thou canst not keep off: misery shall come upon thee suddenly, which thou shalt not know. Is. 47:10 f.

Thou hast failed in the multitude of thy counsels: let now the astrologers stand and save thee, they that gazed at the stars, and counted the months, that from them they might tell the things that shall come to thee. Behold they are as stubble, fire hath burnt them, they shall not deliver themselves from the power of the flames. Is. 44:13 f.

I the Lord have spoken: it shall come to pass, and I will do it: I will not pass by, nor spare, nor be pacified, I will judge thee according to thy ways, and according to thy doings, saith the Lord. Ez. 24:14.

Behold the Lord shall lay waste the earth, and shall strip it, and shall afflict the face thereof, and scatter abroad the inhabitants thereof. And it shall be as with the people, so with the priest: and as with the servant, so with his master: as with the handmaid, so with her mistress: as with the buyer, so with the seller: as with the lender, so with the borrower: as with him that calleth for his money, so with him that oweth. With desolation shall the earth be laid waste, and it shall be utterly spoiled: for the Lord hath spoken this word. Is. 24:1-3.

The earth mourned, and faded away, and is weakened: the world faded away, the height of the people of the earth is weakened. And the earth is infected by the inhabitants thereof: because they have transgressed the laws, they have changed the ordinance, they have broken the everlasting covenant. Therefore shall a curse devour the earth, and the inhabitants thereof shall sin: and therefore they that dwell therein shall be mad, and few men shall be left. Is. 24:4-6.

The vintage hath mourned, the vine hath languished away, all the merry hearted have sighed. The mirth of timbrels hath ceased, the noise of them that rejoice is ended, the melody of the harp is silent. They shall not drink wine with a song: the drink shall be bitter to them that drink it. Is. 24:7-9.

The city of vanity is broken down, every house is shut up, no man cometh in. There shall be a crying for wine in the streets: all mirth is forsaken: the joy of the earth is gone away. Desolation is left in the city, and calamity shall oppress the gates. For it shall be thus in the midst of the earth, in the midst of the people, as if a few olives, that remain, should be shaken out of the olive tree: or grapes, when the vintage is ended. Is. 24:10-13.

27. DESOLATION AND LAMENTATION

I beseech thee, O Lord God of heaven, strong, great, and terrible, who keepest covenant and mercy with those that love thee, and keep thy commandments.

Let thy ears be attentive, and thy eyes open, to hear the prayer of thy servant, which I pray before thee now, night and day, for the children of Israel thy servants: and I confess the sins of the children of Israel, by which they have sinned against thee: I and my father's house have sinned.

We have been seduced by vanity, and have not kept thy commandments, and ceremonies, and judgments, which thou hast commanded thy servant Moses.

Remember the word that thou commandest to Moses thy servant, saying: If you shall transgress, I will scatter you abroad among the nations.

But if you return to me, and keep my commandments and do them, though you should be led away to the uttermost parts of the world, I will gather you from thence, and bring you back to the place which I have chosen for my name to dwell there.

And these are thy servants, and thy people: whom thou hast redeemed by thy great strength, and by thy mighty hand.

I beseech thee, O Lord, let thy ear be attentive to the prayer of thy servant, and to the prayer of thy servants who desire to fear thy name. 2 Es. 1:5-11.

I will take away from them the light of the lamp. And all this land shall be a desolation. Jer. 25:10 f.

There is no knowledge of God in the land. Therefore shall the land mourn. Osee 4:1-3.

The Lord the God of hosts in that day shall call to weeping, and to mourning, and to girding with sackcloth. Is. 22:12.

Joy was taken away from Jacob, and the pipe and harp ceased there. 1 Mac. 3:45.

A voice was heard in the highways, weeping and howling of the children of Israel: because they have made their way wicked, they have forgotten the Lord their God. Jer. 3:21.

Between the porch and the altar the priests, the Lord's ministers shall weep, and shall say: Spare, O Lord, spare thy people; and give not thy inheritance to reproach. Joel 2:17.

Who will give me in the wilderness a lodging-place of wayfaring men, and I will leave my people and depart from them? because they are all adulterers, an assembly of transgressors. Jer. 9:2.

And they have bent their tongue, as a bow, for lies, and not for truth: they have strengthened themselves upon the earth, for they have proceeded from evil to evil, and me they have not known, saith the Lord. Jer. 9:3.

They saw the sanctuary desolate, and the altar profaned, and the gates burnt, and shrubs growing up in the courts as in a forest, or on the mountains, and the chambers joining to the temple thrown down. And they rent their garments, and made great lamentations, and put ashes on their heads. And they fell down to the ground on their faces, and they sounded with the trumpets of alarm, and they cried towards heaven. 1 Mac. 4:38-40.

It shall come to pass in that day, that I will seek to destroy all the nations that come against Jerusalem. And I will pour out upon the house of David, and upon the inhabitants of Jerusalem, the Spirit of grace, and of prayers: and they shall look upon me, whom they have pierced: and they shall mourn for him as one mourneth for an only son, and they shall grieve over him, as the manner is to grieve for the death of the first-born. Zach. 12:9 f.

Now therefore saith the Lord: Be converted to me with all your heart, in fasting and in weeping, and in mourning. And rend your hearts and not your garments, and turn to the Lord your God: for he is gracious and merciful, patient and rich in mercy, and ready to repent of the evil. Who knoweth but he will return, and forgive, and leave a blessing behind him? Joel 2:12-14.

28. THE RECONCILIATION

In those days, saith the Lord, the children of Israel shall come: going and weeping they shall make haste, and shall seek the Lord their God. They shall ask the way to Sion, their faces are hitherward. They shall come, and shall be joined to the Lord by an everlasting covenant, which shall never be forgotten. Jer. 50:4 f.

In the last days many people shall go and say: Come and let us go up to the house of the God of Jacob, and he will teach us his ways, and we will walk in his paths: for the law shall come forth from Sion, and the word of the Lord from Jerusalem. Is. 2:2 f.

We will go with you: for we have heard that God is with you. Zach. 8:23.

The Lord is with you, because you have been with him. If you seek him, you shall find: but if you forsake him, he will forsake you. And many days shall pass in Israel without the true God, and without a priest a teacher, and without the law. And when in their distress they shall return to the Lord the God of Israel, and shall seek him, they shall find him. 2 Par. 15:2-4.

The inhabitants go one to another, saying: Let us go and entreat the face of the Lord, and let us seek the Lord of hosts. I also will go. Zach. 8:21.

Many peoples, and strong nations shall come to seek the Lord of hosts in Jerusalem. Zach. 8:22.

Seek the Lord, all ye meek of the earth; you that have wrought his judgment: seek the Just, seek the Meek: if by any means you may be hid in the day of the Lord's indignation. Soph. 2:3.

They said to him: All seek for thee. Mark 1:37.

This is the generation of them that seek him, of them that seek the face of the God of Jacob. Ps. 23:6.

The Lord is good to the soul that seeketh him. Lam. 3:25.

They came to Capharnaum seeking Jesus. John 6:24.

When thou shalt seek there the Lord thy God thou shalt find him: yet so if thou seek him with all thy heart, and all the affliction of thy soul. Deut. 4:29.

The little ones have asked for bread, and there was none to break it unto them. Lam. 4:4.

In their affliction they will rise early to me: come, and let us return to the Lord: for he hath taken us, and he will heal us: he will strike, and he will cure us. Osee 6:1 f.

Return to me, saith the Lord, and I will receive thee. Jer. 3:1.

And the desolate land shall be tilled, which before was waste in the sight of all that passed by, they shall say: This land that was untilled is become as a garden of pleasure: and the cities that were abandoned, and desolate, and destroyed, are peopled and fenced. Ez. 36:34 f.

Lift up thy eyes round about, and see: all these are gathered together, they are come to thee: thy sons shall come from afar, and thy daughters shall rise up at thy side. Then shalt thou see, and abound, and thy heart shall wonder and be enlarged, when the multitude of the sea shall be converted to thee, the strength of the

Gentiles shall come to thee. Is. 60:4 f.

The multitude of camels shall cover thee, the dromedaries of Madian and Epha: all they from Saba shall come, bringing gold and frankincense: and showing forth praise to the Lord. Is. 60:6.

Say to the faint-hearted: Take courage, and fear not: behold your God will bring the revenge of recompense: God himself will come and will save you. Is. 35:4.

Then shall the eyes of the blind be opened, and the ears of the deaf shall be unstopped. Then shall the lame man leap as a hart, and the tongue of the dumb shall be free: for waters are broken out in the desert, and streams in the wilderness. And that which was dry land shall become a pool, and the thirsty land springs of water. Is. 35:5-7.

They shall not hunger, nor thirst, neither shall the heat nor the sun strike them: for he that is merciful to them shall be their shepherd, and at the fountains of waters he shall give them drink. And I will make all my mountains a way, and my paths shall be exalted. Behold these shall come from afar, and behold these from the north and from the sea, and these from the south country. Give praise, O ye heavens, and rejoice, O earth; ye mountains, give praise with jubilation: because the Lord hath comforted his people, and will have mercy on his poor ones. Is. 49:10-13.

They shall come with weeping: and I will bring them back in mercy: and I will bring them through the torrents of waters in a right way, and they shall not stumble in it: for I am a Father to Israel. Jer. 31:9.

Hear the word of the Lord, O ye nations, and declare it in the islands that are afar off, and say: He that scattered Israel will gather him: and he will keep him as the shepherd doth his flock. Jer. 31:10.

Then shall they say among the Gentiles: The Lord hath done great things for them. The Lord hath done great things for us: we are become joyful. Ps. 125:3.

Turn again our captivity, O Lord, as a stream in the south. They that sow in tears shall reap in joy. Going they went and wept, casting their seeds. But coming they shall come with joyfulness, carrying their sheaves. Ps. 125:4-7.

V

OTHER SACRAMENTS

PENANCE

1. THE VIRTUE OF PENANCE

Unless you do penance, you shall all likewise perish. Luke 13:3.

I say to you that there shall be joy in heaven upon one sinner that doth penance, more than upon ninety-nine just, who need not penance. Luke 15:7.

I came not to call the just, but sinners to penance. Luke 5:32.

Peter said to them: Do penance, and be baptized every one of you in the name of Jesus Christ, for the remission of your sins: and you shall receive the gift of the Holy Ghost. Acts 2:38.

Paul preached first to them that are at Damascus, and at Jerusalem, and throughout all the country of Judea, and to the Gentiles, that they should do penance, and turn to God, doing works worthy of penance. Acts 26:20.

Now I am glad; not because you were made sorrowful; but because you were made sorrowful unto penance. For you were made sorrowful according to God, that in nothing you should suffer damage by us. 2 C. 7:9.

If you turn to the Lord with all your heart, and prepare your hearts unto the Lord, and serve him only, he will deliver you out of the hands of the Philistines. 1 K. 7:3.

Let him do penance for his sin. Lev. 5:5.

If we do not penance, we shall fall into the hands of the Lord, and not into the hands of men. Ecclus. 2:22.

I reprehend myself, and do penance in dust and ashes. Job 42:6.

After thou didst convert me, I did penance. Jer. 31:19.

I have put off the robe of peace, and have put upon me the sackcloth of supplication, and I will cry to the Most High in my days. Bar. 4:20.

Be converted, and do penance for all your iniquities: and iniquity shall not be your ruin. Ez. 18:30.

Do penance, for the kingdom of heaven is at hand. Mat. 4:17.

Bring forth, therefore fruits worthy of penance, and do not begin to say, We have Abraham for our father. For I say unto you, that God is able of these stones to raise up children to Abraham. Luke 3:8.

If they sin against thee (for there is no man who sinneth not), and thou being angry deliver them up to their enemies, then if they do penance in their heart, and being converted make supplication to thee in their captivity, saying: We have sinned, we have done unjustly, we have committed wickedness: and return to thee with all their heart, and all their soul: then hear thou in heaven, in the firmament of thy throne, their prayers, and their supplications, and do judgment for them: and forgive thy people that have sinned against thee, and all their iniquities, by which they have transgressed against thee. 3 K. 8:46-50.

Then began he to upbraid the cities wherein were done the most of his miracles, for that they had not done penance. Mat. 11:20.

The benignity of God leadeth thee to penance. Rom. 2:4.

Be converted, and depart from your idols, and turn away your faces from all your abominations. Ez. 14:6.

If that nation against which I have spoken, shall repent of their evil, I also will repent of the evil that I have thought to do to them. Jer. 18:8.

Do penance from this thy wickedness. Acts 8:22.

Woe to thee, Corozain, woe to thee, Bethsaida: for if in Tyre and Sidon had been wrought the mighty works that have been wrought in you, they would have done penance long ago, sitting in sackcloth and ashes. Luke 10:13.

John was in the desert preaching the baptism of penance. Mark 1:4.

Be penitent, and be converted, that your sins may be blotted out. Acts 3:19.

Him [Jesus] hath God exalted with his right hand, to be Prince and Savior, and to give repentance to Israel, and remission of sins. Acts 5:31.

He came into all the country about the Jordan, preaching the baptism of penance. Luke 2:3.

Be mild towards all men, apt to teach, patient, with modesty admonishing them that resist the truth: if peradventure God may give them repentance to know the truth, and they may recover themselves from the snares of the devil, by whom they are held captive at his will. 2 Tim. 2:24-26.

The Lord delayeth not his promise, as some imagine, but dealeth patiently for your sake, not willing that any should perish, but that all should return to penance. 2 Pet. 3:9.

God indeed having winked at the times of this ignorance, now declareth unto men that all should everywhere do penance. Acts 17:30.

Be mindful therefore from whence thou art fallen: and do penance, and do the first works. Or else I come to thee, and will move thy candlestick out of its place, except thou do penance. Apoc. 2:5.

In like manner do penance: or else I will come to thee quickly, and will fight against them with the sword of my mouth. Apoc. 2:16.

I gave her a time that she might do penance, and she will not repent of her fornication. Apoc. 2:21.

They shall be in very great tribulation, except they do penance from their deeds. Apoc. 2:22.

Have in mind therefore in what manner thou hast received and heard: and observe, and do penance. If then thou shalt not watch; I will come to thee as a thief, and thou shalt not know at what hour I will come to thee. Apoc. 3:3.

Such as I love, I rebuke and chastise. Be zealous therefore, and do penance. Apoc. 3:19.

The publican standing afar off would not so much as lift up his eyes towards heaven; but struck his breast, saying: O God, be merciful to me a sinner. Luke 18:13.

A faithful saying, and worthy of all acceptation, that Christ Jesus came into this world to save sinners, of whom I am the chief. 1 Tim. 1:15.

2. GOD'S MERCY TO REPENTANT SINNERS

A sacrifice to God is an afflicted spirit: a contrite and humble heart, O God, thou wilt not despise. Ps. 50:19.

Behold I will close their wounds and give them health, and I will cure them: and I will reveal to them the prayer of peace and truth. And I will bring back the captivity of Juda, and the captivity of Jerusalem: and I will build them as from the beginning. And I will cleanse them from all their iniquity, whereby they have sinned against me: and I will forgive all their iniquities, whereby they have sinned against me, and despised me. Jer. 33:6-8.

My son, hast thou sinned? do so no more: but for thy former sins also pray that they may be forgiven thee. Ecclus. 21:1.

I am, I am he that blot out thy iniquities for my own sake, and I will not remember thy sins. Is. 43:25.

If your sins be as scarlet, they shall be made as white as snow: and if they be red as crimson, they shall be white as wool. Is. 1:18.

I have blotted out thy iniquities as a cloud, and thy sins as a mist: return to me, for I have redeemed thee. Is. 44:22.

I saw his ways, and I healed him, and brought him back, and restored comforts to him, and to them that mourn for him. Is. 57:18.

I will forgive their iniquity, and will remember their sin no more. Jer. 31:34.

For thy name's sake, O Lord, thou wilt pardon my sin, for it is great. Ps. 24:11.

I will not remember all his iniquities that he hath done: in his justice which he hath wrought, he shall live. Ez. 18:22.

Blessed is thy name, O God of our fathers: who when thou hast been angry, wilt show mercy, and in the time of tribulation forgivest the sins of them that call upon thee. Tob. 3:13.

I know that thou art a gracious and merciful God, patient, and of much compassion, and easy to forgive evil. Job 4:2.

Speak ye to the heart of Jerusalem, and call to her: for her evil is come to an end, her iniquity is forgiven: she hath received of the hand of the Lord double for all her sins. Is. 40:2.

Many sins are forgiven her, because she hath loved much. But to whom less is forgiven, he loveth less. Luke 7:47.

Forgive us our sins, for we also forgive every one that is indebted to us. Luke 11:4.

And when Jesus had seen their faith, he saith to the sick of the palsy: Son, thy sins are forgiven thee. Mark 2:5.

Thy sins are forgiven thee. Who is this that forgiveth sins also? Luke 7:48 f.

Be it known to you, men brethren, that through him forgiveness of sins is preached to you. Acts 13:38.

God indeed was in Christ reconciling the world to himself, not imputing to them their sins. Him that knew no sin, for us he hath made sin, that we might be made the justice of God in him. 2 C. 5:19, 21.

The blood of Jesus Christ his Son cleanseth us from all sin. 1 John 1:7.

He is the propitiation for our sins: and not for ours only, but also for those of the whole world. 1 John 2:2.

Blotting out the handwriting of the decree that was against us, which was contrary to us, he hath taken the same out of the way, fastening it to the cross. Col. 2:14.

I write unto you, little children, because your sins are forgiven you for his name's sake. 1 John 2:12.

In whom we have redemption through his blood, the remission of sins. Col. 1:14.

Go now, and sin no more. John 8:11.

I will love them freely. Osee 14:5.

3. PUBLIC PENANCE

Timotheus came as though he would take Judea by force of arms. But Machabeus and they that were with him, when he drew near, prayed to the Lord, sprinkling earth upon their heads, and girding their loins with haircloth, and lying prostrate at the foot of the altar, besought him to be merciful to them. 2 Mac. 10:24-26.

All the people cried to the Lord with great earnestness, and they humbled their souls in fastings, and prayers, both they and their wives. And the priests put on haircloths, and they caused the little children to lie prostrate before the temple of the Lord, and the altar of the Lord they covered with haircloth. And they cried to the Lord the God of Israel with one accord, that their children might not be made a prey, and their wives carried off, and their cities destroyed, and their holy things profaned, and that they might not be made a reproach to the Gentiles. Jdth. 4:7-9.

Then Eliachim the high priest of the Lord went about all Israel, and spoke to them, saying: Know ye that the Lord will hear your prayers, if you continue with perseverance in fastings and prayers in the sight of the Lord. Jdth. 4:10 f.

Remember Moses the servant of the Lord, who overcame Amalec that trusted in his own strength, and in his power, and in his army, and in his shields, and in his chariots, and in his horsemen, not by fighting with the sword, but by holy prayers: so shall all the enemies of Israel be; if you persevere in this work which you have begun. So they being moved by this exhortation of his, prayed to the Lord, and continued in the sight of the Lord. So that even they who offered the holocausts to the Lord, offered the sacrifices to the Lord, girded with haircloths, and with ashes upon their head. And they all begged of God with all their heart, that he would visit his people Israel. Jdth. 4:12-16.

4. THE REPENTANCE OF NINIVE

And the word of the Lord came to Jonas the second time, saying: Arise, and go to Ninive, the great city: and preach in it the preaching that I bid thee. And Jonas arose, and went to Ninive, according to the word of the Lord: now Ninive was a great city of three days' journey. And Jonas began to enter into the city one day's journey: and he cried, and said: Yet forty days, and Ninive shall be destroyed.

And the men of Ninive believed in God: and they proclaimed a fast, and put on sackcloth from the greatest to the least. And the word came to the king of Ninive: and he rose up out of his throne, and cast away his robe from him, and was clothed with sackcloth, and sat in ashes.

And he caused it to be proclaimed and published in Ninive from the mouth of the king and of his princes, saying: Let neither men nor beasts, oxen nor sheep, taste anything: let them not feed, nor drink water.

And let men and beasts be covered with sackcloth, and cry to the Lord with all their strength, and let them turn every one from his evil way, and from the iniquity that is in their hands. Who can tell if God will turn and forgive: and will turn away from his fierce anger, and we shall not perish?

And God saw their works, that they were turned from their evil way: and God had mercy with regard to the evil which he had said that he would do to them, and he did it not. Jer. 3:1-10.

The men of Ninive shall rise in judgment with this generation, and shall condemn it: because they did penance at the preaching of Jonas. And behold a greater than Jonas here. Mat. 12:41.

5. THE SACRAMENT OF PENANCE INSTITUTED BY OUR LORD

I will give to thee the keys of the kingdom of heaven. And whatsoever thou shalt bind upon earth, shall be bound also in heaven: and whatsoever thou shalt loose on earth, shall be loosed also in heaven. Mat. 16:19.

Amen I say to you, whatsoever you shall bind upon earth, shall be bound also in heaven: and whatsoever you shall loose upon earth, shall be loosed also in heaven. Mat. 18:18.

As the Father hath sent me, I also send you. When he had said this, he breathed on them, and he said to them: Receive ye the Holy Ghost: Whose sins you shall forgive they are forgiven them, and whose sins you shall retain they are retained. John 20:21-23.

All things are of God, who hath reconciled us to himself by Christ: and hath given to us the ministry of reconciliation. 2 C. 5:18.

6. CONTRITION

Now I am glad: not because you were made sorrowful; but because you were made sorrowful unto penance. For you were sorrowful unto God. For the sorrow that is according to God worketh penance steadfast unto salvation: but the sorrow of the world worketh death. 2 C. 7:9 f.

Knowest thou not that the benignity of God leadeth thee to penance? But according to thy hardness and impenitent heart, thou treasurest up to thyself wrath against the day of wrath. Rom. 2:4 f.

O God, be merciful to me a sinner. I say to you, this man went down into his house justified: because every one that exalteth himself, shall be humbled: and he that humbleth himself, shall be exalted. Luke 18:13 ff.

The soul that is sorrowful for the greatness of evil she hath done, and goeth bowed down, and feeble, and the eyes that fail, and the hungry soul giveth glory and justice to thee the Lord. Bar. 2:18.

Thus you have spoken, saying: Our iniquities, and our sins are upon us, and we pine away in them: how then can we live? As I live, saith the Lord God, I desire not the death of the wicked, but that the wicked turn from his way, and live. Turn ye, turn ye from your evil ways: and why will you die, O house of Israel? Ez. 33:10 f.

I will pour out upon the house of David, and upon the inhabitants of Jerusalem, the Spirit of grace, and of prayers: and they shall look upon me, whom they have pierced: and they shall mourn for him as one mourneth for an only son, and they shall grieve over him, as the manner is to grieve for the death of the first-born. Zach. 12:10.

Jesus came into Galilee, preaching the gospel of the kingdom of God, and saying: The time is accomplished, and the kingdom of God is at hand: repent, and believe the gospel. Mark 1:14 f.

This Jesus that God hath raised again, whereof all we are witnesses. Now when they had heard these things, they had compunction in their heart, and said to Peter and to the rest of the apostles: What shall we do, men and brethren? Acts 2:32, 37.

When thou shalt seek there the Lord thy God, thou shalt find him: yet so, if thou seek him with all thy heart, and all the affliction of thy soul. Deut. 4:29.

The things you say in your hearts, be sorry for them upon your beds. Ps. 4:5.

The Lord your God is merciful, and will not turn away his face from you, if you return to him. 2 Par. 30:9.

The Lord is nigh unto them that are of a contrite heart. and he will save the humble of spirit. Ps. 33:19.

Thou hast mercy upon all, because thou canst do all things, and overlookest the sins of men for the sake of repentance. Wis. 11:24.

To the penitent he hath given the way of justice. Ecclus. 17:20.

How good is it, when thou art reproved, to show repentance! for so thou shalt escape wilful sin. Ecclus. 20:4.

7. CONFESSION OF SIN

If we say that we have no sin, we deceive ourselves, and the truth is not in us. If we confess our sins: he is faithful and just, to forgive us our sins, and to cleanse us from all iniquity. 1 John 1:8 f.

Confess your sins one to another. Jas. 5:16.

Go, show yourselves to the priests. Luke 17:14.

For what have I to do to judge them that are without? Do not you judge them that are within? 1 C. 5:12.

Many of them that believed, came confessing and declaring their deeds. Acts 19:18.

With the mouth confession is made unto salvation. Rom. 10:10.

Then went out to him, Jerusalem and all Judea, and all the country about the Jordan: and were baptized by him in the Jordan, confessing their sins. Mat. 3:5 f.

They were baptized by him in the river Jordan, confessing their sins. Mark 1:5.

I will arise, and I will go to my father, and say to him: Father, I have sinned against heaven and before thee. I am not worthy to be called thy son: make me as one of thy hired servants. Luke 15:18 f.

8. CONFESSION OF SIN UNDER THE OLD LAW

Say to the children of Israel: When a man or woman shall have committed any of all the sins that men are wont to commit, and by negligence shall have transgressed the commandment of the Lord, and offended, they shall confess their sin, and restore the principal itself, and the fifth part over and above, to him against whom they have sinned. Num. 5:6 f.

They stood, and confessed their sins. 2 Es. 9:2.

Be not ashamed to confess thy sins, but submit not thyself to every man for sin. For there is a shame that bringeth sin, and there is a shame that bringeth glory and grace. Ecclus. 4:25, 31.

They shall pine away in their iniquities, until they confess their iniquities, whereby they have transgressed against me, and walked contrary unto me. Lev. 26:39 f.

David said to Nathan: I have sinned against the Lord. And Nathan said to David: The Lord also hath taken away thy sin: thou shalt not die. 2 K. 12:13.

He that hideth his sins shall not prosper, but he that shall confess and forsake them shall obtain mercy. Prov. 28:13.

I said I will confess against myself my injustice to the Lord, and thou hast forgiven the wickedness of my sin. Ps. 31:5.

Incline not my heart to evil words, to make excuses in sins. Ps. 140:4.

My son, give glory to the Lord God of Israel, and confess and tell me what thou hast done: hide it not. Jos. 7:12.

9. SATISFACTION FOR SIN AFTER ITS GUILT HAS BEEN PARDONED

Because thou hast hearkened to the voice of thy wife, and hast eaten of the tree, whereof I commanded thee that thou shouldst not eat, cursed is the earth in thy work: with labor and toil shalt thou eat thereof all the days of thy life. In the sweat of thy face shalt thou eat bread till thou return to the earth, out of which thou wast taken. Gen. 3:17, 19.

Because you trespassed against me, and did not sanctify me among the children of Israel: thou shalt see the land before thee which I will give to the children of Israel, but thou shalt not enter into it. Deut. 32:51 f.

The Lord also hath taken away thy sin: thou shalt not die. Nevertheless, because thou hast given occasion to the enemies of the Lord to blaspheme, for this thing the child that is born to thee shall surely die. 2 K. 12:13 f.

You shall not enter into the land over which I lifted up my hand to make you dwell therein. Num. 14:30.

All the children of Israel murmured against Moses and Aaron. And the Lord said to Moses: How long will this people detract me? I will strike them therefore with pestilence, and will consume them. Num. 14:2, 11 f.

David's heart struck him after the people were numbered, and David said to the Lord: I have sinned very much in what I have done: but I pray thee, O Lord, to take away the iniquity of thy servant, because I have done exceeding foolishly. And David arose in the morning, and the word of the Lord came to Gad the prophet and the seer of David, saying: Go and say to David: Thus saith the Lord: I give thee thy choice of three things: choose one of them which thou wilt, that I may do it to thee. And when Gad was come to David, he told him saying: Either seven years of famine shall come to thee in thy land, or thou shalt flee three months before thy adversaries, and they shall pursue thee, or for three days there shall be a pestilence in thy land. 2 K. 24:10-13.

I indeed absent in body, but present in spirit, have already judged, as though I were present, him that hath so done. To deliver such a one to Satan for the destruction of the flesh, that the spirit may be saved in the day of our Lord Jesus Christ. 1 C. 5:3, 5.

Redeem thou thy sins with alms, and thy iniquities with works of mercy to the poor. Dan. 4:24.

10. VICARIOUS SUFFERING

[I] now rejoice in my sufferings for you, and fill up those things that are wanting of the sufferings of Christ, in my flesh for his body, which is the church. Col. 1:24.

In this we have known the charity of God, because he hath laid down his life for us: and we ought to lay down our lives for the brethren. 1 John 3:16.

Jesus turning to them said: Daughters of Jerusalem, weep not over me, but weep for yourselves and for your children. Luke 23:28.

Bear ye one another's burdens: and so you shall fulfil the law of Christ. Gal. 6:2.

You helping withal in prayer for us: that for this gift obtained for us, by the means of many persons, thanks may be given my many in our behalf. 2 C. 1:11.

EXTREME UNCTION

11. INSTITUTION OF THE SACRAMENT

Is any man sick among you? Let him bring in the priests of the church, and let them pray over him, anointing him with oil in name of the Lord. And the prayer of faith shall save the sick man: and the Lord shall raise him up: and if he be in sins, they shall be forgiven him. Jas. 5:14 f.

Going forth they preached that men should do penance: and they cast out many devils, and anointed with oil many that were sick, and healed them. Mark 6:12 f.

12. SICKNESS

Asa fell sick in the nine-and-thirtieth year of his reign, of a most violent pain in his feet, and yet in his illness he did not seek the Lord, but rather trusted in the skill of the physicians. And he slept with his fathers: and he died. 2 Par. 16:12 f.

Their soul abhorred all manner of meat: and they drew nigh even to the gates of death. And they cried to the Lord in their affliction: and he delivered them out of their distresses. He sent his word, and healed them. Ps. 106:18-20.

O Lord my God, I have cried to thee, and thou hast healed me. Ps. 29:3.

A grievous sickness maketh the soul sober. Ecclus. 31:2.

He that sinneth in the sight of his Maker, shall fall into the hands of the physician. Ecclus. 38:15.

His bones shall be filled with the vices of his youth, and they shall sleep with him in the dust. Job 20:11.

My son, in thy sickness neglect not thyself, but pray to the Lord, and he shall heal thee. Turn away from sin, and order thy hands aright, and cleanse thy heart from all offence. Ecclus. 38:9, 13.

Jesus went about all the cities and towns, healing every disease and every infirmity. Mat. 9:35.

Behold thou art made whole; sin no more, lest some worse thing happen to thee. John 5:14.

Lord, behold, he whom thou lovest is sick. John 11:3.

Only say the word, and my servant shall be healed. Mat. 8:8.

All that were sick he healed. Mat. 8:16.

I have heard thy prayer, I have seen thy tears: and behold I have healed thee. 4 K. 20:5.

The Lord hath taken away thy sin. Thou shalt not die. 2 K. 12:13.

He went about doing good, and healing all that were oppressed by the devil, for God was with him. Acts 10:38.

This sickness is not unto death, but for the glory of God, that the Son of God may be glorified by it. John 11:4.

Many are sick among you. 1 C. 11:30.

13. THE PHYSICIAN; THE APOTHECARY

Honor the physician for the need thou hast of him: for the Most High hath created him. For all healing is from God. The skill of the physician shall lift up his head, and in the sight of great men he shall be praised. The Most High hath created medicines out of the earth, and a wise man will not abhor them. Ecclus. 38:1-4.

The virtue of these things is come to the knowledge of men, and the Most High hath given knowledge to men. that he may be honored in his wonders. By these he shall cure and shall allay their pains, and of these the apothecary shall make sweet confections, and shall make up ointments of health, and of his works there shall be no end. Ecclus. 38:6 f.

My son, in thy sickness, give a sweet savor, and a memorial of the fine flour, and make a fat offering, and then give place to the physician. For the Lord created him: and let him not depart from thee, for his works are necessary. For there is a time when thou must fall into their hands. Ecclus. 38:9, 11-13.

HOLY ORDERS

14. INSTITUTION OF THE SACRAMENT

Do this for a commemoration of me. Luke 22:19.

This do for the commemoration of me. 1 C. 11:24.

Receive ye the Holy Ghost. Whose sins you shall forgive, they are forgiven them. John 20:22 f.

The Holy Ghost said to them: Separate me Saul and Barnabas for the work whereunto I have taken them. Then they, fasting and praying, and imposing their hands upon them, sent them away. Acts 13:2 f.

Take heed to yourselves, and to the whole flock, wherein the Holy Ghost hath placed you bishops, to rule the Church of God, which he hath purchased with his own blood. Acts 20:28.

Neglect not the grace that is in thee, which was given thee by prophecy, with imposition of the hands of the priesthood. 1 Tim. 4:14.

For this cause I admonish thee, that thou stir up the grace of God which is in thee by the imposition of my hands. 2 Tim. 1:6.

When they had ordained to them priests in every church, and had prayed with fasting, they commended them to the Lord. Acts 14:22.

Impose not hands lightly upon any man, neither be partaker of other men's sins. 1 Tim. 5:22.

How shall they hear without a preacher? And how shall they preach unless they be sent? I left thee in Crete that thou shouldst ordain priests in every city as I also appointed thee. Titus 1:5.

You shall receive the power of the Holy Ghost coming upon you, and you shall be witnesses unto me in Jerusalem, and in all Judea and Samaria, and even to the uttermost parts of the earth. Acts 1:8.

He that receiveth you, receiveth me: and he that receiveth me, receiveth him that sent me. Mat. 10:4.

Thou art a priest forever. Heb. 5:6.

15. CELIBACY OF THE PRIESTS

They shall be holy to their God, and shall not profane his name. Lev. 21:6.

For they offer the burnt offering of the Lord, and the bread of their God, and therefore they shall be holy. Be ye clean, you that carry the vessels of the Lord. Is. 52:11.

The priests that come to the Lord, let them be sanctified. Ex. 19:22.

I have no common bread at hand, but only holy bread, if the young men be clean, especially from women. 1 K. 21:4.

Labor as a good soldier of Christ Jesus. No man, being a soldier to God, entangleth himself with secular business, that he may please him to whom he hath engaged himself. 2 Tim. 2:3.

He that is without a wife is solicitous for the things that belong to the Lord, how he may please God. But he that is with a wife is solicitous for the things of the world, how he may please his wife, and he is divided. 1 C.7:32 f.

The unmarried woman and the virgin thinketh on the things of the Lord: that she may be holy in body and in spirit. But she that is married thinketh on the things of the world, how she may please her husband. This I speak for your profit: not to cast a snare upon you; but for that which is decent, and which may give you power to attend upon the Lord without impediment. 1 C. 7:34 f.

I would that all men were even as myself: but every one hath his proper gift from God: one after this manner and another after that. But I say to the unmarried, and to the widows: it is good for them if they so continue, even as I. 1 C. 7:7 f.

16. EXHORTATION TO PRIESTS

The Levites are to stand in the morning to give thanks, and to sing praises to the Lord, and in like manner in the evening. 1 Par. 23:30.

Behold now, bless ye the Lord, all ye servants of the Lord: who stand in the house of the Lord, in the courts of the house of our God. In the nights lift up your hands to the holy places, and bless ye the Lord. Ps. 133:1 f.

Cry, cease not, lift up thy voice like a trumpet, and show my people their wicked doings, and the house of Jacob their sins. Is. 58:1.

Let no man despise thy youth: but be thou an example to the faithful.

1. In word,
2. In conversation,
3. In charity,
4. In faith,
5. In chastity.

Attend

1. To reading,
2. To exhortation,
3. And to doctrine.

Neglect not the grace which is in thee, which was given thee by prophecy, with the imposition of the hands of the priesthood. Meditate on these things: be wholly in these things; that thy proficiency may be manifest to all. Attend

1. To thyself
2. And to doctrine:

be earnest in them: for in doing this thou shalt both save thyself and them that hear thee. 1 Tim. 4:12-16.

Keep the good deposited in trust to thee by the Holy Ghost, who dwelleth in us. 2 Thess. 1:41.

Labor as a good soldier of Jesus Christ. 2 Thess. 2:3.

Feed the flock of God which is among you, taking care of it not by constraint, but willingly according to God: not for filthy lucre's sake, but voluntarily: and when the Prince of pastors shall appear, you shall receive a never-fading crown of glory. 1 Pet. 5:2, 4.

No man, being a soldier to God, entangleth himself with wordly businesses; that he may please him to whom he hath engaged himself. 2 Tim. 2:4.

Carefully study to present thyself approved unto God, a workman that needeth not to be ashamed, rightly handling the word of truth. But shun profane and vain babblings: for they grow much towards ungodliness. 2 Tim. 2:15 f.

Flee thou youthful desires; and pursue justice, faith, charity, and peace, with those who call on the Lord from a pure heart. And avoid foolish and unlearned questions: knowing that they beget strifes. But the servant of the Lord must not wrangle, but be gentle towards all men, fit to teach, patient. With modesty admonishing those who resist the truth; if at any time God give them repentance to know the truth; and they recover themselves from the snares of the devil, by whom they are held captives at his will. 2 Tim. 2:22-26.

It is a faithful saying: and of these things I will have thee to affirm earnestly: that they who believe in God may be careful to excel in good works. These things are good and profitable to men. Titus 3:8.

Thou, O man of God, pursue justice, godliness, faith, charity, patience, mildness. Fight the good fight of faith. Lay hold on eternal life whereunto thou art called. Keep the commandment without spot, blameless, unto the coming of our Lord Jesus Christ. 1 Tim. 6:11-14.

I charge thee before God and Jesus Christ, who shall judge the living and the dead, by his coming, and his kingdom: preach the word: be instant in season and out of season: reprove, entreat, rebuke with all patience and doctrine. 2 Tim. 4:1 f.

Be thou vigilant: labor in all things: do the work of an evangelist. Fulfil thy ministry: be sober. 2 Tim. 4:5.

In all things show thyself an example of good works, in doctrine, in integrity, in gravity, the sound word that cannot be blamed: that he who is on the contrary part may be afraid, having no evil to say of us. Titus 2:7 f.

Give no offence to any one, that our ministry be not blamed: but in all things let us exhibit ourselves as the ministers of God, in much patience, in tribulation, in necessities, in distresses, in stripes, in prisons, in seditions, in labors, in watchings, in fastings, in chastity, in knowledge, in longsuffering, in sweetness, in the Holy Ghost, in charity unfeigned, in the word of truth, in the power of God; by the armor of justice on the right hand and on the left, by honor and dishonor, by evil report and good report: as deceivers, and yet true: as unknown, and yet known: as dying, and behold we live: as chastised, and not killed: as sorrowful, yet always rejoicing: as needy, yet enriching many: as having nothing, and possessing all things. 2 C. 6:3-10.

17. PRIESTS MUST BE READY TO SUFFER

Besides those things which are without: my daily instance, the solicitude for all the churches. Who is weak, and I am not weak? Who is scandalized, and I am not on fire? If I must needs glory: I will glory of the things that concern my infirmity. The God and Father of our Lord Jesus Christ, who is blessed forever, knoweth that I lie not.

If I must glory (it is not expedient indeed): but I will come to visions and revelations of the Lord. I know a man in Christ: above fourteen years ago (whether in the body, I know not, or out of the body, I know not, God knoweth), such a one caught up to the third heaven. And I know such a man (whether in the body, or out of the body, I know not: God knoweth): that he was caught up into paradise and heard secret words which it is not granted to man to utter. For such an one I will glory: but for myself I will glory nothing but in my infirmities.

For even if I should have a mind to glory, I shall not be foolish: for I will say the truth. But I forbear, lest any man should think of me above that which he seeth in me, or anything he heareth from me.

And lest the greatness of the revelations should exalt me, there was given me a sting of my flesh, an angel of Satan to buffet me. For which thing thrice I besought the Lord, that it might depart from me: and he said to me: My grace is sufficient for thee: for power is made perfect in infirmity. Gladly therefore will I glory in my infirmities, that the power of Christ may dwell in me. For which cause I please myself in my infirmities, in reproaches, in necessities, in persecutions, in distress, for Christ. For when I am weak, then am I powerful. 2 C. 12:7-10.

They are Hebrews: so am I. They are Israelites: so am I. They are the seed of Abraham: so am I. They are the ministers of Christ (I speak as one less wise): I am more: in many more labors, in prisons more frequently, in stripes above measure, in deaths often.

Of the Jews five times did I receive forty stripes, save one. Thrice was I beaten with rods: once I was stoned: thrice I suffered shipwreck: a night and a day I was in the depth of the sea. In journeying often, in perils of waters, in perils of robbers, in perils from my own nation, in perils from the Gentiles, in perils in the city, in perils in the wilderness, in perils in the sea, in perils from false brethren: in labor and painfulness, in many watchings, in hunger and thirst, in many fastings, in cold and nakedness. 2 C. 11:22-27.

MATRIMONY

18. THE SACRAMENT

This is a great sacrament, but I speak in Christ and in the church. Eph. 5:32.

A man shall leave father and mother, and shall cleave to his wife: and they shall be two in one flesh. Gen. 2:24.

Keep then your spirit, and despise not the wife of thy youth. Mal. 2:15.

House and riches are given by parents: but a prudent wife is properly from the Lord. Prov. 19:14.

A good wife is a good portion, she shall be given in the portion of them that fear God, to a man for his good deeds. Rich or poor if his heart is good, his countenance shall be cheerful at all times. Ecclus. 26:3 f.

He that hath found a good wife, hath found a good thing, and shall receive a pleasure from the Lord. Prov. 18:22.

She is a help like to himself, and a pillar of rest. Ecclus. 36:26.

From the beginning of the creation, God made them male and female. For this cause a man shall leave his father and mother; and shall cleave to his wife. And they two shall be in one flesh. Therefore now they are not two, but one flesh. What therefore God hath joined together, let not man put asunder. Mark 10:6-9.

Every one hath his proper gift from God, one after this manner, and another after that. 1 C. 7:7.

Whilst her husband liveth she shall be called an adulteress if she be with another man. Rom. 7:3.

Whosoever shall put away his wife and marry another, committeth adultery against her. Mark 10:11.

What God hath joined together let no man put asunder. Mat. 19:6.

If the unbeliever depart let him depart. For a brother or sister is not under servitude in such cases. But God hath called us in peace. 1 C. 7:15.

Take heed to keep thyself, my son, from fornication, and beside thy wife never endure to know a crime. Tob. 4:13.

Every one that putteth away his wife, and marrieth another, committeth adultery: and he that marrieth her that is put away from her husband committeth adultery. Luke 16:18.

To them that are married, not I but the Lord commandeth, that the wife depart not from her husband: and if she depart, that she remain unmarried, or be reconciled to her husband. And let not the husband put away his wife. 1 C. 7:10 f.

A woman is bound by the law as long as her husband liveth; but if her husband die, she is at liberty: let her marry to whom she will: only in the Lord. But more blessed shall she be, if she so remain, according to my counsel: and I think that I also have the Spirit of God. 1 C. 7:39 f.

Let women be subject to their husbands, as to the Lord: because the husband is the head of the wife; as Christ is the head of the church. Therefore as the church is subject to Christ, so also let the wives be to their husbands in all things. Eph. 5:22-24.

Hubands, love your wives, as Christ also loved the church, and delivered himself for it: that he might sanctify it. Eph. 5:25 f.

So also ought men to love their wives as their own bodies. He that loveth his wife, loveth himself. For no man ever hated his own flesh: but nourisheth and cherisheth it, as also Christ doth the church. Eph. 5:28 f.

Adam was first formed: then Eve. And Adam was not seduced: but the woman being seduced, was in the transgression. Yet she shall be saved through childbearing: if she continue in faith and love and sanctification with sobriety. 1 Tim. 2:13-15.

Let every one of you in particular love his wife as himself: and let the wife reverence her husband. Eph. 5:33.

Wives, be subject to your husbands, as it behoveth in the Lord. Husbands, love your wives, and be not bitter towards them. Col. 3:18 f.

In like manner also let wives be subject to their husbands: that if any believe not the word, they may be won without the word, by the conversation of the wives, considering your chaste conversation with fear. Whose adorning let it not be the outward plaiting of the hair, or wearing of gold, or putting on of apparel: but the hidden man of the heart in the incorruptibility of a quiet and a meek spirit, which is rich in the sight of God. For after this manner heretofore the holy women also, who trusted in God, adorned themselves, being in subjection to their own husbands. As Sara obeyed Abraham, calling him Lord: whose daughters you are. 1 Pet. 3:1-6.

Ye husbands, likewise dwelling with them according to knowledge, giving honor to the female as to the weaker vessel, and as to the coheirs of the grace of life, that your prayers be not hindered. And in fine be ye all of one mind, having compassion one of another, being lovers of the brotherhood, merciful, modest, humble: not rendering evil for evil, nor railing for railing, but contrariwise, blessing; for unto this are you called, that you may inherit a blessing. 1 Pet. 3:7-9.

19. THE MARRIAGE OF ADAM AND EVE

The Lord God cast a deep sleep upon Adam: and when he was fast asleep, he took one of his ribs, and filled up flesh for it. And the Lord God built the rib which he took from Adam into a woman: and brought her to Adam. And Adam said: This now is bone of my bones, and flesh of my flesh; she shall be called woman, because she was taken out of man. Wherefore a man shall leave father and mother, and shall cleave to his wife: and they shall be two in one flesh. Gen. 2:21-24.

The Divine Blessing on Marriage

There was a marriage in Cana of Galilee: and the mother of Jesus was there. And Jesus also was invited, and his disciples, to the marriage. John 2:1 f.

And the wine failing, the mother of Jesus saith to him: They have no wine. And Jesus saith to her:

Woman, what is to me, and to thee? My hour is not yet come. John 2:3 f.

His mother saith to the waiters: Whatsoever he shall say to you, do ye. Now there were set there six waterpots of stone, according to the manner of the purifying of the Jews, containing two or three measures apiece. Jesus saith to them: Fill the waterpots with water. And they filled them up to the brim. And Jesus saith to them: Draw out now, and carry to the chief steward of the feast. And they carried it. John 2:5-8.

This beginning of miracles did Jesus in Cana of Galilee. John 2:11.

PART V

SIN, JUSTIFICATION, MERIT

I

SIN

1. ORIGINAL SIN

Of the tree of knowledge of good and evil thou shalt not eat. For in what day soever thou shalt eat of it, thou shalt die the death. Gen. 2:17.

The woman saw that the tree was good to eat, and fair to the eyes and delightful to behold: and she took the fruit thereof, and did eat, and gave to her husband, who did eat. Gen. 3:6.

By one man sin entered into this world, and by sin, death: and so death passed upon all men in whom all have sinned. Rom. 5:12.

From the woman came the beginning of sin, and through her we all die. Ecclus. 25:33.

Who can make him clean that is conceived of unclean seed? Is it not thou who only art? Job 14:4.

What is man that he should be without spot, and he that is born of a woman, that he should appear just? Job 15:14.

Behold among his saints none is unchangeable, and the heavens are not pure in his sight. How much more is man abominable and unprofitable who drinketh iniquity like water? Job 15:15 f.

Behold I was conceived in iniquity, and in sins did my mother conceive me. Ps. 50:7.

All have sinned and do need the grace of God. Rom. 3:23.

You, when you are dead in your offences and sins, wherein in time past you walked according to the course of this world, according to the prince of the power of this air, of the spirit that now worketh on the children of unbelief, in which also we all conversed in time past, in the desires of our flesh, fulfilling the will of the flesh, and of our thoughts, and were by nature children of wrath, even as the rest: but God, who is rich in mercy, for his exceeding charity wherewith he loved us, even when we were dead in sins, hath quickened us together in Christ (by whose grace you are saved). Eph. 2:1-5.

Give ear to me, you that follow that which is just, and you that seek the Lord: look unto the rock whence you are hewn, and to the hole of the pit from which you are dug out. Is. 51:1.

Can man be justified compared with God, or he that is born of a woman appear clean? Behold even the moon doth not shine, and the stars are not pure in his sight. How much less man that is rottenness, and the son of man who is a worm? Job 25:4-6.

Not as the offence, so also the gift. For if by the offence of one many died: much more the grace of God and the gift, in the grace of one man Jesus Christ, hath abounded unto many. And not as it was by one sin, so also is the gift. For judgment indeed was by one unto condemnation: but grace is of many offences, unto justification. Rom. 5:15 f.

For if by one man's offence death reigned through one: much more they who receive abundance of grace, and of the gift, and of justice, shall reign in life through one, Jesus Christ.

Therefore as by the offence of one, unto all men to condemnation: so also by the justice of one, unto all men to justification of life. For as by the disobedience of one man, many were made sinners: so also by the obedience of one, many shall be made just. Rom. 5:17-19.

2. MORTAL SIN

The soul that sinneth, the same shall die. Ezech. 18:4.

The fearful and unbelieving, and the abominable, and murderers, and whoremongers, and sorcerers, and idolaters, and all liars, they shall have their portion in the pool burning with fire and brimstone, which is the second death. Apoc. 21:8.

If you live according to the flesh, you shall die. Rom. 8:13.

Sin, when it is completed, begetteth death. Jas. 1:15.

No fornicator, nor unclean, nor covetous person hath inheritance in the kingdom of Christ and of God. Eph. 5:5.

The sin of the young men was exceeding great before the Lord, because they withdrew men from the sacrifice of the Lord. 1 K. 2:17.

He that loveth iniquity hateth his own soul. Ps. 10:6.

If thy right eye scandalize thee, pluck it out and cast it from thee. For it is expedient for thee that one of thy members should perish, rather than thy whole body be cast into hell. Mat. 5:29.

This people hath sinned a heinous sin, and they have made to themselves gods of gold. Ex. 32:31.

All iniquity is sin: and there is a sin unto death. 1 John 5:17.

3. VENIAL SIN

In many things we all offend. Jas. 3:2.

If we say that we have no sin, we deceive ourselves. 1 John 1:8.

A just man shall fall seven times, and shall rise again. Prov. 24:16.

The wise man will make supplication for his sins. Ecclus. 39:7.

Whosoever is angry with his brother shall be in danger of the judgment. And whosoever shall say to his brother, Raca, shall be in danger of the council. And whosoever shall say, Thou fool, shall be in danger of hell fire. Mat. 5:22.

If any man build upon this foundation, gold, silver, precious stones, wood, hay, stubble: he shall be saved, yet so as by fire. 1 C. 3:12, 15.

Why seest thou the mote in thy brother's eye: but the beam that is in thy own eye thou considerest not? Luke 6:41.

He that contemneth small things, shall fall little by little. Ecclus. 19:1.

There is no man that sinneth not. 3 K. 8:46.

Who can understand sin? From my secret ones cleanse me, O Lord. Ps. 18:13.

Your sins have withholden good things from you. Jer. 5:25.

Though he fall, he shall not be utterly cast down; for the Lord upholdeth him with his hand. Ps. 36:24.

4. GOD NOT THE AUTHOR OF SIN

In the morning I will stand before thee, and will see: that thou art not a God that willest iniquity. Ps. 5:5.

Thou hatest all the workers of iniquity. Ps. 5:7.

To God the wicked and his wickedness are hateful alike. Wis. 14:9.

Thy eyes are too pure to behold evil, thou canst not look on iniquity. Heb. 1:13.

They have built the high places of Baalim which I did not command, nor speak of, neither did it once come into my mind. Jer. 19:5.

This is the will of God: your sanctification. 1 Thess. 4:3.

Whosoever committeth sin, committeth also iniquity: and sin is iniquity. And you know that he appeared to take away our sins, and in him there is no sin. Whosoever abideth in him, sinneth not: and whosoever sinneth, hath not seen him, nor known him. Little children, let no man deceive you. He that doth justice, is just: even as he is just. He that commiteth sin is of the devil: for the devil sinneth from the beginning. For this purpose, the Son of God appeared, that he might destroy the works of the devil. Whosoever is born of God, commiteth not sin: for his seed abideth in him, and he cannot sin, because he is born of God. 1 John 3:4-9.

Let no man, when he is tempted, say that he is tempted by God. For God is not a tempter of evils, and he tempteth no man. Jas. 1:13.

By envy of the devil death came into the world: and they that follow him are of his side. Wis. 2:24 f.

He [the devil] is king over all the children of pride. Job 41:25.

They are held captive at his will. 2 Tim. 11:26.

The Lord is holy in all his works. Ps. 144:13.

God is not the God of dissension, but of peace. 1 C. 14:33.

5. SINS ARISING FROM IGNORANCE, PASSION, AND MALICE

If they had known it they would never have crucified the Lord of glory. 1 C. 2:8.

Jesus said: Father, forgive them, for they know not what they do. Luke 23:34.

Brethren, I know that you did it through ignorance as did also your rulers. Acts 3:17.

Jesus said to them: If you were blind, you should not have sin; but now you say: We see. Your sin remaineth. John 9:41.

They leave the right way and walk by dark ways. Who are glad when they have done evil, and rejoice in most wicked things, whose ways are perverse and their steps infamous. Prov. 2:13-15.

The soul that committeth anything through pride, whether he be born in the land or a stranger (because he hath been rebellious against the Lord), shall be cut off from among his people. Num. 15:30.

The beginning of the pride of man is to fall off from God: because his heart is departed from him that made him: for pride is the beginning of all sin. Ecclus. 10:14 f.

Say you, his disciples came by night, and stole him away when we were asleep. Mat. 28:13.

They have a zeal of God, but not according to knowledge. Rom. 10:3.

Yea the hour cometh that whosoever killeth you will think that he doth a service to God. John 16:2.

I before was a blasphemer, and a persecutor, and contumelious. But I obtained the mercy of God, because I did it ignorantly in unbelief. 1 Tim. 1:13.

Every man is tempted by his own concupiscence, being drawn away and allured. Jas. 1:14.

They as it were on purpose have revolted from him, and would not understand all his ways. Job 34:27.

They have labored to commit iniquity. Jer. 9:5.

He hath conceived sorrow, and hath brought forth iniquity, and his womb prepareth deceits. Job 15:35.

Behold he hath been in labor with injustice: he hath conceived sorrow, and brought forth iniquity. Ps. 7:15.

Error and darkness are created with sinners: and they that glory in evil things grow old in evil. Ecclus. 11:16.

In malice be children 1 C. 14:20.

6. HATRED OF SIN

Do not commit this abominable thing which I hate. Jer. 44:4.

You that love the Lord, hate evil: the Lord preserveth the souls of his saints: he will deliver them out of the hand of the sinner. Ps. 96:10.

A fainting hath taken hold of me, because of the wicked that forsake thy law. I have hated all wicked ways. I have hated and abhorred iniquity; but I have loved thy law. Ps. 118:53, 128, 163.

Have I not hated them, O Lord, that hated thee: and pined away because of thy enemies? Ps. 138:21.

Three sorts my soul hateth, and I am greatly grieved at their life: a poor man that is proud: a rich man that is a liar: an old man that is a fool, and doting. Ecclus. 25:3 f.

My mouth shall meditate truth, and my lips shall hate wickedness. The fear of the Lord hateth evil. Prov. 8:7, 13.

Hating that which is evil, cleaving to that which is good. Rom. 12:9.

The deeds of the Nicolaites I hate. Apoc. 2:6.

Let none of you imagine evil in your hearts against his friend: and love not a false oath: for all these are the things that I hate, saith the Lord. Zach. 8:1.

Thou hast hated iniquity: therefore God, thy God, hath anointed thee with the oil of gladness above thy fellows. Ps. 44:8.

Six things there are which the Lord hateth, and the seventh his soul detesteth:

1. haughty eyes,
2. a lying tongue,
3. hands that shed innocent blood,
4. a heart that deviseth wicked plots,
5. feet that are swift to run into mischief,
6. a deceitful witness that uttereth lies,
7. and him that soweth discord among brethren. Prov. 6:16-19.

7. PROSPERITY OF THE WICKED

The earth is given into the hand of the wicked. Job 9:24.

Why then do the wicked live, are they advanced and strengthened with riches? Their seed continueth before them, a multitude of kinsmen, and of children's children in their sight. Their houses are secure and peaceable, and the rod of God is not upon them. Their little ones go out like a flock, and their children dance and play. They take the timbrel and the harp, and rejoice at the sound of the organ. They spend their days in wealth, and in a moment they go down to hell. Who have said to God: Depart from us: we desire not the knowledge of thy ways. Who is the Almighty that we should serve him? and what doth it profit us if we pray to him? Job 21:7-15.

Whilst the wicked man is proud, the poor is set on fire. For the sinner is praised in the desires of his soul: and the unjust man is blessed. Thy judgments are removed from his sight: he shall rule over all his enemies. For he hath said in his heart: I shall not be moved from generation to generation, and shall be without evil. Ps. 9:2 f., 5 f.

Be not thou afraid when a man shall be made rich, and when the glory of his house shall be increased. For when he shall die he shall take nothing away: nor shall his glory descend with him. He shall go into the generations of his fathers: and he shall never see light. Man when he was in honor did not understand: he hath been compared to senseless beasts, and made like to them. Ps. 48:17 f., 20 f.

But my feet were almost moved; my steps had well nigh slipt. Because I had a zeal on occasion of the wicked, seeing the prosperity of sinners. For there is no regard to their death, nor is there strength in their stripes. They are not in the labor of men: neither shall they be scourged like other men. Therefore pride hath held them fast: they are covered with their iniquity and their wickedness. And they said: How doth God know? and is there knowledge in the Most High? Behold these are sinners: and yet abounding in the world they have obtained riches. How are they brought to desolation? they have suddenly ceased to be: they have perished by reason of their iniquity. As the dream of them that awake, O Lord; so in thy city thou shalt bring their image to nothing. Ps. 72:2-6, 11 f., 19 f.

Their storehouses full, flowing out of this into that. Their sheep fruitful in young, abounding in their goings forth. Their oxen fat. . . . They have called the people happy that hath these things: but happy is that people whose God is the Lord. Ps. 143:13-15.

There is success in evil things to a man without discipline, and there is a finding that turneth to loss. Ecclus. 20:9.

Thou indeed, O Lord, art just, if I plead with thee, but yet I will speak what is just to thee: Why doth the way of the wicked prosper; why is it well with all them that transgress, and do wickedly? Thou hast planted them, and they have taken root: they prosper and bring forth fruit. Gather them together as sheep for a sacrifice, and prepare them for the day of slaughter. Jer. 12:1-3.

Woe to you that are wealthy in Sion, and to you that have confidence in the mountain of Samaria: ye great men, heads of the people, that go in with state into the house of Israel. You that are separated unto the evil day: and that approach to the throne of iniquity. You that sleep upon beds of ivory, and are wanton on your couches: that eat the lambs out of the flock, and the calves out of the midst of the herd. You that sing to the sound of the psaltery: they have thought themselves to have instruments of music like David. That drink wine in bowls, and anoint themselves with the best ointments: and they are not concerned for the affliction of Joseph. The faction of the luxurious ones shall be taken away. Amos 6:1-7.

The wicked man is reserved to the day of destruction, and he shall be brought to the day of wrath. Job 21:30.

Therefore hath hell enlarged her soul, and opened her mouth without any bounds, and their strong ones, and their people, and their high and glorious ones shall go down into it. Is. 5:14.

Woe to you that are rich: for you have your consolation. Woe to you that are filled: for you shall hunger. Woe to you that laugh now: for you shall mourn and weep. Woe to you when men shall bless you: for according to these things did their fathers to the false prophets. Luke 6:24-26.

Son, remember that thou didst receive good things in thy lifetime, and likewise Lazarus evil things: but now he is comforted, and thou art tormented. Luke 16:25.

8. DIVINE THREATENINGS

The deceitfulness of the wicked shall destroy them. Prov. 11:3.

He that rendereth evil for good, evil shall not depart from his house. Prov. 17:13.

The wicked shall be punished according to their own devices: who have neglected the just, and have revolted from the Lord. Wis. 3:10.

Humble thy spirit very much: for the vengeance on the flesh of the ungodly is fire and worms. Ecclus. 7:19.

There is no good for him that is always occupied in evil, and that giveth no alms. Ecclus. 12:3.

He that loveth danger shall perish in it. Ecclus. 3:27.

The inheritance of the children of sinners shall perish, and with their posterity shall be a perpetual reproach. Ecclus. 41:9.

Woe to them that are of a double heart, and to wicked lips, and to the hands that do evil, and to the sinner that goeth on the earth two ways. Woe to them that are faint-hearted, and who believe not God: and therefore shall not be protected by him. Woe to them that have lost patience, and that have forsaken the right ways, have gone aside into crooked ways. and what will they do when the Lord shall begin to examine? Ecclus. 2:14-17.

The lofty eyes of man are humbled, and the haughtiness of men shall be made to stoop: and the Lord alone shall be exalted in that day. Because the day of the Lord of hosts shall be upon every one that is proud and high-minded, and upon every one that is arrogant, and he shall be humbled. Is. 2:11 f.

Woe to the wicked unto evil: for the reward of his hands shall be given him. Is. 3:11.

Woe to you that call evil good, and good evil: that put darkness for light, and light for darkness: that put bitter for sweet, and sweet for bitter. Woe to you that are mighty to drink wine, and stout men at drunkenness. That justify the wicked for gifts, and take away the justice of the just from him. Is. 5:20, 22 f.

I turned, and lifted up my eyes: and I saw, and behold a volume flying: this is the curse, that goeth forth over the face of the earth: for every thief shall be judged as is there written: and every one that sweareth in like manner shall be judged by it. And it shall come to the house of the thief, and to the house of him that sweareth falsely by my name: and it shall remain in the midst of his house, and shall consume it, with the timber thereof, and the stones thereof. Zach. 5:1, 3 f.

Woe to them that make wicked laws: and when they write, write injustice. To oppress the poor in judgment, and do violence to the cause of the humble of my people: that widows might be their prey, and that they might rob the fatherless. What will you do in the day of visitation, and of the calamity which cometh from afar? To whom will ye flee for help? and where will ye leave your glory? Is. 10:1-3.

Behold, the day of the Lord shall come, a cruel day, and full of indignation, and of wrath, and fury, to lay the land desolate, and to destroy the sinners thereof out of it. And I will visit the evils of the world, and against the wicked for their iniquity, and I will make the pride of infidels to cease, and will bring down the arrogancy of the mighty. Is. 13:9, 11.

Woe to you that are deep of heart, to hide your counsel from the Lord: and their works are in the dark, and they say: Who seeth us, and who knoweth us? Is. 29:15.

Woe to thee that spoilest, shalt not thou thyself also be spoiled? and thou that despisest, shalt not thyself also be despised? When thou shalt have made an end of spoiling, thou shalt be spoiled: when being wearied thou shalt cease to despise, thou shalt be despised. Is. 33:1.

Woe to him that buildeth up his house by injustice, and his chambers not in judgment: that will oppress his friend without cause, and will not pay him his wages. Jer. 22:13.

Woe to the pastors, that destroy and tear the sheep of my pasture, saith the Lord. Jer. 23:1.

If you will not hear, and if you will not lay it to heart, to give glory to my name, saith the Lord of hosts: I will send poverty upon you, and I will curse your blessings, yea, I will curse them: because you have not laid it to heart. Mal. 2:2.

Every one shall die for his own iniquity. Jer. 31:30.

I will come to you in judgment, and will be a speedy witness against sorcerers, and adulterers, and false swearers, and them that oppress the hireling in his wages, the widows, and the fatherless: and oppress the stranger, and have not feared me, saith the Lord of hosts. Mal. 3:5.

Hear this, you that crush the poor, and make the needy of the land to fail. Amos 8:4.

The day of the Lord is great and very terrible: and who can stand it? Joel 2:11.

For behold the day shall come kindled as a furnace: and all the proud, and all that do wickedly shall be stubble; and the day that cometh shall set them on fire, saith the Lord of hosts, it shall not leave them root, nor branch. Mal. 4:1.

Every tree, therefore, that yieldeth not good fruit, shall be cut down, and cast into the fire. Mat. 3:10.

If any one abide not in me: he shall be cast forth as a branch, and shall wither, and they shall gather him up, and cast him into the fire, and he burneth. John 15:6.

So shall it be at the end of the world. The angels shall go out, and shall separate the wicked from among the just. Mat. 13:49.

And the unprofitable servant cast ye out into the exterior darkness. There shall be weeping and gnashing of teeth. Mat. 25:30.

If that evil servant should say in his heart: My Lord is long a-coming: and shall begin to strike his fellow servants, and shall eat and drink with drunkards: the Lord of that servant shall come in a day that he hopeth not, and at an hour that he knoweth not: and shall separate him, and appoint his portion with the hypocrites. There shall be weeping and gnashing of teeth. Mat. 24:48-51.

It is a fearful thing to fall into the hands of the living God. Heb. 10:31.

Who will render to every man according to his works. To them that are contentious, and who obey not the truth, but give credit to iniquity, wrath, and indignation. Tribulation and anguish upon every soul of man that doeth evil. Rom. 2:6, 8 f.

He that doeth an injury shall receive for that which he hath done unjustly: for there is no respect of persons with God. Col. 3:25.

The countenance of the Lord is against them that do evil things. 1 Pet. 3:12.

And if the just man shall scarcely be saved, where shall the wicked and the sinner appear? 1 Pet. 4:18.

See that you refuse him not who speaketh. For if they escaped not who refused him that spoke upon earth, much more shall not we, who turn away from him that speaketh to us from heaven. Heb. 12:25.

But the heavens and the earth, which are now, by the same word are kept in store, reserved unto fire against the day of judgment and perdition of wicked men. 2 Pet. 3:7.

9. A PRAYER FOR GRACE TO FLEE SIN

O Lord, Father, and Sovereign Ruler of my life, leave me not to their counsel: nor suffer me to fall by them.

Who will set scourges over my thoughts, and the discipline of wisdom over my heart, that they spare me not in their ignorances, and that their sins may not appear: lest my ignorances increase and my offences be multiplied, and my sins abound, and I fall before my adversaries, and my enemy rejoice over me?

O Lord, Father, and God of my life, leave me not to their devices. Give me not haughtiness of my eyes, and turn away from me all coveting.

Take from me the greediness of the belly, and let not the lusts of the flesh take hold of me, and give me not over to a shameless and foolish mind. Ecclus. 23:1-6.

II

JUSTIFICATION

1. THE BLOTTING OUT OF SIN

I will pour upon you clean water, and you shall be cleansed from all your filthiness. Ezech. 36:25.

Thou shalt sprinkle me with hyssop, and I shall be cleansed: thou shalt wash me, and I shall be made whiter than snow. Ps. 50:8.

Unhappy man that I am, who shall deliver me from the body of this death? The grace of God by Jesus Christ. Rom. 7 24.

Such some of you were; but you are washed, but you are sanctified, but you are justified, in the name of our Lord Jesus Christ, and the Spirit of our God. 1 C. 6:11.

As far as the east is from the west, so far hath he removed our iniquities from us. Ps. 102:12.

He will cast all our sins into the bottom of the sea. Mich. 7:19.

Behold the Lamb of God, behold him who taketh away the sins of the world. John 1:29.

Be converted, that your sins may be blotted out. Acts 3:19.

Wash away thy sins. Acts 22:16.

In these days God hath spoken to us by his Son by whom he made the world, making purgation of sins. Heb. 1:2 f.

Christ was offered once to exhaust the sins of many. Heb. 9:28.

For this purpose the Son of God appeared, that he might destroy the works of the devil. 1 John 3:8.

His own self bore our sins in his body upon the tree, that we being dead to sins should live to justice: by whose stripes you were healed. 1 Pet. 2:24.

2. TRUE JUSTIFICATION

Abram believed God, and it was reputed to him unto justice. Gen. 15:6.

In the Lord shall all the seed of Israel be justified and praised. Is. 45:26.

He was taken away from distress and from judgment: who shall declare his generation? because he is cut off out of the land of the living: for the wickedness of my people have I struck him. Is. 53:8.

In those days shall Juda be saved and Israel shall dwell confidently: and this is the name that they shall call him: the Lord our Just One. Jer. 23:6.

Behold he who is unbelieving, his soul shall not be right in himself, but the just shall live in his faith. Heb. 2:4.

To him all the prophets give testimany that through his name all receive remission of sins who believe in him. Acts 10:43.

In him every one that believeth is justified. Acts 13:39.

Christ died once for our sins, the Just for the unjust: that he might offer us to God, being put to death indeed in the flesh, but enlivened in the spirit. 1 Pet. 3:18.

Being justified freely by his grace, through the redemption that is in Christ Jesus. Rom. 3:24.

Not as the offence, so also the gift. For where sin abounded grace has more abounded. Rom. 15:20.

He was delivered up for our sins, and rose again for our justification. Rom. 4:25.

You when you were dead in your sins, he hath quickened together with him, forgiving you all offences. Col. 2:13.

3. INTERIOR SANCTIFICATION

Hope confoundeth not; because the charity of God is poured forth in our hearts, by the Holy Ghost, who is given to us. For why did Christ, when as yet we were weak, die for the ungodly? Rom. 5:5 f.

The light of the moon shall be as the light of the sun in the day when the Lord shall bind up the wound of his people, and shall heal the stroke of their wound. Is. 30:26.

You he hath quickened together with him, forgiving you all your offences. Col. 2:13.

As by the disobedience of one man, many were made sinners: so also by the obedience of one, many shall be made just. Rom. 5:19.

He that confirmeth us with you in Christ, and that hath anointed us, is God: who also hath sealed us, and given the pledge of the Spirit in our hearts. 2 C. 1:21 f.

According to his mercy he saved us, by the laver of regeneration, and renovation of the Holy Ghost; whom he hath poured upon us abundantly, through Jesus Christ our Savior; that being justified by his grace, we may be heirs, according to hope of life everlasting. Titus 3:5-7.

Whosoever is born of God, committeth not sins, for his seed abideth in him. 1 John 3:9.

Because you are sons, God hath sent the Spirit of his Son into your hearts. Gal. 4:6.

Be renewed in the spirit of your mind. And put on the new man, who according to God is created in justice and holiness of truth. Eph. 4:23 f.

If by one man's offence death reigned through one: much more they who receive abundance of grace, and of the gift, and of justice, shall reign in life through one, Jesus Christ. Rom. 5:17.

Whom he foreknew, he also predestinated to be made conformable to the image of his Son; that he might be the first-born amongst many brethren. Rom. 8:29.

As we have borne the image of the earthly, let us bear also the image of the heavenly. 1 C. 15:49.

4. SANCTIFICATION BY FAITH, HOPE, AND CHARITY

By him we have access through faith into this grace wherein we stand. Rom. 5:2.

He that trusteth in the Lord shall be healed. Prov. 28:25.

Hope confoundeth not. Rom. 8:24.

Every one that hath this hope in him, sanctified himself. 1 John 3:3.

If I should have all faith so that I could remove mountains, and have not charity, it profiteth me nothing. 1 C. 13:2.

There remain faith, hope, charity; these three; but the greatest of these is charity. 1 C. 13:13.

We give thanks to God. Hearing your faith in Christ Jesus, and the love which you have towards all the saints. For this hope that is laid up for you in heaven. Col. 1:4.

Charity covereth a multitude of sins. 1 Pet. 4:8.

Many sins are forgiven her because she hath loved much. Luke 7:47.

He that loveth not abideth in death. 1 John 3:14.

5. SANCTIFICATION BY PENANCE AND OTHER GOOD WORKS

Do penance; for the kingdom of heaven is at hand. Mat. 3:2.

Thou hast mercy upon all because thou canst do all things, and overlookest the sins of men for the sake of repentance. Wis. 11:24.

If the wicked do penance for all his sins which he hath committed, and keep all my commandments, and do judgment, and justice, living he shall live, and shall not die. I will not remember all his iniquities that he hath done: in his justice which he hath wrought, he shall live. Ez. 18:21 f.

Let nothing hinder thee from praying always, and be not afraid to be justified, even to death: for the reward of God continueth forever. Ecclus. 18:22.

He that hurteth, let him hurt still: and he that is filthy, let him be filthy still: and he that is just, let him be justified still: and he that is holy, let him be sanctified still. Apoc. 22:11.

Turn to me, and I will turn to you, saith the Lord. Turn ye from your wicked thoughts. Zach. 1:3 f.

Do penance, and be baptized every one of you, for the remission of your sins. Acts 2:38.

The fear of the Lord driveth out sin; for he that is without fear cannot be justified. Ecclus. 1:27 f.

With fear and trembling, work out your salvation. Phil. 2:12.

The sorrow which is according to God worketh penance steadfast unto salvation. 2 C. 7:10.

Put ye on the Lord Jesus Christ, and make not provision for the flesh in its concupiscences. Rom. 13:14.

Do you see that by works a man is justified, and not by faith only? Jas. 2:14.

He said to all: if any man will come after me, let him deny himself and take up his cross daily, and follow me. Luke 9:23.

He that hateth his life in this world, keepeth it unto life eternal. John 12:25.

They that are Christ's, have crucified their flesh with the vices and concupiscences. Gal. 5:24.

We are debtors, not to the flesh, to live according to the flesh. For if you live according to the flesh, you shall die. But if by the Spirit you mortify the deeds of the flesh, you shall live. Rom. 8:12 f.

And every one that striveth for the mastery, refraineth himself from all things: and they indeed that they may receive a corruptible crown: but we an incorruptible one. 1 C. 9:26.

I therefore so run, not as at an uncertainty: I so fight, not as one beating the air: but I chastise my body, and bring it into subjection: lest perhaps, when I have preached to others, I myself should become a castaway. 1 C. 9:27.

Mortify your members which are upon the earth: fornication, uncleanness, lust, evil concupiscence, and covetousness, which is the service of idols. For which things the wrath of God cometh upon the children of unbelief. Col. 3:5 f.

If a man say he hath faith, but hath not works, shall faith be able to save him? Jas. 2:14.

Faith, if it have not works, is dead in itself. Jas. 2:17.

Even as the body without the spirit is dead, so also faith without works is dead. Jas. 2:26.

Not every one that saith to me, Lord, Lord, shall enter into the kingdom of heaven, but he that doth the will of my Father who is in heaven, he shall enter into the kingdom of heaven. Mat. 7:21.

Embrace discipline, lest at any time the Lord be angry and you perish from the just way. Ps. 2:12.

Go not after thy lusts, and turn away from thine own will. If thou give to thy soul her desires, she will make thee a joy to thy enemies. Ecclus. 18:30 f.

Walk in the Spirit, and you shall not fulfil the lusts of the flesh. Gal. 5:16.

Salvation shall be to them that fear thy name. Mich. 6:6.

Because for this end thou hast put thy fear in our hearts, to the intent that we should call upon thy name. Bar. 3:7.

Fear ye him, who after he hath killed, hath power to cast into hell:

Yea, I say to you, fear him. Luke 12:5.

His mercy is from generation unto generation, to them that fear him. Luke 1:50.

Men brethren, sons of the race of Abraham, and whosoever among you fear God, to you the word of this salvation is sent. Acts 13:26.

In every nation, he that feareth him and worketh justice, is acceptable to him. Acts 10:35.

Let us cleanse ourselves from all defilement of the flesh and of the spirit, perfecting sanctification in the fear of God. 2 C. 7:1.

6. ON WHOLESOME FEAR

The fear of the Lord is the glory of the rich, and of the honorable, and of the poor. Ecclus. 10:25.

He that feareth God, will do good. Ecclus. 15:1.

The fear of God is all wisdom. Ecclus. 19:18.

The fear of God is the beginning of his love: and the beginning of faith is to be fast joined unto it. Ecclus. 25:16.

No evils shall happen to him that feareth the Lord, but in temptation God will keep him, and deliver him from evils. Ecclus. 33:1.

The soul of him that feareth the Lord is blessed. Ecclus. 34:17.

The eyes of the Lord are upon them that fear him, he is their powerful protector, and strong stay, a defence from the heat, and a cover from the sun at noon. A preservation from stumbling, and a help from falling: He raiseth up the soul, and enlighteneth the eyes, and giveth health, and life, and blessing. Ecclus. 34:19 f.

There is no want in the fear of the Lord, and it needeth not to seek for help. Ecclus. 40:27.

The fear of the Lord is his treasure. Is. 33:6.

Sanctify the Lord of hosts himself: and let him be your fear, and let him be your dread. And he shall be a sanctification to you. Is. 8:13 f.

Fear God, and keep his commandments: for this is all man. Ecclus. 12:13.

There are just men and wise men, and their works are in the hand of God; and yet man knoweth not whether he be worthy of love or hatred: but all things are kept uncertain for the time to come. Eccles. 9:1 f.

I am not conscious to myself of anything, yet am I not hereby justified; but he that judgeth me is the Lord. 1 C. 4:4.

Judge not before the time: until the Lord come, who both will bring to light the hidden things of darkness, and will make manifest the counsels of the hearts: and then shall every man have praise from God. 1 C. 4:5.

To me it is a very small thing to be judged by you or by any man's day; but neither do I judge my own self. 1 C. 4:3.

Fear the Lord and serve him in truth and with your whole heart, for you have seen the great works he hath done among you. 1 K. 12:24.

Behold the fear of the Lord, that is wisdom: and to depart from evil is understanding. Job 28:28.

The fear of the Lord is holy, enduring forever and ever. Ps. 18:10.

Fear the Lord, all ye saints: for there is no want to them that fear him. Ps. 33:10.

His soul shall dwell in good things: and his seed shall inherit the land. Ps. 24:13.

He hath blessed all that fear the Lord, both little and great. Ps. 113:13.

Blessed are all they that fear the Lord; that walk in his ways. Ps. 127:1.

[The Lord] will do the will of them that fear him: and he will hear their prayer, and save them. Ps. 144:19.

The Lord taketh pleasure in them that fear him: and in them that hope in his mercy. Ps. 146:11.

The fear of the Lord is the beginning of wisdom. Prov. 9:10.

By the fear of the Lord men depart from evil. Prov. 16:6.

The fear of the Lord is honor, and glory, and gladness, and a crown of joy. The fear of the Lord shall delight the heart, and shall give joy, and gladness, and length of days. The fear of the Lord is the beginning of wisdom, and was created with the faithful in the womb, it walketh with chosen women, and is known with the just and faithful. It shall go well with him that feareth the Lord, and in the days of his end he shall be blessed. The fear of the Lord is a crown of wisdom, filling up peace and the fruit of salvation. The fear of the Lord driveth out sin. Ecclus. 1:11 f., 16, 19, 22, 27.

Ye that fear the Lord, wait for his mercy: and go not aside from him, lest ye fall. Ye that fear the Lord, believe him: and your reward shall not be made void. Ye that fear the Lord, hope in him; and mercy shall come to you for your delight. Ye that fear the Lord, love him, and your hearts shall be enlightened. They that fear the Lord will not be incredulous to his word: and they that love him will keep his way. They that fear the Lord, will prepare their hearts, and in his sight will sanctify their souls. They that fear the Lord keep his commandments, and will have patience even unto his visitation. Ecclus. 2:7-10, 18, 20 f.

Because of unbelief they were broken off. But thou standest by faith; be not highminded, but fear. For if God hath not spared the natural branches, fear lest perhaps also he spare not thee. Rom. 11:20 f.

He that thinketh himself to stand, let him take heed lest he fall. 1 C. 10:12.

I chastise my body, and bring it into subjection, lest perhaps when I have preached to others I myself should become a castaway. 1 C. 9:27.

Who shall not fear thee, O Lord, and magnify thy name? For thou only art holy. Apoc. 15:4.

In the fear of the Lord is confidence of strength, and there shall be hope for his children. The fear of the Lord is a fountain of life, to decline from the ruin of death. Prov. 14:26 f.

Strive to enter by the narrow gate. Luke 13:24.

Wide is the gate that leadeth to destruction, and many there are who go in thereat. Mat. 7:13.

I feared all my works, knowing that thou didst not spare the offender. Job 9:28.

7. THE CONFIDENCE OF THE JUST

The Spirit himself giveth testimony to our spirit that we are the sons of God. Rom. 8:16.

Who shall separate us from the love of Christ? Shall tribulation? or distress? or famine? or nakedness? or danger? or persecution? or the sword? But in all these things we overcome because of him that hath loved us. For I am sure that neither death nor life nor any other creature shall be able to separate us from the love of God which is in Christ Jesus. Rom. 8:35-39.

Do manfully, and be of good heart: fear not, nor be ye dismayed at their sight: for the Lord thy God he himself is thy leader, and will not leave thee nor forsake thee. Deut. 31:6.

If armies in camp should stand together against me, my heart shall not fear. If a battle shall rise up against me, in this will I be confident. Ps. 26:3.

The Lord God is my helper, therefore am I not confounded: therefore have I set my face as a most hard rock, and I know that I shall not be confounded. He is near that justifieth me: who will contend with me? Behold, the Lord God is my helper: who is he that shall condemn me? Is. 50:7-9.

It is good to confide in the Lord, rather than to have confidence in man. Ps. 117:8.

Have confidence in the Lord with

all thy heart, and lean not upon thy own prudence. Prov. 3:5.

Blessed be the man that trusteth in the Lord, and the Lord shall be his confidence. Jer. 17:7.

I will look towards the Lord, I will wait for God my Savior: my God will hear me. Mich. 7:7.

The Lord will hear me when I shall cry unto him. Ps. 4:4.

Christ Jesus our Lord. In whom we have boldness and access with confidence by the faith of him. Eph. 3:11 f.

I know whom I have believed: and I am certain that he is able to keep that which I have committed unto him against that day. 2 Tim. 1:12.

Much peace have they that love thy law, and to them there is no stumbling block. Ps. 118:165.

Our glory is this, the testimony of our conscience. 2 C. 1:12.

I will greatly rejoice in the Lord, and my soul shall be joyful in my God; for he hath clothed me with the garments of salvation; and with the robe of justice he has covered me. Is. 61:10.

How great is the multitude of thy sweetness, O Lord, which thou hast hidden for them that fear thee! Ps. 30:20.

Do not lose your confidence, which hath a great reward. Heb. 10:35.

8. THE VAIN PRESUMPTION OF THE WICKED

Say not: How mighty I am? who shall bring me under for my deeds? for God will surely take revenge. Say not: I have sinned, and what harm hath befallen me? for the Most High is a patient rewarder. Be not without fear about sin forgiven, and add not sin upon sin. Say not: The mercy of the Lord is great, he will have mercy on the multitude of my sins. Ecclus. 5:3-6.

They leaned upon the Lord, saying: Is not the Lord in the midst of us? No evil shall come upon us. Mich. 3:11.

I shall have peace, and will walk on in the naughtiness of my heart. Deut. 29:19.

Come, let us take wine, and be filled with drunkenness: and it shall be as today, so also tomorrow, and much more. Is. 56:12.

Say not: God will have respect to the multitude of my gifts, and when I offer to the Most High God, he will accept of my offerings. Ecclus. 7:11.

O God, I give thee thanks that I am not as the rest of men, extortioners, unjust, adulterers, as also is this publican. Luke 18:11.

Let him that thinketh himself to stand take heed, lest he fall. 1 C. 10:12.

They take the timbrel and the harp, and rejoice at the sound of the organ. They spend their days in wealth, and in a moment they go down to hell. Job 21:12.

Who can tell if God will turn, and forgive? Job 3:9.

Do penance, and pray to God, if perhaps this thought of thy heart may be forgiven thee. Acts 8:22.

The hope of the wicked is as dust, which is blown away with the wind; and as a thin froth, which is dispersed by the storm; and a smoke that is scattered abroad by the wind; and as the remembrance of a guest of one day that passeth by. Wis. 5:15.

Destruction and unhappiness are in their ways; and the way of peace they have not known. There is no fear of God before their eyes. Ps. 13:3.

III

MERIT

1. THE PERFECTION OF GOOD WORKS

I

The Lord will reward me according to my justice; and will repay me according to the cleanness of my hands. Because I have kept the ways of the Lord; and have not done wickedly against my God. And I shall be spotless with him; and shall keep myself from my iniquity. Ps. 17:21 f., 24.

I shall always keep thy law, forever and ever. Ps. 118:44.

I have restrained my feet from every evil way; that I may keep thy words. Ps. 118:101.

II

So let your light shine before men that they may see your good works, and glorify your Father, who is in heaven. Mat. 5:16.

Be you perfect, as also your heavenly Father is perfect. Mat. 5:48.

Labor not for the meat which perisheth, but for that which endureth unto life everlasting, which the Son of man will give you. John 6:27.

Having your conversation good among the Gentiles; that whereas they speak against you as evildoers, they may by the good works which they shall behold in you, glorify God in the day of visitation. 1 Pet. 2:12.

God is not a respecter of persons. But in every nation he that feareth him, and worketh justice is acceptable to him. Acts 10:34 f.

2. ACTIONS TO BE DONE FROM SUPERNATURAL MOTIVES

Therein do I endeavor to have always a conscience without offence towards God, and towards man. Acts 24:16.

Be without offence to the Jews and to the Gentiles and to the church of God, as I also in all things please all men. 1 C. 10:32 f.

We exhort you that you receive not the grace of God in vain, giving no offence to any man, that our ministry be not blamed. 2 C. 6:1, 3.

We are his workmanship, created in Christ Jesus, in good works, which God hath prepared that we should walk in them. Eph. 2:10.

Charge the rich of this world not to be highminded, or to trust in the uncertainty of riches, but in the living God (who giveth us abundantly all things to enjoy), to do good, to be rich in good works. To lay up in store for themselves a good foundation against the time to come, that they may lay hold on the true life. 1 Tim. 6:17-19.

What participation hath justice with injustice? or what fellowship hath light with darkness? 2 C. 6:14.

Whosoever abideth in God, sinneth not; and whosoever sinneth, hath not seen him. 1 John 3:6.

In all these things Job sinned not by his lips. Job 1:22.

A man simple, and upright, and avoiding evil, and still keeping his innocence. Job 2:3.

These things have I suffered without the iniquity of my hand, when I offered pure prayers to God. Job 16:18.

If a virgin marry, she hath not sinned. 1 C. 7:28.

3. THE REWARD OF GOOD WORKS

Be ye steadfast and unmovable; always abounding in the work of the Lord, knowing that your labor is not in vain in the Lord. 1 C. 15:58.

God is not unjust that he should forget your work, and the love which you have shown in his name, you who have ministered to the saints. Heb. 6:10.

Do not lose your confidence, which hath a great reward. Heb. 10:35.

I have fought a great fight, I have finished my course, I have kept the faith. As for the rest, there is laid up for me a crown of justice, which the Lord the just Judge will render me in that day. 2 Tim. 4:7 f.

Know you not that they that run in the race, all run indeed, but one receiveth the crown? So run that you may obtain. 1 C. 9:24.

The Son of man shall come in the glory of his Father, and will render to every man according to his works. Mat. 16:27.

Thou treasurest up to thyself wrath, against the day of wrath, and revelation of the just judgment of God, who will render to every man according to his works. Rom. 2:5 f.

They shall walk with me in white because they are worthy. Apoc. 3:4.

If I do this thing willingly, I have a reward: but if against my will, a dispensation is committed to me. 1 C. 9:17.

Abide in me, and I in you. As the branch cannot bear fruit of itself unless it abide in the vine, so neither can you unless you abide in me. John 15:4.

Behold now is the acceptable time, behold now is the day of salvation. 2 C. 6:2.

The path of the just, as a shining light, goeth forward and increaseth even to perfect day. Prov. 4:18.

As you have yielded your members to serve uncleanness, and iniquity unto iniquity: so now yield your members to serve justice, unto sanctification. Rom. 6:19.

Let nothing hinder thee from praying always, and be not afraid to be justified, even to death. Ecclus. 18:22.

Fear the Lord, all ye his saints, for there is no want to them that fear him. Ps. 33:10.

Godliness is profitable to all things, having promise of the life that now is, and of that which is to come. 1 Tim. 4:8.

Every one that hath left house, or lands, for my name's sake, shall receive a hundredfold, and shall possess life everlasting. Mat. 19:28.

4. TO LOVE GOD IS TO OBEY HIM

If you love me, keep my commandments. John 11:15.

He that hath my commandments, and keepeth them, he it is that loveth me. John 11:21.

If any one love me, he will keep my word. John 14:23.

If you keep my commandments, you shall abide in my love: as I also have kept my Father's commandments, and do abide in his love. John 15:10.

You are my friends if you do the things that I command you. John 15:14.

I am the true vine, and my Father is the husbandman. Every branch in me that beareth not fruit, he will take away, and every one that beareth fruit, he will purge it, that it may bring forth more fruit. John 15:2 f.

If you love me, keep my commandments. He that hath my commandments, and keepeth them, he it is that loveth me: and he that loveth me shall be loved of my Father, and I will love him, and will manifest myself to him. John 14: 15, 20.

This is the charity of God: that we keep his commandments. 1 John 5:3.

Love is the keeping of his law. Wis. 6:19.

Fear God and keep his commandments; for this is the whole man. Eccles. 12:13.

Not every one that saith to me, Lord, Lord, shall enter into the kingdom of heaven, but he that doth the will of my Father who is in heaven, he shall enter into the kingdom of heaven. Mat. 7:21.

My meat is to do the will of him who sent me. John 4:34.

Unless your justice abound more than that of the scribes and Pharisees, you shall not enter into the kingdom of heaven. Mat. 5:20.

Christ being consummated, he became to all that obey him, the cause of eternal salvation. Heb. 5:9.

By this, we know that we have known him, if we keep his commandments. 1 John 2:3.

He who saith that he knoweth him, and keepeth not his commandments, is a liar. 1 John 2:4.

He that saith he abideth in him, ought himself also to walk, even as he walked. 1 John 2:6.

Love is the fulfilling of the law. Rom. 13:10.

What doth the Lord thy God require of thee, but that thou fear the Lord thy God, and walk in his ways, and love him, and serve the Lord thy God, with all thy heart, and with all thy soul? Deut. 10:12.

5. THE TEN COMMANDMENTS

The Lord spoke all these words. Ex. 20:1.

And he wrote them on two tables of stone, which he delivered unto me. Deut. 5:22.

First Table of the Law

From Exodus (20:1-11)

I

I am the Lord thy God, who brought thee out of the land of Egypt, out of the house of bondage. Thou shalt not have strange gods before me. Thou shalt not make to thyself a graven thing, nor the likeness of anything that is in heaven above, or in the earth beneath, nor of those things that are in the waters under the earth. Thou shalt not adore them, nor serve them.

II

Thou shalt not take the name of the Lord thy God in vain: for the Lord will not hold him guiltless that shall take the name of the Lord his God in vain.

III

Remember that thou keep holy the Sabbath day. Six days shalt thou labor, and shalt do all thy works. But on the seventh day is the Sabbath of the Lord thy God: thou shalt do no work on it, thou nor thy son, nor thy daughter, nor thy man-servant, nor thy maid-servant, nor thy beast, nor the stranger that is within thy gates. For in six days the Lord made heaven and earth, and the sea, and all things that are in them, and rested on the seventh day: therefore the Lord blessed the seventh day, and sanctified it.

From Deuteronomy (5:6-15)

I

I am the Lord thy God, who brought thee out of the land of Egypt, out of the house of bondage. Thou shalt not have strange gods in my sight. Thou shalt not make to thyself a graven thing, nor the likeness of any things, that are in heaven above, or that are in the earth beneath, or that abide in the waters under the earth. Thou shalt not adore them, and thou shalt not serve them.

II

Thou shalt not take the name of the Lord thy God in vain: for he shall not be unpunished that taketh his name upon a vain thing.

III

Observe the day of the Sabbath, to sanctify it, as the Lord thy God hath commanded thee. Six days shalt thou labor, and shalt do all thy works. The seventh is the day of the Sabbath, that is, the rest of the Lord thy God. Thou shalt not do any work therein, thou nor thy son, nor thy daughter, nor thy man-servant, nor thy maid-servant, nor thy ox, nor thy ass, nor any of thy beasts, nor the stranger that is within thy gates: that thy man-servant and thy maid-servant may rest, even as thyself. Remember that thou also didst serve in Egypt, and the Lord thy God brought thee out from hence with a strong hand, and stretched-out arm. Therefore hath he commanded thee that thou shouldst observe the Sabbath day.

Second Table of the Law

From Exodus (20:12-17)

IV

Honor thy father and thy mother, that thou mayst be long-lived upon the land which the Lord thy God will give thee.

V

Thou shalt not kill.

VI

Thou shalt not commit adultery.

VII

Thou shalt not steal.

VIII

Thou shalt not bear false witness against thy neighbor.

IX

Thou shalt not covet thy neighbor's house.

X

Neither shalt thou desire his wife, nor his servant, nor his handmaid, nor his ox, nor his ass, nor anything that is his.

From Deuteronomy (5:16-21)

IV

Honor thy father and mother, as the Lord thy God hath commanded thee, that thou mayst live a long time, and it may be well with thee in the land which the Lord thy God will give thee.

V

Thou shalt not kill.

VI

Neither shalt thou commit adultery.

VII

And thou shalt not steal.

VIII

Neither shalt thou bear false witness against thy neighbor.

IX

Thou shalt not covet thy neighbor's wife.

X

Nor his house, nor his field, nor his man-servant, nor his maid-servant, nor his ox, nor his ass, nor anything that is his.

Appendix to Each of the Commandments

From Exodus

I am the Lord thy God, mighty, jealous, visiting the iniquity of the fathers upon the children, unto the third and fourth generation of them that hate me: and showing mercy unto thousands to them that love me, and keep my commandments. 20:5 f.

From Deuteronomy

I am the Lord thy God, a jealous God, visiting the iniquity of the fathers upon their children unto the third and fourth generation to them that hate me, and showing mercy unto many thousands to them that love me, and keep my commandments. 5:9 f.

6. GOD REQUIRES THE KEEPING OF HIS COMMANDMENTS

If thou wilt enter into life, keep the commandments. Mat. 19:17.

Thou hast done foolishly, and hast not kept the commandments of the

Lord thy God. Therefore thy kingdom shall not continue. 1 K. 13:13 f.

That eye hath not seen, nor ear heard, neither hath it entered into the heart of man, what things God hath prepared for them that love him. 1 C. 2:9.

Come to me, all you that labor, and are burdened, and I will refresh you. Take up my yoke upon you, and learn of me, because I am meek and humble of heart, and you shall find rest for your souls. For my yoke is sweet and my burden light. Mat. 11:28-30.

The son honoreth the father, and the servant his master: if then I be a father, where is my honor? and if I be a master, where is my fear? Mal. 1:6.

Son, keep my commandments and thou shalt live. Prov. 7:2.

This do, and thou shalt live. Luke 10:28.

God will render to every man according to his works. To them indeed, who according to patience in good work, seek glory, and honor, and incorruption, eternal life. But to them that are contentious, and who obey not the truth, but give credit to iniquity, wrath, and indignation. Rom. 2:6-8.

I will take away the stony heart out of your flesh, and will give you a heart of flesh. And I will put my Spirit in the midst of you, and I will cause you to walk in my commandments, and to keep my judgments, and do them. Ex. 36:26 f.

In the head of the book it is written of me that I should do thy will. O my God, I have desired it, and thy law in the midst of my heart. Ps. 39:8 f.

You have not chosen me, but I have chosen you; that you should go, and should bring forth fruit; and your fruit should remain. John 15:16.

7. THE LIBERTY OF THE SONS OF GOD

You, brethren, have been called unto liberty: only make not liberty an occasion to the flesh. Gal. 5:13.

As free, and not as making liberty a cloak for malice, but as the servants of God. 1 Pet. 2:16.

Where the Spirit of the Lord is, there is liberty. 2 C. 3:17.

When you were the servants of sin, you were free men to justice. But now being made free from sin, and become servants to God, you have your fruit unto sanctification, and the end life everlasting. Rom. 6:20, 22.

I came down from heaven not to do my own will, but the will of him that sent me. John 6:38.

Shall not my soul be subject to God? for from him is my salvation. For he is my God and my Savior; he is my Protector, I shall be moved no more. Ps. 61:1 f.

How sweet are thy words to my palate! more than honey in my mouth. Ps. 118:103.

I have been delighted in the way of thy testimonies as in all riches. Ps. 118:14.

My son, hast thou sinned? Do so no more. Ecclus. 21:1.

Go not after thy lusts. Ecclus. 18:30.

Behold, thou art made whole: sin no more. John 5:14.

Awake, ye just, and sin not. 1 C. 15:34.

Let not sin reign in your mortal body, so as to obey the lusts thereof. Rom. 6:12.

Every man is tempted by his own concupiscence, being drawn away and allured. Jas. 1:14.

Then when concupiscence hath conceived, it bringeth forth sin. Jas. 1:15.

If we sin wilfully after having received the knowledge of the truth, there is now left no sacrifice for sin, but a certain dreadful expectation of judgment. Heb. 10:26 f.

8. GOD'S COMMANDMENTS POSSIBLE IN PRACTICE

I

Keep the law and counsel: and there shall be life to thy soul, and grace to thy mouth. Prov. 3:21 f.

There was not found the like to Abraham in glory, who kept the law of the Most High, and was in covenant with him. Therefore by an oath he gave him glory in his posterity. Ecclus. 44:20, 22.

I can do all things in him who strengtheneth me. Phil. 4:13.

Noe was a just and perfect man in his generation, he walked with God. Gen. 6:9.

The Lord said unto him: Walk before me, and be perfect. Gen. 17:1.

This commandment which I command thee is not above thee. Deut. 30:11.

He [Josue] accomplished all: he left not one thing undone of all the commandments which the Lord had commanded Moses. Jos. 11:15.

My servant David kept my commandments, and followed me with all his heart. 3 K. 14:8.

The king [Josias] stood upon the step and made a covenant with the Lord to walk after the Lord and to keep his commandments, and his testimonies, and his ceremonies with all their heart and with all their soul. 4 K. 23:3.

I have kept the ways of the Lord and have not done wickedly against my God. Ps. 17:22.

I will put my Spirit in the midst of you, and I will cause you to walk in my commandments, and to keep my judgments, and do them. Ez. 36:27.

Thou hast not been as my servant David, who kept my commandments, and followed me, with all his heart, doing that which was well-pleasing in my sight. 3 K. 14:8.

They were both just before God, walking in all the commandments and justifications of the Lord without blame. Luke 1:6.

All these have I kept from my youth. Mat. 19:20.

Remember how I have walked before thee in truth, and with a perfect heart. Is. 38:3.

My yoke is sweet and my burden light. Mat. 11:30.

This is the charity of God, that we keep his comandments: and his commandments are not heavy. 1 John 5:3.

I have run the way of thy commandments. Ps. 118:32.

Give me understanding, and I will search thy law, and I will keep it with my whole heart. Ps. 118:34.

II

He that loveth his neighbor, hath fulfilled the law. Rom. 13:8.

We know that we have passed from death to life, because we love the brethren; he that loveth not, abideth in death. 1 John 3:14.

He that keepeth his word, in him in very deed the charity of God is perfected. 1 John 2:5.

Let us therefore, as many as are perfected, be thus minded. Phil. 3:15.

I am sure that neither death nor life, nor angels, nor principalities, nor any other creature, shall be able to separate us from the love of God. Rom. 8:38 f.

A just man shall fall seven times, and shall rise again; but the wicked shall fall down into evil. Prov. 24:16.

9. PRAYER

Be subject to the Lord and pray to him. Ps. 36:7.

If any of you want wisdom, let him ask of God, who giveth to all abundantly, and upbraideth not: and it shall be given him. But let him ask in faith, nothing wavering: for he that wavereth is like a wave of the sea, that is moved and carried about by the wind. Therefore, let not that man think that he shall receive anything of the Lord. Jas. 1:5-7.

The eyes of the Lord are upon the just: and his ears unto their prayers. The just cried, and the Lord heard them: and delivered them out of all their troubles. Ps. 22:16, 18.

Christ leaving them, went again: and he prayed the third time, saying the selfsame word. Mat. 26:44.

We pray always for you: that our God would make you worthy of his calling, and fulfil all the good pleasure of his goodness and the work of faith in power. 2 Thess. 1:11.

All things whatsoever you shall ask in prayer, believing, you shall receive. Mat. 21:22.

Every creature of God is good, and nothing to be rejected that is received with thanksgiving: for it is sanctified by the word of God and prayer. 1 Tim. 4:4 f.

Behold we come to thee, for thou art the Lord our God. Jer. 3:22.

I set my face to the Lord my God, to pray and make supplication with fasting, and sackcloth, and ashes. O our God, hear the suplication of thy servant, and his prayers: and show thy face upon thy sanctuary which is desolate, for thy own sake. Dan. 9:3, 17.

Pray to the Most High, that he may direct thy way in truth. Ecclus. 37:19.

For thy former sins also pray that they may be forgiven thee. Ecclus. 20:1.

Again I say to you, that if two of you shall agree upon earth, concerning anything whatsoever they shall ask, it shall be done for them by my Father who is in heaven. For where there are two or three gathered together in my name, there am I in the midst of them. Mat. 18:19 f.

He said to them: The harvest indeed is great, but the laborers are few. Pray ye therefore the Lord of the harvest, that he send laborers into his harvest. Luke 10:2.

And now, O Lord Almighty, the God of Israel, the soul in anguish, and the troubled spirit crieth to thee. For thou remainest forever, and shall we perish everlastingly? Bar. 3:1, 3.

This is the confidence which we have in him: that whatsoever we shall ask, according to his will, he heareth us. And we know that he heareth us, whatsoever we ask: we know that we have the petitions which we request of him. 1 John 5:14 f.

Thou shalt pray to him, and he will hear thee. Job 22:27.

Do not multiply to speak lofty things, boasting: let old matters depart from your mouth: for the Lord is a God of all knowledge, and to him are thoughts prepared. 1 K. 2:3.

Far from me be this sin against the Lord, that I should cease to pray for you. 1 K. 12:23.

For the Lord will be entreated in favor of his servants. Ps. 134:14.

You that are mindful of the Lord, hold not your peace, and give him no silence till he establish, and till he make Jerusalem a praise in the earth. Is. 62:6 f.

Every one that calleth upon my name, I have created him for my glory, I have formed him, and made him. Is. 43:7.

I prevented the dawning of the day, and cried: because in thy words I very much hoped. Ps. 118:147.

In what day soever I shall call upon thee, behold I know thou art my God. Ps. 60:10.

The Lord is nigh unto all them that call upon him: to all that call upon him in truth. Ps. 144:18.

Who hath called upon him and he despised him? For God is a protector to all that seek him in truth. Ecclus. 2:12.

He that loveth God, shall obtain pardon of his sins by prayer, and shall refrain himself from them, and shall be heard in the prayer of days. Ecclus. 3:4.

Neglect not to pray, and to give alms. Ecclus. 7:10.

Make thy prayer before the face of the Lord, and offend less. Ecclus. 17:22.

Parable of the unjust judge. Luke 18:1-8.

10. FASTING AND ABSTINENCE

I eat no desirable bread, and neither flesh, nor wine entered into my mouth. Dan. 10:3.

When a man, or woman, shall make

a vow to be sanctified, and will consecrate themselves to the Lord, they shall abstain from wine and from everything that can make a man drunk. Num. 6:2.

The fast of the fourth month, and the fast of the fifth, and the fast of the seventh, and the fast of the tenth shall be to the house of Juda, joy and gladness, and great solemnities. Zach. 8:19.

Can the children of the bridegroom mourn, as long as the bridegroom is with them? But the days will come when the bridegroom shall be taken away from them: and then they shall fast. Mat. 9:15.

If meat scandalize my brother I will never eat flesh. 1 C. 8:13.

A man that fasteth for his sins, and doth the same again, what doth his humbling himself profit him? Who will hear his prayer? Ecclus. 34:31.

When you fasted and mourned did you kep a fast to me? Zach. 7:5.

Prayer is good with fasting and alms, more than to lay up treasures of gold. Tob. 12:8.

I beseech you, by the mercy of God, that you present your bodies a living sacrifice, holy, pleasing unto God, your reasonable service. Rom. 12:1.

Know ye that the Lord will hear your prayers, if you continue with perseverance in fastings and prayers in the sight of the Lord. Jdth. 4:11.

Why have we fasted, and thou hast not regarded? Have we humbled our souls, and thou hast not taken notice? Behold in the day of your fast your own will is found, and you exact of all your debtors. Is. 58:3.

As they were ministering to the Lord, and fasting, the Holy Ghost said to them: Separate me Saul and Barnabas for the work whereunto I have taken them. Then they fasting and praying, and imposing their hands upon them, sent them away. Acts 13:2 f.

When they had ordained to them priests in every church, and had prayed with fasting, they commended them to the Lord in whom they believed. Acts 14:22.

11. VOWS

Vow ye and pay to the Lord your God. Ps. 75:12.

Thou shalt pay thy vows. Job 22:27.

Anything that is devoted to the Lord, whether it be man, or beast, or field, shall not be sold, neither may it be redeemed. Whatsoever is once consecrated shall be holy of holies to the Lord. Lev. 27:28.

Paul when he had stayed yet many days, taking his leave of the brethren, sailed thence into Syria, having shorn his head in Cenchra. For he had a vow. Acts 18:18.

I will pay my vows in the sight of them that fear him. Ps. 21:26.

The victims of the wicked are abominable to the Lord: the vows of the just are acceptable. Prov. 15:8.

If any man make a vow to the Lord, or bind himself by an oath: he shall not make his word void, but shall fulfil all that he promised. Num. 30:3.

When thou hast made a vow to the Lord thy God, thou shalt not delay to pay it: because the Lord thy God will require it. And if thou delay, it shall be imputed to thee for a sin. If thou wilt not promise, thou shalt be without sin. But that which is once gone out of thy lips, thou shalt observe, and shalt do as thou hast promised to the Lord thy God, and hast spoken with thy own will and with thy own mouth. Deut. 23:21-23.

12. VOCATION TO THE PRIESTHOOD AND TO THE RELIGIOUS STATE

Blessed is he whom thou hast chosen, and taken to thee: he shall dwell in thy courts. Ps. 64:5.

If thou wilt be perfect, go sell what thou hast, and give to the poor, and thou shalt have treasure in heaven: and come, follow me. Mat. 19:21.

Behold we have left all things, and have followed thee: what therefore shall we have? Mat. 19:27.

Here am I: for thou didst call me. Speak, Lord, for thy servant heareth. 1 K. 3:9.

The man out of whom the devils were departed, besought him that he might be with him. But Jesus sent him away, saying: Return to thy house, and tell how great things God hath done to thee. And he went through the whole city, publishing how great things Jesus had done to him. Luke 8:38 f.

He said to another: Follow me, and he said: Lord, suffer me first to go, and bury my father. And Jesus said to him: Let the dead bury their dead: but go thou, and preach the kingdom of God. And another said: I will follow thee, Lord, but let me first take my leave of them that are at my house. Jesus said to him: No man putting his hand to the plow, and looking back, is fit for the kingdom of God. Luke 9:59-62.

When he was gone forth into the way, a certain man running up and kneeling before him, asked him, Good Master, what shall I do that I may receive life everlasting? Thou knowest the commandments, Do not commit adultery, do not kill, do not steal, bear not false witness, do no fraud, honor thy father and mother.

But he answering, said to him: Master, all these things I have observed from my youth. And Jesus looking on him, loved him, and said to him: One thing is wanting unto thee: go, sell whatsoever thou hast, and give to the poor, and thou shalt have treasure in heaven: and come, follow me. Who, being struck sad at that saying, went away sorrowful: for he had great possessions. Mark 10:17, 19-22.

It came to pass in those days, that he went out into a mountain to pray, and he passed the whole night in the prayer of God. And when day was come, he called unto him his disciples; and he chose twelve of them (whom also he named apostles). Luke 6:12 f.

You have not chosen me: but I have chosen you: and have appointed you, that you should go, and should bring forth fruit: and your fruit should remain: that whatsoever you shall ask of the Father in my name he may give it you. Follow me. John 15:16, 19.

Lord, and what shall this man do? Jesus saith to him: So I will have him to remain till I come, what is it to thee? follow thou me. John 21:21 f.

We ought to obey God rather than men. Acts 5:29.

I give him thanks, who hath strengthened me, even to Christ Jesus our Lord, for that he hath counted me faithful, putting me in the ministry. 1 Tim. 1:12.

The Lord said to Abram: Go forth out of thy country, and from thy kindred, and out of thy father's house, and come into the land which I shall show thee. Gen. 12:1.

Every one that hath left house, or brethren, or sisters, or father, or mother, or wife, or children, or lands, for my name's sake, shall receive an hundred fold, and shall possess life everlasting. Mat. 19:29.

There are eunuchs who have made themselves eunuchs for the kingdom of heaven. He that can take, let him take it. Mat. 19:11 f.

Fear not, for I have redeemed thee, and have called thee by thy name: thou art mine. Is. 43:1.

After these things he went forth, and saw a publican named Levi, sitting at the receipt of custom, and he said to him: Follow me. And leaving all things, he rose up and followed him. Luke 5:27 f.

Passing by the sea of Galilee, he saw Simon and Andrew his brother, casting nets into the sea (for they were fishermen). And Jesus said to them: Come after me, and I will make you to become fishers of men. And immediately, leaving their nets, they followed him. And going on from thence a little farther, he saw James the son of Zebedee, and John his brother, who also were mending their nets in the ship. And forthwith he called them. And leaving their father Zebedee in the ship with his hired men, they followed him. Mark 1:16-20.

I would that all men were even as myself; but every one hath his proper gift from God; one after this manner, and another after that. 1 C. 7:7.

All they that believed were together, and had all things common. Their possessions and goods they sold, and divided them to all, according as every one had need. Acts 2:44 f.

If any man will come after me, let him deny himself, and take up his cross, and follow me. Mat. 16:24.

It is good for me to die, rather than that any man should make my glory void. For if I preach the gospel, it is no glory to me, for a necessity lieth upon me. 1 C. 9:15 f.

What then is my reward? That preaching the gospel, I may deliver the gospel without charge. 1 C. 9:18.

Religion clean and undefiled before God and the Father is this: to visit the fatherless and widows in their tribulation; and to keep oneself unspotted from this world. Jas. 1:27.

He obeyed, and went out, not knowing whither. Heb. 11:8.

13. ON ALMSGIVING

He that stoppeth his ear against the cry of the poor shall also cry himself, and shall not be heard. Prov. 21:13.

Despise not the hungry soul: and provoke not the poor in his want. Ecclus. 4:2.

He that hath mercy on the poor lendeth to the Lord: and he will repay him. Prov. 19:17.

If one of thy brethren that dwelleth within the gates of thy city come to poverty: thou shalt not harden thy heart, nor close thy hand, but shalt open it to the poor man. Thou shalt give to him: neither shalt thou do anything craftily in relieving his necessities: that the Lord thy God may bless thee at all times, and in all things to which thou shalt put thy hand. There will not be wanting poor in the land of thy habitation: therefore I command thee to open thy hand to thy needy and poor brother, that liveth in the land. Deut. 15:7 f., 10 f.

Give alms out of thy substance; and turn not away thy face from any poor person, for so it shall come to pass that the face of the Lord shall not be turned from thee. Tob. 4:7.

The alms of a man is a signet with him, and shall preserve the grace of a man as the apple of the eye. Ecclus. 17:18.

Neglect not to pray, and to give alms. Stretch out thy hand to the poor, that thy expiation and thy blessing may be perfected. Ecclus. 7:10, 36.

If thou do good, know to whom thou dost it, and there shall be much thanks for thy good deeds. Ecclus. 12:1.

Deal thy bread to the hungry, and bring the needy and the harborless into thy house: and when thou shalt see one naked, cover him, and despise not thy own flesh. Then shall thy light break forth as the morning, and thy health shall speedily arise, and thy justice shall go before thy face, and the glory of the Lord shall gather thee up. Then shalt thou call, and the Lord shall hear: thou shalt cry, and he shall say: Here I am. Is. 58:7-9.

Give to the merciful and uphold not the sinner. After thou hast given, upbraid not. Eccles. 12:4, 28.

Do good to thy friend before thou die. Ecclus. 14:13.

Give to every one that asketh thee. Give, and it shall be given to you: good measure, and pressed down, and shaken together, and running over, shall they give into your bosom, for with the same measure that you shall mete withal, it shall be measured to you again. Luke 6:30, 38.

Remember the word of the Lord Jesus, how he said: It is more blessed to give, than to receive. Acts 20:35.

If I should distribute all my goods to feed the poor, and if I should deliver my body to be burned, and have not charity, it profiteth me nothing. 1 C. 13:3.

Blessed are the merciful, for they shall obtain mercy. Mat. 5:7.

If any of the faithful have widows, let him relieve them. 1 Tim. 5:16.

If a brother or sister be naked, and want daily food: and one of you say to them: Go in peace, be you warmed and filled: yet give them not those things that are necessary for the body, what shall it profit? Jas. 2:15 f.

If thy enemy be hungry, give him to eat; if he thirst, give him to drink. Rom. 12:20.

PART VI

THE FOUR LAST THINGS

I

DEATH

1. MEDITATIONS ON DEATH

SUNDAY

All Must Die

In what day soever thou shalt eat of it, thou shalt die the death. Gen. 2:17.

In the sweat of thy face shalt thou eat bread till thou return to the earth out of which thou wast taken; for dust thou art, and into dust thou shalt return. Gen. 3:19.

It is appointed for men once to die, and after this the judgment. Heb. 9:27.

Yesterday for me, and today for thee. Ecclus. 38:23.

As in Adam all die, so also in Christ all shall be made alive. 1 C. 15:22.

Thou hast made me as the clay, and thou wilt bring me into dust again. Job 10:9.

Thou hast strengthened him for a little while, that he may pass away forever. Thou shalt change his face, and shalt send him away. Job 14:20.

I know that thou wilt deliver me to death, where a house is appointed for every one that liveth. Job 30:23.

The voice of one, saying: Cry; and I said: What shall I cry? All flesh is grass, and all the glory thereof as the flower of the field. The grass is withered and the flower is fallen, because the Spirit of the Lord hath blown upon it. Indeed the people is grass. Is. 40:6 f.

He shall be brought to the graves, and shall watch in the heap of the dead. He hath been acceptable to the gravel of Cocytus, and he shall draw every man after him, and there are innumerable before him. Job 21:32 f.

Who is the man that shall live and not see death? Ps. 88:49.

One generation passeth away, and another generation cometh: but the earth standeth forever. Eccles. 1:4.

Although he lived two thousand years, and hath not enjoyed good things: do not all make haste to one place? Eccles. 6:6.

It is not in man's power to stop the spirit, neither hath he power in the day of death. Eccles. 8:8.

Your fathers, where are they? And the prophets, shall they live always? Zach. 1:5.

The others indeed were made many priests, because by reason of death they were not suffered to continue. Heb. 7:23.

We all die, and like waters that return no more, we fall down into the earth. 2 K. 14:14.

O forgive me, that I may be refreshed before I go hence and be no more. Ps. 38:14.

Thou shalt take away their breath, and they shall fail and shall return to their dust. Ps. 103:9.

[There is] a time to die. Therefore the death of man and of beasts is one, and the condition of them both is equal: as man dieth, so they also die, all things breathe alike, and man hath nothing more than beast: all things are subject to vanity. And all things go to one place: of earth they were made, and into earth they return together. Eccles. 3:2, 19 f.

As he came forth naked from his mother's womb, so shall he return, and shall take nothing away with him of his labor. Job 5:14.

The living know that they shall die, but the dead know nothing more, neither have they a reward any more: for the memory of them is forgotten. Eccles. 9:5.

As by one man sin entered into this world, and by sin death; and so death passed upon all men in whom all have sinned. But death reigned from Adam unto Moses, even over them who have not sinned after the similitude of the transgression of Adam: who is a figure of him who was to come. Rom. 5:12-14.

The body is dead because of sin. Rom. 8:10.

By a man came death. In Adam all died. The enemy death shall be destroyed last. 1 C. 15:21 f., 26.

The sting of death is sin. 1 C. 15:56.

It is appointed unto men, once to die. Heb. 9:27.

As the flower of the grass shall he pass away. For the sun rose with a burning heat, and parched the grass, and the flower thereof fell off, and the beauty of the shape thereof perished; so also shall the rich man fade away in his ways. Jas. 1:10 f.

MONDAY

Preparation for Death

The days of man are short, and the number of his months is with thee: thou hast appointed his bounds, which cannot be passed. Job 14:5.

O Lord, make me know my end, and what is the number of my days: that I may know what is wanting to me. Ps. 38:5.

Thus saith the Lord God: Give charge concerning thy house, for thou shalt die and not live. 4 K. 30:1.

Give ye glory to the Lord your God, before it be dark, and before your feet stumble upon the dark mountains: you shall look for light, and he will turn it into the shadow of death, and into darkness. Jer. 13:16.

It is not in man's power to stop the spirit, neither hath the power in the day of death. Eccles. 8:8.

Our years shall be considered as a spider: the days of our years in them are three-score and ten years. But if in the strong they be four-score years: and what is more of them is labor and sorrow. Ps. 89:9.

Seek not death in the error of your life, neither procure ye destruction by the works of your hands. For God made not death, neither hath he pleasure in the destruction of the living. Wis. 1:12 f.

The life of man upon earth is a warfare, and his days are like the days of a hireling. As a servant longeth for the shade, and as the hireling looketh for the end of his work. Job 7:1 f.

Shall man that is dead, thinkest thou, live again? all the days in which I am now in warfare, I expect until my change come. Thou shalt call me, and I will answer thee: to the work of thy hands thou shalt reach out thy right hand. Thou indeed hast numbered my steps, but spare my sins. Job 14:14-16.

I will add to thy days fifteen years: and I will deliver thee and this city out of the hand of the king of the Assyrians, and I will protect this city for my own sake, and for David thy servant's sake. 4 K. 20:6.

Go and say to Ezechias: Thus saith the Lord the God of David thy father: I have heard thy prayer, and I have seen thy tears: behold I will add to thy days fifteen years. Is. 38:5.

All the days of Mathusala were nine hundred and sixty-nine years, and he died. Gen. 5:27.

There is but one step between me (as I may say) and death. 1 K. 20:3.

Now that he is dead, why should I fast? Shall I be able to bring him back any more? I shall gc to him rather: but he shall not return to me. 2 K. 12:23.

The light is sweet, and it is delightful for the eyes to see the sun. If a man live many years, and have rejoiced in them all, he must remember the darksome time. Eccles. 11:7 f.

Blessed are those servants, whom the Lord, when he cometh, shall find watching. Luke 12:37.

I must work the works of him that sent me, whilst it is day: the night cometh when no man can work. John 9:4.

Converse in fear during the time of your sojourning here. 1 Pet. 1:17.

TUESDAY

Brevity of Life

Behold, short years pass away, and I am walking in a path by which I shall not return. Job 16:23.

We are sojourners before thee, and strangers, as were all our fathers. Our days upon earth are as a shadow, and there is no stay. 1 Par. 29:15.

My days have passed more swiftly than the web is cut by the weaver, and are consumed without any hope. Job 7:6.

Remember that my life is but wind, and my eye shall not return to see good things. Job 7:7.

My days have been swifter than a post: they have fled away and have not seen good. They have passed by as ships carrying fruits, as an eagle flying to the prey. Job 9:25 f.

Shall not the fewness of my days be ended shortly? Suffer me, therefore, that I may lament my sorrow a little. Job 10:20.

Man, born of a woman, living for a short time, is filled with many miseries. He cometh forth like a flower and is destroyed, and fleeth as a shadow, and never continueth in the same state. And dost thou think it meet to open thy eyes upon such a one, and to bring him into judgment with thee? Job 14:1-3.

As a dream that fleeth away he shall not be found: he shall pass as a vision of the night. Job 20:8.

Behold thou hast made my days measurable: and my substance is as nothing before thee. Ps. 38:6.

The time is short: it remaineth that they that weep be as though they wept not, and they that rejoice as if they rejoiced not: and they that use this world, as if they used it not: for the fashion of this world passeth away. 1 C. 7:30 f.

We have not here a lasting city, but we seek one that is to come. Heb. 13:14.

Man is like to vanity: his days pass away like a shadow. Ps. 143:4.

WEDNESDAY

Uncertainty of Life

My strength is not the strength of stones, nor is my flesh of brass. Job 6:12.

Shall man be justified in comparison of God, or shall a man be more pure than his Maker? Behold they that serve him are not steadfast, and in his angels he found wickedness: how much more shall they that dwell in houses of clay, who have an earthly foundation, be consumed as with the moth? Job 4:17-19.

Your remembrance shall be compared to ashes, and your necks shall be brought to clay. Job 13:12.

I am to be consumed as rottenness, and as a garment that is moth-eaten. Job 13:28.

My spirit shall be wasted, my days shall be shortened, and only the grave remaineth for me. Job 17:1.

He knoweth our frame. He remembereth that we are dust: man's days are as grass, as the flower of the field so shall he flourish. For the spirit shall pass in him, and he shall not be: and he shall know his place no more. Ps. 89:14-16.

Lord, what is man, that thou art made known to him? or the son of man, that thou makest account of him? Man is like to vanity: his days pass away like a shadow. Ps. 143:3 f.

A thousand years in thy sight are as yesterday which is past, and as a watch in the night, as things that are counted nothing shall their years be. In the morning man shall grow up like grass, in the morning he shall flourish and pass away: in the evening he shall fall, grow dry, and wither. Ps. 89:4-6.

Remember thy Creator in the days of thy youth, before the time of affliction come, and the years draw nigh of which thou shalt say: They please me not. Before the silver cord be broken, and the golden fillet shrink back, and the pitcher be crushed at the fountain, and the wheel be broken upon the cistern, and the dust return into its earth, from whence it was, and the spirit return to God, who gave it. Eccles. 12:1, 6 f.

All flesh is as grass: and all the glory thereof as the flower of grass. The grass is withered, and the flower thereof is fallen away. 1 Pet. 1:24.

Thou seest that I am old, and know not the day of my death. Gen. 27:2.

Thy life shall be as it were hanging before thee. Thou shalt fear night and day, neither shalt thou trust thy life. In the morning thou shalt say: Who will grant me evening? and at evening: Who will grant me morning? Deut. 28:66 f.

My soul is continually in my hands: and I have not forgotten thy law. Ps. 118:109.

Boast not for tomorrow, for thou knowest not what the day to come may bring forth. Prov. 27:1.

Behold now, you that say: Today or tomorrow we will go into such a city, and there we will spend a year, and will traffic, and make our gain. Whereas you know not what shall be on the morrow. Jas. 4:13 f.

For what is your life? It is a vapor which appeareth for a little while, and afterwards shall vanish away. For that you should say: If the Lord will, and, if we shall live, we will do this or that. But now you rejoice in your arrogancies. All such rejoicing is wicked. Jas. 4:15 f.

THURSDAY

Death of Sinners

The Lord struck Nabal, and he died. 1 K. 25:38.

They that shall be left shall be taken away from them: they shall die, and not in wisdom. Job 4:21.

Let his confidence be rooted out of his tabernacle, and let destruction tread upon him like a king. He shall drive him out of the light into darkness, and shall remove him out of the world. Job 18:14, 18.

The praise of the wicked is short, and the joy of the hypocrite but for a moment. If his pride mount up even to heaven, and his head touch the clouds: in the end he shall be destroyed like a dunghill, and they that had seen him, shall say: Where is he? Job 20:5-7.

As a dream that fleeth away he shall not be found, he shall pass as a vision of the night: the eyes that had seen him, shall see him no more, neither shall his place any more behold him. Job 20:8 f.

How often shall the lamp of the wicked be put out, and a deluge come upon them, and he shall distribute the sorrows of his wrath? They shall be as chaff before the face of the wind, and as ashes which the whirlwind scattereth. Job 21:17 f.

They shall suddenly die, and the people shall be troubled at midnight, and they shall pass, and take away the violent without hand. Job 34:20.

Let mercy forget him: may worms be his sweetness: let him be remembered no more, but be broken in pieces as an unfruitful tree. For he hath fed the barren that beareth not, and to the widow he hath done no good. He hath pulled down the strong by his might: and when he standeth up he shall not trust to his life. Job 24:20-22.

God hath given him place for penance, and he abuseth it unto pride: but his eyes are upon his ways. They are lifted up for a little while, and shall not stand, and shall be brought down as all things, and shall be taken away, and as the tops of the ears of corn they shall be broken. Job 24:23 f.

What is the hope of the hypocrite if through covetousness he take by violence, and God deliver not his soul? The rich man when he shall sleep shall take away nothing with him: he shall open his eyes and find nothing. Job 27:8, 19.

Poverty like water shall take hold on him, a tempest shall oppress him in the night: a burning wind shall take him up, and carry him away, and as a whirlwind shall snatch him from his place. And he shall cast upon him, and shall not spare: out of his hand he would willingly flee. He shall clasp his hands upon him, and shall hiss at him, beholding his place. Job 27:20-23.

If they hear not they shall pass by the sword, and shall be consumed in folly. Their soul shall die in a storm, and their life among the effeminate. Job 36:12, 14.

They shall shortly wither away as grass, and as the green herbs shall quickly fall. For yet a little while, and the wicked shall not be: and thou shalt seek his place, and shalt not find it. Ps. 36:2, 10.

I have seen the wicked highly exalted, and lifted up like the cedars of Libanus. And I passed by, and lo he was not: and I sought him, and his place was not found. Ps. 36:35 f.

He shall not give to God his ransom. Nor the price of the redemption of his soul: and shall labor forever, and shall still live unto the end. Ps. 48:8 f.

He shall not see destruction, when he shall see the wise dying: the senseless and the fools shall perish together. And they shall leave their riches to strangers. They are laid in hell like sheep: death shall feed upon them. And the just shall have dominion over them in the morning: and their help shall decay in hell from their glory. Ps. 48:10 f.

For when he shall die he shall take nothing away: nor shall his glory descend with him. For in his lifetime his soul will be blessed: and he will praise thee when thou shalt do well to him. He shall go in to the generations of his fathers: and he shall never see light. Man when he was in honor did not understand: he hath been compared to senseless beasts, and made like to them. Ps. 48:18-21.

As a tempest that passeth, so the wicked shall be no more: and the years of the wicked shall be shortened. Prov. 10:25, 27.

The lamp of the wicked shall be put out. Prov. 13:9.

When the wicked man is dead, there shall be no hope any more. Prov. 11:7.

The wicked man shall be driven out in his wickedness. Prov. 14:32.

Evil men have no hope of things to come, and the lamp of the wicked shall be put out. Prov. 24:20.

Thy pride is brought down to hell, thy carcass is fallen down: under thee shall the moth be strewed, and worms shall be thy covering. Thou shalt be brought down to hell, unto the depth of the pit. Is. 14:11, 15.

In the time of the evening, behold there shall be trouble: the morning shall come, and he shall not be: this is the portion of them that have wasted us, and the lot of them that spoiled us. Is. 17:14.

Her soul hath fainted away: her sun is gone down while it was yet day. Jer. 15:9.

They shall die by the death of grievous illness: they shall not be lamented, and they shall not be buried. Jer. 16:4.

They shall kill thee, and bring thee down: and thou shalt die the death of them that are slain in the heart of the sea. Thou shalt die the death of the uncircumcised by the hand of strangers: for I have spoken it, saith the Lord God. Ez. 28:8, 10.

All the sinners of my people shall fall by the sword. Amos 9:10.

When they shall say, peace and security: then shall sudden destruction come upon them, as the pains upon her that is with child, and they shall not escape. 1 Thess. 5:3.

FRIDAY

Death Not to Be Feared

Though I should walk in the midst of the shadow of death, I will fear no evils, for thou art with me. Thy rod and thy staff, they have comforted me. Ps. 22:4.

The just perisheth, and no man layeth it to heart, and men of mercy are taken away because there is none that understandeth: for the just man is taken away from before the face of evil. Is. 57:1.

Weep but a little for the dead, for he is at rest. Ecclus. 22:11.

Now thou dost dismiss thy servant, O Lord, according to thy word, in peace. Luke 2:29.

He that believeth in me, although he be dead, shall live. And every one that liveth, and believeth in me, shall not die forever. John 11:25 f.

Fear not the sentence of death. Remember what things have been before thee, and what shall come after thee: this sentence is from the Lord upon all flesh. Ecclus. 41:5.

[Better] is the day of death than the day of one's birth. Eccles. 7:2.

Fear not: I am the First and the Last. Apoc. 1:17.

There remaineth, therefore a rest for the people of God. For he who is entered into his rest, he also hath rested from his own works, as God from his. Let us hasten therefore to enter into that rest. Heb. 4:9-11.

To me, to live is Christ, and to die is gain. Phil. 1:21.

And if to live in the flesh, this is to me the fruit of labor: and what I shall choose, I know not. But I am straitened between two: having a desire to be dissolved, and to be with Christ, being by much the better. But to remain in the flesh is necessary for you. Phil. 1:22-24.

Forasmuch as the children were partakers of flesh and blood, he also himself in like manner partook of the same: that, through death, he might destroy him who had the empire of death, that is to say, the devil; and might deliver them, who, through the fear of death, were all their lifetime subject to slavery. Heb. 2:14 f.

There the wicked cease from tumult, and there the wearied in strength are at rest. Job 3:17.

Who will give me wings like a dove, and I will fly and be at rest? Ps. 54:7.

I will look for thy salvation, O Lord. Gen. 49:18.

All that I have shall go down into the deepest pit: thinkest thou that there at least I shall have rest? Job 17:16.

Let peace come, let him rest in his bed that hath walked in his uprightness. Is. 57:2.

These things he said; and after that he said to them: Lazarus our friend sleepeth; but I go that I may awake him out of sleep. His disciples therefore said: Lord, if he sleep, he shall do well. But Jesus spoke of his death; and they thought that he spoke of the repose of sleep. John 11:11-13.

[The grace of God] is now made manifest by the illumination of our Savior Jesus Christ, who hath destroyed death, and hath brought to light life and incorruption. 2 Tim. 1:10.

The sting of death is sin. But thanks be to God, who hath given us the victory through our Lord Jesus Christ. 1 C. 15:56 f.

We know that if our earthly house of this habitation be dissolved, that we have a building of God, a house not made with hands, eternal in heaven. For we also, who are in this tabernacle, do groan being burdened: because we would not be unclothed, but clothed over: that what is mortal may be swallowed up by life. Now he that maketh us for this very thing is God, who hath given us the pledge of the Spirit. Therefore, having always confidence, knowing that, while we are in the body, we are absent from the Lord: we are confident, I say, and have a good will to be absent rather from the body, and to be present with the Lord. And therefore we labor, whether absent or present, to please him. 2 C. 5:4-9.

SATURDAY

Blessedness of Those Who Die in the Lord

Precious in the sight of the Lord is the death of his saints. Ps. 115:15.

The souls of the just are in the hands of God, and the torment of death shall not touch them. In the sight of the unwise they seemed to die: and their departure was taken for misery and their going away from us, for utter destruction: but they are in peace. And though in the sight of men they suffered torments, their hope is full of immortality. Wis. 3:1-4.

Lord Jesus, receive my spirit. Acts 7:59.

He said to Jesus: Lord, remember me when thou shalt come into thy kingdom. And Jesus said to him: Amen I say to thee, this day thou shalt be with me in paradise. Luke 23:42 f.

Who can count the dust of Jacob, and know the number of the stock of Israel? Let my soul die the death of the just, and my last end be like to them. Num. 23:10.

The just perisheth, and no man layeth it to heart, and men of mercy are taken away, because there is none that understandeth: for the just man is taken away from before the face of evil. Is. 57:1.

The just man if he be prevented with death, shall be in rest. He pleased God and was beloved, and living among sinners he was translated. Wis. 4:7, 10.

He was taken away lest wickedness should alter his understanding, or deceit beguile his soul. For the bewitching of vanity obscureth good things, and the wandering of concupiscence overturneth the innocent mind. Wis. 4:11 f.

Being made perfect in a short space, he fulfilled a long time: for his soul pleased God: therefore he hastened to bring him out of the midst of iniquities: but the people see this, and understand not, nor lay up such things in their hearts. Wis. 4:13 f.

The just that is dead, condemneth the wicked that are living, and youth soon ended, the long life of the unjust. Wis. 4:16.

With him that feareth the Lord, it shall go well in the latter end, and in the day of his death he shall be blessed. Ecclus. 1:13.

Amen, amen I say to you, unless the grain of wheat falling into the ground, die, itself remaineth alone. But if it die, it bringeth forth much fruit. John 12:24 f.

I heard a voice from heaven saying to me: Write, Blessed are the dead who die in the Lord. From henceforth now, saith the Spirit, that they may rest from their labors; for their works follow them. Apoc. 14:13.

2. EXAMPLES OF HOLY DEATHS

1. Our Blessed Lord. Luke 23:46.
2. Stephen. Acts 7:59.
3. Dorcas. Acts 9:39.
4. Abraham. Gen. 25:8.
5. Jacob. Heb. 11:21.
6. Joseph. Heb. 11:22.
7. Aaron. Num. 20:26.
8. Moses. Deut. 34:5.
9. Heli. 1 K. 4:18.
10. David. 3 K. 2:2.
11. Joiada. 2 Par. 24:16.
12. Ezechias. 2 Par. 32:33.
13. Josias. 2 Par. 35:26.

3. THE GENERAL RESURRECTION OF THE DEAD

The hour cometh wherein all that are in the graves shall hear the voice of the Son of God. And they that have done good things shall come forth unto the resurrection of life:

and they that have done evil unto the resurrection of judgment. John 5:28 f.

Now this is the will of the Father who sent me: that of all that he hath given me, I should lose nothing, but should raise it up again at the last day. John 6:39.

It hath not yet appeared what we shall be. We know that when he shall appear, we shall be like to him; because we shall see him as he is. 1 John 3:2.

We will not have you ignorant, brethren, concerning them that are asleep, that you be not sorrowful even as others who have no hope. For if we believe that Jesus died, and rose again, even so them who have slept through Jesus, God will bring with him. 1 Thess. 4:12 f.

Jesus saith to her: Thy brother shall rise again. Martha saith to him: I know that he shall rise again in the resurrection at the last day. Jesus said to her: I am the resurrection and the life: he that believeth in me, although he be dead, shall live. John 11:23-25.

Having hope in God, which these also themselves look for, that there shall be a resurrection of the just and unjust. Acts 24:15.

Except it be for this one voice only that I cried standing among them, Concerning the resurrection of the dead am I judged this day by you. Acts 24:21.

And now for the hope of the promise that was made by God to our fathers do I stand subject to judgment: unto which our twelve tribes, serving night and day, hope to come. For which hope, O king, I am accused by the Jews. Why should it be thought a thing incredible with you, that God should raise the dead? Acts 26:6-8.

With great power did the apostles give testimony to the resurrection of the Lord Jesus. Acts 4:33.

If we have been planted together in the likeness of his death, in like manner shall we be of his resurrection. Rom. 6:5.

To this end Christ died, and rose again: that he might be Lord both of the dead and of the living. Rom. 14:9.

If the Spirit of him that raised up Jesus from the dead, dwell in you: he that raised up Jesus Christ from the dead, shall quicken also your mortal bodies, because of his Spirit that dwelleth in you. Rom. 8:11.

They that shall be accounted worthy of that world and of the resurrection from the dead, shall neither be married nor take wives. Neither can they die any more: for they are equal to the angels, and are the children of God, being the children of the resurrection. Luke 20:35 f.

He shall cast death down headlong forever: and the Lord God shall wipe away tears from every face. Is. 25:8.

When Christ shall appear, who is your life: then also you shall appear with him in glory. Col. 3:4.

4. BELIEF IN THE RESURRECTION UNDER THE OLD LAW

By faith Abraham, when he was tried, offered Isaac: and he that had received the promises, offered up his only-begotten son: to whom it was said: In Isaac shall thy seed be called. Accounting that God is able to raise up even from the dead. Whence also he received him for a parable. Heb. 11:17-19.

Now that the dead rise again, Moses also showed, at the bush, when he calleth the Lord: The God of Abraham, and the God of Isaac, and the God of Jacob. For he is not the God of the dead, but of the living: for all live to him. Luke 26:37 f.

For I know that my Redeemer liveth, and in the last day I shall rise out of the earth. And I shall be clothed again with my skin, and in my flesh I shall see my God. Whom I myself shall see, and my eyes shall behold, and not another: this my hope is laid up in my bosom. Job 19:25-27.

Man when he is fallen asleep, shall not rise again; till the heavens be broken, he shall not awake, nor rise up out of his sleep. Who will grant me this, that thou mayst protect me in hell, and hide me till thy wrath pass, and appoint me a time when thou wilt remember me? Shall man that is dead, thinkest thou, live again? all the days in which I am now in warfare I expect until my change come. Thou shalt call me, and I will answer thee: to the work of thy hands thou shalt reach out thy right hand. Job 14:12-15.

Thy dead men shall live, my slain shall rise again: awake, and give praise, ye that dwell in the dust: for thy dew is the dew of the light: and the land of the giants thou shalt pull down into ruin. Is. 26:19.

God will redeem my soul from the hand of hell, when he shall receive me. Ps. 48:16.

And many of those that sleep in the dust of the earth, shall awake: some unto life everlasting, and others unto reproach, to see it always. But they that are learned shall shine as the brightness of the firmament: and they that instruct many to justice, as stars for all eternity. But go thou thy ways until the time appointed: and thou shalt rest, and stand in thy lot unto the end of the days. Dan. 12:2 f., 13.

I will deliver them out of the hand of death. I will redeem them from death: O death, I will be thy death, O hell, I will be thy bite; comfort is hidden from my eyes. Osee 13:14.

As concerning the dead, that they rise again, have you not read in the book of Moses, how in the bush, God spoke to him, saying: I am the God of Abraham, and the God of Isaac, and the God of Jacob? He is not the God of the dead, but of the living. You therefore do greatly err. Mark 12:26 f.

Shake thyself from the dust, arise, sit up, O Jerusalem: loose the bonds from thy neck. Is. 52:2.

And not only it, but ourselves also, who have the first fruits of the Spirit, even we ourselves groan within ourselves, waiting for the adoption of the sons of God, the redemption of our body. Rom. 8:23.

If by any means I may attain to the resurrection, which is from the dead. Phil. 3:11.

But as for me, I will appear before thy sight in justice: I shall be satisfied when thy glory shall appear. Ps. 16:15.

5. St. Paul's Discourse on the Resurrection

Christ's Resurrection

For I delivered unto you first of all, that which I also received: How that Christ died for our sins according to the Scriptures: and that he was buried, and that he arose again the third day according to the Scriptures: and that he was seen by Cephas; and after that by the eleven. Then was he seen by more than five hundred brethren at once: of whom many remain until this present, and some are fallen asleep. After that, he was seen by James, then by all the apostles. 1 C. 15:3-8.

And last of all, he was seen also by me, as by one born out of due time.

His Resurrection an Argument for Ours

Now if Christ be preached that he rose again from the dead, how do some among you say, that there is no resurrection of the dead? 1 C. 15:10.

But if there be no resurrection of the dead, then Christ is not risen again. And if Christ be not risen again, then is our preaching vain, and your faith is also vain. Yea, and we are found false witnesses of God: because we have given testimony against God, that he hath raised up Christ; whom he hath not raised up, if the dead rise not again. 1 C. 15:13-15.

For if the dead rise not again, neither is Christ risen again. And if Christ is not risen again, your faith is vain, for you are yet in your sins. 1 C. 15:16 f.

Then they also that are fallen asleep in Christ, are perished. If in this life only we have hope in Christ, we are of all men most miserable. But now Christ is risen from the dead, the first-fruits of them that sleep. 1 C. 15:18-20.

The Fruit of the Resurrection

For by a man came death, and by a man the resurrection of the dead. And as in Adam all die, so also in Christ all shall be made alive. But every one in his own order: the first-fruits Christ, then they that are of Christ, who have believed in his coming. 1 C. 15:21-23.

Afterwards the end, when he shall have delivered up the kingdom to God and the Father, when he shall have brought to nought all principality, and power, and virtue. For he must reign, until he hath put all enemies under his feet. 1 C. 15:24 f.

And the enemy death shall be destroyed last, for he hath put all things under his feet. And whereas he saith: All things are put under him; undoubtedly, he is excepted, who put all things under him. 1 C. 15:26 f.

And when all things shall be subdued unto him, then the Son also himself shall be subject unto him that put all things under him, that God may be all in all. Otherwise what shall they do that are baptized for the dead, if the dead rise not again at all? why are they then baptized for them? 1 C. 15:28 f.

Why also are we in danger every hour? I die daily, I protest by your glory, brethren, which I have in Christ Jesus our Lord. If (according to man) I fought with beasts at Ephesus, what doth it profit me, if the dead rise not again? Let us eat and drink, for tomorrow we shall die. 1 C. 15:30-32.

The Manner Thereof

But some man will say: How do the dead rise again? or with what manner of body shall they come? Senseless man, that which thou sowest is not quickened except it die first. And that which thou sowest, thou sowest not the body that shall be; but bare grain, as of wheat, or of some of the rest. But God giveth it a body as he will: and to every seed its proper body. 1 C. 15:35-38.

All flesh is not the same flesh: but one is the flesh of men, another of beasts, another of birds, another of fishes. And there are bodies celestial, and bodies terrestrial: but one is the glory of the celestial, and another of the terrestrial. 1 C. 15:39 f.

One is the glory of the sun, another the glory of the moon, and another the glory of the stars. For star differeth from star in glory: so also is the resurrection of the dead. It is sown in corruption, it shall rise in incorruption. It is sown in dishonor, it shall rise in glory. It is sown in weakness, it shall rise in power. It is sown a natural body, it shall rise a spiritual body. If there be a natural body, there is also a spiritual body, as it is written: The first man Adam was made into a living soul; the last Adam into a quickening Spirit. 1 C. 15:41-45.

Yet that was not first which is spiritual, but that which is natural: afterwards that which is spiritual. The first man was of the earth, earthly: the second man, from heaven, heavenly. Such as is the earthly, such also are the earthly: and such as is the heavenly, such also are they that are heavenly. Therefore as we have borne the image of the earthly, let us bear also the image of the heavenly. Now this I say, brethren, that flesh and blood cannot possess the kingdom of God: neither shall corruption posses incorruption. 1 C. 15:46-50.

Of Them That Shall Be Found Alive at the Last Day

Behold I tell you a mystery. We shall all indeed rise again: but we shall not all be changed. In a moment, in the twinkling of an eye, at the last trumpet; for the trumpet shall sound, and the dead shall rise again incorruptible: and we shall be changed. 1 C. 15:51 f.

For this corruptible must put on incorruption; and this mortal must put on immortality. And when this mortal hath put on immortality, then shall come to pass the saying that is written: Death is swallowed up in victory. O death, where is thy victory? O death, where is thy sting? 1 C. 15:53-55.

6. AN ALLUSION TO THE GENERAL RESURRECTION

The hand of the Lord was upon me, and brought me forth in the spirit of the Lord: and set me down in the midst of a plain that was full of bones.

And I prophesied as he had commanded me: and as I prophesied there was a noise, and behold a commotion: and the bones came together, each one to its joint.

And I saw, and behold the sinews, and the flesh came up upon them: and the skin was stretched out over them, but there was no spirit in them.

And he said to me: Prophesy to the Spirit, prophesy, O son of man, and say to the Spirit: Thus saith the Lord God: Come, Spirit from the four winds and blow upon these slain, and let them live again.

And I prophesied as he had commanded me: and the Spirit came into them, and they lived: and they stood up upon their feet, an exceeding great army.

And he said to me: Son of man: All these bones are the house of Israel: they say: Our bones are dried up, and our hope is lost, and we are cut off.

Therefore prophesy, and say to them: Thus saith the Lord God: Behold I will open your graves, and will bring you out of your sepulchers, O my people: and will bring you into the land of Israel.

And you shall know that I am the Lord, when I shall have opened your sepulchers, and shall have brought you out of your graves, O my people:

And shall have put my Spirit in you, and you shall live, and I shall make you rest upon your own land: and you shall know that I the Lord have spoken, and done it, saith the Lord God. Ez. 37:1, 7-14.

II

JUDGMENT

1. THE DOCTRINE OF THE LAST JUDGMENT

It is appointed unto men once to die, and after this the judgment. Heb. 9:27.

Walk in the ways of thy heart, and in the sight of thy eyes: and know that for all these God will bring thee to judgment. Eccles. 11:9.

And they that have done good things, shall come forth unto the resurrection of life; but they that have done evil, unto the resurrection of judgment. John 5:29.

The Son of man shall come in the glory of his Father with his angels: and then will he render to every man according to his works. Mat. 16:27.

All the hosts of the heavens shall pine away, and the heavens shall be folded together as a book: and all their host shall fall down as the leaf falleth from the vine and from the fig tree. Is. 34:4.

Some men's sins are manifest, going before to judgment: and some men they follow after. In like manner also good deeds are manifest: and they that are otherwise, cannot be hid. 1 Tim. 5:24 f.

There is nothing covered that shall not be revealed: nor hidden, that shall not be known. Luke 12:2.

As he treated of justice and chastity and of the judgment to come, Felix [was] terrified. Acts 24:25.

According to thy hardness and impenitent heart, thou treasurest up to thyself wrath, against the day of wrath, and revelation of the just judgment of God, who will render to every man according to his works: to them indeed, who, according to patience in good work, seek glory and honor and incorruption, eternal life: but to them that are contentious, and who obey not the truth, but give credit to iniquity, wrath and indignation. Rom. 2:5-8.

It is a fearful thing to fall into the hands of the living God. Heb. 10:31.

If God spared not the angels that sinned: but delivered them, drawn down by infernal ropes to the lower hell, unto torments, to be reserved unto judgment: the Lord knoweth how to deliver the godly from temptation, but to reserve the unjust unto the day of judgment to be tormented. 2 Pet. 2:4, 9.

The wicked man is reserved to the day of destruction, and he shall be brought to the day of wrath. Job 21:30.

God shall judge both the just and the wicked, and then shall be the time of everything. Eccles. 3:17.

Behold he cometh with the clouds, and every eye shall see him, and they also that pierced him. Apoc. 1:7.

Every man's work shall be manifest, for the day of the Lord shall declare it. 1 C. 3:13.

Every idle word that a man shall speak, they shall render an account for it in the day of judgment. For by thy words thou shalt be justified, and by thy words thou shalt be condemned. Mat. 12:36 f.

The nations were angry: and thy wrath is come, and the time of the dead, that they should be judged, and that thou shouldst render reward to thy servants the prophets and to the saints, and to them that fear thy name, little and great, and shouldst destroy them who have corrupted the earth. Apoc. 11:18.

If we sin wilfully after having received the knowledge of the truth, there is now left no sacrifice for sins. But a certain dreadful expectation of judgment, and the rage of a fire which shall consume the adversaries. Heb. 10:26 f.

2. THE LAST JUDGMENT AS DESCRIBED BY OUR LORD

When the Son of man shall come in his majesty, and all the angels with him, then shall he sit upon the seat of his majesty: and all nations shall be gathered together before him, and he shall separate them one from another, as the shepherd separateth the sheep from the goats: and he shall set the sheep on his right hand, but the goats on his left. Mat. 25:31-33.

Then shall the King say to them that shall be on his right hand: Come, ye blessed of my Father, possess you the kingdom prepared for you from the foundation of the world. For I was hungry, and you gave me to eat: I was thirsty, and you gave me to drink: I was a stranger, and you took me in: naked, and you covered me: sick, and you visited me: I was in prison, and you came to me.

Then shall the just answer him, saying: Lord, when did we see thee hungry, and fed thee; thirsty, and gave thee drink? And when did we see thee a stranger, and took thee in? or naked, and covered thee? Or when did we see thee sick or in prison, and came to thee? And the king, answering, shall say to them: Amen I say to you, as long as you did it to one of these my least brethren, you did it to me. Mat. 25:34-40.

Then he shall say to them also that shall be on his left hand: Depart from me, you cursed, into everlasting fire, which was prepared for the devil and his angels. For I was hungry, and you gave me not to eat: I was thirsty, and you gave me not to drink: I was a stranger, and you took me not in: naked and you covered me not: sick and in prison, and you did not visit me.

Then they also shall answer him, saying: Lord, when did we see thee hungry or thirsty, or a stranger, or naked, or sick, or in prison, and did not minister to thee? Then he shall answer them, saying: Amen I say to you, as long as you did it not to one of these least, neither did you do it to me. And these shall go into everlasting punishment: but the just into life everlasting. Mat. 25:41-45.

Immediately after the tribulation of those days the sun shall be darkened, and the moon shall not give her light, and the stars shall fall from heaven, and the powers of the heavens shall be moved. And then shall appear the sign of the Son of man in heaven: and then shall all the tribes of the earth mourn: and they shall see the Son of man coming in the clouds of heaven with much power and majesty. And he shall send his angels with a trumpet, and a great voice; and they shall gather together his elect from the four winds, from the farthest parts of the heavens to the utmost bound of them. Heaven and earth shall pass away, but my words shall not pass away. Mat. 24:29-31, 35.

In the time of the harvest I will say to the reapers: Gather up first the cockle, and bind it into bundles to burn, but the wheat gather ye into my barn. Even as cockle therefore is gathered up and burnt with fire: so shall it be at the end of the world. The Son of man shall send his angels, and they shall gather out of his kingdom all scandals, and them that work iniquity. And shall cast them into the furnace of fire: there shall be weeping and gnashing of teeth. Then shall the just shine as the sun in the kingdom of their Father. He that hath ears to hear, let him hear. Mat. 13:30, 40-43.

St. Peter's Account

The heavens and the earth, which are now, by the same word are kept in store, reserved unto fire against the day of judgment and perdition of the ungodly men. 2 Pet. 3:7.

But the day of the Lord shall come as a thief, in which the heavens shall pass away with great violence, and the elements shall be melted with heat, and the earth and the works which are in it shall be burnt up. 2 Pet. 3:10.

Seeing then that all these things are to be dissolved, what manner of people ought you to be in holy conversations and godliness: looking for and hasting unto the coming of the day of the Lord, by which the heavens being on fire shall be dissolved, and the elements shall melt with the heat of fire? 2 Pet. 3:11 f.

3. THE JUDGMENT SEAT; THE GREAT WHITE THRONE

When the Son of man shall come in his majesty, and all the angels with him, then shall he sit on the seat of his majesty; and all nations shall be gathered together before him, and he shall separate them one from another, as the shepherd separates the sheep from the goats. Mat. 25:31 f.

I beheld till thrones were placed, and the Ancient of days sat: his garment was white as snow, and the hair of his head like clean wool: his throne like flames of fire: the wheels of it like a burning fire. A swift stream of fire issued from before him: thousands of thousands ministered to him, and ten thousand times a hundred thousand stood before him: the judgment sat and the books were opened. Dan. 7:9 f.

I saw a great white throne, and one sitting upon it, from whose face the earth and heaven fled away, and there was no place found for them. And I saw the dead, great and small, standing in the presence of the throne, and the books were opened: and another book was opened, which is the book of life: and the dead were judged by those things which were written in the books, according to their works. And the sea gave up the dead, that were in it, and death and hell gave up their dead, that were in them: and they were judged every one according to their works. Apoc. 20:11-13.

We must all be manifested before the judgment seat of Christ, that every one may receive the proper things of the body according as he hath done, whether it be good or evil. 2 C. 5:10.

The kings of the earth and the princes and the tribunes and the rich and the strong and every bondman and every freeman hid themselves in the dens and in the rocks of the mountains: and they say to the mountains and the rocks: Fall upon us and hide us from the face of him that sitteth upon the throne and from the wrath of the Lamb: for the great day of their wrath is come. And who shall be able to stand? Apoc. 6:15-17.

Watch ye, therefore, praying at all times, that you may be accounted worthy to escape all these things that are to come, and to stand before the Son of man. Luke 21:36.

4. CHRIST OUR JUDGE

The Father hath given all judgment to the Son, that all men may honor the Son as they honor the Father. He hath given him power to do judgment because he is the Son of man. John 5:22 f., 27.

He that despiseth me, and receiveth not my words, hath one that judgeth him; the word that I have spoken the same shall judge him in the last day. John 12:48.

It is he who was appointed by God,

to be judge of the living and of the dead. Acts 10:42.

Judge not before the time; until the Lord come, who both will bring to light the hidden things of darkness, and will make manifest the counsels of the hearts; and then shall every man have praise from God. 1 C. 4:5.

Behold, the Lord cometh with thousands of his saints, to execute judgment upon all. Jude 14 f.

The Son of man shall come in the glory of his Father with his angels, and then will he render to every man according to his works. Mat. 16:27.

The Lord is a God of all knowledge, and to him are thoughts prepared. The Lord shall judge the ends of the earth. 1 K. 2:3, 10.

He hath prepared his throne in judgment: and he shall judge the world in equity. He shall judge the people in justice. Ps. 9:8 f.

He cometh to judge the earth. He shall judge the world with justice and the people with his truth. Ps. 95:13.

Thou, why judgest thou thy brother: or thou, why dost thou despise thy brother? For we shall all stand before the judgment seat of Christ. For it is written: As I live, saith the Lord, every knee shall bow to me, and every tongue shall confess to God. Therefore every one of us shall render account to God for himself. Rom. 14:10-12.

I charge thee before God and Jesus Christ, who shall judge the living and the dead by his coming and his kingdom: preach the word. 2 Tim. 4:1 f.

There is laid up for me a crown of justice, which the Lord the just Judge will render to me in that day: and not only to me, but to them also that love his coming. 2 Tim. 4:8.

[You] shall render account to him who is ready to judge the living and the dead. 1 Pet. 4:5.

He shall not judge according to the sight of the eyes, nor reprove according to the hearing to the ears. But he shall judge the poor with justice, and shall reprove with equity for the meek of the earth: and he shall strike the earth with the rod of his mouth, and with the breath of his lips he shall slay the wicked. Is. 11:3 f.

He hath appointed a day wherein he will judge the world in equity, by the Man whom he hath appointed, giving faith to all, raising him up from the dead. Acts 17:31.

Behold, I come quickly, and my reward is with me, to render to every man according to his works. Apoc. 22:12.

5. THE JUDGMENT DAY

God now declareth unto men that all should everywhere do penance. Because he hath appointed a day when he will judge the world in equity. Acts 17:30 f.

As the lightning cometh out of the east, and appeareth even into the west: so shall also the coming of the Son of man be. But of that day and hour no one knoweth, no, not the angels of heaven, but the Father alone. Mat. 24:27 f.

Yourselves know perfectly, that the day of the Lord shall so come as a thief in the night. 1 Thess. 5:2.

The day of the Lord shall come as a thief, in which the heavens shall pass away with great violence, and the elements shall be melted with heat, and the earth and the works which are in it shall be burnt up. 2 Pet. 3:10.

Behold I will send you Elias the prophet, before the coming of the great and dreadful day of the Lord. Mal. 4:5.

The Place of Judgment

I will gather together all nations, and will bring them down to the valley of Josaphat: and I will plead with them there for my people, and for my inheritance Israel, whom they have scattered among the nations, and have parted my land. Joel 3:2.

His feet shall stand in that day upon the Mount of Olives, which is over against Jerusalem, toward the east: and the Mount of Olives shall be divided in the midst thereof to the east, and to the west with a very great opening, and half of the mountain shall be separated to the north, and half thereof to the south. Zach. 14:4.

And you shall flee to the valley of those mountains, for the valley of the mountains shall be joined even to the next, and you shall flee as you fled from the face of the earthquake in the days of Ozias, king of Juda: and the Lord my God shall come, and all the saints with him. Zach. 14:5.

Break forth, and come, all ye nations, from round about, and gather yourselves together: there will the Lord cause all thy strong ones to fall down. Let them arise, and let the nations come up into the valley of Josaphat: for there I will sit to judge all nations round about. Joel 3:11 f.

Put ye in the sickles, for the harvest is ripe: come and go down, for the press is full, the fats run over: for their wickedness is multiplied. Nations, nations in the valley of destruction: for the day of the Lord is near in the valley of destruction. Joel 3:13 f.

The sun and the moon are darkened, and the stars have withdrawn their shining. And the Lord shall roar out of Sion, and utter his voice from Jerusalem: and the heavens and the earth shall be moved, and the Lord shall be the hope of his people, and the strength of the children of Israel. Joel 3:15 f.

And you shall know that I am the Lord your God, dwelling in Sion my holy mountain: and Jerusalem shall be holy, and strangers shall pass through it no more. Joel 3:17.

Allusions to the Judgment

With breaking shall the earth be broken, with crushing shall the earth be crushed, with trembling shall the earth be moved. With shaking shall the earth be shaken as a drunken man, and shall be removed as the tent of one night: and the iniquity thereof shall be heavy upon it, and it shall fall, and not rise again. Is. 24:19 f.

All the host of the heavens shall pine away, and the heavens shall be folded together as a book: and all their host shall fall down as the leaf falleth from the vine, and from the fig tree. Is. 34:4.

I will show wonders in heaven: and in earth, blood, and fire, and vapor of smoke. The sun shall be turned into darkness, and the moon into blood: before the great and dreadful day of the Lord doth come. Joel 2:30 f.

I saw, when he had opened the sixth seal, and behold there was a great earthquake, and the sun became black as sackcloth of hair: and the whole moon became as blood: and the stars from heaven fell upon the earth, as the fig tree casteth its green figs when it is shaken by a great wind: and the heaven departed as a book folded up: and every mountain, and the islands were moved out of their places. Apoc. 6:12-14.

III

HELL

1. HELL, THE ABODE OF THE WICKED

The wicked shall be turned into hell, all the nations that forget God. Ps. 8:18.

If thy hand scandalize thee, cut it off: it is better for thee to enter into life maimed than having two hands to go into hell, into unquenchable fire: where their worm dieth not, and the fire is not extinguished. Mark 9:42 f.

And if thy foot scandalize thee, cut it off. It is better for thee to enter lame into life everlasting, than having two feet, to be cast into the hell of unquenchable fire: where their worm dieth not, and the fire is not extinguished. Mark 9:44 f.

And if thy eye scandalize thee, pluck it out. It is better for thee with one eye to enter into the kingdom of God, than having two eyes, to be cast into the hell of fire: where their worm dieth not, and the fire is not extinguished. Mark 9:46 f.

Whosoever was not found written in the book of life, was cast into the pool of fire. Apoc. 20:15.

Therefore hath hell enlarged her soul, and opened her mouth without any bounds, and their strong ones, and their people, and their high and glorious ones shall go down into it. Is. 5:14.

Let death come upon them, and let them go down alive into hell. For there is wickedness in their dwellings: in the midst of them. Ps. 54:16.

Fear ye not them that kill the body, and are not able to kill the soul: but rather fear him that can destroy both soul and body in hell. Mat. 10:28.

And thou, Capharnaum, which art exalted unto heaven, thou shalt be thrust down to hell. Luke 10:15.

I shook the nation with the sound of his fall, when I brought him down to hell with them that descend into the pit. Ez. 31:16.

Wide is the gate, and broad is the way that leadeth to destruction, and many there are who go in thereat. Mat. 7:13.

For they also shall go down with him to hell to them that are slain by the sword: and the arm of every one shall sit down under his shadow in the midst of the nations. Ez. 31:17.

To whom art thou like, O thou that art famous and lofty among the trees of pleasure? Behold, thou art brought down with the trees of pleasure to the lowest parts of the earth: thou shalt sleep in the midst of the uncircumcised, with them that are slain by the sword: this is Pharao, and all his multitude, saith the Lord God. Ez. 31:18.

The Lord knoweth how to deliver the godly from temptation, but to reserve the unjust unto the day of judgment to be tormented. 2 Pet. 2:9.

Thou shalt make them as an oven of fire, in the time of thy anger: the Lord shall trouble them in his wrath, and fire shall devour them. Ps. 20:10.

The most mighty among the strong ones shall speak to him from the midst of hell, they that went down with his helpers, and slept uncircumcised, slain by the sword. And they shall not sleep with the brave, and with them that fell uncircumcised, that went down to hell with their weapons and laid their swords under their heads, and their iniquities were in their bones because they were the terror of the mighty in the land of the living. Ez. 32:21, 27.

Her house is the way to hell, reaching even to the inner chambers of death. Prov. 7:27.

He did not know that giants are there, and that her guests are in the depths of hell. Prov. 9:18.

The path of life is above for the wise, that he may decline from the lowest hell. Prov. 15:24.

If thy hand or thy foot scandalize thee, cut it off, and cast it from thee. It is better for thee to go into life maimed or lame, than having two hands or two feet, to be cast into everlasting fire. Mat. 18:8.

If God spared not the angels that sinned: but delivered them, drawn down by infernal ropes to the lower hell unto torments to be reserved unto judgment. 2 Pet. 2:4.

2. UNHAPPINESS IN HELL

Then he shall say to them also that shall be on his left hand: Depart from me, you cursed, into everlasting fire which was prepared for the devil and his angels. For I was hungry, and you gave me not to eat: I was thirsty, and you gave me not to drink. Mat. 25:41 f.

He shall say to you: I know not whence you are: depart from me, all ye workers of iniquity. Luke 13:27.

They who obey not the gospel shall suffer eternal punishment in destruction, from the face of the Lord, and from the glory of his power. 2 Thess. 1:9.

He shall not see the glory of God. Is. 29:10.

It shall come to pass, that in that day the Lord shall visit upon the host of heaven on high, and upon the kings of the earth, on the earth. And they shall be gathered together as in the gathering of one bundle into the pit, and they shall be shut up there in prison. Is. 24:21 f.

The angels, who kept not their principality, but forsook their own habitation, he hath reserved under darkness in everlasting chains, unto the judgment of the great day. Jude 6.

The congregation of sinners is like tow heaped together, and the end of them is a flame of fire. The way of sinners is made plain with stones, and in their end is hell, and darkness, and pains. He that keepeth justice shall get the understanding thereof. Ecclus. 21:10-12.

I am counted among them that go down to the pit: I am become as a man without help, free among the dead. Like the slain sleeping in the sepulchers, whom thou rememberest no more: and they are cast off from thy hand. They have laid me in the lower pit: in the dark places, and in the shadow of death. Ps. 87:5, 7.

Shall any one in the sepulcher declare thy mercy: and thy truth in destruction? Shall thy wonders be known in the dark: and thy justice in the land of forgetfulness? Ps. 87:12 f.

Lifting up his eyes when he was in torments, he saw Abraham afar off, and Lazarus in his bosom: and he cried, and said: Father Abraham, have mercy on me, and send Lazarus, that he may dip the tip of his finger in water, to cool my tongue, for I am tormented in this flame. Luke 16:23 f.

The unprofitable servant cast ye out into the exterior darkness. There shall be weeping and gnashing of teeth. Mat. 25:30.

There shall be weeping and gnashing of teeth: when you shall see Abraham and Isaac and Jacob, and all the prophets in the kingdom of God, and you yourselves thrust out. Luke 13:28.

The children of the kingdom shall be cast out into the exterior darkness: there shall be weeping and gnashing of teeth. Mat. 8:12.

They shall come with fear at the thought of their sins, and their iniquities shall stand against them to convict them. Wis. 4:20.

[Wicked men] said to God: Depart from us: and looked upon the Almighty as if he could do nothing: whereas he had filled their houses with good things: whose way of thinking be far from me. The just shall see, and shall rejoice, and the innocent shall laugh them to scorn. Is not their exaltation cut down, and hath not fire devoured the remnants of them? Job 22:17-20.

Many of those that sleep in the dust of the earth shall awake: some unto life everlasting, and others unto reproach to see it always. Dan. 12:2.

Then shall the just stand with great constancy against those that have afflicted them. These seeing it, shall be troubled with terrible fear, saying within themselves, repenting, and groaning for anguish of spirit: These are they, whom we had some time in derision, and for a parable of reproach. Wis. 5:1-3.

We fools esteemed their life madness, and their end without honor. Behold how they are numbered among the children of God, and their lot is among the saints. Wis. 5:4 f.

Therefore we have erred from the way of truth, and the light of justice hath not shined unto us, and the sun of understanding hath not risen upon us. We wearied ourselves in the way of iniquity and destruction, and have walked through hard ways: but the way of the Lord we have not known. What hath pride profited us? Or what advantage hath the boasting of riches brought us? All those things are passed away like a shadow. Wis. 5:7-9.

The sinners in Sion are afraid, trembling hath seized upon the hypocrites. Which of you can dwell with devouring fire? which of you shall dwell with everlasting burnings? Is. 33:14.

There came down fire from God out of heaven, and devoured them: and the devil, who seduced them, was cast into a pool of fire and brimstone, where both the beast and the false prophet shall be tormented day and night forever and ever. Apoc. 20:9 f.

They shall go into everlasting punishment. Mat. 25:46.

The chaff he will burn with unquenchable fire. Mat. 3:12.

If thy foot scandalize thee, cut it off. It is better for thee to enter lame into life everlasting, than having two feet, to be cast into the hell of unquenchable fire. Mark 9:44.

There is none that can deliver out of my hand. Deut. 32:39.

3. THOSE WHO ARE RESERVED TO HELL'S TORMENTS

The Lord knoweth how to deliver the godly from temptation, but to reserve the unjust unto the day of judgment to be tormented: and especially:

1. them who walk after the flesh in the lust of uncleanness,
2. and despise government,
3. audacious,
4. pleasing themselves,
5. they fear not to bring in sects,
6. blaspheming . . . .
7. Rioting in their feasts with you,
8. having eyes full of adultery and of sin that ceaseth not,
9. alluring unstable souls,
10. having their hearts exercised with covetousness. 2 Pet. 2:9 f., 13 f.

Know ye this and understand that

1. no fornicator,
2. nor unclean,
3. nor covetous person (which is the serving of idols),

hath inheritance in the kingdom of Christ and of God. Eph. 5:6.

As they liked not to have God in their knowledge: God delivered them up to a reprobate sense, to do those things which are not convenient, being filled with all iniquity,

malice,
fornication,

avarice,
wickedness,
full of envy,
murder,
contention,
deceit,
malignity,
whisperers,
detractors,
hateful to God,
contumelious,
proud,
haughty,
inventors of evil things,
disobedient to parents,
foolish,
dissolute,
without affection,
without fidelity,
without mercy.

Who, having known the justice of God, did not understand that they, who do such things, are worthy of death: and not only they that do them, but they also that consent to them that do them. Rom. 1:28-32.

Without are dogs, and sorcerers, and unchaste, and murderers, and servers of idols, and every one that loveth and maketh a lie. Apoc. 22:15.

The fearful, and unbelieving, and the abominable, and murderers, and whoremongers, and sorcerers, and idolators, and all liars, they shall have their portion in the pool burning with fire and brimstone, which is the second death. Apoc. 21:8.

IV

HEAVEN

You are come to Mount Sion and to the city of the living God, the heavenly Jerusalem, and to the company of many thousands of angels, and to the church of the firstborn who are written in the heavens, and to God, the Judge of all, and to the spirits of the just made perfect, and to Jesus the mediator of the new testament. Heb. 12:22-24.

It is written that eye hath not seen nor ear heard, neither hath it entered into the heart of man, what things God hath prepared for them that love him. 1 C. 2:9.

1. HEAVEN AS SEEN IN NINE VISIONS

First Vision; St. John's

I looked, and behold a door was opened in heaven, and the first voice which I heard, as it were, of a trumpet speaking with me, said: Come up hither, and I will show thee the things which must be done hereafter. And immediately I was in the Spirit: and behold there was a throne set in heaven, and upon the throne one sitting.

And he that sat, was to the sight like the jasper and the sardine-stone; and there was a rainbow round about the throne, in sight like unto an emerald.

And round about the throne were four-and-twenty seats: and upon the seats, four-and-twenty ancients sitting, clothed in white garments, and on their heads were crowns of gold.

And from the throne proceeded lightnings, and voices, and thunders: and there were seven lamps, burning before the throne, which are the seven spirits of God.

And in sight of the throne was, as it were, a sea of glass like to crystal.

And in the midst of the throne, and round about the throne, were four living creatures, full of eyes before and behind. And the first living creature was like a lion: and the second living creature like a calf: and the third living creature, having the face, as it were, of a man: and the fourth living creature was like an eagle flying.

And the four living creatures had each of them six wings; and round about and within they are full of eyes. And they rested not day and night, saying: Holy, holy, holy, Lord God almighty, who was, and who is, and who is to come. And when those living creatures gave glory, and honor, and benediction to him that sitteth on the throne, who liveth forever and ever; the four-and-twenty ancients fell down before him that sitteth on the throne, and adored him that liveth forever and ever, and cast their crowns before the throne, saying: Thou art worthy, O Lord our God, to receive glory, and honor, and power: because thou hast created all things; and for thy will they were, and have been created. Apoc. 4:1-11.

Second Vision; St. John's

I saw a great multitude, which no man could number, of all nations, and tribes, and peoples, and tongues, standing before the throne, and in sight of the Lamb, clothed with white robes, and palms in their hands.

And they cried with a loud voice: saying: Salvation to our God, who sitteth upon the throne, and to the Lamb.

And all the angels stood round about the throne, and the ancients and the four living creatures.

And they fell down before the throne upon their faces, and adored God, saying: Amen. Benediction, and glory and wisdom and thanksgiving, honor and power and strength to our God forever and ever. Amen.

And one of the ancients answered, and said to me: These that are clothed in white robes, who are they? and whence came they? And I said to him: My lord, thou knowest. And he said to me: These are they who are come out of great tribulation, and have washed their robes, and have made them white in the blood of the Lamb.

Therefore they are before the throne of God, and they serve him day and night in his temple: and he, that sitteth on the throne, shall dwell over them.

They shall no more hunger nor thirst, neither shall the sun fall on them, nor any heat. For the Lamb, which is in the midst of the throne, shall rule them, and shall lead them to the fountains of the waters of life, and God shall wipe away all tears from their eyes. Apoc. 7:9-17.

Third Vision; St. John's

There came one of the seven angels, and spoke with me, saying: Come, and I will show thee the bride, the wife of the Lamb. And he took me up in spirit to a great and high mountain: and he showed me the holy city Jerusalem coming down out of heaven from God, having the glory of God, and the light thereof was like to a precious stone, as to the jasper stone, even as crystal.

And it had a wall, great and high, having twelve gates, and in the gates twelve angels, and names written thereon, which are the names of the twelve tribes of the children of Israel. . . . And the wall of the city had twelve foundations, and in them the twelve names of the twelve apostles of the Lamb.

And he that spoke with me had a measure of a reed of gold, to measure the city and the gates thereof, and the wall. And the city lieth in a four-square, and the length thereof is as great as the breadth: and he measured the city with the golden reed for twelve thousand furlongs, and the length and the height and the breadth thereof are equal. And he measured the wall thereof an hundred forty-four cubits, the measure of a man, which is of an angel.

And the building of the wall thereof was of jasperstone: but the city itself pure gold, like to clear glass. And the foundations of the wall of the city were adorned with all manner of precious stones. . . . And the twelve gates are twelve pearls, one to each: and every several gate was of one several pearl. And the street of the city was pure gold, as it were transparent glass.

And I saw no temple therein. For the Lord God Almighty is the temple thereof, and the Lamb.

And the city hath no need of the sun, nor of the moon, to shine in it. For the glory of God hath enlightened it, and the Lamb is the lamp thereof.

And the nations shall walk in the light of it: and the kings of the earth shall bring their glory and honor into it. And the gates thereof shall not be shut by day for there shall be no night there. And they shall bring the glory and honor of the nations into it. There shall not enter into it anything defiled, but they that are written in the book of life of the Lamb. Apoc. 21:9-27.

Fourth Vision; St. John's

I saw a new heaven and a new earth. For the first heaven and the first earth was gone, and the sea is now no more.

And I John saw the holy city the New Jerusalem coming down out of heaven from God, prepared as a bride adorned for her husband.

And I heard a great voice from the throne, saying: Behold the tabernacle of God with men, and he will dwell with them. And they shall be his people: and God himself with them shall be their God.

And God shall wipe away all tears from their eyes: and death shall be no more, nor mourning, nor crying, nor sorrow shall be any more, for the former things are passed away.

And he that sat on the throne, said: Behold I make all things new. And he said to me: Write, for these words are most faithful and true.

And he said to me: It is done: I am Alpha and Omega: the Beginning and the End. To him that thirsteth I will give of the fountain of the water of life, gratis.

He that shall overcome shall possess these things, and I will be his God: and he shall be my son. Apoc. 21:1-7.

Fifth Vision; St. Stephen's

He being full of the Holy Ghost, looking up steadfastly to heaven, saw the glory of God, and Jesus standing on the right hand of God. And he said: Behold I see the heavens opened, and the Son of man standing on the right hand of God. Acts 7:55.

Sixth Vision; St. Paul's

If I must glory (it is not expedient indeed): but I will come to the visions and revelations of the Lord. I know a man in Christ above fourteen years ago (whether in the body I know not, or out of the body, I know not, God knoweth): such an one rapt even to the third heaven.

And I know such a man, whether in the body or out of the body, I know not: God knoweth: that he was caught up into paradise: and heard secret words, which it is not granted to man to utter. 2 C. 12:1-4.

Seventh Vision; Jacob's

Jacob being departed from Bersabee, went on to Haran. And when he was come to a certain place, and would rest in it after sunset, he took of the stones that lay there, and putting under his head, slept in the same place.

And he saw in his sleep a ladder standing upon the earth, and the top thereof touching heaven: the angels also of God ascending and descending by it, and the Lord, leaning upon the ladder, saying to him: I am the Lord God of Abraham thy father, and the God of Isaac: the land, wherein thou sleepest, I will give to thee and to thy seed. And thy seed shall be as the dust of the earth: thou shalt spread abroad to the west, and to the east, and to the north, and to the south: and in thee and thy seed all the tribes of the earth shall be blessed.

And I will be thy Keeper whithersoever thou goest, and will bring thee back into this land: neither will I leave thee till I shall have accomplished all that I have said.

And when Jacob awakened out of sleep, he said: Indeed the Lord is in this place, and I knew it not. And trembling, he said: How terrible is this place! this is no other but the house of God and the gate of heaven.

And Jacob, arising in the morning, took the stone, which he had laid under his head, and set it up for a title, pouring oil upon the top of it.

And he called the name of the city Bethel, which before was called Luza. Gen. 28:10-19.

Eighth Vision; Isaias'

I saw the Lord sitting upon a throne high and elevated. And his train filled the temple. Upon it stood the seraphim: the one had six wings, and the other had six wings: with two they covered his face, and with two they covered his feet, and with two they flew. And they cried one to another, and said: Holy, holy, holy, the Lord God of hosts, all the earth is full of his glory. And the lintels of the doors were moved at the voice of him that cried. Is. 6:1-4.

Ninth Vision; Daniel's

I beheld till thrones were placed, and the Ancient of days sat: his garment was white as snow, and the hair of his head like clean wool: his throne like flames of fire: the wheels of it like a burning fire.

A swift stream of fire issued forth from before him: thousands of thousands ministered to him, and ten thousand times a hundred thousand stood before him: the judgment sat, and the books were opened.

I beheld because of the voice of the great words which that horn spoke: and I saw that the beast was slain, and the body thereof was destroyed, and given to the fire to be burnt: and that the power of the other beasts was taken away: and that times of life were appointed them for a time, and a time.

I beheld therefore in the vision of the night, and lo! One like the Son of man came with the clouds of heaven, and he came even to the Ancient of days: and they presented him before him.

And he gave him power, and glory, and a kingdom: and all peoples, tribes, and tongues shall serve him: his power is an everlasting power that shall not be taken away: and his kingdom, that shall not be destroyed.

My spirit trembled: I Daniel was affrighted at these things, and the visions of my head troubled me. I went near to one of them that stood by, and asked the truth of him concerning all these things, and he told me the interpretation of the words, and instructed me.

These four great beasts are four kingdoms, which shall arise out of the earth. But the saints of the most high God shall take the kingdom: and they shall possess the kingdom forever and ever. Dan. 7:9-18.

2. THREE GLIMPSES OF HEAVEN

The Transfiguration of Christ

After six days Jesus taketh unto him Peter, and James, and John his brother, and bringeth them up into a high mountain apart.

And he was transfigured before them. And his face did shine as the sun: and his garments became white as snow.

And behold there appeared to them Moses and Elias talking with him.

And Peter answering, said to Jesus: Lord, it is good for us to be here: if thou wilt, let us make here three tabernacles: one for thee, and one for Moses, and one for Elias.

And as he was yet speaking, behold a bright cloud overshadowed them. And lo, a voice out of the cloud, saying: This is my beloved Son, in whom I am well pleased: hear ye him.

And the disciples hearing, fell upon their face, and were very much afraid. And Jesus came and touched them: and said to them: Arise, and fear not.

And they lifting up their eyes, saw no one, but only Jesus. And as they came down from the mountain, Jesus charged them, saying: Tell the vision to no man, till the Son of man be risen from the dead. Mat. 17:1-9.

The Glory of God Shown to Ezechiel

He brought me to the gate that looked towards the east.

And behold the glory of the God of Israel came in by the way of the east: and his voice was like the noise of many waters, and the earth shone with his majesty.

And I saw the vision according to the appearance which I had seen when he came to destroy the city; and the appearance was according to the vision which I had seen by the river Chobar: and I fell upon my face.

And the majesty of the Lord went into the temple by the way of the gate that looked to the east.

And the Spirit lifted me up and brought me into the inner court: and behold the house was filled with the glory of the Lord.

And I hear one speaking to me out of the house, and the man that stood by me, said to me: Son of man, the place of my throne, and the place of the soles of my feet, where I dwell in the midst of the children of Israel forever: and the house of Israel shall no more profane my holy name. Ez. 43:1-7.

The Glory of God Shown to Solomon

It came to pass, when the priests were come out of the sanctuary, that a cloud filled the house of the Lord.

And the priests could not stand to minister because of the cloud: for the glory of the Lord had filled the house of the Lord.

Then Solomon said: The Lord said that he would dwell in a cloud.

Building I have built a house for thy dwelling, to be thy most firm throne forever.

And the king turned his face, and blessed all the assembly of Israel. 3 K. 9:10-14.

3. THE GARDEN OF EDEN A TYPE OF THE HEAVENLY PARADISE

The Lord God had planted a paradise of pleasure from the beginning: wherein he placed man whom he had formed.

And the Lord God brought forth of the ground all manner of trees, fair to behold, and pleasant to eat of: the tree of life also in the midst of paradise: and the tree of knowledge of good and evil.

And a river went out of the place of pleasure to water paradise, which from thence is divided into four heads. . . .

And the Lord God took man, and put him into the paradise of pleasure, to dress it, and to keep it. Gen. 2:8-10, 15.

4. SUPREME HAPPINESS IN HEAVEN

Exemption from all Evils

Death shall be no more. Apoc. 21:4.

He shall cast death down headlong forever. Is. 25:8.

They shall not perish forever. John 10:28.

He asked life of thee: and thou hast given him length of days forever and ever. Ps. 20:5.

If any man keep my word he shall not taste death forever. John 8:52.

Death is swallowed up in victory. 1 C. 15:54.

You shall see and your heart shall rejoice, and your bones shall flourish like an herb, and the hand of the Lord shall be known to his servants. Is. 66:13 f.

They shall no more hunger nor thirst, neither shall the sun fall on them, nor any heat. Apoc. 6:16.

God shall wipe away all tears from their eyes, and death shall be no more, nor mourning, nor crying, nor sorrow shall be any more, for the former things are passed away. Apoc. 21:4.

God shall wipe away all tears from their eyes. Apoc. 6:17.

The redeemed of the Lord shall return, and shall come into Sion with praise, and everlasting joy shall be upon their heads: they shall obtain joy and gladness, and sorrow and mourning shall flee away. Is. 35:10.

The Lord God shall wipe away tears from every face. Is. 25:8.

Thou hast turned for me my mourning into joy: thou hast cut my sackcloth, and hast compassed me with gladness. Ps. 29:12.

I, I myself will comfort you. Is. 51:12.

As one whom the mother caresseth, so will I comfort you, and you shall be comforted in Jerusalem. Is. 66:13.

I will turn their mourning into joy, and will comfort them and make them joyful after their sorrow. Jer. 31:13.

Blessed are they that mourn: for they shall be comforted. Mat. 5:5.

Now he is comforted. Luke 16:25.

Lay not up to yourselves treasures on earth where the rust and moth consume, and where thieves break through and steal. But lay up to yourselves treasures in heaven: where neither rust nor moth doth consume, and where thieves do not break through nor steal. Mat. 6:19 f.

The work of justice shall be peace, and the service of justice quietness, and security forever. Is. 22:17.

No man shall pluck them out of my hand. John 10:28.

They shall be no more for a spoil to the nations, neither shall the beasts of the earth devour them; but they shall dwell securely without any terror. Ez. 34:28.

Fruition of All Goods

With thee is the fountain of life; and in thy light we shall see light. Ps. 35:10.

We know that, when he shall appear, we shall be like to him: because we shall see him as he is. 1 John 3:2.

Thou shalt fill me with joy with thy countenance. Ps. 15:11.

I saw no temple therein. For the Lord God Almighty is the temple thereof, and the Lamb. And the city hath no need of the sun, nor of the moon to shine in it. For the glory of God hath enlightened it, and the Lamb is the lamp thereof. And the nations shall walk in the light of it. Apoc. 21:22-24.

The throne of God and of the Lamb shall be in it, and his servants shall serve him. And they shall see his face: and his name shall be on their foreheads. Apoc. 22:3 f.

To him that shall overcome, I will give to sit with me in my throne: as I also have overcome, and am set down with my Father, in his throne. Apoc. 3:21.

In my Father's house there are many mansions. If not, I would have told you, that I go to prepare a place for you. And if I shall go, and prepare a place for you: I will come again, and will take you to myself, that where I am, you also may be. John 14:2 f.

Father, I will that where I am, they also whom thou hast given me may be with me, that they may see my glory which thou hast given me, because thou hast loved me before the foundation of the world. John 17:2.

The Lamb, which is in the midst of the throne, shall rule them. Apoc. 6:17.

I beheld, and lo a Lamb stood upon Mount Sion, and with him an hundred forty-four thousand having his name, and the name of his Father written on their foreheads. Apoc. 14:1.

In their mouth there was found no lie: for they are without spot before the throne of God. Apoc. 14:5.

The Lord knoweth the days of the undefiled: and their inheritance shall be forever. Ps. 36:18.

There shall not enter into it anything defiled. Apoc. 21:27.

By one oblation, he hath perfected forever them that are sanctified. Heb. 10:14.

Iniquity shall no more be heard in thy land, wasting nor destruction in thy borders, and salvation shall possess thy walls, and praise thy gates. Is. 60:18.

Thy people shall be all just, they shall inherit the land forever, the branch of my planting, the work of my hand to glorify me. Is. 60:21.

White robes were given to every one of them. Apoc. 6:10.

The just shall go into life everlasting. Mat. 25:46.

Israel is saved in the Lord with an eternal salvation. Is. 45:17.

He shall receive in the world to come life everlasting. Mark 10:30.

I give them life everlasting. John 10:28.

The grace of God is life everlasting. Rom. 6:23.

This is the promise which he hath promised us, life everlasting. 1 John 2:25.

God hath given to us eternal life, and this life is in his Son. 1 John 5:11.

He that soweth in the Spirit, of the Spirit shall reap life everlasting. Gal. 6:8.

Great shall be the peace of thy children. Is. 54:13.

My people shall sit in the beauty of peace, and in the tabernacles of confidence, and in wealthy rest. Is. 22:18.

The mountains shall be moved, and the hills shall tremble; but my mercy shall not depart from thee, and the covenant of my peace shall not be moved: said the Lord that hath mercy on thee. Is. 54:10.

The meek shall inherit the land, and shall delight in abundance of peace. Ps. 36:11.

Thus saith the Lord: Behold I will bring upon her as it were a river of peace. Is. 66:12.

The kingdom of God is peace and joy in the Holy Ghost. Rom. 14:17.

I will give peace in your coasts: you shall sleep, and there shall be none to make you afraid. Lev. 26:6.

The redeemed of the Lord shall return, and shall come into Sion with praise, and everlasting joy shall be upon their heads: they shall obtain joy and gladness, and sorrow and mourning shall flee away. Is. 35:10.

Everlasting joy shall be unto them. Is. 61:7.

They that are redeemed by the Lord, shall return, and shall come into Sion singing praises, and joy everlasting shall be upon their heads, they shall obtain joy and gladness, sorrow and mourning shall flee away. Is. 51:11.

They shall rejoice before thee, as they that rejoice in the harvest, as conquerors rejoice after taking a prey, when they divide the spoils. Is. 9:3.

I will see you again, and your heart shall rejoice, and your joy no man shall take from you. John 16:22.

The Lord will give thee rest continually. Is. 58:11.

This is my rest forever and ever: here will I dwell, for I have chosen it. Ps. 131:14.

There the wearied in strength are at rest. Job 3:17.

Thou shalt rest, and there shall be none to make thee afraid. Job 11:19.

Who will give me wings like a dove, and I will fly and be at rest? Ps. 54:7.

You shall find rest to your souls. Mat. 11:29.

There remaineth a day of rest for the people of God. For he that is entered into his rest, the same also hath rested from his works, as God did from his. Let us hasten therefore to enter into that rest. Heb. 4:9-11.

Accessory Goods

You are come to Mount Sion, to the company of many thousands of angels, and to the spirits of the just made perfect. Heb. 12:22 f.

The dwelling in thee is as it were of all rejoicing. Ps. 86:7.

Behold how good and how pleasant it is for brethren to dwell together in unity, as the dew of Hermon, which descendeth upon Mount Sion. For there the Lord hath commanded blessing, and life for evermore. Ps. 132:1, 3.

He prophesied that Jesus should die for the nation. And not only for the nation, but to gather together in one the children of God, that were dispersed. John 11:51 f.

I saw a great multitude which no man could number, of all nations, and tribes, and peoples, and tongues. Apoc. 7:9.

We see now through a glass in a dark manner: but then face to face. Now I know in part: but then I shall know even as I am known. 1 C. 13:12.

In thy light we shall see light. Ps. 35:10.

He gave some apostles . . . for the work of the ministry. . . . Until we all meet into the unity of faith and of the knowledge of the Son of God unto a perfect man. Eph. 4:11-13.

This is eternal life, that they may know thee. John 17:3.

He will raise us up, and we shall live in his sight. We shall know. Osee 6:3.

Thou shalt no more have the sun for thy light by day, neither shall the brightness of the moon enlighten thee: but the Lord shall be unto thee for an everlasting light, and thy God for thy glory. Thy sun shall go down no more, and thy moon shall not decrease: for the Lord shall be unto thee for an everlasting light, and the days of thy mourning shall be ended. Is. 60:19 f.

When one of them that sat at table with him, had heard these things, he said to him: Blessed is he that shall eat bread in the kingdom of God. Luke 14:15.

I dispose to you, as my Father hath disposed to me, a kingdom: that you may eat and drink at my table in my kingdom: and may sit upon thrones judging the twelve tribes of Israel. Luke 22:29 f.

They shall be inebriated with the plenty of thy house; and thou shalt make them drink of the torrent of thy pleasure. Ps. 35:9.

He that hath an ear, let him hear what the Spirit saith to the churches: To him, that overcometh, I will give to eat of the tree of life, which is in the paradise of my God. Apoc. 2:7.

To him that overcometh, I will give the hidden manna, and will give him a white counter, and in the counter a new name written, which no man knoweth but he that receiveth it. Apoc. 2:17.

To him that thirsteth I will give of the fountain of the water of life gratis. Apoc. 21:6.

The Lamb shall lead them to the fountains of the waters of life. Apoc. 7:17.

They that are learned shall shine as the brightness of the firmament: and they that instruct many to justice, as stars for all eternity. Dan. 13:3.

Then shall the just shine as the sun in the kingdom of their Father. Mat. 13:43.

The just shall shine, and shall run to and fro like sparks among the reeds. Wis. 3:7.

The brightness like that of the noonday shall arise to thee at evening: and when thou shalt think thyself consumed, thou shalt rise as the day star. Job 11:17.

If any man minister to me, him will my Father honor. John 12:26.

The wise shall possess glory. Prov. 3:35.

Glory and honor to every one that worketh good. Rom. 2:10.

The glory which thou hast given me, I have given to them. John 17:22.

Walk worthy of God who hath called you unto his kingdom and glory. 1 Thess. 2:12.

It is sown in dishonor, it shall rise in glory. 1 C. 15:43.

If any man love me, my Father will love him. John 14:23.

There appeared also another man, admirable for age, and glory, and environed with great beauty and majesty. 2 Mac. 15:13.

When the Prince of pastors shall appear, you shall receive a neverfading crown of glory. 1 Pet. 5:4.

I saw them that had overcome the beast standing on the sea of glass, having the harps of God. And singing the canticle of Moses the servant of God, and the canticle of the Lamb. Apoc. 15:2 f.

I heard a voice from heaven, as the voice of many waters, and as the voice of great thunder: and the voice, which I heard, was as the voice of harpers, harping on their harps. Apoc. 14:2.

And they sung as it were a new canticle before the throne, and before the four living creatures, and the ancients: and no man could say the canticle but those hundred forty-four thousand, who were purchased from the earth. Apoc. 14:3.

Give praise to the Lord on the harp. Ps. 32:2.

When he had opened the book, the four living creatures, and the four-and-twenty ancients, fell down before the Lamb, having every one of them harps, and golden vials full of odors, which are the prayers of saints. Apoc. 5:8.

Praise the Lord in his holy places. Praise him with psaltery and harp. Ps. 150:1, 3.

O God, I will sing to thee with the harp, thou Holy One of Israel. Ps. 70:22.

At thy right hand are delights even to the end. Ps. 15:11.

I shall be satisfied when thy glory shall appear. Ps. 16:15.

Blessed is he whom thou hast chosen, and taken to thee: he shall dwell in thy courts. We shall be filled with the good things of thy house. Ps. 64:5.

Blessed are they that hunger and thirst after justice, for they shall have their fill. Mat. 5:6.

I will fill the soul of the priests with fatness, and my people shall be filled with my good things, saith the Lord. Jer. 31:14.

The Lord ruleth me, and I shall want nothing. Ps. 22:1.

5. HOW HEAVEN IS TO BE WON

Not every one that saith to me, Lord, Lord, shall enter into the kingdom of heaven: but he that doth the will of my Father, who is in heaven, he shall enter into the kingdom of heaven. Mat. 7:21.

Jesus said to them; Suffer the little children, and forbid them not to come to me: for the kingdom of heaven is for such. The kingdom of heaven suffereth violence, and the violent bear it away. Mat. 11:12.

Lord, who shall dwell in thy tabernacle, or who shall rest in thy holy hill? He that walketh without blemish, and worketh justice: he that speaketh truth in his heart, who hath not used deceit in his tongue: nor hath done evil to his neighbor: nor taken up a reproach against his neighbors: he that sweareth to his neighbor, and deceiveth not, he that hath not put out his money to usury, nor taken bribes against the innocent. He that doth these things shall not be moved forever. Ps. 14:1-5.

Blessed is he whom thou hast chosen and taken to thee: he shall dwell in thy courts. Ps. 64:5.

Blessed is the man whose help is from thee: in his heart he hath disposed to ascend by steps in the vale of tears. Ps. 83:6.

There shall not enter into it anything defiled, but they that are written in the book of life of the Lamb. Apoc. 12:27.

Blessed are the poor in spirit, for theirs is the kingdom of heaven. Mat. 5:3.

Blessed are the meek, for they shall possess the land. Mat. 5:4.

Blessed are they that suffer persecution for justice' sake: for theirs is the kingdom of heaven. Mat. 5:10.

I say to you that many shall come from the east and the west, and shall sit down with Abraham, and Isaac, and Jacob in the kingdom of heaven. Mat. 8:11.

He that hateth his life in this world keepeth it unto life eternal. John 12:25.

The just shall go into life everlasting. Mat. 25:46.

As Moses lifted up the serpent in

the desert, so must the Son of man be lifted up: that whosoever believeth in him may not perish, but may have life everlasting. John 3:14 f.

Who shall ascend into the mountain of the Lord: or who shall stand in his holy place? The innocent in hands, and clean of heart, who hath not taken his soul in vain, nor sworn deceitfully to his neighbor. Ps. 23:3-5.

INDEX